TEACHERS' GUIDE

TO

CHILD DEVELOPMENT

IN THE

INTERMEDIATE GRADES

Prepared under the Direction of the
CALIFORNIA STATE CURRICULUM COMMISSION

Published by the
CALIFORNIA STATE DEPARTMENT OF EDUCATION
Sacramento
1936

372

C 12t

14452

June 1937

CALIFORNIA STATE PRINTING OFFICE
SACRAMENTO, 1936

THE CALIFORNIA STATE CURRICULUM COMMISSION

HELEN M. BARNETT, Santa Barbara State College, Santa Barbara
(Succeeded by Albert R. Lang, July 12, 1935)

JOHN F. BRADY, Principal, Everett Junior High School, San Francisco
(Succeeded Willa M. Marsh, October 4, 1935)

ELLEN R. BREEN, Principal, Lincoln Elementary School, San Diego

L. E. CHENOWETH, Superintendent of Schools, Bakersfield
(Succeeded by John A. Sexson, July 12, 1935)

GERTRUDE M. CROSS, Teacher, Edwin Markham School, Oakland
(Succeeded Gladys Evelyn Moorhead, October 4, 1935)

MARVIN L. DARSIE, Dean of Teachers College, University of California at Los Angeles
(Succeeded John A. Hockett, January 10, 1935)

MERTON E. HILL, Principal, Chaffey Union High School and Junior College, Ontario
(Present position, Director of Admissions, University of California; succeeded by Charles B. Moore, October 2, 1931)

JOHN A. HOCKETT, Lecturer in Education, University of California, Berkeley
(Succeeded by Marvin L. Darsie, January 10, 1935)

A. H. HORRALL, Assistant Superintendent of Schools, San Jose
(Succeeded E. W. Jacobsen, January, 10, 1935)

E. W. JACOBSEN, Assistant Superintendent of Schools, Oakland
(Present position, Superintendent of Schools, Oakland; succeeded Rudolph D. Lindquist, October 2, 1931; succeeded by A. H. Horrall, January 10, 1935)

GEORGE C. JENSEN, Principal, Sacramento High School
(Succeeded Charles B. Moore, January 10, 1935)

ALBERT R. LANG, Dean of Upper Division, Fresno State College, Fresno
(Succeeded Helen M. Barnett, July 12, 1935)

RUDOLPH D. LINDQUIST, Assistant Superintendent of Schools, Oakland, January 31, 1931; President Chico State Teachers College, February 1, 1931, to July 31, 1931
(Present position, Director, The University School, Ohio State University, Columbus, Ohio; succeeded by E. W. Jacobsen, October 2, 1931)

WILLA M. MARSH, Dean of Girls, Alexander Hamilton Junior High School, Fresno
(Present position, Vice Principal, Fresno Technical High School, Fresno; succeeded by John F. Brady, October 4, 1935)

CHARLES B. MOORE, Principal, Franklin High School, Los Angeles
(Present position, Assistant Superintendent of Schools, Los Angeles; succeeded Merton E. Hill, October 2, 1931; succeeded by George C. Jensen, January 10, 1935)

GLADYS EVELYN MOORHEAD, Teacher, Micheltorena Elementary School, Los Angeles
(Succeeded by Gertrude M. Cross, October 4, 1935)

PORTIA F. MOSS, County Superintendent of Schools, Placer County
(Succeeded Ada York, July 12, 1935)

THE CALIFORNIA STATE CURRICULUM COMMISSION—Cont'd

ETHEL I. SALISBURY, Director, Course of Study Division, Los Angeles Schools
(Present position, Associate Professor of Elementary Education, University of California at Los Angeles, and Educational Consultant, Santa Monica Public Schools; succeeded by M. Madilene Veverka, July 12, 1935)

JOHN A. SEXSON, Superintendent of Schools, Pasadena

(Succeeded L. E. Chenoweth, July 12, 1935)

M. MADILENE VEVERKA, Director, Elementary Curriculum, Los Angeles Schools
(Succeeded Ethel I. Salisbury, July 12, 1935)

ADA YORK, County Superintendent of Schools, San Diego County
(Succeeded by Portia F. Moss, July 12, 1935)

VIERLING KERSEY, Superintendent of Public Instruction, *Chairman*

Subcommittee in charge of preparation of *Teachers' Guide to Child Development in the Intermediate Grades*

ETHEL I. SALISBURY, *Chairman*

ELLEN R. BREEN

L. E. CHENOWETH

JOHN A. HOCKETT

FOREWORD

California has no state curriculum, or course of study. It is not the policy of the state to prescribe in detail the content or teaching methods to be followed by individual schools within the state school system. Local school systems have been encouraged to develop their own curricula and courses of study adapted to their local needs in terms of certain requirements either specified in law or established by authority of the State Board of Education and the State Department of Education.

The State Curriculum Commission, established in 1927, was authorized to perform the following functions with respect to courses of study:

> 3.680. The curriculum commission shall study problems of courses of study in the schools of the state and shall have power to recommend to the state board of education the adoption of minimum standards for courses of study in the kindergarten, elementary, and secondary schools.

> 3.681. Courses of study in the public schools must conform to such minimum standards when adopted as provided in this Article.

In accordance with these legal provisions, the State Curriculum Commission and the State Department of Education have endeavored to set up certain standards, objectives, and procedures to guide local school systems in the development of courses of study and curriculum materials. Because of the general sentiment of the citizens of California which demands educational opportunity for childhood and youth of the highest standard of excellence, official publications in the field of curriculum have represented a progressive point of view generally acceptable and practiced throughout the state. Because of the mobility of our pupil population and because of our system of state textbook adoptions, it seems essential that the central authority in the state school system should attempt the formulation of a curriculum organization which will provide a framework indicating the broad scope and sequence of major learnings in the curriculum in order that some desirable uniformity may obtain in the educational program of the state.

The point of view set forth in the curriculum materials developed by the State Curriculum Commission and the State Department of Education represents an ideal toward which it is believed that local school systems should endeavor to work rather than a somewhat inflexible program which must be immediately put into practice. Not all that is suggested will be possible to any school system or to any teacher without considerable study and in some instances reorganization of existing facilities. Many of the suggestions, however, are realizable at the present time. At the outset, however, it should be emphasized that the materials contained in this volume are not imposed upon local school systems or required of individual teachers; instead these materials represent the endeavor of teachers, supervisors, administrators, and professors of education throughout the state to formulate in concrete and definite terms the theory underlying the best practice already existing in many of our schools and to give illustrations of these practices which will be of practical value in guiding teachers to the development of more effective classroom procedures.

This volume is a companion volume to *Teachers' Guide to Child Development—Manual for Kindergarten and Primary Teachers*, prepared under the direction of the State Curriculum Commission and published in 1930. The State Curriculum Commission undertook first to deal with the kindergarten-primary level because this is the critical point at which the influence of the school is first evident. The needs of children in the primary school are generally recognized. Young children are greatly influenced by their early experiences and their personalities are largely determined by the environmental conditions with which they are surrounded. Human development is, however, characterized by continuity. The child in the intermediate school is not greatly different from his younger brothers and sisters in interests and attitudes except as these have been broadened and deepened by experience. The carefully formulated program established for the period of early development is, therefore, continued for the middle grades in its fundamental respects. In preparing similar materials for the secondary level, the State Curriculum Commission will be guided by the same fundamental principles.

The organization of this volume differs in certain important respects from that of the previous volume. The first four chapters are somewhat general in nature and treat the following subjects: the point of view, the organization of the intermediate grades, the teacher, the textbooks and other instructional materials. Following are chapters devoted to the several elementary school subjects. The fact that this organization is utilized here should not be interpreted as a recommendation that the program of the intermediate school should adhere to rigid subject matter divisions. Here, as in the primary school, the trend is toward the organization of learning around centers of human experience. The six curriculum units, offered by way of illustration, indicate the contribution of the subject fields to the understandings and appreciations developed around these centers of interest.

Lack of space prevents the inclusion of many other curriculum units which could be presented to illustrate the principles and teaching procedures of the progressive school. Many excellent units were received and grateful acknowledgment is made to all who furnished such materials whether it was possible to include them in this volume or not. In order to make such additional curriculum units available, however, the State Department of Education has begun the publication of a series of curriculum units for elementary grades which will make available certain of the best materials as they are developed by teachers throughout the state.

Other curriculum materials published by the State Department of Education should also be mentioned. Suggested courses of study are available in science, reading and literature, social studies, and oral and written expression. Beginning with the school year 1934-1935 the publication of a series of bulletins was commenced under the general title: *Science Guide for Elementary Schools*. The titles thus far published in this series are contained in the footnote on page 100.

The Contribution of Modern Science to Education

The growth of modern science has been responsible for profound changes in education. The last three decades have been characterized by tremendous research activities in psycho-biological fields. Biology has investigated the physical basis of the human organism. The social sciences have sought understanding and interpretation of group life under varying environmental influences. Psychology is exploring the conditions essential to the normal human growth and development of the whole organism. Psychiatry is studying aberrant behaviors in an effort to determine the causes for maladjustment in human beings.

The rapidly accumulating knowledge of human growth is profoundly significant to education. Development is coming to be understood as the process of adjustment to the environment. The potentialities of a child are developed through contact with a stimulating environment under wise guidance which will accelerate this interaction. The genetic inheritance of a child may and probably does influence the limits of his possibilities but a suitable environment and intelligent direction will provide the most favorable opportunity for the continuous growth and development of the organism.

The Task of the Modern School

The modern school will take into consideration (1) the nature of the children to be taught, (2) the nature of the society in which they live, and (3) the educational progress of the community it serves. The school must know and meet the needs of the youth it serves; it must fit youth not only to adapt himself to the society in which he lives but must inspire him with a willingness to participate in activities designed to improve that society; and it must interpret to the local community the purposes and ideals of the education with which youth is being provided.

Characteristics of a Progressive Intermediate School

According to John Dewey, education is a continuous reconstruction of experience. A progressive program should, therefore, possess the same general characteristics regardless of the level of maturity of the individual it serves whether he be a child of kindergarten or elementary school age, a youth of high school or college age, or an adult continuously seeking through education the answer to the complex questions of a transitional civilization.

Any attempt to set up the characteristics of a progressive school does not imply standardization. Schools need not be alike, in fact, they will not be alike if they are giving consideration to the individual variations in pupils and the different needs of specific communities. The unique character of each school should be maintained. The fundamental purposes, the materials of learning, and the technique of guiding the experiences of children will be largely the same, however, in schools serving a democratic society.

The school must be organized so children may work and play and live cooperatively in harmonious social groups. Mental, physical, social, and emotional growth should be constantly stimulated, understandings should be broadened, appreciations should be enriched, sympathies should be enlarged. The school is a dynamic institution to the extent that it recognizes the constant growth and development essential to the individuals it serves.

The most significant characteristics of the progressive school are (1) recognition of the motivating influence of purpose, (2) provision for activity, (3) adaptation to individual variation, (4) opportunity for growth in social understandings, and (5) close relationship with the home. These five major characteristics merit somewhat further expansion.

Purpose. The progressive school recognizes the important function served by child purpose. The child is interested in any activity only in so far as he can see its value in meeting his needs. It is the teacher's function to stimulate the development of worthwhile purposes and interests. The child is motivated to learn to write in a clear and interesting manner, not for some remote, adult end but so his story will be worthy of a place in the school newspaper. He learns to speak correctly and forcefully not for some future need as a grown-up but so he may be chosen by his fellows to "broadcast" the "daily news" before the classroom "microphone," or so he may participate in the auditorium program or serve as a class officer. A "felt need" is the drive to effort. The child studies the fundamentals of arithmetic because he is interested in solving a problem which has arisen in a classroom situation. Purposes must be childlike and serve immediate desires to provide the drive necessary for learning.

Activity. The progressive school is characterized by a varied and active program. The single textbook and the formal recitation will no longer suffice to achieve the social purposes of education. Units of work are organized around life situations and involve the use of many books, charts, maps, pictures, and innumerable other aids. Excursions are planned to give that reality and vitality to learning which comes through first hand experiences. Many related fields are brought together around one center of interest. Art, music, literature, history, geography, science have each a contribution to make to a complete understanding of any given cultural epoch or social function. The relationships between the fields are comparable to those which occur in out-of-school situations.

Illustrations of this type of teaching are many. A group of children decide to make a wild flower exhibit to which the parents are to be invited. The situation immediately provides much childlike motivation. Plans must be discussed for the arrangement of an attractive exhibit. Specimens must be collected and correct identification made by consulting many books. Labels must be written or printed. Plans must be made for the entertainment of the guests. A program is planned, wild flower songs are learned, a play is written on the conservation of wildflowers, some of the children are inspired to write original verse. All these activities are rich in vital experiencing and purposeful living and working together. Invitations must be written. The social amenities must be remembered and practiced when the guests arrive. The experience has been full of opportunity for thinking, sharing, cooperating and it has demanded many forms of creative expression.

Adaptation to Individual Variations. The great contribution of psychology to education is the irrefutable evidence that individuals are different. To a certain extent, parents and teachers had always known this but the psychologist provided the proof that the differences are not only great, varied, and persistent but that education to achieve its goal must take into consideration in planning its procedures not only individual differences in native ability but variations in physical equipment, social background and interest.

In the progressive school, teaching begins at each child's level of development and makes possible the fullest realization of his potentialities. The unit of work curriculum provides the finest opportunity for individual adaptation while maintaining all of the advantages of social living in the class group. Reading material, for example, may be carefully adjusted to the individual's reading ability at the same time that it is giving the child information to contribute to the solution of the problem with which the group is confronted.

The special aptitudes of individual children in art, music, and other forms of creative expression have much opportunity for development. Not only may the child experience satisfaction in making his unique contribution to the group but he may learn to exercise leadership in the field in which he is especially gifted. The individual talent of no child need be lost.

The fact that much of the work of the progressive school is carried on independently either by individuals or by groups, frees the teacher's time and makes available intervals in which she has opportunity to help individual pupils solve their particular difficulties. The classroom situation in which the teacher is helping an individual child with his problems, imposes on the group an important discipline to become increasingly self-directed and self-controlled. This self-imposed discipline results in serious concentration upon the purposes the child wishes to accomplish and results in the achievement of the basic purpose of all education, namely, personality development.

Development of Social Understanding. Modern conditions make us unwilling to pin our faith on the acquisition of any fixed body of factual information as the purpose of education. Change is taking place with astounding rapidity in all phases of social life. It would be indeed hazardous to attempt to prophesy the conditions to which children now in school will be required to make adaptation in their adult lives.

The soundest procedure is to lead the child to an understanding of the social, political, industrial, economic, and recreational enterprises of the community in which he lives. By studying the problems inherent in his own social situation, he is stimulated to constructive thinking and learns the technique of group planning in solving the problems of a democratic society.

Only through such a procedure may we hope to help children develop ability in the intelligent appraisal of problems. The ability to do critical thinking, to collect pertinent data, to reserve final judgment until all the information has been canvassed, to interpret data in the light of significant experience is the most indispensable equipment the school may provide for the child in helping him to meet the problems with which he must cope.

Close Relationship with the Home. Sound educational procedure recognizes the totality of the child's experience. The present day school must have the closest possible relationship with the homes of the community. The best conditions for child growth can exist only when the home and the school relationships are characterized by understanding, harmony, and cooperation.

Numerous studies in the field of character education have pointed out the significance of the home in the development of the child's personality. Emotional habits and social adjustments are probably largely developed by family relationships. Under existing and approaching social conditions, it is evident that the major responsibility for the guidance of child development must reside in the home. The school, acting as the best-qualified agency of society, must help parents to give children increasingly better care and to make the home an increasingly more favorable environment for the development of socially desirable personalities.

Transition from Old to New

There are certain characteristics that mark the environment, the teaching procedure, and the attitude of teacher and children in the traditional as well as the new school. Contrasting these characteristics may serve to clarify some of the questions relative to what constitutes the progressive school.

The traditional school is characterized by:	*The modern school is characterized by:*
Formal desks and seats screwed to the floor and arranged in fixed rows.	Informal tables and chairs arranged conveniently for group activity.
Space not occupied by fixed furniture limited.	Some open spaces unobstructed and arranged for such activities as dramatizations, rhythms.
More or less drab interior with blackboards on three sides and limited display space.	Colorful interiors with space to display interesting pictures and other material on a level with the child's eye.
The teacher is a taskmaster.	The teacher is a guide and counselor.
Silence on the part of children except during recitations. Each child expected to remain seated except by permission from the teacher. Whispering and other forbidden activity indulged in secretly.	A natural social situation in which children are free to move about and consult with others as they engage in a variety of worth while activities without interfering with the welfare of others.

Meager equipment consisting largely of standard supplies.	A variety of equipment to meet the needs. Wood, clay, large rolls of paper, paint, tools, and visual aids.
A similar set of books for each child in a particular grade. Recreational reading material and supplementary texts at a minimum.	A variety of books, both texts and recreational, chosen to meet the needs of the individuals within the group. Books and other materials attractively arranged for effective use.
Rigid grade standards. Every child must master the standards for the grade before promotion.	Instruction adjusted to the individual needs and abilities regardless of grade. Children work and play in flexible social groupings.
Short recitations of the question and answer type in the separate subjects are scheduled throughout the day. Recitations consist of giving back to the teacher the statements in the text all have studied. Answers are correct if "that is what the book said."	Longer periods during which study, experimentation, and discussion of a significant worth while central theme are participated in by the group guided by the teacher. References to many authorities, exchange of ideas, and a scientific attitude characterize the period.
Acquisition of factual information, to be used in adult life.	Development of a happy, well adjusted, well rounded individual here and now, who has a life interest in his fact learning.
Casual, parental contacts with school. Responsibilities of home and school widely separated.	Numerous parental contacts. Close cooperation given to insure better understanding of child.
Formal reports of child's achievement in subject matter according to grade standard.	Informal report of child's growth measured against his own previous record.
The inclusion of learning within the four walls of the classroom. School set apart in the community.	The use of educative resources within the community. Pertinent materials brought into the classroom by the children. School an integral part of community.
Conformity.	Creative self-expression.

Modern psychology assumes that *learning* is the most important function of the developing child. The emphasis in this volume is upon a constructive program which provides educational experiences essential to foster learning. A positive program emphasizes the successful handling of children. To be sure, problems must be met, remedial measures must be provided, maladjustments must be dealt with appropriately and judiciously but the greatest progress for education will grow out of the constructive attitude which recognizes and attempts to overcome obvious difficulties but concentrates its effort on a thoughtfully-planned, well-directed effort to secure the greatest possible realization for every child.

Teachers must realize that childhood is the time of adjustment. In order that the child's adjustment to his social situation may be as complete as possible, the life within the school must reflect the life of the social group of which he is a member. The school which can give the child a broad perspective of life and its problems, will equip him to evaluate these problems for himself and to build out of his evaluation a philosophy of life by which he may live.

Acknowledgments

The subcommittee of the State Curriculum Commission in direct charge of the preparation of this volume was headed by Ethel I. Salisbury and included the following members of the Commission: Ellen R. Breen, John A. Hockett, L. E. Chenoweth.

Many persons cooperated in the preparation of materials for this volume. The authorship is indicated in connection with each chapter.

Miss Helen Heffernan, Chief of the Division of Elementary Education and Rural Schools, and Mrs. Gladys L. Potter, Assistant Chief of the Division of Elementary Education and Rural Schools, of the State Department of Education, reviewed materials submitted for publication and made valuable suggestions and additions. They also assisted in the editing of the volume.

Chief editorial responsibility was assigned to Dr. Ivan R. Waterman, Chief of the Division of Textbooks and Publications of the State Department of Education.

Acknowledgment is made to the many publishers for their courtesy in allowing copyrighted materials to be reproduced in this volume. Such materials are indicated by footnotes throughout the volume.

Acknowledgment is also made to the various school systems which supplied illustrations used in this volume. Specific acknowledgment for these materials is indicated throughout the text.

Superintendent of Public Instruction

CONTENTS

CONTENTS—Continued

CHAPTER IV

TEXTBOOKS AND OTHER INSTRUCTIONAL MATERIALS

CHAPTER V

SOCIAL STUDIES

CONTENTS—Continued

Chapter VI

Science

Chapter VII

Units of Work in Social Studies and Science

Chapter VIII

Curriculum Unit—Our Neighbors of the Pacific: Hawaii

Chapter IX

Curriculum Unit—Life of the Sea and Shore

CONTENTS—Continued

CHAPTER X

CURRICULUM UNIT—THE COLORADO DESERT: A REPRESENTATIVE DESERT

CHAPTER XI

CURRICULUM UNIT—SOAP

CHAPTER XII

CURRICULUM UNIT—TRANSPORTATION

A Unit of Work Carried on in Grades 4, 5 and 6

CONTENTS—Continued

Chapter XIII
Curriculum Unit—Mexico

Chapter XIV
Log of the Activities Carried on by a Fifth Grade Class in Developing a Unit of Work on Mexico

Chapter XV
Training in Reading Skills

CONTENTS—Continued

CONTENTS—Continued

CHAPTER XVIII

ORAL AND WRITTEN EXPRESSION

CHAPTER XIX

ARITHMETIC

CONTENTS—Continued

CHAPTER XX

MUSIC

CONTENTS—Continued

Chapter XXI

Art

CONTENTS—Continued

CHAPTER XXII

CREATIVE PLAY AS AN INTEGRATING ACTIVITY

APPENDIX I

APPENDIX II

ILLUSTRATIONS

ILLUSTRATIONS—Continued

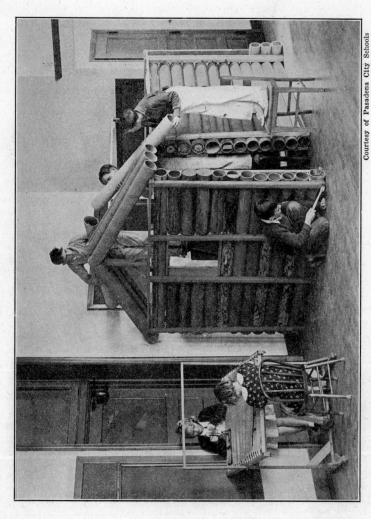

Children in the Fifth Grade, Jackson School, Pasadena, Constructing a Log Cabin in an American Pioneer Unit. A Hooked Rug for the Cabin Is in the Frame.

CHAPTER I

POINT OF VIEW [1]

BASIC EDUCATIONAL PHILOSOPHY

The philosophy of John Dewey is basic in the thought and practice of most advanced schools today. He maintains that education is life; education is growth; education is a social process; and education is a continuous reconstruction of experience.

Education Is Life

Education is life, a continuous process from the beginning to the end of life, both in and out of the school. The child should be treated as an individual with real problems to solve and a real life to live. Education is not only preparation for adult life, it is life itself. Only as this conception is embodied in instruction, will the child be developed to cope with the problems of adult life as he meets them.

Education Is Growth

The great process of education is the change that takes place from day to day. As long as growth continues, education is taking place. The great goal of modern education is growth that begins at birth, is guided through the school years and continues throughout life.

Education Is a Social Process

Education in America must be education for living in democracy. It must go on in a social group. Education is more than learning, it is living. Schools must be democratic societies in which children live natural democratic lives with their companions in order that they may grow into adulthood with good citizenship as a part of their experience.

Education Is a Continuous Reconstruction of Experience

The activities of each day are based on past experiences. Every day of a child's life is conditioned by previous days. When new experience is added to the old, reorganization of all experience takes place in the light of the new experiences. Education is then a present activity and not a product to be striven for in the future. It is life and it is growth in a social environment.

---

[1] Contributed by Helen Heffernan, Chief, and Gladys L. Potter, Assistant Chief, Division of Elementary Education and Rural Schools, California State Department of Education.

PURPOSES OF THE ELEMENTARY SCHOOL

Modern education aims to develop the whole child. It concerns itself with *growth* and *change* in the many sided aspects of child nature. Not only must education provide for the adequate mental development of the child, but provision for the physical, emotional, esthetic, and spiritual progress of the child constitutes equally significant problems.

The multiplicity of kinds of development for which education is responsible may seem to indicate a confusion of the aims or purposes of education. The purposes are complicated because the development of the total personality is an intricate process. Despite their complexity, the purposes lend themselves to considerable clarity of definition in terms of child psychology, scientific education, and the sociological implications of modern life.

In general, the aim of education is to provide opportunity for the fullest development of the thought, feeling, and conduct of each individual, to the end that he may realize his potential possibilities for the greater good of himself and society.

Elementary education has passed through tremendous changes in philosophy, utilization of the scientific method, and reorganization of administrative practices. The concept of knowledge for knowledge's sake is a worn-out fetish. Modern educators know that subject matter is a means to an end, not an end in itself. In the modern school, knowledge is no longer poured in and given back in the formal recitation, but problems are solved, judgments are made, and the child develops through active participation in real life situations. Schools recognize that children come to learning through rich and meaningful experiences.

The environment in the new school is in reality the curriculum. To educate a child, "organize the environment to afford adequate stimuli for the tendencies favorable to development," said De Croly, the great Belgian psychologist. The things we do all through life are to a considerable degree those things the environment suggests and makes possible. The school environment must be selected and controlled in order that it may be full of possibilities for interesting the child, full of stimulation to insure proper growth, full of variety to meet each child's needs and adequately supplement his out-of-school environment, if education for the child is to be complete.

The environment of the modern school is no longer limited to the four walls of a room, but it extends out into the community wherever stimulating activities are going on. A neighboring dairy, a zoo, or an art gallery may be a part of the curriculum of the school.

Experience is a unified thing. Dewey calls it "on-going activity." Professor James speaks of it as "a stream of consciousness." The pigeonholed, isolated subjects of the traditional school had no relation to the life of the child. The so-called "subjects" represent adult attempts to organize the environment so as to give added meaning to significant aspects of our general experiences. Modern education is not concerned with this subject matter as such, but with the child's total experience, his total learnings, his present and potential behavior. All learning is the outcome of things done, and is integrated and unified around wholesome living. It is through participation in living that attitudes and habits are formed, skills are acquired, valuable information is gained, and character is built. The only required or compulsory curriculum is then, after all, practice in living. This problem is as old as man; time and environment may change, human inventions come and go, but to learn to live one's daily life well is still of prime importance as the basic purpose of the educative process.

In the light of modern knowledge of the development of young children an understanding of the specific purpose of the elementary school is essential to an adequate interpretation of a basic curriculum.

It is the purpose of the elementary school to help each child:

1. To establish normal mental attitudes and controlled emotional reactions, and to develop a sound body

2. To develop an understanding of social relationships and a willingness to participate in social activities in ways conducive to the progress of society

3. To develop individual talents and abilities as completely as possible

4. To cultivate habits of analytical thinking

5. To acquire command of the common knowledges and skills essential to effective living

6. To develop appreciation for and desire to seek beauty in its many manifestations.

A brief development of these statements will serve to give them definition.

Purpose 1. To establish normal mental attitudes and controlled emotional reactions, and to develop a sound body. Modern education recognizes and assumes its responsibility in caring for the physical welfare of children and in providing individual success and security which is necessary to insure normal mental attitudes and controlled emotional reactions. The intimate relation between physical and mental health on the one hand and school achievement on the other is definitely established.

The demands of health are imperative. The modern school is vigilant concerning posture, prevention of eyestrain, and the establishment of desirable health habits. Teachers must become increasingly watchful that health is safeguarded by permitting children to move about freely, with opportunity for much activity. If the school situation is not to be positively inimical to children's health, it must eliminate strain and overstimulation, and provide a natural wholesome environment.

Closely allied to physical well-being is mental health. Children must be happy, confident, and successful if they are to have normal mental attitudes. They must know they are growing, must be freed from worry, fear, and any sense of inferiority. The school must adjust its program to insure a measure of success for each child. Repression is the basis of maladjustment. Children must have opportunity to express themselves physically, mentally, and socially. The school must teach control, not through the prevention of activity, but by providing situations in which choice of possible alternative behaviors must be made. The guidance of the teacher is advisory, never dictatorial.

Purpose 2. To develop an understanding of social relationships and a willingness to participate in them in ways conducive to the progress of society. Children enter the elementary school from the smaller social group of the family. They must become socially adjusted to the members of the group. They must learn to work together harmoniously, to use liberty wisely, to participate in group activities in a helpful, socially acceptable way.

The social relationships within the school must provide the natural situation for children to learn to live and work together. Each child has a contribution to make to the group enterprise. He must learn to assume his share of the responsibility; to give directions and to follow directions; to help others; to participate according to his interest and ability; to recognize and appreciate the contributions of others; to feel himself an active, necessary, integral part of his own social situation. No richer opportunity for character development could be afforded him.

Purpose 3. To develop individual talents and abilities as completely as possible. The great variety of contributions made by individuals to society has made life rich and full of interest. It is not the similarity one individual possesses to all others, but the unique differences, which make possible valuable service to the social group.

Modern education purposes to preserve the differences; to develop the varied interests; to cultivate the unique powers of expression; not only that these manifold potential contributions may be secured for society, but in order that the individual may experience vital, satisfying, and complete realization.

This purpose abolishes mass education and the lock step. It means that children will progress at their own rate, whether slow, moderate, or rapid. It means a refusal to gear educational advancement to a mythical "average child." Most profoundly, it means that the interests and purposes of each individual child are important, and it is the function of the school to find ways and means of carrying them out.

There is a vast amount of difference in capacities, experiences, and rates of growth, and no standardized procedure will serve the needs of every child in the complete development for which modern education strives. The individual is the important consideration. Variety is expected and desirable.

Purpose 4. To cultivate habits of analytical thinking. The complexities of modern society can no longer be met by an educative experience based upon the acquisition of a wealth of factual material alone. It is the function of the school to develop powers of analytical thinking by which the problems of today or tomorrow may be evaluated and analyzed. Even the most forward looking educator can not anticipate what conditions will exist in the future. It does lie within the power of education, however, to develop keen, well ordered, analytical habits of thought about genuine problems in preparation for more effective control of future problems. Through a varied program of integrated units of work which demand pupil initiative and responsibility, and which depend upon research by the child for the collection of data essential to thorough understanding, the school may develop habits of analytical thinking.

Purpose 5. To acquire command of the common knowledges and skills essential to effective living. Modern education does not neglect the importance of acquiring command of the common knowledges and skills. These knowledges and skills may be grouped as follows:

1. The *tools of learning*, including reading, writing, spelling, and arithmetic
2. The *motor skills*, involving the use of the hand—crayon, pencil, tools of cutting and measuring, and the manipulation of materials
3. *Oral expression* emphasizing particularly ability to talk correctly and naturally, with clear, pleasing tone quality and careful enunciation
4. Knowledge of the facts essential to an understanding of man's relation to his natural and social environment.

Such skills can not be acquired with equal readiness by all members of a group in a specified time. Such learning should be geared to the individual. Children should be protected from competition with one another because such competition results in feelings of inferiority.

The only competition permissible in the modern school is an effort to improve the individual's own former record.

Purpose 6.   To develop appreciation for and desire to seek beauty in its many manifestations.   The school aims to develop an ever increasing capacity for appreciation of beauty, excellence, and the worthy contributions of all artists to the culture of modern civilization.

The school should develop and stimulate imagination and creative power.   The creative impulse expresses itself most freely in music, in art, in the rhythmic expression of the dance, in literature, in dramatics, but it can express itself in numberless forms, in all the activities of the school day.

Keen sensitiveness to beauty in its myriad forms gives substance and richness to life. We are in a world of beauty, "immersed in beauty," as Emerson puts it, and most of us are missing the beauty around us that might be such a source of solace and joy in helping us meet the problems of life.   Our great cultural inheritance from the past should find us receptive.   Complete development for children must certainly include what is great and beautiful in the world of art— that world in which all may possess the treasure who have eyes to see and ears to hear.

THE INTERMEDIATE GRADE CHILD

Assuming a normal rate of progress, a child will be nine or ten years of age when he reaches the fourth grade.   The present program of adjusting education to individual capacities and needs rather than adjusting the child to artificial standards of attainment in school subjects means unretarded progress through the grades.   By the end of the sixth grade the child will be twelve or thirteen years old.   The physical, mental, social, and emotional characteristics of this period of childhood must form the basis of an educational program scientifically constructed upon biological and psychological foundations.

Physical Development

The child passes through significant modifications in physical structure during these years.   It is a period of rapid growth in the size of bones.   The structure of the bones changes during the period, the mineral content increases and the frame begins to assume the form it will take for life.   The change in stature due to bone development and bone adjustment is the preeminent characteristic of these years.

The period shows a corresponding growth in muscles.   At birth, muscles constitute 23.4 per cent of the weight of the body; at eight years 27.2 per cent; at fifteen years, 32.6 per cent.[1]   The rapid change

---

[1] L. A. Pechstein, and A. Laura McGregor. *Psychology of the Junior High School Pupil.*   Boston: Houghton Mifflin Company, 1924, p. 13.

in bone and muscle structure and the unequal rate of change, frequently results in poor coordination. Many children are awkward, angular, and are physically ineffective. Control results through development of the nervous system.

By the time the child is eight years old, the brain has reached nine-tenths of its final weight. The nervous structure of the child in the middle grades, then, is ready for more minute development.

These years witness a great change in the vital organs. The increased growth of bones and muscles require an increased blood supply. The blood must pass through the lungs in the process of purification, hence a greater lung capacity is required. To provide the additional blood supply, more food must be assimilated, hence larger and stronger digestive organs develop. The increased blood supply throws additional work upon the heart. This period is characterized by a rapid increase in the force of the heart.

The teacher must be aware of the vast physical changes taking place in the child. The prepubescent period is the time when the development of the permanent teeth is completed. Proper attention to the child's teeth at this period is particularly important. Studies of the teeth of school children indicate that this is a period of great neglect. "In New York the ages below ten averaged one-third more carious teeth than the ages above ten. By the age of fourteen, however, so many of the permanent teeth are decayed that the number of defective teeth per child may be as great as at six or seven."[1]

The increased lung capacity is a source of danger. Improper development of the respiratory system may result in pulmonary disorders. The increase in the size of the heart may give rise to various difficulties of which the teacher needs to be aware. An efficient program of health and physical education is profoundly important at this period of child development. One of the most important studies concerning child growth was made by Dr. Bird T. Baldwin. Teachers should be aware of the significant conclusion that there is a wide range in the rate of development in physiological maturity of boys and girls. Children who are chronologically of the same age may vary from four to five years in maturity. It is particularly valuable for the teacher to note that Baldwin definitely establishes the fact that *physical* maturity is usually accompanied by *mental* and *social* maturity. "Rapid, healthy growth favors good mental development, and therefore the healthy growing child should have plenty of physical and mental exercise."[2]

[1] Lewis M. Terman, and John C. Almack. *The Hygiene of the School Child.* Boston: Houghton Mifflin Company, 1929, p. 173.

[2] Bird Thomas Baldwin. *Physical Growth and School Progress.* Washington: United States Bureau of Education Bulletin, 1914, No. 10, p. 97.

The Intermediate Grade Group

A recent writer in the field of educational psychology presents an interesting picture of some characteristics of the intermediate grade group:

The years of the early grades will cover mainly the span from the questioning age of pre-school life to the period of puberty and adolescence —a long stretch sometimes called the "big Injun age." The designation tells a long story. The bodily signs of sex maturity are not yet in evidence, and interests tend to keep boys and girls apart rather than to draw them together. Rivalry rather than cooperation is strong. Boys will still be larger and stronger than girls and will excel them in the muscular dexterities.

Social pressures will have strongly differentiated the behavior and interests of the two groups, boys and girls. In both cases physical and intellectual development will not have reached a point where greater freedom is permitted; children released from the close supervision of the home emerge into the more impersonal supervision of teachers and administrators. This impersonal regime may often be one for which they have been ill-prepared by the fond attentions of parents, uncles and aunts, and considerable rubbing off of the sharp corners of individualism will be required.

The period has been described as one of "competitive socialization." Scorned by the adolescents of their acquaintance, who now seem like grown-ups, and in turn shunned by the younger children who seem now to be "babies," there is a strong tendency for like ages to flock together, and for the environment to be exploited by juvenile groups and "gangs." Play activities will now be very social in the sense that many individuals may take part. But there will be little subordination of individual prowess to the good of the group. Individual competition will be strong, but a keen need for the presence of an audience will be felt.

Boasting, bullying, teasing, showing off may be expected, and on the part of the boys considerable interest in exhibitions of fortitude, speed and strength, cleverness. Concern over features of form, finish, and grace will be low; excitement, speed, and adventure will be preferred. Livelier modes of intellectual play and games will also be appreciated. Collecting activities and interests will be keen and can easily be directed into useful channels.

From the point of view of school "discipline" the middle of the period, the 5th and 6th grades, will be the most taxing on the patience and serenity of the teacher. Sex curiosity, just developing, may lead to disapproved outlets, inquiries, mildly obscene talk and acts. The failure of high intellectual appreciation of the moral criteria of conduct will make behavior strongly influenced by individual loyalties. The general noisiness, roughness, and "savageness" of much of the behavior of this period has led to that quaint notion among early educators that children of this age were "recapitulating the savage pigmy" period in the devolopment of mankind. A large part of this impression is due to the physical vigor and restlessness of the period; to the equivocal status of being neither a baby nor a grown-up; and to the intellectual limitations which fail to grasp the conventional categories of social ethics except in the realm of individual and team interests.

Special influences at home do much to shape the behavior of children during this period. It is then that the effects of being an only child, a spoiled child, are most likely to bring the pupil into an overt clash with the social expectation. Mild neurotic tendencies may begin to show themselves in recognizable form, and the "problem child" and the "delinquent" become objects of school concern.

Excessive egocentricity and selfishness may be expected. Actual or fancied inferiorities of endowment or of social status may lead to indirect modes of adjustment, rather than to a frank facing of reality, and this is a period in which understanding rather than mere control may count for much on the part of the educator. Infantilism of conduct, failure to grow up emotionally, may in this period be frequently encountered and may receive either the proper adjustment or instead be more permanently fixed as the pattern of the individual attitude.

Mild speech disorders and other symptoms of "nervousness" are frequent during the elementary years, and often lead both to refractoriness of conduct and to misunderstanding on the part of teachers. There is likelihood that early tendencies to aggressiveness or to submission will in these years receive that sort of treatment which will either eliminate or fix them as permanent "traits" of the individual, whatever may have been their mode of origin.[1]

Individual Differences

The great contribution of educational psychology to the science of teaching is irrefutable evidence that children differ widely in health and physical vigor; in physiological maturity; in sensory perception particularly in seeing and hearing; in general intelligence; in emotional response; in interests; in out-of-school experiences; in attitudes toward school; in social maturity. The list of differences might be greatly extended but this enumeration will suffice to indicate the complexity of what is meant by the doctrine of individual differences.

Individual differences make of every child a special problem.

> One pupil may need to engage in basic perceptual experiencing, a second pupil may need additional drill, a third may need to be assigned learning exercises commensurate with his capacity to learn, a fourth may need an explanation or certain other remedial instruction and so on. The needs of individual pupils are so varied that a list of types does not seem feasible except when dealing with a restricted subject-matter field.[2]

Interests

The whole field of the interests of children in the intermediate grades is still largely unexplored. The research studies are rare and fragmentary which are available for the guidance of the teacher.

The teacher in the intermediate grades must rely on her own observation of the many interests of this period of childhood and capitalize upon her observation to adjust education to these interests.

The universality of the intermediate grade child's interest in collections is noted by some professional writers.[3] Its usefulness in the

---

[1] Harry L. Hollingworth. *Educational Psychology.* New York: D. Appleton and Company, 1933, pp. 454-457.

[2] Walter S. Monroe, and Ruth Streitz. *Directing Learning in the Elementary School.* Garden City, New York: Doubleday, Doran and Company, 1932, pp. 119-120.

[3] George E. Freeland. *Modern Elementary School Practice.* New York: The Macmillan Company, 1926, rev. ed., Chapter VIII. "The Development of a Natural Interest," pp. 190-204.

immediate processes of education can not be disputed and the influence of an interest in a childhood collection frequently persists through life.

There is no question that dramatic play is a powerful motive in these years.[1] This is a period of rapid emotional development and dramatization affords unequaled opportunity for emotional expression.

The interests of children of this period are authentically portrayed by that inimitable interpreter of boyhood, Mark Twain. No intermediate grade teacher should fail to take frequent advantage of that guide to insight into boy nature provided by Tom Sawyer and Huckleberry Finn.

Education as Personality Adjustment

The new psychology views education as personality adjustment.

> Today we are concerned not only with the academic child, the child who must acquire the skills of language and mathematics, the principles of science and the knowledge of history, but with the whole child, which will include his attitudes and ideals, his conflicts and inhibitions, his unified and integrated outlook on life and the many little habits and skills of social adaptation.[2]

The extent to which a child adjusts successfully to the demands of the school situation will determine his attitudes, interests, and personal integration.

> Many * * * studies indicate a substantial relationship between school achievement and desirable behavior which indicates either that satisfactory achievement has a salutary effect on personal adjustments as evidenced by behavior, or that poor adjustments become reflected in low achievement, and probably indicates both.[3]

Education which concerns itself merely with the academic is not fulfilling its responsibility of educating for a life of satisfactory adjustment. In this connection Watson says:

> There are those who pretend (whether at least they really believe it I never could quite decide) that life will be richer and happier for those who know better how to read efficiently, who know languages, philosophy, and mathematics. It is refreshing to note how little support, even in the academic group itself (of teachers), there is for such assumption.[4]

The mental health of the child is inextricably related to the instructional procedure. Out of the classroom experience will come those feelings of success and security or of failure and inadequacy which will determine the individual's habits of confidence or failure throughout his life. Methods of classroom instruction must be judged at every turn

[1] See Chapter XXII, Creative Play as an Integrating Activity.
[2] Percival M. Symonds. "The Contribution of Research to the Mental Hygiene Program for Schools," *School and Society*, XXXIV (July 11, 1931), 40.
[3] Percival M. Symonds. *Ibid.*, p. 40.
[4] Goodwin B. Watson. "Happiness Among Adult Students of Education," *Journal of Educational Psychology*, XXI (February, 1930), 79-109.

on the basis of their effect on the total results in personality development.

The significance of the mental hygiene problem is of particular concern to the teacher because "most of the problems arising in schools are educational taken in the larger sense, and few are so distinctly pathological as to require the services of a psychiatrist."[1] But that these problems of psychiatric maladjustment have far reaching social effect, is indicated in this authoritative statement:

> The responsibility of the school is apparent when one considers that it has been estimated that one out of every twenty individuals becomes a patient in a hospital for mental diseases during the lifetime of a generation; that the chances of contracting a psychosis or severe incapacitating neurosis whether sent to a hospital or not, are somewhere near one in ten; and that the number of persons in prisons and reformatories at any one time is half as large as those in mental hospitals. A large number of those who in later life become criminal probably showed delinquent tendencies as problem children while in school.[2]

The teacher's attitude toward the child in these important years of his development should be one of scientific study and observation. A knowledge of his IQ is not enough. The teacher must know something of his total situation, of the influences which surround him in his home, of his companions, his games, his work outside of school, his interests, his ideals and his ambitions. The formation of character is in the final analysis the most significant outcome of all education. It is the constant responsibility of the school to provide conditions under which pupils live their school lives as conducive as possible to the best type of character development. "Character education is not a by-product of the educational process; it is the end product, all important, all inclusive."[3] The teacher must maintain an open minded spirit of willingness to readjust the school program and procedures in order to provide more completely for the integration of personality and the wholeness of development which is the goal of the new point of view in education.

THE IMPLICATIONS OF EDUCATIONAL PURPOSES AND THE NATURE OF THE CHILD IN SCHOOL PROCEDURES

The acceptance of these considerations has led to a program based upon units of work or centers of interest, to an integrated curriculum through which first hand experiences and rich vicarious experiences are participated in by every child in the classroom. This type of teaching in which the work is closely integrated was carried on successfully in the lower grades of the elementary schools before the implications on the upper levels were thoroughly accepted. Possibly this fact may be

---

[1] Percival M. Symonds, *op. cit.*, p. 47.
[2] Percival M. Symonds, *op. cit.*, p. 47.
[3] John A. Hockett. "A Point of View in Character Education," *California Journal of Elementary Education*, I (November, 1932), 34.

traceable to the influence of the kindergarten and nursery schools. Today it is interesting to see the evidence pointing toward integration on the high school and college levels. The modern elementary school has accepted the integrated program as the most effective means toward the end desired. How has the integrated curriculum changed the elementary school program?

Long periods of work have replaced the short unrelated periods when lessons were heard. The modern school program is flexible and varies from day to day. Children in the classrooms are grouped according to needs and abilities and old *grade standards* are rapidly losing their former significance. These groups are not static, but vary with the changing activities and with the development of the child.

Textbooks are but a part of the materials necessary to carry on an integrated unit of work; pictures, books of all types, maps, large pieces of paper, paints, scissors, tools, wood, specimens from nature, and music are all necessary. The curriculum is a moving, growing thing.

The establishment of skills in arithmetic, spelling, handwriting, and the formal side of language is handled through individualized instruction. Desirable skills must become automatic. Each child is tested and placed according to his achievement, regardless of the grade to which he may have been assigned, and is allowed to progress at his own rate in these tool subjects.

The content subjects are participated in as a social undertaking, each child contributes to the whole according to his own interests and abilities. The skills acquired in the tool subjects function in this large center of interest, around which the modern program is built.

Reading in an Integrated Program

The reading program is interwoven with the entire curriculum. Reading involves history, geography, spelling, art, literature, number relationships, and oral and written language.

Mastery of the mechanics and establishment of skills in reading are individual problems and must be provided for in a very definite way. Practice must be given in meaningful, interesting situations throughout the day in order that these skills may function. The reading difficulty of material made available to children must be comparable to their reading abilities. The mechanical difficulties must not defeat the purpose for which the material is to be read. Neither meaningful information nor love for reading can be obtained from a book far too difficult in content for the child. If the ultimate goals are sufficiently attractive, obstacles will tend to be surmounted, but the growth must be a gradual one. The day is past in the modern elementary school when reading was in terms of a particular reader with so many pages to cover. The need of quantities of supplementary material in the activity program has made the library the heart of the modern elementary school. It has been truly said: "We learn to read by reading."

Such a reading program implies teaching materials suitable to meet varying needs, a library rich in titles, a standardized testing program, adequate space, library tables, charts, a felt need for information, and, most important of all, it calls for a teacher who sees the value of such a program and is capable of carrying it forward.

Social Studies in the Integrated Program

What are the implications of integration in the field of social studies? In no subject is the teacher of today charged with heavier responsibilities than in teaching of the social studies. For many years the separate subjects which are included in social studies have been taught. But it is no longer sufficient to teach only the factual material from these subjects; schools are charged with the responsibility of functional interpretation of these subjects.

To have one's head stored with facts does not bespeak good citizenship. The ability to make decisions concerning these facts, use judgment, and develop power to think are far more important. Facts of today cease to be facts tomorrow. The development of a broad-minded, tolerant attitude and of a real desire to participate in the solution of the problems of society will be of value today, tomorrow, and all through life. This implies practice in cooperative undertakings, sharing of information, impassionate discussions, a consideration of basic social and economic conditions. Typical units of work undertaken in the more progressive schools and the topics listed in the newer types of textbooks are representative of the problems under discussion today. For example, the development of transportation; cotton over the world; why our country is a good place in which to live; changing civilizations in the modern world; or the chief factors in the high standard of living in the United States, are all familiar inclusive centers of interest.

A social studies classroom in a modern school has an abundance of carefully chosen instructional material available; maps, reference books, pictures, construction materials—it is, in fact, a laboratory. That growth advances only by reconstruction of experience is part of the philosophy of Dewey. In the integrated program children express the history of the race through drama, through art, through music, and through language, recreating until race experience becomes meaningful to them. Socially desirable behavior comes through participation in school life; the child faces real life situations in an environment well within his interest, clubs, banking, sports, or the school newspaper.

The memorizing of the rivers and mountains of Japan or China would have little social value for a child, but the study of Pacific relations would be of inestimable value and have meaning to the child in the schools of California. An understanding of Pacific relations would involve the development of attitudes, an appreciation for the contributions made by Oriental civilizations, the implications of the policies of these Pacific neighbors, all of which would be essential to the active participation of citizens in California. The social studies period probably has more possibilities for integration than any other period in the day.

The auditorium period reflects the social studies, too. The oral and written language is replete with problems of social and economic interest. The school club with its parlimentary procedure, its committees responsible for ways and means, its recognition and consideration of the wishes of the majority, is meaningful experience in social behavior. The attitude in a school, that indescribable something which one feels at once in entering a school, indicates in a very real way the success with which real life values have come from the social studies program under way in that school.

The Language Arts in an Integrated Program

It has been said, ''The degree of mastery of language abilities is an index of the degree of civilization.''[1] The repression of the very skill which we wish to develop in children—the mastery of the mother tongue—was the constant concern of the traditional school. Many lovely bits of childlike expression were no doubt said to a doll or a toy because there was no place for this thing in the classroom of the formal school. The natural literary gift of children is preserved and stimulated in a modern school. The simple beauty of children's speech is too lovely to be lost. It will thrive only where there are ears to hear and the environment furnishes stimulation for practice. The classroom today is relieved of criticism and faultfinding, and is poignant with the earnest enthusiasm and eager interest of children, because there is something to say and a desire to say it.

The opportunities for both oral and written self-expression in an integrated program are rich. A class newspaper, letters of inquiry, a poem, a talk about things of vital interest, letters of invitation, discussion of where to find materials for the social studies, reports and discussions of material found, dramatization, consultations, the school club, are all natural situations in which language in all its beauty is given expression. Language development which is significant can in no way

---

[1] Lois Coffey Mossman. *Principles of Teaching and Learning in the Elementary School.* Boston: Houghton Mifflin Company, 1929, p. 173.

be limited to a set period. It must function throughout the entire program.

Childhood will have no difficulty with literature if it has a chance to develop its own native gifts in language. The truly child-centered school will make this possible.

Writing and spelling as a part of the language arts should be learned in relation to use. The need of the skill should be met in a real situation. The skill itself must be mastered and then given ample opportunity to function in an integrated program.

Formal grammar has been replaced to a great extent by functional grammar that explains errors to pupils and provides an intelligent basis for self correction.

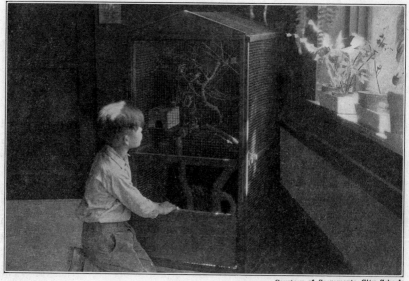

Courtesy of Sacramento City Schools

Education Based on Real Experiences

The Place of Science in the Modern Program

Children naturally love and are interested in the out-of-doors. The new school includes the beauties of the out-of-doors. There are excursions, there are collections in the classroom, there are life cycles evolving under the eyes of interested children. This understanding and appreciation of the beauties and wonders of the natural environment guarantees a solace and a refuge to every child, and can not be neglected in a school where all-round development of children is the basic concern.

Nature education is woven into every part of an integrated program. Social studies must perforce include a knowledge of fauna and flora. How can the silkworm be taught apart from the silk industry? How can the migration of salmon be taught apart from the work of fishermen? How can the glory of the miraculous appearance of Venus in the western sky be taught apart from a study of the globe? How can an appreciation of the majesty of the redwoods be separated from the problem of conservation? The wonders of nature are a part of the creative expression of poetry and prose; art depicts the beauties of nature in the environment.

To lead a child into the realization of his responsibilities for the intelligent use of his own life and his natural environment and to appreciate the beauty and mystery of nature can not be done in an hour set apart for this study, but must be reflected in all the hours of the day.

Esthetic Appreciations in the Intermediate Grades

The interpretation of all learning is influenced by acquaintance with the esthetic. There has accumulated through the ages a wealth of cultural treasures. This storehouse is the rightful inheritance of each individual. As he meets life, much satisfaction can come to him if he knows how others have interpreted similar experiences. It is the province of the school to bring children into this inheritance. This means that there must be much contact with music, art, and literature in the school room. The library, the story hour, rhythmics, and study of lives, customs, and contributions of peoples in other lands, the pictures on the walls of the school room, every activity undertaken should all contribute to a knowledge of this cultural heritage.

Art, music, and literature are a definite part of social studies, of language, of reading, and of dancing. These cultural subjects enrich the entire school program. The techniques of art, of music, and of literature should come when and as they are needed. Children are reading today without knowing the alphabet. They are sewing without knowing all the stitches. They are singing without knowing all the notes. Techniques in the cultural subjects are a means to further enjoyment, not an end in themselves. In attempting to express through the medium of music, art, or literature, children will find the need of the guiding principles of the arts. Such a point of view will make for economy in learning, as well as for joy in the mastery of the processes involved. Knowledge of this cultural heritage constitutes a vital part of education, and colors and enriches every activity in the day's program. The commonplaces of everyday experience are beautiful and satisfying if they have been interpreted to us by the poet and the artist.

Significant Procedures in the Child-Centered School

Such purposes and such a philosophy have profound significance in procedures in the schools. They mean the elimination of the evils of failure and nonpromotion; they guarantee that every child shall work to his fullest capacity and in accordance with his own nature and that the teacher will secure satisfactory results through the child's interest and not by holding over the child the disintegrating fear of failure.

These purposes imply reorganizing the schools so that children may have an opportunity to exercise desirable social relationships; to develop powers of thinking through problems; to cultivate individual interests and aptitudes. They imply an emphasis on that subject matter which makes living a rich, colorful, cultural adventure in the realms of art, music, and literature. They imply watchfulness over every environmental influence which might be subversive to the child's complete physical, mental, social, and spiritual realization.

CHAPTER II

THE ORGANIZATION OF THE INTERMEDIATE GRADES[1]

THE PROGRAM OF ACTIVITIES IN A PROGRESSIVE SCHOOL

The Importance of a Good Program

The making of a program, daily, weekly, or yearly, is one of the most important tasks of every teacher. The program of a school reflects the philosophy of education, the concept of method, and the degree to which the work of the school has been analyzed by the teacher, whether she is conscious of these implications or not. Programs must be adapted to the particular situation in which the teacher finds herself; they can not be turned out "ready made." Program making is a much more difficult task for the teacher in the small rural school, because of the heterogeneous ages and grades, than in the large urban school.[2]

Any well organized, well regulated group of workers finds a workable plan of procedure indispensable to the effective endeavors of every member concerned. A good school program provides appropriate place and desirable emphasis for the various activities to be undertaken as a part of the life of the school, and it encourages related and purposeful work toward desirable educational goals. It recognizes and provides for individual needs through the day.

The Legal Requirements Affecting the Intermediate Grade Program

There are certain legal requirements which must be taken into consideration by the teacher as she plans her schedule.

The minimum school day in grades four to eight, inclusive, in elementary schools is 240 minutes.[3] The school day for the intermediate grades is from 9:00 a.m. until 4:00 p.m., with a noon recess of one hour from 12:00 until 1:00 o'clock, unless otherwise provided for by the local school board.[4]

A minimum of 50 per cent of each school week must be devoted to reading, writing, language study, spelling, and arithmetic in grades one to six, inclusive.[5]

---

[1] Contributed by Ada York, County Superintendent of Schools, San Diego County, and Gladys L. Potter, Assistant Chief, Division of Elementary Education and Rural Schools, California State Department of Education.
[2] Hollis L. Caswell. *Program Making in Small Elementary Schools*. Nashville, Tennessee: George Peabody College for Teachers, 1932.
[3] *California School Code*, section 3.761.
[4] *Rules of California State Board of Education*, section No. 1C.
[5] *California School Code*, section 3.762.

To fail to comply with these legal requirements would be almost impossible, because of the very nature of the school situation. The functioning of skills such as those specified assures their constant inclusion in whatever learning activity may be going on in the classroom. Teachers and pupils together should analyze the large units of work undertaken, and note the scope of the experience in terms of the particular subjects specified by law.

The Implications of a Child-Centered Program

Modern education is based upon a child-centered school. Subject matter is integrated into units of work, large centers of interest or "areas of experience." The modern curriculum is adapted to the needs of the individual child. One of the most significant and far reaching implications of such a philosophy is that program making can not be considered only in terms of a day or even a week, but must take the form of a long time plan, with the desired goals clearly defined. The daily program, if it is to recognize the interests of children, must be flexible and variable, full of purposeful activity, planning, evaluation, research, and creative expression. Long periods of work have replaced the ten minute periods when factual material gathered from a single textbook was given back to the teacher in parrotlike fashion.

Standards and plans are essential to any program, and particularly in the flexible and informal type of program of the progressive school.

In order to insure the greatest educative value in any program, the children should be allowed to cooperate in formulating these standards and to assume responsibility based upon genuine interest in carrying them out. If allowed to be sincere, children will tend to set aside periods of time for "doing" the various things that are to be accomplished.

What an Intermediate School Program Should Include

A well integrated program for the intermediate grades in a child-centered school should include the following:[1]

1. A conference time
2. Time to acquire techniques, skills, and knowledges
3. Time in which to solve problems
4. Time to enjoy the esthetic
5. Time to do creative and constructive work
6. Unassigned time
7. Time for recreation and play

---

[1] Lois Coffey Mossman. *Principles of Teaching and Learning in the Elementary School.* Boston: Houghton, Mifflin Company, 1929, pp. 8-9.

A conference time. This is an opportunity for teachers and children to talk over the plans for the day's work. An evaluation of what has been accomplished in periods, what additional work needs to be done, plans for doing it, materials to be used, and what part each child is to have in the activity, are all problems for discussion in the conference period. Often it seems necessary to have two such periods in the day; one following directly after the activity period, and the other at the beginning of the day. The evaluation which goes on in this period is of inestimable value in keeping the work of the day vital and worth while. Standards should be kept high and any worthless activity or apparent waste of time on the part of individual children should be discussed and passed upon by the group.

During the conference period the teacher has a chance to develop interests and guide the thinking of the children. Responsibility for the use of time and skill in using it are important educative values not to be overlooked in this period.

Time to acquire techniques, skills, and knowledges. Children should learn subject matter in relation to experiences. Skills must be acquired in reading, spelling, language forms, use of reference material, and use of number, in order that their use may be efficient in the activities undertaken.

Because of the wide variety of pupil capacities, individual instruction is most efficient in the tool subjects. This period when each child is progressing at his own rate offers an opportunity for the teacher to guide development in: initiative, as the child goes ahead with his own task; responsibility, as the child assumes the obligation for completing the task; accuracy, as the child checks and compares his work; judgment and habits of analytical thinking, as he appraises his work and decides whether he is ready for a check-up test before beginning new work.

This should be a teaching period for the teacher as well as a work period for the child. To perfect skills, real teaching must have been done; continued testing and checking will not clear up the difficulties. Some schools refer to this as the period for *drills and skills*.

Time in which to solve problems. All life situations are full of challenging questions. Learning to make wise decisions is of supreme value. Problem solving is a daily experience which develops judgment, thoughtfulness, and initiative on the part of children. Science, history, geography, and industry all offer vital problems. Children of intermediate age are curious, eager, investigating, and often skeptical, unless concrete evidence is produced. The place of the teacher in such a period is in guiding, stimulating, encouraging, and challenging pupils to a solution of their own problems. The opinions offered by the class should be kept relevant; facts presented should be authentic; materials must be at hand in which to delve and search for answers to moot questions. The proper guidance of children in problem solving offers an opportunity for real teaching. To form habits of analytical thinking is one of the major objectives of elementary education, and practice must be given in meaningful situations if we are to insure a trained citizenry for tomorrow, able to meet perplexing problems in an analytical way.

Time to enjoy the esthetic. In order to love the beautiful, children must be brought into contact with it. People tend to like the familiar, and it is highly desirable that children of all grades have much contact with music, art, and literature. Acquaintance with the arts should

Courtesy of Sacramento City Schools

Solving Problems Through Wide Reference Reading

come in relation to the experiences they interpret, and the task of the school is to expose "children to the beautiful under conditions that are so satisfying that they will want more." [1]

The gregarious tendencies in children of the intermediate grades and their sensitivity to social approval give the teacher an opportunity to further the love and appreciation for the arts. Association with a teacher and classmates who love the beautiful contributions in the field of art creates a similar appreciation in each child.

This period of enjoyment of the esthetic values should be used as a final interpretation of any worth while experience in the social studies,

---

[1] Lois Coffey Mossman, *op. cit*, p. 255.

nature study, or other content subject. It should be borne in mind that the impulse to express an idea in a beautiful way follows, rather than precedes, a very rich experience. Beautiful interpretations of life experiences are worthy of study, and should be given ample place in the program.

Time to do creative and constructive work. If the time allotment previously discussed has been well filled with experiences with the cultural side of living, the more productive will be this period of creative and constructive work. The more beautiful an experience is, the more desire we have to express it in some satisfying form. Real learning

Courtesy of Sacramento City Schools

A Demonstration Bee Hive

comes in recreating ideas or experiences. The child seeks a medium that will convey his feelings. This period should be in no sense a compulsory one where poetry *must* be written, songs composed, or a picture drawn. The outcomes of this period will depend upon the number of worth while things that are a part of the in and out of school experience of the children. If the outcomes are poor, the teacher should enrich the life of the school, that her group may have fuller and wider experiences upon which to draw for creative expression. Creative efforts should not be limited to the field of the fine arts. Whether working in wood, clay, or reading books and discussing them, the expression of self is a creative art. It is only through being allowed to give his own interpretation and express his own feelings that growth in creative work will come about for a child.

The atmosphere of the school room during this period and at all times should be conducive to unrestrained expression. The child should not be asked to place his creation in unsympathetic hands. There should be true appreciation for the contribution of each one. The school paper may be the medium for expression. The auditorium period affords an opportunity for many contributions. A class period following an excursion may furnish an atmosphere conducive to sympathetic sharing and contributing.

Courtesy of Sacramento City Schools

Editing the School Newspaper

Unassigned time. This should be considered a time when individual children or small groups of children may have an opportunity to do the various things for which they are responsible to the entire group, or to devote themselves to interests that need further time and study.

The conference period should plan carefully with groups and with individuals in order that the fullest possible use of this unassigned time may be made. Interest is the driving force that will make such a period worth while and productive.

The environment of the classroom must offer rich opportunities for growth during this period. An abundance of suitable books, pictures, materials, maps, tools, nature products, must be available for reporting, summarizing, construction, illustration and experimenting. The teacher of the intermediate grades must have varied interests, be active, and dynamic, and alert to the values in the wide variety of children's interests. She should do some of her best teaching during this unassigned period when children are engrossed in their interests.

Time for recreation and play. Human happiness and social usefulness depend upon sound bodies. Health is a primary objective of modern education. The stimulation which comes from a program vitally interesting to every child concerned may be taxing, and it is essential that sufficient relaxation and play shall be provided. The physical education program should include not only the required

Courtesy of River School, Butte County

All Pupils of a One Room School in a Pyramid

twenty minutes of instruction[1] but a plan for a well balanced day.[2] Frequent periods of relaxation when every child lies or sits quietly for a few minutes, occasional provision for rollicking games or songs will break the tension of work. Freedom to move about in an activity type of program, thus using the large muscles of the body, offers one means of physical release. This time provided for recreation and play may be longer some days than others, depending upon the nature of activity going on in the classroom.

---

[1] *California School Code,* section 3.730.
[2] N. P. Neilson, and Winifred Van Hagen. *Manual of Physical Education Activities for the Elementary Schools of the State of California.* Sacramento: California State Department of Education, 1929.

Such scheduling will take care of the sorts of values contained in the traditional subjects, but it places the emphasis upon the functional learning of them.

Terminology

Terminology in a schedule is not of as much significance as the children's attitude toward the use of time. What the teacher *calls* her time allotments is of little note, but to what extent children are developed along desirable lines is highly important.

The place in the daily program accorded the various subject matter is not of as much moment as the time allotment allowed for essential activities to be provided for. On the sample programs submitted indications have been made to the seven periods here suggested, in order that the teacher may be aware at all times of the value of functional learning in her teaching.

SAMPLE PROGRAMS FOR INTERMEDIATE GRADES

It is important that teachers read carefully the discussion under each subject matter head in this volume before attempting to interpret these programs. It has been stated that *programs must be adjusted to particular situations; they cannot be ready-made.* The suggestions given have been used successfully by teachers and are presented for guidance with the thought that they may be adapted to local situations.

Suggestions for Time Allotment in the Intermediate Grade Program

Opening period. (1, 3, 4)[1] Time: 10 to 20 minutes. Routine matters must perforce take a part of this time. The most valuable part of this period should be the friendly greetings and interchange of ideas between members of the group in a natural way.

Provision for individuals to tell about the event or discovery which is consuming their immediate interest will do much to eliminate the problem of divided interest as the work of the day is undertaken. The teacher should be constantly alert to evidences of insecurity or home conflict that may color the entire experience of the day for a particular child unless his mind is relieved or he is put at ease and given a feeling of confidence. This first period should be one of the happiest and most significant in the day if proper use is made of the possibilities inherent in it.

This period may be lengthened to include a more detailed conference period or shortened to allow time for a period of health instruction during the early part of the day.

---

[1] Numbers in parentheses refer to the items listed under "What an Intermediate School Program Should Include," p. 20.

Reading skills. (2, 4, 6) Time: 45 to 60 minutes. This period should be used for establishing skills in reading. It should be primarily a teaching period and the major portion of the time should be devoted to *reading* rather than a recounting of what has been read or futile search for material to be read.

Children should be grouped according to ability in reading. If more than one grade is in a classroom, grade lines should be disregarded in following such a plan. Three groups can be handled efficiently in a 45-minute period in either a graded class of fourth, fifth, or sixth grade pupils, or in an ungraded room by a plan of alteration.[1]

This can well be a period in which data are gathered for a unit of work in the social studies, or a report in the language arts, or for club work. Weaknesses of individuals or groups should be corrected, and needed techniques established during this period. Free reading and use of the library is a legitimate part of the reading period.

Reading is a part of every other subject. Some reading skill is in use every period of the day. These skills must be well established to insure efficient use of this tool of learning.

Language arts. (2, 4, 5) Time: 60 minutes. The teaching of spelling, penmanship, or language should be in relation to its need. For that reason spelling can not be separated from written language, and written language and penmanship in turn are interdependent.[2]

The emphasis in this hour will vary according to needs. Definite spelling teaching, instruction in handwriting, and practice in oral and written language should be provided for during this period. Spelling can be taught most effectively by individual instruction, as can the formal side of language. These are skills that must be acquired, and the rate of acquisition varies with the various capacities of children.

The functioning of these subjects is a part of every other period. An oral report in the social studies should exemplify the teaching done in the language arts period. Legible penmanship should be regarded as important all through the day.

In considering the amount of time which shall be devoted to these subjects, the interrelation and integration with the entire curriculum should be borne in mind. Language arts can in no way be pigeonholed and taught only in a specified period; it must permeate everything done in the school.

---

[1] See complete discussion of Grouping in *Suggested Course of Study in Reading and Literature for Elementary Schools*, State of California Department of Education Bulletin, No. 13, Part II, July 1, 1932, pp. 5, 61.

[2] See *Suggested Course of Study in Oral and Written Expression for Elementary Schools*, State of California Department of Education Bulletin, No. 15, November 1, 1933.

Courtesy of Lone Pine School, Inyo County

A Small Rural School Is Proud of Its Orchestra

Arithmetic. (2, 3) Time: Not more than 40 minutes. Individual instruction is the most efficient way in which to insure mastery of the skills in arithmetic. Group instruction may be used when the number of individuals ready for a particular explanation at the same time makes that method more expedient. The amount of time allowed in the program for arithmetic should vary with the degree of accomplishment of the children concerned. Processes should be automatic. The teacher should plan her time so that she is free to circulate, give help where it is needed, check accuracy of work, and test accomplishments.

Healthful Living. (1, 2, 3, 4, 6, 7) Time: A minimum of 20 minutes. The California School Code requires that at least 20 minutes a day be devoted to physical education.[1] A part of the unapportioned time of the school day may be added to this to provide for rest periods, mid-morning lunch, and definite instruction in healthful living. This period will not always be of the same length.

Healthful living is a vital consideration in each moment of the day, in school and out. This period should supply the necessary knowledge to enable children to put health education into practice. The modern school assumes its full share of the responsibility in caring for the physical welfare of children while entrusted to its care.

Music, art, literature. (2, 3, 4, 5) Time: 30 to 40 minutes. This should be a period in which children become acquainted with as much of the art products as can be included. This does not mean that appreciations or acquaintances shall be limited to this period. Love of beauty should color every experience.

Techniques should always be learned as a means to an end, not an end in themselves; but one cannot go very far in the enjoyment of any field of art without knowing something of technique. Many children will never be creators of art products. They will not need a great deal of technique, but enough to make them intelligent consumers. It is the business of the school to serve both groups. Techniques should not be given in advance of needs. Music reading,[2] rote singing, picture study, art instruction,[3] appreciation lessons, poetry study, dramatics, and enjoyment of literature [4] should be included in this period.

Social studies, including nature study. (1, 3, 4, 5, 6) Time: 60 to 100 minutes. The center of interest around which the entire work of the school should be built is the social studies, including nature

---

[1] *California School Code,* section 3.734.
[2] See Chapter XX, Music.
[3] See Chapter XXI, Art.
[4] See Chapter XVII, Recreatory Reading.

study.[1] This should be the longest period in the day, full of variety of experiences. Children will be grouped according to the tasks in hand, and their individual interests. Construction work, creative expression, research, conference, problem solving, all are integral parts of this period. Frequently teachers have found it successful to place this period early in the day. The skills needed to carry forward this "core of the curriculum" can then be established in relation to this need. Other teachers use the entire afternoon for handling the wide variety of values that accrue from this central theme or unit of work upon which the interest of the entire group is focused.

The results of the reading period, the language arts period, the music or art period, will all function here. The re-creation of the lumbering industry in crayon and poster paint, or other similar expressions where knowledge gained is expressed in artistic and authentic fashion, is legitimately a part of this period. Map making, costuming, dramatics, debates, excursions, all phases of purposeful living are an integral part of this period in the schedule. The teacher must keep her goals in mind, keep the "doing" vital and worth while, and have her daily program serve to acomplish the more complete plan outlined in her weekly and yearly program.

A time for evaluation at the beginning or end of this period is most necessary and helpful to insure effective use of time throughout the period by each individual child.

THE YEARLY PROGRAM

The initial planning done by the teacher is the most significant part of a yearly school program. This initial plan is an essential part of the successful teacher's technique. She must have forethought and foresight and be able to judge the educative value in the activities in which her children are to engage. If children in the modern school are to *search* for information, rather than sit by passively while the teacher supplies it, time must be provided. If *variety* is to be given to insure well rounded development, adequate time must be set aside in the program for pupil planning and evaluation, reports, excursions, and creative expression. No time must be wasted in futile activities. If well rounded development is desirable, adequate provision for its accomplishment is justifiable in the yearly program.

The classroom teacher is guided by a course of study from which she chooses suggested units of work or large centers of interests which have proved applicable to other pupils of like age, grade, and interests as her own.

---

[1] See Chapter V, Social Studies, and Chapter VI, Science.

She must recognize all of the educational implications in the units suggested as they will contribute (1) to the development of her entire group, (2) to the development of individuals within that group.[1]

The nature of the unit will determine, to a great measure, its proportion of time in the year's program. For example: "Cotton Over the World" is a comprehensive, challenging unit which could include an exhaustive study of the cotton growing countries of the world; a detailed study of the cotton industry in all its ramifications in the United States; international trade; the manufacture of cotton cloth; clothing; national costumes; and climate and its relation to cotton production. Such a comprehensive unit would justify several months of time in the yearly program. Careful plans for utilizing all the educative possibilities must be made. The unit must not be carried beyond the point of interest with the children. Inconsequential leads evolving from the activity must be avoided without thwarting individual interests and needs within the group.

"The Life History of Insects" might typify a center of interest in nature study which would represent only a few weeks of time and interest. This latter unit might, however, be a related interest within the larger one just described as "Cotton Over the World," from the facts disclosing the destruction of cotton crops by the boll weevil.

It is evident from these two simple examples that there is a necessity for and a value in initial planning, if efficient use is to be made of school time and if well rounded development of children is to be the outcome of the year's program.

The children should and will take the initiative in many valuable activities that go on in the classroom, but the teacher must be prepared to "set the stage," to stimulate curiosity, to build background, to suggest, and to guide. She must be well informed and familiar with all available material. She must be conscious of the needs of the group. She must know at all times where she is going and why she is going that way.

It is not possible to set down a definite length of time which should be consumed by each unit of work. This must of necessity vary with the needs, abilities, and interests of the group, but an approximation should be made by the teacher on the basis of worth and extent of the unit. The units chosen by the teacher for her year's work must be such that a variety of experiences will be afforded the children engaged in carrying them out.

Check tests to ascertain the amount of worth while factual information gained through the centers of interest should be definitely planned before the units are undertaken.

---

[1] Lois Coffey Mossman, *op. cit.*, p. 13.

Suggestive units of work which might be undertaken by a fifth grade group in a year's time and the subject matter which might be included are given briefly in outline form:[1]

How WE TRAVEL (three or four months)

History of transportation
    Early peoples of Asia, Southern Europe, Africa
    The sea-going Norsemen
How the Old World found the New
The British Empire and its power
How the pathfinders opened the way westward to the Pacific—The Iron Horse
Relationship between inventions and the modern mode of living
How the world has grown smaller
Aviation—Byrd, Amundsen, Scott, Peary, Stefansson, Lindbergh
Aviation and migration of birds
Great rivers of the world and their influence on history

CHRISTMAS CUSTOMS (one month)

How Christmas customs reveal home life, religion, costumes, folk-tales, poetry, music, climate, and art of Germany, France, Italy, Norway, England, Mexico

SKY STUDY[2] (three weeks)

Rotation of the earth on its axis—Standard time belts—Zones
Revolution of the earth around the sun—Seasons
Phases of the moon—Tides
Recognition of planets
Recognition of Orion, Cassiopeia's Chair, Big Dipper, and other familiar constellations
Relationship of stars to travel
Use of compass
Old Greek and Roman stories
    Classic myths
    Poetry about stars

WOOL (three or four months)

Stockraising in Australia, South America, Western United States
Making cloth from wool—In pioneer days and present methods
Importance of wool industry today
Life of shepherds in ancient times—Customs, religion
Pastoral poetry—Twenty-third Psalm

---

[1] See also Chapter VII, Units of Work in Social Studies and Science.
[2] W. T. Skilling. *Sky Study.* Science Guide for Elementary Schools, I (November, 1934). Sacramento: California State Department of Education.

THE WEEKLY PROGRAM

The week's plan should include provision for extra curricula activities. Some of those which should be definitely provided for are:

Club meetings	Gardening activities
Auditorium periods	Library periods at school or at city or county library
Band or orchestra	School games
School newspaper	Community contacts by teachers and
Excursions	principal

To prevent confusion or duplication, the use of the auditorium or extra room in the school building for some of these activities should be scheduled for the week. Often the noise of some activity such as construction, band or orchestra may interfere with other groups engaged in enterprises needing quiet concentration, unless the weekly plans of the teachers are made in advance.

In addition to the value of scheduling extra curricula activities a week in advance, the teacher needs to think through her desired outcomes in relation to the unit of work undertaken. She must provide in advance for an environment with sufficient tools and supplementary reading materials, and plan for necessary committee work, individual responsibilities, and special interests, or other related activities, in order to assure maximum accomplishment of each week's work. This can not be done without a plan. It may be that on Monday the type of activities under way demands the use of the entire afternoon session for social studies. This means that on Tuesday and Wednesday, additional time must be provided for those phases of the program which were omitted on Monday. Or if the interest in making a frieze in nature study was at its height, this interest could be capitalized to include the art appreciation lesson which ordinarily was given on Thursday, and the period lengthened. The teacher may anticipate a need for graphs in social studies and devote a long arithmetic period to a mastery of this subject on Wednesday. She must plan to provide for the experiences omitted from the program at another time in the week. Notations should be made relative to the accomplishment of the week's program to guarantee regular, consistent growth. For example:

No time for this group on Thursday. Give them extra attention on Friday.

Letters written by pupils last week showed need for additional work on question marks, capitals, and paragraphs, before sending them to travel bureaus on Wednesday.

This group (give names) need extra time for spelling on Tuesday because of Monday's excursion.

Plans for auditorium program must be discussed with whole group on Tuesday so that committees may be assigned.

National Geographic Magazines available from library on Wednesday only. Longer period for social studies to include usual penmanship period. Extend penmanship period on Thursday.

A weekly plan, carefully thought through, will give the teacher an opportunity to anticipate her problems and the needs of the pupils. The plan must be flexible to be useful. It may need to be changed, but an initial plan is essential for desired outcomes.

A DAILY PROGRAM FOR INTERMEDIATE GRADES [1]

Time	Monday	Tuesday	Wednesday	Thursday	Friday

9:00 Informal greetings, routine matters, exchange of ideas, music, reports of interesting events, designed to give the teacher an opportunity to observe each child and to give children the chance to express those things in which their interest is great.

9:15 Social studies and nature study

Informal reports of committees or individuals as to the progress of their enterprises. Evaluation of work done. Plans and discussions of the work of the day. Appointing of committees, attention to the arrival of new material such as books from the library, material brought in by class members, notices on bulletin board about subject in hand. Construction work, art work, research work done by groups or individuals as planned. Oral reports or other material to be shared by the group given at the last of this period. Language arts and reading can not be divorced from social studies and nature study.

10:30 Healthful living

Health and physical education activities and free play. Nutrition program and rest period for those who need it.

11:10 Language arts

Oral and written expression, spelling, and handwriting skills and practice in the use of these skills through writing and presenting plays, and puppet shows, writing stories or poetry, reporting for the school newspaper, preparing reports for social studies period.

12:00 Lunch, rest, and directed playground activities

1:00 Arithmetic enterprises

This period should be largely devoted to individual instruction. Establishment of fundamental skills should be the purpose.

1:40 Music skills, appreciations, and rhythms

Harmonica bands, orchestra, glee clubs	Club meetings Use of auditorium Committee meetings	Creative abilities may be a part of work under way in social studies period; or a special interest, as pottery, weaving, or other craft work, or fine arts	Library period (2 days a week)

---

[1] Adapted from "Daily Program in the Child-Centered School," *Teachers' Guide to Child Development.* Compiled by the State Curriculum Commission. Sacramento: State Department of Education, 1930, pp. 355-356. The order of major activities indicated is immaterial.

2:10   Rest and recreation

2:20   Reading activities

> Reading groups on the basis of ability. Remedial work for children with special abilities. Free reading period. Reading research for enterprises in language arts, social studies, or nature study.

BIBLIOGRAPHY

CASWELL, HOLLIS L. *Program Making in Small Elementary Schools.* Division of Surveys and Field Studies. Nashville, Tennessee: George Peabody College for Teachers, 1932.

CLOUSER, LUCY WELLER, and OTHERS. *Educative Experiences Through Activity Units.* Chicago: Lyons and Carnahan, 1932, pp. 31–39.

Suggested Course of Study in Reading and Literature for Elementary Schools. State of California Department of Education Bulletin, No. 13, Part II, July 1, 1932.

Suggested Course of Study in Science for Elementary Schools. State of California Department of Education Bulletin, No. 13, Part I, July 1, 1932.

Suggested Course of Study in Social Studies for Elementary Schools (Revised). State of California Department of Education Bulletin, No. 13, October 1, 1933.

MONROE, WALTER S., and STREITZ, RUTH. *Directing Learning in the Elementary School.* Garden City, New York: Doubleday, Doran & Company, 1932. Chapter XIV.

MOSSMAN, LOIS COFFEY. *Principles of Teaching and Learning in the Elementary School.* Boston: Houghton, Mifflin Company, 1929.

Teachers' Guide to Child Development. Compiled by the State Curriculum Commission. Sacramento: California State Department of Education, 1930. Chapter IV.

CHAPTER III

THE TEACHER [1]

"What shall I have my child study?" asked an anxious mother of a wise friend. "It matters not so much what she studies as with whom she studies," was the sagacious answer.[2] Most of us would agree as to the strong element of truth in this statement, for, in the final analysis, the teacher is the determining factor as to the type of education which goes on in a classroom. We could with considerable justification measure our education by the number of inspiring, stimulating, and "human" teachers it has been our good fortune to have known.

THE TEACHER AND THE TRANSITION

The Teacher's Responsibility

Although the teacher's responsibility has always been heavy, this responsibility is becoming increasingly so as our society becomes more and more complex. We have entered a period when change is even more pronounced and rapid than it has been for generations; a period when society is adjusting and re-adjusting itself to conditions which have had no parallel in history; a period that is referred to as "a period of transition."

The modern teacher is being forced to be sensitive to these changes and also to the leadership that is attempting to guide our society from the chaotic condition of the present to a firmer foundation of a more rational economy. This necessitates, on the part of the teacher, a consciousness of the birth, growth, and convergence of new conceptions, new ideals, and new cultures, and an awareness that human values are undergoing a radical reinterpretation. If the teacher is to survive in the profession, indeed, if the institution of education itself is to survive, those who are active in the work must be willing and able to make effective adaptions to these changes.

Teacher Adaptation

In the total school situation, the teacher has four quite definite adaptations to make: first, the adaptation to each individual pupil's

---

[1] Contributed by Dr. Floyd F. Caldwell, Associate Professor of Education, State College, Chico, California.
[2] Charles McKenny. *The Personality of the Teacher.* Evanston, Illinois: Row, Peterson and Company, 1910, p. 36.

personality; second, an adaptation to the pupils as a classroom group; third, a personal, professional and social adaptation to the faculty and pupils in the total school community; and fourth, a personal, professional, and social adaptation to the immediate community and to the world at large.

The Teacher's Point of View

In making these adaptations, education should be conceived of as a vital, evolving, adventurous enterprise in which the teacher, the pupils, the community, and the nation are cooperatively engaged. If the teacher carries on with this concept uppermost in mind the chances are great that there will be mirrored in that teacher's personality those qualities of eagerness, of willingness, of compassion and cheerfulness, that will in turn generate these same qualities in those with whom that teacher comes in contact. Work will be carried on with the idea in mind that both the pupils and teacher are joint investigators of the fascinating world in which they live. A happy initiative, an originality, and an artful spontaneity of expression will be encouraged. The aim will be toward the development in pupils of a broad, vigorous expansiveness in thought, feeling, and action. There will be no place in the schoolroom for repression, slavish imitation, and fear. The

Courtesy of San Mateo County Schools

Time to Enjoy the Esthetic—The Teacher Is the Guide and not the Taskmaster

teacher will have faith in mankind and particularly in youth; a confidence of success for all children according to their abilities; a belief in and a pride in the task of teaching; a sincerity in the conviction that education is the foundation stone upon which a civilized society is built. The modern teacher knows that

> Real education humanizes man. It does so, not by moulding them into unthinking acceptance of pre-established patterns, but by stimulating them to a continuous reconstruction of their outlook on life.[1]

THE TEACHER IN THE CLASSROOM

As a Student and Guide

In the new education the teacher is no longer an oracle passing out mysterious knowledge to the pupils who in turn memorize it and pass it back with as little change as possible. The new teacher assumes the role of a learner who guides the inquiring minds of the pupils into the highways and byways of problem situations that arise and in which felt needs for solutions appear. Because of the fact that the teacher has acquired certain methods, skills, knowledge, associations, life experiences with the accompanying habits and attitudes, the opportunities are provided for leadership and guidance of the childish minds through the mazes of intricate discovery to the goals of solution and accomplishment.

The teacher who has caught the spirit and vision of the new education will feel an added responsibility and a greater challenge to provide for the pupils a type of guidance that will develop their personalities and characters to the fullest extent. This teacher will know that the processes of child development are extremely complex and will realize the necessity of studying and evaluating all the factors in the child's environment before the behavior of that child adequately can be understood, evaluated, and improved. For instance, merely giving pupils subject matter with a high moral tone will not develop character. It requires teachers with superior personal qualifications and training, a sound technique of teaching, a modern and dynamic curriculum, wise disciplinary measures, and a generally wholesome classroom and community environment.[2] Physical condition, personal interests, ambitions and fears—all play their part in varying degrees in character development.

---

[1] Boyd H. Bode. *The Educational Frontier*, William H. Kilpatrick, Editor. New York: The Century Company, 1933. p. 31.

[2] *The Classroom Teachers and Character.* Seventh Yearbook of the Department of Classroom Teachers. Washington: Department of Classroom Teachers of the National Education Association, 1932, p. 67.

THE TEACHER AND THE CURRICULUM

A Change in Subject Matter

During the next few years, the teacher will see a considerable shift of emphasis in subject matter, and some may feel that subject matter itself is doomed. This however, is not the case. Subject matter is losing its hold upon education, not because it is subject matter but because there is so much in the curriculum that is not vital to our present state of culture. We are not moving away from something to teach but toward something to teach that will be more vital.

A Change of Emphasis

Memorization of subject matter as such has little value unless, through that memorization, transfer and application contributions are made to the solution of life's problems. We have assumed that our past methods of educating the youth would insure that the adult would function intelligently and honestly as a citizen. This is a mistaken assumption. Our present social maladjustments can be attributed in large measure to the fact that our citizenry lacks *personal integrity,* it lacks character. We have not emphasized sufficiently the proper methods or the proper values.

The products of our schools have not had the character to function effectively in a civilization so complex and confusing as ours. Definite study must be made of the multiplicity of relationships which exist, not only upon child levels but upon adult levels as well. Effective methods and techniques must be developed and applied, and curricula content must be selected and organized in a manner that will insure a more effective and efficient product.

Here the teacher should function as an important force in leading society to a richer and more rational culture. To do this effectively, the teacher must have the ability to critically evaluate the socially good and socially bad elements in society and the social viewpoint well enough developed to generate enthusiasms that will create in that society interests for improvement. This can not be accomplished through a militant "reform" attitude but through the sympathetic enlistment of cooperative community effort.

Curriculum Content, Difficulty Level, and the Social Emphasis

The content of every subject in the curriculum should be carefully analyzed and material should be chosen primarily on the basis of its relative value in developing good and useful citizens. In this selection, however, the fact must not be overlooked that the content is on the level of the child's reading ability in order that interests be created and maintained and finer appreciations developed. Furthermore, the teacher must not be content in only getting the children to acquire knowledge and think through problems but it is necessary that the child be made to *feel* the results of events and conditions in terms of good or ill to humanity at large. In other words, the child should be made *conscious of society and its welfare.*

TEACHER-FACULTY RELATIONSHIPS

Social Relationships

A very close relationship exists between a teacher's personal and professional success. Health, happiness, and opportunities for advancement are very closely allied to the social relationships of the teacher. Furthermore, the teacher's life outside the classroom reacts upon and influences greatly the classroom teaching. The best teacher is one who not only is qualified by superior training and teaching skill, but who also is in continuous harmonious relationship with other members of the faculty. A broad knowledge of others' fields of endeavor contributes much to a definite "community of interest." A sympathetic understanding of other teachers' problems, ideals, attitudes, and subject matter objectives makes possible the development and maintenance of congenial relationships.

Professional Relationships

In a society such as ours, when competition is keen and the struggle for security is severe, the general welfare of the total teaching group is sometimes sacrificed on the altar of personal desires, ambitions and greeds. We must remember, however, that before a profession can rightfully be considered as such, there must be an organized body of ethics to which the members of that profession strictly adhere. If teaching is to enjoy the prestige of a profession, if teachers are to enjoy the recognition that is rightfully theirs because of the importance of the work and the training necessary for success, they must adhere carefully to a code which will give them, to some degree, this recognition. In order that teachers may know what is the proper procedure in their professional relationships with other members of their group, the National Educational Association has developed and published a code of ethics. A section of this code as it pertains to professional relationships is given below.

> Section 1. A teacher should avoid unfavorable criticism of other teachers except such as is formally presented to a school official in the interest of the school. It is also unprofessional to fail to report to duly constituted authority any matters which involve the best interests of the school.

Section 2. A teacher should not interfere between another teacher and a pupil in matters such as discipline or marking.

Section 3. There should be cooperation between administrators and classroom teachers, founded upon sympathy for each other's point of view and recognition of the administrator's right to leadership and the teacher's right to self-expression. Both teachers and administrators should observe professional courtesy by transacting official business with the properly designated person next in rank.

Section 4. The teacher should not apply for a specific position unless a vacancy exists. Unless the rules of the school otherwise prescribe, he should apply for a teaching position to the chief executive. He should not knowingly underbid a rival in order to secure a position; neither should he knowingly underbid a salary schedule.

Section 5. Qualification should be the sole determining factor in appointment and promotion. School officials should encourage and carefully nurture the professional growth of worthy teachers by recommending promotion, either in their own school or in other schools. For school officials to fail to recommend a worthy teacher for another position because they do not desire to lose his services is unethical.

Section 6. Testimonials regarding a teacher should be frank, candid, and confidential.

Section 7. A contract, once signed, should be faithfully adhered to until it is dissolved by mutual consent. In case of emergency, the thoughtful consideration which business sanction demands should be given by both parties to the contract.

Section 8. Due notification should be given by school officials and teachers in case a change in position is to be made.[1]

TEACHER-COMMUNITY RELATIONSHIPS

Man Becoming World Minded

The demand that the teacher be conscious of society as well as socially conscious is becoming more and more persistent. Because of the fact that the world is being made smaller, owing to the rapid development of better means of communication and transportation, a familiarity with the culture patterns of a world society is becoming a necessity. Where, in the past, the community's province was largely the community, today the community is in contact with and dependent in large measure upon what goes on in the world at large. The public is becoming, as a result, more world minded than at any time in history. It becomes necessary, therefore, that the teacher's horizon not only extend into the local community environment but must be periscoped into the realm of world affairs.

"Whole Child" Concept and the Community

If a pupil does not have worthy purposes and is failing to profit by the opportunities offered him in the classroom the teacher has an additional task with that pupil. Study must be made of the particular

---

[1] "Code of Ethics of the National Education Association," *Proceedings of the Sixty-seventh Annual Meeting of the National Education Association.* Washington: National Education Association, 1929, pp. 180, 181.

case and situation to see what has caused the failure and through this means determine methods by which the educative process *can* function properly. The responsibility has been broadened to include the whole child's personality as it reacts in a world society. Nothing that effects the welfare of the child can be ignored. If social agencies are failing to function, it is, in part at least, the teacher's concern to aid so that they can function. This broadening of duty entails, of course, the danger of frictions arising in communities where social readjustments are difficult to make, but the skilful and tactful teacher can accomplish much by quiet persistence and careful judgment.

Community Educational and Non-Educational Agencies

The influences which affect the child are often bewildering and extremely difficult to analyze. Among the important items in the environment are the home, the church, out-of-school companions, organized non-commercial recreational, and commercialized agencies such as motion pictures, the press and the radio. Considerable progress is being made in organized study of these influences and the opportunity is provided for the teacher to obtain many helpful suggestions from the published reports of such studies.[1]

Enlistment of Community Cooperation

Likewise, much work is being done in developing ways and means by which the community and the schools can be brought closer together. The following list gives specific ways in which the public schools have been cooperating with the home and other community agencies in furthering a phase of the child's educational development.[2]

a. Creating new interests
b. Helping the less fortunate
c. Using home duties to teach responsibility
d. Securing better opportunities for social contacts
e. Home visitation projects
f. A cooperative courtesy campaign
g. Educating parents through the press
h. Local business firms as visitation laboratories

Ethics and Teacher-Pupil-Community Relationships

As there are certain codes to be considered and adhered to in teacher-faculty relationships, likewise are there codes developed concerning teacher-pupil-community relationships. Space does not permit the inclusion of the complete list but a few of the more important ones follow.

[1] See Bibliography at end of chapter.
[2] For additional suggestions see *Character Education*. Tenth Yearbook of the Department of Superintendence. Washington: Department of Superintendence of the National Education Association, 1932, pp. 337–344.

Section 1.   The schoolroom is not the proper theatre for religious, political, or personal propaganda.   The teacher should exercise his full rights as a citizen but he should avoid controversies which may tend to decrease his value as a teacher.

Section 2.   The teacher should not permit his educational work to be used for partisan politics, personal gain, or selfish propaganda of any kind.

Section 3.   In instructional, administrative, and other relations with pupils, the teacher should be impartial, just, and professional.

Section 4.   The professional relations of the teacher with his pupils demand the same scrupulous guarding of confidential and official information as is observed by members of other long-established professions.

Section 5.   The teacher should seek to establish friendly and intelligent cooperation between the home and the school.

Section 6.   The teacher should not tutor pupils of his classes for pay.

Section 7.   Members of the teaching profession should dignify their calling in every way.   A teacher's own life should show that education does ennoble.

Section 8.   A teacher should not act as an agent, or accept a commission, royalty, or other reward, for books or supplies in the selection or purchase of which he can influence, or exercise the right of decision; nor should he accept a commission or other compensation for helping another teacher to secure a position.[1]

THE TEACHER AND RESEARCH

Value to the Teacher

There has been a growing recognition the last few years of the values to be derived from including classroom teachers in the work of evaluating what is being done in teaching and in finding new ways to improve our present practices.[2]   It seems reasonable to conclude that active interest and participation in research studies creates new interests for the teacher in work that might otherwise become routine; that training and experience gained in research methods results in professional improvement and greater facility in reading educational material.   Furthermore, the teacher is made to feel and actually becomes more a part of the whole educational organization.   If research is properly conceived and pursued, teachers could make a very definite contribution to their own advancement, own interests, and to educational knowledge in general.   Also, through cooperative efforts of teachers in the field and of teacher training institutions much could be done to encourage a rapid readjustment of curricula and teaching practices in answer to the new demands of our present social order.

[1] "Code of Ethics of the National Education Association," *op. cit.*, p. 179.
[2] Bess Goodykoontz. *The Classroom Teacher as a Research Worker.* Fifth Yearbook, Department of Classroom Teachers.   Washington: National Education Association, p. 294.

Types of Research for Teachers

There are certain types of research and certain problems to be studied that fall very definitely within the teacher's province. A few suggestions which may be considered are:

1. Analyzing and organizing the steps in a learning situation
2. Testing the effectiveness of methods of teaching
3. Evaluating new units of curriculum materials
4. Making case studies of pupils' performances
5. Retesting reported experiments of other workers

THE HEALTH OF THE TEACHER AND PUPIL

Mind and Body as Interacting Entities

As the teacher is vitally concerned with the individual pupils in the classroom, it is necessary that there be a comprehensive understanding of the essential elements involved in continuous progressive development. This necessitates a careful study of the principles concerned in both mental and physical hygiene. The teacher must at all times be conscious of the fact that the mind and body are interacting entities each revolving about and dependent upon the other. Modern psychology emphasizes the interdependence of physical and mental functions. The teacher must teach that health is something which everyone must learn to maintain through his own efforts.

Courtesy of San Joaquin County Schools

Recreation Is Essential to Good Mental Health

Mental Balance and Its Relationship to Teaching

There is a constant interplay and clash of personalities in the classroom and the teacher's personality may be responsible for some of the difficulties which arise. Teachers must be able to study critically their own minds, their actions, attitudes and ideals, and to evaluate their effect upon others.[1] For example, the voice is an extremely important factor in the emotional control of children. A high pitched, rasping, nervous voice will create attitudes and emotional behavior in children which are extremely undesirable, while a rich and well modulated voice is identified with calmness, quietness, and self-control.[2] Mental soundness and poise have something contagious about them. Teacher personality balance is the best insurance that desirable characteristics will be maintained in the pupils.

PROFESSIONAL PREPARATION

Need for Comprehensive Professional Preparation

It is quite evident that in this new education, the teacher stands forth in new importance. The task of teaching presupposes a broad background of rich experience and a well rounded professional preparation integrated upon a ground of rich and varied culture. Much emphasis must be placed upon the social sciences but certainly not to the exclusion of other fields of knowledge. In the college preparation, enough of an insight into a large number of fields should be obtained in order that study may be pursued in those fields independently, for, new instruments constantly must be sought that will contribute to a more adequate appreciation of the various aspects of life. It is a far cry from the teacher who thanked the Lord that, "I got my education before I started to teach," to the modern teacher of today.

Importance of Physical and Natural Sciences

The physical and natural sciences have a very definite contribution to make to the elementary teacher, for they provide, to a large extent, the eyes through which the mysteries of life about us may be investigated. Furthermore, these sciences provide definite methods of analysis which make possible a more unbiased approach to study and investigation. These methods and techniques should tend to clear the teacher's thinking of the clutter of magical beliefs which are so common with the population at large and which exist to a surprising extent among teachers.

---

[1] An excellent aid for teachers in self analysis is: Frank W. Hart. *Teachers and Teaching.* New York: The Macmillan Company, 1934.

[2] Daniel Wolford LaRue. "Mental Health and Environment," *Journal of the National Education Association,* XVIII (February, 1929), 51.

Importance of a Knowledge of Psychological and Social Processes

As the teacher must understand individual life processes, so must the principles involved in the interplay of relationships between persons and groups be understood. Many teachers have learned through rather bitter experience that society demands certain qualities of a teacher which it may not demand of others. If prestige is to be maintained with pupils, colleagues, and the community at large, the teacher must give careful consideration to social conventions. These conventions and demands vary, however, from community to community and the teacher who has failed in adaptation to one situation may be successful in adaptation to another, providing there is a willingness to profit by previous experience, providing there is the desire to learn control—self-control.

The teacher should know something about the principles involved in the influence and control of public opinion, the psychological aspects of propaganda, of group, crowd, and mob behavior. In other words, the expert teacher understands life in all its phases. There is an integrated pattern-picture of all of life's processes; a picture of balance which is used as a point of reference when studying the maladjustments caused by man in his gropings for a more complete life, a picture that makes possible intelligent criticism of our institutional life; unbiased, intelligent discussion of controversial issues.

BIBLIOGRAPHY

ADAMS, SIR JOHN. *The Teacher's Many Parts.* Los Angeles: Ivan Deach, Jr., 1932.

CHARTERS, W. W. *Motion Pictures and Youth; a Summary.* The Payne Fund Studies, New York: The Macmillan Company, 1934.

HART, FRANK W. *Teachers and Teaching.* New York: The Macmillan Campany, 1934.

Home and School Cooperation. White House Conference on Child Health and Protection. New York: The Century Company, 1932.

JORDAN, RIVERDA HARDING. *Education as a Life Work.* New York: The Century Company, 1930.

MORRIS, ELIZABETH HUNT. *Personal Traits and Success in Teaching.* New York: Bureau of Publications, Teachers College, Columbia University, 1929.

MORRISON, HENRY C. *Basic Principles in Education.* Boston: Houghton, Mifflin Company, 1934.

Parent Education. White House Conference on Child Health and Protection. New York: The Century Company, 1932.

Preparation and Improvement of Teachers. A Report of a Conference Held at Northwestern University. Evanston, Illinois: School of Education, Northwestern University.

Social Hygiene in Schools. White House Conference on Child Health and Protection. New York: The Century Company, 1932.

The Classroom Teacher and Character Education. Seventh Yearbook of the Department of Classroom Teachers. Washington: Department of Classroom Teachers of the National Education Association, 1932.

Character Education. Tenth Yearbook of the Department of Superintendence. Washington: Department of Superintendence of the National Education Association, 1932.

The Educational Frontier. Edited by William H. Kilpatrick. New York: The Century Company, 1933.

Chapter IV

TEXTBOOKS AND OTHER INSTRUCTIONAL MATERIALS [1]

TEXTBOOKS

The textbook has assumed a prominence in the traditional program of American schools second in importance only to the teacher. In many instances the textbook has represented nearly the entire content of the educational program, has been used as a course of study or in lieu of a course of study, and has determined to a large extent the nature of teaching method. While much of the prominence accorded the textbook may well be attributed to the high standards which have prevailed in textbook construction, undue emphasis and reliance upon textbooks have certainly led to undesirable rigidity and inflexibility of the educational program. It has been true that the textbook has overshadowed other desirable aids to learning and limited the extent to which they have been employed, and has tended even to subordinate the role of the teacher.

Practice with regard to the function of the textbook in the educational program varies widely. There are two extremes of practice, and intermediate practices varying from one extreme to another. On the one extreme, the textbook is used as the sole source of content, as the course of study, and as the chief guide to teaching method. On the other extreme, there is the practice of using no one book strictly as a textbook, but of making available a wealth of instructional material, both books and other aids to learning. This latter practice is in accordance with a progressive point of view and is rapidly gaining headway in practice. In line with the point of view expressed in Chapter I, the "school has become a laboratory, a busy workshop where children actually live and grow." In such a school there must be an abundance and a rich variety of carefully chosen instructional materials available, organized and filed so as to be easily accessible to the children in connection with all types of learning situations. The effectiveness of the educational program depends in large measure upon the adequacy of all types of instructional aids. In a progressive program of elementary

---

[1] Contributed by Ivan R. Waterman, Chief, Division of Textbooks and Publications; Helen Heffernan, Chief, Division of Elementary Education and Rural Schools; and Gladys L. Potter, Assistant Chief, Division of Elementary Education and Rural Schools; California State Department of Education.

education, the textbook, important as it is, must not be considered as the only instructional aid, but must be used together with all the other aids to instruction.

Since the practice of using a basic textbook exists in a vast majority of elementary schools, it is important to consider its proper function in a program of instruction. The textbook is primarily an aid to learning—one of many types of aids. It should not be regarded as a complete course of study; it can not possibly represent the total content of a course; and it can not be a complete guide to teaching method. It is, however, one of the chief instruments through which the learning activities of pupils will be facilitated. Textbooks and also reference books should be regarded as source material to which pupils will eagerly turn to seek answers to questions and problems which have arisen in the normal course of their learning activities.

It is pertinent to discuss at this point the place of a uniform series of state or school district textbooks in a progressive program of education. Two points should be emphasized in this connection; the proper function of the textbook, and the dangers and abuses to be avoided. A uniform series of textbooks should perform the following functions:

1. It will constitute one of the chief of a variety of aids to the learning activities of pupils.

2. It will indicate the general nature of the content of the course of study and of the learning activities to be expected of the pupils.

3. It will indicate, for certain subjects (for example, spelling, writing, and arithmetic), a desirable minimum uniformity as regards teaching method.

It is to be presumed, of course, that textbooks to perform the above functions will have been selected on the basis of carefully developed purposes and upon their fitness to aid in previously determined learning activities.[1]

Some of the dangers and abuses of textbooks to be avoided are:

1. Textbooks should not be followed so slavishly and inflexibly that the proper growth and development of the pupils is subordinated to learning the text.

2. The natural interests of children and their abilities should not be overlooked.

3. Textbooks should be so used that the individual differences among children in interests, capacities, and needs are properly recognized.

---

[1] For a detailed discussion of textbook selection see *Selection and Distribution of Supplementary and Library Books in California Counties*, State of California Department of Education Bulletin, No. 10, May 15, 1934, pp. 17–32. *Evaluation of Arithmetic Textbooks*, State of California Department of Education Bulletin, No. 19, October 1, 1932. Ivan R. Waterman and Irving R. Melbo, "Selection of Sixth Grade Reading Textbooks for California Adoption," *California Journal of Elementary Education*, III (February, 1935), 133–141.

4. The activities of the teacher should not be subordinated to the textbook. Textbooks or any other instructional aids can not supplant the science and art of teaching. Textbooks and all other aids to learning are merely tools or instruments to be skilfully employed by one of the two human agents in the educational process—the teacher.

A few examples may serve to illustrate the foregoing statement of purposes of textbooks. *Our California Home* [1] is a recently adopted social studies reader for the fourth grade. It was adopted after careful consideration of the materials contained and was revised somewhat and additional material included before being published and distributed to the schools. This book does not pretend to be a course of study in California history and geography. Very little of teaching method is included in the book. There is, however, an abundance of information about California, presented in interesting story form, which children are anxious to learn, which should be the possession of every California child. This book could be misused by setting aside a certain period of each day and requiring every pupil to read and master a certain fixed assignment, and continuing the procedure until the book was "learned." On the other hand, this book can be used in connection with the total program of projects and learning activities of the children and together with other instructional aids in such a manner that the pupils, as a part of the natural learning process, will acquire not only the information, but also certain desired ideals and attitudes.

The use of arithmetic textbooks presents a somewhat different problem than the example previously cited. The state series arithmetic textbooks are intended to indicate the arithmetic skills and number concepts which pupils should acquire as a part of their school experience, to contain the necessary explanatory and drill material to be used in acquiring these skills and concepts, and to indicate the teaching methods which may be employed. Because of the very nature of the subject, an arithmetic text will indicate more completely the content and methods of teaching than will textbooks in certain other subjects. Even so, the teaching of arithmetic should not become completely formalized, and the textbook should not lead to inflexibility in the learning activities of the pupils.

The skilful teacher will find numerous opportunities in the projects and activities of the pupils where number concepts and arithmetic skills are needed in the activity or project to bring in the somewhat formal study of arithmetic as a normal part of the pupils' activities.

---

[1] Irmagarde Richards. *Our California Home* (California State Series). Sacramento: State Department of Education, 1933.

For example, in a learning unit on the industries of some region, quantitative concepts are essential. This will very naturally lead to certain drill with number for the proper development of these concepts.

To be more specific, a learning unit involving a study of the California raisin crop might lead to a consideration of the proportion of the world's raisin supply contributed by California. This of course involves the concept of percentage. The introduction of the study of percentage in a problem situation growing out of this study of the California raisin crop leads naturally and logically to the drill and practice necessary to properly understand percentage and to develop an adequate amount of skill in computation with percentage.

Rather than setting aside a certain time allotment for the study of arithmetic without reference to its relation to normal learning activities of children, good practice demands that drill in arithmetic should grow out of other situations where number concept is involved.

OTHER AIDS TO LEARNING

No attempt will be made here to show how the many aids to learning may best be employed. Many illustrations of the use of different types of aids are contained in the chapters on the various subjects. A large number and rich variety of aids are essential to effective learning. Those to be selected in connection with a particular activity will depend both upon the nature of the activity and upon the characteristics and previous background of the children. It is evident that certain types of aids are more appropriate for certain activities than others. For example, if the children are engaged for the time in an activity involving acquaintance with California wild flowers, it would be the height of folly to confine their study to a beautiful book of wild flowers, if a few minutes walk from the classroom would bring them to a field of live, growing flowers in which they were interested. Similarly, a collection of flowers brought by some member of the class or by the teacher would in most instances be far more appropriate than a book.

After the direct experience with the flowers, the book might very properly be used to aid in answering questions and solving problems arising from the children's first-hand experience with the flowers. The book also would serve a useful purpose in regions or in seasons when the exhibits or growing flowers were not at hand.

The printed page can not take the place of real experience. It enriches experience, however, and aids in integrating learning. The skilful teacher will succeed in stimulating and vitalizing learning activities with a host of materials adapted both to the nature of that to be learned and to the characteristics of the children.

Following are a few suggestions regarding the use of certain of the more important aids to instruction other than textbooks.

Maps, Globes, and Charts

Maps and globes are a part of indispensable equipment in the teaching of the social studies. These formal materials may be purchased from reliable publishers. Excellent maps may be made by the children themselves.

Maps. Maps for elementary schools should be of physical, social, or industrial nature. The political map, which shows only boundaries and locations, is of little value to young children. A set of wall maps, political on a physical base, is essential for the grades. The initial cost is high, but the sets last until they become out of date because of political changes. Among recommended maps are:[1]

Courtesy of Riverside County Schools

An Outline Map Made by a Group of Intermediate Grade Children on the School Grounds

The Goode Series.   Rand McNally & Company
The Kuhbreist Series.   A. J. Nystrom and Company
The Denoyer-Geppert Series.   Denoyer-Geppert Company

For elementary schools the following maps should be acquired in the order named. The projection indicated is considered the most desirable for each particular map:

United States, Polyconic projection
World, Interrupted Homolographic or Homolosine
North America, Polyconic

---

[1] See also, *Suggested Course of Study in the Social Studies for Elementary Schools (Revised).* State of California Department of Education Bulletin, No. 13, October 1, 1933, p. 21.

Europe, Conic or Lambert's Azimuthal
California, Conic or Polyconic
South America, Lambert's Azimuthal or Sansome's Sinusoidal or Polyconic
Asia, Lambert's Azimuthal
Africa, Sinusoidal or Lambert's Azimuthal

Outline maps for individual use may be obtained from the firms listed above, also from McKinley Publishing Company, Philadelphia.

Pictorial, product, relief, and outline maps may be made by upper grade children. While many inaccuracies may exist in these school made maps, they serve many purposes and can be made of many different materials. Cloth, wrapping paper, clay, sand, paper pulp, or salt and flour mixture are possible mediums. A corner of the playground may lend itself to a large map to be used temporarily to illustrate a passing problem. Pictorial maps offer excellent opportunities for both group and individual work with older children. All the earlier maps of exploration and travel were of this type, with miniature pictures of ships, houses, or other objects used, instead of the dots or symbols of the modern map.[1] Pictorial maps may be purchased as well as made by school children.[2]

Globes.[3] A pendant physical globe with political outlines 16 to 18 inches is preferable. A 12-inch size showing names, meridians, and parallels may be used advantageously. Blackboard globes on standards showing outlines of continents and lines of latitude and longitude are desirable. Small 6-inch globes for individual use are valuable.

Charts. Much complicated data can be reduced to simple terms much more easily understood by children through the use of charts. The adoption of this method of learning by the commercial world has shown its value.

Reference Material

The following reference materials are recommended:

PERIODICALS

American Forests. Washington, D. C.: The American Forestry Association, 1727 K Street, N. W. Subscription, $4.00.

Asia. New York: Asia Magazine Incorporated, 461 Eighth Avenue. Subscription, $4.00.

Current Events. Columbus, Ohio: American Education Press, Inc. Subscription, 75¢.

Current History. New York: New York Times. Subscription, $3.00.

---

[1] Rose B. Knox, *School Activities and Equipment.* Boston: Houghton, Mifflin Company, 1927, p. 39.
[2] Reproductions of delightful old historical maps and mariners' charts cost $1 at the Sea Arts Guild, Milwaukee, Wisconsin.
[3] *Suggested Course of Study in the Social Studies for Elementary Schools, op. cit.,* p. 21.

Economic Geography. Worcester, Massachusetts: Clark University. Subscription, $3.00.

Japan. San Francisco: Toyo Kaisha Company. Subscription, $1.50.

Junior Red Cross News. Washington, D. C.: American Junior Red Cross. Subscription, 50¢.

My Weekly Reader. 40 South Third Street, Columbus, Ohio. American Educational Press, Inc. Subscription, 75¢.

The National Geographic Magazine. Washington, D. C.: National Geographic Society. Subscription, $3.50.

Nature Magazine. Washington, D. C.: American Nature Association. Subscription, $3.00.

Scholastic. Pittsburgh, Penn.: Scholastic, Wabash Building. Subscription, $1.00.

Spyglass. A quarterly. New York: American Child Health Association, 450 Seventh Street. Subscription, 75¢.

Travel. New York: Robert McBride Company. Subscription, $4.00.

Western Journal of Education. San Francisco: Harr Wagner Publishing Company. Subscription, $1.50. (Material for observance of special holidays)

Western Nature Study. A quarterly. San Jose, California: Natural Science Department, San Jose State College. Subscription, $1.00.

ENCYCLOPEDIAS

Britannica Junior. (12 volumes) New York: Encyclopaedia Britannica, Inc., 1934.

Compton's Pictured Encyclopedia. (15 volumes) Chicago: F. E. Compton and Company, 1934.

The World Book Encyclopedia. (18 volumes) Chicago: W. F. Quarrie & Company, 1934.

ATLASES

GOODE, J. PAUL. *Goode's School Atlas, Physical, Political, and Economic.* Chicago: Rand McNally & Company, 1923.

YEARBOOKS

New York World Almanac and Book of Facts. Edited by Robert Hunt Lyman. New York: New York World.

The Chicago Daily News Almanac and Yearbook. Chicago: Chicago Daily News Company.

American Yearbook. New York: D. Appleton & Company.

International Yearbook. New York: Dodd, Mead & Company.

DICTIONARIES

The Thorndike-Century Junior Dictionary. Chicago: Scott, Foresman and Company, 1935.

The Winston Simplified Dictionary. Philadelphia: The John C. Winston Company.

Webster's Elementary Dictionary. New York: American Book Company, 1935.

GOVERNMENT PUBLICATIONS

HENDRICKS, GENEVIEVE POYNEER. *Handbook of Social Resources of the United States.* Washington: The American Red Cross, 1921.

Visual Material [1]

Pictures. Beautiful pictures are an important part of the education of children. They supplement, enrich, and enliven both real and vicarious experiences, and develop appreciation in art and nature. They may be of all kinds, each valuable in its particular use. Bright, colorful pictures of sufficient size to lend themselves to an artistic hanging should be a part of the decoration of every classroom. Lovely small pictures may be used on the bulletin board, mounted and collected on the reading table, or kept in a scrap book. Those which form a permanent display should be few, well chosen, and hung at the eye level of those who are to enjoy them as a part of their classroom environment. Pictures should be planned for the space they are to decorate.

Picture collections may be made by a class, a school, or a group of schools for use in connection with various centers of interest. These collections may cost little or nothing, while others may be expensive. Magazines, rotogravure supplements of newspapers, advertising material, catalogues, travel folders, and post cards may be possible sources for such a collection. The following firms have pictures plain or in colors at 10 cents upward:

The Detroit Publishing Company. Detroit, Michigan. (Post cards, pictures in color)

United States Lithographing Company, Fine Arts Section. 6 East 39th St., New York, N. Y. (Pictures, post cards)

Brown-Robertson Company, 8–10 East 49th St., New York, N. Y. (Educational art publishers)

Elson Art Publication Company, Inc. Belmont, Mass. (Miniature pictures)

Art Extension Society. Westport, Conn. (Pictures)

Curtis and Cameron. Boston, Mass. (Pictures)

Emery School Art Company. 372 Boylston St., Boston, Mass. (Colored reproductions of famous paintings)

A. J. Nystrom & Company. 2249–53 Calumet Avenue, Chicago, Ill. (Large colored history and geography pictures)

N. C. Rom. Copenhagen, Denmark. (Pictures of Vikings)

F. A. Owen Publishing Co., 24 Bank St., Dansville, New York. (Full-color Prints of Art Masterpieces 97 subjects—Large Pictures and Miniatures)

George Phillip and Son. 32 Fleet Street, London, England. (Historical pictures, especially Types of Nations and Story of Civilization)

Perry Picture Company. Malden, Mass. (Miniature pictures)

The London Electric Railway, Publicity Manager, 55 Broadway, Westminster, London, S.W.S., and London Midland and Scottish Railway, 220 Fifth Ave., New York City, will send a list of travel poster titles on receipt of a stamped envelope.

---

[1] A special list of visual materials applied to geography, history and civics, natural science, fine arts, and health is found in Anna V. Dorris, *Visual Instruction in the Public Schools.* Boston: Ginn and Co., 1928, Appendix B, pp. 447–470.

The following reproductions of modern pictures are suggested as suitable for an intermediate classroom:[1]

Sunset and Splendor—Inness. 17 x 28. $15
Rocks and Sea—Bower. 16 x 20. $6
Autumn Gold (Landscape)—G. Weigand. 16 x 12. $2
The Grand Canal, Venice—J. M. W. Turner
A New England Harbor—Vincent. 16 x 20. $6
Autumn Oaks—Inness. 11 x 17. $2
The Lifting Fog (Ships)—H. A. Vincent. 20 x 28. $10
The Flower Market (Dutch)—F. Van Vreeland. 14 x 20. $10
Song of the Lark—Breton. 21 x 16. $3
Joan of Arc—Boutet de Monvel. 8 x 20. 75¢
Wild Heliotrope (Landscape)—Gamble. 20 x 30. $10

Old favorites which are always acceptable in classroom pictures may be chosen from among the following:[2] They may be purchased through any reliable dealer in various sizes and at various prices:

Feeding her Birds—Millet
The Sower—Millet
Sistine Madonna—Raphael
Madonna of the Chair—Raphael
The Nativity—Correggio
Boy with the Torn Hat—Sully
The Blue Boy—Gainsborough
Boy with a Rabbit—Raeburn
The Strawberry Girl—Reynolds
The Fruit Girls—Murillo

Collections of pictures for use in nature study or social studies are valuable teaching aids. The following are suggestive:

Compton's Pictured Teaching Units. Chicago: F. E. Compton & Company, 1933.

Pickwell, Gayle. *Natural History Pictures.* Los Angeles: Publishers Distributing Service, Inc., 1934.

Photographic Historical Study Units. 5537 Hollywood Blvd., Hollywood, California: Educational Research Studies, Ltd., 1933.

Screen Pictures and Stereographs. The film has come to the school room from the world of entertainment and has brought many limitations as well as advantages. The educational value of visual material is recognized, but it is generally conceded that this should supplement rather than substitute in the school program. In most instances the pictures shown should follow the work and study done in connection with the subject, in order to insure sufficient background for a full use of the material.

There are many sources of films, slides, stereopticons and similar materials. Teachers may find it convenient to rent or borrow slides or motion picture films. Firms distributing films and slides frequently provide suggestive materials to promote the use of these aids. Publi-

---

[1] Rose B. Knox, *op. cit.*, p. 252. Sizes and prices quoted are from United States Printing and Lithograph Company, Fine Arts Section, 6 East 39th Street, New York, N. Y.

[2] Rose B. Knox, *op. cit.*, p. 252.

cations dealing with visual instruction should be consulted by the teacher before purchasing screen or stereograph materials.[1]

Exhibits and Models. There is much interesting and valuable material which can not be a part of the permanent equipment of the school, but which may furnish a fine educational experience for children. Members of the class may bring in cherished bits of art or a collection from home. Museums, organizations, firms, local celebrities may lend or bring their collections to the school.

Usually such material is loaned and explained by the collectors with great pleasure.

Industrial exhibits are often sent upon request. The teacher should be sure of cost, terms, time limit, methods of shipping, and so forth, before sending for this material.[2]

The Metropolitan Art Museum of New York, Henry W. Kent, Secretary, has a rent collection of textiles, electrotype reproductions of ancient coins, original paintings and reproductions, etchings, and post cards.

The Chicago Art Institute, Chicago, Illinois, has an exhibit of post cards, photographs, color prints.

The Elson Art Publication Company, Inc., Belmont, Mass., has a picture exhibit which may be rented.

The Bureau of Forestry, Washington, D. C., will send an exhibit of commercial woods if the postage is sent.

Careful arrangement and handling of these materials is important.

The fullest value from these exhibits and models is insured only if the children are prepared beforehand so that they may observe intelligently. A free discussion should follow while the interest and impressions are still fresh.

Supplementing Activities of the Classroom

The walls of the classroom no longer encompass the learning area of a modern school. Teachers are taking advantage of the many opportunities for educative experiences in and about the community. Museums, zoos, parks, points of historic importance, unusual formations, or industrial enterprises available through excursions supplement the activities of the classroom. Teachers should familiarize them-

[1] *Visual Education Through Stereographs and Lantern Slides.* Meadville, Pennsylvania: The Keystone View Company, 1917.
Visual Education Service, Inc., 7024 Melrose Avenue, Los Angeles, California.
1001 Films. Educational Screen Magazine, 5 South Wabash Avenue, Chicago, Illinois.
Nature Study Illustrated. San Jose, California: San Jose State College.
Anna V. Dorris. *Visual Instruction in the Public Schools.* Boston: Ginn and Company. 1928. pp. 437-446.
Rose B. Knox, *op. cit.,* pp. 240-245.
[2] Anna V. Dorris, *op. cit.,* pp. 433-437.

selves with all the possibilities of the neighborhood and direct the attention of pupils to these spots of interest for holiday trips with parents and friends as well as for school excursions.

Miscellaneous Materials for Constructive Activities

Expression through making and constructing is a universal impulse. The broadening of outlook and social understanding which comes from "taking nature's materials and making them into a form"[1] which can be useful to man is not to be overlooked. Constructive activities are not ends in themselves, but a part of a large center of interest for the child.

Courtesy of San Jose City Schools

Expression Through Making and Constructing Is a Universal Impulse

In a modern school program there is need for a great variety of materials. Only a few from an exhaustive list are discussed here.

Boxes. Boxes of wood, cardboard, and tin may be easily obtained at little expense and are useful in a variety of ways in carrying on activities such as the study of homes, doll houses, doll furniture making, play communities, puppet theaters, and peep shows.

Cement or Concrete. Cement has many possibilities. Small children get satisfactory results with it. Cement is valuable in much out-of-door work, such as the construction of aquaria, bowls, reliefs and

---

[1] Rose B. Knox, *op cit.,* p. 49.

other art objects, and can be secured from building supply firms. The teacher may wish to consult one or more of the following references for suggestions and guidance in the use of cement:

Lemos, John T., and Lemos, R. A. *Color Cement Handicraft.* Worcester, Massachusetts: Davis Press, Inc., 1922.

Seaton, Thomas. *Concrete Construction for Rural Communities.* New York: McGraw, Hill Company, 1918.

U. S. Department of Agriculture, S. B. 1279, *Plain Concrete for Farm Use.* Washington, D. C.: United States Printing Office. (Five cents)

Clay. Clay is especially good material for creative work and can be used in any type of classroom for free play, for illustration work, and for art work.

Natural clay may sometime be found in the vicinity of the school. Children will enjoy working with materials from their own environment.[1]

Clay flour may be obtained inexpensively and mixed as needed. Clay should be kept in an air-tight container. Any large can or jar with a close fitting top will serve. If a tin receptacle is used it should be painted inside and out to prevent rust. The bottom should be covered with a two-inch layer of mixed plaster of Paris. If the plaster of Paris is kept damp, the clay will be kept in perfect condition for use. Keep a damp cloth over the top of clay. Scraps of dry clay should not be thrown back into the jar without being worked into the supply. For complete directions for firing clay objects the teacher will need to consult more extensive sources.[2]

Cloth. Many practical uses can be made of cloth in dressing dolls, furnishing doll houses, costuming plays and making maps, etc.

Composition Wallboard. Composition board has many uses. It is light and easily cut. Composition board may be secured from any local supply firm. This board may be used as a base for relief maps, for walls in doll houses, for screens, bulletin boards, and a variety of purposes.

Crayons. Wax crayons are needed in every grade. A full set of eight colors is desirable for each child. If the paper wrappers are given two coats of shellac, the crayons will not break easily. Crayons may be obtained from any reliable firm.

---

[1] For an account of children working with native clay see *Teachers' Guide to Child Development.* Compiled by State Curriculum Commission. Sacramento, California: State Department of Education, 1930, pp. 101–113.

[2] L. L. Winslow. *Elementary Industrial Arts.* New York: The Macmillan Company, 1922.
Charles Fergus Binns. *The Potter's Craft.* New York: D. Van Nostrand Company, 1922.

Dyes. Many kinds of handwork need to be dyed to complete them. Costume problems are often solved by dyeing old as well as new materials. For such a use it is not often necessary to boil the material. Dipping in two colors, one then the other, often gives a much better effect than a plain dye.

Baskets or other reed work are colored by soaking in a strong, hot dye. Paper and articles made from wood may be colored many beautiful shades with dye.

Salt dyes are the most permanent. Familiar makes may be purchased by the pound or package at small cost.

Aniline dyes are best for the clear strong colors needed in costumes. The cost varies according to color.[1] One ounce of the primary colors will be sufficient under ordinary circumstances, as they are highly concentrated.

Other materials which may be used for dying are crepe paper, powdered blueing, ink, and coffee or tea.[2]

Inks. Higgins' waterproof ink is among those recommended for drawing, and can be obtained from any school supply firm. Printers' ink is needed for linoleum or wood block printing or for the printing press. Both of the inks mentioned above can be obtained in colors as well as in black. A small amount of ink goes a long way for school purposes.

Paints and Brushes. The results from the use of paint by children are quite permanent and satisfying. The materials are expensive if a good quality is used, but because of the practicality of this activity, the children should be given a wide experience in the use of paints, varnishes, stains, and shellacs.

For school use, a four-inch brush is best for most purposes. Other sizes may be kept on hand for special needs. Brushes should be clean and paint well mixed.

The care of paints and brushes is important. Keep paint in a tightly sealed container. Oil or turpentine poured over the surface will prevent a scum forming and the paint drying. Brushes must be well cleaned and never allowed to dry with the paint still in them. Kerosene is cheaper than turpentine for cleaning brushes, though not quite as effective. Alcohol should be used to clean shellac from a brush. If a paint brush is to be used again the next day, it may be

---

[1] Aniline dyes may be obtained from Chicago Apparatus Company, 701 West Washington Boulevard, Chicago, Illinois, or Eimer & Amend, Third Avenue at 19th Street, New York, New York.

[2] For complete directions as to the use and handling of dyes see:
Rose B. Knox, *op. cit.*, p. 81.
Frederick G. Bonser, and L. C. Mossman. *Industrial Arts for Elementary Schools.* New York: The Macmillan Company, 1923.

wrapped in several thicknesses of paper to prevent drying and not washed.

Paper. A big roll of wrapping paper is indispensable for use in making charts, friezes, "movies," or maps, and in construction work. It is not only practical but economical. The roll should be secured in a convenient place on wall, table, or shelf where it can be cut and handled efficiently. Bogus, building, and kraft papers are also useful papers for writing, drawing, or painting. Colored papers are somewhat expensive, but are valuable for art and craft use.

Paper Pulp and Papier-mâché. Paper pulp is used for relief work, puppetry, and various kinds of craft work. To make this, newspapers or other paper may be torn into single pieces and the pieces covered with boiling water. Soak for a day or two. Drain and work or pound the material with a stick until a mass of pulp is made.

The following recipe for the preparation of papier-mâché has been found serviceable:[1]

> (a) Preparation of the pulp: Use deadening felt paper such as builders use. Pieces can often be obtained when a house is being built. Old pieces of cardboard can also be used. Tear the dry felt into small pieces, place the pieces in a pan, and heat them on a stove. As they dissolve, work the mass with the fingers until there are no lumps. Squeeze it dry with the fingers. Keep it until it is needed.
> (b) Preparation of the glue: Take one cupful of dry, ground fish glue and one cupful of water. Heat the mixture in a double boiler until the fish glue melts.
> (c) To make the papier-mâché: Put into a pan one cupful of dry pulp; one-half cupful of water; one cupful of liquid glue; one-third cupful boiled linseed oil to give pliability. Mix thoroughly, and add whiting or pulverized gypsum for strength. Keep mixing until three cupfuls of whiting have been mixed. This is the moist papier-mâché.
> Note: Keep a dry cloth over the pan when it is not in use. If the pulp hardens, heat the pan over hot water to melt the glue. If necessary add a little water.

Tools and Appliances. All instructional equipment should be chosen carefully. Most classroom work can be adjusted so that only a few children at a time work with the tools and appliances if the supply is limited.

There are certain materials which every teacher should have available. Some of these materials may be a part of the building equipment while other items should be in each classroom. A few suggestions follow:

> Paper cutter. A reliable cutter with a blade 12" to 24" in length costs about $20.

---

[1] Given by the Industrial Arts Cooperative Service, 519 West 121st Street, New York, N. Y. Directions and recipes for the preparation of materials for the craft work of all kinds are published in pamphlets by this company. Send a stamped, addressed envelope.

Punch. This should be strong, simply made for punching thick paper, leather and tin.

Carpenter's tools. The number and kind depend upon conditions. A minimum list of equipment of this kind is suggested.[1]

- 2 claw hammers (flat head, 12-ounce)
- 4 tack hammers
- 2 cross-cut saws (10 points to one inch, 18–22 inches long, for intermediate children)
- 1 keyhole saw
- 1 brace with bits ($\frac{1}{4}$ to 1 inch) or 1 gimlet No. 18
- 2 vises or 2 C-clamps (8-inch opening)
- 1 table or 1 work bench, or 2 sawhorses
- 1 miter box

THE LIBRARY IN THE ELEMENTARY SCHOOL [2]

The library has a new significance in modern education. Gone are the days when acquisition of the meager facts of a textbook represented realization of the educational ideal. The program of integrated activities around large centers of interest requires wide reading, the consultation of many references, investigation of extensive sources of information.

Every phase in current educational use contributes to an acceptance of the concept of the library as the heart of the modern school. The ''reading program'' replaces the deadening repetition of ''finish'' the grade reader. The ''reading program'' implies reading many interesting books, of widely varying content, at the level of reading ability the child possesses.

The ''unit of work'' in the social studies means a comprehensive experience centering around a definite topic rather than a few pages mastered from the geography or history book. It means consulting many books and periodicals to accumulate the necessary data essential to recreate for the child the specific experience involved in the unit.

The modern philosophy of education elevates the library to a position of supreme importance. The use of the library by the children of a school is an accurate criterion of the school's educational progress. Kathleen Norris unconsciously expressed the modern school's attitude toward the meaning of developing in children ability to use and appreciate books when she said: ''Once get in the habit of really enjoying books and you have put into your life something that is pure gain.

---

[1] Rose B. Knox, *op. cit.*, pp. 129–130.
For more extensive equipment see *ibid.*, ''Liberal Equipment for Classroom,'' p. 130.
Teachers' Guide to Child Development. Compiled by State Curriculum Commission. Sacramento, California: State Department of Education, 1930, pp. 420–425. Also has suggestive lists for purchase of equipment.
[2] For an extended treatment of this subject see:
Effective Use of Library Facilities in Rural Schools. State of California Department of Education Bulletin, No. 11, June 1, 1934.
The Library in the Elementary School. State of California Department of Education Bulletin, No. 18, September 15, 1935.
Selection and Distribution of Supplementary and Library Books in California Counties. State of California Department of Education Bulletin, No. 10, May 15, 1934.

Nothing restores a sense of true proportion, the true value of our harassed and undignified lives, like a background of books. Little detached flashes of life they are—a Russian interior here, a cold bit of New England ice poetry there, they begin to build themselves together, to take form, to give an expanding interest in the big world and a willingness at least to decrease one's own ignorance.''

Not only is the library the indispensable tool of modern instructional procedure, but its habitual use determines the cultural level a human being will maintain in adult life. The library is the most powerful influence in promoting the ideal of education as a process which begins at birth and continues throughout life both in and out of school.

The Place of the Library in the Modern Elementary School

The library has a place (1) to provide an enriched program so that effective attitudes and habits of reading for pleasure, for information, and for study may be developed; (2) to stimulate a desire for use of books through contact with various kinds of good literature; (3) to develop skill and resourcefulness in the use of books and libraries as "the tools of intellectual growth"; (4) to help the child "to discover the unity of knowledge" and to learn many important things not contained in the regular courses.

The Library Atmosphere

Sometimes (although not often) there is an extra room; it may be a small room or an unused classroom; ideally it will be a real library room separated from the classroom with a glass partition so that it may be continually under the supervision of the teacher. The school trustees, the local parent-teacher association, the teachers, and the children can be encouraged to cooperate in an enterprise to convert this room into a library; decorating this room so that it will appeal to the children, contribute to the development of their esthetic sense, and yet not interfere with the calm atmosphere conducive to concentration.

Perhaps a separate room is out of the question. Certainly a library corner can be arranged in the classroom where books may be kept and where children may gather around a table to enjoy books.

Necessary Furnishing

Without attempting to be exhaustive, the library should certainly have: books, book shelves, tables, chairs, catalog, file for pictures, and a file for fugitive material. Other special features which are desirable might be added: magazine rack, world globe, bulletin board, art study board, poetry corner, display case, children's periodicals, dictionary stand, et cetera.

Although the reference and reading materials may come from a central depository, there are other library materials of almost equal value that can constitute the permanent cumulative possession of the school: well mounted and filed collections of pictures, post cards, copies of favorite poems, children's original books, and other fugitive material.

Use of Books and Libraries

All children in the school should use the library in varying degrees. The children in third to sixth grades should have at least two library periods a week in which they are free to pursue their interests under the guidance of the teacher. Home circulation of books should be encouraged.

One city school system [1] has been devoting much energy to the guidance of individual reading in the library situation. Through the cooperative effort of teachers, simple tests of the supplementary reading books have been devised, multiple choice or completion in type, which the child will fail completely if he has not read the book. It is appropriate to be warned that there is danger in testing children too minutely or the reading will be slowed down in order to remember details.

Instruction in the Use of the Library

Another problem of significance in the extension of the library is the way in which definite instruction shall be given in the use of the library. This training should be integrated with the regular work of the school day, but for children in grades five and six some general library instruction will prove immeasurably valuable. Probable mediums for this instruction are units of work, informal talks, dramatizations, demonstrations, assembly programs, book contests, etcetera.

The problem of selecting books for the elementary school library is one which must be faced and solved to a greater or lesser degree of satisfaction. Very definite criteria must be established and adhered to rigidly. The factors to be included should certainly be: children's interest, literary style, suitability of vocabulary, reading difficulty, quality of illustrations, style of topography, quality of paper, and binding.

The following titles are suggested to guide the teacher in the selection of the proper materials:

Beust, Nora, and Others. *Graded List of Books for Children.* Chicago: American Library Association, 1930.

Effective Use of Library Facilities in Rural Schools. State of California Department of Education Bulletin, No. 11, June, 1934.

---

[1] Sacramento, California.

The Library in the Elementary School. State of California Department of Education Bulletin, No. 18, September 15, 1935.

Selection and Distribution of Supplementary and Library Books in California Counties. State of California Department of Education Bulletin, No. 10, May 15, 1934.

Terman, Lewis M., and Lima, Margaret. *Children's Reading.* New York: D. Appleton and Company, 1931.

The Right Book for the Right Child. A graded buying list of children's books. New York: The John Day Company, 1933.

Aids in Book Selection for Elementary School Libraries. U. S. Office of Education, Department of the Interior Circular No. 69, January, 1933. Washington: United States Government Printing Office.

CHAPTER V

SOCIAL STUDIES[1]

I. THE PLACE OF SOCIAL STUDIES IN THE CURRICULUM

In growing from infancy to maturity, an individual spends a large share of his time and energy learning about and adjusting to the world of nature and the world of people. There is, in fact, nothing else that he can learn about or make adjustment to. Social studies and elementary science, broadly conceived, comprise the whole field of significant content of the school curriculum. Subject matter of study always involves people, their activities, aspirations, and achievements or the phenomena of nature, if not both. The subjects of the elementary school curriculum do not, consequently, stand upon one plane of importance; nor are they coordinate in scope or type. The social studies in particular occupy a unique position in the school program, since their purpose is fundamentally the central purpose as well as the justification of the whole school. The school is a social institution, one of the major social institutions of mankind. All that is included in the curriculum must be justified in terms of its social value. The child reads, and learns to read, in order to share in the experiences and thoughts of other members of society. He writes and spells according to socially approved standards in order to communicate with others. He learns arithmetic that he may understand the quantitative aspects of social situations and participate in the business and technical affairs of the community. Similarly, music, art, and even health instruction are largely determined by social motives and standards. Development of the highest type of citizenship is the basic goal of the school. Since this goal is peculiarly the aim of social studies instruction, it is clear that the social studies constitute the very heart of the curriculum.

In broadest terms, the objectives of teaching social studies is to help children understand the world they live in, in order first, that they may adjust themselves to it successfully and happily, and secondly, that they may contribute to its welfare and participate intelligently in its improvement. It is obvious that the older type of instruction in history and geography failed to achieve this aim. In fact, no such worthy and inclusive goal was commonly recognized. Widespread civic illiteracy is consequently one of the great shortcomings of American citizenship today. Well-disposed individuals and groups act in accord with shibboleths, slogans and illusions to defeat rather than

---

[1] Contributed by Dr. John A. Hockett, Department of Education, University of California.

further the progress they desire, and become prey to selfish and unscrupulous manipulators who exploit them for their own anti-social purposes. Such is always the reward of ignorance, not of course ignorance of certain hallowed facts of history and geography, but ignorance of the crucial realities of contemporary life.

Civic illiteracy is unbearably costly in social results. No less intolerable is civic indifference. Business men who boasted they could make money faster than the politicians could steal it from them, and the fifty per cent of the voters who couldn't be bothered to cast a vote on election day were, a few years ago, shocking evidence of our tragic civic indifference. The school can not be satisfied with its efforts to build an adequate understanding of the world of men and their affairs unless it simultaneously strives to develop strong interests in cooperative endeavor and lifelong attitudes of concern for the welfare of all men, women, and children. Enthusiasm for human welfare and active opposition to political, economic, and social injustice—these are as essential in the good citizens as enlightened intelligence. Unless we teach faith in human nature, in democracy, and in the possibility of progress through intelligent cooperation, our pupils are likely to lack the impelling drive that makes their citizenship effective.

If we accept adequate civic understanding and a socialized conscience as two basic objectives of social studies instruction, a third major aim inevitably follows: development of permanent habits, skills, and attitudes of cooperation and participation in worthy group enterprises. Effectiveness in cooperation is not merely a matter of insight and of disposition; it also involves well established habits and skills. These abilities are acquired only through long experience in working with others in the attainment of shared objectives. No school which emphasizes individualism and competition to the neglect of cooperative endeavor can succeed in building these essential habits.

Development of Civic Competence Is a Challenging Goal

The teaching of social studies so that it results in effective civic functioning is the most difficult, the most challenging, and the most rewarding of the teacher's responsibilities. It is distressingly easy to carry on textbook recitations of the facts of history and geography. To widen the social outlook of pupils, to deepen their human sympathies, to kindle lifelong enthusiasm for positive social and civic behavior, and to practice them daily in the fine art of living together in a democratic social group is infinitely more difficult—and worth while. Tact, skill and patience in large measure are required of one who would liberate children from prejudice and provincialism, from unthinking acceptance of superficial opinion, and from smug complacency and self-satisfied individualism. To have a part in the moulding of superior personalities who combine social vision, understanding and zeal with personal integrity and effectiveness is the greatest reward any teacher can ask.

Without the attainment of such goals as those suggested above, the contribution of the school to society and to the individual is a meagre and relatively futile thing, unworthy of the respect and support it receives from the American people.

II.   WHAT WE TEACH IN SOCIAL STUDIES—CONTENT

Objectives Determine Both Content and Method

The field of social studies is as broad as life itself.   In this respect, it contrasts sharply with many other subjects of the elementary curriculum.   In spelling, in arithmetic, in handwriting, even in reading and language, it is possible to designate minimum essentials in terms of facts, processes, and skills.   In arithmetic, for example, each objective is achieved through the mastery of a certain specific content.   Skill in long division is acquired through practice in specific types of exercises. Success in spelling comes through the masterly of a definite list of words which have been proved to be more commonly used in writing than any other words.   In social studies, however, there is no body of specific content that is supremely valuable in producing good citizenship.   Each social objective may be achieved through various means and through a great diversity of content.   Young people may grow in open-mindedness, in tolerance, in critical judgment, or in human sympathy, for example, through studying any significant social condition or problem, past or present.   They should, in fact, grow in these respects in every such study.   As teachers, therefore, our primary ment of our objectives rather than we merely "cover" certain specified concern should be that we make continuous progress in the achieve-subject matter.

Minimum Essentials in Social Studies

If we wish to define minimum essentials in social studies, we must state them not in terms of bare facts but in terms of understandings. These understandings concern the relationships that exist between facts and the significance of facts for human welfare and progress. They concern the conditions under which men live and work and play. They concern the institutions, the conventions and traditions that liberate or restrict the individual in his striving for self-realization. Understanding reveals the problems or maladjustments in the relationships of man to man and group to group.   Understanding requires definite knowledge of facts; it must be based upon adequate and accurate information, but it involves much more than mere accumulation of information.   It signifies perception of the significance of facts.

Unfortunately, much acquiring of information by children stops short of understanding, and hence is a futile and exhausting exercise. The acquisition of facts is not educative unless the learner can use the facts in interpreting experiences, perceiving relationships, answering questions and solving problems which are of concern to him. Children as well as adults need facts but they need them only as they contribute to the development and expansion of significant experiences. Bare facts, isolated and unused, are to the mind what indigestible food is to the body. The ask-me-another conception of learning may serve occasionally to help while away an idle hour; it does not promote the growth of socialized intelligence, which requires the digestion and assimilation of mental food. Social studies teaching has been guilty of much overfeeding at the expense of wholesome assimilation. Let us be quite clear and emphatic: facts are absolutely indispensable but are valuable only when they are used to promote understanding.

Principles for Organizing Content

If understanding rather than mere memory is our goal, certain principles must be observed in the organization of the social studies curriculum.

First, the intensive study of a few things is better than a smattering of information about everything. Understanding requires looking at a matter from all sides, having a variety of experiences related to it, attempting to go to the bottom of things. In our discussion of method, we shall point out that the habits and attitudes developed in the attempt to study some important matters thoroughly are of paramount importance. Nothing but superficial memory-stuffing can result from the requirement that children "learn" the myriad facts of geography and history as formerly organized.

Second, the materials of social studies must be organized into inclusive units of activity and understanding, which represent important aspects of life and which utilize as needed the subject matter academically classified as history, geography, civics or any other study. These classifications are the work of advanced specialists. They do not correspond to the needs of everyday life or of the learner who seeks to gain an understanding of some significant theme. No condition, custom, relationship, or problem of contemporary life can be truly understood except as we bring together at one time the geographic influences, historical antecedents and civic implications that are pertinent to it. Organization of materials must promote integration of experience and thought, not artificially restrict it.

Third, major emphasis should be on the here and now. Children in the schools must live their lives in the world as it is. Stories of distant places and past times may be entertaining and may add to one's cultural background, but unless they are related to the life the child sees about him in such a way as to deepen and broaden his understanding of it, they do not further the objectives of civic education. The present can not be understood apart from a knowledge of the important past events and movements which have made the present what it is.   Children may, however, and often do, acquire much information about the past which does not contribute in any vital way to their understanding of the world they live in.   Similarly, remote parts of the earth have numerous connections with our own country and even our local community.   Unless these connections and their significance are perceived, the study of distant places and peoples loses its functional value.   Comparison and contrast of the activities of our own community with those of other peoples leads to a richer understanding of the life of both groups.   Provincialism declines as one realizes that the mores of his little group fall far short of exhausting the possibilities of group life.   In these times when the whole world is being more and more intimately tied together, and when economic, political, and cultural changes take place with ever increasing rapidity, a broad social perspective is urgently needed. Perspective is gained only through understanding the here and now in its relations to the remote in both space and time.

Fourth, since the phenomena of social life are complex and interrelated, the organization of subject matter must be such as to simplify complicated trends and conditions through the emphasis first of one aspect of the matter, then of another until sufficient background is acquired to enable the pupil to perceive the complexity of the whole. Skill is required to maintain emphasis on the significant phases of a unit and to use the mass of possible details to vivify and clarify the essential relationships rather than to bewilder and confuse.   Unless the detailed materials of history and geography are definitely organized to reveal and emphasize important relationships, that which is significant will be lost in a mass of trivial detail.   Unfortunately, many textbooks present masses of information without interpretation or relative emphasis, leaving to teachers and pupils the difficult problem of interpreting and appraising the significance of the material.   No effort should be spared, however, in aiding boys and girls to evaluate and interpret their reading, for such abilities are essential in all their future reading as adults and citizens.

Fifth, the curriculum must provide for the continuous and gradual development of meanings and understandings.   Such conceptions as "democracy" and "freedom" are not acquired through a sudden flash of insight, but are broad, inclusive concepts built up by the gradual accumulation of meanings over a long period of time. Realization of the complexity of modern economic and political life, of the interdependence of individuals, groups, communities, and nations, and all such fruitful understandings are the products of long series of experiences during which the essential relationships are perceived more and more clearly as the individual gradually matures in background and wisdom. Children in the kindergarten may study the life of their community, and learn the obvious functions of butcher, baker, fireman and policeman. The next year, and each succeeding year, they can penetrate somewhat more deeply into the hidden relationships of group life and the motives and activities of people. The school must insure that children study the essentials of social life over and over again in different situations, from various points of view, and on successively more mature levels of understanding.

Courage to Face the Realities of Life Is Needed

The increasing tendency to teach the realities of social life, present and past, is a hopeful trend in social studies instruction. Refusal to face reality is as unwholesome educationally for teacher and pupil alike as is the same tendency in the personal life of the individual. The values of civilization need not be bolstered up with falsehoods. History as the record of man's achievements and failures, his progress, slow and uneven though it has been, in spite of obstacles without and weaknesses within, is both more edifying and enlightening than any pseudo-history manufactured to "inculcate" certain ready-made viewpoints. If we have not the courage to teach the truth about present conditions as well as past events, we had best not "teach" at all. Courage is, indeed, required for there is a very widespread sort of ignorance which fears and opposes the searching attitude necessary to pursue truth. Silence, moreover, regarding things which should be understood may be a more serious form of falsehood than the perpetuation of a few harmless myths about bygone heroes. Realism in social studies means teaching the actual functioning of human institutions and processes, not romantic, sentimental speculation regarding how they might operate in a perfect world. If we wish pupils to have faith in democracy and courage to strive for human progress we must help them understand the conditions under which democracy and progress are to be achieved. They will meet only frustration in attacking the windmills of unreality.

The Local Community Is a Social Studies Laboratory

The content of social studies includes the facts and principles contained in books but also, and more basically, the experiences and activities of life about us. The local community of every school constitutes a challenging laboratory of social relations. The true function of books is to supplement, enrich, and extend the first hand experiences of life. In no other field is this fact so important as in the study of social life. If our instruction is not to be bookish and remote, it must continually enlighten and be enlightened by the day-by-day activities of the real world. Many teachers are already making use of the local environment as a laboratory of first hand experience.

Still more immediate and vital are the experiences of the pupil in his own school and classroom groups. This experience is the most basic of all social studies content as will be emphasized in the discussion of method which follows.

Rituals Can Not Take the Place of Realities

Forms and rituals have long held a prominent place in instruction for citizenship. There is undoubtedly value in permitting children to express loyalty to their country and to the principles of democracy for which it stands. It must be borne in mind, however, that the reiteration of a formal statement soon becomes a ritual performed with a minimum of thought as to its significance. Moreover, the repetition of a memorized generality carries no assurance that the pupil understands the application of the general creed in the many practical situations of life, not to mention the actual practice of those principles in behavior. One may proclaim devotion to his country in a loud voice and yet be a civic incompetent or hypocrite. There is yet another deficiency and possible danger in excessive reliance on rituals for civic education. If teacher and pupils think they are performing a significant part of their civic responsibilities by merely engaging in formal exercises, they deceive themselves as to the true nature of citizenship. The good citizen continually serves the people of his community, state, nation, and humanity in general by wise and well-disposed behavior in the many situations of practical daily life. He spends little time proclaiming to the world his own civic virtues.

III.   HOW WE TEACH SOCIAL STUDIES—METHOD

Treatment of Children Is of Utmost Significance

The school exerts two major influences in education for citizenship : (1) the all-important influence of the school life it provides for pupils, and (2) the influence of its organized civic instruction. The way we treat children is vastly more important than what we attempt to "teach" them. Unless we can set up a school environment in which pupils willingly and happily practice day by day the characteristics of good citizenship, it is futile to expect them to be greatly influenced by our words or lessons. The teacher's words may roar loudly in their ears, but the kind of citizenship they experience in school will mould their lives. Children must learn to cooperate through years of practice in cooperation. They must learn self-control through a long process of gradual emancipation from external control, as under wise guidance they develop greater capacity for freedom and responsibility. They become group leaders through exercising initiative and through deserving the confidence of their fellows. They learn to choose and follow the best leadership only through a long period of active participation in group enterprises. Democracy is a way of life, implying respect for each person in the group and involving the most complete sharing of purposes and activities. Such a way of living is not learned in a despotic or autocratic school, wherein dictator-teachers issue arbitrary commands to obedient subjects. Children must be respected as human personalities and as school citizens and must share fully in the life of the school if they are to learn and to love the democratic way of life. To practice the principles of democracy in the daily work and play of the school is the first principle of effective method in educating for citizenship.

Purposeful Self-Activity Is Basic to Learning

In the organized work in social studies the most important principle of method is that pupils be aggressors in purposeful activity directed towards the understanding of the world they live in. The importance of such a conception of method is very great. The most valuable outcomes can be achieved in no other way. In the first place, this method transforms the whole spirit of the classroom. Intellectual curiosity is preserved and stimulated. Interests are utilized and extended. Group work is promoted, with mutual sharing of aims, experiences and achievements. Initiative, resourcefulness, open-mindedness, habits of questioning, problem solving, and critical thinking are all made possible. Pupils have an opportunity to learn what it really means to study. With wise guidance they grow in habits of intellectual thoroughness and mental integrity. A wide variety of worth while experiences is involved in the active study of an important phase of life: the formulation of group objectives, planning and sharing of investigational work, recognition and formulation of problems and questions, actual first hand investigation of social phenomena, reading and research in textbooks and books of reference, reconciliation of conflicting desires, opinions and evidence, continual evaluation, revision and improvement of goals, plans and activities. These are some of the profitable experiences possible through a dynamic program of teaching. The race has developed civilization through the learning that came in connection with the active pursuit of worthy purposes. Children must learn by the same process.

Teaching and Learning Procedures Must Be Flexible

Flexibility in method, as in content, is essential if pupil experiences are to be most educative. The methods of work of teacher and pupils must be continually modified in the light of current developments if experiences are to be kept vital and progressively enlightening. There is no one best way to organize subject matter or to carry on learning activities. Any way is good in so far as it promotes in children desirable behavior leading toward the realization of at least some of the fundamental objectives. Any way is good to the extent that it makes use of the background, interests and abilities of a particular group of children and leads on to the development and enrichment of their social experiences. Teaching procedures can never be rigidly standardized, but must always be adjusted to the level of development of the pupil group, the background and particular abilities of the teacher, the special opportunities of the local environment, and the significant current developments in the social world as a whole.

Teachers Cannot Be Propagandists

Teaching is not indoctrination, and the methods of the propagandist will not serve the ideals of democratic citizenship. Propaganda and indoctrination are the methods of the despot, for they promote unthinking allegiance to predetermined points of view. These methods deny the basic principle of democracy, i.e., maximum development of the individual. True education strives to develop competence in the individual, equipping him with such attitudes and abilities that he can and will deal intelligently with each situation in life as it arises. The propagandist distrusts both intelligence and the unrestricted development of individual ability, and makes adherence to certain specific dogmas superior to individual and to social progress. One of the most searching questions a teacher can ask herself is whether her methods promote competence in the individual pupil or blind acceptance of some creed. The unreasonable demand for quick, visible results to be displayed on tests and otherwise, exerts a constant and pernicious influence on teachers to teach their pupils what to think instead of how to think. The propagandist wishes, and is satisfied with, quick, external results. The educator knows that human development is a long, slow process.

Not only must teachers guard against the danger that their own methods will indoctrinate rather than educate, but they must also equip their pupils to meet and deal with widespread attempts at indoctrination by outside agencies. The skilful use of propaganda is one of the major arts of modern life. Hundreds of groups and organizations constantly seek to secure acceptance of certain points of view through the manipulation of public and private opinion. The motives of these groups range from the noblest to the most unworthy, but in so far as their methods suppress a part or all of the truth, and in so far as they limit the freest exercise of intelligence by the individual, to that extent is their influence inimical to democracy. Since the presence of propaganda is so all-pervasive that no one can escape its influence for a single day, the only hope of education is to build up a sensitiveness to its presence, and a critical attitude towards its assertions and the motives of its sponsors. This the school can and must accomplish through its program of social studies. A large part of this work should be done in the junior and senior high schools. Pupils in the intermediate grades, however, are subject to many propagandizing influences, and are not too young to begin to appreciate the methods and dangers of these forces.

The Methods of Effective Teachers

Teachers who accept as their goal the maximum development of worthy civic attitudes, interests, habits, and understandings are primarily concerned:

That children continually engage in activities and experiences that are significant to them,

That children have abundant first hand contacts with the realities of social life,

That children constantly set up purposes, plan procedures, carry out activities, and evaluate results on successively more mature levels,

That children form habits of intellectual thoroughness and mental honesty that come from the vigorous effort to see things through,

That pupils learn to integrate their experiences and their knowledge,

That pupils be encouraged to raise questions and recognize problems rather than merely learn answers to questions asked by someone else,

That each experience of pupils leads on and out to wider perspective and to other worthy experiences,

That the life of the school provides abundant opportunities for the practice of initiative, responsibility, cooperation, openmindedness, critical judgment and the other habits and attitudes that characterize the good citizen.

IV. THE UNIT OF WORK IN SOCIAL STUDIES

A Social Studies Unit Includes Many Types of Experiences

All teachers must organize their work into units of one sort or another. In arithmetic, the study of a specific process such as addition of fractions may be considered a unit. In social studies, teachers sometimes think of the specific information which is to be learned in connection with the study of some period of history or some region in geography as constituting a unit. A more helpful conception, how-

Courtesy of San Diego City Schools

A Social Studies Unit Includes Many Types of Experiences

ever, sums up in the phrase "unit of work" all of the activities and experiences of whatever nature that are involved in the cooperative investigation of some important aspect of social life, such as transportation, books and records, food, or colonial life. Both historical and geographical subject matter are generally included, but in addition all the experiences of the group in purposing, planning and evaluating the various activities. The raising of problems and questions for study and the attempts to give expression to the insights gained through constructive, dramatic and artistic means are also important aspects of the unit.

Selecting and Initiating the Unit

Some courses of study rigidly prescribe the specific units which are to be included in the work of each grade. In such situations, the teacher's first responsibility is to be alert for, and to utilize, all interests of the children which may be directed toward the required unit. She may also do many things to stimulate interest in the field which is to be explored. She will provide appropriate books, articles and illustrative materials. She may read selected materials to the children. Slides and other visual aids may be secured. A qualified person may be invited to visit the class and discuss the topic or problem. In many cases an excursion is useful. Class discussions will be held in which pupils and teacher pool their knowledge about the subject and together raise questions which they would like to have answered. The variety of means employed to develop interest in and introduce the unit are limited only by the ingenuity and resourcefulness of the teacher.

Some of the recent progressive courses of study permit greater leeway to the teacher and pupils in the choice of units. Where this freedom exists, it is often possible to make a better selection of units in terms of the previous experiences of the particular group of pupils, the background of the teacher, the resources of the local environment, and the important current developments. Increased freedom, here as always, entails greater responsibility. The teacher must, with this freedom, make certain that the pupils have a balanced assortment of units, taking into consideration their whole program for the year and over a period of years. She must also insure that any unit selected possess, in fact, abundant opportunities for the growth of each and every child in the class. With freedom to exercise choice, teacher and pupils together find it profitable at first to spend some time in exploring the various possibilities open to them and in coming to an agreement on what seems the most significant and challenging field of study. Here, as in every other phase of the work, the wise guidance of a farseeing teacher is indispensable.

Criteria for Evaluating Units of Work

Criteria or standards for the selection and evaluation of units of work have recently been suggested in various books.[1] Only a brief list will be given here. It should be borne in mind that such criteria serve as guides in the development of the unit as well as in its selection.

1. The unit should involve intimate contact with aspects of social life that are of fundamental significance today. By this criterion, it would be more valuable to study China or the British Empire than

[1] See for example *Teachers' Guide to Child Development*, compiled by the State Curriculum Commission. Sacramento: California State Department of Education, 1930, pp. 25–43, 87.

the Eskimos or Hottentots, because the former are of vastly greater importance in world affairs.

2. The unit should be so developed as to acquaint pupils with the crucial data, relationships, conditions, problems and the significance

Courtesy of San Diego City Schools

The "Santa Maria" Was Designed and Made by These Fifth Grade Children

for human welfare of the field studied. This standard demands proper relative emphasis on the important and the trivial, and a continually broadening social outlook and ever more penetrating social insight. It requires more than a hasty, superficial study of any important topic which is selected.

3. The unit should provide for a large amount of actual experiencing by pupils, and for abundant contact with first hand source materials. The aim is to broaden and enrich the experiences of pupils; not to build up a body of information remote from and alien to the pupils' own activities and the social life he sees going on about him.

4. The unit should provide pupils with abundant opportunities for clarifying and enriching the conceptions gained, through various forms of individual and group expression. Creative expression through meaningful dramatization, construction, drawing, sketching, painting, modeling, pageantry, puppetry, music and other means is a significant part of the process of acquiring understanding.

5. The unit should continually stimulate mental activity on the part of pupils. This should reveal itself in the recognition of problems and in their thoughtful consideration. It is revealed in purposing, planning, executing, and evaluating on ever higher levels.

6. The unit should provide for continuous sharing of purposes, activities, and achievements in an atmosphere of cooperative effort. Pupils should be living the democratic life as well as learning about it.

Things the Teacher Does in Carrying Out a Unit

1. The teacher builds up for herself a rich background in the subject matter of the unit, both before its initiation with the class and during its development.

2. She lists possible approaches to the unit that would make use of the pupils' previous experiences and challenge their interest in the new field.

3. She thinks through questions, problems, reports, excursions, dramatizations, and other activities of all types that might profitably be involved in carrying on the unit.

4. She keeps constantly in mind the immediate and the more ultimate objectives, expressed in terms of the changed understandings, attitudes, interests and habits of boys and girls.

5. She lists and thinks through the social relationships, generalizations, conditions, trends, etc., which should be emphasized in the unit.

6. She chooses and makes available books, articles, pictures, and other types of materials useful to pupils in their work on the unit.

7. She helps her pupils purpose more wisely, plan more thoughtfully, carry out more effectively, and evaluate more critically, in each aspect of the work.

8. She assists the children in organizing themselves into groups and committees for investigation of special phases of the topic, and makes sure that each individual knows what he is to do and how he is to go about it.

9. She insures that the work of each group and each individual contribute to a better understanding of the whole unit.

10. She leads and takes part in group discussions, in which pupils, with her guidance, determine goals, plan procedures, and evaluate achievements. She will frequently challenge assumptions, point out misconceptions, encourage more careful thinking, and suggest higher attainable standards.

11. She makes provision for definitely organized, effective drill on the skills found useful in furthering the work of the unit.

12. She provides for frequent review and simultaneously for the new view that comes from perceiving the details of daily work through the perspective of a growing background.

13. She continually interrelates the direct first-hand experiences of pupils and the information gained from second-hand sources, to the mutual enrichment of each.

14. She plans for a concluding activity which will serve to integrate and emphasize the important outcomes of the unit. In many cases, this culminating phase will involve sharing experiences with others in an exhibit, play, or other type of program.

V.   SOCIAL STUDIES ARE THE INTEGRATING CENTER OF THE CURRICULUM

The Value of Integrated Experience

Since the school has a social purpose, the content of instruction must be chiefly concerned with man and his society, present, past, and future. The units of work which constitute the curriculum inevitably relate to various aspects of social life and to the phenomena of nature. Social studies are necessarily the core of the curriculum. There is no other subject which can possibly occupy that strategic position. Reading, writing and the other skills enter as necessary tools in carrying on the socialized units, and together with music, art, and dramatics, also provide pupils with means of giving expression to the social insights and appreciations acquired. Only through such integration of the skill, the informational, and the esthetic and expressive aspects of the curriculum does each become most educative. Each subject has its own distinctive value in the development of an integrated personality, but no subject can make its rightful contribution in isolation. Skills and processes are significant only in relation to individual and social purposes. Each subject emphasizes one phase of the integrated experience of living, and should be understood in that relationship.

If this reasoning is valid, pupils in the intermediate grades will spend a considerable portion of each school day in the various activities involved in the development of a unit of work having significant social content. They will utilize every skill the school teaches in effectively investigating the chosen field of interest. They will extend and deepen their understanding and appreciation of that aspect of life by giving expression to their discoveries through as wide a variety of media as the school can provide. This is the true meaning of integration or correlation in the school program. Social studies must be its center.

Emphasis upon integration of the school program is not intended to suggest the abolition of school subjects. There is very great need for systematic, well planned practice in each useful skill. Definite time must be provided for mastering the tools of learning, as well as for diagnostic and remedial measures, designed to eliminate difficulties. There must be no sacrifice or neglect of any worth while contributions which have been made to the child's development by the older methods of teaching each subject separately. There need be no such sacrifice, but on the other hand there should result increased appreciation of the values and improved command of the techniques of all subjects when they are continually utilized in the prosecution of socially motivated enterprises. It is insisted, however, that academic skills are but the tools with which the individual may achieve an education. The motive for mastering the skills should come from a realization of their usefulness in carrying on group and social activities, and as they are progressively acquired they should make participation in such activities more effective. Perfecting skills is, after all, a subordinate part of the elementary school's function.

VI. EVALUATING RESULTS IN SOCIAL STUDIES

The Inadequacy of Information Tests

What constitutes success in the teaching of social studies? The obvious answer is: successful attainment of the fundamental objectives. But the objectives are broad and inclusive, involving desirable changes in the civic attitudes, interests, and behavior of the individual. Certainly mere knowledge of isolated facts does not indicate successful teaching of social studies. Yet this is virtually the only outcome measured by most commonly used tests. Not only informal tests made by the teacher for her own group of pupils but standardized tests used in great numbers throughout the country likewise emphasize memory of isolated, unrelated, and often comparatively unimportant scraps of information. The reasons for this practice are apparent. In the first place, facts have been traditionally emphasized as the almost exclusive outcome of instruction in history and geography. The second reason is the ease of devising a test of facts and the difficulty of measuring the most intangible and more important outcomes.

Dangers in Overemphasis of Test Results

The misuse of information tests threatens very serious consequences to the teaching of social studies. Teachers' efforts to attain the fundamental objectives will be frustrated if their success in teaching is judged wholly or primarily by the scores of their pupils on such tests. On this basis, the best teacher is the one who most persistently drills her pupils on the answers to specific questions of fact, i.e., isolated fragments of information. Where this type of testing is emphasized, any attempt to develop civic understandings, ideals, attitudes, and dispositions becomes professional suicide for the teacher. Whenever standardized social studies tests of the factual type are regularly given throughout a school for any purpose, it is difficult to convince teachers that their work is not judged by the scores of their pupils. In view of this situation, the wisdom of using such tests may well be questioned, for they also give pupils the wrong conception of achievement in social studies.

We are not suggesting that children can get along without facts. If a class has devoted several weeks or months to the study of China, for example, the pupils should have a great amount of definite, organized, accurate information about China. The teacher should frequently evaluate the accuracy and range of information acquired by means of tests of various types. She should also attempt to evaluate the pupils' ability to use that information in solving problems, clarifying relationships, and drawing generalizations, as well as attempting to "size up" their attitudes and interests in regard to the Chinese. Such testing for definite factual knowledge in the specific field of study is very different from that secured through the shotgun type of test which demands a smattering of information about everything and no real understanding of anything.

Other Outcomes Must Be Evaluated

The use of factual tests would be less pernicious if tests of other important outcomes were available. Since we can not measure attitudes, interests and behaviors through paper-and-pencil tests, we are obligated to evaluate them in other ways. Behavior can be observed, and accurate observation is the first step in measurement. Interests are revealed through the spontaneous activities of pupils when free from the pressure of teacher or of classmates. When pupils do more work in a chosen field than is expected of them, when they continue to study and discuss a vital topic after the organized study of it has been concluded, they reveal an intensity and permanence of interest that should delight the heart of the teacher. Attitudes toward the peoples of other races, nationalities and groups, toward civic and social conditions and problems, toward the efficacy or futility of intelligent cooperative effort, attitudes of open-mindedness and tolerance, these and many other attitudes are of supreme importance in determining the behavior of the individual. Although subtle and only partially understood, attitudes can be rather accurately estimated from the specific statements and actions of individuals. If teachers will persistently watch for evidence of growing interests and attitudes, they will find that these outcomes can be measured with considerable reliability, and that their development can be guided along desirable lines.

VII. THE CHALLENGE TO TEACHERS OF SOCIAL STUDIES

The success of a social studies program depends upon the teacher. The course of study, textbooks, supplementary materials, and local environment are educationally valuable only as the teacher makes them so. In the development of constructive citizenship there is no substitute for a wise and skilful teacher. No other factor compares with this one in determining the quality of experience that pupils have. The conception of civic education here presented makes heavy, but legitimate, demands upon one who would achieve its goals. Four types of demands may be indicated: (1) A clear vision of the objectives of civic education, combined with skill and resourcefulness in making all experiences and subject matter contribute to their attainment. (2) Faith in human nature, in democratic living and in the possibility of a better world through intelligence and good will. (3) Sympathetic insight into children's interests and recognition of the significance of their activities. (4) Interest in, and a growing understanding of, the world the teacher is trying to help children understand and appreciate.

The first of these four demands explains the difficulty of teaching social studies. To follow specific directions and fixed rules is comparatively easy for teachers, as for others. Much more difficult to conceive

8—17050

and to practice is the viewpoint that effective teaching consists in the continual modification of materials and methods, in the light of the developing experiences of boys and girls, in order to achieve, gradually but progressively, the true objectives of social education. This makes teaching a fine art, indeed. Some teachers are forever wanting to be told just what to do and how to do it. Such requests are essentially futile, for if the what and the how do not grow out of an adequate realization of the why, they lose their significance. Procedures in themselves have no value; only as they contribute to the attainment of worthy goals do they gain importance. If as teachers we will work first to define and and redefine our objectives, not on paper merely, but in actual practice, then we can ourselves evaluate methods and materials, and our work will gain in significance as well as in effectiveness.

In recent years, teachers have, by some, been charged with civic and economic illiteracy. Certainly, no such indictment should be deserved by those whose chief function is leading boys and girls to an understanding of their world and its problems. Teachers should be among the best informed and socially alert citizens of each community. Their behavior ought to show that education not only has made them law abiding but also improves aggressive citizenship. This obligation of teachers should be considered a privilege rather than a burden, however, for it brings its personal rewards as well as its professional compensations. Life is much more interesting to one who knows what is going on in the world and who takes part in civic activities. The danger of preoccupation with one's own petty affairs and of overconcern for the trivial annoyances of the classroom are lessened. Because of the nature of their work, teachers need this protection against the development of unwholesome mental states. Contacts and friends are formed that are valuable in themselves and that enrich one's background for professional service. The issue confronting teachers of social studies is clear. Shall the school lag hopelessly behind its civic opportunities and obligations, serving as a brake upon the wheels of progress, or shall it contribute both motive power and guidance to the progress of society as it labors up the rough road toward a higher civilization and a finer life for humanity?

BIBLIOGRAPHY ON SOCIAL-ECONOMIC PROBLEMS FOR THE TEACHER

ADAMS, J. T.   *The Epic of America.*   Boston: Little, Brown and Company, 1931.

BURNS, C. D.   *Leisure in the Modern World.*   New York: The Century Co., 1932.

CHASE, STUART.   *The Economy of Abundance.*   New York: The Macmillan Company, 1934.

COLE, G. D. H.   *The Intelligent Man's Review of Europe Today.*   New York: Alfred A. Knopf, 1933.

COUNTS, G. S. *Dare the School Build a New Social Order?* New York: The John Day Company, 1932.

EDDY, G. S. *The Challenge of the East.* New York: Farrar & Rinehart, Inc., 1931.

Elementary School Libraries. Twelfth Yearbook. National Education Association. Department of Elementary School Principals. Washington: National Education Association, 1933.

FORMAN, H. J. *Our Movie Made Children.* New York: The Macmillan Company, 1933.

HAMBIDGE, GOVE. *Time to Live.* New York: McGraw-Hill Book Company, 1933.

JACKS, L. P. *Education Through Recreation.* New York: Harper and Brothers, 1932.

JUDD, C. H. *Problems of Education in the United States.* New York: McGraw-Hill Book Company, 1933.

KILPATRICK, W. H. *Education and the Social Crisis.* New York: Liveright Publishing Corporation, 1932.

KILPATRICK, W. H.; BODE, B. H.; DEWEY, JOHN, AND OTHERS. *The Educational Frontier.* New York: The Century Co., 1933.

LEAGUE OF NATIONS. Secretariat. *Ten Years of World Cooperation.* Boston: World Peace Foundation, 1930.

LIES, E. T. *The New Leisure Challenges the Schools.* New York: National Recreation Association, 1933.

LIPPMANN, WALTER, and SCROGGS, W. A. *The United States in World Affairs.* New York: Harper and Brothers, 1932–34. 3 Vol.

MARTIN, E. D. *The Meaning of a Liberal Education.* New York: W. W. Norton & Company, Inc., 1926.

MOULTON, H. G., and PASVOLSKY, LEO. *War Debts and World Prosperity.* New York: The Century Co., 1932.

OVERSTREET, H. A. *We Move in New Directions.* New York: W. W. Norton & Company, Inc., 1933.

POWYS, J. C. *The Meaning of Culture.* New York: W. W. Norton & Company, Inc., 1929.

RUGG, H. O. *Culture and Education in America.* New York: Harcourt, Brace & Company, 1931.

RUGG, H. O., and SHUMAKER, ANN. *The Child Centered School; an Appraisal of the New Education.* New York: World Book Company, 1928.

SALTER, SIR JAMES ARTHUR, and OTHERS. *The World's Economic Crisis, and the Way of Escape.* New York: D. Appleton-Century Company, 1932.

SIMONDS, F. H. *Can America Stay at Home?* New York: Harper and Brothers, 1932.

WASHBURNE, C. W. *Remakers of Mankind.* New York: The John Day Company, 1932.

CHAPTER VI

SCIENCE [1]

THE PLACE OF SCIENCE IN MODERN LIFE

The present world is unintelligible to one ignorant of science. No realm of human activity or thought can be adequately considered apart from the influence of science. Whether we think of our miraculous modern methods of transportation and communication, the well-nigh automatic machinery which each year produces a larger percentage of the goods we consume, the safeguarding of health and elimination of disease and suffering, the mind-stretching findings of astronomers and physicists who explore the vast stretches of the universe and the minute complexity of the atom, or the baffling social and economic problems which plague us as we attempt to adjust our ideas and habits to the economy of abundance which scientific technology promises us, the significant role of science is apparent on every hand. If the major purpose of the school is to orient children in their world, it can not neglect to give them an understanding of the subject matter and the method of science.

Science has been defined as knowledge at its best, knowledge in its tested and surest form. Science is tested thought, but it is also a method of thinking, not merely one among many methods of thinking, but the only method of rigorous, critical thinking. As John Dewey has said, "It *is* thinking so far as thought has become conscious of its proper ends and of the equipment indispensable for success in their pursuit."

The importance of science in life and in education will be more apparent, if we stop to analyze its contributions to the modern world. First and most obvious, is the role science has played in remaking the physical basis of life. Not only have the age-old threats of famine and pestilence been virtually banished, but, we are assured, science has given mankind, for the first time since man existed on this earth, the means of abolishing poverty, want, hunger and insecurity. Science offers us the means if we can but learn to make use of them. On the other hand, it threatens to destroy us with its too effective instruments of warfare, even with its highspeed automobiles, if we fail in subordinating its power to humane ends. Our use of science depends upon our system of values, our philosophy of life.

---

[1] Contributed by Dr. John A. Hockett, Department of Education, University of California.

The mental and spiritual values of science, while less evident, are no less important. The development of science has done much to eliminate mankind's inferiority complex. Without science, man is a cringing, terrified creature, overwhelmed by the caprices of a hostile universe, doomed to a life of toil and insecurity. Science gives man confidence in his ability to understand and control nature for his own purposes. It assures him that he can find ways of satisfying his needs and desires. It convinces him not only that he can learn, but also that he can learn how to learn, nature's secrets. It gives him hope that he may solve his problems in the social sciences by the same use of intelligence that has proved so fruitful in the natural sciences. Science enlarges man's vision of the possibilities of human experience, at the same time that it places in his hand instruments of tremendous potentiality for good or ill.

THE PURPOSE AND SCOPE OF SCIENCE IN THE ELEMENTARY SCHOOL

If we are to live in a world permeated by science, we must be aware of the potentialities and dangers which it presents to us both individually and collectively. This fact suggests the functions of the school in teaching science. The inclusive aim is to help young people understand the significance of science, its method and spirit, the problems and difficulties which its rapid growth has caused, and the possibilities for human welfare in its rational control and its extension to other aspects of life. The elementary school can do much to further the attainment of this objective. Boys and girls in the intermediate grades can know, and value, the difference between idle guesswork, mere speculation, and ignorant opinion on the one hand and verified knowledge on the other. They can sense the difference in attitude of the scientist and the propagandist or promoter. With their love of biography and adventure, they can thrill to the stories of pioneers in science who have revealed to men the potentialities of their own intelligence. Hopeful and forward looking as youth is, it can be enthusiastic over the possibilities of extending the role of intelligence in human affairs. Science study can be for young people a thrilling adventure, richly educative in the deepest sense.

Science has much to contribute to the life of every boy and girl, much of adventure, of enjoyment, of beauty, and of understanding. We should help children enjoy their exploration of the world of nature in its many aspects. They will do so if we lead them in an eager quest of investigation and understanding of nature's phenomena, and avoid fixed and formal lessons about science subjects which are but facts to be memorized. One of our first objectives will be to keep alive their native interest and enthusiasm in nature and science. In California especially, no child should grow up without an abiding love of the great out-of-doors, and its beauty, its perennial freshness, its wholesome recreative power.

Throughout the elementary school program, we must plan for the two important phases of science instruction; learning about and enjoying nature and natural phenomena, and growing in understanding and appreciation of the scientific method.

The potential content of science for the elementary school child is vast and inclusive. The objective is to insure his acquaintance with all important aspects of his environment, rather than make him a specialist in one restricted area. Because of special interests, however, some children will study some areas much more than others. Here, as in social studies, a moderately intensive study of certain important units will yield values that can never be achieved by superficially skimming the surface of everything under, and beyond, the sun. Intensive study of significant units does not necessitate a one-sided or provincial curriculum.

Children should certainly study living things, beginning perhaps with pets, and including such life forms as birds, insects, animals, flowers, and trees. They can perceive the adaptation of living things to diverse environments, the struggle for existence, the survival of the fittest, the balance of nature, the conditions necessary to life and the economic and other values to men of the different species. They should know something of earth science, the geologic forms and forces, the physical geography of continents, the nature of ocean tides and currents, and the composition and movements of the atmosphere, with their influences on weather and climate.

Intermediate grade pupils are interested in the sun, moon, planets, and stars, and should be aided in orienting themselves not only in the world but in the universe. It is enlightening to learn of the vastness of space, the inconceivable duration of astronomic time, and the magnitude of the forces that exist in suns and nebulae. Physical and chemical forces and their simple manifestations will also be investigated: sound, light, heat, magnetism, and electricity. These present numerous opportunities for original investigation and experimentation.

Biological science must not be neglected, for one needs to understand the elementary principles of biology to live hygienically and to safeguard one's health and safety. It may be that health instruction is best given in connection with the study of life needs and processes.

Finally, man's applied uses of science in the daily work and play of the world need study. These applications in agriculture, industry, health, and all realms of human activity are too numerous to list. Some conception of the historical development of science and the scientific attitude might well be gained, as well as a recognition of the present conflicts between scientific and non-scientific practices and points of view.

THE INTERRELATIONS OF SOCIAL STUDIES AND SCIENCE

In the preceding chapter was emphasized the necessity of understanding the motives, ideals, and activities of human beings. It is well to consider that activities of people are determined by the nature of the world they live in. The story of civilization is the record of man's efforts to use the materials and forces of nature in fulfilling his own needs and desires. Man's very aims and purposes, indeed, grow out of the conditions of his natural environment. Aspirations which do not take into account the limiting realities of the world as it is, are visionary day-dreams. All this is but to say that the study of social life necessitates a correlative study of the forces and materials of nature; social studies and science are inextricably interwoven. Every unit or topic in social studies involves science. Transportation is a major social activity, but its modern development involves ten thousand applications of scientific principles. Such is true also of communication, the provision of shelter, the manufacture of clothing, the processing of food, the furnishing of entertainment, the generation and distribution of electrical power and light. Conservation of health, life and natural resources are significant human purposes achieved through the applications of science. Every important social activity is permeated with science. Young people can not grow in an understanding of social life without simultaneously studying the possibilities and limitations set by science.

Similarly, every unit in science involves social considerations. The study of birds, plants, animals, insects, magnetism, electricity, weather or any other science topic is superficial and miseducative if it fails to include the implications of the subject for human welfare. A major source of present-day difficulties is our facile application of scientific principles, in industry and otherwise, without thinking through their social effects. Science must be humanized; science study in our schools must be humanized.

Some units of work will be classified as social studies, others as elementary science, but there can be no rigid separation of the two fields of study. In both fields the important outcomes will be in terms of understanding rather than mere factual information. The perception of relationships, sensing of cause and effect sequences, exercise of originality in discovering problems and critically collecting evidence for their consideration—these are the typically educative experiences in both fields. Reading will be used to extend and to stimulate first-hand experience in science as in social studies. Literature will help children not only to understand the mysteries of nature but to appreciate its beauties, as with John Muir they thrill to the ecstatic charm of the singing waterfall or the courageous tenacity of the rugged conifer. So too, will writing and art be freely drawn upon as means to clarify, record, and express the intellectual and emotional experiences of pupils. There is much art in nature; children's experience can be greatly enriched and refined through a close correlation of art and science. Arithmetic, too, is essential in dealing with many phases of science, physical science in particular.

From the teaching viewpoint, science has one marked advantage over social studies. The materials of science can be seen, touched, and experimented with. They are less abstract and more amenable to manipulation than the subject matter of social studies. This distinction

Courtesy of Sacramento City Schools

The Materials of Science Can Be Seen, Touched, and Experimented With

suggests the wisdom of beginning with the concrete or science phases of many units, and subsequently leading on to the more abstract and hidden social implications.

MATERIALS AND ACTIVITIES IN ELEMENTARY SCIENCE

Materials for science study lie about us on every hand. There is no school without its trees, flowers, birds, and insects. Every group of children has its pets. Every community contains countless applications of science, in its industries, power distributing system, water supply, and health precautions. Many communities have their hills, or fields, mountains, seashore, desert, or river. All have the starry heavens above and the clouds, winds, and rain. Most classes can find space for at least a small flower or vegetable garden. Every room may contain potted plants, jars for caterpillars, beetles, and "bugs" of all kinds. Any group may improvise an aquarium and find pollywogs and water plants, if not turtles and fish to stock it.

Every school should provide some sort of laboratory where tinkering and experimenting can be carried on. A corner, an alcove or a cubbyhole in the basement will suffice if nothing better can be devised. If no funds for equipment are available, let it be known that contributions will be accepted as materials can be found. Dry cells, electric wire, small light globes, a magnet and iron filings, thermometer, alcohol lamp, glass tubing, magnifying glass, prism, pieces of metal, cork, wood, screen, seeds and other equipment will accumulate rapidly. Much equipment may be purchased for a few cents, if not secured gratis. Children can profitably make much of the equipment needed for their investigations.

A science museum, possibly only an exhibit case or a shelf, is useful for the display of collections of rocks, insects, leaves, flowers or any other science materials. It can be used to exhibit models or apparatus made by the pupils, or for charts, diagrams, blue prints, drawings, paintings, and booklets illustrating science subjects.

Pictures, picture books, slides, film strips and moving pictures dealing with science materials are all of great usefulness in every phase of science study.

Pupils will engage in a wide variety of activities in pursuing their science studies. Children ten to twelve years old are almost universally fond of collecting. The making of science collections can be very profitable as well as interesting. This activity may well serve as an introduction to many of the units in science. The teacher's guidance is necessary in helping children determine what specimens to include in their collections, how to organize, preserve, and label the specimens, and in observing desirable standards of conservation.

Much of the study of living plants and animals is best carried on in the natural habitat of the life form. Excursions or field trips for observation and study are, therefore, of great importance in science study. Definite preparation should be made for each trip, including a decision regarding the purposes of the trip and the methods of study. Further discussion should summarize the findings and conclusions of the excursion and determine the next steps to be taken in answering the questions and satisfying the interest growing out of the trip. Let us reemphasize the importance of trips, for science deals with things and involves first-hand investigation, and can not be rightly learned from books alone.

Book study is important, however, as a supplement to first-hand experience. Books contain answers to questions that personal observation and investigation can not answer. Books suggest further possibilities of experimentation and research. Books serve to extend and enrich experience, but can not take the place of actual experience.

Children ought to care for pets, make gardens, and experiment with the growth of seeds and plants. They should experiment with electricity, magnetism, heat, light, harmless chemicals, metals, woods and various substances. A certain amount of apparently aimless tinkering is often valuable in building up a familiarity with materials and in leading to more thoughtful questioning. Pupils can profitably construct toys and models illustrating scientific principles.

Courtesy of Inyo County Schools

Children Can Profitably Construct Toys and Models Illustrating Scientific Principles

Expression of new or beautiful conceptions can be made in other ways, too. Sketching, diagraming, drawing, and painting are forms of expression available to all. Modeling of animals, natural formations, and engineering achievements such as dams or canals is another profitable activity. Photography may be used in many phases of science work. Photographic studies may be made of birds, plants, or animals. Snapshots of machines made on excursions serve to explain their construction and operation to others, and to recall the essential features to those who took part in the experience.

METHODS IN ELEMENTARY SCIENCE

Science is not so much a subject to be taught as a fascinating realm to be discovered and explored. The elementary school child has a keen interest in the scientific aspects of his environment. The first principle of effective method is to maintain and strengthen his curiosity as to the hows and whys of things. His eager, sensitive mind is like that of the true scientist who is unsatisfied with obvious or superficial explanations and ceaselessly strives to push back the frontiers of knowledge. It is contrary to the whole spirit of science to substitute fixed lessons to be learned from a book for this joyous quest for experience and enlightenment. The teacher's role is to stimulate new interests and encourage children to go beyond the mere learning of names and characteristics to the discovery of causes, relationships, principles, and laws.

The teacher can well afford to place the cultivation of the scientific spirit first in her thinking. The emphasis given this factor by Dewey some years ago is more sorely needed now than ever:

> One of the only two articles that remains in my creed of life is that the future of our civilization depends upon the widening spread and deepening hold of the scientific habit of mind: and that the problem of problems in our education is therefore to discover how to mature and make effective this scientific habit.

While no tricks of pedagogy can substitute for a sincere scientific mindedness on the part of the teacher, all of us can cultivate in ourselves and our children certain methods of thinking which further growth in this all-important characteristic of mind. The child's tendency to question must, as we have suggested, be kept alive and stimulated to grow. Each child must be encouraged to sense problems as he observes and investigates nature's ways. In many cases, help will be needed in formulating the problem so as to make its consideration most fruitful. Plans for solving the problem will be considered and evaluated. Hypotheses to explain various phenomena will be suggested. Evidence will be accumulated, and that which is irrelevant discarded. The different hypotheses, theories, or explanations will be critically considered in the light of the evidence. Tentative conclusions will be drawn as justified by the evidence. Open-mindedness will be encouraged, however, and the fact recognized that further evidence might modify or contradict the apparent conclusion. The quality of thinking carried on by the pupils is the primary consideration. Long years of practice are required if the individual is to become thoroughly imbued with the spirit of science. The school seriously hinders the achievement of this goal if it substitutes the authoritarian acceptance of textbook information for the embryonic research attitudes characteristic of children.

It need hardly be emphasized that the problems to be considered should be primarily those arising in the experiences of the children rather than those posed by some writer of textbook or course of study. Throughout the study of science care should be observed to prevent the development of a gap between the experiences of daily life that might be illuminated by science, but are not, and the piling up of information that does not relate to any life activities of the pupil. The skilful teacher recognizes possibilities in the simplest experience or question of the child to lead on to a better understanding of some phase of science, and so of life.

The ideal teacher of science has retained much of childhood's interest and enthusiasm for the world of nature. By her own attitude she maintains an atmosphere conducive to exploration and discovery. If she is well versed in nature lore and science she can greatly enrich children's experiences by suggesting and leading on into fascinating by-paths and little known fields. Lacking such a background, she may be almost if not fully as effective by joining with her young explorers in a common quest for adventure, beauty, and understanding in the enchanting realm of science.

CHAPTER VII

UNITS OF WORK IN SOCIAL STUDIES AND SCIENCE[1]

PROGRAM OF UNITS

Is there a series of best units which if allocated to the grades will insure the child who passes through the elementary schools the greatest possible number of rich experiences for the time spent? Without doubt some units are more profitable for the majority of children of a given grade than are others. Compare People of the Middle Ages and Homes, for example, as units for third grade children. The concepts involved in the former are beyond the normal eight year old child. Furthermore, the content of such a unit would not be useful to the child in any of three fundamental types of activities: dramatic play, construction with materials, and experimentation. Unless he engages repeatedly in such activities he is not placed in situations for learning the techniques of cooperation and problem solving. A unit on People of the Middle Ages would not acquaint the child with a modern institution which has any bearing on his life; nor would it afford art experiences leading to the development of appreciation of beauty.

The unit, *Homes,* on the other hand, is suitable for the third grade level for the reason that the concepts involved relate to the basic and elementary needs of the child himself, and of society; namely, *food, shelter, clothing, tools* and *utensils,* and *records.* In reliving the daily experiences of these primitive people the children find innumerable opportunities for expression through creative play and simple constructive activities. It is in the situations and informal relationship provided by such activities that the children under proper guidance learn to work and play happily and cooperatively together.

Even though it be true that certain units are richer in educative possibilities than are others, does this fact point to the conclusion that there should be a fixed program of units? Such standardization is invariably stultifying. For many years courses of study made definite assignments of subject matter and even indicated the number of weeks to be devoted to each topic. The result was an emphasis on the memorization of specific items of subject matter rather than the use of facts

---

[1] Contributed by Ethel I. Salisbury, Associate Professor of Elementary Education, University of California at Los Angeles, and Educational Consultant, Santa Monica Public Schools.

Courtesy of Sonoma County Schools

Children Relive the Experiences of Primitive People

in solving problems, carrying out enterprises and gaining understandings.

Should, then, the program of units for a class be determined entirely by the teacher who, knowing the ability and background of her pupils, applies the criteria for selecting a unit to whatever makes an appeal to the children? To leave the choice entirely to the individual teacher seems hardly feasible for several reasons.

First, successful guidance must always be anticipated months in advance by carefully planned book orders and adoptions as well as the purchase and collection of suitable materials. Otherwise when the teacher and children come together there may be nothing with which to work. Furthermore, unless there is a general program of broad topics assigned to each grade it is conceivable that one class might study the same topic in several successive years. Lastly, it is not to be expected that the teacher will have personal knowledge of the many books, their content and reading difficulty which should serve as instructional material.

To avoid rigidity and over-organization on the one hand and chaos on the other it seems best to indicate for each grade level certain broad topics to be subdivided into many units, each of which is rich in possibilities for study. For example, the United States may be allocated to the low fifth grade. Every experienced teacher knows that the possibilities of such a topic can be little more than tapped by children of this grade. The United States is, therefore, subdivided into such units as Manufacturing, Farming, Cities, Clothing, Shelter, Westward Trails, Forestry, and others listed on page 102. One or two, not more than three of these units, should be the basis for the work of a semester. A class that studies the first three mentioned above with constant reference to maps can hardly fail to derive many facts and geographic principles, both of which are important outcomes. The primary objective of the teacher, however, is the same no matter what subject matter is involved, namely, to guide children so that they will have frequent opportunities to plan, to carry out their plans, to evaluate, to cooperate, to practice the techniques of thinking, or problem solving, to see and create beauty.

If the child in his working hours is really engaged in these activities he will acquire an enormous amount of information. Obviously, each child may not, probably will not, become intimately acquainted with all the countries of the world or with all the periods of history. Such a feat is not the goal of social studies. Even in the days when several continents were assigned to each grade to prevent gaps in subject matter the objective of comprehensive knowledge was never realized.

There must be time for experiencing. For this reason, excellent teachers frequently limit the work of a semester to one unit in order that the children may carry out plans that take hours for execution and also that they may follow interesting leads or digressions as long as these prove educative. Such digressions often involve much of the content of related units.

The outline on pages 100–103 offers a choice within rather broad limits. A few teachers with good libraries at hand or with the ability to write and facilities for duplicating informational material may wish to take the children into an intensive study of some local project such as a unit on paving, if this activity happens to be going on in front of the school, or a project relating to the construction of a nearby bridge or dam. Local projects of this type offer a wealth of experiences for children, particularly along civic lines, providing the teacher can make the study more than a sightseeing tour, obviate hazards, prevent the children from becoming a nuisance to the workers, enlist the cooperation of those who can explain things in detail to the children and answer their questions, guide the activities of the children in such ways that they derive real values, provide related materials, and extend the study beyond its local aspects. Any curriculum should be flexible enough to permit such departures with the counsel of the supervisor.

There is a certain amount of preliminary work necessary on the part of a teacher if she is to guide a class into profitable activities related to a unit. For this reason and others, it is usually not feasible for her to come before a class on the first day of the semester and ask "What unit would you like to study?" Such a procedure brings forth many different and often superficial replies. If the teacher and children have worked together on a previous unit she can probably see opportunities to make a natural outgrowth of a former unit.

If, however, teacher and children are new to each other, she should try to get acquainted with the personnel of the class as early as possible even before school begins. She will need to know their general background, the units they have had, and the range and distribution of ability within the class. With these data in mind the teacher will examine available reading material. Subjects should be within their everyday experience such as pets, the post office, and the like. These units can be very short.

TYPES OF SOCIAL STUDIES UNITS

During any one year pupils are led into units emphasizing different types of content and different techniques of study. Probably groups of people, contemporary and historical, should most frequently be the central theme for the social studies activities of the intermediate grades.

Contemporary groups include national and tribal peoples, such as the Japanese, Italians, Germans, and Pueblos, as well as occupational and regional groups including such workers as Miners, Fishermen, and Manufacturers. The study of contemporary groups tends to stress geographic principles and adaptation of peoples to environment, and more important still, relationships among peoples.

Historical groups, of which Ancient Greece, Medieval Life, Phoenicians, and Pioneers are examples, offer a different point of emphasis. They show the beginnings of things and afford perspective on modern institutions and achievements. While these units are rich in opportunities for children to gain geographic principles, they are most valuable for the appreciations they develop. Narrative and dramatic phases are capitalized and the life of other days is made vivid and concrete.

Industrial arts units approach directly the "study of the ways and means by which we are efficiently supplied with the materials and products which we use in daily life." In these units children are concerned with the processes through which raw materials must go to become valuable merchandise. Food, shelter, clothing, and pottery are typical industrial arts units.

Science units offer a content especially adapted to experimentation and problem-solving with first hand materials as contrasted with problem-solving from books alone. Children who are indifferent to the study of remote places and peoples frequently find a challenge in the activities related to science units. The techniques involved are so different from those of other units that science should sometimes be the central theme for class room work. It is true that there are science aspects to other types of units, for example, silk worm raising in connection with the unit on China.

Science teaching in the elementary school has been somewhat handicapped because of a scarcity of adequate instructional materials. There is a definite need and growing demand both for suitable reference material for pupils and for suggestions on instructional content and methods for teachers. To assist in meeting the latter need, the California State Department of Education, in 1934, began the publication of a series of bulletins entitled *Science Guide for Elementary Schools.* The publication of this series is a cooperative project; the materials being written by members of the science faculties of the California State Colleges who are specialists in the subjects treated, and the bulletins being edited and published by the State Department of Education. Each bulletin of the series deals with a selected science subject suitable for the elementary school program. Ten bulletins in this series are published each year.[1]

Other types of units could be listed. If selections are made from the groups here named, however, children will be exposed to a variety of content and have practice in different techniques of study. There is no thought that the teacher will feel restricted to the suggestions given here.

SUGGESTED ALLOCATION OF UNITS BY GRADES

The units listed below are classified according to the major emphasis in each. They are included because their values have been repeatedly demonstrated. A unit classified under one heading, however, may include many activities which if emphasized would place the unit under another heading.

GRADE 3

PRIMITIVE LIFE, AND CHILD LIFE IN FOREIGN LANDS

Social Studies

Holland	Pueblo Indians
Japan	Prairie Indians
Polar Regions	Appropriate Holidays
Indians of California	Food
Yuroks (Wooded Valley)	Homes
Maidu (Great Central	The Postman
Valley Foothills, and	Milk and the Milk Man
Mountains)	Trains
Mojaves (Desert)	
Chumash (Santa Barbara	
Islands) Extinct	

Science

Pets	Animals	Sea Life	Wild Flowers
Dogs	Birds	Garden	Frogs

---

[1] Following are the titles of this series for 1934–35 and 1935–36.
No. 1, August, 1934. *Suggestions to Teachers for the Science Program in Elementary Schools*
No. 2, September, 1934. *Pets and Their Care*
No. 3, October, 1934. *Common Insects*
No. 4, November, 1934. *Sky Study*
No. 5, December, 1934. *Weather*
No. 6, January, 1935. *Frogs, Toads, and Salamanders*
No. 7, February, 1935. *School and Home Gardens*
No. 8, March, 1935. *Trees*
No. 9, April, 1935. *Birds*
No. 10, May, 1935. *Snakes, Lizards, and Turtles*

No. 1, August, 1935. *Tide-Pool Animals*
No. 2, September, 1935. *Man's Tools*
No. 3, October, 1935. *Spiders*
No. 4, November, 1935. *How the Energy of Nature Has Been Harnessed for Man's Use*
No. 5, December, 1935. *How Living Things Get Food*
No. 6, January, 1936. *Mushrooms and Other Fungi*
No. 7, February, 1936. *Desert Life*
No. 8, March, 1936. *Wild Flower Roads to Learning*
No. 9, April, 1936. *Ornamental Shrubs*
No. 10, May, 1936. *Fresh Water Animals*

GRADE 4

CALIFORNIA, AND CHILD LIFE IN OTHER LANDS

Social Studies	Science
Harbors of California	Weather
California National Parks	California Animals
California Highways	Sun, Moon, and Stars
China, African Congo,	California Wild Flowers
Arabia, Switzerland	Desert Life
Spanish Days in California	Bees and Butterflies
Pioneer Days in California	California Trees
Appropriate Holidays	
Farmers in California	
Citrus Fruit Growers in	
California	
Manufacturers in California	
Fishermen in California	
Water Supply in California	
Ships	
Trains	

Courtesy of Los Angeles County Schools

Fifth Grade Boys Reliving Pioneer Days

GRADE LOW 5

THE UNITED STATES

Social Studies	Science
Farming	Aquariums
Cattle Raising, Dairying,	Horses
Midwest Farming, Truck	Rocks
Farming, Cotton Raising	Magnets
Manufacturing	
Automobiles	
Textiles	
Shoes, Paper	
Mining	
Coal, Gold, Iron, Oil, etc.	
Forestry	
Fishing	
Cities	
Exploration	
Pioneer Life	
Westward Trails	
Great Men	
Shelter	
Clothing	
Modern Air Travel	
History of Travel	

GRADE HIGH 5

OUR NEIGHBORS NORTH AND SOUTH

Social Studies	Science
Mexico	Animals
The People and the Land	Ants
South America	Cotton
Life in Contrasting Areas	Bats
such as City and Jungle	
Canada	
Mexico before the Spaniards	
Spanish Explorers of Mexico	
The Buccaneers	
French Explorers in Canada	
Fur Trappers of Canada	
Pottery	
Industries in Canada	
Lumbering	
Farming	
Fishing	
Paper Making	

GRADE LOW 6

THE ANCIENT WORLD

Social Studies	Science
Prehistoric Man	Light
Babylonians	Electricity
Hebrews	Flies
Phoenicians	
Vikings	
Ancient Egypt	
Ancient Greece	
Ancient Rome	
Records	
Time Telling	
Ships	
Money	
Toys and Toy Making	

GRADE HIGH 6

MEDIEVAL AND MODERN EUROPE

Social Studies	Science
The British Empire	Aviation
France	Communication
Germany	
Rivers of Europe	
The Middle Ages	
Castle Life	
The Crusades	
Craftsmen of the Towns	
and Villages of Medieval	
Europe	

HOW TO GUIDE CHILDREN THROUGH A UNIT OF WORK

The teacher must think through the unit of work which is to be undertaken by the group. A brief statement of the steps through which she must move in her planning may be of value. The illustration is applicable to a unit of work on Mexico.

1. The first steps in guidance are for the teacher to saturate herself with information about Mexico and to collect books and materials on the topic.

2. A list of profitable activities in which the children should engage at some time during the progress of the unit should be made. Such a list will include:

Problems to be solved. Example: Why are there 50 different languages spoken in Mexico?

Things to Make. Example: A Mexican Costume, Charcoal Burner.

Letters and Compositions to Write. Example: Letter to Mexican Consul, Stories About Mexican customs.

Pictures to Draw and Paint. Example: Frieze of Mexican Village Life.

Process to carry out. Example: Making Pottery, Weaving Serapes.

Programs to Give. Example: The Conquest of Tenochitlan.

Phases of Mexican Life Suitable for Dramatic Play. Example: Fiesta, Life on a Hacienda.

3. The topic should be opened with the children in order to discover what background they have for it, where their interests lie in connection with the unit, and what they wish to find out. If the teacher discovers the children have no background, she may proceed in one of several ways. She may show visual materials to them, introduce them to map study, read a story, or invite some well informed person in to give information on the subject. The teacher should also encourage the children to bring in materials. This approach to the unit may occupy several days.

4. The teacher should now organize available material. The children should have a share in this if possible. For example, suppose the general topic is The Mexican Children and the class has asked many different questions about Mexico. Among these questions may be the following five:

1. What are Mexican houses made of?
2. How do the Mexicans cook tortillas?
3. Does the Mexican child sleep on a bed?
4. Do the Mexicans have stoves?
5. Do the Mexicans have three meals a day?

The teacher shows them that all these questions may be answered if they read about Mexican homes. Other questions will follow under the subjects of clothing, food, etc. The teacher and class together may write a simple outline to guide their study, answering the children's questions as they come to the appropriate topic. Example:

The Mexican children
   Types of homes
   Food
   Shelter
   Clothing
   Tools and utensils

5. The teacher should lead the class into the study of one of the minor topics which is a part of the general theme; for example, The Peon's Home, or Aztecs. Here is the place for definite reading assignments. Different books should be used with specific page assignments for individual children, where necessary. The use of different books gives the children a real reason for giving information, knowing that the remainder of the class has not read all the references. Children should be encouraged to speak of authors and titles. Sometimes the reading lesson for particular groups will be concerned with some phase of a study of Mexico. The different types of reading lessons can be used to further the unit and at the same time give definite skill in the subject matter field.

6. The teacher and children should discuss what they have learned, answer questions that have been asked and list further questions which grow out of their reading.

7. The work continues on other minor topics. During the study of a topic the teacher or children may suggest things to do, such as carrying out the paper making process, writing letters, giving dramatizations, writing stories or poems. Before the children engage in any one of these minor activities, the teacher should lead them to set up standards for the particular thing they are going to do. For example, if they are writing a letter to ask for advertising material, they decide:

a. To make it brief
b. To have a heading, salutation, and closing
c. To spell all words correctly
d. To write legibly

When one of these minor activities is completed the teacher leads the children to judge whether or not they have reached the standards. The emphasis is placed on the individual's estimate of his own achievement, guided by the group and the teacher. Constructive suggestions should be encouraged. Undue criticism is to be avoided. The spirit of the group should be kept on a high level.

In rare instances the teacher may allow the class to go ahead even though she knows the results will be inadequate. For example, making a map. The teacher will then use these efforts as a point of departure and develop the class standards based on the criticisms of their efforts; for example, they may evolve the following: Maps should be large enough to be useful. Only a few things should be shown on any one map. Every map should have a legend.

In the use of appreciation materials such as pictures, literature, and music, the teacher does not set up standards. Children and teacher simply enjoy the artistic things without effort to reach goals.

8. The teacher should introduce to the children each day or week those visual materials which apply to the topic under discussion. Materials no longer of use are removed. It is highly desirable that the room should have an orderly appearance.

9. The teacher should provide for drill at intervals to fix the skills necessary to the successful carrying out of activities in connection with the unit. For example, the children, in studying Mexico as a land of contrasts, need to know the elevations and climates, condition of peons, etc., to make the work intelligible.

10. The teacher and children should plan and carry out an assembly program or other summary of the unit. This should not be a long, monotonous recital of everything studied. It should be a varied and interesting program of the high spots of the study. For example: Dramatization of a fiesta scene.

11. Informal and standard tests to measure definitely the outcomes in reading, writing, spelling, arithmetic and other subjects should be used by the teacher as she feels the need.

OUTCOMES

Children's participation in the activities of curriculum units should result in definite growth and development in many respects. The teacher should have in mind the outcomes to be expected from the various experiences in which the child engages. Following are listed certain of the more important of these outcomes in terms of the approximate grade level at which they may be expected to develop. The outcomes listed emphasize behavior traits and habits more than knowledge and skills. Although such outcomes are more difficult to measure, they are among the most important.

GRADES THREE AND FOUR

Group Discussions. The child:

Shares information with others.

Suggests class, group, or individual enterprises.

Makes helpful suggestions in the conference which follows a work period.

Helps to formulate standards for group behavior.

Asks intelligent questions.

Helps to evaluate questions asked by the children and to organize them under large headings, when possible.

Brings material when he agrees to do so.

Getting Information. The child:

Enlists the interest of his parents and friends in the class work.

Gets information by asking people, by going to see for himself, by experimenting, by looking at pictures, and by reading from books.

Is able to select from a page or paragraph statements that have some bearing on the subject.

Uses table of contents effectively.

Listens attentively when others speak.

Asks questions when he does not understand, or does not believe the information given to be correct.

Tries to solve problems without asking help unnecessarily.

Giving Information. The child:

Gives an intelligible report of information obtained by asking someone, by experimenting, or by observing.

Reproduces information that he has read, in such a way as to answer a class question satisfactorily.

Sticks to the point under discussion.

Takes his turn and does not monopolize the conversation.

Shows poise and self-reliance when speaking to the class or when speaking in assembly.

Shows increasing ability to speak freely and naturally without notes.

Shows increasing ability to evaluate all contributions impersonally.

Suggests sentences for group-composed stories.

Writes interesting paragraphs for class or individual booklets.

Takes part in assembly programs which are based on class work.

Creative Experiences. The child:

Records his impressions after a class experience, such as an excursion or an assembly program.

Vivifies his impression through dramatizing situations and experiences pertaining to the class interest, through art work, through modeling, through building.

Satisfies curiosities through observation and through experimentation.

Orientation Experiences. The child:

Can draw a simple floor map of the playground upon which directions are correctly indicated.

Is able to locate Los Angeles, and San Francisco, California, and the United States of America upon a large wall map of the world.

Is able to distinguish between land bodies and water bodies on a map or globe.

Knows what and where the Pacific Ocean is.

Is able to face or point toward the north, the south, the east, and the west.

Knows directions on a wall map.

Knows at least one major street in the neighborhood which runs east and west; another which runs north and south.

Can locate and name some of the interesting landmarks which can be seen from the school; for example, the City Hall, the Public Library, Mount Shasta or Mount Wilson, San Francisco Bay or Catalina Island.

Can locate on the world map the countries which are discussed in class.

Additional Orientation Experiences for Grade Four. The child:

Can locate on a world map all countries or other places referred to in class work.

Can locate on the map of California, Sierra Nevada Mountains, Coast Range Mountains, Mount Whitney, Mount Shasta, and Mount Lowe.

Courtesy of San Diego City Schools

Fifth Grade Children Gain a Knowledge of the Lives of the Pioneers, Their Work and Play, the Homes They Live in, the Clothes They Wear, and the Food They Eat, Through Dramatization

Can locate on map of California, Los Angeles River, Owens River, San Joaquin River, Sacramento River, and Colorado River.

Can locate Lake Tahoe, Mono Lake, and Salton Sea.

Can locate the Great Valley, Death Valley, Imperial Valley, Mojave Desert.

Can locate Los Angeles, San Francisco, Sacramento, San Diego, and Fresno.

Can locate Los Angeles Harbor, San Diego Bay, and San Francisco Bay.

GRADES FIVE AND SIX

Information. The child:

Has knowledge of lives of the people, their work and play, the homes they live in, the clothes they wear, the food they eat, the ways they travel, their art, music, and literature.

Knows how the lives of the people are usually affected by the amount of rainfall, the elevation of land, the distance from the equator, nearness to bodies of water, the quality of the soil and the supply of natural resources.

Can use such geographical and historical and scientific terms as city, state, country, continent, island, ocean, lake, canal, harbor and zone, pioneer, colonial, weather and the like.

Knows the causes of natural phenomena as day and night, heat and cold.

Interests and Appreciations. The child:

Through his comments, his class contributions, or his voluntary reading shows an interest in and an appreciation of:

The ways in which people depend upon one another in matters of every day living, i.e., food, clothing, homes, tools, and utensils.

The contributions of people in the past to living today.

The everyday life of the people studied.

Responsibility. The child:

Takes part in class discussion.

Contributes helpful material from the newspaper, the branch library, the encyclopaedia or from home.

Works cooperatively with a group of his classmates.

Questions statements made by other members of his class.

Takes part in class programs and dramatizations.

Interprets illustrative material made by other members of the class.

Conducts himself courteously on an excursion, a visit to another class room, or the school yard.

Assists in class planning by contributing suggestions.

Contributes from his experiences in previous units material relating to the present unit.

Skills and abilities. The child:

In using books:

Locates material by using the contents or index of a book.

Selects from two or more books only the parts needed for his topic.

Makes a simple bibliography of the books used in his work, giving only the author and title.

Interprets charts, graphs, and pictures found in the books suitable to his grade.

Uses the author's last name and the title when speaking of a book.

Is familiar with the organization of a book so that when the need arises he may use the title page, copyright and date, contents, index, word list or glossary or other helps.

Uses a simple school dictionary when needed.

In preparing reports:

Reads from two or more books in preparing a report.

Takes a few notes in words and phrases in preparation for a report.

Aids in making a class outline or plan, to be used in the work.

Chooses a subject narrow enough for him to handle with success.

Gives an interesting oral report on a subject after content has been built up in class.

Writes in his own words a report rich in content at least one half page long.

Illustrates his report with maps, charts, graphs, diagrams, pictures, simple experiments or constructed articles when they will be useful in explaining points and adding interest.

In using maps, through repeated reference to wall maps, maps in books and globes, understands:

How to use the legend and scale of miles.

How to interpret the key to elevations of land.

That the top of the map is north, the bottom south, the right-hand side east, and the left-hand side west.

Locates on the map the places mentioned in the social studies period, and locates on any map the important places to which the class continually refers. For example:

During a study of Our Cotton Clothes, the children repeatedly locate:
   The states of the cotton belt
   The states of the United States that raise cotton
   The cotton shipping ports

The large cities where cotton is manufactured into cloth
The large cities where our clothes are made
The section of the United States where manufacturing began
The countries of the world that raise cotton

During a study of Egypt the children repeatedly locate:
The Nile River
   The mouth and source
   The section of the six cataracts
   The Assuan Dam
The Suez Canal
Alexandria
Cairo
Port Said
The area of the pyramids
The Mediterranean Sea
The Red Sea
The fertile area where crops are raised
The desert area
The bodies of water to be crossed in going to Egypt

Improving Standards. The child:
Shows improvement in standards of workmanship.
Neatness of written work.
Neatness and accuracy of map work.
Intelligent arrangement of classroom exhibits.
Neatness and suitability of illustrative material.
Selection and rejection of material bearing on a subject under discussion.
Organization of material for an oral or written report.

EXAMPLES OF CURRICULUM UNITS

In the chapters immediately following are presented examples of several curriculum units with which teachers have had highly successful experience. Certain of these units emphasize social studies content; others emphasize science.

The units are reproduced here in approximately the same form in which they were prepared and used, and with a minimum of editorial revision. Since these units were written by different authors, it is to be expected that they will differ widely in organization, nature of content included, and form. While with certain types of material it is highly desirable to employ uniformity of form and style, in the case of curriculum units it appears desirable to include examples representing different practices. There are no generally accepted standards for organization, content, and form of curriculum units. However, certain elements such as a statement of objectives or expected outcomes, informational material for the teacher, suggestions for introducing pupils to the unit, suggestions on instructional methods, suggested pupil activities, and a bibliography are probably essential.

The units which follow contain these elements, but with varying degrees of emphasis. They should serve not only as material which the teacher can use directly, but also as illustrative of several methods and plans which the classroom teacher may well employ in preparing additional curriculum units to fit the local classroom situation.

The following curriculum units are presented :[1]

Our Neighbors of the Pacific: Hawaii

Life of the Sea and Shore

The Colorado Desert

Soap

Transportation

Mexico

---

[1] In addition to these curriculum units, the State Department of Education has undertaken the publication of a series of curriculum units for elementary schools emphasizing social studies content, beginning with the school year 1935–1936. The first of these curriculum units is entitled *Community Life in the Harbor* and is published as State of California Department of Education Bulletin, No. 16, August 15, 1935.

Attention is also directed to the series of bulletins, *Science Guide for Elementary Schools*, published by the State Department of Education. A list of the bulletins of this series appears on page 100.

Chapter VIII

CURRICULUM UNIT

OUR NEIGHBORS OF THE PACIFIC: HAWAII[1]

OUTLINE OF SUBJECT MATTER

A. Hawaii Before the Coming of the White Man
1. Physical Features
   a. Hawaiian Archipelago—midway of the Pacific Ocean—is of volcanic origin.
   b. Eight major islands lie in a chain from northwest to southeast, nearly four hundred miles long.
   c. Combined area is equivalent to that of Rhode Island and Connecticut.
   d. Surface varies from smooth seashore and level plains to rugged volcanic peaks.
   e. Northeast trade-winds prevail throughout most of the year.
   f. Exceptional climate—no seasons.
   g. Temperature at sea level rarely falls below 65 degrees or rises above 85 degrees.
   h. Rainfall—sharp contrasts, from copious amounts on windward slopes to scanty rainfall on leeward slopes.
   i. Rich soil. Tropical jungles. Desert wastes.
   j. Scenic beauty. Flowering trees, tree ferns, filmy water falls, active volcanoes, wonderful moonlight, gorgeous flowers, blue waters, colored fishes, coral sands, royal palms, and night-blooming cereus.
2. Native Hawaiians—Polynesians
   a. It is generally believed that the Polynesians came from the southeastern corner of Asia.
   b. Remarkable race. Tall, finely proportioned, and dignified. They had well-formed features, wavy black hair, and a kind and gentle disposition.
   c. The men and women did all the work, because they had no beasts of burden.
   d. Ancient occupations. Pounding taro root to make poi, weaving mats, hollowing trunks of koa trees to make boats, building grass houses, fishing in the surf with spear and throw-net.

---

[1] Contributed by Mrs. Blanche West, Teacher, Rockridge Elementary School, Oakland.

e. Tools were stone hatchets, hardwood digging tools, knives of sharks' teeth or bamboo, since they lacked metals for either tools or weapons.

f. Food. Fish, poi, sweet potatoes, yams, sugar cane, bananas, coconuts, breadfruit, chelo berries, pigs and fowls.

g. Preparation of food. Fish, fowls, pork, vegetables, and fruits were wrapped in leaves and cooked in earth oven. Luau, or native feast, was prepared in this way. (Same principle as our fireless cooker.)

h. Houses, furnishings, utensils were made of grasses, leaves, bamboo, gourds, coconut shells, hardwood and olona—a hemp-like plant.

i. Lights were made by burning kukui nuts.

j. Clothing. Inner bark of paper mulberry, dyed and gummed from juices of roots, and leaves, bark and pitch of trees.

k. Royal robes were works of art constructed from feathers woven into net.

l. Games. Sports were swimming, surf-riding, sledding on grassy hills, and throwing of lava discs.

m. Festivals, feasts, and dances. Religious ceremonials, native feast-days, and hula dances.

n. Religion. Idolatry. The Hawaiians worshipped four great deities and many lesser ones. These deities were conceived of as beings who lived in or above the clouds and also appeared on the earth in human form. There were temples in which to worship these gods and a priesthood to conduct the ceremonies.

Tabus. A tabu might be declared on anything by a priest or chief. The thing tabued was consecrated to the gods until the tabu was removed. Violation of the tabu aroused the wrath of the gods and could be atoned for only by death. The tabu had its good side, but could become a terrible weapon in the hands of unscrupulous priests and chiefs. The tabu kept the people in a state of terror.

o. Government. For centuries the islands were divided into independent kingdoms, each under a native ruler. These rulers were constantly fighting and the number of kingdoms always changing.

B. The Coming of the White Man to Hawaii

1. Captain Cook makes known the Hawaiian Islands

a. January 18, 1778, Captain Cook sighted Oahu while searching for a water passage from Europe to Asia north of the continent of North America.

b. Captain Cook traded with the Hawaiians who thought he was their god Lono, who had come to minister to them.

c. Captain Cook was killed by Hawaiians because of misunderstandings.

2. Captain Vancouver

a. Captain Vancouver, who came after Captain Cook, treated Hawaiians with kindness, brought useful seeds, cattle and sheep, and gave friendly counsel.

b. Captain Vancouver's name is honored among Hawaiians to this day.

3. Trade in Sandalwood

a. New England navigators developed big trade in Hawaiian sandalwood.

b. Lives were lost and terrible cruelties endured in collecting sandalwood.

c. Habits of reckless extravagance developed.

d. Sandalwood is now almost extinct in the Hawaiian Islands.

4. New England Missionaries

a. Christian missionaries, with the utmost sincerity and earnestness, sought to prevent evil influences of the white people among the child-like natives.

b. American Board of Commissioners for Foreign Missions established a school for pagan boys at Cornwall, Connecticut. (1816)

c. Hawaiian boys were educated there.

d. The missionaries established schools, constructed written languages, taught the elements of health and sanitation, and sought to develop the best and suppress the worst in Hawaiian life and character.

e. To the descendants of early missionaries, the Islands owe the remarkable development of their natural resources and the fact that the Islands are now a part of the United States.

5. Hawaii Becomes a Territory of the United States

a. Hawaiian authorities had frequent clashes with official agents of France and Great Britain.

b. United States befriended Hawaii by inducing other nations to recognize her independence.

c. United States entered into treaty with Hawaii whereby Hawaiian sugar, coffee, and certain other products were admitted to United States without duty.

    d. Hawaii asked to be annexed to the United States. Her request was granted in April, 1900.

    e. Young people who are born in the Islands are United States citizens, for the Constitution of the United States provides that every child born in the United States and subject to its jurisdiction is a citizen.

C. Hawaii Today

1. Hawaiian Islands called "Crossroads of the Pacific." Center of trade and commerce

    a. Central position midway of the Pacific surrounded by great nations and civilizations.

    b. Trade and travel routes of the world converge at its splendid harbors where both fuel and water can be obtained.

    c. It is the logical port of call for both tourists and traders.

    d. Foreigners of many nationalities lured by trade, adventure, or to work in the fields, have drifted in or been brought into Hawaii.

    e. Representatives of most of the races of mankind live together in mutual friendliness, an object lesson for all the world.

2. Hawaiian Culture

    a. Hawaii has its age-old traditions. Hawaiian culture is built upon these traditions and found in the "Aloha" spirit—that simple, charming, heart-warming courtesy of a kindly and lovable race.

    b. Throughout the islands one hears the soft speech of the laughter-loving native folk, a liquid language for which an alphabet of twelve letters suffices.

3. Hawaii For All

    a. Hawaii is for every one. She offers a delightful climate, rest and relaxation, invigorating sports, social gaiety, smart, fascinating shops, distinguished hotels, industrial and educational opportunities of high standard, melodious hymn singing, rhythmic dances, melting song melodies, native rites, hulas, colorful festivals, slumbering volcanoes, coral lagoons, flower-blanketed hills, forests of giant ferns, mighty cliffs, "barking sands," and rainbows that appear at night.

4. Hawaiian Transportation

    a. Transportation about the islands and between the islands is carried on by means of paved highways—with never a billboard—or by means of speedy amphibian planes, interisland steamers, and transpacific liners.

5. Hawaiian Industries
   a. Production of sugar
      (1) Each of the four principal islands is girdled by a belt of cane which extends from the seashore up the sides of the mountain slopes to the 2000 foot level. Sugar cane grows best on the lowlands where an abundance of water can be had.
      (2) Cuba, British India, Java, and Hawaii rank as named in producing the world's yearly yield of sugar.
   b. Production of pineapple
      (1) Pineapples thrive best at high altitudes where the soil is porous and good drainage exists.
      (2) The picking and canning of pineapples is over before the grinding season for the cane begins.
      (3) During twenty-five years the pineapple industry has grown until its production is one-half as valuable as sugar.
   c. Coffee, rice, banana, and vegetable raising rank among important industries.
   d. Hawaii buys fruits, vegetables, eggs, meat, and dairy products from the United States because she does not raise enough to supply her needs. She exchanges her tropical products which we can not raise in abundance because of climate.

6. Scientists Solve Difficult Problems
   a. Hawaiian scientists give help wherever the study of tropical agriculture, of certain tropical diseases, and the control of tropical insect pests is needed throughout the world.
   b. Hawaiian scientists have solved the problem of destroying insect pests which attack the sugar cane.
   c. They have experimented to find the best soil for pineapples.
   d. They are experimenting with fertilizers to find the food most needed by cane and pineapples.
   e. A distinguished authority resides at Kilauea for the purpose of studying the volcano.

7. Education
   a. Today the islands possess a system of schools ranging from the elementary through junior high school, industrial training schools, business schools, foreign language schools, teacher training college, and university, which will stand comparison with the development in our most progressive states.
   b. There is no place under the American flag where more interesting racial and educational forces are at work than on these islands.

    c. They represent a great experiement in the development of social accord and cooperation which is worthy of emulation in other parts of the world.

    d. Hawaii is a philosophy of life, a new spirit of living—the absorbing product of blending the South Seas with both the Occident and Orient.

8. Hawaiian Influence

    a. Students from countries around the Pacific are turning to Hawaii, particularly to the university, for their education. It is not impossible that the University of Hawaii is destined to become the University of the Pacific.

    b. Young people of Oriental parentage, born and educated in Hawaii, go to the countries of their parents carrying with them the culture and ideas of the Islands.

    c. Young people of Hawaii who speak both English and Oriental languages are being obtained by firms engaged in business between the United States and the Orient.

    d. Hawaii is the center of investigations now being carried on in the Pacific to learn the origin of the Polynesian race and to trace its migrations.

    e. The headquarters of the Pan-Pacific Union are in Honolulu. The active president of this organization is the Governor of Hawaii.

9. Religion

    a. The number of churches in the Islands reveals the peoples' attitude toward the higher and finer things of life. We find Protestant or Catholic churches, the Church of Christ Scientist, and even the Buddhist and Shinto Temples, also the Mormon church.

10. Hawaii—Strategic Key to Pacific

    a. The United States has wisely established the Schofield Barracks, the Pearl Harbor Naval Base, and the Luke Field Airport in order to render service to mankind in times of great distress such as war, famine, earthquake, tidal wave, shipwreck, and plagues.

11. Government

    a. The United States Congress passed the famous Organic Act defining the rights and privileges of the Hawaiian people. This document became the first constitution of the Territory of Hawaii.

    b. The President of the United States appoints the governor and the major judges. The people have a voice in their government by electing their own legislature, the duties of which correspond to those of our own states.

WAYS TO LAUNCH A UNIT

The teacher may tell of Dr. Jagger, the world's most famous volcanologist, broadcasting the phenomenal eruption of Kilauea at Hilo, Hawaii, from the crater's brink on December 28 during the 1931 eruption.

The story of the first California-to-Hawaii flight made by Lieutenant Lester J. Maitland and A. F. Hagenberger from Oakland, California, to Honolulu, Hawaii, will be found in *Air Travel*, by James E. Mooney,[1] and will stimulate interest in Hawaii.

Some member of the class or the teacher may tell the story of the "Southern Cross" as piloted by C. E. Kingsford-Smith and Charles Ulm across the Pacific via California, Hawaii, and Fiji Islands to Australia.[2]

The children may be shown Hawaiian leis, a grass skirt, a ukulele, steel guitar, or listen to "Aloha Oe," composed by Queen Liliuokalani, to arouse their interest in our neighbors of the Pacific.

A box of C and H sugar or a can of Hawaiian pineapple may be brought to school and the children asked if they use it, and if they know of the land where it grows.

The teacher may show the children the colorful bulletins, pamphlets, and maps of Hawaii from the Hawaii Tourist Bureau, Monadnock Building, San Francisco, California; or the Matson Navigation Company, Matson Building, 215 Market Street, San Francisco, California.

The children will enjoy a picture of the palatial liner "Lurline."[3] They may take an imaginary voyage 2091 miles across the Pacific to Hawaii to visit the "Paradise of the Pacific."

Some child may bring the *National Geographic Magazine* for February, 1924, Hawaii issue. The colorful illustrations of volcanoes will immediately arouse interest.

If any child has visited the Hawaiian Islands, let him tell of his experiences.

The teacher may ask the children what they know about the surf board, an outrigger canoe, coral, lava, poi, and luau. Lead them to satisfy their curiosity by an interesting study of Hawaii.

The class may turn to a map of the Pacific Ocean and locate the Hawaiian Islands. Ask the children what they think the plant life, animal life, and human life would be on the islands due to location.

The children may be led to give reasons for these Islands being called "The Crossroads of the Pacific."

[1] James E. Mooney. *Air Travel*. New York: Charles Scribner's Sons, 1930.
[2] *Ibid.* See also story, maps, and illustrations found in *National Geographic Magazine*, LIV (October, 1928), 371.
[3] Colored folders may be obtained from Matson Navigation Company, Matson Building, 215 Market Street, San Francisco.

SUGGESTED ACTIVITIES

The teacher should plan in a *general* way before meeting the children with whom she is to develop a unit of work. She should plan in a *specific* way after discovering the childrens' interests.

The following suggested activities will provide many experiences in the study of Hawaii:

Make a large map of the Hawaiian Islands. Name each island and locate the principal cities. Show pictorially[1] the famous volcanoes, popular resorts and beaches, the leading industries, the invigorating sports, the native plant life, the colorful coral gardens and fishes, the means of transportation, "barking" sands, deep sea fishing, bird life, lighthouses, jungle lands, desert wastes, native villages, scenic drives, United States' largest army post (Schofield Barracks), Pearl Harbor Naval Base, and Luke Field Airport.

Courtesy of San Jose City Schools

Huts of Primitive People Are Constructed by Children During Their Study

Make a map of the Pacific Region and trace in Captain Cook's voyages.[2]

Make a cable map of the Pacific showing the principal stations. What countries own the lines? Choose a member of the class to write Postal Telegraph-Cable Company, Postal Telegraph Building, San Francisco, California, for a "World Pictorial Map."

---

[1] See Ruth Taylor While. *Cartographs of Hawaii.* San Francisco: Hawaii Tourist Bureau.
[2] *National Geographic Magazine,* LI (January, 1927), 87.

Make a map showing the world-wide radiogram system of R.C.A. Communications, Inc. Appoint a member of the class to write to the Radio Corporation of America, 28 Geary Street, San Francisco, California, for a map showing the existing circuits.

Make a map of the Pacific Region showing the surrounding nations. Locate the Islands and draw in the routes of leading Steamship Companies which justify giving Hawaii the name "Crossroads of *the Pacific*."[1]

On an outline map of the world, color in the countries from which people have emigrated to Hawaii.

Collect newspaper notices of the arrival of ships from Hawaiian ports. List cargoes.

Construct an exhibit of native life in Polynesia. Dress dolls to represent native Hawaiians at work and at play. Make primitive tools, grass houses, furnishings, utensils, bark cloth, earth oven, outrigger canoe, surfboard, stone discs for rolling contests, hardwood sled for sledding on grassy slopes, grass mats, carve or model wooden idols and temple images.

Make a class scrap book of pictures showing types of natives living in the islands of the South Pacific, showing their occupations and illustrating their lives.

Locate the Hawaiian Islands by means of latitude and longitude.

Use the scale of your map and estimate the distances from Hawaii to the principal cities of the leading nations bordering on the Pacific Ocean.

Make graphs showing comparative sizes of the islands in square miles.

Make graphs showing sugar production in Hawaii and in other countries.

Make graphs showing the food value of sugar as compared with other staple foods.

Make graphs showing beet sugar production.

Make graph showing production of pineapple.

Make graphs showing value of sugar and pineapple crops.

Compute the costs of radiograms from the United States to the Hawaiian Islands.

Make a colored poster of Mauna Kea.

Make a poster showing a sandy beach, palms, blue water, distant mountains and native boy on surfboard.

Make paintings and designs of colorful butterflies and fishes native to the Islands.

Make a painting of a night visit to the crater of Kilauea.

Make a painting of the burning of a cane field at night.

[1] For map see back of booklet *Story of Sugar in Hawaii.* Honolulu: Hawaiian Sugar Planters' Association.

Make a painting or crayon sketch showing growing fields of rice, sugar cane, and pineapple with trees and mountains as a background and natives at work as center of interest.

Make a poster, painting or crayon sketch of sea, land, and palms in the moonlight.

Illustrate native Hawaiian fisherman spearing fish and using the throw net.

Make designs suitable for bark cloth.

Make a painting or crayon sketch of a steamer loading with sugar and pineapple for the United States Coast.

Make a painting or crayon sketch of a native Hawaiian girl in tapa cloth bark costume.

Make a painting or crayon sketch of American-Hawaiian girl with flower leis and grass skirt.

Plan attractive covers for scrap books, using colorful butterflies, tropical fish, flowers or ferns as the design motif. Use also scenes of Hawaii for cover designs.

Make a collection of pictures of interest on Hawaii, carefully cut and mounted with suitable colored background mats, remounted on heavier chipboard.

Tell the story of "Pele and the Ocean Spirits." [1]

Dramatize the story of Princess Kapiolani entering the crater of the fire-mountain. [2]

Write the story of cloth made from bark.

Write a paper telling of the changes in Hawaii during the last one hundred years.

Tell the story of a visit to a volcano.

Tell the story of Captain Cook's voyages.

Give an oral talk on "Life in Honolulu."

Write a composition on Hawaiian courtesy.

Prepare written materials on the pineapple and sugar industries.

Dramatize the pineapple and cane sugar harvest.

Make a list of the adjectives used in presenting descriptions of Hawaii.

Make a list of all the proper names used in studying Hawaii and a pronouncing vocabulary for them.

Write poems about the beauties of Hawaii, the volcanoes, the people at work and play.

Read about the leper colony on Molokai Island and report it to the class.

Read in *The Book of Knowledge* [3] the story of Father Damien's life among the lepers and tell it to your class.

---

[1] George A. Mirick. *Home Life Around the World.* Boston: Houghton, Mifflin Company, 1929, p. 116.
[2] *Ibid.*, p. 118.
[3] *The Book of Knowledge.* Edited by Holland Thompson and Arthur Mee. New York: Grolier Society, 1929.

Read Mark Twain's [1] book in which he describes Haleakala. Tell what you read to the class.

Debate the question: "Resolved, That contact between primitive races and the white race has been bad for the former."

Debate the question: "Resolved, That the greatest good requires that the primitive races give their land up to those who can and will develop and use it."

Read, enjoy, and discuss the poems of Padraic Colum, the famous Irish poet, on native folk-lore; also his poem, "Sandalwood." [2]

Plan a class room or assembly program where other classes and parents may enjoy a visit to Hawaii with your class. Plan attractive invitations and programs in the form of tropical fish, colorful flower, or surfboard. Read, tell, or dramatize your stories. Show your exhibits, scrap books, graphs, maps, interesting pictures, and your paintings. Make a paper lei as a favor for each guest.

Sing or play "Aloha Oe" composed by Queen Liliuokalani, as the concluding number on your program.

Study the ukulele, steel guitar, and gourd drums which are the principal Hawaiian instruments.

Enjoy phonograph records of Hawaiian music. "Aloha Oe," "Hilo" (Hawaiian March), "Kiluea Waltz," "Wailana Waltz."

Tell of the origin of the Hawaiian Islands.

Find out where the principal lines of weakness in the earth's crust are according to the scientists and locate them on a map of the world.

Find pictures of Hawaiian birds, fishes, and plant life for a scrap book.

Study and report the effect of the prevailing northeast trade winds on rainfall, crops, jungle lands, and desert wastes.

Tell how the sub-tropical climate has affected plant life.

List flowers and vegetables found in Hawaii.

Find out what the Southern Cross looks like and make a sketch of it in your scrap book.

Give evidence that Punchbowl was once an active volcano.

Give reasons why American youths do not practice surf riding along our coasts.

Tell the story of how the scientists have controlled insect pests in Hawaii. Compare with the control of the cottony-cushion scale in California.

Have a report made on the coral polyp, its life, and the results of its activities.

---

[1] S. L. Clemens (Mark Twain pseud.). *Roughing It.* New York: The American Book Co., 1899.
[2] *The Best Poems of 1922-1926.* Selected by Thomas Moult. Padraic Colum, "Sandalwood," pp. 14-15. New York: Harcourt, Brace and Company, 1927.

Primitive natives long anticipated the radio in their methods of signaling over great distances. Investigate and report.

Report on the use of the airplane in Hawaii.

The natives of Polynesia lacked metals, beasts of burden, and domestic animals, except the dog, hog, fowl. Cereals were also unknown. Find out how they supplied these deficiencies.

Describe the whaling industry. Find out what caused its sudden decline. Determine how this business and its decline affeected Hawaii.

Decide what tabus declared by Hawaiian chiefs and priests served a good purpose. Compare their tabus on the catching of fish with the efforts made in our country to protect the fish of our waters.

Make a list of the native activities and practices that have ceased because of the influence of civilization.

Courtesy of San Jose City Schools

Much Information Must Be Acquired Vicariously Before Children Can Reconstruct the Experiences of Peoples Who Live Across the Seas

Trade in sandalwood is made much of in *The Crater,* by James Fenimore Cooper.[1] Have the story read and reported upon.

Cuban cane land yields two tons per acre while Hawaiian land yields range from four to eight tons. It costs more to produce sugar in Hawaii than in Cuba. Tell why Hawaii produces more. Tell why it costs more to produce it in Hawaii.

Read about the scientists' work in improving growing things. Read about Luther Burbank's work in California in improving growing things. Report to the class the methods that they employed.

---

[1] James Fenimore Cooper. *The Crater.* New York: D. Appleton and Company, 1889.

TYPE TESTS FOR EVALUATING PROGRESS

These tests are suggestive of the means which may be utilized to test the unit on Hawaii. Teachers may wish to develop similar tests based on the unit as carried out within their own classrooms.

TRUE—FALSE EXERCISE

Are the following statements true or false? *Underline the correct answer.*

1. The Hawaiian Islands are rich in valuable metals_____   True   False
2. The climate of the Hawaiian Islands is not pleasant as it varies from extreme heat to extreme cold_____   True   False
3. It is believed that the native Hawaiians came from the southeastern corner of Asia_____   True   False
4. The native Hawaiians were a remarkable race, of attractive, kind, and lovable people_____   True   False
5. The native Hawaiians were Christians_____   True   False

MULTIPLE CHOICE OR RECOGNITION EXERCISE

Read each statement carefully and make a choice of the answers offered. *Underline the one you think is correct.*

1. We connect the name of Magellan; Balboa; Captain Cook; Columbus; with the Hawaiian Islands.
2. Early navigators carried on trade in Hawaiian sugar; sandalwood; pineapples.
3. The first missionaries to the Hawaiian Islands were from England; China; New England States; Spain.
4. Hawaii became a protectorate of the United States; a territory of the United States; a possession of the United States.
5. Persons born in the Hawaiian Islands are Japanese citizens; American citizens; Portuguese citizens.

YES—NO EXERCISE

Read carefully and decide on yes or no. *Underline the correct answer.*

1. Hawaii occupies a central position midway of the Pacific and is surrounded by great nations and civilizations_____   Yes   No
2. Trade and travel routes of the world find Hawaii's location to be a disadvantage _____   Yes   No
3. Representatives of most of the races of mankind live together in mutual friendliness in Hawaii_____   Yes   No
4. Hawaiian culture, courtesy, friendliness, kindliness, and charm is felt throughout the Islands_____   Yes   No
5. Means of transportation throughout the islands is slow, inefficient, inadequate _____   Yes   No

COMPLETION EXERCISE

An important word or group of words has been omitted from the following statements. *Supply in the blank spaces the word or group of words that you believe is correct.*

1. The two leading industries of the Hawaiian Islands are the_____ industry and _____ industry.
2. Scientists in the Hawaiian Islands study _____ and _____.
3. The educational system of the Hawaiian Islands includes _____ schools, _____ schools, _____ schools, and _____ schools.
4. The Hawaiian Islands have peoples from many nations. Four nations represented are _____, _____, _____, _____.
5. The United States has established great defensive strength in the Hawaiian Islands. This strength includes _____, _____, and _____

BIBLIOGRAPHY

General

SUGGESTED REFERENCES FOR TEACHERS

BUNKER, FRANK. *Hawaii and the Philippines.* Philadelphia: J. B. Lippincott Company, 1928.
Complete, interesting general history and geography.

CASTLE, WILLIAM R. *Hawaii, Past and Present.* New York: Dodd Mead and Company, Inc., 1927.

FREAR, MARY EMMA. *Our Familiar Island Trees.* Boston: Richard D. Badger, 1929.

GRIFFISS, T. *When You Go To Hawaii, You Will Need This Guide to the Islands.* Boston: Houghton Mifflin Company, 1930.

KUYKENDALL, RALPH SIMON, AND GREGORY, HERBERT ERNEST. *History of Hawaii.* New York: The Macmillan Company, 1926.
Excellent, interesting history of Hawaii and how it came to be what it is today.

LILIUOKALANI, LYDIA KAMAKAEHA. *Hawaii's Story by Hawaii's Queen.* Boston: Lothrop, Lee & Shepard Company, 1898.
The fortunes of Hawaii's royal family; the overthrow of the dynasty and the creation of a republic.

NEAL, MARIE C. *In Honolulu Gardens.* Publication No. 13, Honolulu, T. H.: Bishop Museum Special, 1928.
Describes the commonest and most conspicuous herbs, vines, shrubs, and trees that are seen in gardens and parks and along roadsides. Many legends of the plants are included.

PALMER, ALBERT WENTWORTH. *The Human Side of Hawaii.* 14 Beacon Street, Boston: Pilgrim Press, 1924.
Study of the race question in Hawaii by a former pastor of Central Union Church, Honolulu.

POPE, WILLIS THOMAS. *Wayside Plants of Hawaii.* Honolulu, T. H.: Advertiser Publishing Company, Ltd., 1929.
A new book devoting 290 pages to descriptions and illustrations of about 200 species of plants growing in the Hawaiian Islands.

TAYLOR, ALBERT PIERCE. *Under Hawaiian Skies.* Honolulu, T. H.: Advertiser Publishing Company, Ltd., 1926.
Sketches of Hawaiian history by an experienced journalist, with emphasis on the romantic features.

THORPE, CORA WELLS. *In the Path of the Trade Winds.* New York: G. P. Putnam's Sons, 1924.

WRISTON, ROSCOE C. *Hawaii Today.* Garden City, New York: Doubleday, Doran & Company, 1926.
Deals with description of travel in, and history of, Hawaiian Islands.

SUGGESTED REFERENCES FOR PUPILS

ALEXANDER, MARY CHARLOTTE. *The Story of Hawaii.* New York: American Book Company, 1912.

> Excellent, interesting history of Hawaii, past and present. Splendid illustrations. Grades 4–8.

All About Hawaii. Honolulu, T. H., Honolulu Star-Bulletin.

> Description and travel. Grades 5–9.

BAILEY, ALICE COOPER. *Sun Gold.* Boston: Houghton Mifflin Company, 1930.

> Story of Hawaiian Islands. Grades 7–9.

BALDWIN, CHARLES WICKLIFFE. *Geography of the Hawaiian Islands.* New York: American Book Co., 1920.

> Grades 4–8.

BLANDING, DON. *Stowaways in Paradise.* New York: Farrar & Rinehart, 1931.

> Grades 7–9.

BUNKER, FRANK FOREST. *Hawaii and the Philippines.* Philadelphia: J. B. Lippincott Company, 1928.

> Complete, interesting, general history and geography. Grades 6–9.

CARPENTER, FRANK G. *Australia, The Philippines, and Other Islands of the Sea.* Garden City, New York: Doubleday, Doran & Company, 1927.

> Grades 5–9.

CARROLL, CLARENCE FRANKLIN. *Around the World.* Book III. New York: Silver, Burdett and Company, 1908.

> Simple, interesting story of Hawaii. Grades 3–6.

Centenary Number. Honolulu, T. H.: Honolulu Star-Bulletin, 1920.

> Grades 5–6.

CHAMBERLAIN, J. F., AND A. H. *The Continents and Their People. Oceania.* New York: The Macmillan Company, 1925.

> General history. Grades 5–6.

Compton's Pictured Encyclopedia. Chicago: F. E. Compton and Company, 1932.

> Grades 3–9.

Encyclopedia Britannica Junior. 12 v. Chicago: Encyclopedia Britannica, Inc., 1934.

FAIRGRIEVE, JAMES, AND YOUNG, ERNEST. *Our Pacific Lands from the World.* Book III. New York: D. Appleton and Company, 1925.

> Good general story of Hawaii. Grades 3–6.

GEORGE, MARIAN MINNIE. *Little Journey to Hawaii and the Philippines.* Chicago: A. Flanagan Company, 1927.

> Descriptive travel. Grades 5–6.

GILSON, JEWETT CASTELLO. *Wealth of the World's Waste Places, and Oceania.* New York: Charles Scribner's Sons, 1913.

> Interesting story of Hawaii within an interesting book. Grades 5–9.

GIST, ARTHUR. *New Stories from Eskimo Land.* San Francisco: Harr Wagner Publishing Company, 1930.

HILL, MAURICE. *Golden Shower.* Honolulu, T. H.: Honolulu Star-Bulletin Press, 1929.

Poetry. Grades 5–9.

KROUT, MARY HANNAH. *Alice's Visit to the Hawaiian Islands.* New York: American Book Company, 1900.

Excellent, interesting, complete and simple story. Grades 5–9.

McFEE, INEZ NELLIE. *Visit to Hawaii: Boys and Girls of Many Lands.* New York: T. Y. Crowell Company, 1917.

Grades 6–7.

MISICK, LILLIAN S. *A Visit to Hawaii.* Dansville, New York: F. A. Owen Publishing Company, 1922.

An account of a visit in Hawaii. Mrs. Misick is a teacher in Likelike School, Honolulu. Grades 5–6.

MOONEY, JAMES ELLIOTT. *Air Travel.* New York: Charles Scribner's Sons, 1930.

Interesting, history making flights. Grades 5–9.

PERDUE, HANNAH AVIS. *How Other Children Live.* Chicago: Rand, McNally & Company, 1927.

' Descriptions of Hawaii and Hawaiian child life. Grades 3 and up.

SMITH, JOSEPH RUSSELL. *Human Geography.* Book One, Part One. (California State Series) Sacramento: State Department of Education, 1926.

"Our Island Possessions." General geography and history of Hawaiian Islands. Grades 5–7.

TAYLOR, ALBERT PIERCE. *Sesquicentennial Celebration of Captain Cook's Discovery of Hawaiian Islands.* Honolulu, T. H.: Advertiser Publishing Company, 1929. Grades 5–9.

THOMPSON, HOLLAND, AND MEE, ARTHUR. *Book of Knowledge.* Vols. X and XV. New York: Grolier Society, 1930.

. General information on Hawaiian Islands. Grades 5–9.

THOMPSON, J. EARLE. *Our Pacific Possessions.* New York: Charles Scribner's Sons, 1931.

Complete, interesting, and new book on Hawaii and islands of the Pacific. Grades 5–9.

THRUM, THOMAS G. *Hawaiian Annual of 1929.* Honolulu, T. H.: T. G. Thrum, Box 205, 1929.

Contains an immense amount of information and statistics and many valuable historical articles. Grades 7–9.

WADE, MARY HAZELTON. *Our Little Hawaiian Cousin.* Boston: L. C. Page & Company, 1902.

Simple story of Hawaii. Grades 4–6.

WINSLOW, ISAAC OSCAR. *Our American Neighbors.* Boston: D. C. Heath & Company, 1921.

Description and travel. Grades 4–6.

World Book Encyclopedia. 19 v. Chicago: W. F. Quarrie & Company, 1934.

Industrial Hawaii

SUGGESTED REFERENCE FOR TEACHERS

The Story of Cane Sugar. Honolulu, T. H.: University of Hawaii, 1928.

SUGGESTED REFERENCE FOR PUPILS

The Story of Sugar in Hawaii. Honolulu, T. H.: Hawaiian Sugar Planters' Association, 1926.
>   Grades 5–9.

Primitive Hawaiian Life

SUGGESTED REFERENCES FOR TEACHERS

EMERSON, OLIVER POMEROY. *Pioneer Days in Hawaii.* New York: Harper and Brothers, 1928.
>   Biography of John S. Emerson. Life in Waialua nearly a century ago. Primitive Hawaiian life.

THRUM, THOMAS G. *Hawaiian Folk Tales.* Chicago: A. C. McClurg & Company, 1907.
>   A collection of native legends.

SUGGESTED REFERENCES FOR PUPILS

BAILEY, ALICE COOPER. *Kimo, the Whistling Boy.* Joliet, Illinois: P. F. Volland Company, 1928.
>   Beautifully illustrated in color. Old folk tales and legends beautifully told. Grades 4–6.

COLUM, PADRIAC. *At the Gateways of the Day.* New Haven, Connecticut: Yale University Press, 1924.
>   Grades 4–6.

METZGER, BERTA. *Tales Told in Hawaii.* New York: Frederick A. Stokes Company, 1929.
>   Stories which reveal the manners, customs, and life of the early Hawaiians. Grades 4–6.

MIRICK, GEORGE ALONZO. *Home Life Around the World.* Boston: Houghton Mifflin Company, 1929.
>   Excellent stories of primitive Hawaiian life. Grades 5–6.

Bulletins, Pamphlets, and Miscellaneous Materials

DOLLAR STEAMSHIP LINES, Robert Dollar Building, San Francisco, California.
>   Bulletins, booklets.

HAWAIIAN TOURIST BUREAU, 1107 Monadnock Building, San Francisco, California.
>   Bulletins, maps.

HONOLULU STAR-BULLETIN, 125 Merchant Street, Honolulu, T. H. *All About Hawaii.* Section Edition. 1930.

MATSON NAVIGATION COMPANY, Matson Building, 215 Market Street, San Francisco, California.
>   Bulletins, maps, pamphlets. *Hawaii Romantic, Beautiful.*

POSTAL TELEGRAPH-CABLE COMPANY, Postal Telegraph Building, 470 Market Street, San Francisco, California.
>   World pictorial map.

RADIO CORPORATION OF AMERICA, 28 Geary Street, San Francisco, California.
>   Map of world wide radiogram system.

UNITED STATES DEPARTMENT OF THE INTERIOR, National Park Service, Washington, D. C., *Hawaii National Park.*

Articles from the National Geographic Magazine

A Bird City. XV (December, 1904), 494–498. 6 Illustrations.

GROSVENOR, GILBERT. *The Hawaiian Islands.* XLV (February, 1924), 115–238. 106 illustrations in black and white, 21 illustrations in color, 6 maps, 1 diagram.

HILDEBRAND, J. R. *The Columbus of the Pacific.* LI (January, 1927), 85–132. Excellent early map. Cook's voyages and story of Cook's discoveries and death.

KINGSFORD-SMITH, CHARLES E., AND ULM, CHARLES T. P. *Our Conquest of the Pacific.* LIV (October, 1928), 371–402. Excellent map of aerial trail blazed across Pacific by *Southern Cross,* Skipper C. E. Kingsford-Smith. Slight history of Hawaiian Islands.

PERKINS, GEORGE C. *The Key to the Pacific.* XIX (April, 1908), 295-298. One-half page map.

WETMORE, ALEXANDER. *Bird Life Among Lava Rocks and Coral Sands: The Chronicle of a Scientific Expedition to Little-Known Islands of Hawaii.* XLVIII (July, 1925), 77-108. 36 Ills. One-half page map.

WOOD, H. P. *Hawaii for Homes.* XIX (April, 1908), 298-299.

CHAPTER IX

CURRICULUM UNIT

LIFE OF THE SEA AND SHORE[1]

THE REASON THIS UNIT WAS CHOSEN

A class of low fifth and high fourth grade children ranged from eight to thirteen years of age. The children lacked group unity and interest in cooperative undertakings. The teacher's problem was to find a common meeting ground for their diversified interests, which also offered cooperative exercise for the wide range of their abilities. She chose the study of the sea and the shore; first, because of the close proximity of the ocean; secondly, because the life and the activities of the sea and the shore offered inexhaustible material for interesting study; and thirdly, because the subject matter was of such a nature as to insure an enthusiastic response from the entire class.

OUTLINE OF THE UNIT

Topics to be Studied

    A. Sea Life in Local Waters
    B. Life of the Deep Sea
    C. Products of the Sea
    D. Local Industries

Pupils' Experiences and Activities

1. Excursions	7. Exhibits
2. Oral Reports	8. Visual Aids
3. Reading	9. Art
4. Problem Solving	10. Music
5. Experiments	11. Poetry
6. Written Language	12. Dramatization

APPROACH TO THE UNIT

A motion picture was projected in the classroom, beginning with a view of waves dashing upon a rocky shore, and from there carrying the audience, step by step, to the finding, collecting, and close examination of the commonest of seashore life.

THE ACTIVITIES

Some of the children's questions following the showing of the picture were: "Does anything like what we have seen in these pictures

---

[1] Carried on under the guidance of, and reported by Miss Lela McCoy, Fourth and Fifth Grades, Garfield School, San Diego. Report contributed by Miss Emma A. Baldwin, Supervisor of Elementary Education, San Diego.

live on the rocks of our beaches?" "Does anything live under the sand?"

The teacher in her turn asked a question, "What have you seen on the sand and the rocks of our beaches?"

Some of the children had seen crabs, and some sand fleas, while others mentioned kelp and other seaweed. A few had gathered shells. One little girl knew the sea anemone. One child asked: "Does the sea anemone die when the tide goes down and leaves it out of the water?" The discussion brought out the fact that though the children had been at the beach many times they really did not know much about its life. But they were all eager to overcome this limitation.

One child suggested: "My mother could take some of us to the beach some day after school." Another said: "Oh, we were out at the beach last Saturday, and the water was so high that we couldn't even get down to the rocks and the sand." Someone suggested that the tide must have been too high. Then came the question, "When is the tide low?" So the necessity of first studying the tide tables was brought out, together with the fact that a tide table could be found in the daily papers.

One boy, whose father worked at a sporting goods house, said that he could bring a tide table. When it came next day it proved to be a yearly schedule of the tides, published for those who fish for sport. The teacher explained that the "minus-O-point-one" (—0.1) and lower tides are the best tides for collecting specimens of sea life. Little pools of water are left among the rocks at low tide, wherein many sea creatures may be found for observation and collection and great stretches of sand are left where one usually sees only water. She also explained the advantage of not getting wet by the incoming waves when it is ebb tide. The best low tide of the year according to the tide table came one week from that date. Of course everyone wanted to go to the beach on that day.

The Excursion

Preparations should include the planning of transportation by autos, street car, or bus; admonishing the children regarding behavior, emphasizing courtesy and obedience; a special note to parents requesting permission to make the excursion. The discussion period centered around these preparations to be made for the excursion.

Such planning is the prerequisite of success in undertaking an excursion. The consent and the cooperation of the parent is of vital importance. The following note is one way of securing good results:

Dear Parents:

It is our custom to take classes on excursions to places of interest in connection with the regular work. This term we have planned many

instructive trips. It is not possible to take every child every time.
Interest, conduct, and attention are important items to be considered in
choosing pupils for our excursions.

We will appreciate your cooperation in our plans and feel that both
parents and pupils will enjoy this method of learning about our environment.

Most cordially yours,

Signed :_____

Teacher

NOTICE

1. _____ is invited to go on an excursion on _____, to _____.
2. Can the parent go? (Answer yes or no) _____.
3. Can parent take a car? (Answer yes or no) _____.
4. How many passengers is your car built to carry? _____.
5. Kindly sign and return this blank.
   My child has my permission to go on this excursion.

Signed :_____, Parent.

Discussions were carried on by the class on the following items.

Dressing for comfort and efficiency. Bathing suits seemed advisable (the weather permitting) with heavier outer garments to be worn
in transit. Tennis shoes seemed desirable, as they provided a better
footing on the rocks.

Lunches. The children decided that this excursion was not to be a
picnic, and that they would therefore neither lunch nor swim, but
would devote the entire time to the search for plant and animal life.

Containers for collections. For collecting the children decided to
bring small pails and other unbreakable containers. The teacher
advised small paring or putty knives for detaching live shells from the
rocks.

Finally the forty-five boys and girls with eight mothers and the
teacher boarded the street car chartered for the occasion.

Every precaution was taken for the children's safety. A street
car for transportation was chosen instead of a number of privately
owned and operated automobiles. The school nurse drove her own car
to be on hand in case of an emergency. The life guard met the excursionists at the rocks where there might be danger of slipping on the sea
weeds or wet rocks and of being cut on the sharp shells.

On their arrival at the beach the children's first reaction was to
stretch out their arms and call at the top of their voices, and in some
instances they ran, as if the presence of the ocean and its tremendous
energy called to them and helped them to release their own pent-up
energies.

The Children's Observations

The moving life was without exception the first to catch the
children's attention, the crab holding the center of the stage with the

more active and determined ones. The timid and less persistent children soon turned from the too active crab to the colorful tide pools.

Courtesy of San Diego County Schools

Collecting Specimens on the Muddy Bay Shore

The small swimming creatures and the open sea anemones held their interest. Then the closed anemones above the tide level were discovered. An experiment proved that the little grey bunches of shell-covered life were the same creatures as the open sea anemones in the tide pools. Pails of sea water were poured upon some closed sea anemones until they were covered with the water and opened their tentacles. Bits of chopped-up mussel were held against the open tentacles of the anemone. The sea anemone closed about this morsel of food. The children were greatly interested in this feeding experiment.

Live California spiny lobster were found at the very low tide level. They could be picked up by their long front spines and carried to the tide pools. The pupils watched them move about on their ten feet and swim swiftly backward with a strong flip of their fan like tails.

A live eel had been caught by a man nearby. This animal's sharp teeth and lively movements under the captor's spear showed he was no catch for child's play. However the eel's fear of the searcher would eliminate all danger of children encountering him.

Under the right tide conditions, the stimulus of some knowledge and with a group interest, the collections of an elementary class can eclipse the more sophisticated efforts of older groups of students. Early acquaintance with necessary favorable conditions for searching for sea life may also lead to greater future achievement in this field.

To illustrate, both the sea pen and the sea palm are only to be found at sufficiently low tide levels. The sea pen buries itself deep in the sandy shore leaving only a wire-like projection visible above the surface. This breaks off or disappears entirely if an effort is made to pull it up. One small boy, with no idea of the importance of his find, persevered until he had *dug up* several of this rare specimen for the class exhibit.

The delicate sea palm is so tiny that it is easily overlooked in the eager rush of the less observant seekers, but one child, less hurried, was so fascinated by the movements of this interesting specimen that he took his treasure home and introduced it to the class the next day.

Preparing Shell Specimens

Back at school the live creatures were put into glass bowls and jars containing sea water, so that the children could watch their antics. The barnacles remained alive a long time. When the water was agitated near them the feet were extended and the vivid coloring of the inner surfaces could be seen.

The hermit crab made an attractive display of himself when he deserted his shell. The siphons of the clam timidly came to view while the wild careening of "Mr. Pecten" in his effort to swim in a small space was startling as well as enlightening. Other discoveries too numerous to mention were enjoyed by individuals who called the attention of the class to their findings.

After twenty-four hours very little was left to enjoy for then the disagreeable odor became very noticeable. Time now for the children to begin to remove the animal life from all the shell specimens. For this purpose a sharp knife was used. Then the shells were washed and set to dry.

Some of the children cleaned their shells at home by boiling them, and by scrubbing them with scouring powder. But when these were compared with the shells done at school it was found that the process had dimmed and changed their naturally delicate coloring.

Star fish, sea urchins, live sand dollars and similar specimens which live both inside and outside their skeletons were soaked for twenty-four hours in a solution of equal parts of sea water, formaldehyde, alcohol and glycerine. Then the children placed them in a wire case and put them in an airy but shady place to dry as the direct sun dims their colors. When thoroughly dry, they were given a coat of shellac to protect them from the dust. Now they were ready to be classified and mounted for exhibition.

Preparing Seaweed Specimens

The seaweeds were floated in sea water (which preserves their natural coloring) in the process of mounting. Hydrant water has a bleaching effect upon them.

A piece of white paper was slipped under each floating specimen and it was lifted out to a blotter to dry. The natural mucilage in the algae makes the specimen adhere to the paper in most cases. The blotting or newspapers were changed every day until the specimens were entirely dry.

The children found that a suitable press could be made by strapping a board on either side of the stacked pile of specimens. Then the straps were tightened to produce pressure.

Very delicate weeds were floated in shallow sea water, then covered with a cloth and sand sifted over the cloth to absorb the water. The weight of the sand held the specimen in the desired position. When the sand was completely dry the cloth was removed and the specimen was attached to the mounting papers with a combination of library paste and glue. The mixture is spread on a smooth surface, such as marble or enamel. The sea weed is then dropped on the glue mixture. With slight pressure enough adheres to paste the specimen firmly to the paper.

Heavy white paper having a smooth finish was found to be ideal for mounting the sea weed, though other kinds such as those used for typing, or common manila paper, may be used.

The classification of sea weeds is simple for elementary use. The color classifications, green, brown and red, are all that are necessary for this purpose. Very attractive arrangements of these sea weeds may be made. (The children experimented and expressed varied individual taste and ideas in mounting their collections.)

Exhibiting Specimens

Various experiments were tried in displaying exhibits to advantage. One method followed was that of numbering each shell and dried specimen and placing it in a box with an accompanying card numbered and named to fit the number on the shell:

Some children arranged their exhibit on cotton in a large flat box and placed the typewritten slip of paper with the individual name by each specimen. The box lid was cut to form a frame and cellophane fitted into the opening, thereby keeping dust from the objects and allowing a clear view of each.

The most elaborate method tried was to put each specimen into an individual box. The entire class helped by preparing the specimen and the finished exhibit was given to the school museum. Sewing thread boxes of the approximate size 6″ x 3″ x 1″ were secured in large numbers from the department stores. The top was cut to a quarter-inch frame and a piece of glass the desired size placed beneath this. A child had his father cut the glass from pieces contributed by the class. Ordinary brown gummed paper held the cover of the box in place. Typewritten information was attached to the reverse side and the entire box shellacked. This insured longer wearing as well as attractiveness. At least three or more specimens of a given variety were put into each box, showing the upper, lower and side views, as the peculiarity of the specimen could best be shown in this way.

Classification

It was impossible for the entire class to get the desired information from books for the classifying of their specimens. The pictured material was practically all that was usable and that had its limitation. The teacher knew the local Natural History Museum contained exhibit cases of all local shells but considered it of more value to have the information introduced to the class by a child who happened to visit there with his parents on Sunday. An excursion was planned with the usual discussion of points to be considered. A letter to the Director of the Museum requesting permission to make the visit was composed by the class. The one written the best was sent.

Since the distance was short and the traffic light, automobile transportation seemed advisable. Cars were available, and this eliminated expense to the child. Because it was difficult for all the class to see the exhibits and hear the explanations at the same time it was decided to go in two groups. One group remained at the school and worked at assigned tasks. This was a self-imposed responsibility for the good of the whole. It met the approval of the principal and brought satisfying comment from teachers who seemingly "happened to look in" during the absence of the teacher. Their praise stimulated the desired response in the pupils. The start at eight thirty in the morning enabled the excursionists to return by ten o'clock.

After the reports of the first group, the second group was extremely anxious to find additional material. The second group, left at school, had a standard to live up to in conduct and accomplishment established by group one.

Exhibits receiving particular attention at the Natural History Museum were:

1. Cases of local shells
2. Shells from all over the world

3. All forms of sea life
4. Birds of the seashore
5. Seaweed collections
6. Fossils
7. Model of ocean depths

List of Specimens

Following is a list of the objects that were found on a rocky shore and brought back to school for identification and study. The scientific names of many of the specimens were learned and used freely by the children.

1. Gray Littorine
2. Alectrion Tegula
3. Limpets:
   a. Horseshoe
   b. Owl
   c. File
   d. Volcano
   e. Keyhole
   f. Slipper
   g. Cup-and-Saucer
   h. Scabra
   i. Finger and others
4. Turban Shells
5. Unicorn
6. Basket Shells
7. Chiton
8. Mussels
9. Barnacles:
   a. Acorn
   b. Goose
10. Clams
11. Lithoranium
12. Sea Urchins
13. Sea Anemones
14. Starfish
15. Brittle Stars
16. Abalone
17. Worm Tubes
18. Sponge
19. Crabs
20. Oysters
21. Seaweed

Some of the things that were found on the sandy bay shore were:

1. Sand Dollars
2. Sea Pansies
3. Bubble Shells
4. Pectens
5. Swimming Crabs
6. Worm Tubes
7. Horn Shells
8. Moon Snails
9. Sand Collars
10. Sea Anemones
11. Dead shells washed in by tide.

Some of the things that were found on a muddy bay shore were:

1. Horn Shells
2. Periwinkles
3. Fairy Sea Palms
4. Sea Pens
5. Worms
6. Fiddler Crabs
7. California Cone Shells
8. Clams

Aquarium and Museum at the Institute of Oceanography

The interest and cooperation of parents was a large item in contributing to the class interest and accomplishment in this study at the Institute of Oceanography. The report of one child of a trip his family made one Sunday afternoon to the Institute opened an entirely new field of interest to the class. Another excursion was desired by all. Letters were written to the bus company for rates, which were found prohibitive. As there was no other public conveyance the private machine was considered. The distance to be traveled was over fifty miles, involving traffic congestion and grades. Through the class discussion all these points were brought out, together with State regulations as to the responsibility of the driver of a private car.

Several children finally gained the consent of their parents to invite other children to ride with them. Invitations were written to these children and they answered, giving their parents' consent to the trip. Fifteen members of the class took the trip the following Saturday afternoon.

Sending groups of six or seven children on an excursion under the guidance of a parent places a peculiar responsibility of conduct and attention on the child. He is responsible for a good report of himself, as well as for bringing back information to the class, as he can not rely on the teacher for either of these.

Reports of the trip showed interest in the following:

Aquarium Specimens

Goldfish of the sea	Sea Anemones
Sharks	Starfish
Other strange fishes	Lobsters
Octopus	Eels
Stingarees	

Museum

Largest fish	The many different starfish
Seaweed collection over 30 years old	Model of local coast line and adjoining land and sea levels

The museum collection did not interest the children as did the aquarium due to the great amount of material presented with no one to guide their attention to particular objects.

A Salt Water Aquarium

Following the trip to the Institute of Oceanography the children asked the following questions: "Why couldn't we have an aquarium like the one we saw Saturday?" "Why hadn't our specimens lived that we had brought from our beach excursion?" "What is necessary for a good salt water aquarium?"

In order to answer their questions such items as the following were discussed:

1. What is necessary to sustain life of the sea in its natural seashore home?

2. What do we provide for our goldfish to eat?

3. Could we make a salt water aquarium by adding salt to hydrant water?

Experiments followed but the animals always died, one reason being that animals were placed together which were natural enemies. Our manufactured salt water lacked the chemicals of the real sea water.

Finally the following plan brought satisfying results: Water was taken by a fishing boat in five-gallon bottles from the sea outside the bay and was therefore unpolluted by sewage disposal. The natural life in this sea water furnished food for our animal life. Sand from the sea was placed on the bottom of an oblong ten-gallon glass aquarium. Sea lettuce that was growing on a rock was carefully transported in an enamel pail in plenty of sea water to add the necessary vegetable growth for a balanced aquarium.

A special committee went to the seashore equipped with numerous glass jars to get the desired sea life. Each specimen was placed in a clean glass jar by itself. The following specimens were secured:

2 California Ghost Shrimps
3 Hermit Crabs
2 Tide-pool Fish
a rock containing Marine Worms
a group of Acorn Barnacles.

By careful aeration of the water each day (dipping the water up by cupfuls and pouring it back into the tank) and feeding with dried, unsalted shrimp and other goldfish foods the balanced aquarium flourished.

After three weeks an ambitious collector who had been absent during the weeks of experimentation added a number of half-dead specimens in stale sea water and that was the end of the experiment! It was too late in the term to start another aquarium.

Map Making

One morning a child had an interesting story to tell of a visitor in his home. This guest was a member of the crew of the *U. S. S. Ramapo* who had actually helped construct the model of the ocean bed the class had all seen at the Natural History Museum.

The children who had been to the Institute of Oceanography told again of seeing the models representing the local coastline and adjoining land and sea levels. Maps of this region were consulted to see where the river reached the ocean. Other places the children were interested in finding on the map were the bay, adjoining towns, and the islands.

From the school building the bay, islands and peninsula could be seen. In the work period three children traced the outline of the bay and the adjoining land in the sand table as they looked from the school building. The class wanted something more permanent and this desire led to the construction of relief maps from the following materials: salt and flour, paper and clay, drawings and tracings (to represent the correct forms).

Physical features represented were: continent, ocean (continental shelf), bay, peninsula, island, and river.

The suggestion came from a satisfied map maker that an exhibit of maps in the halls would be interesting to others. Other children in the class had made things they wished to exhibit. The shell collections, the pressed seaweeds and the large calcimine pictures were all interesting. Since many questions had been asked about our pictures and exhibits by visitors to the class room it was decided that written explanations should accompany them when they were displayed in the halls.

Little by little a summary was made of the material covered in the study of "Life of the sea and shore" and an assembly program took form without a definite start in that direction.

The following is a list of the subjects discussed in the assembly program:

1. Shell Life in General
2. Bivalves and Univalves
3. Oysters, Clams and Mussels as Food
4. Stories of Pectens
5. About Limpets
6. The Moon Snail
7. How to Collect Sea Animals
8. The Starfish and Its Cousins
9. Mr. Octopus
10. Birds of the Seashore
11. The Penetration of Light Into the Sea
12. Seaweeds
13. Ocean Depth
14. Deep Sea Life
15. Original Poems
16. Songs by the Class

Writing Poetry

The first attempt to describe a sunset on the ocean as projected on the silver screen brought out the fact that the class was extremely limited in the use of descriptive words. Later especial attention was given to this problem when discussing pictures, telling experiences, or selecting passages from reading material.

Occasionally someone wrote a poem, but not of a type to be read to the class. Then one afternoon when the class had been talking about how the sea had looked on the day of the excursion the children decided to write poetry about it. The result was an acceptable verse from each child. The accompanying poems are representative of their work.

CALL OF THE OCEAN

The dashing
The splashing
Of the foamy spray
As it clashes on the rocky shores,
The mystery shadows of the waves,
It is night on the ocean shore.

The peaceful waves are running in ripples,
The sanderlings are piping,
As they chase the merry waves.
The sand is a yellow crystal color.
It is quiet.
It is dawn on the ocean shore.

The shouts of merry children
As they collect the pretty shells,
The mothers are spreading the lunch.
It is noon on the ocean shore.

The sunset is spreading on the sea,
The water is a sparkling turquoise color,
It is all quiet.
It is twilight on the ocean shore.

The waves are yellow from the sunset,
The light from the campfire flows
It is dark on the ocean shore.
                              —*Twila Evey*

SUNSHINE ON THE SEA

When the sun shines on the sea
It's as pretty as can be.
I like to see the water hit the rocks.
And sometimes it hits me.
But still it is pretty as can be.
                              —*Robert Klicka*

STORMY DAYS

On stormy days
The sea is rough,
And to sail a boat
    It is pretty tough.
Some boats will sink,
Some will stay up.
    Oh, that sea,
When it is rough! !
                              —*Charles Miller*

Ho—Mystery of the sea!
Why do you not tell your thoughts to me?
What do you keep under your waves?
And on your sandy shores,
    Oh, gorgeous sea,
Will you tell me?

                              —*Howard Seay*

SLASHING, SPLASHING, DASHING WAVES

Slashing, splashing, dashing waves,
    You have so many creatures in you.
You wash the wavy top through and through.
    Then you wash it up to shore,
Little people and big people
    Pick you up and listen to you.
You keep singing all the time,
    It is just like a rhyme.
                              —*Phyllis Ann Douthit*

SEA, O SEA

Sea, O Sea, will you tell me?
What is under the water
Where I can't see?
O please tell me—
Of what animals live in the waters deep.
I would like to know these things
Sea, O Sea.
Please tell me why
The misty shadows
Crept in and out on the waves?
—*Mary Scudder*

THE WONDERFUL SEA

As I was watching the sea,
I could see the waves splashing, splashing
And the breakers roaring
And the ships sailing so gay.
What a wonderful sight that was,
The mysterious shadows of the
Ship sailing down the sea.
The sparkling fishes swimming down the sea,
What a wonderful sight that was.
—*Billy Aicinena*

THE SEA AT SUNSET

The sea at sunset,
  Is of golden hue.
With colors that look
As though they were
  Set with jewels
Jewels of beautiful colors
Red, orange, and yellow.
  Oh, sea at sunset!
—*Josephine Small*

A'SAILING

Oh, to go a'sailing,
A'sailing on the sea.
And watch the boats go rowing,
A'rowing on the sea.
While the waves are splashing
As happy as can be,
That's the happy life for me.
—*Lucile Fleiss*

THE SEA

Sea, oh Sea!
Please play with me!
Show me the things
I desire to know.
Show me the things
You hide in the sea.
The sea holds so many things,
I would like to know.
Show me the mystery
Of the shadows below.
—*Howard Miller*

SHELLS

Pretty shells down by the sea,
Roaring waves and raging sea,
Aren't you afraid, oh pretty shells?
When you've never heard the city bell,
Aren't you afraid down in a
Deep sand well?

—*Jean Smith*

THE ROCKY SHORE

I like to sit and watch,
The waves pounding against the rocky shore.
The big and little waves.
When splashing, dashing, flashing,
Sending the salt spray in my eyes;
The cool refreshing spray!
I like to sit all day.

—*David Price*

Writing Stories

Some of the stories given in the assembly program are reproduced here.

PECTEN STORIES

Do you know the rhyme,

"Mary, Mary, quite contrary,
How does your garden grow?
Silver bells and cockle shells
And pretty maids all in a row."?

Did you know that "cockle shells" were really pectens or scallops as they are sometimes called? If you went to a cafe or to a fish market to buy pectens you would call them scallops.

Maybe you do not know that the founder of the Shell Oil Company was very much interested in shells and chose the pecten shell as the sign for his big business organization.

In the olden times the scallop shell was often worn by pilgrims to the Holy Land. Once one of these pilgrims picked up a pretty pecten shell and stuck it in his hat. From then on it became a symbol. Now many old families in England have this shell in their coat-of-arms. No other sea shell has been so honored.

LIMPETS

All the limpets live in little tent-shaped houses. The keyhole limpet has grown very curious and made a hole in top of his house so he can see out. The horeshoe just trusts to luck and doesn't care what happens. Of course the owl likes the dark. But how would you like to have tea with the fairies from the cup-and-saucer limpet or go for a walk in a slipper limpet? You can imagine lots of stories about the shells if you take time to look at them and wonder.

THE MOON SNAIL

On the bay shore you often find the sand collar. It is really the egg case of the moon snail. This queer creature has a very large foot and in that foot is the mouth. Instead of teeth it carries a file in its mouth. As the moon snail goes plying through the sand with his foot he feels a clam or some other shell creature alive and immediately makes a neat round hole in the shell with the file and has a good dinner.

We don't like the moon snail very well and maybe the other sea creatures don't either. That is why she must hide her eggs in a collar of sand so nothing will eat them.

THE BED OF THE OCEAN

(A talk from a diagram)

The seashore we know is a very small part of the ocean bed. We see the surface of the sea and where the waves wash the shore. This area is called the "tidal zone" and is the distance between the very highest tide and the very lowest tide. Under the sea the land slopes gently from the shore along most of the continents and this is called the continental shelf. Then the deep part begins rather suddenly. The deepest place that has been found in the ocean is over nine miles, and this is out in the Pacific Ocean. This greatest depth is deeper than the highest mountain is high. Men have gone into the ocean as deep as one and one-half miles and over the earth to an altitude of over ten miles.

The Visit to a Fish Market

Some of the questions asked by the audience of 4th, 5th and 6th grade children after the assembly program showed that in the active interest in the environment the commercial side of the study had been neglected. Some of the questions the children could not answer were:

1. Do our fish markets sell oysters from the local shores?
2. Do they catch salmon near here?
3. Is the swordfish good to eat?
4. Are the pearls found in oysters at the fish markets of any value?

To answer these questions it was decided to visit a fish market. A committee was appointed to make the trip and obtain the information.

The committee found the answers to the questions, but the class wanted additional information, such as:

1. What different kinds of fish are sold at a fish market?
2. Are all the fish caught in local waters?
3. How much is fish a pound?

Products of the Sea

The class listed all the possible sea foods. The following list was compiled:

fish
anchovy
crab meat
clams
lobsters
mussels
oysters
salt
sardines
shrimp

turtle soup
gelatin products
octopus and squid (considered delicacies by those who know how to prepare them)
sea hares (eaten by natives of the Friendly and Society Islands)
eggs of sea birds (eaten by Eskimos)
seaweed (eaten by Japanese)

Many items were found from reading that were not foods, so these lists were gathered also:

ORNAMENTATION
buttons
coral
ivory
jewelry of abalone
mother-of-pearl
pearls

MEDICINE
iodine
kelp products
cod liver oil

OTHER UTILITIES
chalk
eider
fertilizer
fur
potash
sponge
whalebone

WHAT FISHES GIVE US TO USE
oils
fertilizers and meals
glue
isinglass
leather

WHY WHALES WERE ONCE HUNTED
oils
crude
sperm
spermaceti for face creams
ambergris for perfumes
whalebone
meat
fertilizer

Recipes

The class tried to think of all the possible ways of preparing fish for serving. Even with the help of the mothers they could suggest only fried and baked fish and recipes taken from canned sea foods. This was probably because in this school district few parents were associated with the fish industry.

One child brought a booklet called *Five Hundred Ways to Prepare California Sea Foods.*[1] He had secured this book from a local market. It gave such an abundance of information that each child wanted to have one to take home.

---

[1] *Five Hundred Ways to Prepare California Sea Foods.* State Fish Exchange, State Division of Natural Resources. 450 McAllister Street, San Francisco: State Fish Exchange, 1932.

In reply to a request to the State Fish Exchange, State Department of Agriculture, Sacramento, California, fifty free copies were received.

The Plans for a Play

The class proposed to have a party, entertain the parents and give them the lovely booklets containing the recipes. This seemed quite an undertaking. Discussion finally swung to a play. "We could have scenery and costumes," was the unanimous suggestion. Plans were at once under way!

After listening to a Standard Broadcast that morning a little girl described the music as suggesting the "dipping, sailing and soaring sea gulls." No one else saw the picture but her suggestion was appreciated and though the music of the program was not available several Victrola records were tried. In imitation of this music a "Sea Gull" dance was originated to use in the play.

What to do next? "Sometimes children scare the gulls away!" one child suggested. What could the children be doing near the sea gulls? "Studying the sea life, of course," exclaimed several.

Stage Scenery and Costumes for the Play Program

The stage was prepared to represent the seashore. The backdrop was made of ten yards of cheesecloth and was painted with calcimine colors to represent an ocean scene. The cloth was stretched over newspapers on the floor of the classroom. The calcimine was mixed with cold water and spread on with brushes, every member of the class taking a turn with the painting. This gave the children an opportunity for friendly criticism of their own and each other's work. After everyone had "painted and painted" to his own satisfaction, a committee was appointed to put on the finishing touches.

The "sea gull dancers" planned the color and style of their costumes. They measured themselves for the material and had help from their mothers with the sewing and fitting.

The boys prepared their own shell costumes from large sheets of light weight chipboard fastened with brass brads and painted with calcimine.

A strip of green and a strip of purple crepe paper were sewed together and made into a ruffle about the neck of each little girl representing a sea anemone.

With these simple arrangements the setting was complete.

Following is the playlet prepared by the class.

Some of the Characters in the Play "At the Seashore"

AT THE SEASHORE

Place: At the seashore.

Stage: A back drop of a sunset on the sea. Right side a large pile of rocks. Left—smaller rocks. Front—a low wall of rock to represent edge of tide pool. Left (at extreme front) a large white shell.

Characters: Four girls as sea anemones sit in tide pool at front of stage. Three girls as sea gulls stand on rocks and sail about as soft music plays (Victrola record). Anemones move about a little to add color and motion to scene, but do not leave places. Other characters given as they enter.

Two children enter right dressed in bathing suits, frightening sea gulls away and sea anemones settle to tide pools. Boy slips on rocks and falls.

BONNIE: Oh Billy! Be careful! These rocks are wet and slippery.

BILLY: Oh! Agh! Better go slowly Bonnie. We don't want to get hurt the very first day of our summer vacation.

BONNIE: Ouch! Oh! I hurt my foot on one of those sharp shells. Look Billy, it's bleeding.

BILLY: (Looking at Bonnie's foot) That's nothing. The salt water will make it well in no time.

BONNIE: (Crying) It hurts.

BILLY: Well, come up here on the rocks. We can't swim now anyway for it's low tide.

BONNIE: Why Billy, it's all rocks here. We can't ever swim on a rocky beach.

BILLY: (Standing up and talking very emphatically) What a terrible place! Does Grandmother expect us to spend all summer here and never go swimming?

BONNIE: Mother said it would be so lovely here and now look, there is hardly any sand, just rocks, rocks, rocks. Boo-Hoo!

BILLY: Don't cry, baby. Here comes someone.

(Eight children appear from left. Some carry small pails for collecting.)

DAVID: (Skipping to front of stage) Goody goody! It's a fine low tide.

PEGGY: Maybe we will see the starfish today.

WILLA: What lovely sea anemones.

FRED: There are some children. Hello! Are you studying sea creatures too?

BILLY: Studying! Creatures! What do you mean?

DAVID: Don't you know? It's such a lovely rocky beach we have come to see the little sea creatures that live in the rock pools.

BONNIE: Live there! Does anything live on these awful rocks?

ALL CHILDREN: Yes! Yes! (Laughing) Let us tell you.
(Children sit about near Bonnie and Billy on the rocks.)

LUCILE: (Recites poem "The Invitation.")

HUGH: (Dressed as a crab—two large paper pincers tied to his arms, comes from behind rocks children are sitting on. He recites his lines[1] and exits left.)

ESTELEN: (A starfish comes from behind rocks.)

MARY: (Recites lines about a starfish.) (Starfish places herself against curtain at left of stage.)

CALVIN: (Comes in as sea urchin.)

WILLA: (Recites lines about urchin and takes center back stage.)

CHARLES: (A large shell on back appears as "shell.")

DAVID: (Tells of shells and settles on right side of stage.)

DAVID C.: (Comes on as old sand dollar.)

LAWRENCE: (Comes on as a live sand dollar.)

JAMES: (Recites lines about each.) (Sand dollars place selves on either side of sea urchin.)

JOHN B.: (Enters as hermit crab and sits on left stage in shell already placed there, leaving his shell center stage.)

FRED: (Recites lines about hermit crab.)

JOSEPHINE: (As sandpiper enters from left dancing on toes quite close to children.)

TEACHER: What a dear little sandpiper. It reminds me of the poem by Celia Thaxter.

PEGGY JO: Oh I know that poem.

TEACHER: Please say it for us.

PEGGY JO: (Recites "The Sandpiper." Sandpiper dances to soft music and leaves stage at end of recitation.)

BONNIE: Isn't the rocky seashore wonderful? Billy, I would like to know more about sea life.

TEACHER: Then come to our school and see our exhibit in the halls.

BILLY: Say! that would be fine. We should like to come!

Curtain

Note: Children who found it difficult to speak took the part of sea urchins, shell, sand dollars and other characters in order to have every child appear on the stage sometime during the program.

---

[1] Lines referred to here were adapted from E. C. Brown, *Green Gate to the Sea.* New York: Silver, Burdett and Company, 1924.

OUTCOMES

1. Appreciation of the beauty and the mystery of the sea and its manifold life as seen in form, color, light and sound; and the child's individual reaction to these which was expressed in terms of art, music, literature, or drama.

2. Curiosity leading to personal investigation of the seashore to study the habits of the sea creatures.

3. Interest in the multitudinous life of the sea and shore. This interest sustained by making collections. Studying pictures, other exhibits, and reading to make it possible to classify and label the collections.

4. Knowledge of the various products of the sea, conducive to greater appreciation of the wealth of material which lies at our door, for our enjoyment and use.

5. Understanding of the uses which man has made of all sea products in industries yielding economic support.

6. Group participation in thinking, acting and living the experience promoted greater harmony, mutual understanding and orderliness in the classroom.

7. Leisure activities of the entire family group was influenced by this interest and knowledge.

8. Preparation of the class for the study of related subjects. The study of Polar exploration, the early explorers and the shipping activities of the local harbor are all linked with the theme, "Man's Use of the Seas."

BIBLIOGRAPHY

Books

ANDERSON, CHARLES J. *Lincoln Readers*. Chicago: Laurel Book Company, 1922.
    Where Fishes Spend the Winter, pp. 95–98. A Peep Into the Deep, pp. 137–140. A Test for Iodine, p. 253. A Shipwrecked Sailor, pp. 273–279.
ARNOLD, AUGUSTA F. *The Sea Beach at Ebb Tide*. New York: The Century Co., 1903.
    Reference for the teacher and pictures for children.
ATWATER, EMILY PARET. *In Ocean Land*. Fourth Grade. Chicago: Albert Whitman & Co., 1902.
BAMFORD, MARY E. *My Land and Water Friends*. Boston: Lothrop, Lee & Shepard Company, 1886.
BERRIDGE, WALTER S. *Animal Curiosities*. Boston: Small, Maynard & Company, 1923.
BROWN, E. C. *Green Gate to the Sea*. Third Grade. New York: Silver, Burdett and Company, 1924.
    Fine for children.

BURGESS, THORNTON W. *Seashore Book for Children.* Boston: Little, Brown & Company, 1929.
>Covers things most likely to catch eye and interest of child. Written about Atlantic Coast but equally good for Pacific. Scientific identification. Algae, Birds, Animal Life.

BUTLER, EVA. *Along the Shore.* Fourth Grade. New York: The John Day Co., 1930.

CARPENTER, FRANK G. *How the World is Fed.* New York: American Book Company, 1923.
>"Fish in General," p. 167. "Salmon," p. 177. "Oysters," p. 184. "Lobsters, Shrimps, Crabs and other Shell Fish," p. 195. "Sea Food in Other Lands," p. 200.

CHAMBERLAIN, JAMES FRANKLIN. Geographical Readers. Fifth Grade. New York: The Macmillan Company, 1924.

>*How We are Fed.*
>>"The Fishing Industry," pp. 58–64.
>>"Oyster Farming," pp. 65–70.
>>"Where Salt Comes From," pp. 93–98.

>*How We are Clothed.*
>>"A Summer with the Seals," pp. 111–116.
>>"What the (Pearl) Buttons Told," pp. 154–158.

Compton's Pictured Encyclopedia. Chicago: F. E. Compton and Company, 1932.

CROWDER, WILLIAM. *Dwellers of the Sea and Shore.* New York: The Macmillan Company, 1923.
>Good for teachers. Illustrations for children.

DAGLISH, ERIC FITCH. *Fishes and Sea Animals.* New York: William Morrow and Co., 1929.

DAWSON, WILLIAM LEON. *The Birds of California.* San Diego: South Moulton Co., 1923.
>Wonderful illustrations.

DUNCAN, F. M., AND DUNCAN, L. T. Wonders of the Sea Series. Six volumes. New York: Oxford University Press, 1912–1923.

>*Wonders of the Shore*
>*Lobster and His Relations*
>*Starfish and His Relations*
>*Dwellers in the Rock Pools*
>*Life in the Deep Sea*
>*The Sea Birds*

>These six small books comprise the most concise information available on the subject. Though written of English sea life, it is applicable to our local studies. Children can read selections from third to sixth grade reading levels.

EDWARDS, CHARLES LINCOLN. *Nature Study.* Parts I and II. Los Angeles: Hesperian Press, 1924.
>Part I. "Sea Shells and the Animals Who Made Them"; also "Fishes," pp. 164–182.
>Part II. "Seaside Life," pp. 139–149. "Fishes," pp. 180–187.

Encyclopedia Britannica Junior. 12 v. Chicago: Encyclopedia Britannica, Inc., 1934.

FAIRBANKS, HAROLD W. *Home Geography.* Fifth Grade. San Francisco: Educational Publishing Co., 1915. Revised Edition.
"Where Water Comes From," pp. 43–46. "The Ocean," pp. 76–79. "The Work of the Ocean," pp. 80–83. "Inhabitants of the Water," pp. 121–125. "The Home by the Ocean," pp. 233–236. "The Wanderer" (Poem), p. 103. "The Tides," p. 235.

FAIRBANKS, HAROLD W. *Stories of Our Mother Earth.* Fourth Grade. San Francisco: Educational Publishing Co., 1908.
"A Handful of Sand," pp. 29–36. "A Story of San Francisco Bay," pp. 41–46. "An Ancient Oyster Bed," pp. 47–53. "Something About Salt," pp. 80–85. "What We Saw on an Ocean Cliff," pp. 101–106. "How Islands Are Formed," pp. 106–114.

FREEMAN, FRANK N. *Wonder Stories,* Book III. Child-Story Readers, California State Series. Sacramento: California State Department of Education, 1929.
"The Little Water Fairy," pp. 13–30. "'A Sea Diver," pp. 286–290. "Queen Fishes," pp. 321–326. "Poems," pp. 356–359. "Fairy Gardens of the Sea," pp. 360–365.

GAYLORD, ILSIEN NATHALIE. *Sea Creatures.* Boston: Little, Brown and Co., 1924. Charming story for children to read. Fine questions at end of chapters.

GOULD, ALLEN WALTON. *Mother Nature's Children.* Fourth Grade. Boston: Ginn and Company, 1900.
"How Fish Cradle Their Babies," p. 15. "How Fish Tend Their Babies," pp. 49–52. "How Mother Nature Clothes the Mollusks," pp. 105–112.

HARDY, M. E. *Sea Stories.* Boston: Ginn and Company, 1904.

HENDERSON, D. M. *Children of the Tide.* New York: D. Appleton and Co., 1925.

HOWES, EDITH. *Sandals of Pearl.* New York: William Morrow and Co., 1928. Good fourth grade story of romantic type.

INGERSOLL, ERNEST. *Book of the Ocean.* New York: The Century Co., 1928.

JOHNSON, MYRTLE E. *Seashore Animals of the Pacific Coast.* New York: The Macmillan Company, 1927.
Very scientific. Excellent illustrations.

MANLY, JOHN M.; RICKER, EDITH; AND TEUBRIE, NINA. *Good Reading.* California State Series. Sacramento: State Department of Education, 1930.
State text for fifth grade. Poems and stories of excellent value, pp. 284–300.

MAYER, ALFRED GOLDSBOROUGH. *Sea Shore Life.* Chicago: A. S. Barnes Co., 1916.

National Geographic Society. *The Book of Birds.* Washington: National Geographic Society, 1927.
For identification.

PITKIN, WALTER B., AND HUGHES, HAROLD F. *Farm and Field.* Book I. Seeing America. New York: The Macmillan Company, 1929.
"On Boston Fish Docks," pp. 1–9. "Boys for Fishing Cod," pp. 10–28. "Description of a Salt Mine," pp. 172–174. "Salmon Cannery," pp. 301–304.

RICE, LUCIA WEBSTER. *Box in the Sand.* Second Grade. Boston: Ginn and Co., 1927.
Pp. 1–4, 32–46, 59–66, about seashore.

ROGERS, J. E. *The Shell Book.* Garden City, New York: Doubleday Page & Co., 1908.
A good story for fifth grade boys. Deep sea life studied.

Schoolroom Aquaria. Lincoln School of Teachers College. New York: Lincoln School of Teachers College, Columbia University, 1925.

TRAFTON, GILBERT H. *Nature Study and Science for Intermediate Grades.* New York: The Macmillan Company, 1927.
A textbook in fourth, fifth, and sixth grades. "The School Aquarium," pp. 84–96.

WALKER, ALBERTA, AND PARKMAN, MARY R. *Study Reader.* Fourth Year. New York: Chas. E. Merrill Co., 1924.
"The Lobster and the Crab," pp. 286–289.

Choice Literature. Compiled by SHERWIN WILLIAMS. New York: American Book Company, 1912.
"Capture of a Whale," by James F. Cooper, pp. 109–111. "The Wreck of the Hesperus," by Henry W. Longfellow, pp. 162–165. "Sweet and Low," by Alfred Tennyson, pp. 177.

WOOD, THEODORE. *Little Naturalist at the Seashore.* New York: E. P. Dutton & Co., 1905.

World Book Encyclopedia. 19 v. Chicago: W. F. Quarrie & Company, 1934.

WRIGHT, J. M. *Seaside and Wayside Nature Readers.* Boston: D. C. Heath & Co., 1900.

Articles from the National Geographic Magazine

ADAMS, GREENWOOD. "Australia's Wild Wonderland." XLV (March, 1924), 329–356.

"A Wanderer Under the Sea." LXII (December, 1932), 741–758. (Color plates.)

BEEBE, WILLIAM. "Depths of the Sea." LXI (January, 1932), 65–88.

"Crabs and Crab Like Curiosities of the Sea." LIV (July, 1928), 57–72. (Color plates.)

CROWDER, WILLIAM. "The Life of the Moon-Jelly Fish." L. (August, 1926), 187–202.

ELLISON, NORMAN. "Shark Fishing." LXII (September, 1932), 369–386.

"Living Jewels of the Sea." LII (September, 1927), 290–304. (Color plates.)

"Luminous Life in the Depth of the Sea." LIX (June, 1931), 666. (Eight paintings.)

"Our Friend the Frog." LXI (May, 1932), 629. (Color plates.)

"Tropical Toy Fish." LIX (March, 1931), 287–318. (Color plates.)

Motion Picture Films

Name of Film	*Source*
Beach and Sea Animals	Bell & Howell Company 1801 Larchmont Avenue Chicago, Illinois
Elementary Animals	University Film Foundation Harvard University
Fish in the Southern California Biological Station	Robert Barkley 3214 Trumbull San Diego, California
Fishing in San Diego	Robert Barkley 3214 Trumbull San Diego, California
Grunion, The Mystery Fish	Eastman Kodak Company Rochester, New York
Nesting of the Sea Turtle	University Film Foundation Harvard University

Name of Film	*Source*
New England Fisheries	Eastman Kodak Company Rochester, New York
Nomads of the Sea (Sea Fowls of Canada)	Canadian Pacific Railroad Co. Montreal, Canada
Salt	Robert Barkley, 3214 Trumbull San Diego, California
Salmon of Pacific Coast	Eastman Kodak Company Rochester, New York
Sea Elephants	Robert Barkley, 3214 Trumbull San Diego, California
Seashore Animals	Eastman Kodak Company Rochester, New York
Sea Urchin and Starfish	Bell & Howell Company 1801 Larchmont Avenue Chicago, Illinois
Simple Forms—Animals	Eastman Kodak Company Rochester, New York
The Corals	Bell & Howell Company 1801 Larchmont Avenue Chicago, Illinois
Tiny Water Animals	Bell & Howell Company 1801 Larchmont Avenue Chicago, Illinois
Tuna Fishing	Robert Barkley, 3214 Trumbull San Diego, California
Water Insects	Eastman Kodak Company Rochester, New York

Stillfilms

Available from Stillfilm Incorporated,
1052 Cahuenga Ave.
Hollywood, California

Birds of Coronado Islands
Canadian Fishing
Catalina Islands
Crabs of the Pacific Coast
Elephant Seals Part I & II

Elephant Seals in the Zoo
Fishing (U. S.)
Weather
Whaling
Seashore Animals

Lantern Slides

Available from Keystone View Co.,
Meadville, Pennsylvania

Fishing
Marine Life

Mollusks
Salt
Starfish and Sea Urchins

Songs ·

McConathy, Osbourne; Miessner, W. Otto; Birge, Edward Baily; and Bray, Mabel E. *The Music Hour.* Third Book. California State Series. Sacramento: California State Department of Education, 1931.
  "Seashore Days," p. 9. "The Shell," p. 75.

McConathy, Osbourne; Beattie, John W.; and Morgan, Russell V. *Music of Many Lands and Peoples.* California State Series. Sacramento: California State Department of Education, 1933.
  "Sea Fever," p. 69.

Tomlins, W. L. *Laurel Music Reader.* Boston: C. C. Birchard & Company, 1925.

CHAPTER X

CURRICULUM UNIT

THE COLORADO DESERT: A REPRESENTATIVE DESERT[1]

I. PREVIEW OF THE UNIT

The Colorado Desert in California is located in the southeastern part of the state. It was formerly an arm of the Gulf of California, but the Colorado River built a delta and cut off the land. There are abundant traces of the ancient sea life.

This desert is generally below sea level increasing in depth as you go north as much as three hundred feet. The Colorado River flows on a raised river bed and this endangers life and property because of the danger of flood.

The first known inhabitants of this region were nomadic Indians. Colonel Kearney, of the United States Army, marched through in 1846 and left a detailed army report. It was not until the gold rush of 1849 that people visited this region in great numbers.

In 1892 Charles Rockwood began his efforts to have the waters of the Colorado River used for irrigation. His efforts were successful in 1901 when the first water flowed through canals into this desert.

The unreclaimed part of the desert is rich in mineral formations and much characteristic desert plant and animal life is found.

The reclaimed part of the desert is called the Imperial Valley, which is a rich agricultural region. A study of this district gives one an idea of what water does for the desert.

In 1907 a break occurred in the Colorado levees and the entire valley was flooded. This began a movement for better flood control, until at the present time the United States Government is directing the building of the Boulder Dam and All-American Canal project, which will irrigate and protect the largest irrigation project in the world.

II. APPROACH

A collection of desert pictures will provide a stimulating beginning. Point out similarities in pictures. Why is sand usually shown? Read descriptions of sand dunes.

---

[1] Prepared under the direction of Clara H. Smith, Director of Rural Education, Ventura County, by Esther Surface, Teacher, Seventh and Eighth Grades, Pleasant Valley, California State Demonstration Rural School, Camarillo.

Discuss what an oasis is. This may lead to the question why there are so few trees on the desert.

Encourage pupils to tell about their experiences on the desert.

Read newspaper clippings regarding the Boulder Dam.

Read Bible stories dealing with shepherds and flocks. Were not the herdsmen living on the fringe of deserts? How did these people adapt themselves to their environment?

Name and locate the principal deserts of the world.

Read poetry about the desert and encourage pupils to write original poetry.

Have the pupils write a story about something characteristic of the desert. These may be compared with compositions written at the end of the study.

III. OUTLINE OF UNIT
GEOGRAPHY OF THE DESERT

Content	*Teaching Aids*
A. Topography of the land.	
1. Deserts are the valleys between mountain ranges.	Have you ever visited a desert? Where?
2. Deserts differ materially from other lands only in lack of water.	Point out the principal deserts of the world on a map. Name the mountains surrounding these deserts.
3. Land is not a permanent affair because of shifting sand.	Does this make the desert a dangerous place? Why?
B. Temperature and Rainfall.	
1. Severe summers.	Where is the hottest place in the United States? How hot does it get there?
2. Winter mid-day heat; nights cold.	What is absent in the air to cause this great change in temperature?
3. Temperature may vary as much as eighty degrees in a few hours.	What effect does this have on health? Point out the fact that pneumonia is a common desert disease.
4. Practically no rain. Moisture falls on the coast side of the mountains.	Why does the rain fall on the coast side?
5. Rain that does fall often evaporates before it reaches the ground.	Why does the rain evaporate in the air?
C. Air.	
1. Severe winds caused by hot air rising. Other wind is continually rushing in to take its place.	Severe windstorms are characteristic of all deserts.
2. Air is very clear—no moisture or humidity.	Why are the reclaimed portions of the desert sometimes humid?
3. Glare—sand is a reflector; everything has color.	How has this caused many desert tragedies?

PLANT LIFE OF THE COLORADO DESERT—CHAPARRAL

Content	Teaching Aids

A. Sahuaro

1. 20 to 50 feet in height. — Locate the Sahuaro forest on a map.

2. Branches form columns from stems. — Collect pictures of this plant.

3. Purple flower—edible fruit. — Fruit used as food by the Indians and animals.

B. Cholla

1. Tree like branches. — "Cactus of the Southwest." *The National Geographic*, September, 1925.[1]

2. Does not often grow higher than twelve feet. — Cactus wrens use this plant to nest in. Protection.

3. Red or yellow blooms. — Used as food by the mountain sheep.

C. Prickly Pear

1. Spade-like jointed stems — Most pupils familiar with this variety of cactus.

2. Moisture held in the stems. Needs more moisture than some varieties. — What confection is made from this plant?

Discuss Luther Burbank's work with cacti. Do the spines ever return? *Stories of Luther Burbank*—Slusser.[1]

D. Ocotillo

1. Trunk grows in the ground like a beet. — Show pictures of this plant.

2. Stem reaches just above the ground.

3. Stems grow as long as eighteen feet.

4. Scarlet flowers.

5. When heat shrivels the leaves they develop thorns. — How is the plant protected by the thorns?

E. Barrel

1. Called the desert water tank. — Mexican people make candy from it.

F. Agave—called the century plant

1. Leaves cluster at the top of ground.

---

[1] See Reading Materials on page 165 for complete references.

Content	*Teaching Aids*

2. Flowers rise at center.

3. Mescal made from sap.

4. Fiber is sisal hemp. — Name the industries that are dependent in some way upon rope.

5. Spines are at end of leaves. — How have the cacti family adapted themselves to their environment?

G. Yucca

   1. Spanish Bayonet type—giant. — *Touring Topics*, September, 1933.[1]

   2. Indians used roots for baskets. — Found in the foothills.

   3. Flour made from the seed pods. — How does this state protect the Yucca?

   4. The green stalk may be eaten like asparagus. — What is the Spanish name for Yucca?

H. Palo Verde

   1. Smooth bark. — What is the Spanish meaning?

   2. Soft green in color.

I. Mesquite

   1. Similar to Palo Verde in shape and size. — Usually found along old water courses. Why?

   2. Wood is very hard. — How is this wood used commercially?

   3. Has long tap roots.

J. Sage

   1. Very profuse.

   2. Protected by its smell. — Animals will not go near it.

K. Joshua Tree

   1. Limbs all point in one direction. — Joshua seeking the holy land lost his way and looked to heaven for a sign.

   2. Some as large as three feet across. — Joshua Tree not found in the Colorado Desert; in the Mohave.

Discuss other desert plants not found in the Colorado Desert.

L. Conclusions

   1. Plants are protected by nature to resist heat and drought. — Palo Verde leaves hang diagonally to avoid direct rays of sun.

   2. There is no unnecessary exposure of leaf surface.

[1] See Reading Materials on page 165 for complete references.

Content	*Teaching Aids*
3. Plants have thick coating of spines and hairy growth.	
4. No large leaves on desert bushes.	Greasewood and Ocotillo.
5. Some plants have a shellac—makes evaporation impossible.	
6. Long powerful tap roots.	Mesquite roots have been known to go through granite.
7. Plants provide a covering for a desert that would otherwise be barren.	What benefit does a brush covering contribute to a land?
	Try to imagine the condition that would exist if there were no covering on the desert.
8. Desert plants are strong and healthy, adapting themselves in every way to their environment.	*Wild Flowers and Trees of California*—Saunders.[1]

ANIMAL LIFE OF THE COLORADO DESERT

A. Tortoise.

1. Eats grass, clover and herbs.	*Nature's Wonderland*, Hornaday.[1]
2. Can go as long as two months without water.	
3. Sense of touch is in the end of his nose.	Why is this of great value to him?
4. Sleeps all winter like a bear.	
5. Grown ones weigh about 20 pounds.	Name all the ways this animal has adapted himself to his environment.

B. Rats.

1. Kangaroo and Pack.	Discuss how these animals get their names. *Denizens of the Desert*, Jaeger.[1]

C. Lizards and Reptiles.

1. Chuckawalla. Tail is his defense weapon.	Indians used them for food.
2. Gila monster. Controversy over deadliness of poison.	Indians used the designs on their backs as designs for their baskets.
3. Horned lizard.	How is this animal protected?

[1] See Reading Materials on page 165 for complete references.

Content   *Teaching Aids*

4. Gridironed tailed lizard.

5. Rattlesnake.
   Sidewinder strikes on the run.   How does the Sidewinder get his name?

                                         Stress fact that reptiles lack cunning and
                                         swiftness of flight and some are provided
                                         with poison.
D. Roadrunner.

   1. Lives in the mesquite.   Point out that his protection is his speed.

   2. Eats a variety of food.

   3. Poor ability in flight, smell and
   song.

   4. Will dare attack a rattlesnake.

E. Cactus Wren.

   1. Lives in cactus.   How is Cactus Wren different from the
                                         wrens here?

F. Rabbits.

   1. Powerful hind legs and endurance.

G. Coyote.

   1. Highly developed cunning.   Is this necessary in order to live on the
                                         desert?
   2. Keen nose, good ears and eyes.

H. Mule deer

   1. Found in edge of mountains.   Isn't it true that only the hardy survive?

I. Mountain Sheep.

   1. 300 head in California.

   2. No open season since 1883.   Stress the fact that California protects its
                                         game.

   3. Golden Eagle principal enemy.

   4. Light steel grey in color.   California Fish and Game Commission
                                         Bulletin, January 1931.[1]

[1] See Reading Materials on page 165 for complete references.

Content   *Teaching Aids*

J. Conclusions.

1. Desert animals are wary.

2. Desert animals are lean and gaunt.

3. Desert animals are fierce.   Is this a result of the constant danger?

4. Desert animals gain moisture   Compare desert animals with animals of
from animal blood and plants.   same family living in other surroundings.

                                       Draw and color these animals on card-
                                       board; cut them out and arrange on
                                       grooved board.

GEOLOGICAL FORMATIONS—MINERALS

A. Sand is chipped rock.

1. Rock is poor conductor; heat and   Why is sand characteristic of a desert
cold penetrate only a little way;   country?
chips off rock.

2. Rain cools hot rock and one part
shrinks away from the other.

3. Wind turns rock over and grinds
them together; sand.

B. Non-metallic minerals—Gypsum.

1. Contributes most of m i n e r a l   Stress economic value.
wealth of desert.

2. Plaster City Plant employs 80
men and mines 300 tons daily.

3. Specimens of clay, cyanide, lime-   Valuable gems have been collected in
stone, marble, pumice, soda, stron-   Southwest part of desert.
tium, sulphur, turquoise, silica and
sodium sulphate found.   Is no borax mined here? Where is
                                       borax an important mineral in the des-
                                       ert?

C. Metallic minerals.   California Bureau of Mines: *Mining in
                                       California*, April 1926.[1]

1. Gold
Many abandoned mines here, "Pi-   Recently some of these abandoned mines
chacho," "American Girl" and   have been reopened? Why?
"Tumco."

2. Copper, iron, lead and s i l v e r, Make a collection of typical desert min-
nickel and zinc.   erals.

_____

[1] See Reading Materials on page 165 for complete references.

Content	*Teaching Aids*

D. Salton Sea.

1. An inland sea 250 feet below sea level.

Dinosaur's tracks found imprinted in rocks here.
Indian relics found in abundance.

2. Mullet Island
Mud pots—oxide springs, paint deposits.
Average 50 eruptions in every 20 acres.

Water line is plainly visible on rocks.
What does this prove?

3. Oyster beds
Sandstone creations; odd figures.
Easy to find fish fossils.

Dispute theory that some of these figures are petrified water lilies.
What does this prove?
Make a collection of these formations.

E. Painted gorge.

1. Curious shapes and formations on cliffs.

Sea urchins reputed to be a million years old have been found here.

2. High coral reefs and oyster shells.

3. Highly colored rocks typical of desert.

F. Petrified Forest.

1. Extends for an area of 10 acres.

Locate this and other petrified forests in California and Arizona.

G. Conclusions.

1. The Colorado desert is rich in mineral formations.

Conduct an imaginary tour to the places of interest in this desert.

2. The Colorado Desert has a variety of mineral formations.

3. Many evidences of a n c i e n t life found in mineral formations.

RECLAIMED SECTION OF THE COLORADO DESERT—THE IMPERIAL VALLEY

In studying this region we wish to show what water will do for the desert. For that reason we are particularly interested in the agricultural aspect of the Valley.

A. Date culture.
1. There are as many as 119 varieties.
2. Male palm produces the pollen.
3. Blossoms are dried and pollen dusted on other blooms.
4. One plant may produce between 100 and 350 pounds annually.
5. Dates do not ripen in cluster—must be picked as they ripen.

Why is this a representative d e s e r t crop?
Where in other parts of the world are dates an important crop? Where did the original plants in California come from? Discuss pollinization. "Date Romance," Sheilds, Indio.[1]
Visit the Highway Date Gardens, El Centro, California. Make a pictorial display of the history of the date culture in this country.
Make a collection of different varieties of dates.

---

[1] See Reading Materials on page 165 for complete references.
13—17050

Content	*Teaching Aids*

B. Dairying.
1. 24,000 head of cattle in the Valley.
2. Six million pounds of butter fat produced annually.
3. Feed conditions ideal.
4. Mild winter temperature.

Point out fact that desert people of all ages have been dependent on their flocks—pastoral.
Discuss how people of Gobi and Arabian deserts used their flocks for food, shelter and clothing.
How does this industry depend on the climate?
Why may hogs be profitably grown as a side line?

C. Alfalfa.
1. Largest crop.

Why may so many crops be grown in one year?
What industry is dependent on alfalfa?

2. Seven to ten crops yearly.
3. Land produces 6 to 10 tons per acre.
4. 200,000 acres acreage.
5. Supports the livestock industry.
6. Annual value ranges from two to three million dollars annually.

D. Lettuce.
1. 10,000 carloads shipped out of Valley in 1933.
2. Imperial Valley ranks first in value and production of crop.

Is the soil fertile? Where does it come from?
Imperial County Board of Trade, "Imperial Valley—America's Winter Playground." [1]

E. Cantaloupes and other melons.
1. Imperial County ranks first in value and production of cantaloupes in the United States.
2. Annual shipment of about 15,000 carloads.

Imagine you were working for the Chamber of Commerce of one of the Imperial Valley cities; what points would you stress?

F. Conclusions.
1. Imperial County is a rich agricultural region.
2. A desert region differs materially from other regions only in absence of water.

Compare irrigated section with unreclaimed section.
Make a product map of Imperial County.
Write to the El Centro Chamber of Commerce for literature.

IV. TOPIC CONCLUSIONS

In the desert there is great need of water control, not only for irrigation but to protect people against floods.

California deserts have a wealth of characteristic desert plant and animal life.

California deserts have many unusual geological formations.

Desert lands differ materially from other lands in absence of water.

Desert lands are productive if water is obtainable.

[1] See Reading Materials on page 165 for complete references.

Desert plants and animals adapt themselves to their environment. The Colorado Desert is valuable for study because of the large section of reclaimed land.

V. PROJECT WORK COMPLETED

Make a frieze showing a desert oasis. This can include plant and animal life, varied rock formations and rugged appearance of the region.

Make a product map of the irrigated section.

Cut out characteristic desert animals and arrange a desert scene.

Paste desert pictures on a background to make a wall hanging. This is a good activity for pupils who are not gifted in art work.

Write compositions about some phase of desert life. Compare the ones written at the first with those written at the close of the study. Accept this as a measure of what has been gained.

Write original poetry about the desert.

Make a collection of desert wild flowers.

Collect minerals and unusual formations.

Outline the desert regions on a map of California.

Trace the routes used by the early pioneers in going across the desert.

VI. READING MATERIALS

Books

BOLTON, HERBERT EUGENE. *De Anza's California Expeditions*. Berkeley: University of California, 1930.

BONKER, C. E. *Sage of the Desert and Other Cacti*. Boston: The Stratford Company, 1930.

CHASE, J. S. *California Desert Trails*. Boston: Houghton Mifflin Company, 1919.

Compton's Pictured Encyclopedia. Chicago: F. E. Compton and Company, 1932.

DITMARS, RAYMOND. *Reptiles of the World*. New York: The Macmillan Company, 1927.

DITMARS, RAYMOND. *The Reptile Book*. Garden City, New York: Doubleday, Doran and Company, 1907.

DUPUY, W. A. *Our Plant Friends and Foes*. Philadelphia: The John C. Winston Company, 1925.

Encyclopedia Britannica Junior. 12 v. Chicago: Encyclopedia Britannica, Inc., 1934.

FAIRBANKS, HAROLD. *The Western United States*. Boston: D. C. Heath and Company, 1908.

FREEMAN, LEWIS R. *The Colorado River, Yesterday, Today and Tomorrow*. New York: Dodd, Mead & Company, 1923.

HAWKSWORTH, H. *Adventures of a Grain of Dust*. New York: Chas. Scribner's Sons, 1925.

HAWKSWORTH, H. *Adventures of a Pebble*. New York: Chas. Scribner's Sons, 1921.

HORNADAY, W. T. *Tales from Nature's Wonderland*. New York: Chas. Scribner's Sons, 1924.

HORNADAY, W. T. *Campfires on Desert and Lava.* New York: Chas. Scribner's Sons, 1908.

HORNADAY, W. T. *Wild Animal Interviews.* New York: Chas. Scribner's Sons, 1918.

JAEGER, E. C. *Denizens of the Desert.* Boston: Houghton Mifflin Company, 1922.

JAEGER, E. C. *The California Desert.* Stanford University, California: Stanford University Press, 1933.

KOCH, FELIX JOHN. *Little Journeys Through the Great Southwest.* Chicago: A. Flanagan Co., 1907.

LEE, BOURKE. *Death Valley.* New York: The Macmillan Company, 1930.

LUMMIS, C. F. *Strange Corners of Our Country.* New York: The Century Company, 1898.

PERKINS, EDNA B. *The White Heart of the Mohave.* New York: Boni & Liveright, 1922.

SAUNDERS, C. F. *Wild Flowers and Trees of California.* New York: McBride Publishing Co., 1914.

SLUSSER, A. *Stories of Luther Burbank and His Plant School.* New York: Chas. Scribner's Sons, 1920.

VAN DYKE, JOHN CHARLES. *The Desert.* New York: Chas. Scribner's Sons, 1930.

UNTERMEYER, LOUIS. *Modern American Poetry.* Third Revised Edition. New York: Harcourt Brace & Company, 1925.

World Book Encyclopedia. 19 v. Chicago: W. F. Quarrie & Company, 1934.

Pamphlets and Magazines

"Canyons and Cactus of the Southwest." Natural color photographs. *The National Geographic Magazine,* XLVIII (September, 1925), pp. 275–290.

"Imperial Valley—America's Winter Playground." El Centro, California: Imperial County Board of Trade.

JOHNSTON, PHILIP. "Death Valley Canyons, The Squeaking Saurian." *Westway,* XXVI (March, 1934), p. 10.

LAKEN, ANNA BELLE. "Edible Wildings." *Touring Topics,* XXVIII (September, 1933), p. 26.

OBER, E. H. "Mountain Sheep of California." *California Fish and Game Commission,* XVII (January, 1931), pp. 27–39.

"Romance of the Date." Indio, California: C. F. Sheilds.

"Scenic Wonders of Imperial Valley." El Centro, California: Imperial County Chamber of Commerce.

"Story of the Conquest of the Colorado." Las Vegas, Nevada: Boulder Dam Association.

TUCKER, W. BURLING. "Imperial County." *Mining in California.* San Francisco: California State Bureau of Mines, XXII (April, 1926), pp. 248–254.

CHAPTER XI

CURRICULUM UNIT

SOAP[1]

HOW THIS UNIT WAS APPROACHED

The fifth grade were studying wild flowers. Every Monday morning the children brought in new specimens. Betty Jo brought a specimen of soap root plant from a Sunday trip. She asked her teacher to identify it for her. This was done and then the teacher read the story about soap root or amoli in *The Wild Flowers of California* by Mary E. Parsons to the class. Since the soap root plant was used by the early Spanish Californians, it occurred to Betty Jo that the specimen would be interesting to the A4's who were studying about California. She came to the A4's room and asked the class if they knew what wild flower the early Spanish Californians used for soap. No one knew; so instead of showing them the soap root plant, she left *The Wild Flowers of California* and said, "There is a story about the plant in this book. It is interesting. See if you can find it. If you can, I will bring you the plant."

She had aroused the curiosity of the class just enough. What plant could it be? All day the book was on someone's desk and by three o'clock no one had found the answer. "But we will tomorrow," said some of the boys.

The next morning when Group I was busy reading a story, suddenly Clifford called out, "I have it. Here it is. It's the soap root plant." Then he read the story to the class. Immediately they wanted him to tell Betty Jo and to get the soap root plant. Clifford went to the Fifth Grade Room and made the following report to Betty Jo and her class.

"Betty Jo wanted us to find out what plant the early Spanish Californians used for soap. I was the first one to find out; so I have come to tell you about it. The name of the plant is soap root or amoli. It grows two and one-half feet tall and has white blossoms. The Indians and the Spaniards were not interested in the flowers. They wanted the root. The root looks like an onion bulb and the Indians discovered that the bulb made a fine lather and made things clean. The Spanish

---

[1] This unit of work was developed by Mrs. Nelva C. Harrington Poor, Principal Chapman Avenue School, Los Angeles, under the direction of Ethel I. Salisbury, Associate Professor of Elementary Education, University of California at Los Angeles, and Educational Consultant, Santa Monica Public Schools; formerly Director of Curriculum, Los Angeles City Schools.

women also used it when they washed their clothes in the creek. The outer covering of the bulb is stiff and the Indians used it for stuffing mattresses. Could we see the plant you found, Betty Jo?"

Betty Jo was so pleased with this report that she gave him the plant to keep in his room.

When Clifford returned to his class with the plant the children began talking about soap and asked many questions. These were written on the board and the class was encouraged to find answers to them.

The following questions were asked:

When did people first begin using soap?
How do they make soap in a factory?
How many kinds of soap are there?
How did the pilgrims make soap?
Could we make soap?
Who were the first people to have a soap factory?
How do they make it into so many shapes?
How did the Spanish people discover that the soap plant was good to use as soap?
Where is a common place to find the soap plant in California?
What is soap?
Why does soap make a suds and lather?
Why does soap make our faces and hands clean?
Why are soaps yellow, green, red, pink and other colors?
Why do some soaps float?
Is one kind as good as another?
How can you tell which to buy?
Why are some soaps marked Laundry Soap and some Toilet Soap?
Why do some soaps say "99% pure"?

ACTIVITIES UNDERTAKEN BY THE CLASS

Before they knew it the class was busy with the study of soap and everyone was trying to bring in some information.

Exhibits

So many interesting things came in, the class decided to have an exhibit table and by the time the study was finished, the following things were on the table:

Exhibits of 15 different kinds of soap.
Wrappers from 20 different soaps—telling for what use each was best suited and why.
Laundry soap made by class.
Pink perfumed toilet soap made by class.

Soap root plant.

Potash solution made by boys.

A coconut in shell to illustrate use of coconut oil.

Palm leaf—with a story of palm oil used in soaps.

Two books with typewritten material written by teacher which helped in answering some of the questions.

An exhibit of soap builders
  a. Rosin
  b. Sodium Silicate
  c. Borax
  d. Naphtha
  e. Washing soda
  f. Bluing
  g. Bleach

A set of recipes for mother to use when washing
  a. Wool
  b. Silk
  c. Cotton
  d. Linen
  e. Rayon
     (A set went home to each mother)

Experiments

Making Potash Solution. The boys built a wood fire to make ashes. They secured a small wooden keg and bored holes in the bottom of it. They put the ashes in the keg. Water was poured over the ashes and when this drained out slowly through the ashes the boys had a potash solution. They knew that if they added lime they would have lye. But on account of the dangers of handling lye, they did not take this step.

Making Laundry Soap. Two children worked as partners. Each couple had ½ pound of melted fat which they weighed and ½ cup of lye solution which was prepared for them by the teacher. (The directions on the can of lye for making lye solution were followed.) One child of each couple slowly poured the lye into the fat while the other child stirred the mixture. One child fixed a mold for the soap by lining a match box with oiled paper. This recipe just filled the match box and gave each child a good sized piece of soap to take home when it was hard.

The partners took turns stirring the mixture. Some of them stirred as long as 30 minutes. When the mixture was thick, almost the consistency of fudge, it was ready to turn out into the molds. It was left in the molds until the next afternoon and then cut into two parts with a piece of fine wire.

Each pair of children who were making the soap read the following directions.

Two people worked together helping each other with the measuring and weighing.

SOAP RECIPE

One-half pound of melted fat (pure lard will do nicely).

One-half cup of lye solution (following directions on can of lye for making lye solution).

Pour the melted fat into the bowl.

Add the lye solution, one person pouring very slowly while the other one stirs.

While one person is stirring, the other may line a cardboard box with waxed paper.

Stir the mixture for some time, probably 30 minutes.

When the fat and lye blend into a thick creamy mass then the soap is ready to pour into the mold.

Set aside to harden. Tomorrow it will be ready to cut in half to take home.

Use a piece of sharp wire to cut the cake of soap.

How the Glycerine is Taken from the Soap at the Factory. The children had found out that glycerine was taken from the soap at the factory. They had also learned that when salt is added to soap, the latter is broken into small pieces and comes to the top of the kettle while the glycerine and most of the lye solution stays in the bottom of the kettle. In the factory the mixture is run off in pipes to the glycerine refinery.

The children took two pans of water and made a good lather with their own soap in one pan and a lather with Ivory Soap in the other. Then they added the same amount of salt to each pan. In the pan containing their own soap—the soap came to the top broken up into small chunks. In the other pan very little effect of the salt was noticed.

The children drew the conclusion that glycerine had already been taken from the Ivory Soap, while some was still in their own soap.

Why Soap Cleanses. The girls and boys were given some pieces of soiled muslin which the girls were told to wash in clear water, while the boys washed their pieces in soapy water. In a few minutes, time was called and each held up his piece—the girls were not so proud of their work, but immediately said, "Well the boys had soap. Why is it that soap takes out the dirt?" To help them in finding out the teacher directed another experiment.

First, the children smeared a thin film of oil on one side of a small strip of glass. Then they placed a drop of clear water on the glass and near by on the glass one drop of the soapy solution. The children noticed at once a difference in the shape of the drops. The drop of clear water was round and high and the drop of soapy solution spread out flat.

The same experiment was tried on the other side of the glass and again the soapy solution spread out farther than the water.

The children took a glass tumbler and spread oil around the inside. They filled it with water and then shook out the water. But still the water clung to the glass in places. They then filled the glass with a soapy solution and shook that out. Now there were no clinging drops; the soap had spread over the whole glass.

They were asked these questions: "If your dishes or clothes are greasy, which will spread more quickly and evenly over them, soapy water or clear? Which will get farther and more evenly into the fibers of our clothing?"

Then they wanted to find out just how the soap removed the grease in the pieces of muslin the boys washed.

Another experiment was carried out.

The teacher brought out two bottles. A boy put the same amount of water and oil in each bottle. To one bottle he added soapy solution. The oil came to the top in both bottles. Now the boy was told to shake the second bottle hard for a minute. The bottles were then placed where all could see. In one bottle the oil was still on the top, but in the other no oil could be seen. "Where is the oil?" the children asked.

Then the teacher explained that the oil had been broken up into

Experiments in Making Soap

tiny bits and the soap solution was around all these little drops keeping them apart.

The teacher asked, "What did you do to make the soap solution surround the oil?" The answer, of course, was, "We shook it together." The teacher then told the children that the soap had emulsified the oil, and the mixture was an emulsion.

The class now came to the conclusion that work was necessary to break up the grease and dirt in small pieces and to help the soap surround these pieces and pry them loose.

Value of Washing Powders. The teacher had asked several children to prepare reports on hard and soft water. After these reports the following experiment was carried out.

Two basins containing equal amounts of water were on the table. Equal amounts of limewater were added to each. George made a soap solution in a third pan. The teacher dissolved a little washing soda in one of the pans of clear water. Then George was told to beat in a tablespoonful of his soap solution to each pan. "Keep on adding and stirring until you get a suds in each basin. Count the tablespoonfuls you use for both," said the teacher.

George began, soon he was getting a good suds in the basin where the washing soda had been added, but no suds in the other. He kept on adding soap to the second basin. At last the suds came. He had used six times as much soap in the basin without the washing soda as he had used in the one with the washing soda.

The children were led to the conclusion that when there was no washing soda the lime in the water surrounded the soap. When there was washing soda the lime did not surround the soap. That was why the soap could make a suds—so it really kept the lime away from the soap.

Washing soda does not cost as much as soap and less soda than soap is required to soften water. So it pays to use just enough washing soda in the water to get the lime out of the way before putting in the soap.

What Makes Some Soaps Float? Several pans of water were on the table and several kinds of soap. The children placed the various kinds of soap in the pans and asked at once, "Why do some float?" "Why does some of our own soap float and some sink?" "What do you think?" asked the teacher. The following guesses were made:

The one that floats is smaller in size
One has more grease, grease floats on water
One has more lye
The bar that floats weighs less
One was stirred longer

The teacher suggested that they try to find out which, if any, of their guesses was correct.   First: "How could we find out if the size makes it float?"   Take a small piece of Palm Olive and a big piece of Ivory and see what happens.   This was tried, the Ivory floated so a line was drawn through the first guess.

The second guess was immediately crossed out by the class since some of their own soap floated and some did not even though all had been made by the same recipe.   The third guess fared the same.

Since the fourth guess referred to the weight, the children decided to cut two pieces until they both weighed exactly the same and try floating them.   This was done but the Ivory still floated while the White King went to the bottom of the pan.   The children proved that the weight of a piece of soap was not what makes it sink or float.

The last guess sounded as if it might be true but there was no way to test to find out.   The teacher then passed out some typewritten sheets with information about floating soap.   Two systems were fully described here.   One, the "Tower System" and the other "The Crutching Machine." [1]

The children were told to read carefully and when they could tell what they had found out to raise their hands.

In a few minutes nearly everyone was ready to tell.   The two systems were then described and it was decided the last guess that had been made was the right one.

Informational Material Given the Children About the "Tower System" and "The Crutching Machine."   The manufacture of a soap which would float on the water is said to have originated with the Chinese.   They sent this soap to England.   It was made entirely from coconut oil.

Long ago various ways were suggested and many experiments made to try to make soap lighter than water so that it would float. One was the insertion of a cork or other light material, or the insertion of a metal plate in such a way as to enclose air in the body of the soap bar, but these methods proved to be failures.

There are now two methods used by most soap manufacturers and both are successful.

One way is to have a high tower 17 feet in height built in an open place where the air surrounding it is kept in motion by fans and the soap is dropped from this tower to a big tank below.   In falling through this stream of air the soap becomes full of air or we say aerated.   When it lights in the tank below it is light and fluffy and looks much like egg whites do when beaten.

---

[1] The teacher had secured her information by a trip through a soap factory and had written it for the children.

It is immediately put into the soap press and left for four or five days to harden. Now the soap is light and will float for the simple reason that it is aerated, or filled with air.

The other system of making soap float is really used more commonly than the "Tower System." This is the large crutching machine idea. This machine looks like a big dish washing machine from the outside. This machine has a slightly cone-shaped bottom and is fitted inside with several blades which move in different directions, churning the soap upward. The soap is pushed to the top of the machine, and then dropped to the bottom and is pushed to the top again. In this case, too, it is just like beating eggs, and before long the soap is as light and fluffy as can be, as it is filled with air. Now it is taken out and put in the soap press to harden just as other soap, but because the air has been beaten into it, it is light and will float.

Floating soaps will not lather as well as other soaps, and they are wasteful in use.

How to Wash Various Kinds of Material. Different children had been chosen to find out just how each kind of material should be washed.

Reports and demonstrations were given in the following order:

a. Wool   d. Linen
b. Silk   e. Rayon
c. Cotton

The following materials were experimented upon:

a. Clean soft wool   h. Silk hose
b. Balls of wool yarn   i. Bright pieces of silk
c. Skeins of silk   and cotton
d. Cotton balls.   j. Strong muslin
e. Woolen hose   k. Soft white lawn
f. Woolen sweaters   l. Linen—several shades
g. Baby clothes   m. Rayon

One child suggested it would be helpful to their mothers if directions were prepared on a card that told how to wash each material.

For several days the language period was spent fixing these recipes for mothers. The teacher then had them mimeographed and they were mounted on cards and taken home.

A Soap Bubble Party. Several children had been asking for a soap bubble party. Each child brought his own glass and the teacher brought two packages of soda straws. Each child was allowed three. A soapy solution was made and each child came to the pitcher and filled his glass half full. Then the fun began. It was only a few minutes until one after another said, "Now I see what makes the bubbles." It was fun seeing who could get the largest bubble, the prettiest one, the one that lasted the longest.

BIBLIOGRAPHY

For Children

BAILEY, CAROLYN SHERWIN. *Boys and Girls of Colonial Days.* Chicago: A. Flanagan Company, 1917.
> Story of soap making.

CHANDLER, KATHERINE. *Stories of Wild Flowers Children Love.* Philadelphia: P. Blakiston's Son & Co., 1923.
> The soap plant.

DAVIDSON, ISOBEL, and ANDERSON, CHARLES. *The Lincoln Reader.* Book III. New York: Laurel Book Company, 1925.
> "Soap-Making" p. 250.

FREEMAN, FRANK, and OTHERS. *Child-Story Readers.* Book IV. California State Series. Sacramento: California State Department of Education, 1929.
> "Soap" p. 349.
> "Blowing Bubbles" p. 355.

HALLECK, GRACE TABER. *A Tale of Soap and Water.* 45 East 17th Street, New York: Cleanliness Institute, 1928.

HORN, ERNEST, and OTHERS. *Learn to Study Reader.* Book III. Boston: Ginn and Company, 1926.
> "Soap Making in Pioneer Days" p. 120.

McGOWAN, ELLEN AMELIA. *Soap Bubbles.* New York: The Macmillan Company, 1929.

SCHWARTZ, JULIA AUGUSTA. *Five Little Strangers and How They Came to Live in America.* New York: American Book Company, 1924.
> Only one page.

SMITH, EDITH LILLIAN. *Everyday Science Projects.* Boston: Houghton Mifflin Company, 1925.

STONE, GERTRUDE LINCOLN, and FICKETT, M. G. *Everyday Life in the Colonies.* Boston: D. C. Heath & Company, 1905.
> Story of soap making.

WERTHNER, WILLIAM BENJAMIN. *How Man Makes Markets.* New York: The Macmillan Company, 1917.
> The oils used in soap and where they are found.

For Teachers

BONSER, F. G., and MOSSMAN, L. C. *Industrial Arts in the Elementary School.* New York: The Macmillan Company, 1923.

DARROW, F. L. *The Boys Own Book of Science.* New York: Silver, Burdett and Company, 1926.
> Making many kinds of soap.

PARSONS, MARY E. *The Wild Flowers of California.* San Francisco: Harr Wagner Publishing Company, 1925.

PIEPER, CHARLES J., and BEAUCHAMP, WILBUR L. *Everyday Problems in Science.* Chicago: Scott, Foresman and Company, 1925.

SIMMONS, WILLIAM HERBERT. *Soap; Its Composition, Manufacture and Properties.* New York: Sir Isaac Pitman & Sons, n. d.

WINSLOW, LEON LOYAL. *Elementary Industrial Arts.* New York: The Macmillan Company, 1922.

CHAPTER XII

CURRICULUM UNIT

TRANSPORTATION[1]

A Unit of Work Carried on in Grades 4, 5, and 6

LAUNCHING THE UNIT

During the first week of the semester, the social science room had exhibits and pictures of almost every form of transportation. The exhibit included a perfect model of the DeWitt Clinton locomotive, a sedan chair, stage coach, royal coach, covered wagon, trains, trucks, aeroplanes, and gliders.

Representing transportation by water were outrigger canoes from Samoa and Hawaii, Egyptian, Greek, Roman, Viking and Clipper ships, and samples of the modern liner.

Pictures on the wall showed the less familiar ways of travel— the "karak" and "umiak" of the Eskimo; the "koofah" of the Tigris River, historic ships such as the "Mayflower," "Santa Maria," "Old Ironsides," "Clermont," "Savannah" and "Monitor," the "palanquin" and "jinrikisha" of the Orient, the wheelbarrow of China, and chariot of an earlier civilization, beasts of burden of other countries, such as elephant, camel, yak, water buffalo, and llama.

Pupils who came to the social science room for their class work examined these at their leisure and their reactions were extremely interesting. The boys wanted to build ships or stage coaches. Some of the girls also expressed the desire to build stage coaches or sedan chairs. In the discussion that followed, pupils told of visits they had made to museums and the boats they had seen there. Others told of boat, railway, or aeroplane trips they had taken. The coming visit of "Old Ironsides" to San Pedro was discussed and all decided to visit it if possible.

After hearing the various experiences of pupils, all the classes were eager to start working on transportation. This, of course, introduced several problems which had to be solved before any work could start. Several of the girls wanted to study the people and dress figures in the costumes of other times and other lands. Other pupils wanted to study France, or England, or Holland, or Italy. After a general

---

[1] Prepared under the direction of Elizabeth Hamlin, Elementary Supervisor, Santa Monica City Schools, by Harriet MacKay, Helen Warde, Anna M. Devine, Ellen Moreland, Catherine Crippen, Irma Glanfield, Dora May Priester, Elsie Miller, Mae K. Siddell, and Winifred Neeley, Teachers, John Muir School, Santa Monica.

discussion, taking up these points, the various classes arrived at the following conclusions:

1. That pupils who could bring tools, odd pieces of lumber, nails, etc. should do so.

2. That a study of transportation must include a study of the life of the people.

3. That such a study must also include a study of the countries. The statement "The ways of living and travel fit the country" helped greatly in clarifying this point.

4. That to complete the study of transportation, pupils should know something of how the world's trade is carried on today and what part the more important countries take in this trade. They must know the chief products and industries, exports and imports, seaports and trade routes of these countries.

5. To study the progress of transportation in the period of history appropriate to the grade; for example:

Low 6: Prehistoric times to 476 A. D.
High 6: 476 to 1933
Low 5: United States; Colonial Life
High 5: United States; Pioneer Life
Low 4: Transportation in Distant Lands
High 4: Transportation in Early California
Low 4 and High 4: The History of Transportation

It was suggested further that other groups might undertake special problems such as, "Travel In Literature."

6. To make a large "Time Chart" to show graphically the development of transportation.

7. To work in groups on different phases of the work for about two weeks, when a different arrangement of the work may be made.

As the pupils in each class had already formed themselves into five committees to take care of their room, materials, citizenship, social and dramatic activities, it was decided to let these five committees form the groups which should work together under their leaders. The work of the groups varied slightly in the different sections, but it was along these lines:

Group   I: Preparing oral or written reports to present to the class.

Group   II: Dramatizing suitable material and presenting it to the class.

Group III: Constructing boats, stage coaches, etc.

Group IV: Studying the lives and dress of the people and making and dressing figures.

Group V: Work on maps.

To encourage responsibility in the groups, it was agreed to check the progress made, every two weeks. Each group agreed to report concerning the work done at that time, the class to evaluate the reports and make constructive suggestions to the various groups.

As each section has a different period and had different problems to solve, the way in which the activities relative to transportation were carried on has been recorded here according to the work done by the various grades.

LOW 6—TRANSPORTATION FROM EARLIEST TIMES TO 476 A. D.

The very earliest form of transportation by water was first discussed. From books pupils had already read and from drawing on their imaginations, they pictured the first boat, a rude log. Two problems arose here: "What would happen to the log if there was a swift current?" and "How could you get across a stream where there was a strong current?" Answers volunteered by pupils were noted and books were read to determine whether answers were right or wrong. From this problem it was easy to attack the various steps in the progress of boatmaking—log, raft, dugout, canoe, sailboat. At this point some boys were anxious to construct types of early boats. This led to further reading and research. Branches of trees and small logs were brought to school and one group of boys made a raft, a dugout, and a canoe.

Meanwhile, land transportation was not neglected. A very animated discussion arose as to why man began to carry burdens. As none of the books told the reason, some solution had to be worked out. Other early modes of transportation were read about and discussed, as ox pack, ox drag, horse, camel, wheels, ox cart, litter, and palanquin. One group of children was directly responsible for making reports to the class. Another group dramatized the beginning of water travel.

From the reading and research, the pupils had learned that the Egyptians were among the first people to make progress in their methods of transportation. It was found that the Egyptians were using sailboats about 3000 B. C. This introduced the question of dates, which had to be thoroughly discussed, especially B. C. and A. D.

An interesting problem arose at this point. One child asked, "Why was Egypt civilized so soon?" After a study of maps of

Egypt and the world, various answers were given and later verified or rejected by research and reading about the Egyptians. In this study, the importance of the Nile Valley and Egypt's contribution to the world's progress were specially noted. The study of Egypt finished with the completion of two Egyptian boats of the type in use about 2000 B. C.

A study of the life of the Babylonians and Phoenicians brought many interesting contributions to our study of transportation. Here the problem arose as to why the Phoenicians were such great sailors and traders. This was solved. Phoenicians were traders, and their ships, their trade and influence were discussed and studied.

Europe presented several interesting problems to be solved. "Why was Greece the first country in Europe to be civilized?" led to a study of Greek life and trade. A group of boys decided to make a Greek ship, while other groups chose to find out how the Greeks lived and what they did for the world. A similar study of the Romans followed, in order to answer the questions, "What contributions were made to Roman civilization by the Greeks?" "Were the Greeks and Romans very much alike?" "Why did the Romans build such a great Empire?" "What caused the fall of the Roman Empire?" A model was made of a Roman ship and the "Time Chart" was kept up to date.

HIGH 6—TRANSPORTATION FROM 476 A. D. TO 1933

The class became extremely interested in the different kinds of ships. After discussing the period to be considered, it was decided to begin the study with the Vikings and make a Viking ship. Many questions arose, such as "Why were Viking ships ornamented with dragons?" "Why did they have the round shields on their boats?" "Why were they called Vikings?"

Interest in the early history of France and England up to the time of the coming of the Normans and the Danes grew out of the study of the Vikings. Alfred the Great's navy, the ships of William the Conqueror, and the ships of the Crusaders were links to connect our history. The "Time Chart" was used to show the various steps in the progress of transportation. The girls were studying the life and the dress of the people, so the class was able to get a fairly complete picture of castle life, knights and knighthood, life of the serfs, growth of the monasteries and towns, the Crusades, and the expansion of trade. Venetian ships were studied in this connection, and later the type of merchant ship needed because of the great increase in trade.

Problems which arose in this study were, "What started the first navy?" "Why was Venice so important in the Middle Ages?" "What effect did the Crusades have on trade?" "How did the growth of

14—17050

the towns affect trade?" "Who were the robber barons and how did they hinder trade on the Rhine?"

Transportation by land (from 1492–1933),—pack horse, horse caravan, sedan chair, coach, stage coach, bicycle, train, and automobile was studied by different groups. It was decided to make a sedan chair and a stage coach and to show the other ways of transportation on the "Time Chart."

Famous ships of this period (1492–1933) were discussed and read about. These were added to the "Time Chart." The class chose the "Clipper," "Savannah," "Monitor," and "Tramp Steamer" as being the most interesting ship models to make. The clipper ships were found to be especially interesting, and many questions arose in this study. Reasons for their beauty and speed were talked about. The problem arose, "Why did the clipper ships disappear from the seas so suddenly?" This problem required more research. Its solution led to a study of the ships of today, their crew, speed, cost, and reliability.

To complete the study, some time was given to air transportation.

LOW 5—TRANSPORTATION IN THE UNITED STATES DURING COLONIAL TIMES

As a part of the interest of the class in Colonial life a study was made of the earliest forms of transportation, such as canoes, drags, settler's carts, runners on Indian trails, horse and pillion, Conestoga wagon, and stage coach. A group of boys made a Conestoga wagon and others worked on the "Time Chart."

The need for better means of transportation to carry on extensive trade became apparent to this group, following a discussion of the various means of modern transportation. The class listed those things necessary for trade, such as: products, exports, imports, harbors, vessels and trade routes, trains and railways, airplanes and air lines. A large outline map was used to show the location of various products exported and imported, and the trade routes, harbors, and methods of transporting them.

Pupils found that the New England states, particularly Massachusetts, manufactured so many of the commodities we use every day, as shoes, cotton and woolen clothes, watches, paper, machinery, and jewelry, that interest was focused on this group of states. Suggested reasons for the extensive manufacturing were listed and further research was made to find the correct solution.

A similar study was made of the Middle Atlantic, South Atlantic, and Southern States, during which the following problems arose, were discussed and solved; "Why is New York such a large city?" "How is each group of states dependent on every other group?"

HIGH 5—TRANSPORTATION IN THE UNITED STATES
DURING PIONEER DAYS

Some of the problems that arose were, "Why was the building of the Erie Canal so important?" "Who were the great trail blazers to the West?" "What part did the covered wagon and the Pony Express play in our history?" These problems led to study of the building of the first transcontinental railway in 1869, and from that to transportation of today.

To complete the study it was decided to hold an open house for parents and friends. Pupils would show the work they had done and tell the story of transportation. Each class invited another class to visit their room and see what had been accomplished. Invitations were written, some of them in rhyme. This is one of them:

AN INVITATION

We send to you this invitation,
To see our program on transportation,
In John Muir School, room number one,
Where we will show the work we've done.
Our raft, our dugout, and canoe,
Our Viking ships and others too,
Stagecoach and chariot, sled and chair,
We have constructed with great care,
So please accept our invitation,
And come and see us before vacation.

Courtesy of Alameda County Schools

Children Undertook Many Activities in Relation to Modes of Travel

LOW 4—TRANSPORTATION IN DISTANT LANDS

Introduction

Discussion of the necessity of various modes of travel in different regions due to differences in climate, physical features, etc., stimulated interest in problems of transportation. The teacher added further to the interest by showing pictures of typical modes of travel used throughout the world, and films depicting means of travel in different countries.

Purpose

It was the purpose of the teacher in undertaking this study to provide a situation in which children would become acquainted with the various means of travel in the regions and countries studied. The following regions were included in this study:

Cold Regions
  Eskimos
  Reindeer and dog-sledges
Temperate Regions
  United States
  England
  France
  Germany
  Japan—jinrikishas
  Switzerland—goat, St. Bernard

Desert Regions
  Africa
  Sahara Desert—camel
Jungle Regions
  Africa—elephant
Indian lands
  Dugout
  Canoes
  Travois

Activities

The children undertook many activities in relation to modes of travel.

For example:

1. Reports of stories read in school library

2. Illustrations of ways of travel by various members of the class

3. An outline of the world was sketched on a large piece of wrapping paper 5' x 8'. As the different countries and regions were studied, the particular mode of travel common to that location was placed in its respective place. These were drawn in crayola as the study progressed by members of the class.

4. Illustrations were drawn in colored chalk on the board relative to country or region studied at the time.

Bibliography Used by Children

CARPENTER, FRANCES. *The Ways We Travel.* New York: American Book Company, 1929.

CARPENTER, FRANK. *Around the World with the Children.* New York: American Book Company, 1917.

CHAMBERLAIN, J. F. *How We Travel.* New York: The Macmillan Company, 1924.

CHANCE, L. M. *Little Folks of Many Lands.* Boston: Ginn and Company, 1904.

HEADLEY, E. A. *How Other People Travel.* Chicago: Rand McNally and Company, 1926.

PERDUE, H. A. *Child Life in Other Lands.* Chicago: Rand McNally and Company, 1918.

SHAW, E. R. *Big People and Little People of Other Lands.* New York: American Book Company, 1900.

HIGH 4—TRANSPORTATION IN EARLY CALIFORNIA

A class discussion of the coming of the first people to California leads to an interest in the various routes followed, as well as the means of transportation.

Purpose

1. To become acquainted with the various means of transportation having a part in the growth and development of California.

2. To develop an interest in the historical importance of this growth.

Activities

1. Oral reports from stories read

2. Illustrations

3. A number of outline maps were sketched on large sheets of wrapping paper size 5' x 8'. Several children worked together on them until completed.
   a. A United States Outline Map
   Indicated coming of the pioneers; across the plains in covered wagon and prairie schooner; across the Isthmus of Panama and around the Horn.
   b. Upon a California map was drawn in crayola, the coming of Cabrillo's ship, a Spanish ox-cart (or carreta) coming up from Mexico, a covered wagon coming from across the plains, and Jedediah Smith crossing the Sierras. John C. Fremont, the pathfinder, was also included.

4. A number of early Spanish galleons were constructed from cardboard

5. A long strip of wrapping paper was used to illustrate the march across the plains of the prairie schooner enroute to California.

Bibliography

BAILEY, CAROLYN. *Untold History Stories.* Dansville, New York: F. A. Owen Publishing Company, 1927.
>   El Camino Real, p. 166
>   The Pathfinder, p. 154
>   The Pony Express, p. 173

BANDINI, HELEN E. *History of California.* New York American Book Company, 1908.

BASS, FLORENCE. *Stories of Early Times in the Great West.* Indianapolis, Indiana: Bobbs-Merrill Company, 1927.
>   The Overland Stage, p. 47
>   The Pony Express, p. 153
>   The Iron Horse, p. 158

CARPENTER, FRANCES. *The Ways We Travel.* New York: American Book Company, 1929.

CHAMBERLAIN, J. F. *How We Travel.* New York: The Macmillan Company, 1924.
>   How the Mail is Delivered, pp. 145–157
>   Pony Express, pp. 154–157

EATON, JEANETTE. *Story of Transportation.* New York: Harper and Brothers, 1927.

FAIRBANKS, H. W. *Geography of California.* California State Series. Sacramento: California State Department of Education, 1927.
>   Main Routes of the Explorers, Chapter II.

FOX, EDITH K. *In Old California.* New York: The Macmillan Company, 1927.
>   On the Way to Monterey, p. 60 (play)

FOX, F. C. *How the World Rides.* New York: Charles Scribner's Sons, 1929.

RICHARDS, IRMAGARDE. *Our California Home.* California State Series. Sacramento: California State Department of Education, 1933.
>   Overland Immigrants, Chapter X
>   The Ways Men Travel, Chapter XVIII
>   Redwood Highway, Chapter XX
>   El Camino Real, Chapter XXI

WAGNER, HARR. *Pacific History Stories.* San Francisco: Harr Wagner Publishing Company, 1918.
>   Cabrillo, Chapter III
>   March of Portola, Chapter VI
>   The First Ship to Enter Golden Gate, Chapter VIII
>   Canoe and Saddle, Chapter XXIV

WAGNER, HARR, and KEPPEL, MARK. *Lessons in California History.* San Francisco: Harr Wagner Publishing Company, 1922.
>   Cabrillo, Chapter III
>   Jedediah Smith, Chapter XV
>   John C. Fremont, Chapter XVI
>   Transportation, Chapter XXIX

LOW 4 AND HIGH 4—THE HISTORY OF TRANSPORTATION

Objectives

To give children some idea of the development and progress man has made throughout the centuries in his gradually improved methods of transportation.

1. By land
2. By air
3. By water

To encourage pupils to develop the library habit, in order to familiarize themselves with library atmosphere, rules, catalogues, shelf arrangement of books, and to gain ability in choosing the correct type of book to meet their needs so that they will become better silent and oral readers.

The slow child was encouraged to select easy books with short sentences until he felt success, increased his vocabulary, and read fluently to the end of every sentence.

The child of medium ability was led to choose more difficult books, while the best readers selected still more difficult ones.

To develop initiative and power in English work through:

1. Oral and written reports—stories, book reports
2. Written letters to friends or relatives, telling of their imaginary travel experiences in different parts of the world, or in different times
3. Writing simple poetry as a cooperative class activity.

To interest children in learning to spell words pertaining to transportation, for use in their written work.

Launching the Unit

A section of *Facts and Fun*,[1] pp. 150–204, was read silently or orally by both classes.

Class discussion on material followed. Study assignments and directed activities at the close of the different stories were worked out. Much interest was stimulated in knowing more about travel.

The teacher brought interesting public library books on different phases of transportation, read stories from *How Other People Travel*, by E. A. Headley;[2] *Clear Track Ahead*,[3] and part of *Robinson Crusoe*.

---

[1] Frank N. Freeman and Others. *Facts and Fun.* Child-Story Readers, California State Series. Sacramento: California State Department of Education, 1929.

[2] E. A. Headley. *How Other People Travel.* Chicago: Rand McNally and Company, 1905.

[3] Henry Lent. *Clear Track Ahead.* New York: The Macmillan Company, 1932.

Activities

Reading

1. Five groups selected according to their reading ability in the
   B4 class, and four groups in the A4 worked with their respective
   leaders in reading orally and silently, books and stories on
   transportation.

2. Home reading on the subject in books, encyclopedias, such as
   the World Book, and in magazines and newspapers, was encouraged.

3. Short stories typed and mounted by the teacher, were read by
   groups.

English

1. Whole class made up a few poems relating to travel.

2. Some individuals composed short poems.

3. Oral and written book reports were given.

4. Letters written.

5. Stories written.

Spelling

1. Word lists made of simple transportation terms, as names of
   different animals or conveyances.

Outcomes

Information

This project encouraged the children to gain the library habit.
In fact, nearly all the pupils of both groups now have and use their
own library cards.

Most of the books in the following list were brought from the Santa
Monica Library, or its branches, by the children, the teacher getting
but eight when first launching the activity.

One little girl, who was leader of a slow group and especially interested in the subject of transportation, brought very appropriate books
from the city library for her group. Other children did the same but
A __ seemed to lead the class, both in choosing good material and assisting the slow children of her group to gain power and ability in reading.

Individuals have gained knowledge about a particular phase of
transportation in which they were most interested.

Habits and Skills

Abilities

1. Read better, both silently and orally

2. Scan and choose outstanding information pertaining to a particular topic

3. Give oral reports in acceptable, concise sentences

4. Recognize, indent, and arrange paragraphs

5. Recognize, construct and punctuate better written sentences

6. Write stories, book reports, and letters using knowledge and facts gained

7. Compose simple verses. (Class enterprise, with teacher's suggestions, and a few written by especially able individuals.)

Appreciations

1. An increased interest in reading

2. An appreciation of the value of public library service

3. An appreciation of the fact that the United States leads the world in improved methods of travel

4. An appreciation of the advantages we have today over those of early man, pilgrims, pioneers, etc.

5. Desire to continue reading of public library books and to gain more information on the development of transportation in this and other countries

Books Used

These books were especially enjoyed by the children.

Bock, G. E. *What Makes the Wheels Go Round.* New York: The Macmillan Company, 1931.

Campbell, H. M. L. *Story of Little Metzu.* Chicago: Educational Publishing company, 1905.

Chamberlain, J. F. *How We Travel.* New York: The Macmillan Company, 1924.

Dobias, Frank. *The Picture Book of Flying.* New York: The Macmillan Company, 1928.

Dopp, Katherine E. *Early Cave Men.* Chicago: Rand McNally and Company, 1904.

DUKELOW, J. H., and WEBSTER, H. H. *The Ship Book*. Boston: Houghton Mifflin Company, 1931.

EATON, JEANETTE. *Story of Transportation*. New York: Harper and Brothers, 1927.

FOX, F. C. *How the World Rides*. New York: Charles Scribner's Sons, 1929.

FRANCK, HARRY A. *Travels in Many Lands*. (China) Dansville, New York: F. A. Owen Publishing Company, 1927.

GIMMAGE, PETER. *Picture Book of Ships*. New York: The Macmillan Company, 1930.

GRANT, GORDON. *The Story of the Ship*. Springfield, Massachusetts: McLoughlin Brothers, Inc., 1931.

HADER, BERTA, and HADER, ELMER. *Picture Book of Travel*. New York: The Macmillan Company, 1928.

HARDY, MARJORIE. *Best Stories*. Chicago: Wheeler Publishing Company, 1926.

HARPER, WILHELMINA, and HAMILTON, A. J. *Winding Roads*. New York: The Macmillan Company, 1927.

HEADLEY, EDIA A. *How Other People Travel*. Chicago: Rand McNally and Company, 1926.

HOLLAND, R. S. *Historic Railroads*. Philadelphia: Macrae Smith Company, 1927.

JONES, PAUL. *An Alphabet of Aviation*. Philadelphia: Macrae Smith Company, 1928.

KEELOR, KATHERINE L. *Working with Electricity*. New York: The Macmillan Company, 1929.

KUH, CHARLOTTE. *A Train, A Boat, and An Island*. New York: The Macmillan Company, 1929.

LENT, HENRY B. *Clear Track Ahead*. New York: The Macmillan Company, 1932.

LENT, HENRY B. *Full Steam Ahead! Six Days on an Ocean Liner*. New York: The Macmillan Company, 1933.

McNAB, ALLAN. *Picture Book of Rivers*. New York: The Macmillan Company, 1932.

McSPADDEN, JOSEPH WALKER. *How They Carried the Mail*. New York: Sears Publishing Company, 1930.

MEIGS, CORNELIA. *The Wonderful Locomotive*. New York: The Macmillan Company, 1928.

MORY, W. A., and MORY, A. M. *American Inventions and Inventors*. New York: Silver, Burdett and Company, 1900.

MULLER, C. G. *How They Carried the Goods*. New York: Sears Publishing Company, 1932.

PRYOR, WILLIAM CLAYTON. *Train Book*. New York: Harcourt, Brace and Company, 1933.

READ, HELEN S. *An Airplane Ride*. New York: Charles Scribner's Sons, 1928.

READ, HELEN S. *An Engine Story*. New York: Charles Scribner's Sons, 1928.

Rocheleau, William Frances. *Transportation*. Great Industries Series. Chicago: A. Flanagan Company, 1928.

Rowe, Dorothy. *Traveling Shops*. New York: The Macmillan Company, 1929.

Scantlebury, E. E. *Little World Children*. Boston: Ginn and Company, 1928.

Smalley, Janet. *How it All Began*. New York: William Morrow and Company, Inc., 1932.

Stephenson, Mary B., and Wood, Lawrence. *Wheel, Sail and Wing*. Chicago: Follett Publishing Company, 1932.

Van Metre, T. W. *Trains, Tracks and Travel*. New York: Simons-Boardman Publishing Company, 1931.

Washburne, Heluiz Chandler. *Letters to Channy; A Trip Around the World*. Chicago: Rand McNally and Company, 1932.

Wells, Rhea. *Ali, the Camel*. Garden City, New York: Doubleday, Doran and Company, 1928.

Wonder Book of Ships for Boys and Girls. Edited by Harry Golding. New York: Frederick A. Stokes Company, 1914.

TRAVEL IN LITERATURE

A special committee of intermediate grade children became in addition to their other topics much interested in the reflection of travel in literature. Sea travel held a particular charm. "The Argonauts,"

Sea Travel in Spain and Scandinavia Holds Particular Charm for Intermediate Grade Children

and "The Skeleton in Armor," and the Biblical story of "Noah's Ark" were all enjoyed by the group. The following anthology of sea poems was made. Many of the poems were read by the teacher to the class, while others were read by the children themselves.

AN ANTHOLOGY OF SEA POEMS

Anonymous. "A Wanderer's Song"
Anonymous. "The White Squall"
Arnold, Mathew. "Dover Beach"
Beddoes, Thomas L. "Sailor's Song"
Bennett, Rowena Basten. "Boats"
Brodie, E. H. "The Sea"; "In Shore"
Browning, Robert. "Home Thoughts From the Sea"
Cunningham, Allan. "A Sea Song"
Cunningham, Allan. "At Sea"
Harrington, Sarah Jane S. "My Little Boat"
Holmes, Oliver Wendell. "Old Ironsides"
Hovey, Richard. "The Sea Gypsy"
Joyce, James. "The Noise of Waters"
Longfellow, Henry W. "Seaweed"
Longfellow, Henry W. "The Secret of the Sea"
Masefield, John. "Roadways"
Masefield, John. "Sea Fever"
Miller, Joaquin. "Columbus"
Morton, David. "Old Ships"
Rossetti, Christina G. "Boats Sail on the Rivers"
Rossetti, Christina G. "O Sailor, Come Ashore"
Sandburg, Carl. "The Harbor"
Sargent, Epes. "A Life on the Ocean Wave"
Sargent, Epes. "On Deck"
Southey, Robert. "The Inchcape Rock"
Stephens, James. "The Shell"
Stevenson, Robert Louis. "At the Seaside"
Stevenson, Robert Louis. "Visit from the Sea"
Tennyson, Alfred. "Break, Break, Break"
Tennyson, Alfred. "The Eagle"
Wheelock, John Hall. "The Sea is Wild"
Whitman, Walt. "Oh Captain, My Captain"
Whitman, Walt. "The Dismantled Ship"
Widdemer, Margaret. "Sea Call"
Wolfe, Robert. "Open Ocean"

Material in various books bearing on the following topics was much enjoyed during the library hour: The Pony Express, The Covered Wagon, The Story of Robert Fulton, The Denver Flier, Conquest of the Air, and Modern Radio Communication. The books the children enjoyed particularly were:

BROWN, C. L. M. *The Conquest of the Air.* New York: Oxford University Press, 1927.

CARPENTER, FRANK G. *Around the World With the Children.* New York: American Book Company, 1917.

CHAPMAN, ARTHUR. *The Pony Express.* New York: G. P. Putnam's Sons, 1932.

CURTIS, NELL C. *Boats.* Chicago: Rand McNally and Company, 1927.

DUKELOW, JEAN H., and WEBSTER, H. H. *The Book of Ships.* Boston: Houghton, Mifflin Company, 1931.

FOX, F. C. *How the World Rides.* New York: Charles Scribner's Sons, 1929.

GRANT, GORDON. *The Story of the Ship.* Springfield, Massachusetts: McLoughlin Bros., 1931.

GRAVATT, LILA. *Pioneers of the Air.* New York: Mentzer, Bush and Company, 1928.

HADER, BERTA, and HADER, ELMER. *The Book of Travel.* New York: The Macmillan Company, 1928.

HOUGH, EMERSON. *The Covered Wagon.* New York: D. Appleton and Company, 1928.

LEONARD, THOMAS HENRY. *From Indian Trail to Electric Rail.* Atlantic Highlands, New Jersey: M. R. Shale Journal, 1923.

REYNER, J. H. *Modern Radio Communication.* New York: Pitman Publishing Corporation, 1932.

STOCKTON, FRANK. *Buccaneers and Pirates of Our Coast.* New York: Grossett and Dunlap, 1898.

The World Book. (10 volumes) Chicago: F. E. Compton and Company, 1923.

THE EFFECTIVE USE OF THE LIBRARY IN A STUDY OF TRANSPORTATION

As a preliminary preparation for the integrated activity on Transportation a bibliography was compiled by the librarian for all the classes participating, of the information on the subject to be found in the school library. Several copies were made of this list, anticipating a request which was soon forthcoming.

At the beginning of the semester, different types of boats were brought in by the children and displayed in the library. Several of them were made by the children or their parents. The children were allowed to wander around and handle these boats, and eventually they began to notice the display of books about boats which has been placed at various places in the room.

The social science display noted on page 176, and the library display soon aroused intense interest, and requests began pouring in for books on transportation other than by boat. The bibliography prepared beforehand made it possible for the library to give immediate service.

Time was taken during library period to explain fully the use of these lists. The word "bibliography" was developed and different books examined for this list. From that time on at any hour during the day a child or group of children could be found in the library doing research work. Frequently the information was taken to the classroom and the books returned at the close of the period. The children have made the library theirs.

Eventually the question was asked, "What can the library do with all this information about transportation?" It was suggested that the bibliography be compiled into a book, to be kept in the library to help other children who may study transportation in the future.

The classes were then divided into groups to organize and record this information as it was submitted by the children. A gifted group took charge of designing the cover and the arrangement of the book. The other groups took charge of the following modes of transportation:

land, air, and water, respectively. One child suggested that the story book she was reading was about transportation. From this suggestion was developed a list of fiction dealing with different modes of transportation.

The children have advanced greatly in the use and understanding of the library. They are able to locate and use books. Each child has taken an active part in making a bibliography. The non-fiction books were listed by titles, authors, and the call numbers used in the John Muir library were indicated by the children. The fiction books were listed by author and title and the call number was given. The making of this bibliography on the transportation unit was one of the most interesting enterprises experienced by the children.

OUTCOMES OF THE STUDY OF TRANSPORTATION

Subject Matter

1. Knowledge of the methods of transportation from the earliest times to the present.
2. Knowledge of the peoples whose ways of transportation were studied.
3. Knowledge of travel routes by land, sea, and air.

Habits

1. Ability to use and understand the library.
2. Accuracy in looking up materials.
3. Ability to evaluate materials.
4. Mastery of material in order to:
   a. Present it in oral or written form, or
   b. To construct models of ships, etc.
5. Skill in using tools, wood, or other concrete material.

Attitudes

1. Appreciation of the obstacles man has had to overcome to attain his present civilization.
2. Appreciation of the progress of other nations and their contributions to us.
3. Greater interest in our present modes of transportation.
4. Increased development of the social attitude through working and planning in groups.
5. Some development of the scientific attitude in searching for authentic information.

Chapter XIII

CURRICULUM UNIT

MEXICO [1]

INTRODUCTION

Mexicans make beautiful things as a matter of course. The words that you hear on the street most often, especially in little towns, are "Qué bonita" (How beautiful), and any villager is always willing to have a conversation with you about "How beautiful is" a church, a piece of pottery, the mountains, a flower, a painting, an idol, a saint, a serape, or a song.

Everything in Mexico that is "corriente"—that is, in common use among the people—is beautiful and personal and made with intention.

No two markets in Mexico are exactly alike. But it is the markets of the small towns that have most charm—in the tierra caliente an exotic oriental charm of color and movement.

WAYS IN WHICH TEACHERS AND CHILDREN STARTED THE UNIT OF STUDY ON MEXICO

I. Our children have very little background in the way of home training or books, but some children in the class had lived in Mexico and a few had been there. They immediately offered to bring things to class that they had brought from Mexico. The articles brought in by the children aroused the interest of the whole class and laid a good background for real questions on the country of Mexico. This is a partial list of articles brought to school:

> A real tortilla baked by a Mexican woman
> Bowl made of volcanic rock used for grinding corn to make tortillas
> Little images of monks, Diaz, bullfighter
> Mexican drawn work
> Money used in Mexico
> Several pieces of Mexican pottery
> Mexican jumping beans
> Reboso, serape, sombrero
> Mexican flag

Pictures were displayed and some reading followed.

---

[1] Prepared under the direction of Janie P. Duggan and Mary Lothrop, Supervisors of Grades Five and Six, Los Angeles City Schools. The material of this chapter was contributed by Ethel I. Salisbury, Associate Professor of Education, University of California at Los Angeles, and Educational Consultant, Santa Monica Public Schools.

193

During a discussion of the pieces exhibited, stories read, and pictures studied, some of the children suggested that they would like to know more about the Mexican people. The suggestions were written on the board.

We should like to know more about:

> How the dark skinned Indians look
> Why the Indians are so poor when they once had so many rich mines
> Why they are not educated
> How they dress
> Why they eat such simple food
> How many Spaniards are living in Mexico now
> The Mexicans' love of music
> Life in the plaza
> The Mexican holidays
> Life on a hacienda
> Why so much fighting goes on in Mexico
> How they make sombreros and pottery
> Their homes; their markets
> How they make a living
> What they sell the United States and other countries

We reorganized these topics under a few headings and formed research groups. In the meantime the teacher's part consisted in preparing definite materials on each main topic. The children were thrilled over these descriptions and talks which supplemented their limited reading. After each talk we had a class discussion. The discussions were followed with planned tests. As a final summary of the study, we decided to leave something for another class so that their study of Mexico would be interesting.

Group One mounted pictures showing Mexican industries, markets, mines, and people. These were classified and left in a neat folder.

Group Two wrote lectures on the exhibits. A third grade, also engaged in the study of Mexico, was invited in to hear the lectures.

Group Three became map makers. They made a picture map of Mexico, showing the people at work.

II. In another class the teacher showed the children a Mexican water jar. She talked to the class about the jar, explaining the design and the reason for the small openings. "I will place this water jug on the table and if other Mexican articles are brought in, we may arrange them into an exhibit," she said. Bowls, rugs, cactus candy, serapes, and many other things Mexican found a place in the school

Class Room Exhibit Developed by Children in Connection With Unit on Mexico

room. Due recognition was given each child's contribution as it was brought. Gradually questions came from the class and interest in Mexico was launched.

III. The children knew that we were to study Mexico, but a situation arose which brought it about most naturally. Over half the children in one of the two A5 groups were absent on September 16, and when they returned the following day they were given the opportunity to tell about why they had had a holiday. They told us about going to Lincoln Park where great crowds were gathered in celebration of September 16, and about the speeches, songs, etc. The other children were much interested, asking many questions, and the discussion which followed brought up questions such as these:

> What is an Independence Day?
> Is it like our Fourth of July?
> From whom did the Mexicans get free?
> Why didn't they want Spain to rule them longer?
> Why did the speakers all mention Hidalgo?
> Why do so many Mexicans come to Southern California?
> Why did the people at the celebration sing "The Star-Spangled Banner"?

Real interest was stimulated, and we decided to find out just what led up to the rebellion of the people against Spanish rule. One boy asked how the Spanish happened to be in Mexico in the first place, and we started from there by finding out about Cortez and his expeditions.

The activity started naturally by our looking up material to find answers to the questions and in so doing, many other problems presented themselves, also topics for reports and discussions.

Questions and problems raised:

> Who were the people living in Mexico when the Spaniards came?
> Who lived there before the Aztecs? What happened to them?
> Which tribe was the more ferocious and warlike, the Toltecs or the Aztecs?
> How did the Aztecs treat the Spaniards when they came? How do you explain this?
> What kind of king was Montezuma? How was he killed?
> Is the Mexican government as good as ours? Is it getting better? Who is the president?
> Do the children go to schools? What kind of schools have they?
> Why have so many Mexicans come to southern California?

How has the United States helped Mexico?

What are some of the things in our own stores that come from Mexico?

What are some of the things we would see in a Mexican market?

Why has Mexico sometimes been called a "beggar sitting on a bag of gold"?

How has the story of Mexican independence been different from our own?

Why are most of the mines developed by Americans?

Do the people have good machinery on the farms such as our farmers have?

Are the Mexicans religious?

Why is Benito Juarez called the "Lincoln of Mexico"?

Why did the conquering tribes occupy the tablelands and drive the conquered to the plains?

IV. Current items on the new west coast highway led to such questions as:

Are there many highways in Mexico?

Why is this highway being built?

Who furnishes the machinery and materials used in its construction?

How do the Mexican people feel about highways?

What provisions will be made for accommodations for tourists?

What is the appearance of the country through which the highway passes?

Travel and transportation in Mexico form the basis for a clear understanding of the people from before the days of the Spanish highway to the present time. A cartograph map picturing modes of transportation, with the various forms of burden bearing, will be of interest to both the makers of the map and those to whom it is interpreted by the children. Harry Carr's *Old Mother Mexico* [1] gives the teacher excellent material, and *The Burro's Moneybag* [2] and *Pancho and His Burro* [3] charm the children.

V. On the brown bulletin board, covered with mustard colored paper, a few newspaper articles on Mexico, colored pictures, and photographs of Mexican people were placed in orderly arrangement. On the front blackboard, written with yellow chalk were these quotations:

---

[1] Harry Carr. *Old Mother Mexico*. Boston: Houghton Mifflin Company, 1931.
[2] Margaret Loring Thomas. *The Burro's Moneybag*. New York: The Abingdon Press, 1931.
[3] Zhinya Gay and Jan Gay. *Pancho and His Burro*. New York: William Morrow & Co., Inc., 1930.

"The Land of Contrasts"
"The Land of the Sombrero"
"The Mineral Storehouse of the World"
"The Land of Mañana"

In the front of the room were three tables conveniently arranged for working. Table one contained the materials we use every day—different kinds of paper, pens, pencils. The long table was covered with a strip of mustard colored paper. On it were arranged a few childish articles from Mexico, and in the center a bouquet of yellow flowers. On the third table were a few colorful magazines, photo cards, and programs, written in Spanish, from Mexico.

Along the window side of the room were three low tables. In the drawers of these tables paints, brushes, pans, crayons, and colored inks were kept handy. Two of these small tables were covered with black oil cloth and were to be used for work tables. On the third were two bright colored books, *Made in Mexico* [1] and *Pancho and His Burro*. In the center of each table was a blue and yellow bowl with yellow flowers.

On his desk each child found a book containing material on Mexico.

The children were allowed to walk around and talk about the pictures, books, and bulletin board. Many questions were asked naturally and informally. After taking their seats, the children began looking at the pictures in their books and reading explanations under the pictures. They exclaimed over pictures that interested them.

The teacher, who had visited Mexico City, told them about the lovely open air "Don Quixote Library" in Chapultepec Park. She also told them about some of the Mexican schools she had visited, and played a Mexican folk song "Pregientale á las Estrallas" on the victrola. A child found in a National Geographic magazine a picture of the Don Quixote Library.

Thus was launched our activity of the open air library under the trees on our playground. We too called ours "The Don Quixote Library." The working out of the unit required much planning, reading, and questioning.

What is the Don Quixote Library like?
Why is it so called?
Why do they never lose any books when there is no librarian?
Do the people use the library much?
Where did some of the tile come from?
What are the pictures on the tile?
How are the books protected from the rain?
Can we make a drawing plan of our library?

---

[1] S. C. Smith. *Made in Mexico.* New York: Alfred A. Knopf, Inc., 1930.

Where shall we place the fountain?
Benches and book cases?
Where plant the lilies?
What pictures shall we paint on the backs of benches?
How shellac them for protection?
What books shall we place in the library?
Who shall use this library?

We enjoyed such poems as Susan Gregory's "I Want a Garden in the Sun."

As we planned we made many large colored pictures of details of the garden as we hoped it would be.   Some of the titles of these pictures were:

"A Patio Is Planned"
"Preparing the Sail"
"The Turtle's Name was Don Quixote"
"Mixing Clay"
"A Finished Bowl"
"Making Mexican Pottery"

Courtesy of Los Angeles City Schools

Making a Garden of Mexican Plants and Molding Mexican Pottery

As we worked and planned we were confronted with many, many more questions concerning the patio:

What are the plants found in nearly every Mexican garden?
How do the Mexicans use their gardens?
What are the floating gardens?
How are the vegetables and flowers planted?
How do the Mexicans market them?
How shall we plant our garden?
What shall we plant?

Questions particularly concerning pottery were:
Why do we see pottery in nearly every picture of Mexico?
What are the uses of pottery?
Where does the clay come from?
How is pottery fired?
What is glaze?
Where do the Mexicans get their designs?
Why are some of their designs like those of the Spanish, and even Egyptian, Grecian, and Oriental?
How do they paint and color the pottery?
How can we distinguish pottery from Pueblo, Guadalajara, and Oaxaca?
What is tile used for?

Questions particularly concerning murals were:
What is a mural?
Who are some of the great modern artists of Mexico?
Where may we find paintings by Diego Rivera?
What murals would be suitable for us to paint?

The enthusiasm and interest led our group into organizing a Spanish Club. We learned Mexican songs and dances, played on stringed instruments, acquired a simple vocabulary for introductions, greetings, courting, and names of things. We dramatized scenes from Mexican history, market scenes, and amusements.

VI. A very interesting article appeared in the *Los Angeles Times*, by a Spanish archaeologist. He claims that he has absolute proof that the first civilized people lived in America; that the Aztec and the Maya Indians were civilized long before the ancient Egyptians. He claims also that the Chinese were in America before the Aztec and Maya. He is publishing a book which will be released soon.

Our A5's became very much interested in this account and of course wanted to find out more about these people. This gave an approach to Mexico, through history.

These are some of the questions asked:

> Who were the Mayas?   Aztecs?
> Where did they live?   How do we know?
> Which race was the most civilized?   Give your proof.
> What was their religion?
> Who conquered them?
> Why was Cortez able to conquer them?
> What has become of them?
> What Indians are in Mexico today?

This led to the study of present day Indians, and other people in Mexico.

Here are some of the things we wanted to know:

> Some Spanish words
> How do Mexicans work, play, and live?
> What do they eat?
> How do they dress?
> What are their houses like?
> Why do they have so many fiestas?
> Where did they learn to make such beautiful pottery and drawnwork?
> What are Mexican cities like?
> Why are so many Americans interested in Mexico?
> Why is the Auto Club building a road through Mexico?
> What cities would be interesting to visit? Why?
> Why has Mexico had so many revolutions?
> Who are some of their heroes?
> Who is the George Washington of Mexico?
> Who is the Abraham Lincoln of Mexico?
> What is Mexico doing today for her people?

VII. Last February a new pupil entered our class from Mexico City. After his introduction to the class, he read us a story from his Spanish reader and then graciously tranlated it for us. It happened to be a Spanish fable and very interesting.

Immediately questions came from the class concerning the adobe hut, the home of the Mexican child in the story, and the pigs, chickens, ducks, and turkeys, which rambled through the home. Other questions followed and were listed on the board for study. Gradually through discussion many questions were added to the list.

> What kind of school did you attend in Mexico? Did you study at home, at school, or both?
> Did you live in an adobe house? What other kind of homes do they have?

Is Mexico City as large as Los Angeles? Do they have a mayor like ours?

Is there a president in Mexico? Where does he live? What is his name?

What do the people do when they want a new president?

Who lived in Mexico first? Was that before the Pilgrims came here?

In Tia Juana there are saloons. Are there saloons in all Mexico?

What do they like best to drink?

Are the streets in Mexico City wide or narrow? Do they have parks there?

Where do the riches come from?

Is Mexico a rich or poor country?

Do they mine there like they do in Colorado?

Where is the money made? How many kinds of coins have they? Do they put their money in savings banks?

How much does a good meal cost in a Mexican cafe? What food do Mexicans like best to eat?

Is Mexico bigger than the United States? Has Mexico states like we have?

Do Indians live in Mexico? What do they do for a living?

How do they say "Hello" in Mexico?

What fruits do they grow in Mexico?

What wild animals live there?

What do the Mexicans do to have a good time? Do they dance as fast as some of the radio music we hear?

Each child has made his own book with stories and illustrations of Mexico.

The girls made bead bracelets with rings to match, while the boys made an export map and a "Sketch Book on Mexico." They kept a "Current Events" folio with news from Mexico, especially the operations of the engineering party working upon the International Highway.

THINGS THE CHILDREN DID IN A UNIT OF STUDY ON MEXICO

I. Gave dramatizations

SYNOPSIS OF A HISTORICAL DRAMATIZATION
"THE WHITE GOD," OR
"THE CONQUEST OF TENOCHTITLAN"—AZTEC PLAY—TRAGEDY IN 7 ACTS

Act I—Scene—Montezuma's palace—Mexico City—1519

An Indian runner from Cortez arrives and asks Montezuma if Cortez may pay him a visit. The runner describes Cortez as being a white man from the East. He had arrived in Vera Cruz a few days before with ten ships. Montezuma calls his chiefs and discusses the proposed visit with them. He confesses that he believes the newcomer to be the White God, and reminds them of the Legend. The chieftains discuss it but finally decide to tell Cortez the roads are too rough—that he'd better not try to come. This message is sent by the runner.

Act II—Same scene—A week later

The Indian runner returns saying that Cortez is coming anyhow, and wants Montezuma to give up his throne. Montezuma's chiefs decide to try and make friends with Cortez, so plan to meet him at Amecameca.

Act III—Amecameca—A few days later

Cortez is greeted by Montezuma who tells him that he's been expecting him for years, that the Legend had prepared him for his arrival. Cortez realizes, then, why his invasion is meeting with so little resistance.

Act IV—Montezuma's palace—A few weeks later

Chiefs arrive, and tell Montezuma some of the outrages that Cortez has been perpetrating since his arrival. Montezuma sends for Cortez, who charges the King with the death of some Spanish soldiers at Vera Cruz. To prove that his soldiers are innocent, Montezuma agrees to go as hostage until the real culprit is found.

Montezuma's chiefs are horrified, and decide to follow him to Cortez's palace to try to bring him to his senses.

Act V—Cortez's palace—Immediately

While the chiefs are reasoning with Montezuma, the Aztec people are heard clamoring outside. Their spokesman accuses Montezuma of cowardice and the people stone him.

Act VI—Cortez' palace—Two weeks later

Cortez paces up and down congratulating himself that the last of the Aztec kings has gone (Montezuma having died of a broken heart), and Mexico City is at last his. At this moment, Cuatemoc enters stating that he is the new King. He knows that Cortez is not the fair God and tells him that he and his soldiers are to be destroyed, that the bridges leading to the main land are guarded, and not one shall escape. Cortez calls his captains together to decide upon a plan of escape. They decide to build a bridge of boats and escape at midnight.

(Just preceding the next act, the chairman explains that the Aztecs discovered the Spaniard's plan to escape and surprised them. A great battle took place. So many men were killed that this night is called The Sad Night, La Noche Triste. Cortez and his men fled to the Tlascallan Indians, who, because of Montezuma's cruelty to them, were glad to help Cortez return and lay siege to Mexico City.)

Act VII—Cuatemoc's palace—Six weeks later

Cuatemoc is grieving over his starving people, when a Spanish soldier enters with a flag of truce, saying that if Cuatemoc will give himself as prisoner, Cortez will give the Aztec people food and freedom. Cuatemoc consents. As he is being bound (he and his faithful servant) Cortez asks him where his gold is hidden. When he refuses to tell, Cortez orders two pots of hot coals brought in, over which the prisoners' feet are held. After torturing them, with no success, Cortez orders Cuatemoc and his servant destroyed.

They are taken away, and Cortez, surrounded by his staff, at last claims Mexico in the name of Spain.

DESCRIPTION OF CLASS WORK IN PLANNING A CHRISTMAS SCENE

At a teachers' meeting it was decided to give the usual Christmas program and party for the children of the building. Volunteer numbers were called for by the principal. The teacher of the group that had been studying Mexico made the announcement to the children and asked if they felt there was anything their group might contribute as an outgrowth of their work on Mexico. One boy suggested getting slides on Mexico and giving talks about them. The children felt that this would be too much like a lesson and not exactly in keeping with the spirit of a Christmas program. Further suggestions were called for. A little girl proposed that the class show how Christmas is celebrated in Mexico. This met with the approval of all.

The next step was to find out how Christmas really is celebrated in Mexico. Two or three of our reference books had material on the subject, but the *Mexican Twins* proved to be the most helpful; so, after reading the chapter on Christmas on the hacienda, it was decided to base the dramatization on that material.

The class chairman next appointed four capable children to confer with the teacher. As a committee, they decided to divide the presentation into two scenes, one showing the religious and the other the social aspect of the Christmas celebration. Characters were chosen and the scenes planned. Since nothing very definite or in detail was given in the book about *Las Posadas*, it was left to the teacher to find out what she could about that part of the program. The rest of the committee wrote the short dialogue that was to be used in the second scene, basing it almost entirely upon the conversation found in the story.

The first scene was to be given in the patio, as in the story, and a shrine was needed. The sloyd teacher felt that the boys of the group were not quite equal to making the frame-work, so kindly offered to let some older boys do that. When it was finished it was brought to the room where boys in the group measured off paper, covered it, and painted the shrine with calcimine. Real candles were taboo, of course, so the girls made paper ones of manila drawing paper, coloring the flame brilliantly and mounting the whole thing on heavy cardboard so that it would stand erect on the shelf in front of the shrine.

The story says the priest carried images of Mary and Joseph and placed them in the shrine. It somehow seemed inappropriate for us to try to make crude sacred images, none of the children had any at home, and they were too expensive to buy. Paul, a Mexican boy, said his cousin had some we might borrow, but next day disgustedly announced that his cousin wouldn't let us use them. Jessie, a Mexican girl, said in her home was a fine picture of the Virgin that she might be allowed to bring to hang in the shrine. So the picture with heavy gold frame was brought and hung in the shrine where, with its vivid colors, it looked very impressive.

The teacher's task in getting the necessary material for *Las Posadas* presented its difficulties also. The children knew nothing about it. The libraries in Los Angeles and Pasadena had nothing to offer. At Olvera Street it was suggested that the Plaza church might have it. There they had *Las Posadas* in a small booklet in Spanish, a rather long service such as is used in church, but no music. A message came by phone that a young Spanish woman in the music department of the Los Angeles library knew of a Spanish record called "Las Posadas" that might help us. The larger music houses did not carry it but referred us to a North Main Street music store that carries foreign records. That store had no such record but could send to Mexico City for the music. There was not time to wait for that, so the teacher was sent to another North Main Street music store. At this place we were successful in getting the Columbia record "Las Posadas."

The record, a peculiar combination of sacred and secular music, was played for the children, but the Mexican children were unable to express the Spanish lines in English sufficiently well to use them. As a last resort, appeal was made to the citizenship teacher who works among the Mexican mothers. She finally reported that a Spanish woman in another district had the words of *Las Posadas* in Spanish. This lady, with the help of the citizenship teacher, kindly translated them for us. The next step was to get the music to fit the words. From the record the teacher set down the notes used in the chanting of the priest for the first part of the litany, and chose two of the more tuneful melodies for the last two sections. So with accompaniment supplied by the teacher, we at last had music and words for the first scene.

The children brought in as much green shrubbery as they could, and large palm leaves, in order to make the stage look as much as possible like a corner in the

LAS POSADAS*

In the name of Heav'n I ask you for shel-ter, for my be-lov-ed wife is so ver-y tired.

This is not a room-ing house, keep on your way. I am a-fraid to o-pen, It might be high-way men.

Don't be so in-hu-man. Have pit-y up - on us, that God in Heav'n may re-com-pense you.

You can keep on go-ing and don't both-er me, For if I get ang-ry you will be sorry soon.

We are very tired, com-ing from Naz-ar-eth. I am a car-pen-ter. My name is Jos-é.

I don't care about your name. Please do let me sleep, For a-gain I tell you I won't o-pen.

For shel-ter is pray-ing, my dear house-keep-er, for only one night, The Queen of Heav'n.

Is it you, Jos-é? Your wife is Ma-ry. Come in dear pil-grims, I had not re-cog-nized you.

God pay you, dear folks, your char-i-ty, that you had pit-y on these pil-grims.

Hap-py the house that shel-ters this day the pure Vir-gin, the beau-ti-ful Ma-ry. En-ter,

sa-cred pil-grims. Ho-nor my poor man-sion, And as I give you my hum-ble house, Re-ceive my

heart al - so. You are wel-come, wel-come are you, Beau-ti-ful Ma - ry, flow'r of Gal-i-lee.

And in these moun-tains that want-ed to see you, Thou art wel-come, wel————come art thou.

*Edited by Louis W. Curtis, Director, Music Division, Los Angeles City Schools.

patio. No one child had strong enough voice or sufficient courage to sing the part of the inn-keeper on the stage alone, so seven of the best singers were chosen to be on the stage and were to represent the hacienda owner, his family, and friends. The rest of the class sang the part of Mary and Joseph behind the curtain. The procedure is indicated below. At the words, "Enter sacred pilgrims," the procession entered the patio, placing the candles, two at a time, in the rack before the shrine during the singing of the rest of the song. When the last candle had been placed, the scene ended with the priest's pronouncing a blessing upon the kneeling group.

Scene two represented a room in the "big house" of the hacienda. The owner and his family welcomed the people of the hacienda to the celebration. The dialogue used followed closely the one in the book. A Mexican girl in the class made a beautiful piñata. This is a bag filled with toys and suspended over the heads of children. Sticks are used to break the bag and the children scramble for the scattered toys. This piñata was made by covering an ordinary shopping bag very artistically with crepe paper. The girl said her family was in the habit of using that kind of piñata. The teacher had imagined that the bag might not break easily and cut several slits on the inside but even so, there was some trouble in breaking it. We learned that it would be better another time to use a bag of lighter weight paper. The question arose, "What if someone should accidentally be struck by the stick used in breaking the piñata, or suppose the first person who tried should really break it?" (Tonio was the one who was to succeed in that.) In order to prevent either of these disasters, it was decided to use as a blindfold a cloth thin enough to see through.

The matter of costumes was the least satisfactory part of our program. It was a real problem to try to costume forty children, and our district is one where the hard times have been keenly felt, so asking children to buy anything in the way of a costume was out of the question. The only thing we could do was to fall back on the school costume supply, not overly large, and to ask the children to bring in what they could from home. We managed to have a few sombreros and to costume nicely the main characters. The boys were urged to wear overalls and all to look as much like peons as possible.

After the piñata had been broken and the children had had time to gather up the contents from the floor, Carmen invited two of the girls to present a dance. They gave a Spanish dance, accompanied by the teacher and a Mexican boy from the school orchestra playing a violin. After the dance, there were some solos played on the accordion, by a boy from another grade, who had wanted to be on the program so was included. With his performance the Christmas party at the hacienda ended.

Stanzas 1, 2, 3, 4, 5, were sung by a group of 7 of the best singers of the room. 1A-2A-3A-4A-5A—Sung by rest of room standing behind curtain.

Stanza 6 was sung by the seven singers as the procession entered the patio on stage.

Stanza 7 was sung by everyone as candles were being placed before shrine.

A MARKET SCENE

After browsing through many books on Mexico we had a lesson on how to find information in books by inspecting table of contents, table of illustrations, index, glossary, and skimming through books. We found that Mexican markets were most often mentioned, and that the most outstanding feature of each large or small town is its market. So we decided to have a real Mexican market. First we made a list on the board of the things that are seen in Mexican markets. This list was made through the use of books, a visit to the Mexican market in Olvera Street, Los Angeles, questioning Mexican friends and parents, and looking at pictures. The list formed a basis for dividing the class into working groups. To actually make the Mexican baskets, pottery, foods, serapes, a great amount of research was necessary. After the things were made we set up our market scene and gave a program.

Courtesy of Los Angeles City Schools

Painting Scenery for an Outdoor Mexican Play

Setting for the dramatization:

Children sitting on Navajo rugs on the floor in front of classroom, with pottery, potted cactus plants, baskets, bead work, rugs, serapes, sombreros, fruits, vegetables, tamales, chili beans, and tortillas on rugs in front of them, just as in a real Mexican market.

The program:

After the Mexican national dance, children of various groups explained how they had made or collected their wares, and what part these things play in the life of the people. An outline will show the nature of the simple talks.

Pottery

Shaping pottery	Designs on pottery
Baking pottery	Uses of pottery
History of pottery making	

Weaving

Serapes	Rugs

Basketry

History of basketry	Sisal baskets
Raffia and reed baskets	Palm leaf baskets

Clothes

How peons dress (demonstration)
How wealthy Mexicans dress (demonstration)

Foods

Tamales   Tortillas
Chili beans

Actual sale of our pottery, baskets, and food followed. The money was used in purchasing materials with which to work.

A FIESTA SCENE

To complete our term's work on Mexico, we decided to hold a Fiesta and invite other fifth grade classes and the mothers.

We chose the chapter named Judas Iscariot Day in *The Mexican Twins*, and dramatized it. Two of the girls wrote out the play and directed it. Since the main event in this chapter takes place in the village on a Saint's Day and Market Day, it seemed necessary for us to represent a street scene in Mexico. Booths for food, flowers, pottery, and baskets were erected. Awnings were placed over the cloak room doors with signs "Pottery" and "Baskets." A white canvas awning was made for the food booth, then decorated with colored crepe paper. The Pottery group exhibited the articles they had made and demonstrated modeling. The basket booth sold reed and raffia and demonstrated basket weaving. The flower booth, arranged in one of our wide ledged windows, displayed a variety of colorful posies. Each bunch was sold for a few centavos. The popular place was the food booth where tortillas, enchiladas, tamales, and chili con carne were on sale.

As the families representing the characters in the play entered the market there were many interesting things for them to see. Then groups of dancers made merry by dancing one of the Mexican folk dances. A group of minstrels sang "In Gay Seville."

All the children in the class were in costume, each one choosing the type of Mexican he wanted to represent.

Before the play was presented several children gave reports on the topics which we considered most important in our study of Mexico.

II. Made maps showing:

Plant life and animal life of Mexico.

Typical scenes of the work and play of the people. The border of the carto-graph map was made up of many rectangular pictures giving scenes from the history of Mexico.

The varied elevations of the land.

The principal railroads and the prospective highways to be built from the United States to Mexico City.

The routes of Diaz, Vasco de Gama, Columbus, Cortez, Magellan, de Soto, and Coronado, the landing of Ponce de Leon in Florida and the point where Balboa sighted the Pacific Ocean.

Spanish territory in the new world about 1600.[1]

Location of chief cities, territory occupied by ancient Indian tribes, sites of six major dam projects.

The natural resources and agricultural products—silver, copper, oil, truck crops, alfalfa, corn, maguey, and fruit. (Cartograph map.)

Cities about which we studied. Each city (or section) is illustrated by its outstanding feature, i.e., Mexico City is marked with a picture of the cathedral—Guadalajara by people making pottery—Oaxaca by people making serapes, with a background of the houses typical of that region—Vera Cruz shows oil wells—et cetera.

III. Learned songs and dances

MARTENS, FREDERICK H. *Mexican and Spanish Songs.* Boston: Oliver Ditson Co., 1928.

STURGIS, M. H., and BLAKE, W. P. *Songs of the Pyrenees.* Boston: The Arthur P. Schmidt Co., n.d.

---

[1] See Marion G. Clark and A. F. Gordy. *What Men From Europe Brought to America.* New York: Charles Scribner's Sons, 1929, p. 244.

We learned one song in Spanish and the others with English words. The ones we chose were "The Breeze," "Ask of the Stars," "Linda Mia," "Teresita Mia," (which was sung as a serenade), and "Carnations." The latter was sung as a solo by a Mexican boy dressed in sombrero, serape, and red sash. He carried a basket of fresh carnations and distributed them as he sang.

Records and songs purchased at Mauricio Calderon, 408 No. Main Street, Los Angeles, California.

Dances

El Jarabe Tapitio—Brunswick record No. 40402
    Mexican typical dance—easily picked up by the children if some one can be found who knows the many steps. Danced by a girl and boy. Used in the Mission Play.
La Jota—Record is La Madre del Cordero—Victor record No. 79364B.
    Difficult typical dance, usually a solo.
Las Manzanitas—Record is Morir Sonando or Quatro Milpas—Victor record No. 78984B. Very simple. All the children can do this.
El Chocolo—Victor record No. 21393B.
    A few easy tango steps make this an effective dance and give the children much pleasure. The use of castanets adds much.

IV. Prepared booklets

A Mexican recipe book.
A stamp book with a paragraph giving the history represented on each stamp.
A clippings booklet organized topically.
A series of booklets on Mexican people, dress, homes, travel, arts and crafts, customs, and holidays.
A booklet of stories giving the life of the people. This was illustrated with maps and pictures.
A booklet giving the history of Mexico.

V. Made a collection of things from Mexico

Bright colored handkerchiefs embroidered in Mexican characters or the Eagle of Mexico; Mexican drawn work.
Paper masks used at the Christmas celebration.
Filigree jewelry of silver; hammered silver jewelry.
Hand made baskets woven of plant fibers; metate; straw envelopes, horses, and figures.
Pictures of Spanish characters and birds made of bright colored feathers; copies of Mexican paintings.
Pottery typical in shape and design.
A large sombrero and serape; sandals of braided leather.
A petate; cooking dish; gourd bowls.
A string of red peppers.

VI. Illustrated in crayola or calcimine paints

Street Scenes—In Pueblo, at one corner a petate—covered ox-cart carrying a load of clay to the factory; at another corner, a train of burros loaded with wood for the furnaces; in the street beyond, a man carrying a crate of pottery on his back to market.

At Tepalcingo, in the tierra caliente, awnings spread over the hot stony road that lies between the plaza of the cathedral and the portales of the town hall of justice—a space of a quarter mile square, crowded with every sort of ware and marked off by little lanes between the piles of merchandise.

A Railway Station Scene—Women in blue rebozos and men in big peaked straw hats crowding up to the car windows to sell their wares—white cheese on green leaves, enchiladas, tortillas, toys, tropical fruits with their beautiful shapes and names.

A Plaza Scene in Oaxaca—A procession—Indian women wearing white cotton blouses and pink or purple cotton skirts, full and long and ruffled, like gypsies' skirts: their long black braids finished with bright pink ribbons; a quiet round-eyed baby looking out at the world from the blue rebozo. Indian men, barefooted or wearing sandals made of strips of crossed leather; dressed in white cotton clothes and either huge brimmed, high peaked straw hats or funny little peaked black felt hats; a serape thrown over their shoulder.

Market Scenes and Fair Booths—Booths of hats, the great peaked straw hats of Mexico, hanging in rows on the walls, piled in stacks on the floor; and the people who sell the hats holding half-finished ones on their laps as they go on plaiting them.

Booths of chairs—the straight slot-backed chairs, with seats of woven colored rope, and the wooden shelves with doves or flowers carved at the top and made for kitchen dishes.

Booths of Oaxacan pottery—great black jars of a size and shape that suggest Ali Baba and the Forty Thieves, and beside the jars a basket of penny whistles made of black pottery in the shape of birds and animals; blue and yellow home made pottery—plates, cups, pitchers, bowls, platters, vases, flower pots.

Booths of Ignalan pottery—water jars, some left in the natural color of clay and decorated with beautiful designs in blue or red, others with no decoration, only the most perfect shape.

Mexican Types of Houses—The cathedral that is found in every town. In Oaxaca, adobe houses thatched with palm. In the tierra caliente, a kitchen detached from the house and thatched with straw or palms; walls of bamboo reeds open on at least two sides. The native inns—great dreary yards with little sheds, and little rooms around.

Interiors of Homes—A house in Oaxaca where serapes are made—at one end a picture of the Virgin of Guadalupe, with a bunch of flowers on the table underneath

Dramatization of a Mexican Market Scene

it, the petate on which the family sleep rolled up in a corner; at the other end the loom at which the owner of the house is at work.

A Mexican kitchen—the stove of red unglazed tiles, a woven straw fan hanging near for fanning the charcoal; earthen "casuelas" hung on the walls beside the stove or arranged on "trastes"; turkeys and chickens strolling about the kitchen.

Mexican Types of People—Women of Tehauntepec wearing a short, straight, embroidered blouse that comes just to the waist, and a full, long skirt. For special occasions, beautiful pleated lace head-dresses that stand out in a stiff wide frill around their lovely faces.

Indians of Oaxaca (see plaza scene).

Zapotec Indians: small men with lifted chests and quick, lifted knees; quiet, small, round-headed, barefooted women with blue rebozos round their shoulders, and a baby in the fold.

By the Roadside—Women at the river filling beautiful big jars with two handles, or walking like a procession bearing the filled jars home on their shoulders or heads.

Lawrence [1] gives a vivid description of such a picture:

"From the valley villages and from the mountains the peasants and the Indians are coming in with supplies (market day), the road is like a pilgrimage; dark-eared asses and running men, running women, running girls, running lads, twinkling donkeys ambling on fine little feet, under twin great baskets with tomatoes and gourds, twin great nets of bubble-shaped jars, twin bundles of neat-cut faggots of wood, and neat as bunches of cigarettes, and twin net-sacks of charcoal. Donkeys, mules, on they come, great pannier baskets making a rhythm under the perched woman, great bundles bouncing against the sides of the slim-footed animals."

In the Fields [2]—Just across the state line between Sinaloa and Sonora, in the heart of the sugar cane country, plantations operated with American efficiency.

Burros stepping aside to let an American tractor pass.

Peons plowing the corn with an old fashioned wooden plow.

VII. Made things typically Mexican in clay

Before working with clay the children studied distinctive shapes of Mexican pottery, listed the questions which arose and looked them up in their research period.

Why has the water jug two openings?
Why are the vases irregular?
Where did the Indians get their designs?
Where did they get their paints?

The teacher also took part in the research work and reported to the class that the Indians used sticks with bits of wool or soft animal skin tied on one end for brushes. They used sharp edged porous bone for making the fine lines. They used clay from the natural clay banks which they found in many colors. These colors were used for paints. Later they used animal and vegetable dyes such as cochineal insects, the indigo plant, and the bark of trees. These gave the colors, red, blue, and yellow. The Indians baked the pottery in an open wood fire or in a crude outdoor oven. The baking was quite an event and was celebrated with a ceremony consisting of songs and dances.

Pottery [3]

Bowls, cups, plates, cooking dishes, and pitchers, typical kitchen ware.
Beautifully decorated and glazed vases, bowls, and water jugs from Puebla.

[1] David H. Lawrence. *Mornings In Mexico*. New York: Alfred A. Knopf, Inc., 1927.
[2] Detailed farm scenes are given in *Lucita, Mexican Twins, The Burro's Money-bag*, and Franck's *Mexico and Central America*. See Bibliography for complete references.
[3] For a description of the coil method see Ida Willsea Wheeler. *Playing With Clay*. New York: The Macmillan Company, 1931.

16—17050

Water jars with two handles used by the women in carrying water from the streams.

Bowls for cacti.

Miniature dishes and vases of all kinds.

Toys

Pink pigs, blue cats, orange tigers, white rabbits, ducks, chickens, turkeys, birds, cows, horses, and donkeys.

Tiles

Tolavera tiles, beautiful in design with colors of blue, green, and yellow.

Figures

Women carrying water jars, sitting in the market place, and caring for their babies.

Men transporting goods to market, wearing the dress of a rich hacienda owner, and riding on donkeys.

Children at work or play.

VIII. Made articles from gourds

Bowls painted in bright colors.

Water jugs with cork stoppers.

Birds with long legs and sharp bills.

IX. Mounted pictures from magazines showing various industries of Mexico, markets, mines, people, transportation. Classified all these pictures and left them in a neat folder for the next class.

X. Wrote and gave talks on our exhibit materials and invited a third grade to hear these lectures.

XI. Selected holidays to write about with the understanding that the best story should be published in the school paper. A committee from the class read the stories, choosing the four excellent ones to read to the entire class who voted on the best one.

XII-a. Constructed a model of the Cathedral of Guadalupe with plastic figures depicting the life of the people.

Interest was aroused by

Showing pictures comparing the Aztecs and the Mexicans of today.

Taking children out on the lawn for discussion periods in which our principal who had visited Mexico the previous summer told many interesting stories of true life there.

A visit to Olvera Street.

Stories of Aztec religion.

Displaying many interesting story books such as the *Painted Pig, Pancho and His Burro, Lucita, Manuel in Mexico, The Talking Bird, Made in Mexico,* etc.

Exhibit of baskets, pottery, sombreros, lace, books, pictures, brought to the children.

In trying to find answers to the questions that were asked it became evident that the life of Mexico seemed centered around the church and the markets. Some one found the story of Our Lady of Guadalupe. Finding this an interesting story we decided to take Guadalupe as a type study. Questions were asked as to where it was located and suggestions made as to what they would like to do to make the study more interesting. Someone found that this is the only cathedral in Mexico City which has a market place in front of it.

A postcard picture of the Cathedral was brought and the children tried to model it in clay, but found that they could hardly make it as large or as durable as they wished to have it. They then drew a plan of it to scale, but after trying to figure out all the dimensions, they came to the conclusion that it was too difficult for them. So they drew up a plan the actual size they wished to have the cathedral. This solved their difficulty.

This plan was taken to the sloyd shop and used as the blue-print in building the cathedral. Scraps of boards and boxes were used in the construction. The cathedral was taken to the art room where it was covered with a stucco composition. Religious pictures were painted with oil paints on glass for the windows. The altar was made and the whole interior was carefully painted and gilded as the class learned of the beautiful pieces of statuary and painting done by the masters of art and brought from Europe. They learned of the three hundred feet of solid silver railing around the altar. This led to an interesting study of the mines and of the Indian workers of Mexico.

So bit by bit as they read and talked they added the tapestry of Guadalupe; the pilgrims coming to pray; the market along the walk; the products offered for sale and how they were used in the home; the straw rain coats worn on rainy days, etc.

The boys wanted to light the interior so a book on electricity was consulted and dry batteries used.[1]

Each child was able to add his little bit so that each child felt that it was indeed his own creation.

Art periods were used in illustrating stories, making the clay figures, booklets, baskets, shawls, pottery.

Language periods were used for oral reports and writing short stories of what we had read in our research periods. Some of these stories were read and commented upon. The best ones were chosen, written upon the board and corrected in class. Finally they were copied, mounted, and pasted in our large class book, together with the best illustrations.

Most of the reference books were much too hard for these children so the teacher wrote short stories and mounted them on cardboard for reference.

XII-b. Constructed a model of a peon's home

Our class decided to make a small model of a Mexican home, using materials close at hand. We planned three rooms and a patio. Patterns for bricks, $1\frac{1}{2}''$ x $3\frac{1}{4}''$, were made of stiff paper. The boys got mud from under the viaduct between Long Beach and Wilmington. The bricks were made of this adobe mud, mixed with dry grass and molded by hand. Every child made at least two bricks. The tiles for the roof were also molded by hand. They were $1''$ x $3''$. After the tiles and bricks had dried for about three days, four of the boys built the house. It took 145 tiles and 200 bricks. The dried bricks were put together with wet adobe and carefully smoothed. The walls of the house were painted with thick white calcimine and the tile roof with red. While the boys were building the house the rest of the class furnished it. Some girls made tiny serapes and strung red peppers. Others made furniture, clay figures, chickens, animals, and pottery. We planted real cactus from Olvera Street in tiny handmade pottery bowls, and placed them around the home.

XIII. Made index files

Topics were listed and placed on the board—markets, sports and amusements, pottery, travel and transportation, homes, holidays, Mexican emblem, pyramids ruins, Guadalupe, volcanoes, dress and customs, plants, schools, weaving. References were found, verified and placed on index cards.

XIV. Solved problems

Why is it possible to grow corn, wheat, and other temperate products in Mexico? How our farms in the United States compare with a Mexican hacienda.

---

[1] Catherine Louis Kellor. *Working With Electricity.* New York: The Macmillan Company, 1929, pp. 93–98.

What products are raised in both the United States and Mexico.
What is raised there that we can not grow here.
How to tell the climate of a place when we know the crops.

XV. Prepared Mexican food

Salad made of little green beans, tomatoes, strips of alligator pears, and shredded cabbage and lettuce.

Tortillas, tamales, and chili with frijoles.

XVI. Edited a newspaper

"La Estrella de Mexico" (Mexican Star) is a newspaper edited by a 5A class. The articles are typed and mounted in an orderly fashion on the four sides of a large folded white sheet of paper 26" x 20". Five crayola drawings are inserted. The titles of the articles suggest the richness of content.

Main headings:

Travel Bureau (Sights)
    Chapultepec Park
    Xochimilco or Floating Gardens
    National Theater
    Pyramids
    Volcanoes

    Market Places
    Flower Market
    Military Academy
    Open-Air Schools

Industries
    Coffee
    Henequen
    Gathering Chicle
    Mexican Mining
    Comparing Mines

    Oil
    Pottery
    Productions of Mexico
    The Maguey Plant

History of Mexico
    Anahuac of Mexico
    The Story of the Fair God
    Mayan History

    Aztec History
    Spanish History

Legends—Stories—Book Reviews
    Guadalupe
    Pancho and Lola
    Food

    Cocoa
    Houses
    Peon Baths

XVII. Wrote stories

These reports were taken from children's booklets.

WHAT THE PEOPLE EAT

The people of Mexico eat tortillas at every meal. The poorer people have no knives, forks, and spoons. When they eat their meals they roll up a tortilla and scoop up their food. In this way they eat their spoons.

The Mexicans often have chile con carne for dinner, chile means a kind of a pepper, con means with, and carne means meat. The meat is chopped fine and cooked with the chile.

Another dish the Mexicans sometimes have is frijoles. Frijoles are nothing but brown beans. The Mexicans boil the beans in earthenware pots and then fry them in fat. When the Mexicans have roast beef they serve it with a sauce as hot as chile and peppers will make it.—Vivian.

UNDER THE GROUND IN MEXICO

Near the city of Guanajuato there are many mines. Indian peons work in these mines. The miners are put in a huge iron bucket, a man blows a whistle and they are lowered into a kind of well or shaft dug about a thousand feet deep. At the bottom there are a lot of little hallways leading into parts of the mine. In some parts there are miners digging out ore. Other hallways lead into very hot parts of the mine, where the men wear little clothing, but they always wear a big straw hat. You might wonder why they wear the straw hat. They wear it because sometimes they work in pairs, one has a chisel and hits it with a hammer to chip off the ore, and the other holds his big hat under the chisel, to catch the ore as it drops.

Sometimes as the men work they have bad fortune, and a big piece of jagged rock may fall upon their heads. Inside the mine they stack up dynamite boxes for a church and have a cross or picture of Virgin Mary. Most of them have a little wallet, with a prayer written on a paper folded up inside.—Sol.

REFERENCES THAT PROVED MOST HELPFUL IN A UNIT OF STUDY ON MEXICO

In Making Pottery

GAY, ZHINYA and GAY, JAN. *Pancho and His Burro.* New York: William Morrow & Co., Inc., 1930.

MORROW, ELIZABETH REEVE. *The Painted Pig.* New York: Alfred A. Knopf, Inc., 1930.

PURNELL, IDELLA, and WEATHERWAX, J. M. *Talking Bird.* New York: The Macmillan Company, 1930.

SMITH, S. C. *Made in Mexico.* New York: Alfred A. Knopf, Inc., 1930.

SPINDEN, HERBERT JOSEPH. *Ancient Civilizations of Mexico and Central America.* New York: American Museum of Natural History, 1928.

WHEELER, IDA WILLSEA. *Playing with Clay.* New York: The Macmillan Company, 1931.

In Understanding the History of the People

BANKS, HELEN WARD. *Boy's Prescott: The Conquest of Mexico.* New York: Frederick A. Stokes Company, 1916.

CHASE, STUART, and OTHERS. *Mexico.* New York: The Macmillan Company, 1931.

LANG, ANDREW. *Conquest of Montezuma's Empire.* New York: Longmans, Green & Company, 1932.

MORRIS, ANN. *Digging in Yucatan.* Garden City, New York: Doubleday, Doran & Company, 1931.

SMALLIDGE, OLIVE E., and PAXSON, F. L. *Finding America.* Boston: Houghton Mifflin Company, 1929.

In Becoming Familiar With Life in Mexico Today

BARROWS, HARLAN H., and PARKER, E. P. *Geography, Southern Lands.* New York: Silver, Burdett & Company, 1929.

CARR, HARRY. *Old Mother Mexico.* Boston: Houghton Mifflin Company, 1931.

FRANCK, HARRY A. *Mexico and Central America.* Dansville, New York: F. A. Owens Publishing Company, 1929.

GEORGE, MARIAN MINNIE. *Little Journey to Mexico and Central America.* Chicago: A. Flanagan Company, 1929.

LEFFERTS, WALTER. *Our Neighbors North and South.* Philadelphia: J. B. Lippincott Company, 1926.

In Giving Pleasure and Understanding Through a Story

BAYLOR, FRANCES COURTENAY. *Juan and Juanita.* Boston: Houghton Mifflin Company, 1930.

GAINES, RUTH LOUISE. *Lucita.* Chicago: Rand McNally & Company, 1913.

GAINES, RUTH LOUISE. *Village Shield.* New York: E. P. Dutton & Co., Inc., 1916.

MCDONALD, ETTA AUSTEN, and Others. *Manuel in Mexico.* Boston: Little, Brown and Company, 1909.

MOON, GRACE. *Nadito (Little Nothing).* Garden City, New York: Doubleday, Doran & Company, 1927.

PERKINS, LUCY FITCH. *Mexican Twins.* Boston: Houghton Mifflin Company, 1915.

THOMAS, MARGARET LORING. *The Burro's Moneybag.* New York: The Abingdon Press, 1931.

Magazines

National Geographic Magazine. LI (May, 1927); LVII (June, 1930).

CHAPTER XIV

LOG OF THE ACTIVITIES CARRIED ON BY A FIFTH GRADE CLASS IN DEVELOPING A UNIT OF WORK ON MEXICO[1]

PURPOSE OF THE REPORT

This chronological report is given to reveal the careful techniques involved in successful activity work with a large class in a public school. The criteria applied in using the word successful are two: Children should work cooperatively in informal relationships, and they should accomplish something as they carry out plans they themselves have had a large part in making.

This skeleton report is for the purpose of making clear:

1. The continuity between the activities of one day and those of the next. The best learning goes on when the children see the relationships between what they have done and what they are going to do for the reason that the latter is an outgrowth of the former.

2. The frequent grouping and re-grouping necessary in carrying out the variety of activities connected with one unit and the devices used in order that the re-grouping may not result in chaos. This grouping is not made arbitrarily by the teacher, but is based on the tasks to be done as the need for workers becomes apparent.

3. The progress made by a class whose prose reading was done in a variety of books to gain information for carrying out definite activities.

4. The activities actually carried out by one class in four months under the guidance of an experienced teacher with progressive ideas of education.

THE CHILDREN

This class consisted of twenty-six American children from poor homes, and nine Japanese children speaking their native language at

[1] Prepared by Marcia Bonsall, Teacher Sawtelle Boulevard School, observation school for the University of California at Los Angeles.

home. Three of the thirty-five children were on the free lunch lists and two boys were from a home where only boys from broken homes are enrolled. A number of others had parents entirely lacking in home-school cooperation.

In the main the class was one with remarkable unity of purpose and initiative. It had come up through the grades where industrial arts activities and dramatic play had been stressed. There was, however, need of improvement in the citizenship qualities of several individuals. For example, one boy with an intelligence quotient of 120 had been a problem case in several previous grades. He was irresponsible and was interested in nothing except map making, and even in this work he failed to profit by suggestions for improvement. He was also inclined to be cruel, pinching children as he moved about the room and in other ways displaying a negative attitude. At the close of the unit on Mexico he had become markedly more cooperative and participated helpfully in the activities of the room. Lack of space forbids a detailed account of the incidents in his change and that of several other children in different respects.

Improvement in character traits is always considered more important for children than progress in academic ratings. Both, however, are essential and they should be attained together.

The following distribution indicates the intelligence quotients of the members of this class:

I Q	Number of Children
80 to 85	2
86 to 90	3
91 to 95	3
96 to 100	13
101 to 105	3
106 to 110	4
111 to 115	1
116 to 120	4
121 to 125	1
Total	34
Median	99.0

LEADING-ON-NESS OF THE PREVIOUS UNIT

The unit on Mexico was an outgrowth of the one preceding it in the Low Fifth grade relating to the Westward Movement. The territorial expansion of the United States and the trails across the country, the clothing and utensils of the early pioneers, and their mode of transportation had been studied. The children had relived some of the experiences of the pioneers in their dramatic play, making the necessary clothing, weapons, and the like, themselves. The last trail to the unexplored West to be studied was the Santa Fe Trail. It led into Mexico and back into California. The children saw Mexico always as the next place to study, for trails from the interior of that country led to the Santa Fe.

The unit on Westward Movement was so real to the children that since they remained with the same teacher throughout the year, the subject was continued for one month of the new semester. This of course allowed only four months for the new unit.

The development of the unit on Mexico as it progressed day by day has been recorded here to guide the teacher who may lack experience in carrying out the activity technique. The "log" presents problems raised by the children, what the teacher did to direct the solution of these problems, the construction work undertaken, and the ways in which the language arts, arithmetic, reading, etc., are brought in as an integral part of the unit of work.

DAY BY DAY DEVELOPMENT OF UNIT

March 2—Friday

When the children came into the room on the day the unit was to be launched, they found the environment suggestive of Mexico. The following Mexican exhibits were attractively placed as follows: a large straw basket, and a straw soldier on a straw horse in the high transom spaces above the blackboard; a picture of a burro rider made of dyed feathers over an exhibit table where a gaily painted pig stood beside Elizabeth Morrow's book *Painted Pig*,[1] together with a few other choice books about the country, and a metate; a group of pictures of burros and their masters at the top of the back blackboard above a bookcase filled with sets of books on Mexico.

The children were surprised and pleased and began to ask questions about the exhibits and pictures. The many pictures of burros stimulated interest and some of the children told of their experiences with the woolly creatures. The teacher said she had a new book about a burro and began reading *The Burro's Moneybag*.[2] The story called forth many comments and questions. After the first chapter was finished Floyd said, "I think it would be fun to know more about Mexico." "And so do I," said a number of the children. Other comments followed. "I know that all Mexican boys seem to want a burro." "I know that Mexico is in North America." "The people eat tortillas as their main food." "They have pretty pottery." "The country has lots of cactus." "Many of the people go barefooted." "The money is different from ours." "The poor people live in adobe houses."

[1] Elizabeth Reeve Morrow. *Painted Pig; a Mexican Picture Book.* New York: Alfred A. Knopf, Inc., 1930.
[2] Margaret Loring Thomas. *The Burro's Moneybag.* New York: The Abingdon Press, 1931.

These contributions were listed on the board by the teacher under the heading, "Some Things We Know About Mexico." At last the ideas were exhausted and one child noticed that eleven of the twenty-five items had been suggested by the chapter read from *The Burro's Moneybag.*

Other questions raised were soon grouped on the board under the heading, "Some Things Our Class Wishes to Know About Mexicans." These numbered fifty. Upon examining the list the children decided that all questions of one kind should be grouped together if we intended locating all of the answers. These were placed under such topics as food, clothing, shelter, industries, products, physical environment, history, amusements, government, and education. The classifications were checked upon the board and the class elected a secretary to copy them into a permanent notebook. The class decided to try to answer the questions one group at a time.

Later, the teacher put the questions in each group on a large sheet of 18" x 24" newspaper and these were clipped to an easel. For instance, the questions on *Food* included:

1. What kinds of food do the Mexican people eat besides tortillas?
2. Do they eat out of dishes like ours?
3. What fruits grow in the country?
4. What crops can they raise?
5. Out of what materials do they make tortillas?
6. What animals can they use for food?
7. Where do they get their water supply?
8. Do they use machinery in their fields?

Some of the questions on *Shelter* were:

1. How do they make their homes?
2. Where do they get adobe for their houses?
3. Are the houses in the cities the same as those of the poor people in the country?
4. Do they have beds?
5. What kinds of furniture do country and city houses have?
6. What kind of a climate do they have?

March 5—Monday

Since one of the children was absent on Friday, Jean volunteered to tell her about the story which the teacher had read that day. The class wished to play the story. Characters were chosen and the play began. After a second group had an opportunity to play, the teacher asked, "Do you think of anything which we could do to make our play better?" When classified, the answer came under two headings. (1) Materials needed: a house, clothing, and furniture, and (2) English suggestions, such as: be the character you say you are; speak distinctly; try to get more action into the play; and learn some Mexican expressions.

At the spelling period the class decided that the words *Mexican, Mexico, burro, carreta,* and *metate* should be included in the spelling list for the week. Since the class secretary and her helper had had difficulty when making up the notebook, perhaps the other children would need to use those words also.

March 6—Tuesday

The subject of the need for a house if the class wished to be Mexicans for the rest of the semester was discussed. No one was sure to what kind of a house *The Burro's Moneybag* referred because there had been no description. Furthermore, someone knew that there were several kinds of houses in Mexico, but no one had any definite information—not even the girl who had lived in Mexico City when she was a small child. Discussions as to why there would be several kinds of houses in one country which most of the class supposed to be largely desert covered with cactus—led to the answer that it must be the climate. Then came the question, "Why are there different kinds of climate? Mexico is all close to the equator." This brought the decision to study the maps of the country.

Research reading and a brief examination of a physical map showed that there were three kinds of climate—*tierras caliente, tierras templada, tierras frias*—in three kinds of territory. The children decided that if they could find out more about the climate and the topography of the country they would be able to find out what kinds of houses the country had, and in turn decide what kind the class would build, for in past studies they knew that a very cold climate called for a better constructed house than a hot one would.

March 7 to 9—Wednesday to Friday

The remainder of the week consisted of filling in 8"x14" outline maps of Mexico to show topography, and putting them into permanent booklets; playing scenes about an Indian's home, such as gathering and sorting tomatoes for market, gathering flowers to sell, taking the flowers to the depot to sell to passengers, making tortillas, (concluded each time with discussions for their improvement in number and accuracy of details); reading the second chapter of *The Burro's Moneybag* solving the problem, "Why does Mexico have three kinds of climate?" planning to make a set of 24"x36" pictorial maps of Mexico. The outlines of the maps were to be made with a still film slide. Maps were made by the children showing certain physical features, kinds of vegetation and animal life in various regions, cities, and industrial centers.

March 12—Monday

The need of a house in order to make the play better was evident and the class decided that they still did not know what kinds of houses could be built. The problem was stated, "What kinds of houses are there in Mexico?" The teacher had prepared a two page article which served for the research reading. The answers were found and the class planned to make an adobe house like those used by the Indians and the Mestizos of the free village in the tierras templadas. This type, they thought, was the most representative.

The teacher read the legend of "The Finding of Corn" and "The Man and the Balam" from *The Bright Feather*[1] by Rhoads.

The spelling list for the week included the words *mestizos, Indian, miniature, framework,* and *adobe.*

March 13—Tuesday

At the discussion period the problem was raised: "What would the Indian home in the tierras templada look like?" The teacher had prepared an article from source materials which answered this question. The children then formulated a plan of study for their home, clothing, furniture, and utensils, so that individual work could be carried on at leisure as well as during directed lessons, as follows:

> To have furniture and utensils for our Mexican house, we must:
> 1. Read to find out what kinds of furniture and utensils the Mexicans have.
> 2. Plan the kinds we want in our house.
> 3. Make plans and drawings of them.
> 4. Make the articles.
> 5. Use them.
>
> To wear Mexican clothing, we must:
> 1. Read to find out what kinds of clothes the Mexicans have.
> 2. Plan our own clothes.
> 3. Make patterns for ourselves.
> 4. Make the clothing.
> 5. Wear them.

These brief plans were copied into loose-leafed notebooks, to be referred to by the children when they chose. Their problem for Wednesday grew out of this planning.

March 14—Wednesday

The class made definite plans for their adobe house.

> 1. Size, and general appearance of the frame work.
>   a. Floor—8' x 6'. Use 2" x 4"s.
>   b. Back—6' high.
>   c. Front—7' high.

---

[1] Dorothy M. Rhoads. *The Bright Feather.* Garden City, New York: Doubleday, Doran and Company, 1932.

  d. Slanting roof.
  e. Open toward the front door of our classroom, with a door.
  f. Side open, so the other children can see the play if they choose.

2. Roof.
  a. Use tiles made of cardboard dipped in red calcimine and dried around oatmeal boxes.
  b. Make a frame work of lath to hold the tiles.
  c. Clip the tiles together and lay them on the frame.

3. Walls.
  a. Use the pieces of wallboard and cover them with wrapping paper painted to look like adobe which had been painted yellow.
  b. The other walls would not have the wallboard, but have the wrapping paper stretched across and painted the same.
  c. The entire sections would be painted yellow and then the bricks lined in with brown to represent mortar.
  d. Since the framework committee needed the space, the walls committee would have to work outside. They would pin the correct length of paper to the cork above the blackboard and paint it to look like bricks painted yellow. As each strip was completed it was to be rolled up and put away until all were finished. Then they would be put together with butcher's tape and hung in the house.

As the children planned, they drew lines on the floor with chalk so they would be ready to begin as soon as the lumber arrived, and their plans were completed.

The teacher read "The Corn that Flew Away" from *The Wishing Owl*.[1] There are several legends built around corn, as that is the staple food of Mexico.

March 15—Thursday

The class decided that the house could not be the size of a real Mexican house, but that they would make it as large as possible in the classroom. There was no room for garden space, or yard, or sheds. In order to have a complete Indian home, one group of children wished to make the house in miniature showing the furniture and occupants. This house could be constructed of real adobe bricks. Three members of the class had come from a grade where they had made a South American house of real adobe. They took charge of the brick making group and directed their activities. The plans which developed were:

To Make a Miniature House out of Real Adobe:
1. Mix the adobe
  a. Bring adobe from a neighboring vacant lot
  b. Pound it with a mallet
  c. Sift the adobe into a bucket, with the same amount of school clay
  d. Cut straw into fine pieces and add to the adobe
  e. Mix with water
  f. Let set over night

---

[1] Idella Purnell. *The Wishing Owl*. New York: The Macmillan Company, 1931.

2. Make brick molds
  a. Cut two strips 7″ x ½″ x ¼″.
  b. Cut four strips 1″ x ½″ x ¼″ (called blocks for convenience).
  c. Make molds for three bricks by nailing the blocks to the strips at equal intervals. Each brick then will be 2″ x 1″ x ½″.

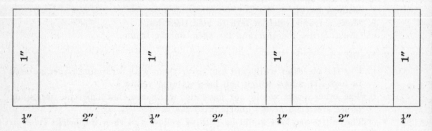

3. Make the bricks
  a. Press the adobe-clay mixture into the molds
  b. Smooth the bottom and top
  c. Run a knife around the edges so the brick will loosen easily when dry
  d. Let dry for twenty-four hours in the sun
  e. Tap the molds and the bricks will fall out

4. Build the house
  a. Lay the bricks alternately, beginning at one corner with the side of a brick in the first row and the end of a brick in the second row, etc. When placing the bricks at the corners make a whole brick come to the end, rather than using a half brick
  b. Mix a thin mortar of adobe to put the bricks together
  c. Make careful plans for the house
  d. Construct the house
  e. Use corrugated cardboard for the roof. Paint it red so it will resemble tiles
  f. Paint the house yellow

5. Make furniture for the house

6. People the house and yard with figures made of pipe-stem cleaners
  a. Wind the arms, legs, and body with yarn to make the figures more durable
  b. Use a large bead (wooden) for the head
  c. Pieces of wood or pliable lead for feet
  d. Make the appropriate clothing

The teacher re-read parts of the third chapter of *The Burro's Moneybag* to help in playing a market scene. The class played going on the long trek from the hills to the market which ends in a procession by the time of the arrival at the final destination.

March 16—Friday

In order to begin actual construction of the large house and the miniature, it was necessary for the children to supplement the teacher's materials. Various members promised to bring oatmeal boxes, adobe, a piece of door screen to use when sifting the adobe, straw, and a bucket. These were listed on the board and left all day as reminders.

Groupings were made for the work period on Monday. The children decided that there must be groups to be responsible for each of the following:

1. House—framework
2. Tiles
3. Plans for the miniature house
4. Brick samples for the walls
5. Brick molds
6. Cut straw
7. Pound adobe to get the lumps out
8. Work on the large 24" x 36" map

The teacher chose a captain for each working group and the captain called for volunteers or chose particularly good workers. The captain then made a list of his helpers for Monday.

In addition, small sheets of pencil paper were passed upon which each child wrote his name and (1) What I expect to do Monday for work period, and (2) Materials I think I shall need which I cannot find. These slips were returned to the teacher in order that she might check materials which she had to furnish or procure from the supply closet, and to know exactly what each child would do on Monday morning.

The teacher read from *The Burro's Moneybag*.

March 19—Monday

The list of committee members was written on the board by the teacher to help poor memories, and to assist the teacher in keeping an accurate check on the work. This device was used almost every day during the work period.

The class worked in the groups mentioned above, for 40 minutes. A ten minute clean-up period followed, in which each captain was responsible for his committee and their materials. A discussion period followed, at which time the class considered the work done, brought up problems which had to be settled before work could continue the next day, and talked over any problems of discipline which had come up during the period. The class worked out a set of standards which they hoped they would be able to attain.

STANDARDS FOR OUR WORK PERIOD

We will:

1. Talk only to our group
2. Talk only about our work
3. Speak softly
4. Try to find our own materials
5. Use our time wisely
6. Clean up when it is time

These standards were printed in manuscript writing on a large piece of tagboard and pinned to the top of the blackboard as a reminder. If someone were too noisy he was quietly and courteously reminded by a classmate at the time, or if the offense was great, the subject was brought up at discussion time and disposed of by the children in so far as possible. A number of cases of sufficient severity or continued offenses caused the children to decide that since it was a privilege to have a free work period nearly every day, the loss of that period would make the offender realize what he had been doing and try to remedy his mistakes. Depriving a child of the privileges was found to be very effective in improving his conduct.

A suggestion was made by the teacher that if during the work period any child had a problem which had to be settled at that moment in order that he might continue his work, he should ring the bell and present the problem to the class at that time and ask for a solution. Often a time-keeper was chosen who rang the bell at the proper time for clean-up. This relieved the teacher.

Again slips of paper were given to the class on which each wrote his name, and (1) What I expect to do tomorrow, (2) Materials I will need. This procedure was carried out every day for a while. Later it was done only when new groupings were made, or when the teacher felt it was necessary for her to check groups or provide materials.

Spelling words for the week included *mañana, adobe, adios, muchas gracias.*

The teacher read from *The Burro's Moneybag.*

A scene showing the activities about the Mexican home was played for the Third Grade class. Of course there were very few materials which could be used, as the class had had only one work period. The children decided that they really needed to know more Mexican expressions. The teacher brought a railroad folder in which were the ordinary expressions needed by those who travel in Mexico. Some of them were listed on the board to be learned, such as:

Como esta usted?_____How are you?
Muy bien, gracias_____Very well, thank you.
Buenas dias_____Good day.
Muchas gracias_____Many thanks.
Bueno _____Good.
El libro_____The book.
Adios _____Good bye.
Amigo _____Friend.

March 21 and 22—Wednesday and Thursday

Some of the children became so interested in the furniture to be made for the house that the problem of, "What kind of furniture do the lower class homes have?" was asked and *The Mexican Twins*[1] was read by the class to find an answer. Lists of furniture were made and discussed by the class. Then each child tried to decide the problem, "What furniture shall we have in our house?" The space limited the furniture and definite plans began as to the actual construction. The

---

[1] Lucy Fitch Perkins. *The Mexican Twins.* Boston: Houghton Mifflin Company, 1915.

class wanted a rough table, chair, cupboard, a shelf for a shrine, a brasero, a metate, (which they already had), petates, an oil can for storage purposes, and decorations of peppers and corn hanging from the rafters.

An oil can seemed to be all that was necessary for the children to furnish, beyond the materials which were already in the room.

The work period continued both days with the same groupings as indicated on Monday. As usual, questions, problems, discussions, and comments upon citizenship followed each period.

The children were not satisfied with the map slide which Floyd had made, and when one arrived from the Visual Education Department they decided that he should use it in the still film machine to improve his map.

When reading from *The Burro's Moneybag* on Monday, reference had been made to "Popo," causing a great deal of interest. Included in the box with the map slide was one of the volcano Popocateptl which answered previous questions. The teacher read the legend of the "Moon Princess" from *The Talking Bird* [1] which tells of the volcanoes Iztaccihuatl and Popocatepetl.

March 23—Friday

The work period continued as before, followed by discussion.

The children played scenes which centered about the trips into the mountains to get charcoal to use in the brasero. Since little was known about charcoal, research reading was done in order to make the play better. The teacher had prepared a card file of annotated references for her own benefit. The children had access to this and often found the book and page references for themselves.

The teacher continued reading from *The Burro's Moneybag*.

March 26 to 30—Easter Vacation

April 2 to 6—Monday to Friday

The work period continued each day. Some of the work was being brought to completion by various groups, so Friday's discussion period was given to the reorganization of groups by the children and the teacher. This included personnel of the groups as well.

This week's spelling included the words *samples, time-keeper, discussion, metate, petate, brasero, shrine.*

The teacher read more from *The Burro's Moneybag*. The last chapter read told of the hero and his grandfather going to visit a wealthy uncle in Mexico City. This gave the children the idea that

---

[1] Idella Purnell and J. M. Weatherwax. *The Talking Bird*. New York: The Macmillan Company, 1930.

they would like to have another kind of house in which to play, but space in the classroom did not permit. They decided that a frieze might be painted upon some large sheets of wrapping paper and pinned to the top of the blackboard. This might be a courtyard scene, since the finer homes in Mexico always include one. They had seen pictures of these homes and they seemed very inviting. Someone asked the question, "Why do the hacienda and city homes have these courtyards?" This was answered by reading from books and by the teacher reading "The Queen and the Giant" from *The Talking Bird*.

The play of the week included selling the charcoal which was secured in the mountains, and playing market.

During the free reading hour in the school library the teacher read "The Prince and the Humming Bird" (The Ceremony of the Corn) from *The Wishing Owl*.

April 9—Monday

The work period was carried on by groups centered about the following outline placed on the board by the teacher:

1. Furniture
   Make the brasero and the shelf for the shrine
2. Tiles
3. Adobe bricks
4. Miniature house
   Construct it. Draw definite plans.
5. Walls
6. Dishes
   Clay and adobe mixed
7. Molds
8. Maps
9. Plans for the middle class frieze

On this day the children played going for charcoal, for they enjoyed the long trip up the mountain, watching the charcoal burners, and bringing the fuel down to be used in the home and to sell, and played it often. Members of the family who remained at home carried on such household duties as cleaning the house, making tortillas, getting vegetables ready for market, and caring for the livestock. The spelling included *chili peppers, furniture, storage, bueno.*

April 10—Tuesday

The work period continued the same as on Monday. The house was progressing nicely and the class began to wish for the clothing they had planned to make. The teacher had rearranged the bulletin board and pinned up pictures of the five types of clothing which are typical of the Mexican plateau section; the every-day clothes of the working class, for both men and women; the national fiesta dress for women, (called China Poblona); the national fiesta dress for men (Charro); and the beautiful party dresses, including the lace mantillas and elaborate shawls for those who can afford them. The problem arose, "Why do the Mexican people wear different kinds of clothing?" Reading from books followed.

Other words were added to the spelling for the week—*serape, reboso, poncho, sombrero, fiesta.*

April 11 to 13—Wednesday to Friday

The work groups had to be reorganized slightly before tasks were begun for the day. The following guide was put on the blackboard:

1. Furniture
2. House in general (repairs)
3. Make back walls
4. Brasero
5. Make front outside walls
6. Molds
7. Tiles
8. Plans for middle class house (frieze)
9. Cupboard

The class decided to study the clothing of the men of the working class first. They listed the articles worn and each chose one of the following subjects about which to write a report: (1) serapes, (2) sombreros, (3) shirts, (4) trousers and sash, (5) sandals. The teacher passed books marked with small slips of paper to the children, according to their reading ability. Each child made brief notes on small sheets of paper. On Thursday the reports were written from the notes while the teacher went about the room helping and correcting when needed. The following day the reports were copied in ink in note-books, and illustrated by drawings two inches square. The children who wrote upon the same subject met in a committee to read the reports and select the one to present to the class. When it was approved by the class it was put into a Clothing Booklet as a permanent record.

On Wednesday the teacher read "The Bird of Love" from *The Talking Bird.*

April 16 to 19—Monday to Thursday

This week's work consisted of a work period each day, as indicated in the previous week's write-up. During Monday's work, two boys were making a bowl out of a gourd and had sawed off the neck. George brought the end of this tan, dried up gourd to the teacher and said, "It looks like a wild tulip just about ready to bloom." Several children heard him and agreed that it did.

The same procedure was used for writing reports on the Indian women's clothing as was used in writing on the men's. Each child was required to use at least two reference books. On Thursday the best report for a reboso, a dress, and sandals was read to the class and put into the Clothing Booklet.

The teacher read from *The Burro's Moneybag.*

The children made up some adventures similar to those of the hero and played a street scene in Mexico City.

April 20 and 23—Friday and Monday

The class worked so steadily and efficiently that the house and furniture were nearly finished.

In making their first reports on clothing the children had written on only one article of clothing. When they came to the reports on the *Charros*, they felt that by using at least two or more books they could write a complete description of that costume. The reports of the Charro costume were begun Friday and continued on Monday. These reports gave an opportunity for learning paragraphing.

The records *La Golondrina*[1] and *La Paloma*[2] were played during the music period. On Monday, the words for *La Golondrina* were taught as a rote song.

Spelling words included *gourd, chili peppers, storage, tortillas, Charro, China Poblona.*

April 24—Tuesday

One wall of the house became torn and it was necessary to make another one. This time no one was working on the frame-work and the paper was pasted together, fastened to the frame, and the painting was done inside the house. The plan for the middle class courtyard was made. Samples of calcimine colors to use on the frieze were tried on a sheet of daily newspaper.

Research work continued on the Charro reports.

April 25—Wednesday

During the work period those groups which had finished made samples of tile designs for the courtyard floor of the frieze. Another group finished and worked on designs to put around the edge of the yellow cloth on the table made by the boys.

During the research period a few finished their reports and devoted the remainder of the period to free reading about Mexico in general.

The class was given mimeographed copies of the words to *Cielito Lindo*[3] to put into the music section of their loose-leafed notebooks. This helped the children to learn the song. *La Golondrina* was also practiced.

The teacher read "The Vegetable Tree" from *The Bright Feather.*

April 26—Thursday

Another grouping was made and posted on the blackboard, although it was to last only a few days. Each group was responsible for one of the items:

1. Side walls
2. Pictures of designs for the tile courtyard
3. Designs for the tablecloth
4. Map
5. Bricks
6. Miniature house

---

[1] *La Golondrina.* Victor Phonograph Record No. 21235.
[2] *La Paloma.* Victor Phonograph Record No. 20172.
[3] *Cielito Lindo.* Victor Phonograph Record No. 21235.

Most of the Charro reports were finished, checked for neatness, and read to the class. The best one was chosen for the booklet. Those who had not finished their reports continued working while the choosing was being done.

The class divided into two parts to write reports on the China Poblona and upper class party dresses. The same standards were used as for the Charro reports. Research work was begun.

April 27 and 30— Friday and Monday

The China Poblona and upper class party dress reports were completed, checked, and chosen for the book.

Since there had been some difficulty about using the best words when writing the reports, the teacher planned a specific learning lesson to give the children practice in selecting the best word to express a given meaning. The children were asked to read from Franck's *Mexico*[1] about city houses. They were then given a mimeographed sheet with a list of sentences offering multiple choice of words to underline. Following are two of the sentences:

The daytime living room of a Mexican house is called:

> patio
> porch
> sun-parlor
> courtyard

The roof of the house is made of:

> tiles
> bricks
> lath
> shingles

The victrola was brought and *La Golondrina* played during the music appreciation period.

The work period each day continued as on Thursday.

Spelling for this week included *sandal, bolero, mantilla, reports.*

May 1 and 2—Tuesday and Wednesday

The type of clothing which each person wished to make was listed in detail on the board by the teacher as the children recalled what they had learned from writing their reports. Following is a list of the articles which were made.

---

[1] Harry Alverson Franck. *Mexico.* Dansville, N. Y.: F. A. Owen Publishing Company, 1929.

EVERY DAY CLOTHING OF THE WORKING CLASS

Men

1. Serape
2. Sandals
3. White cotton pants
4. Blouse
5. Sash
6. Sombrero

Women

1. Reboso
2. Skirt
3. Waist
4. Sandals
5. Sash

NATIONAL FIESTA DRESS

Men—Charro

1. Coat of bolero type
2. Trousers
3. Shirt
4. Sash and tie
5. Sombrero
6. Serape

Women—China Poblona

1. Reboso
2. Blouse
3. Skirt
4. Sash
5. Jewelry
6. Vest

UPPER CLASS PARTY DRESS

Women

1. Mantilla
2. Shawl
3. Dress with ruffled skirt
4. Comb
5. Jewelry

In preparation each child drew a 9″ x 12″ illustration in crayola of the clothing which he expected to make. Five members of the class chose to finish the miniature house and work on the frieze rather than make clothing. It so happened that four of the five members of the class were Japanese children who were very timid and self-conscious and did not care to enter into the play "If I have to say anything." Later on they were persuaded to join their classmates in the play, although they lacked the proper clothing.

Since the house and its furnishings were now completed, the children wanted to play more often than before. Free play of household duties was carried on Tuesday.

May 3—Thursday

The general plan for making the clothing was:

1. Make the designs of the way the clothing should look
2. Make the patterns
3. Dye your own materials (if you need to)
4. Make your own clothing

Since some of the clothing, such as a reboso, or a sash, did not require the use of a definite pattern, actual work was begun during Thursday's work period. The class was now reorganized in groups for the seventh time. Each group was responsible for one of the following tasks:

1. Every day clothing of men. Make designs for the serapes on 12" x 18" manila paper.
2. Fiesta clothing of men. Make designs for the serapes as above.
3. Every day clothing of women. Dye rebosos or skirts.
4. Fiesta clothing for women. Make waist patterns, or dye waist material if the color wanted is in the dye pot.
5. Upper class party dresses for women. Draw designs for yard-square shawls.
6. Miniature house.
7. Courtyard frieze.

May 4 to 8—Friday to Tuesday

The same grouping continued, although the work within a group rapidly changed as the various articles were finished.

Courtesy of Oakland City Schools

Children-Made Native Costumes for Use in Dramatization

A roll of still films on Tuesday clarified ideas on clothing—the general appearance, and the way it is worn.

A sewing machine was made available in the room and the consent of parents was required before the children were allowed to use it. Only one parent refused permission. Most of the children had had a little experience with a machine, although a few had to be taught how to use it. The boys, of course, made their own clothing and most of them became as proficient with the machine as some of the girls.   As we only had one machine and there were thirty children wanting to use it, some of the sewing necessarily was done at home.

Spelling words—*permission, sewing machine, patterns.*

May 9 to 11—Wednesday to Friday

The first part of the library hour was devoted to the teacher reading a few pages from *Lucita*[1] by Gaines, to introduce the book on Mexico to the children.

The work period each day continued as before.   When there was a play period, the children eagerly donned finished articles of clothing.

The teacher read "The Eagle and the Snake" from *The Talking Bird,* which tells of the Aztecs finding the site for their new home.

Because of the interest aroused about the capital, the class wanted to know "Why is Mexico City such an interesting city today?"   They had enjoyed writing clothing reports to put into a booklet, and now wished to write another one telling about the sights near Mexico City. This time they planned a program in which one child from each group would tell the rest of the class what his group had learned on the topic. Thus, each child was allowed to choose the thing he thought was the most interesting.   Topics to choose from were: (1) Pyramids, (2) Xochimilco, (3) Markets, (4) National Theatre, (5) Chapultepec Park, (6) Records left by the Aztecs.

May 14—Monday

The work period continued as outlined, and research reading from two or more books about the sights near Mexico City was begun.

Interest in the clothing had been so great that *The Burro's Money-bag* had been neglected, but not forgotten, and it was called for again.

More things to play with called for more time to play, and no one lost an opportunity.   This morning two different groups played freely. The first played in the house, followed by the second group, who gave their version of a typical street scene.   The class liked to play market and street scenes, as it gave so many a chance to play, and to use all the different costumes.

Spelling for the week included *pyramids, cactus, eagle, Aztecs, records, designs.*

May 15 to 18—Tuesday to Friday

By this time several children had finished their clothing and the eighth grouping of the class was made as follows:

---

[1] Ruth Louise Gaines.   *Lucita.*   Chicago: Rand McNally and Company, 1913.

Each group was to be responsible for one of the following tasks:

1. Clothing
2. Miniature house
3. Frieze
4. Repair house
5. Illustrations for the new booklet
6. Put the design on the tablecloth

Spelling for this week included—*exhibits, important, illustrate, repair.*

During the play period, a group of girls made the outline of a story which would include all classes of people. They called it "Visiting the Poor."

Work on the reports went on as before. As the reports were completed the children looked for illustrative materials to use when the talks were given. They looked through cans of still films, boxes of slides, books for pictures, a large box of loose pictures, and exhibits.

The principal came in and told the children a story about Montezuma.

May 23—Wednesday

Work on the clothing, frieze, and miniature house continued.

The reports were copied into the notebooks and illustrations drawn on each. Pictures and other illustrative materials were selected and the class met in the groups formed about their topics, with their chairmen. Each child read his story to his committee and the best was chosen to be presented to the class.

May 24—Thursday

One of the teachers in the school had been to Mexico and loaned us her set of photographs, consisting of some 100 pictures. Part of them were shown to the class in a picture game.

The work period continued in the same grouping as before.

The children wished to paint Mexican scenes. Three groups of children in costume were posed: (1) *Going to Market*—A boy with seven sombreros piled one on top of the other, another boy carrying a heavy bag of charcoal, and a girl with a huge basket of tomatoes on her head. They stood on tables at the side of the room. (2) *Fiesta Dancers*—A Charro man and a China Poblona girl stood on another table. (3) *In the Courtyard*—A Charro gentleman in a black and red suit stood playing a guitar to entertain two upper class ladies in their party finery who were seated in the courtyard of the middle class home. The figures were filled in, but no attempt was made to put in an appropriate background. The class was to try to:

1. Fill the figures in solidly without any linings.
2. Make the figures overlap.
3. Think of dark against light.
4. Keep the colors bright.

Afterward, others dressed and played "Visiting the Poor."

May 25—Friday

This morning the children had a work period; examined the rest of the pictures left by the visitor; listened to a chapter from *The Burro's Moneybag;* and did some research reading on the important cities and towns of Mexico.

The latter information gained from the reading was to be used on the pictorial map.

During the music appreciation period, the records of *La Golondrina* and *La Paloma* were played, and later some of the children began to learn the folk dance for *La Paloma.*

The class worked on their paintings again, by filling in the appropriate background.

May 28—Monday

The story of "The Chewing Gum Tree" was read by the class and as a result of the discussion which followed and the research reading on Friday, came the question, "What are the principal industries or products of these important cities?" and "What makes them so important?" These were listed and when a visitor (the lady who loaned us the photographs) came in she told about the industries and products which she had seen in various towns, cities, and villages of Mexico. The children asked her many questions and were particularly interested in the woman who came with her—a Mexican lady of the neighborhood who had lived most of her life in Mexico City. She, too, talked to the children a little, and offered to bring some things for them to see.

One member of the class brought some other Mexican records for us to hear—*The National Anthem* of Mexico, and *Las Cholas.* The class again practiced the folk dance for *La Paloma* in the classroom.

The paintings which had been done on Thursday were pinned above the blackboard and discussed by the teacher and the children. Suggestions for improvements were made, such as: "Put in an outline to make the scene stand out." "Repaint that section with a brighter color." "Put in more detail." "Cut off that poor part." Since there were some suggestions for each person, the papers were given out and improved. The best were mounted on large sheets of bogus by the teacher and pinned to the large section of cork above the blackboard. Others were put into the Finished Art Book, a large 12" x 18" cardboard folder, and those not completed were left in the Unfinished Book for the owner to work on during free time.

May 29 to June 4—Tuesday to Monday

These days continued with the work period; research reading on the principal cities and the oral reports about the sights near Mexico

City. Jean told the legend of the pyramids with her report—"The Dwarf Who Became King," from *The Wishing Owl*. Others showed pictures, drawings, exhibits, and one group showed slides in the still film machine.

Work on the city map was begun.

Spelling words included—*miniature, charcoal*.

The end of the term was drawing near and the class became interested in having a fiesta.

On Wednesday the teacher read the Aztec story about pulque, "The Green Serpents," from *The Talking Bird*.

The Mexican woman who previously visited brought a complete Indian dress, some money and typical Mexican toys for the children to see. She told about the things and left them for the children to see later.

June 5—Tuesday

Many of the children were finished with their clothing and a new work grouping had to be made. Tasks in connection with the following were to be undertaken by each group:

1. Clothing.
2. Miniature house.
3. Frieze.
4. Adobe for a miniature market.
5. Gourds (a string of them to be painted for decorations).
6. Illustrations (for the gourds).
7. Map—showing the principal cities and their industries or products.

The class wished to give a play of "Visiting the Poor" when they had their fiesta day. As the children decided on the continuity the teacher made notes on the board.

Scene I. American tourists come to visit a Mexican family on the outskirts of Mexico City. They are met at the station by members of the family. They remark on the sights as they walk the two blocks from the station to the house where they are greeted by the rest of the family and sit in the cool courtyard to rest. A servant brings them glasses of pulque to drink. A neighbor lady comes to call and relate the news of the village. They all decide to take the Smith family with them the next day to visit a poor family who live on the extreme edge of the village.

Scene II. The Smiths and Varelas go through the village the next morning on their way to the Gonzales home. They shop in the market, and since it is Wednesday there is a great deal of activity about the plaza. Part of the family return to their home with their purchases and the rest go on their way. They travel in the family automobile. When they arrive, the Indian family is engaged in various household tasks, and since Pedro has worked at the Varela home he is much pleased at their visit. They present the family with corn for their tortillas, vegetables, fruit, charcoal, and clothing. In return, the Indian boys, although awed by the presence of the Americans, play on their guitars and sing for their guests. The Varelas invite the Gonzales family to come to their home the following Saturday for a fiesta, and hire the Gonzales to cook the tortillas for the entire company. They leave and return by the way of the market place.

Scene III—Fiesta Day. The class got to this scene and had to confess that they did not know what went on at a fiesta. They supposed the Mexicans probably ate and danced, but what else? The question was left open until the children could find out.

The children thought it would be fun to make a miniature market out of the adobe and clay mixture and began to make plans. "How shall we make our market? Where? Just how does a real Mexican market look?" These and other questions were answered by some mimeographed material, "The Mexican Shopping News," and by books and pictures. The teacher had rearranged the back bulletin board so that it contained only pictures pertaining to markets.

Plans for the market were developed, both for work and personnel:

1. A sombrero market
2. Pottery
3. Fowls
4. Serapes
5. Food
6. Baskets and toys
7. Burros
8. Customers
9. Salesmen
10. Other livestock

Each group would be responsible for making the articles, the salesman or saleslady, and the awnings or place to display the wares. Anyone who finished might make a miniature customer. The customers and salesmen were to be approximately six inches high and the other things in proportion. The awnings might be of the umbrella type, rectangular, square; made of wood, or just a mat on the ground without a covering. These things were made of heavy paper painted with calcimine. The market was to be placed on two primary tables and each group was responsible for arranging their articles.

June 6—Wednesday

Plans were made for the fiesta on Tuesday of the last week, with only a few invited guests; the principal, the university supervisor, and the physical education teacher.

The first scene of the play was practiced in costume.

The *La Paloma* dance was practiced and a child who knew the dance *La Cucharacha* began to teach it to the class.

Reading for information about the market was continued.

The teacher read "The Ants and the Milpa" from *The Bright Feather,* another legend of corn.

June 7—Thursday

The work period was carried on with the ninth grouping of responsibilities:

1. Clothing—a few children still had not finished
2. Miniature house
3. Invitations and place cards. Each child was to make his own card, but a committee was making samples.
4. Clay modeling for the miniature markets. (See sub-grouping for June 5)
5. Awnings for the markets
6. Finish the paintings from pose
7. Gourds

A table was arranged with a number of very lovely pieces of Mexican pottery. These were admired by the children, who soon asked, "How do the Mexicans make their pottery?" Reading from a mimeographed article called "Bowls, Bottles and Jugs" followed.

The second scene of the play was practiced and the class wished to go on with the third. It was decided to find out about a fiesta on Friday.

The two folk dances were practiced.

By this time Joe Bill had become so proficient with his harmonica that he often accompanied the children when they decided to sing while playing.

June 8—Friday

The work period went on with the same groupings as on Thursday. Of course the personnel of the groups changed slightly as a child would complete the clay articles, but it remained very much the same for a few days.

"What do the Mexicans do at a Fiesta?" was answered by the teacher reading the last chapter of *The Burro's Moneybag,* and the children reading from mimeographed material, "Fiesta Time in San Miguel." The class planned the last scene for their play.

> *Scene III—The Fiesta.* There would be great excitement in the courtyard, for guests would be arriving; the Gonzales family with their baskets of tortillas and Senora Martinez coming to help. Later, Senor Martinez would arrive from his journey to Mexico City and tell about the bull fight he had attended, the boys of the family would go into the yard to play, others would chat about the doings of the day, the noted fiesta dancers would come from Mexico City to dance, and there would be food, more dancing, and songs.

June 11 to 20—Monday to Wednesday

The last eight days of the term the groups were changed daily, because:

1. The market required:
   - a. Clay modeling
   - b. Painting, with calcimine
   - c. Making awnings
   - d. Setting up of the markets

2. As an individual finished or waited a turn to model, paint or shellac, he often worked on designs for place cards, which he made later; or, played with a few others in the house in free play; or, played with the clay articles in free market play; or, played with the miniature house and its occupants.

3. Plans were necessary to:
   a. Arrange for the fiesta day
   b. Prepare the menu for the fiesta

4. "Thank-you" letters were written to people who had helped with the study of Mexico.

Each child wrote on his slip of paper what he expected to do the next day. Each day the teacher put the work-groups on the board according to the choices.

The spelling words for the week included—*shellac, awning, place-cards.*

The class practiced the play in costume each day. This included the songs and dances which had been learned.

The Fiesta Day committee made plans for Tuesday, working out the schedule and duties for each member of the class, including the teacher. The question arose, "What foods would the Mexicans really eat if they were at a fiesta?" To get the answer to this question the children went to the Mexican grocery in the next block, inquired from their Mexican visitor, and read from the books in the room. Then the following meal was decided upon:

tortillas	vegetable salad
chili sauce	watermelon
frijoles	fruits for the end of their fiesta

Two of the mothers were asked to cook the beans and help serve, and the Mexican visitor volunteered to make the chili sauce and serve it in a real stone chili bowl from Mexico City.

The foods were to be brought on Monday. So much was brought that the teacher did not have to purchase anything extra or call on the mothers who had volunteered to supply the extras!

Committees for Fiesta Day were assigned to perform the following tasks:

1. Move part of the desks, which were screwed on runners with two sections to a row, out into the hall, then bring in tables and chairs to seat forty. These committee members were also to return the tables, chairs, and seats afterward.
2. Make the vegetable salad with the help of the two mothers. This committee was to go to the cafeteria.
3. Make the salad dressing. This committee would go to the cafeteria also.
4. Wait on the tables. The members of this committee would have to make their caps and aprons early in the morning. They would use crepe paper.

5. Set the tables. This committee would put crepe paper on the tables for tablecloths, using red, green, and white, which are the national colors of Mexico. They would use figures from the market for decorations in the middle of each group of tables.
6. Clean off the tables before returning them to the library.
7. Wash the forks. Paper plates would be used to avoid too much dish washing, although there were many volunteers.
8. Straighten up the house.
9. Clean the blackboards.
10. Run errands.

June 19—Tuesday: Fiesta Day

Dawn arrived bright and early for many that morning, for when the teacher arrived before eight children loaded down with watermelons and fruits were waiting to get into the building. The various bags of fruits and vegetables were sorted to turn over to the various committees. Those needing caps and aprons made them and the seats were moved.

Children who were unoccupied at the time read, drew, or played in the house. Everyone soon had on his best fiesta clothes in anticipation.

By 11:30 everything was ready and the guests had arrived. Lunch was a merry time and extra rebosos or mantillas were found for all of the guests, who were soon caught in the spirit of the occasion. Those who were not on clean-up duties went out at 12:30 with the physical education teacher for their regular lesson, still in fiesta clothing and spirit.

From one to three o'clock the fiesta continued with the play, its freedom of action, conversation, dance, and song. Only the two mothers looked on. The afternoon was concluded with fruit and the cactus candy which the teacher passed as a surprise. The fiesta might have lasted on into the night as true fiestas do, but three o'clock came and the children wore their Mexican clothing home for the last time.

The next morning it took only one hour to take down a typical Mexican Indian home and distribute the furnishings, which had taken four months of careful planning and long hours of hard work to build.

CONCLUSION

Although this chronological report has been given to clarify the points made on page 217, it should be recognized that there were certain academic outcomes of the work as a result of the integration of the skills with the socialized activities of the group. Through the daily reading, either in problem solving activities or specific reading enterprises, as well as free reading, the class gained ten months on the average in reading skill from February to June. Normal gain would have been five months.

BIBLIOGRAPHY [1]

For Children

AITCHISON, A. E. *North America by Plane and Train.* Indianapolis: Bobbs-Merrill Company, 1931.

ALLEN, N. B. *Geographical and Industrial Studies: North America.* Boston: Ginn and Company, 1922.

ATWOOD, W. W. and THOMAS, H. G. *The Americas.* Boston: Ginn and Company, 1929.

BANKS, H. W. *Story of Mexico Including the "Boys' Prescott."* New York: Frederick A. Stokes Company, 1926.

BARROWS, H. H. *Geography, Southern Lands.* New York: Silver, Burdett and Company, 1929.

BAYLOR, F. C. *Juan and Juanita.* Boston: Houghton Mifflin Company, 1926.

CARPENTER, F. G. *North America.* New York: American Book Company, 1922.

CHAMBERLAIN, J. F. and CHAMBERLAIN, A. H. *North America.* New York: The Macmillan Company, 1927.

CLARK, M. G. and GORDY, W. F. *What Men From Europe Brought to America.* New York: Charles Scribner's Sons, 1929.

COATSWORTH, E. J. *Boy with the Parrot.* New York: The Macmillan Company, 1930.

ECKFORD, EUGENIA. *Wonder Windows.* New York: E. P. Dutton and Company, 1931.

FRANCK, H. A. *Mexico and Central America.* Dansville, N. Y.: F. A. Owen Publishing Company, 1927.

GAINES, RUTH. *Lucita.* Chicago: Rand McNally and Company, 1913.

GAINES, RUTH. *Village Shield.* New York: E. P. Dutton and Company, 1917.

GAY, ZHENYA. *Pancho and His Burro.* New York: William Morrow and Company, 1930.

HALLECK, R. P. and FRANTZ, JULIETTE. *Founders of Our Nation.* New York: American Book Company, 1929.

HUNTINGTON, ELLSWORTH. *Living Geography, Book I.* "How Countries Differ." Book II, "Why Countries Differ." New York: The Macmillan Company, 1932.

JANVIER, T. A. *Aztec Treasure House.* New York: Harper and Brothers, 1890.

KELTY, M. G. *Beginnings of American People and Nation.* Boston: Ginn and Company, 1930.

KELTY, M. G. *Growth of American People and Nation.* Boston: Ginn and Company, 1931.

LANG, ANDREW. *Conquest of Montezuma's Empire.* New York: Longmans, Green and Company, 1928.

LEFFERTS, WALTER. *Neighbors North and South.* Philadelphia: J. B. Lippincott Company, 1926.

McLEAN, R. N. and CRAWFORD, M. L. *Jumping Beans; Stories about Mexicans in the United States.* New York: Friendship Press, 1929.

McMURRY, K. F. and PARKINS, A. E. *Advanced Geography I.* New York: The Macmillan Company, 1922.

MITCHELL, L. S. *North America.* New York: The Macmillan Company, 1931.

MOON, G. P. *Nadita.* Garden City, New York: Doubleday, Doran and Company, Inc., 1929.

MORROW, E. R. *Painted Pig.* New York: Alfred A. Knopf, Inc., 1930.

---

[1] Prepared by Rosemary Livsey, Los Angeles Public Library.

NIDA, W. L. and WEBB, V. L. *Our Country Past and Present.* Chicago: Scott, Foresman and Company, 1930.

O'SHEA, M. V. and Others. *World Book Encyclopedia,* Vol. 7. Chicago: W. F. Quarrie and Company, 1931.

PERDUE, H. A. *How Other Children Live.* Chicago: Rand McNally and Company, 1927.

PERKINS, L. F. *The Mexican Twins.* Boston: Houghton Mifflin Company, 1915.

PURNELL, IDELLA and WEATHERWAX, J. M. *The Talking Bird.* New York: The Macmillan Company, 1930.

PURNELL, IDELLA. *The Wishing Owl.* New York: The Macmillan Company, 1931.

RHOADES, DOROTHY. *The Bright Feather.* Garden City, New York: Doubleday, Doran and Company, 1932.

SMALLIDGE, O. E. *Finding America.* Boston: Houghton Mifflin Company, 1929.

SMITH, N. A. *Bee of the Cactus Country.* Boston: Houghton Mifflin Company, 1932.

SMITH, J. R. *Human Geography.* Philadelphia: John C. Winston Company, 1931.

SMITH, S. C. *Made in Mexico.* New York: Alfred A. Knopf, Inc., 1930.

STARR, FREDERICK. *Strange Peoples.* Boston: D. C. Heath and Company, 1901.

THOMAS, M. L. *The Burro's Moneybag.* New York: The Abingdon Press, 1931.

WHEELER, I. W. *Playing with Clay.* New York: The Macmillan Company, 1927.

For Teachers

BANCROFT, H. H. *History of Mexico.* New York: Bancroft-Whitney Company, 1914.

BARNARD, E. F. *How the Old World Found the New.* Boston: Ginn and Company, 1929.

BEALS, CARLETON. *Mexican Maze.* Philadelphia: J. B. Lippincott Company, 1931.

BIART, LUCIEN. *The Aztecs.* Chicago: A. C. McClurg and Company, 1900.

BRENNER, ANITA. *Your Mexican Holiday.* New York: G. P. Putnam's Sons, 1932.

BYNNER, WITTER. *Indian Earth.* New York: Alfred A. Knopf, Inc., 1929.

CARPENTER, F. G. *Mexico.* Garden City, New York: Doubleday, Doran and Company, 1924.

CARR, HARRY. *Old Mother Mexico.* Boston: Houghton Mifflin Company, 1931.

CHASE, STUART. *Mexico.* New York: The Macmillian Company, 1931.

COOK, K. M. *The House of the People; an Account of Mexico's New Schools in Action.* (U. S. Bureau of Education Bulletin, 1932, No. 11.) Washington, D. C.: Government Printing Office, 1932.

d' HARNONCOURT, RENE. *Mexicana, a Book of Pictures.* New York: Alfred A. Knopf. Inc., 1931.

GODOY, MERCEDES. *When I Was a Girl in Mexico.* Boston: Lothrop, Lee and Shepard Company, 1919.

HASBROUCK, L. S. *Mexico from Cortez to Carranza.* New York: D. Appleton and Company, 1918.

JAMES, G. W. *Indian Basketry, and How to Make Other Baskets.* Pasadena: Author, 1903.

JORDAN, D. S. and CATHER, K. D. *North America.* Yonkers-on-Hudson, New York: The World Book Company, 1925.

LAWRENCE, D. H. *Mornings in Mexico.* New York: Alfred A. Knopf, Inc., 1927.

MORRIS, A. A. *Digging in Yucatan.* Garden City, New York: Doubleday, Doran and Company, 1931.

National Geographic Magazine. XXI (December 1910) ; XXX (July 1916) ; XXXVI (October 1919) ; XXXVIII (July 1920) ; XLI (February 1922) ; XLII (November 1922) ; XLIII (March 1923) ; XLIV (August 1923) ; LI (May 1927) ; LVII (June 1930) ; LXV (March 1934).

Pageant of America. Vol. 1, pt. 3, "Spain and the New World." New Haven : Yale University Press, 1929.

PAN AMERICAN UNION. *Mexico City.* Washington, D. C. : Government Printing Office, 1924.

PAN AMERICAN UNION. *Mexico.* Washington, D. C. : Government Printing Office, 1923.

PRESCOTT, W. H. *The Conquest of Mexico.* N. Y. : The Junior Literary Guild, 1934.

QUINN, VERNON. *Beautiful Mexico.* New York : Frederick A. Stokes Company, 1924.

RUSSELL, PHILIP. *Red Tiger.* New York : Brentano's, 1929.

SHAMBAUGH, M. E. *Folk Festivals for Schools and Playgrounds; Folk Dances and Melodies.* New York : A. S. Barnes and Company, 1932.

SPINDEN, H. J. *Ancient Civilizations of Mexico and Central America.* New York : American Museum of Natural History, 1922.

STULL, DE FOREST. *Our World Today.* Boston : Allyn and Bacon, 1931.

TERRY, T. P. *Guide to Mexico.* Boston : Houghton Mifflin Company, 1930.

WINTER, N. O. *Mexico and Her People of Today.* Boston : L. C. Page and Company, 1907.

WINTERBURN, R. V. *Spanish in the Southwest.* New York : American Book Company, 1903

WYMAN, A. L. *Chef Wyman's Daily Health Menus.* 717 Commercial Exchange Building, Los Angeles : Wyman Book Company, 1927.

CHAPTER XV

TRAINING IN READING SKILLS [1]

GENERAL PROCEDURE

Period for Definite Training

A satisfactory reading program for children in the middle grades provides a separate period each day for definite training in the reading skills. This reading period is always a time of concentration and earnest effort, but care is taken to make it also a period that yields satisfaction even to the slow child. To this end materials are selected to meet his interests and needs; and an attitude of cooperation rather than impatience or censure is established, with each child using material adapted to his interest and his needs.

Grouping [2]

The first step in initiating the program of definite training is to test the children, in order to determine their reading grade placements. Standardized reading tests are recommended for the initial testing and for a formal check up later in the term. Resourceful teachers, however, who are not furnished standardized tests, use informal tests. Some of the comprehension checking exercises found at the close of selections in the worktype readers are helpful. Manuals for the basic readers also supply suggestions. The important consideration is that accomplishment should be checked regularly and individual records kept on graphs, or other effective means of recording pupils' progress.

Following an analysis of the results of the test, the children are divided into groups. More than three groups are not practical for the average classroom, but there may be one or two individuals who present special problems and must be handled alone. Instruction should be fitted to the needs of each group. Social characteristics of children need to be taken into consideration in the groupings. The sectioning is flexibly administered, permitting a child to be shifted into whatever division he can work with immediate profit. The number in the slower section should be limited. Assignments to sections should be made with the full cooperation of the children; thus no stigma

---

[1] Contributed by Huberteen Kueneman, Elementary School Supervisor, Santa Ana City Schools.
[2] For a more complete description of grouping children see *Suggested Course of Study in Reading and Literature for Elementary Schools*, State of California Department of Education Bulletin, No. 13, Part II, July 1, 1932, pp. 4–6, 60–61.

is attached to assignment to the slower group, and conversely, no cocksureness results from membership in the superior group.

Range in Abilities

The tests and added observation of the study habits of the children will reveal the range of ability represented in the class. Some children will be unable to read simple content material effectively. Diagnosis must be made to find the cause of the difficulty.[1] Difficulties caused by an impoverished environment, or a foreign language handicap, and those caused by the lack of familiarity with the mechanics of reading should be distinguished. These types of difficulties require different treatment. To remedy the first there should be opportunities for conversation, for observation and experimentation, and the reading of much easy informational material. Children in the second group need also to read easy and interesting material, but have the language background necessary to begin development of reading skills. Pupils who have unusual difficulty in learning to read need the services of a specialist but 90 per cent of the poor readers are in need of the kind of guidance which skillful teachers employ in developmental teaching of reading [2] and should be handled in the classroom.

A certain portion of the class, the Macaulays and the Carlyles, who greatly exceed the normal expectancy in reading, will need little formal drill. Their reading periods may be used for research reading in order to gain varied points of view on a topic, and for the reading of literature, and also for reading to broaden interest. The middle group, too, will read widely in the content fields to gain deeper meanings and to widen their reading interests. Free reading privileges for all children should be liberally provided.

Reading for Specific Purposes

After a study of the range of abilities it will usually be found that for the large majority of children it is necessary to provide a training period in reading which is definitely a teaching period. The teacher devotes all of her time of the period to training children to read for specific purposes and to check their accomplishment. It cannot be over emphasized that the success of this work period depends largely upon the teacher's realization that the development of an ability to read for a given purpose is individual and specific. Following is a list of purposes for which pupils of the intermediate grades should have frequent opportunities to read in the definite training period.

Finding answers to questions

Finding facts related to a given problem

---

[1] *Ibid.*, pp. 85–91.
[2] William S. Gray. "Remedial Reading." *Journal of the National Education Association*, XX (May, 1931), 163.

Grasping main points and supporting details
Selecting passages that describe given characters
Verifying a statement or an opinion
Following directions
Discovering the general significance of a selection
Drawing conclusions from facts presented
Answering judgment questions
Selecting the facts relating to a given problem
Listing steps in a sequence
Preparing an outline
Preparing a summary
Preparing a bibliography
Locating material
Evaluating material
Making notes

Many of the purposes listed above break into several minor purposes. The items given are isolated from all content and the list merely affords a check for the teachers. It is important to remember that a child is taught to read for a given purpose as that purpose develops in a natural situation or shortly afterward, while he still feels the need for practice. It would, therefore, be a questionable procedure for the teacher to follow the order of the above list in determining the exercises for a series of definite training periods. The account below may serve to show how purposes for reading arise in natural situations and that each involves the achievement of several subordinate purposes.

A class has been inducted into the study of the life of the Greeks through the reading and telling of stories by both teacher and pupils. The class decides to carry out some of the activities of the early folk in dramatic play, or rhythmic pantomime. Definite information in regard to costumes, other properties and movements is necessary. In securing this information the children become aware of their need to know how to use the following skills:

Finding and reading titles and authors of books
Locating and using tables of contents and indices
Locating pages quickly and skimming to find content that in general relates to the problem at hand
Reading carefully to find a specific item of information related to a general problem
Judging when to skim and when to read carefully
Drawing conclusions from facts presented
Following directions
Interpreting
Summarizing

Much of the practice on these skills should come as the pupils seek further information in relation to new but real purposes, but if the children are fully conscious of their need and the skill is a complicated one, then it should be made the basis of drill in the definite training reading period. Such a period affords opportunity for the bunched drill essential in the initial learning of a skill. The minor skills involved in using the index, such as naming the letters of the alphabet in consecutive order, locating the letters in the alphabet in relation to each other, arranging words in alphabetical order, etc., must be practiced. They should not be treated as unrelated elements, but practiced in relation to the main skill, the value of which has been established in the minds of the pupils. The reading skills involved in arithmetic, a subject which is not often a part of an integrated program, are usually taught as a regular part of that subject.

Vocabulary Development

A steadily increasing vocabulary aids comprehension. Two elements are significant in vocabulary development; knowledge of word meanings, and speed of recognition. We must distinguish between these two elements in the methods and materials which we use to develop them.

There are two ways in which meanings are acquired; by direct experience, and by reading. Both sources need to be cultivated in the school, especially do meanings through direct experience need to be increased. The problem for the teacher is to interrelate these two types of training.

If children have the opportunity to observe water birds, for example, and to discuss these observations, the words which describe the habits of those birds, their adaptations to their mode of life, and the distinguishing characteristics of the species will present little difficulty. Likewise the observation can stimulate related reading on the part of the children to find more information about the birds.

The constructive activities, which now play an important part in progressive classrooms would be justified if for no other reason in the fact that they clarify meanings for children and make concrete the related reading.

The importance of oral language and fluent speech should not be overlooked in vocabulary building.

Teachers will find many worthwhile devices for vocabulary building in the newer readers. They may be used as patterns for building additional exercises with the material the children are reading.

The vocabulary, technical in many respects, which is needed in the unit of work must be kept up systematically during the life of the unit. Some teachers find it helpful to keep vocabulary charts. They are large sheets of oak tag on which are printed words, phrases, and expressions as they are encountered in the study. The list is not restricted to words difficult to pronounce. Here are some words and expressions used in a Colonial and Pioneer Life study:

puncheons	New England	circuit rider	homemade moccasins
tavern	Massachusetts	Conestoga wagons	buckskin breeches
pewter	New Amsterdam	gap	coarse homespun
infare	New York		linsey-woolsey dress
tithing	Virginia		knitted wristlets
hornbook			

The speed with which the child recognizes words affects, of course, the speed and comprehension with which he reads. Speed in recognizing a word depends upon the number of times the child has met that word in situations meaningful to him. Gates has shown through experiment that the average child must encounter a word thirty-five times or more to recognize it readily.[1] Formerly this repetition was provided by making lists of the difficult words and drilling on them in isolation of content. The better way to provide this repetition for the child is for him to meet the words again and again in new situations.

The best aid to rapid recognition of words is the reading of much easy material. The newer emphasis is upon reading many books in which relatively few difficulties are encountered, rather than a few books in which many difficulties are encountered. The former affords the child more satisfaction and distributes practice to better advantage than does the latter.

Skill in attacking unfamiliar words must be developed. Children should not be restricted to any one method of attack. Words are recognized through context, through word form, through general configuration, and through phonetic characteristics. Instruction in all these techniques should be given in some degree to the children. Not all children, however, will need the same amount of each type. The teacher should discriminate.

Helping the child to recognize new words through context or phonics frequently presents one of the most difficult problems in teaching reading. Directing the child to read the rest of the sentence and to guess the unknown word is one appropriate means of aiding in context clues. Wild guesses are precluded somewhat if the child has sufficient phonetic ability to sound the initial syllable. The teacher will find it important to give definite instruction in the differences and similarities of words such as *through, though, thought,* for example.

---

[1] A. I. Gates. *Interest and Ability in Reading.* New York: The Macmillian Company, 1930, pp. 35-36.

After the similarities and differences in the words have been adequately demonstrated, subsequent drill on recognition should come in context.

Children should be encouraged to ask for the meanings of words or expressions which they do not understand during the silent reading period. The use of the dictionary should be encouraged also in determining meanings of words, but should not be made such a burden that interest in context is lost.

Comprehension

Comprehension is the most important outcome of reading. Comprehension should always be stressed as a part of oral and silent reading from the first. Speed and comprehension in silent reading can be increased by providing an ample amount of easy material within the interest of the children.

Oral Reading Standards

Oral reading in audience situations with standards set up by pupils for both reader and listeners should be provided for in the definite training period. Such standards will include:

For the Reader

1. Giving the audience satisfaction and pleasure
2. Reading distinctly
3. Pronouncing the words accurately
4. Standing correctly and holding the book properly

For the Audience

1. Cooperating
2. Asking sincere questions or making interesting reactions
3. Offering helpful suggestions

Procedure for Definite Training Periods

All definite training to develop an ability, a habit or a skill should proceed as follows:

1. The child sees the need and wishes to practice the ability, habit or skill
2. The teacher leads the child into the exercise calculated to give practice on the ability, habit or skill
3. Accomplishment is checked
4. Additional practice is given if necessary

Maintenance and Extension of Reading Habits Initiated in Primary Grades

The scope of the reading training period includes maintaining the reading habits initiated in the primary grades, and also giving drills necessary to promoting their growth.

Reading Habits Begun in the Primary Grades Must Be Maintained Throughout the Intermediate Grades

Warning needs to be given in regard to the way in which this part of the reading program is handled. An overemphasis upon the skill side of reading often arouses in children an aversion to all reading. Skills are always taught in relation to the functions which they serve in reading. They are never taught for their own sake.

Teachers in the middle grades often experience difficulty in adjusting to the range of ability represented in a class. The important thing to be remembered in this connection is that we start with a child at whatever stages of development we find him. Otherwise, he is hampered at the outset by the teacher's preconceived notion of his accomplishment in the specific skills.

Teachers should study constantly the reading methods employed by successful primary teachers.

The reading habits which are begun in the primary grades must be maintained throughout the intermediate grades. Important among these are the following:

Silent reading

1. Reading with little or no lip movement.
2. Reading with a fair degree of speed.
3. Reading increasingly larger units.
4. Recognizing new words through context or phonics.

Oral reading

1. Reading to give pleasure to others.
2. Pronouncing words accurately.

Care of books

1. Handling books carefully.
2. Turning pages so as not to soil them.
3. Keeping books clean.
4. Placing books in an orderly manner in desks, on tables and book-shelves.

MATERIALS [1]

Sources

Materials from the following sources can be used to improve reading skills and techniques:

Selections from readers

Selections from history, geography, science and arithmetic textbooks

Work books

Teacher-made practice exercises

Dictionaries, encyclopedias, and other reference volumes

As to type, the materials may be either literary or factual, or a combination of literary and factual, and should represent a variety of ungraded selections. Too much can not be said about the importance of ample ungraded material well within the interest and ability of the children. The day has passed when the reading program means the completion of a certain reader designated for a particular grade. A wide variety of suitable material should be available for groups and individuals within the group.

The content should relate to the experiences of the children directly concerned. If the experiences of the group or individuals within the group have been meager the first responsibility of the teacher is to provide opportunities for developmental experiences which will make the printed page meaningful.

Organization of Materials to Support Units

Organizing the reading program about broad topics or centers of interest suggests one way to overcome the loss of momentum in interest that results from the day by day reading of isolated, unrelated selections. The first step in such a project is to survey the available

---

[1] See also *Suggested Course of Study in Reading and Literature for Elementary Schools.* State of California Department of Education Bulletin, No. 13, Part II, July 1, 1932.

material within the ability of the children and list related selections under topical headings. If readers from third grade in addition to those from grades four, five and six are used for a particular group it is helpful to have the readers unmarked as to grade placement.

In the mechanics of the plan is involved some scheme for keying the readers. Roman numerals or the initials of the books are efficient keys.

Here is an abridged sample outline of topics[1] related to social studies and science:

OUTLINE OF TOPICS

Our People at Work
- Those who provide us with things we eat and drink
- Those who provide us with things we wear
- Those who provide us with homes, conveniences, and protection

Our Outdoor World
- Native wild animals
- Domestic animals and pets
- Wild animals of the jungle
- Plants

Our Favorite Sports
Our Music
Our Cities and Towns
Our Money
Our Museums
Natural Wonders in Our Country
Transportation In and From Our Country
Our Highways and Travel
Our Mail and Other Means of Communication
Some Important Men and Women

The present dearth of easy reading material relating to centers of interest for children has to be faced. Clever and able teachers are meeting this situation by writing selections themselves. This work is certainly desirable if satisfactory standards of composition are maintained. Authenticity of factual content should be checked. Gifted teachers should be given more time to continue this work. Since the material is developed in the classroom in response to definite needs, there is a greater probability that it will answer the need for detail than does some of the material written by those remote from the children.

---

[1] Los Angeles City Schools Bulletin No. 322, Division of Course of Study, Ethel I. Salisbury, Director. This bulletin contains a list of selections from 21 readers which have been grouped under 25 broad topics.

The sample which follows shows the directness of style and the wealth of concrete detail which is demanded of informational material if it is to help children in carrying out their activities.

CHUMASH CANOES [1]

The Yurok Indian used a canoe dug out of a big log. The Maidu also used this kind of a canoe up in the mountains but in the valleys the balsa made of rushes was used. The Chumash had a still different kind of canoe. This tribe of Indians tied heavy boards or planks together to make their canoe. They filled the cracks with asphalt to keep the water out. The asphalt was easy to get. The Indians found it on their beaches.

The Chumash canoe was not as strong as the Yurok's dugout. However the Chumash used their boats only on calm quiet waters and not on rushing rivers as the Yurok did. Though these boats were not as strong they were much lighter and swifter. Two Indians could lift them in and out of the water. With one stroke they covered a great distance.

There seems to have been a very good reason why the Chumash canoes were made out of boards rather than logs. Most of the big trees in Chumash land grew on the mountains. The streams were not large enough to float a heavy log down to the ocean. Logs large enough to make a canoe were too clumsy and heavy for the Indians to carry down from the mountains. However, a long board was quite easily carried down a trail by two Indians.

The canoes were all sizes. Some were large enough to carry six passengers. A boat this size was most likely paddled by about eight Indians. The largest Chumash canoes were about twenty-five feet long and four feet wide. The paddles had a double blade. The Chumash Indians and the Eskimo are the only tribes in North America that always used a double bladed paddle. The Yurok paddle was long and narrow and much like a pole.

You may wonder how the Chumash made nice planks or boards for their canoes. They split their boards with a wedge. A wedge must have a nice thin edge. Many of the California Indians used the antler of the deer for a wedge. But the Chumash Indians used the rib of a whale. They also used an adze to cut their planks. The blade of their adze was a heavy shell with a sharp edge and the handle was a piece of wood.

Practice Exercises

Teachers frequently prepare exercises for directed reading. Following are three sample exercises taken from a set of twenty, all prepared by a regular classroom teacher.[2] The directions suggest that similar exercises might be worked out using other readers.

These exercises for directed reading are suitable for a class of good readers in the third grade or for weaker readers in the fourth grade. They have been tested and found interesting to children.

Each of the statements in the following exercises should be placed on a separate card. The answers in the first exercise should be cut apart from the questions and the children asked to match correct answer to the question. In the second exercise the card containing the statements should be cut apart as indicated and the children asked to match the parts.

[1] Contributed by Ethelyn Yount Weida, Principal, Willowbrook Grammar School, Willowbrook, California.
[2] Jean H. Dukelow, Alexandria Avenue School, Los Angeles.

EXERCISE ON "THE GOLDEN FISH"

1. Who was fishing for many hours? An old man.
2. Who was kind to the fish? The fisherman.
3. Who was very angry? His wife.
4. What was the oven full of? Loaves of bread.
5. Who wanted a great many servants? The wife.
6. Who did the fisherman never see again? The fish.

EXERCISE ON "HOW DOUGHNUTS CAME TO BE MADE"

1. The little/cook had a long spoon hanging in his belt.
2. The little cook made/some turtle soup, spice cake and other good things.
3. The fairy said/that the toast was too dark.
4. They needed/a preacher to marry them.
5. The little cook had/no ring.
6. He made a/ring out of dough.

EXERCISE ON "GRETCHEN'S CHRISTMAS"

1. Gretchen came from far across the_____. (ocean)
2. She lived away upstairs in a_____house. (boarding)
3. She wore_____shoes. (wooden)
4. She could not_____English. (speak)
5. A_____lady took Gretchen down to look in the store windows. (kind)
6. The thing Gretchen liked best was a_____. (baby doll)
7. It looked as if it wanted to be_____. (loved)
8. Margaret was a kind little_____girl who wanted to make somebody happy. (American)
9. Margaret put the baby doll in Gretchen's_____. (shoe)
10. Margaret and her father were_____because they had been kind. (happy)

SUGGESTIONS FOR PUPILS WITH FOREIGN LANGUAGE DIFFICULTIES

Some of the problems in teaching reading which will be encountered by teachers of foreign groups are indicated, and a brief hint as to ways and means of meeting the difficulties are suggested below:

1. Insufficient vocabulary
   a. Develop vocabulary by much free conversation, by conference periods in which children make plans, examine and talk about exhibit articles, discuss stories and pictures.
   b. Teach new words by planning definite time for presentation of words and what they mean. New objects that come into the room or into the school experiences of the children should be discussed and named.
   c. Dramatize stories children have read in order to furnish opportunity for expressions found in the books.

2. Word readers (halting reading—without getting meaning)
   a. Choose easy material.

b. Prepare children for the reading by talking about the pictures, titles, and possible contents of story before children start to read.

c. Supply troublesome words, and explain meanings of any children do not know before or during reading lesson.

d. Emphasize meanings; do not be too insistant that every word be read correctly if thought is correct.

e. Emphasize big points of story. Do much talking *about the content*.

f. Show children how to group words into thought phrases.

g. Read aloud to the children. Stop occasionally and let the children tell what they think will come next.

h. Let the reading hour be a happy time for both children and teacher.

3. Poor pronunciation and enunciation

a. Set a particularly fine example. The teacher is very definitely setting the speech models for her children.

b. Read to the children frequently.

c. Afford an opportunity for the best readers in the group to read aloud to the other children occasionally.

d. Drill the children who need it on words that are difficult for them to pronounce, as *every, very, this*.

e. Give much ear and lip training to small groups or individual children who need it. Show them how to place the lips and tongue when enunciating certain difficult sounds.

4. Colorless voices

a. Set a good example in the proper use of voice. The children's voices reflect the tones of the teacher.

b. See that the classroom is a happy place where children laugh and sing often.

c. Have much free dramatization.

READING PROBLEMS IN RELATION TO SOCIAL STUDIES

Reading is an integral part of the entire school program. Social studies cannot be taught as a thing apart from reading. The difficulties encountered in reading are reflected in the ability to understand content, use reference materials effectively, skim contents to answer particular questions, etc., relating to a problem in the social studies field. Practical suggestions are included here to aid the teacher in meeting the situation in her own classroom if social studies materials adapted to the reading abilities of children are not readily available.

1. Children who cannot read the material
   a. Some books may be used effectively if the pictures are particularly revealing.
   b. The teacher may read a great deal of the material herself and then tell it to the children.
   c. The teacher may mark particular sections that children can read for special reports.
   d. The teacher can use much of the material to get information for her own use. She can then rewrite (in long hand if necessary) some of this information in a simpler vocabulary to be used by children of limited ability.

2. Children who are not interested
   a. Interest may be stimulated through visual materials, pictures, stories, excursions and observation.
   b. Provide for many first hand experiences, and fewer that are vicarious.
   c. Let the children have many experiences in making but see that they get the information about how a thing is to be made *before* they make it. Thus they will do purposeful reading.
   d. Do not overemphasize the need of reading. We learn in many other ways.

TYPE LESSONS

I. Instruction for Poor Readers

This lesson suggests a procedure for making assignments to ability groups during the reading training period and using selections in readers below grade for the slow group.

The situation. A class of 37 fifth-grade pupils; under the usual grade organization with all subjects taught by one teacher; grouped in ability sections, with 22 average and superior readers, and 11 poor readers.

Background of the lesson. A unit of work, "Life in the Early Days of America," was in progress in the class room. Questions raised by the pupils in the course of the activity of this unit furnished a guide to the reading undertaken. The average and superior readers were concerned with the following questions: What did the colonists learn from the Indians, and what thing could the Indians do better than the colonists?

Reading materials. During their unsupervised study time on the day of this lesson the children read for information on the question suggested, the following selections: "Food in Early Colonial Days,"[1] "Indian Canoes,"[2] "Early American Methods of Transportation,"[3] and "From Cow Path to Highway."[4]

Purposes. The following specific purposes were the basis of the instruction for pupils who were poor readers:

To let these pupils experience the thrill of getting information on the topic of general interest to the class.

To improve ability to comprehend through reading to find the answers to definite questions.

To provide word drill in content after the selection has been read.

To help make notes on the story which will be serviceable when the information gained is shared with the class.

Arrangement. The teacher and children in the group of poor readers were seated around the library table in one corner apart from children who were studying independently.

Reading selection. For this lesson the children studied "The Town Crier."[5]

THE LESSON

TEACHER: How have we found out things about the way people lived a long time ago?

PUPILS: Read stories. And you read stories to us.

TEACHER: Yes, where did Mary Jo find out about "Ten Broeck?"

PUPILS: From her grandmother.

TEACHER: Yes, but was it her *grandmother* who first knew about this man?

PUPILS: No, her great great grandmother.

TEACHER: Yes, Mary Jo told us there were three "greats"—great, great, great grandmother.

In the story we are going to read now Betty and David, two children, find out something very interesting from their great grandmother about the people of long ago.

Find page 392. Close your books over your finger, and listen to my first direction.

Begin on the first page and read until you find out something about the people in the days when Grandmother was a little girl.

(As they read different pupils ask for pronunciation of *trolley, remarked, notice* without disturbing others.)

[1] Paul Spencer and Others. *Thought Study Readers.* Book IV. Chicago: Lyons and Carnahan, 1929, pp. 121-133.

[2] Frank Freeman and Eleanor Johnson. *Facts and Fun.* Child-Story Readers. California State Series. Sacramento: California State Department of Education, 1930, pp. 161-167.

[3] Ernest Horn and Others. *Learn to Study Readers.* Book V. Boston: Ginn and Company, 1926, pp. 344-358.

[4] Isobel Davidson and Charles Anderson. *The Lincoln Readers.* Fourth Reader. New York: Laurel Book Company, 1922, pp. 181-187.

[5] Frank Freeman and Eleanor Johnson. *Wonder Stories.* Child-Story Readers. California State Series. Sacramento: California State Department of Education, 1930, p. 392.

PUPIL: People couldn't read.

TEACHER: Everybody? Couldn't anybody read?

PUPIL: Yes some, but not very many.

TEACHER: Do you suppose that they had newspapers then?
(Pupils are undecided)

TEACHER: We shall try to decide that after we finish the story.
Remember you said that hardly any of the people could read. Read on now to find out what they did when they wanted to know about something.

PUPIL: Here, this tells. (Points and reads) "The Town Crier."
(Teacher helps pronounce *crier*.)

TEACHER: Read on beginning at the top of the next page to find out what a town crier is.

PUPIL: He has a blue coat and a tall hat.

TEACHER: Does that tell what a town crier is, that is, what he does?

PUPIL: He has a big bell and he rings it and says things and everybody listens.

TEACHER: Yes, now if you will read on from that place about an experience which Granny had with the Town Crier, you will find out in another way why he rings the bell and why he makes announcements.
(Words on which help with pronunciations is asked are: *allowed, reins, sly, hostler, interested, particularly, legged, lonely.*

TEACHER: (Encourages some pupils to continue through the two pages of reading matter with the question) "Have you found out yet about Granny's experience with the Town Crier?"

PUPIL: Yes, she got lost.

TEACHER: Yes, lost from her father. Did she ever find her father? Read on to the end of the story to find out.
(Words on which help with pronunciation is asked: *twinkling, shy, courage.*)

PUPIL: Yes, he put her up on the steps, and rang his bell, and then, her father came up and got her.

TEACHER: What do we do when we have lost something and want to let people know so that they can bring it back to us if they find it?

PUPIL: We tell people.

TEACHER: Can almost everybody read today?
Do we have any way to tell people all over the city that we have lost something?

PUPIL: Yes, you put it in the paper.

TEACHER: Yes, do you know in what section of the newspaper?
(None do) The want ads.

PUPIL: They announce it over the radio lots of times when people lose things.

TEACHER: Why didn't they put a want ad in the newspaper when they lost something when Granny was a little girl?

PUPIL: They didn't have newspapers.

TEACHER: And why didn't they have newspapers or pin up notices for people to read?

PUPIL: Because only a few people could read.

WORD DRILL IN CONTENT

TEACHER : Let us turn back to the beginning of the story and get some help on some of the words which bothered us.
How did David know someone had found a little gray kitten?

PUPIL : Notice pinned up on a post.

TEACHER : What word in that part means the same as street car?

PUPIL : Trolley car.

TEACHER : Why is a street car sometimes called a trolley car?
Since no one in this group knows, teacher says that the question will be referred to the rest of the class later.

TEACHER : I want to call your attention to four words or expressions on the first page which we should be able to recognize from now on. The story is talked and told by some one; so it's all conversation.
How do you know that Betty said, "That's a good place to get off?"

PUPIL : It says, "Said Betty."

TEACHER : Who says, "When I was a little girl?"

PUPIL : "Grandmother."

TEACHER : Read the part that told you.

PUPIL : "Remarked Grandmother."

TEACHER : That word, *remarked*, is used instead of what other word?

PUPIL : "Said."

TEACHER : Skip down to the question David asks, after Grandmother says it wouldn't have been much good putting up a notice, and notice the word used instead of "Said David."

PUPIL : "Asked David."

TEACHER : What expression is used to tell you that Granny says "Because it wasn't everyone who could read in my day?"

PUPIL : "Was the reply."

TEACHER : What expression tells you that Betty asked the next question?

PUPIL : "Betty inquired."

TEACHER : What four expressions did we find on this page that can be used instead of using "said" all the time?

PUPIL : "Remarked, asked, was the reply, inquired."

TEACHER : Do you have information now that you can report back to the class?

PUPIL : Yes, about the Town Crier.

TEACHER : We shall not be able to report this until tomorrow. Perhaps it would be well for us to make a few notes to help us remember what we want to say.
Paper was passed and the following notes written by the pupils under the guidance of leading questions asked by the teacher.

THE NOTES

The Town Crier
No newspapers
How they made important announcements
    What the Town Crier looked like
    Granny's experience with the Town Crier
How they traveled to town in those days
    Where they put their horse
    What the man is called who has charge of the horses at
        the inn ("hostler")
(When this information was shared with the class it was
    reported in three parts by three pupils.)

Follow-up assignment. Rereading of the story was checked during an unsupervised study period by the comprehension test exercise which occurs at the end of the selection.

II. Observation of Reading in the Fifth Grade [1]

The class was divided into three groups: The good readers, the fair readers, and the poor readers. It was the teacher's purpose to present material suitable to the abilities of each group and to have each child study according to the directions given.

A study of this report will reveal, among other things, that definite training in other reading skills (using the index, for example) has preceded the lesson reported.

GROUP II

The following material was written on the blackboard before class time.

Find out:
1. Why the corn from which tortillas are made is soaked a long time?
2. Whether Mexico's corn products are more or less valuable than her minerals.
3. Which city of Mexico is one of the famous mining centers of the world?
4. What product changed Yucatan from one of the poorest to one of the richest states of Mexico?
5. What has made the city of Guadalajara wealthy and beautiful?
6. In what part of Mexico is the petroleum industry carried on?
7. How the houses of the hacienda owners differ from that of the peon who works for him.
8. What fraction of the people can neither read nor write.
9. Which mountain range of Mexico is higher, the one on the western coast or the one on the eastern?
10. What guaijule is?

Reference: Nellie B. Allen. *North America*[2]

DISCUSSION

TEACHER: If you have any question about the indexes you wrote yesterday,[3] use the book index instead.

TEACHER: Wait for directions, using your index to find out.
Question 1—"Why the corn from which tortillas are made is soaked a long time?"
Pupil read the answer in one sentence.

TEACHER: Write the first and last word of the sentence on your paper. She showed them what to do.
This_____grain.

TEACHER: If the pages for the references are 305, 306, 307 must I read each page to find the answer?

---

[1] Contributed by Eva M. Danielson, Teacher, Sawtelle Boulevard School, Los Angeles.
[2] Nellie B. Allen. *North America.* Boston: Ginn and Company, 1922.
[3] The key words to questions about Mexico and page numbers from Allen's *North America* had been copied.

PUPIL: No, skim through it.

TEACHER: How many think that you could do the next one and all the rest alone?

GROUP III

The following material was written on the blackboard before class time.

1. Why Bear Cubs are So Amusing
2. The Playfulness of Bear Cubs
3. Older Bears at Play
4. A Puzzled Grizzly
5. The Size, Color and Habitat of Grizzly Bears
6. The Intelligence of Grizzly Bears
7. What Grizzly Bears Eat
8. The Grizzly Bear's "Sweet Tooth"
9. A Strange Ladder
10. Private Property
11. The Bears' Meeting Place
12. Finding a Den for Winter
13. Preparation for a Long Sleep
14. The Time When Grizzly Bears Begin Their Sleep
15. A Long Fast
16. The Arrival of Cub Bears
17. Mother Bear and Cubs Leaving Their Den
18. Breaking a Winter's Fast
19. Watchful Mothers
20. An Unexpected "Dip"
21. How Long Cubs Depend Upon Their Mothers

Reference. "Grizzly Bears"[1]

DISCUSSION

TEACHER: How many reading the story? How many found the story? Raise your hand if you were able to find any titles matching the paragraphs. How did you find them? Skim quickly through the first paragraph and see if you can find the title that matches this paragraph.

(The children read quickly through the first paragraph.)

PUPIL: "Why Cubs Are So Amusing."

(This same procedure was followed through four or five paragraphs, when the teacher was confident that the children understood the work, they were left alone to complete the assignment matching each paragraph with a title.)

GROUP I

The following material was written on the blackboard.

Answer the following questions with *yes* or *no* and give proof.
1. Is gold the most important mineral in Mexico?
2. Does a sugar cane field look like a field of corn?
3. Can you tell from the looks or taste whether the sugar on your table is cane sugar or beet sugar?
4. Can Mexico grow a great variety of products?
5. Is Mexico one-half as large as our country?
6. Do most of the people of Mexico live on the low hot seacoast?

---

[1] Frank Freeman and Eleanor Johnson. *Facts and Fun.* Child-Story Readers. California State Series. Sacramento: California State Department of Education, 1930, pp. 215–223.

7. Are there any sisal factories in Yucatan?
8. Are bananas grown in Mexico?
9. Is it difficult to keep the jungle growth from covering the railway tracks in Mexico?
10. Does Mexico have many climates?
11. Does Mexico have much coal?
12. Is petroleum found in large quantities in Mexico?
13. Does Mexico have more than five thousand mines?
14. Are golf and tennis as popular in Mexico as in our country?
15. Is the climate along the seacoast of Mexico healthful?

DISCUSSION

TEACHER : You may be able to answer the questions on the board by *yes* or *no*. You may have to look in all four books for your proof, and you may only be able to find the answer in one book.

PUPIL :   Reads the second question : "Does a sugar cane field look like a field of corn?"

TEACHER : What do you suppose you would look up?

PUPIL :   Sugar cane.

TEACHER : Now where do you suppose you are going to be able to look this up?

PUPIL :   In the index.

TEACHER : Franck's *Mexico and Central America*[1] has no index.
(Teacher gave a short drill on looking up material in books which had no index but had a table of contents.)

TEACHER : Now let us take the first question.

PUPIL :   Is gold the most important mineral of Mexico?

TEACHER : What words would you look up?

PUPIL :   Gold and mineral.

The children were then instructed to try to find the answer to the above questions in any one of the four following books.

CARPENTER, FRANK G. *North America.* New York : American Book Company, 1922.

FRANCK, HARRY A. *Mexico and Central America.* Dansville, New York : F. A. Owen Publishing Company, 1927.

HORN, ERNEST, and Others. *Learn to Study Readers.* Boston : Ginn and Company, 1926.

SMITH, J. RUSSELL. *Human Geography.* Philadelphia : The John C. Winston Company, 1922.

III. Reading With Definite Questions in Mind

The lesson is based upon the selection "Dairying in the United States."[2] The selection follows :

Dairy products, such as milk, butter, and cheese, are among the most common articles of our diet. Scarcely a meal is prepared without using one or more of these products. Of the money spent for food in our country, about one-fifth goes for milk, butter, and cheese. Considerably over one-half of this amount is for milk alone. The average amount

---

[1] Harry Franck. *Mexico and Central America.* Dansville, New York : F. A. Owen Publishing Company, 1927.
[2] De Forest Stull and Roy W. Hatch. *Our World Today.* Boston : Allyn and Bacon, 1934, pp. 174-175.

of milk per person consumed in the United States yearly is about fifty gallons, or nearly one gallon per week. Wisconsin now leads in the number of dairy cows, while New York is second.

Dairies are usually located near the city where the milk is to be sold or near transportation lines leading to that city. Great care is taken of dairy cattle and of the milk in transit. Cows are regularly inspected, and milk trains are given right of way in the same manner as passenger trains.

Butter and cheese do not need to be made near the cities, as these products are more easily transported than milk. Cheese factories especially are located in the northern states, where the nights are cool and water is abundant. They will also be found in the highlands in the western states and in North Carolina, Virginia, and Tennessee. Wisconsin alone makes about two-thirds of all the cheese made in the United States.

Dairying is carried on very extensively in the middle western states, where food for the cattle is abundant and cheap. Formerly butter making was the work of the farmer's wife, who poured the milk into pans and later skimmed off the cream. Now the cream separator automatically separates the cream from the milk right after milking. The farmer may then take the cream to the butter factory or creamery, and sell it. The skim milk is retained for feeding to the swine or other animals, and some of it may be used in the household.

Questions Based upon the Material Read

1. How much of the money spent in our country for food goes for dairy products?
2. How much milk does each person in the United States drink per week?
3. Which state has the most dairy cows?
4. Where are farms that sell fresh milk usually located?
5. Which is more difficult to ship—milk, butter, or cheese?
6. For what two reasons are cheese factories located in the northern states?
7. How much of the cheese made in the United States is made in Wisconsin?
8. Why are so many dairy cattle raised in the middle western states?
9. To whom does the farmer sell the cream?
10. What is left after cream is taken off the milk?

Procedure in Developing Lesson

The following steps indicate the procedure followed in conducting the lessons.

1. The above questions were written on the blackboard before class time and covered by drawing down a map over them or pinning newspapers across them.
2. Children number lines of both sides of paper from 1 to 10.
3. Purpose of reading is not explained at this point.
4. The children start reading on signal. They close their books and stand quietly beside desks when finished. They wait until all have finished.
5. Questions are then exposed and children are directed to answer them without referring to the book. Time is called without waiting for the slower ones to finish.
6. Answers are checked by calling on various children for their answers, each child checking his own paper. If some questions are missed by all children, do not tell the right answer.

7. Count one for each correct answer. The highest possible score is 10, in this case.
8. Record on the blackboard all scores in order beginning with the highest.
9. There will be as many scores as there are children.
10. Find the median score.
11. Tell the children that as a class they have made ____ (the median) on this exercise.
12. Cover the questions again.
13. Direct the children to open their books and begin reading the same selection again when the signal is given.
14. Follow the same procedure used before.
15. Use the opposite side of the papers for writing the answers this time.
16. When the new median score is found, compare with the first to see if there has been improvement.
17. Ask children who improved their scores to raise their hands.
18. By asking, "Why did you have more correct answers the second time?" lead the children to see the value of reading with a definite question in mind when studying.

PROBLEM SOLVING AS STUDY READING

A fifth grade class in a unit of transportation had made boats. They had heard that a shipbuilder and owner had a ceremony for launching a new boat. The question arose, "What is done at a launching?" The children launched their little boat, *bow first*, without success. The teacher than made the statement that at the launchings she had attended and in all the pictures she had seen, the boat was launched *stern first*. The children promptly asked "Why should the stern go first?" There were several guesses, among them the statement that the stern is broader. Other answers were fairly random.

The teacher supplied material, which she had prepared entitled "Stern First," and the children read to find the correct answer to their question. The reading was followed by dramatic play centered about the ceremony of launching a ship, using one of the boats which had been constructed. The next period for creative play included the ceremony and the launching of the boat with corrected detail.

Reading factual material in this close relationship to an activity gives meaningful practice on the skills, and no doubt will become more frequently a part of the integrated program when reading materials are developed by or with teachers in the classroom for specific units.

STERN FIRST[1]

The stern of a ship is much wider and heavier than the bow, and therefore weighs much more. The sliding ways are always fixed so they slant down toward the water. When the vessel has been moved from the keel blocks to the cradle and the sliding ways, the ship must be slanted enough so it will slide into the water. Now, since the stern is *downhill* and is *heavier than the bow* this extra weight will pull the vessel into the water without any help from the workmen. Once in a while, but not often, the workmen have not slanted the ways enough or not put

[1] Contributed by Marcia Bonsall, Teacher, Fifth Grade, Sawtelle Boulevard School, Los Angeles.

enough grease and soap on the ways and a huge piece of machinery must give the vessel a push in order to start it sliding toward the water.

The stern is wider and when it goes into the water there is more surface of the boat in the water than if the bow went in first. Shipbuilders say that the stern of a ship is more buoyant. They mean that it can float better than the bow, merely because it is wider. Then too, when the ship's bow is still on the sliding ways and the stern is in the water, the vessel wouldn't be as likely to tip over as it might if the narrow bow had been put into the water first.

There is still another reason for launching a ship stern first. Think how the back of a toy boat sinks in the water while its other end is out of water. The farther you push your toy into the water the higher up out of the water the back of it comes. It begins to float. A vessel does the same thing. Water pushes *up* against the stern to make it float. If the shipbuilder has put a good strong keel on the ship the bow pushes against the sliding ways with a great force. Unless the ways are as strong as possible they might break. So the builder makes them of oak, which is the strongest wood he can get.

Just imagine what might happen even to oak if the bow were launched first! The stern might be so heavy that neither the ways nor the keel could stand it. A ship costs a large amount of money, and neither the shipbuilder nor the owner can afford to have anything damage the new vessel when it is being launched.

SURVEYING AND CHECKING ACCOMPLISHMENT

The measurement of pupil accomplishment in reading through the administration of general survey or special diagnostic tests has become an essential part of the instructional process. It is primarily through the results yielded by tests that individual needs in reading are first recognized, then diagnosed in greater detail, and later given the special treatment which will best aid each child in the development of his reading ability.

Perhaps the most common error to guard against in using tests for the measurement of reading accomplishment and the diagnosis of special difficulties is the tendency to use a given test in a capacity for which it is not suited. If the need is for diagnosis of individual reading difficulties, only truly diagnostic tests should be used. Tests which have the greatest diagnostic value measure not only specific abilities but also indicate the type of instruction, if any, which is especially needed. Great care should be exercised in interpreting the scores made by pupils on reading tests in that many important factors in reading may not be measured by the tests. Generally speaking, the interpretation of test scores and the uses to which tests are put should be limited strictly to the purposes and functions for which they were designed.

It is desirable that each teacher should plan to check the accomplishment of her pupils at regular intervals throughout each school year. In planning this phase of the reading program, careful attention should be given to at least two major types of testing which are somewhat apart from the more general survey type of testing program:

1. The brief informal test or check-up which follows a study period. This should be definitely related to the assignment for that period and should provide a genuine purpose for reading during the study period. It may be either oral or written or both. If the assignment is written, the papers should be carefully checked and the results put to some use.

2. The more extended test or check-up which follows a given block or unit of special reading instruction. The test exercise may be one devised by the teacher[1] or it may possibly be one prepared commercially. Only those children who received the special instruction should be tested.

Effective use of the results revealed by such tests is dependent largely upon the teacher's ability to organize her class into working groups for purposes of special instruction designed to improve the conditions revealed by the tests.

Courtesy of Oakland City Schools

Individual Reading Difficulties Must Be Discovered and Remedied

REMEDIAL READING

Almost every teacher of reading will encounter each year a number of pupils who present special problems. The recognition and treatment of problem cases in reading is now generally recognized to be a part of each teacher's work. Consequently, every teacher must be reason-

---

[1] The types of tests are illustrated in *Suggested Course of Study in Reading and Literature for Elementary Schools.* State of California, Department of Education Bulletin, No. 13, Part II, July, 1932, p. 64.

ably well informed and skilled in the treatment of the more common types of such problem cases.

It is essential that individual reading difficulties be discovered and remedied before they became firmly fixed as a part of the pupil's reading habits. One of the first points to consider is the possible relationship between special reading difficulty and the pupil's mental ability. While there appears to be some general relationship between reading ability and mental ability, great care must be exercised in interpreting the scores on mental tests and in making inferences therefrom. By no means should the teacher assume that all pupils in need of special reading instruction are mentally dull.

Quite often pupils who present special reading difficulties are really the victims of ineffective teaching. Many who may be classified as nonreaders possess satisfactory mental ability, but their previous instruction has produced only a mechanical familiarity with the words read rather than an essential comprehension of what is read. Continued increases in the amount of remedial instruction which is necessary is usually an indication that the regular day-by-day teaching is lacking in one or more particulars. Effective reading instruction should prevent special difficulties from developing and reduce remedial instruction to a minimum.

When the teacher has determined the nature of the pupil's reading difficulty, instructional materials and methods which will aid in overcoming the deficiency must be selected. Much of the success of the remedial work depends upon this step. If the materials and methods chosen are too easy, they may do nothing but dull the pupil's interest. If the reading tasks and abilities required are too difficult, the pupils may be discouraged. The instructional materials and methods should be so skilfully selected that the pupil comes to experience the stimulating thrill of an initial success which will be followed by repeated successes in reading activities other than the special remedial period. Obviously, the selection of materials and methods for remedial instruction must be conditioned by each pupil's own peculiar needs.

Frequently it is helpful to make the pupil aware of the special difficulty which a particular task is designed to correct. This often secures better cooperation from the child than could otherwise be obtained. Checking results regularly and recording improvement on individual graphs is also a valuable aid in stimulating children to greater interest and effort in improving their reading.

A Behavior Problem Which Was Also a Reading Problem

A type of behavior problem, which is also a reading problem, is present when the individual withdraws from reality and lives in the realm of fancy in books. Such a case, while often hard for the untrained person to recognize, is usually found among the "good readers"—so called because they need no instruction in the mechanics of word recognition. He may be actually weak in the study activities involving reading. Pointing out the possibility of such a case arising may stress in another way the necessity of a proper balance between reading to develop right study habits and reading for pleasure.

A recent case of this sort which was brought before a behavior clinic was that of a nine and one-half years old in the low fifth grade with an intelligence quotient of 143. He was referred to the clinic because of his unsocial behavior on the playground, in physical education classes, in the corridors, and in the classroom when group work was in progress. He was given to striking children, making faces, and acting in a silly manner during class periods. The children disliked him. He preferred to read undisturbed or talk to his teachers privately about his reading. His arithmetic teacher had no complaint to make of his behavior because he was able to do all the work assigned both in arithmetic processes and reasoning. He had been allowed to devote most of his time to reading for his own amusement, because, as his teachers said, he finished his assignments quickly, and recreatory reading was a legitimate occupation for spare time.

The tendency of this boy to seek the realm of fancy through reading and the dangers attached to this tendency in personality development were pointed out by members of the clinic staff. The clinic recommended placing the boy in a situation where his reading might be of the study sort and more purposeful. He was shifted to a sixth grade group then engaged in a study of Castle Life. At the conclusion of this unit, modern Italy and Ancient Rome were studied. The boy in this case was given much responsibility in searching through reference books for information bearing on class problems and was constantly challenged by the teacher's questioning to bring before the class other questions and problems which this reading raised. He continued to read many adventure stories, but this time he was guided to include such as *Ivanhoe, When Knights Were Bold,*[1] *The Honor of Dunmore,*[2] as sources of information. Without aid or suggestion, he made a full-sized armor at home and appeared at school one morning wearing it. He believed his armor to be an improvement over that worn by real knights because he had, as he said, improved the hinge arrangement at the elbows and knees. His armor precipitated the dramatization of a joust from which grew a more elaborate dramatization of Gareth and Lynette with the tournament scene playing a prominent part.

---

[1] Eva March Tappan. *When Knights Were Bold.* Boston: Houghton Mifflin Company, 1911.
[2] Hawthorne Daniel. *Honor of Dunmore.* New York: The Macmillan Company, 1927.

Suggestions for Helping Slow Readers

The practice of providing very simple material for the slow reader is obviously sound. If a story has information bearing on the topic of general class interest which those children can report to the class, its value is enhanced by a genuine motive for reading. A sixth-grade class is making a study of pottery, for example, and it is satisfying to the slow readers in the group to read and report on "How the First Dishes Were Made."[1] This information may be contrasted with that found in the stories about "An Indian Water Jar."[2]

In one school charts of material correlated with other subjects than reading were used successfully with the slower readers. A content for the charts was dictated by the children following class discussion. The following is an example of a chart made by a fifth-grade class.

A PIONEER HOME

The pioneer made his home of logs.
The furniture was made from logs.
Every home had a fireplace.
The women cooked in the fireplace.
The fire lighted the home and warmed it.
Every home had a spinning wheel.
The women made the clothing.

Two copies of the chart were printed by the teacher on large sheets of paper. The sentences on one chart were cut apart, passed to the group, and the story reconstructed by placing the sentences in a chart holder. Later the sentences were cut into phrases and these phrases matched with the master chart. This procedure is that followed by primary teachers.[3]

Upper grade teachers who have used this device have varied it by writing the story on the blackboard and having the children respond by pointing to the words and phrases. They report results from this variation less satisfactory than when charts are made.

Science material will furnish interesting content for the charts such as those described above.

In the cases where a single child in a group is retarded the device of keeping a picture notebook has been used successfully. The virtue of the device appears to lie in the fact that it provides a means whereby the teacher with a large class can give more individual help. The device is worked this way: The child cuts whatever pictures he wishes from magazines. He pastes a picture in his notebook and under it

---

[1] W. H. Elson; L. E. Runkel; and W. S. Gray. *The Elson Basic Readers*. Book II. Chicago: Scott Foresman and Company, 1931, pp. 137-143.
[2] Arthur Irving Gates, and Others. *The Work Play Books*. New York: The Macmillan Company, 1931, p. 149.
[3] Those interested will find an adequate account of the method in the *Suggested Course of Study in Reading and Literature for Elementary Schools*. State of California Department of Education Bulletin, No. 13, Part II, July, 1932, pp. 28-31.

writes a story about the picture. He keeps a "word box" for help with spelling. The stories are also typewritten. It requires two or three periods of close supervision and help from the teacher in order to get this plan working.

An Extreme Case of Reading Disability

An analytical report of one extreme case of reading disability may serve to make concrete some principles of instruction which apply both to development and to remedial reading instruction.

The case is of a boy with a chronological age of 12 years, 2 months, and a mental age of 12 years, one month.

Due to his extreme retardation in reading, he had repeated every grade in school. He was believed to be incapable of learning to read.

On the basis of a standard test[1] his reading ability was about of first grade level. The clinic report showed:

An analysis of his reading errors shows that he apparently does not recognize the letters, for he made a great many consonant and vowel errors. He seems not to know one letter from another and is unable to repeat the alphabet. Faulty reading habits are shown even in the reading of a short selection by frequent omissions or additions of sounds, and many wild guesses as to what the words are, etc.

Intensive remedial instruction was given during summer vacation. Thirty hours instruction over a period of five weeks were given. At the end of that time the Gates Primary Reading Test[2] was given. From the composite score on the three types of reading tested, the boy made a grade placement of 2.35. At the present time the instruction is being continued by the regular classroom teacher in fifth grade. The plan is to repeat the Monroe Diagnostic Test immediately and to give the second form of Gates Primary Reading Test at the end of the third month.

Further diagnosis showed this boy to be without an adequate method of word attack. He showed an extreme disregard for the initial sounds of words.

The instruction. Two sources of material were used at the outset of the instruction. A regular first reader, the workbook accompanying it, and stories from the child's experience. The latter were dropped after the first few lessons because the child's reticence and apparent dearth of vivid experiences made it appear best. At a later time

---

[1] W. S. Monroe. *Monroe's Standardized Silent Reading Tests.* Bloomington, Illinois: Public School Publishing Company.

[2] Arthur I. Gates. *Gates Primary Reading Test.* New York: Bureau of Publications, Teachers College, Columbia University.

pictures and stereographs were used to stimulate stories, with much better success.

Words which presented difficulty were put into practice exercises. The exercises were designed to give practice in perceiving the differences and similarities in words and recognizing words in context.

Here is a sample of one of the first of the exercises emphasizing similarities and differences in words. The content is taken from a story dictated by the child and from the first story in a reader.

I $\begin{cases} \text{made} \\ \text{mad a wagon} \\ \text{nab} \end{cases}$

My wagon has four $\begin{cases} \text{when} \\ \text{wells} \\ \text{wheels} \end{cases}$

I live in a $\begin{cases} \text{horse} \\ \text{house} \\ \text{home} \end{cases}$

The big elephant is $\begin{cases} \text{fuzzy} \\ \text{fine} \\ \text{funny} \end{cases}$

Tom $\begin{cases} \text{was} \\ \text{raw four elephants} \\ \text{saw} \end{cases}$

The elephant can $\begin{cases} \text{sat} \\ \text{sleep on his head} \\ \text{stand} \end{cases}$

The elephant $\begin{cases} \text{saw} \\ \text{sat down} \\ \text{see} \end{cases}$

Jumbo $\begin{cases} \text{thanks} \\ \text{thin he is a big elephant} \\ \text{thinks} \end{cases}$

An exercise on part of the same content illustrates drill in getting context clues.

I _____ a wagon.
My wagon has four _____.
I put the wheels _____ the axle.
I made my wagon out of _____.
The elephant can _____ on his head.
The elephant _____ down.
A big elephant is very _____.
"I _____ Jumbo could do tricks," said Polly.
A little elephant is called a _____ elephant.
You do not need all these words:

wheels	elephants	wagon	put
sat	stand	funny	baby
wish	want	pony	boy
in	made	boards	on

The exercise was introduced in this way. The child read the sentence to himself and then aloud, inserting the word left out. Afterwards he was given a slip of paper on which the words, which now appear below the exercise, were written and he was asked to write them in the proper places.

The interest in elephants already referred to in a previous section, was used as the basis for other reading.

Five stereographs showing pictures of elephants in their native habitat and at work carrying burdens and plowing were found and used as the subject of a story. The boy was first directed to arrange them in the order in which he thought they would tell the best story about the elephants. This direction was given to aid organizing the story.

The story which he dictated appears below. He is able to read such stories.

> An elephant takes a shower with his trunk. He likes to sleep by the water in the afternoon.
> The driver pushes him with a stick to make him go. They make them lift heavy poles. He pulls the plow and lifts heavy blocks. He likes to eat palm wood.

He was also able to make a perfect score on the following exercise the next day:

An elephant $\begin{cases} \text{takes a shower} \\ \text{likes a shower with his trunk.} \\ \text{likes to sleep} \end{cases}$

The $\begin{cases} \text{driver} \\ \text{rider pushes him with a pole.} \\ \text{native} \end{cases}$

They make elephants $\begin{cases} \text{push} \\ \text{take heavy poles.} \\ \text{lift} \end{cases}$

He pulls the $\begin{cases} \text{pole} \\ \text{plow for the farmer.} \\ \text{blocks} \end{cases}$

He likes to eat palm $\begin{cases} \text{trees} \\ \text{leaves.} \\ \text{wood} \end{cases}$

Other details in the picture not so obvious were turned into questions, and reading exercises made to answer them.

> What are the men doing in the river?
> What is growing in the field?
> What are the two elephants doing in the back of the (one) picture?

The following stories were composed after content was developed with the child by the instructor. Comprehension exercises emphasizing similarities and differences in words follow each story.

> The men were sitting on the elephants' backs. The men are going across the river. They do not go on the bridge. There is no bridge across this river.

The men are $\begin{cases} \text{sitting} \\ \text{standing on the elephants' backs.} \\ \text{slipping} \end{cases}$

The men are going $\begin{cases} \text{around the river} \\ \text{above the river.} \\ \text{across the river} \end{cases}$

Is there a bridge across the river? Yes No
Did the elephants sit on the bridge? Yes No
Did the men go across the bridge? Yes No
Did the men go across the river? Yes No
The elephant pulls the plow for the farmer. The farmer planted rice.

What is the elephant doing? $\begin{cases} \text{planting the rice} \\ \text{pushing the plow.} \\ \text{pulling the plow} \end{cases}$

What is the farmer doing? $\begin{cases} \text{pushing the plow} \\ \text{planting rice.} \\ \text{pulling the plow} \end{cases}$

The two elephants are working together. One elephant pushes up the log with his tusks. The other elephant puts his trunk around one end of the log. They take the log away together. They always work together.

How many elephants are working? $\begin{cases} \text{two} \\ \text{ten} \\ \text{one} \end{cases}$

The elephant $\begin{cases} \text{pulls} \\ \text{pushes up the log.} \\ \text{points} \end{cases}$

He pushes up the log $\begin{cases} \text{with his teeth} \\ \text{with his trunk.} \\ \text{with his tusks} \end{cases}$

The boy had other questions to ask.
Does an elephant weigh a ton?
How big (tall) are elephants?
What else do they eat?
Do they eat meat?

Parts of the informational stories about elephants, *Learn to Study Readers*, Book III,[1] were read to obtain the answers to these questions.

Other exercises which were used with this boy were:

A baby elephant is as big as the $\begin{cases} \text{greatest} \\ \text{largest dog.} \\ \text{smallest} \end{cases}$

Elephants are the $\begin{cases} \text{smallest} \\ \text{wildest animals we have on land.} \\ \text{biggest} \end{cases}$

Bolivar was $\begin{cases} \text{ten} \\ \text{two feet high.} \\ \text{twelve} \end{cases}$

Bolivar weighed $\begin{cases} \text{one thousand pounds} \\ \text{twelve thousand pounds.} \\ \text{ten thousand pounds} \end{cases}$

Jumbo was more than $\begin{cases} \text{seven} \\ \text{eight feet high.} \\ \text{eleven} \end{cases}$

A baby elephant weighs about $\begin{cases} \text{one hundred and four pounds} \\ \text{one hundred and five pounds.} \\ \text{one hundred and fifty pounds} \end{cases}$

---

[1] Ernest Horn, and Others. *Learn to Study Readers*, Book III. Boston: Ginn and Company, 1926.

An elephant grows up in about {twenty-five years / twenty-six years. / twenty-four years}

A baby elephant is _____ than a dog.
      big bigger biggest

Elephants are the _____ land animals.
      big bigger biggest

A baby elephant is as big as the _____ dog.
      large larger largest

How do elephants keep together in a circus parade?
  {hide behind each other / hold each other's tails / march together}

How do elephants march along?
  {very funny / very quickly / very quietly}

How does the man guide the elephant?
  {with his long stick / with his long hooked stick / with his heavy pole}

Where does he touch the elephant?
  {on his hand or head / on his ear or shoulder / on the hind legs}

What four tricks can circus elephants do?
  {stand up on the table legs / stand up on their hind legs / step up in the tree top}

  {sit on big stools / sit on big spools / sing in the school}

  {run a big ball around / roll a big bell around / roll a big ball around}

  {sleep on his head and front legs / stand on his head and hind legs / stand on his head and front legs}

How do elephants help after the circus is over?
  {pump heavy washers / push heavy wigwams / push heavy wagons / cart heavy poles / carry heavy poles / march in the parade}

How do elephants learn?
  {three things / very quickly / very quietly}

Simpler forms of the elephant stories were prepared by the teacher. Each was accompanied by comprehension checks designed to focus

20—17050

attention on the words which presented the greatest difficulty. Examples of this material which will illustrate how teachers may stimulate interest in reading by adapting materials to individual needs follow:

CIRCUS ELEPHANTS

Circus elephants do many tricks.
They stand on their heads.
They can dance.
They can play music.
They can even learn to walk tight ropes.

Elephants can $\begin{cases} \text{sit} \\ \text{sleep} \\ \text{stand} \end{cases}$ on their heads.

They can $\begin{cases} \text{say} \\ \text{play} \\ \text{pay} \end{cases}$ music.

They can $\begin{cases} \text{walk} \\ \text{talk} \\ \text{wash} \end{cases}$ tight ropes.

What tricks can elephants do?

1. _____
2. _____
3. _____
4. _____
5. _____

CLEVER CIRCUS ELEPHANTS

Barney was a clever circus elephant.
Barney could dance on a box.
Barney could play a mouth organ.
He played his own tunes while he danced.
Barney also worked after the circus was over.
He pushed the heavy circus wagons.
He hauled hay for the other elephants.
He played his mouth organ while he worked.
He looked very funny when he worked this way. He pushed the wagons with his head and held the mouth organ in his trunk. He played the same tune over and over.

Barney could $\begin{cases} \text{dance on a box} \\ \text{bance on a box.} \\ \text{dance on a dox} \end{cases}$

He could $\begin{cases} \text{pay a mouth organ} \\ \text{pray a mouth organ.} \\ \text{play a mouth organ} \end{cases}$

He played $\begin{cases} \text{his own tunes} \\ \text{his one tunes.} \\ \text{his our tunes} \end{cases}$

He also $\begin{cases} \text{walked} \\ \text{washed} \\ \text{worked} \end{cases}$ after the circus was over.

He { played the wagons / pushed the wagons. / pointed the wagons

He { had hay / helped hay for the other elephants. / hauled hay

What things could Barney do?

1. _____

2. _____

3. _____

4. _____

JUMBO

Jumbo was the greatest of all circus elephants.

He was the biggest elephant in any circus.

He weighed more than six tons.

He weighed as much as four big automobiles.

Jumbo was very tall. When he was twenty-six years old he was eleven feet and two inches tall.

Jumbo belonged to the Barnum and Bailey Circus. Mr. Barnum got Jumbo when he was a baby elephant. He was only four feet tall then.

Do you know what happened to Jumbo? He was killed by a train. He was crossing the railroad tracks and a train hit him.

Jumbo was the _____ of all elephants.

He weighed as much as _____ big automobiles.

He was 11 feet and 2 inches tall when he was _____ years old.

When a baby, Jumbo was _____ feet tall.

He was _____ by a train.

ANOTHER CLEVER ELEPHANT

One elephant learned to guide an automobile. He sat in the front seat. He steered the car with his front feet. His big brother pushed the car from behind.

This elephant learned { to get the automobile / to give the automobile. / to guide the automobile

He { steered the car / stopped the car with his front feet. / stole the car

His big brother { pulled the car. / pushed the car. / played the car

JUMBO   BARNEY   ALL ELEPHANTS

Cut out the phrases below and paste them under the right words.

the biggest elephant

played a mouth organ

have big trunks

have short tails

was killed by a train

hauled hay

have big feet

drink water

eat hay

push heavy wagons

danced on a box

weighed about twelve thousand pounds

a clever elephant

more than eleven feet tall

liked peanuts

belonged to the Barnum and Bailey Circus

have big ears

1. Was Jumbo the biggest elephant? Yes No
2. Did Jumbo weigh more than one automobile? Yes No
3. Did Jumbo weigh more than a horse? Yes No
4. Did Jumbo guide an automobile? Yes No
5. Was Jumbo in the circus with Barney? Yes No
6. Was Barney hit by a train? Yes No
7. Did Jumbo play a mouth organ? Yes No
8. Did Barney haul hay? Yes No
9. Was Jumbo six feet tall when Mr. Barnum got him? Yes No
10. Could Jumbo dance on a box? Yes No
11. Was Jumbo twelve feet tall? Yes No
12. Was Jumbo twenty-six feet tall? Yes No
13. Did Barney belong to Mr. Barnum? Yes No
14. Did Barney steer an automobile? Yes No
15. Did Barney dance on a box? Yes No

Word Recognition Devices

In order to work toward independence in word recognition definite training was given to this boy with particular reading difficulties. Certain features of these lessons are discussed in the following examples for the benefit of the teacher wishing to adapt them to her own situation.

I. Example of lessons to give ear training in hearing initial sounds. Teacher pronounces the three words at a time. Pupil responds *Yes* if he thinks they sound alike and *No* if he thinks they do not sound alike.

All combinations of initial sounds were tried in order to select those which presented the greatest difficulty.

candy	can't	big	(No)
cattle	catch	captain	(Yes)
did	dishes	dim	(Yes)
dig	dip	dress	(No)

The following initial sounds presented greatest difficulty: *he, ne, la, le, ti, sti, whi, sli, slee.*

The fact that training in recognizing "final blends" must complement stress on "initial sounds" was not overlooked nor is it minimized here. With this case, the only method the child used for getting new words was that of sounding by "final blends." This device worked for the boy when the instructor aided. For example when he attacked "ball" the instructor said, "What little word do you see?" and the pupil responded, "All," and then perceived *ball*. Spend, "end," *spend*. Reversing words and responding to an element near the end of the word when guessing seemed attributable to his having had but this one method for attacking new words.

II. Perceiving similarities and differences in words presented in thought exercises. (For examples see preceding exercises checking comprehension of the stories about elephants.)

III. Tracing words. Especially helpful in this case in learning to spell and in fixing the recognition of polysyllabic words.

IV. A "word box" was kept. As words were learned they were filed alphabetically in a box with index cards. These words were referred to often for spelling help.

V. A picture dictionary was kept in a notebook. Pictures were cut from magazines to illustrate the words and phrases which presented difficulty. If a suitable picture could not be found in the magazines, the boy drew a small one of his own, which would help to recall the word for him. The words were kept in alphabetic order with the illustration pasted beside the word. The word was written in script and typewritten. Beside the word itself an illustrative phrase or sentence about the picture was often written. No gain in word recognition can be directly attributable to these latter devises. They served mainly to keep up the boy's interest.

BIBLIOGRAPHY

Books

DOLCH, EDWARD WILLIAM. *The Psychology and Teaching of Reading.* Boston: Ginn and Company, 1931.

GATES, ARTHUR IRVING. *The Improvement of Reading; a Program of Diagnostic and Remedial Methods.* New York: The Macmillan Company, 1927.

GATES, ARTHUR IRVING. *Interest and Ability in Reading.* New York: The Macmillan Company, 1931.

GATES, ARTHUR IRVING. *Reading for Public School Administrators.* New York: Bureau of Publications, Teachers College, Columbia University, 1931.

GRAY, WILLIAM SCOTT. *Summary of Investigations Relating to Reading.* Chicago: University of Chicago Press, 1925. Continued by an annual summary in the *Elementary School Journal*, 1926–32, and in the *Journal of Educational Research*, 1933.

MONROE, MARION. *Children Who Cannot Read.* Chicago: University of Chicago Press, 1932.

The Principal and Supervision. Tenth Yearbook. Department of Elementary School Principals. National Education Association. Washington: National Education Association, 1931.

PATTERSON, SAMUEL WHITE. *Teaching the Child to Read; Practical Studies in Reading Method.* Garden City, New York: Doubleday, Doran & Company, 1930.

Report of the National Committee on Reading. Twenty-fourth Yearbook, Part I. National Society for the Study of Education. Edited by Guy Montrose Whipple. Bloomington, Illinois: Public School Publishing Company, 1925.

Report of the Society's Committee on Silent Reading. Twentieth Yearbook, Part II. National Society for the Study of Education. Bloomington, Illinois: Public School Publishing Company, 1921.

SMITH, NILA BANTON. *One Hundred Ways of Teaching Silent Reading.* Yonkers-on-Hudson, New York: World Book Company, 1925.

"Special Classes for Non-readers." *Fourth Yearbook, 1931.* CCXI (School Publication, 1931), 99–105. Los Angeles: Division of Psychology and Educational Research.

ZIRBES, LAURA. *Comparative Studies of Current Practice in Reading, with Techniques for the Improvement of Teaching.* Contributions to Education, No. 316. New York: Bureau of Publications, Teachers College, Columbia University, 1928.

Periodical Articles

BEATTY, WILLARD WALCOTT. "Teaching of Reading: Modern Reading Technique and Its Results." *Grade Teacher.* L (April, 1933), 594–5.

BLACKHURST, JAMES HERBERT. "Nature of the Reading Process." *Elementary English Review.* X (April, 1933), 3–5.

BONAR, HUGH SAMUEL. "Systematic Versus Incidental Training in Reading." *Elementary English Review.* X (April, 1933), 90–4.

GATES, ARTHUR IRVING. "Improved Methods Suggested by Recent Research." *Indiana University School of Education Bulletin.* IX (September, 1932), 70–80.

GRAY, WILLIAM SCOTT. "Reading; Special Methods in the Elementary Schools." *Review of Educational Research.* I (February, 1931), 247–60.

GRAY, WILLIAM SCOTT. "Summary of Reading Investigations: July 1, 1931, to June 30, 1932." *Journal of Educational Research.* XXVI (February, 1933), 401–24.

MONROE, MARION. "Remedial Treatment in Reading." *Elementary English Review.* X (April, 1933), 95–7.

MURPHY, PAUL G. "Role of the Concept of Reading Ability." *Elementary English Review.* X (April, 1933), 86–9.

PARKER, CLAUDIA M., and WATERBURY, E. A. "Reading Disability." *Educational Method.* XII (April, 1933), 411–19.

SMITH, MADORAH ELIZABETH. "Direction of Reading and the Effect of Foreign Language School Attendance on Learning to Read." *Pedagogical Seminary.* XL (June, 1932), 422–51.

SMITH, NILA BANTON. "Functional Reading Objectives." *Educational Method.* XII (April, 1933), 427–32.

SMITH, NILA BANTON. "Sucessive Emphases in American Reading Instruction." *Teachers College Record.* XXXIV (December, 1932), 188–203.

THAYER, BEATRICE. "Pupil-teacher Group-work: How to Provide for Individual Differences in Reading." *Grade Teacher.* L (September, 1932), 34–5.

TINKER, MILES ALBERT. "Diagnostic and Remedial Reading." Bibliography. *Elementary School Journal.* XXXIII (December, 1932), 293–306; XXXIII (January, 1933), 346–57.

WITTY, PAUL ANDREW, and LEHMAN, H. C. "Study of the Reading and Reading Interests of Gifted Children." Bibliography. *Pedagogical Seminary.* XL (June, 1932), 473–85.

Chapter XVI

READING IN THE CONTENT FIELDS[1]

GENERAL PROCEDURES

In the content subjects, pupils receive guidance in reading for purposes to which they have been introduced in the reading period and for purposes peculiar to a subject. For example, while pupils apply to history suitable reading techniques, they also determine the time order of events and read and interpret maps. Pupils develop the kind of thinking inherent in the subject. For example, in arithmetic they sense relationships between numbers presented in problems, and in geography they think in terms of the relationship of human items to the environment. They could not effectively interpret materials of these fields if this were not true. They become familiar with the meaning and pronunciation of important new words peculiar to the subject and with new meanings of many already familiar words. Furthermore, pupils continue to read voluntarily on the many interesting subjects to which they are introduced in the content subjects. Instruction is adjusted to individual needs, and remedial training is given in applying in the content fields abilities developed in the reading period. Materials used during other periods should be carefully chosen and of such a type that it will insure thinking and establish centers of reading interest for each child. Text books, books containing detailed information, fiction and non-fiction of the literary type, should all find a place in a well arranged program. The reading difficulty of these materials should as a rule be somewhat easier than those used in the reading period, since the pupil must employ reading as a tool in developing new concepts in the content field.[2]

The following skeleton of objectives, procedures, and outcomes has been set up to guide the teacher in developing reading abilities and interests in children:

A. Objectives

    1. To establish interest and attitudes

        a. Arouse interest in reading activities

        b. Stimulate good thinking

        c. Extend the pupil's experiences through worthwhile reading

        d. Link pupil's reading with the content subjects

---

[1] Contributed by Lillian Lamoreaux, Supervisor of Elementary Schools, Burbank, California.

[2] Bulletin 334, 1932. Los Angeles City Schools, Division of Course of Study, Ethel I. Salisbury, Director.

2. To develop habits and skills
   a. Comprehension and interpretation
      recognizing main ideas
      recognizing contrasting or conflicting ideas
      drawing valid conclusions
      analyzing and understanding characters and events
      organizing and outlining
      making judgments
      comparing actions and results
   b. Application and Use
      retention of facts
      reproduction—oral reading
      dramatization
      productions—manual and art
   c. Mechanics of reading
      independence in the use of study helps, glossary, maps,
        references, charts, graphs, etc.
      acquisition, development, and refinement of vocabulary

B. Procedure
   Provide reading tables or book shelves.
      A wide variety of books and reading materials.
      A challenging problem.
      Proper guidance.

C. Outcomes[1]
   As a result of the periods devoted to the content subjects the pupil:
   Reads widely in the fields by free choice.
   Acquires wide information which assists in interpreting new
   content.
   Thinks actively when reading, employing the kind of thinking
   appropriate to the subject matter.
   Reads effectively for many different purposes, materials relating
   to the content subjects.
   Utilizes illustrative material for the light it throws upon the
   context.
   Interprets accurately a wide variety of graphic materials, such as
   line and bar graphs, rainfall, relief and population maps; and tabular
   data.
   Understands clearly basic words which occur in reading materials
   relating to the content subjects.
   Pronounces such words correctly.

---

[1] *Ibid.*

Recognizes the general time placement of dates met in the content subjects.

Attends first to the situations described in arithmetic problems rather than to the numbers presented.

Gives evidence of concrete concepts of the magnitude of numbers met in reading.

In order to use effectively the materials presented in the content subjects children need certain types of reading skills as: ability to read intensively to get information from texts; ability to skim to secure points which have a definite bearing on the problem and reject all other information; ability to read widely for background relating to a particular problem. Particular study habits are needed in order to do this and these are best developed in connection with the content subjects themselves and the activities relating to them. Examples of these needed habits are suggested here:

1. Locating information in a paragraph, on a page, in a selection, in a number of books, in a library. These involve the use of tables of content and indices, the use of a card index, cross references, footnotes, and dictionaries.

2. Collecting and organizing information for some purpose. These involve note taking, outlining, organizing, and gathering facts in sequence.

3. Formulating questions raised during study.

4. Recognizing when the problem has been solved. This involves a knowledge of inferences, conclusions, summaries.

5. Reading and interpreting graphs, charts, tables and other forms in which data are presented.

6. Recognizing equivalent statements in spite of changes in terminology or sentence structure.

The National Committee on Reading recommends two types of reading for most school subjects.[1] First, the textbook material which is centered around a problem or unit of work. Here the habits and attitudes of preliminary training are applied and further developed and specialized as in map reading or in attacking an arithmetic problem.

The second type is the simple supplementary recreatory book which relates to the unit of work. This type of work individualizes, enriches and broadens the experiences of the children and calls forth much voluntary reading, due to interest and pure enjoyment.

[1] National Society for the Study of Education. *The Twenty-Fourth Yearbook.* Part 1. "Report of the National Committee on Reading." Bloomington, Illinois: Public School Publishing Company, 1925.

Reading in the content fields needs to be guided and needs to be purposeful. The materials should be well organized in order that each child may read and contribute. Various and numerous checks should be given to test the outcomes of the reading program. This may be done by informal tests, culminations of units in form of reports, dramatizations, making of still film, illustrations, etc.

Courtesy of Lodi Public Schools

Every Content Subject Is Called Upon to Furnish Reading Experiences

Interest and Attitudes

Almost every content subject is called upon today to furnish reading experiences to the children in order that they may learn to solve problems and do good thinking. No longer can teachers say, "this is a reading period; this is a geography period, a language, science or a history period." The program of work in a modern school is so integrated that many of the content subjects are grouped as social studies and social studies material becomes reading material and reading material becomes good social studies material. This is equally true of the language arts, nature study or health. Even arithmetic offers a type of reading material and teachers must definitely give children training in interpreting arithmetic content.

Children read to find out or to get correct ideas for a felt need, to help solve a problem, or to express themselves. Pupils may read only a portion of a book which applies to the problem at hand or they may read the complete book or article. A felt need for reading stimulates and motivates reading and expedites the learning process. Children become aware of the need of reading skill as a necessary tool. The content of the printed page has a value to them and the use they make of what is read offers them satisfaction.

Some illustrations of ways in which reading may be guided in connection with the integrated program of work follow:

EXAMPLE I

A UNIT OF WORK ON EGYPTIAN LIFE [1]

Ways in Which Interest in Reading Activities Was Aroused

The class approached this unit through the story of Azir Girges.[2] They read aloud chapters from the book, describing Azir's trip up the Nile, his jaunt to the desert, and other typical Egyptian experiences. The children asked many questions, such as, "What did the house boat look like?" "Can you still see those pyramids?"

Beeby's history [3] was found interesting and helpful in answering the questions. A day or two was spent in reading and in informal discussion, then two sets of films were secured and shown to the children showing ancient Egypt. These films stimulated the thinking and furthered the interest of the children to the extent that they were now eager to work in earnest.

Ways in Which Good Thinking Was Stimulated

At this point the children were asked if they would like to prepare a brief story of Egypt. They were eager to do so. The question was asked, "If you were talking to someone who had never studied this land, what are some of the interesting things you would wish to tell him?" Some of the responses were, "We could tell him what the people look like," "We could show him the pyramids." As these suggestions were made, they were placed on the board. Then the children were asked to look at the list to see if it was in logical order. It was not, so they tried to reorganize it. As a child would suggest, "We could tell about modern Egypt last," the teacher wrote "Modern Egypt" at the bottom of the board. When someone suggested a topic to be reported upon first it was written at the top of the board. Gradually the remaining topics were placed in proper order. After the reorganization was satisfactory to the children they were asked, "When

---

[1] Contributed by Miss Elizabeth Feeley, Sixth Grade Teacher, William McKinley School, Burbank, California.
[2] W. S. Perry. *In Egypt With Azir Girges.* Chicago: Mentzer, Bush and Company, 1913.
[3] Daniel J. Beeby and Dorothea Beeby. *America's Roots in the Past.* New York: Charles E. Merrill Company, 1927.

you have told your friends of these things do you think they would have a clear picture of Egypt?'' The group felt satisfied with their arrangement after some thought of the material noted in the topics.

The children divided the topics into sections and were allowed to choose the section upon which they wished to work in committee formation. Their names were written on the board opposite the chosen topic. Groups which were not experienced in committee work were given specific aid in organization within the group and help was given in adapting the work to the individual children within each group.

When the groups reported to the class on work completed it was interesting to see that every child on a committee was eager to contribute something to make the work a success. Some of the contributions were meager but each one felt he had a part. For example, in the case of the group reporting on music, one child made the report, another child held the chart showing the musical instruments, and a third wound the victrola while another put on the record. All contributed to the success of the whole.

Ways in Which the Pupil's Experiences Were Extended Through Worthwhile Reading in the Content Subjects

Much time was spent, before attempting to read for their reports, in discussing a bibliography. ''What books would be likely to give us information on Egypt as a whole?'' ''What books would be likely to give us information on our particular topic'' were questions discussed.

The children were allowed to go to the library to secure any books they found relating to the subject. The bibliography and references were placed on the board.

When the groups were well along in their reading they were told that they might order the materials for their maps, charts, or posters when they had decided what they would need.

Before the reports were due the captains of each group were asked to prepare an outline of the topics covered by their committees. They did this by collecting all the reports within their group, reading or talking them over with the persons who wrote them. Then the outline was compiled.

The reports were given before the class with the teacher, the principal and the supervisor as special members of the audience. The reports were well prepared, although not too well delivered. The children had read widely and in most cases were so familiar with their material that they were able to speak without notes. They told their stories simply and in their own words. Charts and pictures made by the children were vivid and very interesting.

From a consideration of the oral reports which were given came certain specific suggestions as to improvement in delivery. The children were praised for the good work they had done in preparing their talks but were told that the guests had not been able to hear everything. The class worked out cooperatively simple suggestions which would improve their delivery as—

> Stand up straight.
> Speak clearly and slowly.
> Hold heads up.

During this study the class had difficulty in finding many desert songs to sing. As no suggestions came from the children the teacher asked them if they had ever tried to write a song. No one had but the idea seemed to strike their fancies. They were invited to experiment. They had little trouble with the verses but the music was difficult. After a time this method was used; the verse was written on the board with the staff above it.

Volunteers were called for to sing the first line. As a child would sing a line that pleased the audience and seemed to express the feeling of the Egyptians, the notes were written on the staff. The following song was finally completed.

AN EGYPTIAN DAY

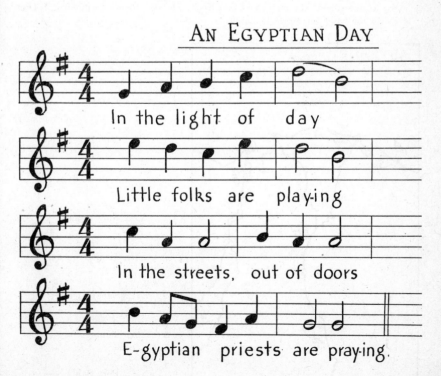

The following check-test prepared by the teacher at the conclusion of the project reveals the type of experiences the children had and shows integration of the content fields.

EGYPT

1. The Nile overflowing caused:
   a. Many people to lose their lives.
   b. Rich soil to be deposited.
   c. Poor crops because the water ruined them.
   d. A shortage of water each year.
2. The boats had sails and when sails did not work they had _____ which they could use.
3. What did the farmer do when he threw the seed on the top of the ground?
4. The Nile Valley was:
   a. Very high.
   b. Rather low.
   c. Rather high.
   d. Quite low.
5. How often did a rich Egyptian lady comb her hair? _____.
6. What kind of clothes did the laborers wear?
7. What kind of clothes did the rich man wear?
8. What kind of houses did the laborers live in?
9. The pyramids were made to be used as _____.
10. What took the place of the practice of leaving food in the tombs?
11. What was the purpose of the carvings on the sides of the tombs?
12. The Egyptian paper or papyrus was made from _____.
13. On the following map there are numbers instead of the names of places. At the side of the map there is a list of places. Place the number in front of the name for which it stands.

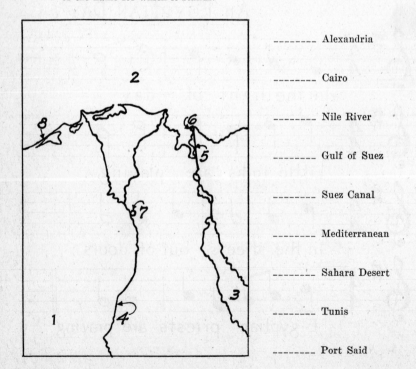

_____	Alexandria
_____	Cairo
_____	Nile River
_____	Gulf of Suez
_____	Suez Canal
_____	Mediterranean
_____	Sahara Desert
_____	Tunis
_____	Port Said

14. What did the Egyptians use for writing?
15. Check the musical instruments in the following list which were used by the Egyptians:
    a. lyre
    b. cornet
    c. horn
    d. piano
    e. trombone
    f. harp
16. Write 345 using the Egyptian numbers.

Bibliography Used by the Children

BARNES, F. *Man and His Record.* Chicago: Thomas S. Rockwell Company, 1931, pp. 42-50.

COMPTON, F. E. *Compton's Pictured Encyclopedia.* Chicago: F. E. Compton and Company, pp. 1098, 1092, 101, 2939, 1101.

GREGORY, J. W. *Africa.* Chicago: Rand McNally and Company, 1928, p. 456.

HALL, N. M. *Tales of Far-Off Days.* Boston: Ginn and Company, 1922, pp. 107, 165.

HALLOCK, G. T. *Grain Through the Ages.* Chicago: Quaker Oats Company, 1929, pp. 19-24.

HALLOCK, G. T. *Hob O' the Mill.* Chicago: Quaker Oats Company, 1929, p. 39.

HARDING, S. B. *Old World Background to American History.* Chicago: Scott, Foresman and Company, 1919, pp. 3-11.

HARPER, W., and HAMILTON, A. J. *Far-Away Hills.* New York: The Macmillan Company, 1929, p. 46.

KELLY, R. T. *Egypt.* London: A. & C. Black, 1902.

NIDA, W. L. *Dawn of American History.* New York: The Macmillan Company, 1912, pp. 17-35.

PERRY, W. S. *In Egypt with Azir Girges.* Chicago: Mentzer, Bush and Company, 1913.

STARR, L. B. *Mustafa, the Egyptian Boy.* Chicago: A. Flanagan Company, 1905, p. 146.

THOMPSON, H. and MEE, A., (eds.) *The Book of Knowledge,* Vol. 11, p. 3710, Vol. 3, p. 806. New York: Grolier Society.

VAN LOON, H. W. *Story of Mankind.* New York: The Macmillan Company, 1931, pp. 16-19, 21-25.

WEST, R., and WEST, W. M. *The New World's Foundations in the Old.* Boston: Allyn and Bacon, 1929, pp. 18-39.

EXAMPLE II
A READING LESSON IN "EVALUATING" [1]

In preparation for this lesson the teacher listed the following:
Evaluating consists of:

1. Comparing and contrasting—synonyms and antonyms
2. Seeing cause and effect—how or why
3. Predicting outcomes

---

[1] Contributed by Alice Gratrix, Teacher, Grade 6A, Joaquin Miller School, Burbank, California.

4. Judging character and deeds
5. Noting literary qualities
6. Relating what is read to personal experience
7. Supplementing data (using other reference books)
8. Planning illustrations for texts

It was found possible to bring into this lesson several of the above types of work. The story of the ''Warrior Ants''[1] was chosen because of the interest in ants in our Nature Study Club.

The following procedure was used with the children:

The introductory note about Jean Henri Fabre was read by this group of ten children of varied reading abilities. The children were asked to recall as they read the story if they had had a similar experience. (See 6 above). While they read, paper was passed, and as each child finished he did the True-False Test at the end of the story, consisting of twenty statements.

When most of the children had finished the written work, the class talked about some of their experiences with ants. One told of a battle he had seen between red and black ants, with the red ants victorious. Another child said she had found it true that ants always followed the same trail, despite possible short cuts. Several other children contributed equally interesting details about ants.

The attention of the whole group was called to paragraph 3 in the story, which said, ''Long ago the Greeks told stories of a strange country inhabited by terrible women warriors. They were called *Amazons*. Can you tell why the writer calls the Red Ants Amazons?''[2]   In considering the answer to this question the children brought out the fact that warrior ants are female. One child recalled a magazine article in which women communists in Los Angeles were called Amazons. This application of previously gained information to a new situation was gratifying to the teacher.

''Did you notice, on page 195, the part of the story that said, 'They are unable to bring up their own families, to look for their food, to take it even when it is within their reach?' What do you suppose is the reason for that?'' One child explained it was because they were so used to being waited on that they were not equipped to eat coarser food, and had to have it fed to them in liquid form. The teacher compared this with the story of the measuring worm, who had lost his middle feet because he used only the ones on either end. This offered an opportunity for discussion of character development. The children

---

[1] Alberta Walker and Mary R. Parkman. ''The Warrior Ants.'' *The Study Readers, Sixth Year.* New York: Charles E. Merrill Company, 1925, pp. 194–199.
[2] *Ibid.,* p. 199.

were impressed with the fact that if a thing is not used it disappears or becomes valueless.

The teacher suggested that if some child could find more on inability of warrior ants to provide for themselves, he could report to the class. This provided an opportunity for use of other data and reference books, as well as for using judgment and observing cause and effect relationships.

One boy read excerpts from *The Prince and His Ants*,[1] which he had enjoyed. Another child commented that from his own personal experience he found June and July to be the best months for watching ants.

A True-False Test was given as a culmination to the lesson and any doubtful points were clarified by the teacher.

EXAMPLE III

EVALUATION OF MATERIAL READ[2]

Class: 4B Social Studies
Subject: "Desert Life"
Book: Carpenter, F. G. *Around the World With the Children.* New York: American Book Company, 1917, Chapter 11, pp. 93-103.

Procedure

The following five questions were compiled by the teacher which might be answered by any member of the class who understood the significance of the factual material in the chapter assigned. The group was referred to the sections of the chapter which dealt with the desert and town homes, the clothes of the Arabs and travel on camels. None of these questions are suggested in the reading matter, but all the information necessary for discovering the answers is given.

1. Why do the Arabs have so little furniture?
2. Why is the camel often called the "ship of the desert?"
3. How do the Arabs know that a place is good for a well?
4. Why do the people in the desert wear so many more clothes than those in the jungle even though it is very hot?
5. Why are the houses in the towns not built of wood?

The results of this directed study were as follows:

1. Every answer included the fact that Arabs move often and that furniture could not be burdensome for the camels to carry. One person in the group also thought that the scarcity of trees, and consequently of wood, was another reason for the lack of furniture among these

---

[1] Lugi Bartelli (Vambda, *pseud.*) *The Prince and His Ants.* New York: Henry Holt and Company, 1910.
[2] Contributed by Mrs. Esther Earl Lindley, Teacher, Burbank, California.

people. The class decided that this was a plausible reason why the more permanent homes in the towns did not have much furniture.

2. The majority of the group decided that the camel was given the name because he rocked back and forth, or swayed from side to side, much as a ship would on waves. Two children suggested that it was because he was used so much for travel on the sand and could travel longer than any other animal.

3. Only one person in the group failed to recognize that grass and trees indicated the presence of water and, therefore, such a location would be a good place to dig a well. That person said he would dig for a well in an oasis, so he probably had the right idea rather vaguely in mind.

4. All of the group agreed that the danger of sunburn caused Arabs to wear many clothes, since their skin was not as dark as the jungle people's. Two children suggested that clothes were a protection during sand storms. The class decided that the coverings on the heads would be a protection against sunstroke as well.

5. All except one in the group said that houses were not built of wood because of lack of trees in the desert. That person thought that mud brick houses would be cooler than wooden ones. He had probably heard someone say this of brick houses in this country.

EXAMPLE IV

A READING LESSON IN FINDING SPECIFIC DATA [1]

There are several types of lessons which are included in the big objective of finding specific data, such as finding isolated facts; finding enumerated facts; grouping scattered facts; using pictures of data and interpreting data; using maps for data; making questions.

A teacher attempted to apply this method to a lesson in the *Triangle Arithmetic Book VI*,[2] "How Interest is Paid." Previous experiences of the class were used to introduce this lesson. The teacher said, "In our class bank we have been talking about interest and how it is paid. I am going to give you a reading assignment which, if read carefully, will show you how to figure interest. Study page 241. Raise your hand when you have finished."

Following is a shortened version of what all the children studied:

When Harry's class began to deposit money in the savings bank, his teacher told the pupils that the bank would pay 4% interest a year

[1] Contributed by Alice Gratrix, Teacher, Joaquin Miller School, Burbank, California.
[2] Leo J. Brueckner, and Others. *The Triangle Arithmetics*. Grade Six. "How Interest is Paid." California State Series. Sacramento: California State Department of Education, 1932, pp. 241, 242.

for the use of the money. Banks usually pay half the yearly interest every six months, although some pay by the year.

　　1. Suppose that you lent someone $50 at 4% a year interest. For the use of the money for one year, he would pay 4 per cent of $50. How much is 4% of $50? Think 4% of $50 = .04 × $50 = $2.00 interest for 1 year.

　　2. If he kept the money for two years, how much would be the interest on $50 at 4%? Think 4% of $50 = $2.00, the interest for one year.

　　2 × $2.00 = $4.00, the interest for 2 years.

　　3. Find the interest on $100 for 6 months at 4% a year. Think 6 mo. = ? year _____

As soon as most of the class had signalled they had read the page, the teacher said, ''If you do not yet feel sure you would know how to work a problem in interest, re-read the page.'' Some half-dozen felt they understood after one reading but the others re-read the selection. One child in particular studied by trying to work out some of the examples as the book did. Then the teacher said, ''If you have read carefully you will know *what* interest a bank pays, *when* it pays interest, and *how* to find interest for one year, two years, or more. Now we'll have paper passed and see if you understood what you read.'' While the children were putting headings on their papers, she asked, ''What do you have to know in order to figure interest?'' And these responses were given: ''What interest is paid?'' ''For how long is the money borrowed?'' ''How much money is borrowed?'' (This illustrates ''making questions'' noted under the several types of lessons to be included under Finding Specific Data, page 292.)

The questions suggested were put on the board in this manner:

　　a. How much money?
　　b. For how long?　　　　　　Finding enumerated facts.
　　c. Find the answer.

The children were asked to answer each question for problems 7 to 13 on page 242 in the text.

While they were working the teacher walked about the room to help where necessary. Some children had not read carefully enough to see that *4% of* means *.04 times,* although they should have remembered from previous work in percentage. Some children made careless mistakes in answering the questions, consequently they had the wrong results. This work had purposely been planned to call attention to the three different parts of an interest problem, namely, principal, interest, and time, so that they would keep these in mind for accurate results.

Some children were able to do more than the seven problems assigned. Before the close of the period, answers for the seven problems were read and the papers corrected. It developed that eighteen of the thirty-nine children understood the work without being helped in any way; many others retained the idea after being helped once.

EXAMPLE V

HOW TO TEACH PUPILS TO OUTLINE

The general plan of this lesson is similar to that suggested by Anderson and Davidson.[1] When pupils are being taught to outline, all material should be easily read and the selections should be short. Experiences in outlining should be provided over a period of years, the difficulty of the assignment increasing with the ability of the children.

Lessons in developing outlining should include the following steps:

1. Teacher and pupils working together select the main topics. (Many English teachers prefer main headings *stated in good, short sentences.*)
2. Pupils select the main topics.
3. Teacher and pupils select the main topics, but space is left for sub-heads. Teacher and pupils fill in these sub-topics.
4. Main topics selected by teacher and pupils and written on the blackboard, or placed on the board by the teacher, or provided by the text. Pupils fill in sub-topics.
5. Pupils write main topics and sub-heads.
6. Pupils organize in outline form, data gathered from many sources.

The following lessons are suggested for training pupils to find and place in outline form the main topics.[2]

1. Use books with paragraph headings. Read the paragraphs. Discuss the headings. Suggest other possible headings. Decide why the author selected the heading.
2. Match a given list of paragraph headings to paragraphs that have been numbered.
3. Have pupils suggest paragraph headings.
4. Have pupils read a paragraph with this question in mind. "What is the main idea in this paragraph?" Write a number of suggested answers on the blackboard. Rewrite the best answer as number I under the title of the story. Do the same for the remaining two or three paragraphs. Discuss the form of the outline and why outlines are important. Have pupils copy the outline.

---

[1] Charles J. Anderson and Isobel Davidson. *Reading Objectives.* Chicago: Laurel Book Company, 1925.
[2] Contributed by Mrs. Rebecca Farley, Teacher, Abraham Lincoln School, Burbank, California.

5. Have the pupils select the main topics in answer to the question, "What is the central thought in this paragraph?" Discuss the outlines with the group. Write the best topics on the board.

6. Continue these lessons until the pupils are capable of selecting and writing in outline form the main topics.

Lessons for training pupils to fill in the sub-topics.

1. Teacher and pupils write main topics on the board, teacher writes main topics on board, or use a text that has the main headings. Teacher and pupils fill in sub-heads.

2. Have pupils fill in sub-heads.

3. Have pupils fill in both main topics and sub-heads.

Lessons for training pupils to organize, in outline form, data gathered from many sources.[1]

1. Have pupils read about the subject in one book, select main topics, and, perhaps, one sub-head. Leave room for more sub-heads and main topics.

2. Have pupils skim other articles for more information. Read carefully when additional sub-heads are found and add these. Do the same for new main topics.

3. When pupils have gathered sufficient data, have them re-read the complete outline, and if necessary, rearrange the order of the topics.

4. Have pupils use this outline in preparing and giving an oral report.

SUGGESTED FORM

Title

I. Main topic—a short sentence, if desired.
   A. Sub-head—a word or phrase.
      1. Second sub-head—a word or phrase.
II. Main topic.

EXAMPLE VI

LEARNING TO FILL IN AN OUTLINE [2]

Below is an outline on parts IV, V, and VI of the lesson "Life in the Sahara Desert." Each main topic is the name of one part of the lesson. Topic I is about part IV. Find topic I. Topic II

---

[1] *Note:* When pupils are doing this type of outlining the teacher should pass from pupil to pupil, giving individual instruction. When necessary, group discussion should be held.

[2] Taken from Ernest Horn and Ruth M. Moscrip. *Learn to Study Readers.* Book IV, Grade V, pp. 165–166. Boston: Ginn and Company, 1926.

is about part V. Find topic II. Topic III is about part VI. Find topic III.

Under topic I there are two parts. These parts are A and B. Read A. Read B. Can you put in the information under A?

One animal which the desert people use in traveling is the camel. The word *camel* would be 1 under A. What other animals are used for traveling? The names of these animals would be after 2 and 3 under A.

Can you fill in the rest of the outline?

I. *How these desert people travel*—

    A. Animals used in traveling
      1.
      2.
      3.

    B. What the camels carry
      1.   3.
      2.   4.

II. *What these people do for a living*—

    A. What the people who travel raise
      1.
      2.

    B. What the people raise in an oasis
      1.
      2
      3.
      4.

    C. What caravans carry to trade
      1.
      2.
      3.
      4.

III. *Where the great deserts are*—

    A. Deserts in the United States
      1.
      2.
      3.
      4.

B. Deserts in other parts of the world
  1.
  2.
  3.

EXAMPLE VII

ORGANIZATION OF FACTS [1]

Some of the different methods used to teach 6A classes to summarize and organize facts have been as follows:

1. In the preparation of a program
2. In the making of a class booklet
3. Through dramatizations
4. In the giving of reports
5. In the making of diagrams, charts, or illustrative material.

After one of the 6A classes had finished reading about early civilization, they made a class booklet called "The Beginning of Things," in which were saved the stories about the first fire, the first tools, the first home, etc. It was necessary to summarize by a discussion all that had been learned before the plan for the book could be completed.

The organization of the material which had been collected in the unit on the architecture of Greece occurred in a program, prepared for a school assembly. Short talks were given, while large wall pictures were used to illustrate the following topics: The Origin of the Olympic Games; The Purpose of the Ancient Games; The Religion of the Greeks; The Acropolis; The Parthenon. A dramatization of the "Myth of Demeter and Persephone" followed. These two characters had been pointed out among the immortals in the sculpture of the Parthenon.

During the study of modern Europe it has been necessary to summarize and organize material frequently. This has been taken care of partly by journeys to the land of each child's choice. For example, Jean had recently made a trip to England so she gave the first report. When she had finished, the class outlined her report together on the board. From this, topics for discussion were put into a working outline for the rest of the class to use, in gathering material for their reports.

Sometimes these reports were very meager, sometimes highly imaginative, but they summarized the knowledge the child had been able to gather for himself.

---

[1] Contributed by Miss Arline Dunne, Teacher, Ralph W. Emerson School, Burbank, California.

EXAMPLE VIII
READING FOR INFORMATION [1]

Class: 4B Social Studies.

Subject: "Desert Life."

Book: Carpenter, F. G. *Around the World With the Children.* New York: American Book Company, 1917, Chapter 11, pp. 93–103.

In making plans for the construction of a desert scene on a sand table, the class compiled a list of eleven questions to be answered before beginning work.

1. What kind of country is Arabia?

2. What is an oasis?

3. What kind of trees are there?

4. What kind of people live there?

5. How do the people dress?

6. What kind of homes do they have?

7. How do they get water?

8. What kind of food do the people have?

9. How do they travel?

10. What animals are there in Arabia?

11. What do the animals eat?

The wording of some of these questions indicated that the pupils had some vague notions about a desert, and their questions were consequently directed to certain things, such as the scarcity of water in desert regions, which they needed to understand more fully.

The second reading group was assigned the task of answering these questions for the benefit of the class. Each member of the group was given one question and directed to read the pages indicated in Carpenter's book. He was told that probably all the information about his question would not be located in the same paragraph or page, that it would be necessary for him to read the entire section and pick out those points which would help him to answer the question fully.

The answers which were reported to the class the next day are as follows: [2]

---

[1] Contributed by Mrs. Esther Earl Lindley, Teacher, Burbank, California.
[2] The italicized portions were added by other members of the reading group or the class in general discussion.

1. Arabia is very sandy. It is very hot and dry. There is very little grass and a few trees. Water is scarce. It hardly ever rains. It is quite level. There are small hills and dunes.

2. An oasis is a place in the desert where there are grass and trees and water. *It is sometimes large enough for a town.*

3. They have orange trees, lemon trees, pear trees, peach trees, fig trees, and date palms. *There are more palm trees than others.*

4. They are brown people and have straight black hair. *They really belong to the white race, but are tanned by the sun.*

5. They wear a cloth around their heads and a long gown from their neck to their feet. *They also wear leather sandals.*

6. In the desert they live in a tent made of cloth. It is divided into two rooms, one for the men and one for the women of the family. *The cloth is made of camel's hair and sheep's wool. In towns they have houses made of mud brick dried in the sun. The houses have flat roofs.*

7. They get water from a well or a spring. *The towns are located where they can get water this way.*

8. The people eat dates, figs, roast kid, flat round cakes, cheese and coffee. *They also eat oranges and peaches sometimes. The cheese is made of goat's milk.*

9. They travel on camels, donkeys, or horses. *They use camels mostly. The donkeys are used more in the cities. The camel is best for desert travel because it can go without food or water for a long time and because its feet are wide and keep it from sinking into the sand.*

10. The animals found in the desert are: sheep, goat, camel, horse, jackal, hyena, donkey, leopard, and lion. *There are also ostriches.*

11. The animals eat the grass that grows in some parts of the desert and the leaves from bushes. *They also eat alfalfa which is grown in the towns and also dates and figs.*

EXAMPLE IX

A MAP READING LESSON [1]

In the 6A class, our course in social science consists of a study of the modern European nations. We need to use maps frequently for physical, economic, and political references. We also make our own maps to show trade lines, travel itineraries, etc.

[1] Contributed by Miss Elizabeth Feeley, Teacher, William McKinley School, Burbank, California.

Children, therefore, need to be able to use the map as a familiar tool. And so we have an occasional short drill in the mechanics of map reading.

The following map lesson was given to the sixth grade class.

A large wall map of Africa was used to introduce the lesson.

The children were asked:

"Suppose this is the first map you have used. What are some of the questions you would ask about it?"

The following questions were asked by the children and were written on the board.

1. What country is that?
2. What kind of people live there?
3. What do they raise?
4. What do those lines mean?
5. What kind of homes do the people live in?
6. Is that a cold country?
7. What ocean is that?

The group went to work to answer these questions.

Question number one was easy. The name of the country was written across the map.

Question number two raised a difference of opinion. A few children felt that in some way—they didn't know how—you could tell what kind of people lived there from the map. Most of the class felt, however, that this question could not be answered from a map. Each child had a copy of *Nations Beyond the Sea* [1] in his desk. We turned to page 49, and found two small maps of Africa. One showed the population, the other showed rainfall. The class discussed the key, and then looked to see where there were many people, and where there were only a few. In order to understand this distribution the second map was studied, and it was found that in the areas where there was the heaviest rainfall, there were also the most people.

On the desert there was little rainfall and few people. The kind of a land it must be was then discussed and it was decided that the desert must be very hot, that it would be impossible to raise crops there, and that the people were probably wandering nomads, and lived in tents. These opinions were confirmed by reading in the text.

Along the Nile there was abundant rainfall, and many people. The group decided that these people were probably farmers. After this very interesting discussion the children felt that it was possible to tell something about the people, from the map.

---

[1] W. W. Atwood and H. G. Thomas. *Nations Beyond the Sea.* Boston: Ginn and Company, 1930.

Questions two, five and six were now answered and question three was attacked.

"What do they raise?"

The children saw that they would need another kind of map. This was found on page 140, *Nations Beyond the Sea*,[1] "A Political and Economic Map of Central Europe."

Here the key was discussed again and it was discovered that in this map could be found boundaries of countries, seaports, capitals, rivers, canals, products, and mineral resources.

The teacher said, "In what country is silver mined?" or "In what country do you find dairy products?" The children enjoyed this. It was a game to them.

The class then turned to question four. The meanings of the lines were explained by the teacher. Greenwich Village was found and one or two cities in different degrees of latitude and longitude were located.

Then to emphasize a point, the teacher said, "We have had to use different kinds of maps to answer different kinds of questions. How many kinds of maps have we used?" The children answered, "We used one that showed the people." (Economic) "We used one that showed countries." (Economic and Political) "There is one more. Let us find a map that shows what the land looks like." (Physical)

This the class found on page 13, *Nations Beyond the Sea*,[2] "A Physical Map of Europe, Showing Natural Regions." Here the children again turned to the key, and spent a minute or two locating different regions, such as low, moist, rugged lands, etc.

The children were told that they would be asked some questions that they would have to think hard about. The answers were not to be found in the key. They were asked to locate a country in which they would expect to find a mild, pleasant climate, etc. They pointed to the lowland country. Then they were asked the reason for their choice, and this stimulated a discussion about the effects of geographical features on climate.

The value of this lesson was that it provided experience in interpreting and making use of map keys; the children became familiar with the map index, and learned to use the figures at the side of the map to locate cities, etc.; the lines of latitude and longitude, the degree sign, were interpreted to them; the children realized, perhaps for the first time, that a map answers many different kinds of questions; and important, also, was the experience in reasoning; in taking a map and reading into it a meaning.

---

[1] *Ibid.*
[2] *Ibid.*

Chapter XVII

RECREATORY READING [1]

If children are asked why they read, two reasons are always given; for fun and for facts. They find it impossible to separate the two, because acquiring information is often a real pleasure, while recreational reading adds to their stock of information. "I read for knowledge," one twelve year old boy said, seriously, "and even when I am reading a story I am getting knowledge. Now in *Silent Scot*,[2] didn't I learn how people lived at that time, and about the battle of King's Mountain? And when I read *Swift Rivers*,[3] I learned about the Mississippi and lumbering and the Louisiana Purchase." Unconsciously, this boy had learned the secret of one of life's richest pleasures, for his recreational reading opened new vistas to him.

Of course no one will expect all books to serve all purposes. Some splendid books deepen and extend experience while at the same time they present patterns of behavior and factual information. Usually, however, different volumes are chosen for different needs, and the fortunate child and the discerning teacher make constant use of the variety of books provided for recreatory reading.[4]

Most children are eager to read. Dr. Terman's study of unselected California children showed that before they are eight years old they are struggling with the mechanics of reading, but after that age they enjoy reading to themselves. They read because they are curious about the world around them; they imitate their elders and other children in reading to satisfy their curiosity or to identify themselves with the characters and to satisfy subconscious desires. Many schools report a greater number of books read for pleasure than Dr. Terman's investigation reports. In some classes the average is fifteen books per pupil each term. Some children at a certain age, around eleven to fourteen,

---

[1] Prepared by Marion Horton, Traveling Librarian, Los Angeles Public Schools, under the direction of Jasmine Britton, Supervising Librarian, Los Angeles Public Schools. The following teachers in the Los Angeles city schools have contributed accounts of their experiences to this survey of recreatory reading: Miss Irma Coleman, Sheridan Street; Mrs. Hazel Colyer, Melrose Avenue; Mrs. E. R. Magagnosc, Ford Boulevard; Mrs. Josie Magee, Ford Boulevard; Mrs. Ruth M. Myers, Sawtelle Boulevard; Mrs. Nelva C. Poor, Principal, Chapman Avenue; Miss Gertrude Stephens, Ninety-ninth Street; Miss Rose Taber, Trinity Street; Miss Ruth Walser, Malabar Street; Miss Charlotte Wardell, Pacoima School.

[2] Constance Lindsay Skinner. *Silent Scot*. New York: The Macmillan Company, 1927.

[3] Cornelia L. Meigs. *Swift Rivers*. Boston: Little, Brown and Company, 1932.

[4] *Effective Use of Library Facilities in Rural Schools*. State of California Department of Education Bulletin No. 11, June 1, 1934.
  Selection and Distribution of Supplementary and Library Books in California Counties. State of California Department of Education Bulletin, No. 10, May 15, 1934.
  Pleasure Reading for Boys and Girls. State of California Department of Education Bulletin, No. 17, September 1, 1935.

read as many as three books a week, while on the other hand some
read nothing beyond the required school texts.[1]

AIMS OF RECREATORY READING

To Fill Leisure Time

If recreatory reading did nothing more than to prepare for a wise
use of leisure time, it would have its place in the school day. Economists
and social workers are concerned with the problem of the use of the
hours of leisure that have come with the shorter week and with unemployment. Leisure is a boon which may easily prove a curse unless
one knows what to do with it. If masses continue to use their leisure

Courtesy of Oakland City Schools

Recreational Reading Opens New Vistas for Children

hours merely for mass recreation, for viewing the combats of professional gladiators and screen dramas, and choking the streets with
crowds whenever a much-touted nonentity comes to town, or for reading the funnies, the pornographic magazines, and other fiction of the
western and detective types, then obviously they might as well, perhaps better, be at work at the old grind.[2]

To Extend Experience

Reading, however, is infinitely more than a way of spending leisure hours. How it may deepen and extend experience is shown each

---

[1] L. M. Terman. *Children's Reading.* New York: D. Appleton and Company,
1931, pp. 17-26.
[2] Arthur Pound. "Out of Unemployment into Leisure." *Atlantic Monthly.*
CXLVI (December, 1930), 784–92.

day in schools where the integrated program expands the children's mental horizon. Curiosity about the world around them leads the children to wonder about stars, and shells, and earthquakes, to ask why the days are longer in summer than in winter, how man learned to tell time, to keep records, to make tools, and a thousand similar questions. Books about nature, about other countries, and other ages serve to extend experience. A sixth grade class, for example, seemed actually to live in the middle ages while they read *Gabriel and the Hour Book.*[1] Reading eagerly for authentic details, they designed an abbey, fashioned coarse brown cotton robes and sandals to wear, made the parchment and illuminated Books of Hours, wrote a play based on the story, sang Latin hymns, addressed each other punctiliously with "thee" and "thou," and even cooked a lamb stew according to a mediaeval recipe. These boys and girls have learned to transcend the limitations of time and space and to live in an ampler world through the medium of books.

Form Patterns of Behavior

That reading has definite effects—positive and negative—on the formation of character, is unquestioned. On one side are the reports of psychologists who have found that many delinquent boys do not know what to read and do not use libraries. One boy who read regularly the magazines containing western thrillers stole the money to buy them if he could not get them in any other way. He also stole the money in order to see western movie serials, explaining "Boy, when you get started on them, you just can't bear to miss one!"[2]

On the other side, the ideals fostered by good reading make a definite contribution to the building of character. From nine to twelve is the age of hero worship, and stories of heroes of today and of earlier periods set standards without moralizing and inspire boys and girls to aim for nobility of character. School clubs like the Argonauts foster ideals of citizenship and set patterns of behavior, while at the same time they widen the children's mental horizon through acquaintance with the world's great literature. The children become familiar with the classic story of Jason and the Argonauts as related in Kingsley's *Greek Heroes,*[3] and *The Golden Fleece,*[4] by Padraic Colum. *The*

[1] Evaleen Stein. *Gabriel and the Hour Book.* Boston: L. C. Page and Company, 1906.
[2] Norman Fenton. "Reading Interests of Delinquent Boys." *Journal of Juvenile Research,* XV (January, 1931), 28–32.
  The motion picture as a cause of delinquency is well discussed in Henry James Forman, *Our Movie Made Children.* New York: The Macmillan Company, 1933.
[3] Charles Kingsley. *Greek Heroes.* Philadelphia: Henry Altemus Company, Inc., 1907.
[4] Padraic Colum. *The Golden Fleece.* New York: The Macmillan Company, 1921.

Life and Death of Jason,[1] by William Morris, gives them suggestions for their ritual. All the members of the class rank first as members of the Orpheus crew. Later they may belong to the Nestor, Herakles, or Jason crew, always with all members of the class holding the same rank. The distinguishing characteristics of the heroes, whose names are given to the crews, were set down by one of the club members:

> Jason brave,
> And Herakles strong,
> Nestor full of wisdom,
> Orpheus with his lyre and song,
> Charmed all mortals weak and strong.

The original honor points devised by the clubs at Breed Street School, Los Angeles, included fair play, dependableness, good order, respect for law, respect for the feelings, rights and property of others, right use of time, control of temper, cooperation and perseverance.

Some of the ideals gained from reading and fostered by the club are expressed in the Jason salutation:

> No wall so high but it may be climbed at last, no wood so thick but it may be crawled through, no serpent so wary but it may be charmed, no witch queen so fierce but spells may soothe her, and I may win the *Golden Fleece.*[2]

The recognition of such ideals and the aspirations stimulated by group action contribute to that intangible factor, character building.

To Find Inspiration and Refreshment of Spirit

Children appreciate the spiritual quickening, like new life from a cup of sparkling water, that comes from great literature. There is nothing more refreshing than the pure delight that comes from reading De La Mare's magical verses or Masefield's sea chanteys. When poetry is read not only with the mind, but with the ear, the imagination and the emotions, it becomes a permanent possession. What is more inspiring than to hear a class speak in unison and with understanding some great song, or the haunting cadences of a psalm, or verses from Ecclesiastes:

> Cast thy bread upon the waters, for thou shalt find it after many days.
> Give a portion to seven and also to eight, for thou knowest not what evil shall be upon the earth.
> In the morning sow thy seed and in the evening withhold not thy hand, for thou knowest not whether shall prosper this or that,
> Or whether they shall both be alike good.

---

[1] William Morris. *Life and Death of Jason.* New York: E. P. Dutton and Company, 1911.
[2] *Ibid.*

After a fifth grade choir had spoken their favorite poems, one of the audience asked, "Isn't it fun?" One boy replied, "And a pleasure, too," while another said, "Think how we will enjoy saying these poems to our grandchildren." They know that the enchantment of poetry is not a transitory thing, but something that will illuminate and enrich many life experiences.

To Discover Facts and Items of Information

While children read first for pleasure, they soon discover that books give directions for doing things; for making ships and castles and clay bowls, for collecting stamps and coins and insects, for identifying shells and leaves and wild flowers. They may read for information about archaeological excavations, or about Beebe's explorations as eagerly as they read pirate stories. This type of recreational reading often appeals to boys and girls who are not interested in imaginative literature.

THE TEACHER'S RESPONSIBILITY

To Create and Stimulate Interest in Reading

While Dr. Terman's investigations show that most children want to read, the desire in some cases is dormant. When the children do not see books as living things glowing with possibilities of delight and charm, the teacher can do much to arouse the pupils' interest and to improve the amount, variety and scope of their recreatory reading. The experience of a sixth grade in the Ford Boulevard School shows what can be accomplished by a skillful teacher. Before the term began, she consulted the children's records and grouped the class according to comprehension. She obtained a list of books used for the browsing table the term before, so that there would be no duplication. Since the forty pupils varied in reading ability from 2.3 to 8.5, expressed in terms of grade norms, the forty-nine books chosen from the school and county libraries and from the teacher's own collection ranged from very easy titles in large print to books of eighth grade difficulty. The books were placed on a browsing table at the back of the room, and during their reading period the children with low IQ's were given the first choice of books. While the class was reading, the teacher studied the pupils. Some read steadily, some read a little, some merely looked at the pictures. The teacher made a list of the children who did not read. At the close of the library period the pupils who wished to continue reading their books kept them at their desks. No books were taken home, but each day when the children had finished their work they read whatever they chose. The assignments for the entire day had been placed on the board before the children assembled.

When the teacher was free, the children reported to her for their individual records. Knowing the child's IQ and comprehension record, and having read or skimmed through the books, the teacher judged without subjecting the pupil to an inquisition, whether he could reasonably have read and enjoyed the book. When they found that more books could be borrowed from the school library, the children wrote letters to the librarian, telling her what kind of books they liked best and making individual requests. Books on Indians, cowboys, the world war, submarines, dogs, camels, whales, pirates, shipwrecks, earthquakes, dolls, and funny books were asked for, and one boy quite honestly wrote to the librarian, "I do not want any books." Letters of thanks for the books and other requests followed and the books were exchanged frequently. By the middle of the term, two-thirds of the class were reading freely. The others were individual problems. Three needed glasses and two who seemed lazy were really poorly nourished. When their physical defects were corrected, the children's interest in reading increased. One boy liked nonsense. He was introduced to *Just So Stories*.[1] Several boys had never before read a book through to the end until they investigated the books on the library table. One child from the south began with one story from *Uncle Remus, His Songs and His Sayings*,[2] and then finished the book. A boy who had helped his uncle in trapping read Seton's *Lobo*[3] and later read the other stories about Rag and Vixen. The cryptic code in Poe's *Gold Bug*[4] intrigued another boy with a high IQ who had never been interested in reading. Finally each member of the class was reading with interest; some were still reading easy books, but there was a decided improvement in the type of book requested. The boy who had written to the librarian that he did "not want any book" read four. The children began to ask for the entire story when their readers gave a selection from a book, and best of all, everyone was enjoying what he read.

To Cultivate Good Taste

The verse-speaking choir may play an important part in cultivating the exquisite and intangible delight that is called appreciation. Choric verse in which the whole class takes part bears no resemblance to the old agony of speaking a piece. On the contrary, the children enter into a spontaneous and joyful experience, losing self-consciousness and gaining a real understanding of verse forms, rhythm, and the meaning of poetry. They are divided into groups according to the

---

[1] Rudyard Kipling. *Just So Stories.* Garden City, New York: Doubleday, Doran and Company, 1902.
[2] Joel C. Harris. *Uncle Remus, His Songs and His Sayings.* New York: D. Appleton & Company, 1902.
[3] Ernest T. Seton. *Lobo, Rag, and Vixen.* New York: Charles Scribner's Sons, 1899.
[4] Edgar Allan Poe. *The Gold Bug.* New York: A. L. Burt Company, Inc., n.d.

pitch of their voices. Sometimes they speak in unison, or the high
voices ask a question and the lower voices reply, as in Kipling's *Big
Steamers*:[1]

> Oh, where are you going to, all you big steamers,
> With England's own coal up and down the salt seas?
>
> We are going to fetch you your bread and your butter,
> Your beef, pork and mutton, eggs, apples and cheese.

One group may tell the story of a ballad, and the other group give
the refrain, or several children may take different parts, as in *King's
Breakfast*,[2] by Milne, where there is the King, the Queen, the Dairy-
maid and the Cow, or different voices different lines as in Vachel Lindsay's *The Mysterious Cat*:[3]

I saw a proud, mysterious cat	(low voice)
I saw a proud, mysterious cat	(high voice)
Too proud to catch a mouse or rat	(chorus of low voices)
Mew, mew, mew!	(high voices in chorus)

There is no deliberate learning of the verses by heart; the children memorize the lines unconsciously after repeating the words with
due attention to meaning, rhythm, and tone color. The poems selected
have a refrain or a swinging rhythm, vivid images, and meaning
within the grasp of the children. Appropriate verses are found in
Silver Pennies,[4] an anthology edited by Blanche J. Thompson, and in
poetry collections by Rudyard Kipling, Henry Newbolt, Alfred Noyes,
A. A. Milne, Christina Rossetti, and Walter De La Mare. Two books
useful to the teacher who directs a verse-speaking choir are *Spoken
Poetry in the Schools*,[5] by Marjorie Gullan, and *The Teaching of
Choric Speech*,[6] by Elizabeth E. Keppie.

The following books contain poems that children read with genuine delight:

CHISHOLM, LOUEY. *The Golden Staircase*. New York: G. P. Putnam's Sons, 1920.
DE LA MARE, WALTER. *Peacock Pie*. New York: Henry Holt and Company, 1924.
FISH, HELEN D. (ed) *Boys' Book of Verse*. New York: Frederick A. Stokes Company, 1923.
FYLEMAN, ROSE. *Fairies and Chimneys*. Garden City, New York: Doubleday, Doran and Company, 1920.

---

[1] *Rudyard Kipling's Verse*. Inclusive Edition 1885-1932. "Big Steamers," pp. 811–812. Garden City, New York: Doubleday, Doran and Company, 1934.
[2] Alan A. Milne. *King's Breakfast*. New York: E. P. Dutton and Company, 1925.
[3] Vachel Lindsay. *Collected Poems*. "The Mysterious Cat," pp. 226-227. New York: The Macmillan Company, 1925.
[4] Blanche J. Thompson. *Silver Pennies*. New York: The Macmillan Company, 1926.
[5] Marjorie Gullan. *Spoken Poetry in the Schools*. London: Methuen and Company, Ltd., 1930.
[6] Elizabeth E. Keppie. *Teaching of Choric Speech*. Boston: Expression Company, 1932.

GROVER, EULALIE O. (ed) *My Caravan*. New York: Laidlaw Brothers, 1931.

HARRINGTON, MILDRED P. (ed) *Ring-Around*. New York: The Macmillan Company, 1930.

HUTCHINSON, VERONICA S. (ed) *Chimney Corner Poems*. New York: Minton, Balch & Company, 1928.

LEAR, EDWARD. *The Jumblies and Other Nonsense Verse*. New York: Frederick Warne and Company, 1919.

LINDSAY, VACHEL. *Johnny Appleseed and Other Poems*. New York: The Macmillan Company, 1928.

MILNE, ALAN A. *When We Were Very Young*. New York: E. P. Dutton and Company, 1924.

RICHARDS, LAURA E. *Tirra Lirra*. Boston: Little, Brown and Company, 1932.

ROSSETTI, CHRISTINA. *Sing Song*. New York: The Macmillan Company, 1924.

STEVENSON, BURTON E. (ed) *Home Book of Verse for Young Folks*. New York: Henry Holt and Company, 1915.

TEASDALE, SARA (ed) *Rainbow Gold*. New York: The Macmillan Company, 1922.

THOMPSON, BLANCHE J. (ed) *Silver Pennies*. New York: The Macmillan Company, 1926.

TILESTON, M. W. (ed) *Sugar and Spice and All That's Nice*. Boston: Little, Brown and Company, 1910.

TURNER, N. B., and MERWIN D. *Magpie Lane*. New York: Harcourt, Brace and Company, 1927.

UNTERMEYER, LOUIS (ed) *This Singing World*. New York: Harcourt, Brace and Company, 1923.

WIGGIN, K. D., and SMITH, N. A. (eds) *Posy Ring*. Garden City, New York: Doubleday, Doran and Company, n.d.

To Develop Discrimination

The delicate art of discrimination and the ability to set standards is best developed by reading and comparison of many books. Children can be directed to reading the books that have received the Newbery Medal and then discussing the qualities that make each book distinctive in its own field. The Newbery Medal is awarded each year by the American Library Association to the author of the most important children's book of the year. Since the first award was made ten years ago, books of different types—history, folklore and legend, stories of animals, adventure and fancy—have been chosen. Beginning in 1922 the following books have received the Newbery Medal:

1922, *Story of Mankind,* by Van Loon [1]
1923, *Voyages of Doctor Dolittle,* by Lofting [2]
1924, *Dark Frigate,* by Hawes [3]
1925, *Tales from Silver Lands,* by Finger [4]

---

[1] Hendrik W. Van Loon. *Story of Mankind.* Garden City, New York: Garden City Publishing Company, 1931.

[2] Hugh Lofting. *Voyages of Doctor Dolittle.* London: Jonathan Cape, Ltd., 1931.

[3] Charles B. Hawes. *Dark Frigate.* Boston: Little, Brown and Company, 1925.

[4] Charles J. Finger. *Tales from Silver Lands.* Garden City, New York: Doubleday, Doran and Company, 1931.

1926, *Shen of the Sea*, by Chrisman[1]
1927, *Smoky*, by James[2]
1928, *Gay Neck*, by Mukerji[3]
1929, *Trumpeter of Krakow*, by Kelly[4]
1930, *Hitty*, by Field[5]
1931, *Cat Who Went to Heaven*, by Coatsworth[6]
1932, *Waterless Mountain*, by Armer[7]
1933, *Young Fu of the Upper Yangtze*, by Lewis[8]
1934, *Invincible Louisa*, by Meigs[9]

When the children in the fifth grade in the Trinity Street School read the *Cat Who Went to Heaven*, they thought it was the saddest, most beautiful and most exciting story they had ever read. They were sure that it deserved the medal in 1931. They began at once to read the books published in the following year to see which was the best. A committee of the class wrote to the children's librarian and to Frederic G. Melcher, who gives the medal, to ask what points should be considered in judging a book.

We are children in the fifth grade of Trinity School. We are reading to choose the best children's book of the year and when we have decided we are going to make an award to the winning author. But we would like some help. We like adventures, mystery, and humor. We want a story so interesting that we can hardly put the book down. We like it to be said beautifully. Is this the way to judge books? What other points shall we look for? Please advise us. We shall appreciate your help very much. We have just read *The Cat Who Went to Heaven*. We love that story. We think the committee surely knew what they were about when they chose it for the Newbery Medal.

Yours sincerely,
Library Committee of Room Fifteen.

Mr. Melcher replied:

Of course, you understand that there is no one and perfect way to judge books. To be a good judge, you have to read well and widely, keep your mind open and your opinion sensitive to the good and the beautiful in whatever form it is presented. Back of the book is the writer, and the writer's mind and heart and knowledge come through to you, and if the book moves you by its humor, by its imagination, by its fine feeling, then it is a good book. To judge a good book of today you must know a good book of the past, and both are needed if we are to get the full value and the full experience that books can give us.

After reading fifteen of the outsanding books of the year, the children decided that *Waterless Mountain*,[10] by Laura Adams Armer,

[1] Arthur B. Chrisman. *Shen of the Sea.* New York: E. P. Dutton and Company, 1925.
[2] Will James. *Smoky.* New York: Charles Scribner's Sons, 1930.
[3] Dhan G. Mukerji. *Gay Neck.* New York: E. P. Dutton and Company, 1928.
[4] Eric P. Kelly. *Trumpeter of Krakow.* New York: The Macmillan Company, 1928.
[5] Rachel L. Field. *Hitty.* New York: The Macmillan Company, 1929.
[6] Elizabeth J. Coatsworth. *The Cat Who Went to Heaven.* New York: The Macmillan Company, 1930.
[7] Laura Adams Armer. *Waterless Mountain.* New York: Longmans, Green and Company, 1931.
[8] Elizabeth F. Lewis. *Young Fu of the Upper Yangtze.* Philadelphia: The John C. Winston Co., 1932.
[9] Cornelia Meigs. *Invincible Louisa.* Boston: Little, Brown and Company, 1933.
[10] Laura Adams Armer, *op. cit.*

was the best. They wrote letters to Mrs. Armer, telling her the reasons for their decision, and presenting her the Trinity certificate, adorned with a gold seal and blue ribbon, "For the book we love the best." Their decision was not influenced by the teacher's judgment, but was based on principles of discrimination which they had evolved. Great was their delight when the American Library Association awarded the Newbery Medal to Mrs. Armer a few weeks later.

Activities

Among the activities in which children engage, which involve books very directly and which afford children satisfactions which lead to further reading, are book reports and book reviews, puppet shows, picture shows and peepshows, book maps, illustrations, cartoons, and book clubs. Of course the children should not be led into any of these activities so often or so continuously that it becomes monotonous or deadens the interest. If the pupil is expected to read books which he ought to like and is compelled to write a series of the deadly things called book reports, he is quite likely to acquire an aversion to all kinds of reading.

Book Reviews

The most important characteristic of a book review is something that will capture the essence of the book and present it so that others will be intrigued into reading the book for themselves. Reports have endless variations. They may be oral, written, or dramatized, or presented in picture or peepshow. If the school publishes a paper, reviews may be printed there. They may be written or typed on cards and filed for other members of the class.

Those reports written by children in the third, fourth, fifth, and sixth grades have the merits of brevity, spontaneity, and point. The teachers have insisted on correct spelling of the names of the authors and the titles of the books, but the summary of the chief feature of the book is individual and complete. The following are examples:

Wee Ann,[1] by Ethel C. Phillips.
> I like surprises, don't you? Wee Ann thinks they are great.

Snow-White and the Seven Dwarfs,[2] by the Brothers Grimm.
> Little Snow-White lived with the dwarfs. One day an old woman came to the door. She had an apple in her basket, and she said, "Will you try a piece of my apple?" Snow-White said, "Yes." Snow-White took the piece that had the poison on it. What do you suppose happened?

---

[1] Ethel C. Phillips. *Wee Ann*. Boston: Houghton Mifflin Company, 1919.
[2] *Snow-White and the Seven Dwarfs*. Tales from the Brothers Grimm. New York: Oxford University Press, 1930.

Trail of the Sandhill Stag,[1] by Ernest T. Seton.

Yan was trailing the sandhill stag. Yan saw a track that he had never seen before. So Yan kept on traveling for a number of long white miles. The snow was bitter cold. Will you read the rest for yourself?

Jungle Book,[2] by Rudyard Kipling.

Mowgli understands the snakes hiss, the hunting call, and bothers nobody if nobody bothers him. He was brought up in the jungle by a mother wolf and went hunting with the pack.

Little Women,[3] by Louisa May Alcott.

Jo lived in a big house with her three sisters. They were very poor and their mother had to work, but there was love and happiness in the family and Jo kept the house laughing.

Boy Knight of Reims,[4] by Eloise Lownsbery.

I especially enjoyed the book, "Boy Knight of Reims." It seemed as if you could see a picture of life in an old French village. As Jean and Marcel were on the way to the castle it seemed as though I were walking along with them.

A book review in the form of printed questions or a completion test is often useful as a game or for remedial reading. Cards are given to the children, while the teacher uses a master test with answers. The following test on the *Terrible Nuisance*[5] has been used in the fifth grade:

1. The terrible nuisance was (a) a boy (b) a girl (c) a dog (d) a cat.
2. The puppy annoyed (a) Mr. Montgomery (b) the children (c) Mr. Avon (d) Mrs. Avon.
3. Juliana spent her allowance for (a) books (b) sweets (c) clothes (d) presents.
4. Juliana earned twenty-five cents (a) weeding a garden (b) washing dishes (c) caring for the baby (d) helping her mother.
5. The reward for Sammy's kitten was (a) fifty cents (b) five dollars (c) two dollars (d) ten cents.
6. Benjy wanted (a) a puppy (b) a rabbit (c) a squirrel (d) a kitten.
7. Out of the hole in the ground came (a) a baby rabbit (b) a little puppy (c) a fox (d) a cat.
8. The Avon children went to the Fair with (a) their parents (b) their teacher (c) Mr. Montgomery (d) Mrs. Badger and Sammy.
9. Benjy made some clay (a) guinea pigs (b) rabbits (c) dogs (d) lions.
10. For his birthday Benjy got (a) a dog (b) two guinea pigs (c) one guinea pig (d) a rabbit.

An individual record of books read and others to be read is worth keeping. In one fifth grade each child wrote in a little notebook pithy quotations and kept two lists of books: "Good books to read" and "Books I want to read." Many classes keep reading charts which have space for the children's names and tiny paper squares represent-

---

[1] Ernest T. Seton. *Trail of the Sandhill Stag.* New York: Charles Scribner's Sons, 1899.

[2] Rudyard Kipling. *Jungle Book.* Garden City, New York: Doubleday, Doran and Company, 1932.

[3] Louisa May Alcott. *Little Women.* New York: A. L. Burt Company, Inc., 1932.

[4] Eloise Lownsbery. *Boy Knight of Reims.* Boston: Houghton Mifflin Company, 1927.

[5] Peggy Bacon. *Terrible Nuisance.* New York: Harcourt Brace and Company, 1931.

ing the covers of the books they have read. When a boy or girl reads
a book, the title is written on the gay paper and pasted opposite the
reader's name. Frequently ten, twenty or even more books are read
by each child in a single term. Sometimes the colors of the miniature
book represent the type of book; green for adventure, flame for
geography or travel, blue for fairy tales, red for animal stories, pale
green for art and poetry, purple for history. Or the color may indicate the difficulty of the book, a yellow square standing for a short,
easy book, blue for a long, hard one, and red for a book of average
difficulty. The reading charts may be decorated with sketches of
bookshelves or children reading, or with an appropriate quotation.
One class lettered their chart with the motto:

> The wise fly away to the best of all climes,
> Which you enter with history, memories or rhymes,—
> That most wonderful country of books.

At the Chapman Avenue school, a bulletin board in the sixth grade
room is headed "Have you read these fun books?" Below are pasted
bright sheets of paper folded to represent the covers of a book. Each
is lettered with a book title. Inside is a sheet of white paper where
the children write their names when they have read the book. If the
teacher finds that some book is not read, she reads a part of the story
aloud, or tells a bit of it until the children's interest is aroused.

In a combination record of books read and book reports, the children drew pictures representing some incident in each book they had
read; a horse for *Rusty Pete of the Lazy AB*,[1] a little cat, black, white,
and yellow, for the *Cat Who Went to Heaven*;[2] and snowy mountain
peaks for *Heidi*.[3] These illustrations are sometimes finished sketches,
sometimes crude, but always a spontaneous interpretation of the book.
Boys often prefer to draw cartoons without pretense of artistic value,
but vivid in their characterization.

A book map is another satisfactory method of recording books
read. It may be made on a large scale by the entire class, revealing
the setting of stories in all parts of the world or the United States, or
each child may make his own map, indicating the location of the books
he has read, and showing the author and title in the legend below
the map.

A fascinating project is the making of a book for other children.
The children in the fifth grade at Chapman Avenue school, most of
them Japanese, wanted their little brothers and sisters to enjoy the
Japanese fairy stories written by Teresa Peirce Williston.[4] The book

---

[1] Doris Fogler and Nina Nicol. *Rusty Pete of the Lazy AB.* New York: The Macmillan Co., 1929.
[2] Elizabeth Coatsworth. *Cat Who Went to Heaven.* New York: The Macmillan Company, 1930.
[3] Fran J. Spyri. *Heidi.* New York: A. L. Burt Company, Inc., 1932.
[4] Teresa Peirce Williston. *Japanese Fairy Tales.* Chicago: Rand McNally & Company, 1911.

was too difficult for the younger children to read, so the fifth grade decided to rewrite and illustrate the story of Peach Boy. After much discussion they decided on the most important events to be pictured. They condensed the story into briefer paragraphs and simpler phrasing and finally chose the minimum essentials as captions to the pictures, so that the very youngest could enjoy the story. The skills in outlining and condensing, in writing, spelling and art work were important, but equally vital was the joyous expression of a real pleasure and the spontaneous sharing of it.

Advertising Books

Accounts of books read and enjoyed often intrigue other children into reading the same books. Book-lovers of all ages delight in sharing their experiences, and a variety of programs for classroom or assembly may be created. Picture shows, puppet shows and plays may be planned to advertise books of merit.

Picture Shows and Peepshows

The sixth grade in the Melrose school gave a picture show based on the books that have received the Newbery Medal. The children made pictures showing the most dramatic moment in each book, and these were pasted in a long strip and mounted on reels. The class told the stories in an assembly program that was repeated four times to different appreciative audiences.

Another type of illustration is the peepshow. Miniature stage settings and tiny figures appropriately costumed are mounted in shoeboxes. Books with a foreign setting such as *The Red Howling Monkey*,[1] or *The Lance of Kanana*,[2] are effectively illustrated in this way.

Puppet Shows

An Eskimo puppet show was given as the climax of the year's work of an A3 class in the Malabar school. The children had heard that the Eskimos of Alaska were descendants of emigrants from Siberia. They wanted to know if Eskimos and Siberians were alike. Many books were consulted and many types of activity were integrated in an absorbing unit of work. Before giving the puppet show, the children recorded the information they had found in their notebooks, collected pictures and clippings and made individual dictionaries of the new words they had learned. They dramatized the story first in order to get as many facts into it as possible, then wrote three scenes and speeches for famous explorers to give as an introduction. Pictures were drawn to

[1] Helen Tee-Van. *The Red Howling Monkey.* New York: The Macmillan Company, 1929.
[2] Henry W. French. *The Lance of Kanana.* Boston: Lothrop, Lee & Shepherd Company, 1932.

show how the puppets should look, and patterns were made for their costumes. The puppets were made of cloth with bath towels dyed in different colors to represent fur. Scenery was painted with kalsomine and the stage properties were made of papier mâché and clay. The program, repeated several times for parents and other classes, included Eskimo songs, speeches by children representing the explorers— Captain Peary, Mrs. Peary, the Snowbaby, General Nobile and Admiral Byrd—as well as the puppet show in three scenes, the Angakok's visit to the twins' igloo, the mothers at their sewing, and the children at play out of doors. The children showed marked improvement in reading, spelling, oral and written English skills; they learned something of the relationship between environment and methods of living, and acquired a feeling of respect rather than of superiority for a simple people.

Assembly Program

In the Chapman Avenue school assemblies have been arranged as often as every three weeks, first one group entertaining and then another. The desire to give reports on books in novel ways has developed among the children. Each group tries to have surprises and an interesting program. In one assembly, each number was introduced by printing on a large chart. The program began when a child entered, carrying a chart on which was written "Program for Today. Dramatization of Dr. Dolittle, by Georgia." When the second number was ready, another child appeared with a second chart. All of the audience read because they wished to know what would happen next.

Another assembly was presented by the sixth grade. The boys had built a large book in which the children posed as living pictures. The assembly had been advertised on all the classroom blackboards by the sixth grade as follows:

Come to the Auditorium tomorrow and see your friends. Heidi, Huckleberry Finn, Tom Sawyer and Dr. Dolittle will be there.

As the pages of the book in the frame were turned, the child posing spoke. One said, "Do you know me? I am a little Swiss girl. I lived for several years with my grandfather on the top of the mountain. One day . . . ."

INTRODUCTION TO BOOKS

Reading Clubs

In many schools club meetings are scheduled regularly. The Argonaut clubs are not primarily book clubs, but reading is an important factor in their success. In some book clubs the children give oral reports on whatever they have read recently. The secretary's record of one club indicates the variety and type of books read by an average group of fifth and sixth grade children:

October 15. The Book Club was called to order by the president. The minutes of the last meeting were read and approved. Jimmy reviewed *The Boy With the Parrot*.[1] Mary told about *Juan and Juanita*.[2] The rest of the program was as follows: *Master Simon's Garden*,[3] by Sue; *Dusty Star*,[4] by Gladys; *The New Moon*,[5] by Joseph; *The Young Trailers*,[6] by Herman.

Instead of general programs, the clubs may concentrate on special subjects. In the sixth grade at the Ford Boulevard school, each child belongs to one of three clubs, the Archaeologists, the Poetry Lovers, or the Nature Club. Each member keeps a notebook in which he pastes clippings or copies interesting items, as well as a list of the books he has read. On certain days the Archaeologists give a program to the class. One program included reports of what they had discovered about excavations in New Mexico, Crete, Egypt, and Chaldea, a review of *Digging in Yucatan*,[7] by Anne Morris, and plans for making clay tablets. They decided that the symbols on their bricks must be authentic copies, and a member joyfully reported that Jack and Jill in cuneiform characters could be found in *The Story of Writing*,[8] published by the American Council on Education. On other days the Poetry Lovers meet, to read favorite poems to the class and to report on the life of different poets. Later in the week, the naturalists present their program, perhaps general items of interest, a review of the book entitled *The Earth for Sam*,[9] accompanied by a display of rocks gathered from far and near, or a report on tropical fish, supplemented by an account of Beebe's adventures on the Galapagos Islands, or an account of the animals of Alaska, with book reviews of *Ood-Le-Uk the Wanderer*,[10] and *Baldy of Nome*.[11] The chairman, club members and audience develop an amazing familiarity with current events in these three fields, and the children's genuine enthusiasm and resourcefulness continues as they go into junior high school.

Reading Aloud

One of the most delightful ways of stimulating an interest in books is to read aloud. Books that children can read for themselves

---

[1] Elizabeth Coatsworth. *The Boy With the Parrot*. New York: The Macmillan Company, 1930.
[2] F. C. Baylor. *Juan and Juanita*. Boston: Houghton Mifflin Company, 1930.
[3] Cornelia L. Meigs. *Master Simon's Garden*. New York: The Macmillan Company, 1929.
[4] Olaf Baker. *Dusty Star*. New York: Dodd, Mead and Company, Inc., 1922.
[5] Cornelia L. Meigs. *The New Moon*. New York: The Macmillan Company, 1929.
[6] Joseph Altsheler. *The Young Trailers*. New York: D. Appleton Company, 1907.
[7] Anne Morris. *Digging in Yucatan*. Garden City, New York: Doubleday, Doran and Company, 1931.
[8] *The Story of Writing*. Achievements of Civilization, No. 1. Washington: American Council on Education, 1933.
[9] William M. Reed. *The Earth for Sam*. New York: Harcourt, Brace and Company, 1920.
[10] Alice Lide and M. Johansen. *Ood-Le-Uk the Wanderer*. Boston: Little, Brown and Company, 1930.
[11] Esther Birdsall Darling. *Baldy of Nome*. Philadelphia: Penn Publishing Co., 1916.

are happily introduced when a dramatic incident is read by the teacher. More difficult books are enjoyed when the teacher or one of the children reads a part of the book each day. A brief introduction will lead children to read books like *Poppy Seed Cakes*[1] and *Voyages of Doctor Dolittle*,[2] for themselves, but the charm of such books as the *Tangle-Coated Horse*,[3] *Wind in the Willows*,[4] *I know a Secret*,[5] *Rose and the Ring*,[6] *Peacock Pie*,[7] *Slowcoach*,[8] *The Lance of Kanana*,[9] and *The Boy Who Knew What the Birds Said*,[10] is assured when they are read aloud. Their magic is never lessened by repetition. They are still lively and odd and mysterious and wonderful after many readings. In a new anthology for children Walter De La Mare indicates some of the reasons for reading aloud. "The sounds of the words of poetry resemble the sounds of music," he says. "They are a pleasure and a delight merely to listen to, as they rise and fall and flow and echo—like the singing of birds at daybreak or a little before the fall of night when the daffodils 'take the winds of March with beauty.' It is a great pleasure to say the words aloud as well and clearly and carefully as one possibly can. I have always found, even after reading a poem twenty times, that the next time I read it, there was not only a new meaning to be found in it, but also a new music, something I had not noticed before. For as we ourselves change and become a little different every year, and grow older every day, so poems change with us. In reading a poem we change its words into something of our own. This indeed is the only way we can get anything out of a book. And the more of ourselves, of our senses and feelings and dreams and thoughts, and what we love and what we hope for, and what we believe in, we put into the words of a poem, by so much better will that poem be.'"[11]

The following books are enjoyed by children in the third and fourth grades, when they are read aloud:

BENNETT, JOHN. *Pigtail of Ah Lee Ben Loo.* New York: Longmans, Green and Company, 1928.

BROWN, ABBIE F. *John of the Woods.* Boston: Houghton Mifflin Company, 1909.

[1] Mary F. Clark and M. C. Quigley. *Poppy Seed Cakes.* Garden City, New York: Doubleday, Doran and Company, 1924.
[2] Hugh Lofting. *Voyages of Doctor Dolittle.* London: Jonathan Cape, Ltd., 1931.
[3] Ella Young. *Tangle-Coated Horse.* New York: Longmans, Green and Company, 1929.
[4] Kenneth Grahame. *Wind in the Willows.* London: Methuen and Company, Ltd., 1931.
[5] Christopher D. Morley. *I know a Secret.* Garden City, New York: Doubleday, Doran and Company, 1927.
[6] William M. Thackeray. *Rose and the Ring.* New York: Coward, McCann, Inc., n.d.
[7] Walter De La Mare. *Peacock Pie.* New York: Henry Holt and Company, 1924.
[8] Edward V. Lucas. *Slowcoach.* New York: The Macmillan Company, 1910.
[9] Henry W. French. *The Lance of Kanana.* Boston: Lothrop, Lee and Shepherd Co., 1932.
[10] Padraic Colum. *The Boy Who Knew What the Birds Said.* New York: The Macmillan Co., 1918.
[11] Walter De La Mare. (Comp.) *Tom Tiddler's Ground.* New York: William Collins Sons and Company, Ltd., 1931.

CARROLL, LEWIS. (Pseudonym of Charles L. Dodgson.) *Alice's Adventures in Wonderland.* New York: William Collins Sons and Company, Ltd., 1931.

CASSERLY, ANNE T. *Whins on Knockattan.* New York: Harper and Brothers, 1928.

CLARK, MARY E., and QUIGLEY, M. C. *Poppy Seed Cakes.* Garden City, New York: Doubleday, Doran and Company, 1924.

COATSWORTH, ELIZABETH. *Cat Who Went to Heaven.* New York: The Macmillan Company, 1930.

DALGLIESH, ALICE. *Relief's Rocker.* New York: The Macmillan Company, 1932.

FARJEON, ELEANOR. *Italian Peepshow.* New York: Frederick A. Stokes Company, 1926.

FISHER, DOROTHEA F. *Made-to-Order Stories.* New York: Harcourt, Brace and Company, 1925.

GRISHINA GIVAGO, NADEJDA J. *Peter-Pea.* New York: Frederick A. Stokes Company, 1926.

HARRIS, JOEL C. *Uncle Remus.* New York: D. Appleton and Company, 1908.

KIPLING, RUDYARD. *Just So Stories.* Garden City, New York: Doubleday, Doran and Company, 1912.

LATHROP, DOROTHY P. *Fairy Circus.* New York: The Macmillan Company, 1931.

LEAMY, EDMUND. *Golden Spears.* New York: Baker and Taylor Company, 1930.

LOFTING, HUGH. *Voyages of Doctor Dolittle.* London: Jonathan Cape, Ltd., 1931.

MARTINEAU des CHESNEZ, ELIZABETH L. *Lady Green Satin and Her Maid Rosette.* New York: The Macmillan Company, 1927.

MEIGS, CORNELIA L. *Willow Whistle.* New York: The Macmillan Company, 1931.

MILNE, ALAN A. *Winnie-the-Pooh.* New York: E. P. Dutton and Company, 1926.

MOON, GRACE. *Chi-Wee.* Garden City, New York: Doubleday, Doran and Company, 1925.

PARISH, ANNE. *Floating Island.* New York: Harper and Brothers, 1930.

PETERSHAM, MAUD, and PETERSHAM, MISKA. *Miki.* Garden City, New York: Doubleday, Doran and Company, 1929.

PYLE, HOWARD. *Wonder Clock.* New York: Harper and Brothers, 1904.

RANSOME, ARTHUR. *Old Peter's Russian Tales.* New York: Thomas Nelson and Sons. n.d.

SHANNON, MONICA. *California Fairy Tales.* Garden City, New York: Doubleday, Doran and Company, 1926.

THACKERAY, WILLIAM M. *The Rose and the Ring.* New York: William Collins Sons and Company, Ltd., 1929.

For children in the fifth and sixth grades, the following are excellent choices for reading aloud:

ARMER, LAURA A. *Waterless Mountain.* New York: Longmans, Green and Company, 1931.

BALDWIN, JAMES. *Story of Roland.* New York: Charles Scribner's Sons, 1930.

BALDWIN, JAMES. *Story of Siegfried.* New York: Charles Scribner's Sons, 1931.

BARRIE, JAMES M. *Peter Pan in Kensington Gardens.* New York: Charles Scribner's Sons, 1926.

CLEMENS, SAMUEL L. (Pseudonym of Mark Twain.) *Prince and the Pauper.* New York: Harper and Brothers, 1931.

COLUM, PADRAIC. *Adventures of Odysseus and the Tale of Troy.* New York: The Macmillan Company, 1918.

DAVIS, MARY G. *Truce of the Wolf.* New York: Harcourt, Brace and Company, 1931.

DE LA MARE, WALTER J. *Three Mulla-Mulgars.* New York: Alfred A. Knopf, 1925.

FIELD, RACHEL L. *Hitty.* New York: The Macmillan Company, 1929.

FRENCH, ALLEN. *Sir Marrok.* New York: Century Company, 1902.

FRENCH, HENRY W. *The Lance of Kanana.* Boston: Lothrop, Lee and Shepard Company, 1932.

GRAHAME, KENNETH. *Wind in the Willows.* London: Methuen and Company, Ltd., 1931.

HALE, LUCRETIA P. *Peterkin Papers.* Boston: Houghton Mifflin Company, 1924.

HUDSON, WILLIAM H. *Little Boy Lost.* New York: Alfred A. Knopf, 1920.

KELLY, ERIC P. *Trumpeter of Krakow.* New York: The Macmillan Company, 1928.

KIPLING, RUDYARD. *Puck of Pook's Hill.* Garden City, New York: Doubleday, Doran and Company, 1906.

LOWNSBERY, ELOISE. *Boy Knight of Reims.* Boston: Houghton Mifflin Company, 1927.

LUCAS, EDWARD V. *Slowcoach.* New York: The Macmillan Company, 1910.

PYLE, HOWARD. *Men of Iron.* New York: Harper and Brothers, 1930.

STOCKTON, FRANK R. *The Bee-Man of Orn and Other Fanciful Tales.* New York: Charles Scribner's Sons, 1908.

YOUNG, ELLA. *Wonder Smith and His Son.* New York: Longmans, Green and Company, 1927.

ZOLLINGER, GULIELMA (Pseudonym of William Zachary Gladwin). *The Widow O'Callaghan's Boys.* Chicago: A. C. McClurg and Company, 1898.

Book Week

Each year children, teachers, librarians, authors and publishers unite in celebrating Book Week in November. Special exhibits and programs during the week serve to point the way to new book discoveries and the fun of year-round reading. An infinite variety of activities have books as their theme during the week—book plays or pageants, assemblies, exhibits, book reviews, oral and written, hobby book exhibits, lists of book chums, the making of bookplates and posters.

In the book parade staged by the Micheltorena school, boys and girls from each room were costumed to represent characters from favorite books, and marched in a colorful procession. Each child told the story of the book he had chosen, and together they presented a pageant of vivid interest.

Suggestions for the celebration of Book Week may be found in the *Elementary English Review*,[1] *The Library Journal*,[2] and other professional magazines.

Teachers' Reading

The most effective way of arousing and cultivating the children's interest in reading is the contagious example of a teacher who reads widely and enthusiastically. Her own pleasure in books will be reflected and magnified in her pupils. Something more than a knowledge of subject matter and a casual acquaintance with books for recreational reading is needed. For her own satisfaction she reads on one subject to give greater depth and power to the units of work in which the children are then engaged. She also reads generously on subjects

---

[1] *Elementary English Review.* C. C. Certain, Editor, 6505 Grand River Ave., Detroit, Mich.

[2] *The Library Journal.* Editors, Bertine E. Weston, Frederic G. Melcher, 62 W. 45th St., New York: R. R. Bowker Company.

Courtesy of Los Angeles City Schools

The Modern Classroom Requires a Rich Collection of Books and Magazines

of current importance. She hopes to orient herself in the world in which she lives, while at the same time she accepts her responsibility in working for a better social order. She reads books and articles on current educational practices, on world affairs and on the experiences of the past that will help in shaping the future. Books like *Education for a Changing Civilization*[1] and *Remakers of Mankind*[2] contain the ideals that lie beneath curriculum making and foreshadow desirable readjustments. In reading *War Debts and World Prosperity*[3] and *Can America Stay at Home*[4] it is possible to prepare for the rebuilding of our civilization, and never again can one take a narrow view of the universe after reading *The Meaning of a Liberal Education*,[5] or *What We Live By*.[6]

PROVISION OF BOOKS

Classroom Collections and Library Rooms

If reading for pleasure is to become a habit, the right books must be constantly available. The modern school requires a rich collection

[1] William H. Kilpatrick. *Education for a Changing Civilization.* New York: The Macmillan Co., 1926.
[2] Carleton Washburne. *Remakers of Mankind.* New York: The John Day Company, 1932.
[3] Harold Glenn Moulton. *War Debts and World Prosperity.* Washington: The Brookings Institution, 1932.
[4] Frank H. Simonds. *Can America Stay at Home?* New York: Harper and Brothers, 1932.
[5] Everett Dean Martin. *The Meaning of a Liberal Education.* New York: W. W. Norton and Company, Inc., 1926.
[6] Ernest Dimnet. *What We Live By.* New York: Simon and Schuster, 1932.

of books to supplement the textbooks and to stimulate and satisfy mental curiosity. "The veritable foundation of the child's whole educational development rests in large measure upon the book tables of the primary school. The meat of the matter is to expose the primary pupil to an abundance of good material which he may utilize for free reading."[1]

It is estimated that a satisfactory collection for a six-grade school of 900 pupils numbers 5,000 volumes, that is, between five and six books per pupil.[2]

In describing the classroom of a modern school, a superintendent says:

> A library table should be provided. It should be large enough to accommodate at least eight children, should be equipped with comfortable chairs, should have an ample supply of books and magazines and should be made attractive by an appropriate cover or runner and fresh flowers, a potted plant, or a centerpiece of pottery or glass. Bookcases should be provided both for the supplementary readers which accompany each unit of work and for the miscellaneous titles not needed on the library table. Supplemental sets should have from five to twenty copies per set varying with the material and the needs of the moment. Supplemental equipment of this kind should include 100 to 150 copies. It is wise to allow the children to make the room bookcases from such simple materials as can be found around any school. When finished, the bookcases should be painted in attractive colors, to be retouched from time to time, to keep them looking neat and clean. Articles from magazines, folders, etc., should be placed in a convenient box, arranged alphabetically.[3]

A number of schools have established library rooms in addition to the classroom collections. Because the principals feel that the library is essential, they appropriate sums ranging from $10 to $200 a year from their own funds for the purchase of books. Money is sometimes raised at a May festival or through the Parent Teacher Association and books are purchased to supplement those purchased by the school district in accordance with the school law which requires that a minimum of forty cents per child be expended for books annually.[4]

The arrangement of the library rooms is informal and inviting. Bookcases, painted gray or soft green, bright curtains, tables large and small, rocking chairs, gay foreign prints, posters made by the children themselves, make the rooms individual. When the library of the Thirty-sixth Street school, Los Angeles, was planned, the art teacher asked the sixth grade boys who were studying mural decoration to work out a design for the library windows. They chose a vine motif to symbolize the qualities of continuous growth and beautiful spirit to be found in the room. This they painted on the casing of the arched

[1] H. C. Morrison. *The Practice of Teaching in the Secondary School.* Chicago, Illinois: University of Chicago Press, 1926, pp. 336-8.
[2] L. F. Fargo. *The Program for Elementary School Library Service.* Chicago, Illinois: American Library Association, 1930, p. 104.
[3] R. L. Lane. *Bulletin to Elementary Principals,* No. 1, Los Angeles Public Schools, 1931-32.
[4] *California School Code,* section 6.552.

windows. The library furnishings include filing cases for pictures, stereographs and catalog cards, exhibit cases for special treasures, a globe and pictorial maps.

Explicit and stimulating directions for making over an old classroom into a library, based on experience in the Long Beach elementary schools will be found in *A Handbook for Teacher-Librarians*,[1] published by the American Library Association. Teachers will also find much helpful material in *Effective Use of Library Facilities in Rural Schools*.[2]

The following statement by Mrs. Nelva C. Poor, principal of the Chapman Avenue school, indicates how the school library has contributed to recreatory reading:

> We have tried in the entire school to provide a natural social grouping of the children. We know in our own lives that the social grouping of people around a fireside or reading table tends to promote a desirable atmosphere, while straight rows of seats in a barren auditorium check any desire to participate in friendliness. If we are influenced by these things, surely children are just as sensitive. We have arranged one room in the school as a library. Each class has a schedule of twenty minutes every day when the children may use the room for their own pleasure. Here we have arranged book exhibits, toys representing book characters, inviting reading tables with attractive books, low cases full of fiction, low chairs and straw rugs where the children may get close together in a cultural atmosphere for a story hour, poetry hour, or dramatization.

BIBLIOGRAPHY

Books

BAMBERGER, FLORENCE EILAU, and BROENING, ANGELA M. *A Guide to Children's Literature.* Baltimore: Johns Hopkins Press, 1931.

Children's Catalog. 4th Rev. Edition. Compiled by Minnie Earl Sears. New York: H. W. Wilson Company, 1930. Second Supplement, 1932.

DALGLIESH, ALICE. *First Experiences with Literature.* New York: Charles Scribner's Sons, 1932.

$400 Elementary School Library. Bibliography. Selected Articles on School Library Experience; Second Series. Compiled by Laura C. Bailey. New York: H. W. Wilson Company, 1932.

GARDNER, EMELYN E., and RAMSEY, ELOISE. *A Handbook of Children's Literature.* Chicago: Scott, Foresman & Company, 1927.

Graded List of Books for Children. Compiled by Nora Beust. Chicago: American Library Association, 1930.

A Handbook for Teacher-Librarians. Prepared by the Elementary Sub-Committee on the Education Committee. Bibliography. Chicago: American Library Association, 1931.

MAHONEY, BERTHA E., and WHITNEY, ELINOR. *Contemporary Illustrators of Children's Books.* Boston: Bookshop for Boys and Girls, 1930.

MOORE, ANNIE CARROLL. *Cross-roads to Childhood.* Garden City, New York: Doubleday, Doran & Company, 1926.

---

[1] *A Handbook for Teacher-Librarians.* American Library Association. Education Committee. Chicago: American Library Association, 1931.
[2] *Effective Use of Library Facilities in Rural Schools.* State of California Department of Education Bulletin, No. 11, June 1, 1934.

MOORE, ANNIE CARROLL. *The Three Owls; a Book about Children's Books: Their Authors, Artists and Critics.* New York: The Macmillan Company, 1925.

MOORE, ANNIE CARROLL. *The Three Owls; Second Book; Contemporary Criticism of Children's Books.* New York: Coward, McCann & Company, 1928.

MOORE, ANNIE CARROLL. *The Three Owls; Third Book; Contemporary Criticism of Children's Books, 1927–1930.* New York: Coward, McCann & Company, 1931.

Realms of Gold in Children's Books. Compiled by Bertha E. Mahoney, and Elinor Whitney. Garden City, New York: Doubleday, Doran & Company, 1929.

Right Book for the Right Child: A Graded Buying List. New York: John Day Company, 1933. Selected and annotated by a Committee of the American Library Association, graded by the Research Department of the Winnetka Public Schools.

TERMAN, LEWIS MADISON, and LIMA, MARGARET. *Children's Reading; a Guide for Parents and Teachers.* Second Edition. New York: D. Appleton and Company, 1931.

White House Conference on Child Health and Protection, 1930. Subcommittee on Reading. (Children's Reading; a Study of Voluntary Reading of Boys and Girls in the United States; Report.) New York: The Century Co., 1932.

Magazines

"Child's Own Library." Compiled by Nora Beust. *Journal of the National Education Association.* XXI (December, 1932), 289–90.

DALGLIESH, ALICE. "Literature and Children's Interests." *Childhood Education.* V (May, 1929), 475–8.

HILL, MAY. "The Place of the Folk Tale Today." *Elementary English Review.* VIII (November, 1931), 123–28. Bibliography by Eloise Ramsey.

MAHONEY, BERTHA E., and WHITNEY, ELINOR. "A Pick and Choose Book-list for Summer Reading." Part II. *Horn Book.* VIII (May, 1932), 96–100.

SAYERS, FRANCES CLARKE. "Bibliography for Children." *Elementary English Review.* IX (October, 1932), 197–9.

SHEA, AGATHA L. "New Placement of Emphasis in Histories Written for Young People." *Children's Library Year Book.* Number Four. 7–15. Chicago: American Library Association, 1932.

Teacher's Lesson Unit Series. (Numbers 1–40.) Bibliographies Edited by William A. McCall, and Lelah Mae Crabbs. New York: Bureau of Publications, Teachers College, Columbia University, 1931-32.

Partial content:
Spanish Trail. Grades IV-V. No. 7
Story of Lighting. Grade IV. No. 22
Ancient Athens, Rebuilt and Relived. Grade IV. No. 32
Hopi Indians. Grade III. No. 33
China. Grade III. No. 36
Travel on Land, on Sea, and in the Air. Grade VI. No. 40

Books for Children

An annotated bibliography of recreatory reading for boys and girls is presented in Appendix II, Bibliography on Recreatory Reading.

CHAPTER XVIII

ORAL AND WRITTEN EXPRESSION[1]

To be a child is:

> "To see a World in a Grain of Sand,
> And a Heaven in a Wild Flower,
> Hold Infinity in the palm of your hand
> And Eternity in an hour."
>
> —*William Blake*

I am the child.
I inhabit the Earth and inherit her loveliness,
Her singing trees, her cooling winds,
Her fragrant blossoms, her swaying grasses.
Her furry creatures, her winged birds,
Her dripping rains, her luscious fruits,
All these belong to me.

Life offers me:
The joy of being myself,
That my spirit may be free to soar,
The joy of companionship,
That I may share my life with others,
The joy of surprises and discoveries along my way,
The joy of sensing ideals
That I may reach out toward Beauty beyond myself.
Life is a challenge, for I am the child!

My classroom is my whole world for a portion of the
day.
I am happy there, for within its walls I find Earth's
Beauty.
My teacher, my proven friend, knows me,
A seeing, thinking, feeling, active person.

My world is not dimmed for me by barred paths nor
closed windows.
Avenues of adventure open before me—colorful and
inviting.

---

[1] Prepared by Marie L. Burgess, Teacher, Rockridge Elementary School; Gertrude Cross, Teacher, Burbank Elementary School; Regina M. Kent, Teacher, Durant Elementary School; Eveline P. Marcous, Teacher, Jefferson Elementary School; and Doris E. McEntyre, Supervisor of English and Dramatic Art, Oakland Public Schools, under the supervision of Dr. E. W. Jacobsen, Assistant Superintendent, Oakland Public Schools.

Bright pictures surround me on every hand.
I find shelves of good books where old Earth waits for
　me in all her splendor.
I pause there to refresh myself at a cool mountain
　stream
Or to walk bronzed autumn paths and hear the
　crackle of fallen leaves beneath my feet.
I live in igloos, travel in mid-air, dance with fairies
　or visit the haunts of furry forest folk.
My world grows day by day.

My teacher, my proven friend, banishes my fears.
She helps me to share this world of mine with others.

Often at work or play I find my way to the highest
　hilltops.
There I rest and count the treasures which are mine.

So I live, I feel, I sing,
　　I am a happy child!

Since the English language is the chief means for communicating
our thoughts and our feelings to other people, every classroom which is
an adequate place for girls and boys to grow provides for the spontaneous interchange of feelings and ideas. Children brought together
in a wholesome, friendly atmosphere will *want* to exchange experiences
and to relive together their adventures. Their natural inborn desire
for communication is the soundest possible foundation for further
growth in expression through language.

To be sure, some children in any group will be slow in expressing
their thoughts and feelings for others. Their natural desire for communication has perhaps been thwarted. The inhibiting factors must be
recognized by the teacher before she is able to call out the desire for
sincere communication from each one of her pupils.

Some girls and boys have been led to believe at home or at school
that their personal experiences are of no special value, that their own
observations are trivial and that their own feelings about things should
be carefully concealed. Others have been led to think that their imagin-
ings are silly and infantile. Still others have been impressed with the
fact that children "should be seen and not heard." An even larger
number of the group have perhaps been required to write fragmentary
"compositions" on dictated topics beyond their experience before they
were really ready to "compose" at all. The emphasis was placed
upon the way they wrote, upon the *form* rather than upon the content.

This fact that their form was so often faulty has perplexed them and led them to withdraw from class conversation and written comment because they feared the teacher's negative criticism or the ridicule of the group. Any one of these situations may prove to be a wall, shutting a pupil away from freedom in the expression of his thought.

The skillful teacher recognizes the conditions which may have temporarily strangled a desire for communication in the classroom. She takes time to establish an atmosphere of friendliness and sincere interest. She does not violate the privacy of her shy pupils. She does not demand response. She waits for it. She arranges situations in which each pupil will feel somehow impelled to contribute his own experience. Her own genuineness and her skill in relieving tensions by an expectant and sincere appreciation gradually break through the walls and open the way for expression for the most shut-in pupil who covers his fear with sullen silence.

As time goes on she develops interesting units of activity with her pupils and as the boys and girls explore together in forest or field or in far places, their opportunities for enjoying and sharing their adventures increase rapidly. When art, music, industrial arts, language expression and nature study swing together naturally *into whole and satisfying experiences,* power in the interchange of opinion and feeling is sure to develop rapidly, for interest will push it forward. Each pupil will find that he has some part in planning, discussing, and

Courtesy of Riverside County Schools

Child-Like Situations Impel Pupils to Talk Naturally and Freely

developing the activity. He will realize that he may make a unique contribution to the work of the group. As the teacher who guides the work recognizes the smallest contribution she will observe that capacity for expression is released. The very situations developing day by day in the classroom impel each pupil to talk naturally and freely.

When the teacher realizes fully that the fragmentary, isolated language study of the past must give way to vital language expression which grows out of the living interests and the planned activities of her group, some of the difficulties which have beset her path will disappear. Conversation and the exchange of opinion will take the place of glib question and tentative answer. The desire to communicate interesting discoveries will drive out hesitancy and fear. English learning will take the place of English teaching.

NATURAL SITUATIONS FOR ENGLISH EXPRESSION

We need not search for situations adaptable for the teaching of English. Innumerable appropriate activities suggest themselves in which oral and written expression play a part. Boys and girls take delight in recreating the life experiences of people in other lands and other times; they enjoy exploring the land of books for stories that have been beloved by children of their own ages, and they find no end of pleasure in bringing those stories to life for an audience.

Countless opportunities for sincere expression present themselves in everyday social life of the classroom. Jack extends a courtesy to a classmate; Mary relates to the group her happy experience at a Puppet Show; Lois tells how a new game was played at her birthday party; Frank introduces a favorite book; Louise presents a workable plan for her group in Social Studies; Helen gives her observations on the habits of butterflies or the class sends a packet of friendly notes to John who is ill. Out of such natural everyday happenings in the classroom will grow the power to speak and to write effectively.

FINDING THE WAY INTO THE FIELD OF CREATIVE WRITING

Of all the possible experiences in the use of English, creative adventures are the most satisfying to children. With the slightest accomplishment in this field, the personality seems to expand. Even one well-turned phrase or a single expressive line which he makes for himself gives the child a positive sense of power and the joy of ownership.

There is nothing mysterious nor strange about creative expression. The individual's own unique response to some aspect of his world forms itself within his consciousness. This response may never pour itself out in words to be shared with others, indeed it is frequently locked away. But when children are encouraged by a genuine, patient, sympathetic teacher who is herself sincere and expressive, these responses may be readily evoked from an individual or from a harmonious group.

The expression may be brief or extended, prose, poetry, or drama, even a mere group of words. *It is truly creative if it springs from the sincere, inward response of the individual.* John P. Frederick has given us the following lucid definition of creative writing:

> Creative writing occurs when the pupil recognizes the dignity and the value of his own experience and when he imposes upon that experience the discipline necessary to an attempt to transfer it to others. * * * In creative writing the aim is the transfer of experience and the reason for that transfer lies not in some material benefit to be attained by the writer but in his interest and pleasure in the experience itself.[1]

We sense its arrival, this creative work, by a flash of the owner's eye, a consciousness of absolute possession, "This is mine!" We note that as he shares it with others who are appreciative, he experiences a sense of fellowship, a feeling of well-being.

The outward, tangible result of creative effort may be halting and stumbling, its inward beauty scarcely discernable, but if it has about it a freshness, a vigor, an originality, we may be sure of its high spiritual origin. Whatever form of creation the pupil's effort may take, if it bears the mark of his own individuality, it satisfies a universal and profound urge to make something new—to create.

The creative effort springs from the unseen and often unsuspected imaginative life which is the heritage of every boy and girl. If this life is to develop fully it must be given every possible opportunity for expression.

Creative composition is not to be thought of as a decoration to be applied after language skills have been acquired nor is it to be considered as a special activity limited to a selected group of gifted pupils. Its purpose is not the development of a few specially gifted authors but rather the awakening in each boy and girl of a realization of an inherent power to communicate in a vivid fashion his own quickened reactions to the fascinating outer and inner world in which he lives. Hughes Mearns has expressed the universal presence of this gift for creative communication, perhaps better than any other teacher in our time.

> Deep within us all is a vast imaginative power varying in quality and in intensity but probably the same in each of us; it finds for itself, in devious unreasonable ways, an artistic expression.[2]

---

[1] John P. Frederick. "Creative Writing in American Schools." *The English Journal.* XXII (January, 1933), 1.
[2] Hughes Mearns. *Creative Youth.* Garden City, New York: Doubleday, Page & Company, 1925, p. 3.

It is just as important for every pupil to take delight in the color, the fragrance and the manifold exquisite sounds in the world about him as it is for him to recognize a complete sentence. It is just as important for him to recognize the value of his own vivid imaginative experiences as it is for him to know the correct form for a friendly letter.

EVOKING A CREATIVE MOOD FOR WRITING

Although latent creative and imaginative power is aroused to some extent by the interesting manifestations of life that surround children, the teacher who wishes to make the most of these innate abilities must do more than provide real experiences with life and beauty for her pupils. She must see to it that through her tactful guidance they become increasingly awake and aware of and increasingly responsive to the covered beauty that lies all about them. When she has accomplished this, she has provided riches for them that will last a lifetime and will gradually lead them to appreciate more and more keenly the recorded experiences which are stored away in literature.

Those children who live in the city have perhaps more need for a quickened observation of beauty than have those fortunate youngsters who live close to the forests and the hills. Their lives are often drab and humdrum. There is beauty available for them in the pyramids of color in the vegetable stands, the teasing rhythms of passing railway trains, and in the pounding pulse of the occasional speeding airplane. The shabbiest window in the drabest house frames a surprising square of blue when evening lights are lit just after sundown. The cool, fresh smell of the pavements on a rainy day and those magic rivers of blackness that give back the lamplights on damp evenings have a quality that is worth recording. But they may be missed altogether just as the richness of bird songs and the music of hurrying water may pass unnoticed by those who live in the country. Lethargy and dulled perceptions are not uncommon in an age when materialism and industrialism have dominated the thinking of our people. When wages and profits have been men's chief concern, there has been but small time for emphasis on the subtle appreciations which bring their only return in the realm of the spirit.

The teacher who is keenly aware of the beauty that surrounds her boys and girls communicates it through her own response and through her own sharing with them. Her appreciations are sure to quicken their reaction. As she plans ahead for her group, she will set about widening their horizons deliberately. After she has opened their eyes to the treasures close at hand she will lead them beyond their own door-

steps. She will frequently read aloud to them the best available literature written for children—both poetry and prose. She will select this
background material with the greatest care realizing that her pupils
will respond to her own appreciation of vivid writing and that their
taste will be influenced in part by her presentation. She will see to
it that they share the incomparable rhythm and the humor of Lear
and A. A. Milne, the music and the magical pictures of Walter de La
Mare, and the whimsical narrative of Rose Fyleman. In proportion
as she herself enters into the feeling, making the words "come alive"
for her group, her reading will lead her boys and girls to want to
bring their own experiences to life through vivid written expression.

Children respond so quickly to the surprising and unusual in their
immediate world that in a group the greater number are caught up
by the stimulating experience even before the teacher is aware of the
presence of these experiences. This consciousness of surprising things
happening, the pushing wind bending the trees double, the quick sharp
patter of hail on the windows, the unexpected Tootle-de-Tum of a
carnival band may start responses that could find expression in vivid
verse or prose if the teacher were on the alert for every opportunity.
A drab preoccupation with immediate tasks, may sometimes shut the
teacher's ears to these magical tunes.

For the boy and girl, who are somewhat slow when it comes to
sensing interesting things about them, the school environment must be
skillfully arranged. Live creatures, colorful flowers, pictures, and
books must be provided to lead out his interest.

A series of excellent verses was evoked in a fifth grade made up
largely of stolid Chinese children when they became interested in the
habits and the engaging antics of a pet squirrel and a collection of
flashing goldfish.

Some pupils may be genuinely moved by the beauty about them
but their feelings are blocked in expression by their loss or lack of
words. Their powers of expression can be released only when the
appropriate words for saying what they feel have been recalled or
pointed out. If the north wind is whistling about the schoolroom,
rattling the windows, blowing clouds of leaves about and pushing
with all its strength against small bodies at recess time that is the
time to help him find "windy words" that he may tell the feeling
which the north wind stirs in him.

If the rhythm of pattering rain on the schoolroom windows calls
his attention to its hurried movements then that is the very time to
lead him to build his impression into poetry or descriptive prose.

At times boys and girls want to search for the appropriate word
just as the adult does. At this point the teacher or other classmates

may be of real service. New and unusual words may be discovered, the very sound of which suggest ideas, and the child is off adventuring. Thus the feeling for beautiful verse or expressive prose may be gradually and naturally established as the desire to create them develops.

Experiences in creative writing are perhaps of greatest value because they quicken the powers of observation and appreciation through which the surrounding world becomes more truly a home. The senses one by one awaken to the manifold stimuli in the colorful world and the child becomes increasingly aware of the riches in nature's world. The successful search for things which speak to his spirit will lead him on to new discoveries. As he captures those discoveries in words and shares them with a few sincerely appreciative people they become fixed in the heart as well as in the memory and a sense of ownership is established which is a permanent part of the young author's joy.

HELPING GIRLS AND BOYS TO ESTABLISH THEIR POWER IN CREATIVE WRITING

In order that each child may gain genuine satisfaction from his own writing, whether it be verse or prose, and at the same time feel justified in claiming the finished product as his own, a certain amount of carefully directed suggestion must be given by the sympathetic teacher without any violation whatever of the writer's sense of ownership. This is a delicate and an important step which requires the utmost tact and understanding as well as genuine appreciation and discrimination on the part of the teacher.

To be sure, some few children in the fourth grade need but little assistance in expressive writing, unless it be a suggestion as to a more fitting form for a particular story or a choice of more vivid words with which to cloak ideas. But by far the greater number need much oral practice in the expression of their feelings and ideas before they attempt to write at all. Then, as their ability to formulate stories and poems develops, sometimes the incidents are so fleeting or indistinct that the children lack the courage to set them down. Encouragement is needed every step of the way. When the vocabulary is drab, concrete help should be at hand. The wise teacher will attempt to discover hidden beauties in somewhat incoherent first efforts, searching for and selecting a well-chosen word, an appropriate phrase, a singing line or a longer selection upon which to build. From very small beginnings, indeed, she may help girls and boys to produce short selections that really satisfy them.

It is important from the first that finished perfection in detail according to adult standards should not be the aim but rather growth toward better and better standards which are understood and accepted by the pupils themselves. The first slow steps in helping pupils to gain confidence in the creation of their written verse or prose are very important indeed. They are a necessary foundation for all further growth in expressive writing.

For example, in the creation of a poem by the group, the teacher will do well to work with the children, adding a word here or suggesting an appropriate phrase there. All share in the finished accomplishment and because of the guidance and the stimulation of the teacher a long, forward step may be taken by the entire group through the satisfaction they feel in their product.

After several satisfying stories, poems, or plays have been accomplished by the group, individual children are able to create independently, experiencing the joy of complete ownership in their lines whether they be few or many. As time goes on and each pupil feels his power to work with words to express his feelings and ideas he will want to search for exactly the word which makes his picture or his feeling clear. But the desire for revision must come from him. He has a right to his own choice of phrase. His work has now become completely his own and he experiences the joy of that unique ownership which is authorship.

EXPRESSIVE WRITING AND WORK WITH COLOR

A group of girls and boys in a low fourth grade were enjoying their first experiences with water color. Their teacher helped them to discover that they were living in a world filled with color where glorious hues surrounded them on every hand. Nature's vivid displays of color in the rainbow, in the early morning sky, and in the frequent sunsets, were pointed out to them. They, themselves, soon began to observe and to point out the color in the flowers, the grasses and the hillsides.

They attempted to catch the glory of color first through their paints. The best of their pictures were selected and mounted. Then the group composed together a number of poems telling the wonders of color. Each poem which was finally accepted was given its appropriate water color illustration and every child made for himself a booklet which he kept, his record of a journey to color-land. The following poems are illustrative of the children's work:

THE FAIRY CHAIRS

In the deep dark forest
Where the fairies play
The brownies give parties
For the pixies so gay.

Did you ever know what
These fairies used for chairs?
Just tiny toadstools
To sit on and rest from daytime cares.

And if you will go to this silent dark forest
You will find—
Rings of toadstools
That the fairies left behind.

THE RAINBOW FAIRIES

I know where the rainbow fairies hide
When the sky is a turquoise blue.
I know that they
Are peeping out of windows wide.
You can't see these fairies small
For behind the rainbow wall
They watch and wait
For the next faint rainbow's call.

Is it a fairy cave—
Or is it the bridge of the fairies
Stretching across the sunset sky?
And will this bridge lead
The fairies to Fairyland?

AT SUNSET

The fiery sun as it sends
Its flood of light across the sky
Tells the fairies that they
May go to their fairy haunts
In the mossy green trees on high.

THE GYPSIES

The brownies are like gypsies
And steal the pixies away.
They creep around the rainbow
Till they come to their secret doorway,
And down into the cave of the rainbow
They hide those pixies away.

FAIRIES OF THE RAINBOW

Fairies of the Rainbow
Playing in the sky
I know that I can see you
Way up high.

FAIRIES IN THE NIGHT

The sun, when he goes to rest,
Leaves a russet wheel of light
So the fairies can see their way
Thru the night.

LULLABY TREES

As the breeze goes gently
Past the lullaby trees
When the twilight lights are dim
I walk silently thru the quiet grass
And listen to the breeze
As it gently passes the lullaby trees.

A JOURNEY TO COLOR LAND

Color-Land

From sunrise morn to starlit sky
Just anywhere you go,
You can see the rainbow colors bright
Are nodding to you so.

They are calling you to color-land
Where color fairies live
Who paint the blossoms, trees, and birds
That happiness do give.

To go to color-land you know
Just open wide your eyes
And look at hillside fields and sky
That are everywhere you go.

Sunrise

At early morn
When the sky is clear blue
We look thru the grasses
All sparkling with dew
For blossoms just like
The sky's dainty hue
That come in the springtime
To gladden our view.

Sunset

At sunset time
When the sky is all red
We know those same blossoms
Have crept into bed
They have snuggled down low
In the grasses so tall
To wait till tomorrow
For the sun's merry call.

The Rainbow

The Rainbow's such a pretty sight
With all its colors set
Red, orange, yellow, green and blue and violet.

Did you ever see a rainbow
With its colors bright?
Isn't it a lovely thing
When its colors are alight?

SHARING ENJOYMENT IN CREATIVE WORK

Children love to share the achievements of other children. They enjoy listening to the verses that their classmates have made. It is surprising with what wholehearted concentration and interest they listen again and again as each child contributes his sincere effort to the group or to some visitor who has come into the school to enjoy it with them. With this joy of listening they often appropriate the richness that a friend has discovered and make his words their own. And if a thought is beautiful, who can measure the growth that comes from its possession, its release, and the genuine enjoyment of it?

Many boys and girls find their way naturally and easily into the realm of poetry when they are once awakened to the realization of its simplicity, both in form and in content. After all, poetry is simply the expression of beautiful feeling and beautiful thought in beautiful words.

TELL ME WHAT IS POETRY?

Tell me, what is poetry—
Wind in the pines along the sea,
Wind in the forest-browned lanes of sedge,
Lying close to the sand's white edge;
Song of the wave and the muttering roar
Of breakers lashing a wintry shore,
Tinkling sounds where waters slip
Through blue sea caves, drip by drip.

Tell me, what is poetry—
The earth's unceasing melody;
Dawn song, night song, birds awhir,
Fields where the bee is worshipper;
Drowsy drone of the summer rain,
Chirruping calls from ripening grain,
Cicada, cricket, shrilling low;
Nature's music in ebb and flow.

Tell me, what is poetry—
The heart's undying ecstasy,
Songs of our faith, our hopes, our tears,
Songs of the joys of passing years,
Laughter of children, glory of spring,
Tenderness for each blind dumb thing;
Praise when we bend 'neath the chastening rod;
Music that leads us up to God.

—*Jeanne Robert Foster*

VERSE FORMS

Verse forms are quickly understood and only a few lines have to be written before the child feels the appropriate beat so strongly that he writes his own original lines as the rhythm of each experience suggests. When the proper background has been established through the reading of appropriate children's verse, very few boys and girls will write meaningless jingles or limericks that have conspicuous end rhymes. Most children will want to express their genuine feelings in an appropriate pattern that will sing. If the teacher continually stresses communication of genuine feeling and picture rather than mere form, she will have little to fear from stereotyped patterns.

The form for poetic expression is neither complex nor difficult when we get away from fixed rhyme patterns. It is actually the simplest possible written English since it records feeling briefly and the rhythm of each line naturally measures the thought as it should be written down.

The following "beautiful pictures in beautiful words" which we call poetry have grown up in the classrooms of fourth, fifth, and sixth grade children. They are examples of expressive unrhymed *verse*, *showing different types of rhythm*.

Fourth grade children have written these brief poems:

THE SEASHORE

The rocks near the seashore
Are swept away by the waves.
Deep in the sea they are lying
While the waves are angrily lapping
And playing with the wind.

THE GLEN

Way down in the glen
Where the fairies dance and play
There are many toadstool umbrellas
Tucked away
In case of rain.

TREES

The trees are happy in the summer
The birds come and build nests in their branches.
But when winter comes the trees have no leaves.
The birds fly far, far to the south.
Then the trees are sad.

BUTTERFLIES AND BIRDS

Did you ever see the butterflies
Sail thru the sky?
Did you ever see the birds
As they pass the butterflies by?
Did you ever hear
A bird singing in the sky?
Did you ever see a butterfly close his wings
To say goodbye?

RAINDROPS

Raindrops thumping
On my window pane
Are like
Clumsy brownies
Playing in the rain.

THE SILVER MOON

The silver moon up in the sky
Is like a bed where
Fairies lie
And sleep till dawn.

PLAYING IN THE SNOW

Whenever it snows
On the garden walls
I like to go out
And make snowballs
And then to make
A big snowman
And for a hat
Add an old tin can

One child's impression of a stream gives us the sense of the rapid movement of the water.

O STREAM

Hop, skippety, jump, down its rock-dotted bed it flowed,
Hitting rocks and sending rainbow sprays.
Moss bent over and drank from its cool water.
Its jagged banks were lined with smooth white clay.
I asked of this foaming stream,
"Where do you come from so high?"
It answered, laughingly,
"I come trickling down the mountain-side, many of us side by side."
"Where do you go?" I asked again.
It answered with a smile,
"Don't you know?
I run down the canyon for miles and miles
Laughing all the while."

A girl in the sixth grade whose classroom windows face a young grove of eucalyptus trees has made her own picture of these neighbors.

SLIM EUCALYPTUS TREE

Tall eucalyptus tree,
With your leaves hanging from your branches
In clusters of green
With tiny snatches of leaves,
All curly
All crackly
And whirly,
Young boughs and limbs wave in the air,
Like long, green tresses of hair.

Another sixth grade girl has caught the secret of a pine tree in words that hold a whimsical smile in their pattern.

THE BIG PINE TREE

Oh, big pine tree
Why are you growing so tall,
Are you trying to reach the yellow moon?
He may pull you up.
You must wish to be a beautiful pine tree in heaven.

Although the surest form to insure the preservation of the child's feeling is the unrhymed poem, there are boys and girls, especially those at the fourth grade level, who naturally express their reactions in rhymed lines. This may be because their earliest association with poetry was Mother Goose or because the musical fascination of rhymed words captures them.

Their own natural use of rhyme is perfectly safe provided they are not led to sacrifice story or thought to mere jingle of sounds.

Following are examples of poetic expression from fourth and sixth grade children who use rhymed words and whose writing conveys not only mood and feeling, but thought as well.

RAIN

It's been raining all day long,
Pitter, patter is the song.
And I can't go out to play
On this muddy rainy day.

I just have to stay inside
And watch the raindrops hide
Among the blades of grass—
I hope this rain won't last.

THE WITHERED ROSES

Yesterday the roses were gay
But now they're withered and thrown away.
Yesterday the house was bright
But now it's dull—dull as night—
Because of those bright-colored roses
That were withered and thrown away.

THE VIOLET

One bright and early morning
Before the sun arose
I looked down in the grasses
And what do you suppose?

A pretty little violet
Lay cuddled in the green
Drinking falling dewdrops
Thinking itself unseen.

I watched and saw the violet
Turn its head up high
It peered up at the orange sun
Blinking his big round eye.

Soon it curled beneath its leaf,
A parasol of green
And there it rested through the day
Thinking itself unseen.

ON A RAINY DAY

Off to school on a rainy day,
Sorry for those who indoors stay.
Rain coat snug around me wrapped,
Warmly gloved and cosily capped.
Rain drops on my umbrella tapping,
Galoshes thru the water flapping.
"Oh what fun," I always say
When I walk to school on a rainy day.

FOG

The fog comes gliding on misty feet,
Filling up every space on the street,
Making its way to the villagers' town
Hanging its heavy mist
    Down, down, down!

THE MOON

The moon is hanging like a lantern in the sky.
Like a gorgeous emerald swinging on high.
Like a great big orange hanging round and bare,
Suspended by silver chains in the light brisk air.

A CREATIVE ADVENTURE

Creative work with children is a captivating adventure for the experienced and the inexperienced teachers alike. Even the first harvest proves a revelation. Perhaps from a page of writing, John has contributed but one original feeling or produced but one poetic thought. Sympathetic recognition of this contribution, however slight, provides further seed for a second yield and each harvest proves more bountiful than the last.

City children often seem a bit removed from many of the stirring beauties of nature that would lead them naturally to an expression of beauty. The racing brooks, the warbling birds, and the talking trees are sometimes beyond their immediate horizon. To be sure their own city streets have beauties to offer and these may be easily discovered. Sometimes the teacher may bring the out-of-doors that is not close at hand into her classroom that they may enjoy it.

We shall do well to remember that different groups need different types of inspirational stimuli to set them free, so, for beginners, care must be taken to have the environment carefully arranged. The feeling and thought should be stimulated and to some extent directed by questions. In other words, a mood should be created and as many of the child's senses as possible be called into play by the use of color, pictures, word-sounds, music, imaginary trips, references to home ties, and the reading aloud, in a well-modulated, expressive voice, of beautiful stories, plays or poems.

It is of special importance that the teacher's presentation "sing" with her own enthusiasm for that which she is attempting to convey. She should be enthusiastic to the point of contagion. Her questions which follow will help the children bring to a focus the emotional experiences they have enjoyed and lead them to reveal their inner feelings eagerly and sincerely.

LEADING FIFTH AND SIXTH GRADE BOYS AND GIRLS TO ATTEMPT CREATIVE WRITING

The following describes a sixth grade teacher's effort to get a sincere child-like verbal or written emotional reaction (either through stories or poems) to the swaying, gnarled, leafy trees that lend their rich beauty to the earth.

Beauty is found where beauty abides, so the classroom was first changed from one of orderly precision to one of beauty. Colorful pictures of tree-adorned landscapes were hung on the walls. Vases were filled with brilliant, scented blossoms. Pungent needled branches of evergreens were arranged to offer their spiciness. All was planned to create a stimulating atmosphere of beauty.

The teacher then directed her efforts toward leading her group to find beauty in trees, or to voice that which they had already sensed. Branches were held up for recognition. The characteristic size, form, trunk, and verdure of each tree was discussed. A picture then held up by the teacher assisted the children to vizualize whole trees.

Different children were asked what they considered beautiful about the oak, the elm, the fir. Such responses as: "I like the fir because each time I see it, it looks to me as though it were waiting with outstretched arms to hold my Christmas gifts and ornaments"; "I think the elm is beautiful because I feel cooler when I look at those green leaves on a hot, summer day"; "The oak seems to bend to one side or the other as though it were making a bow. I think its spotted leaves are beautiful in autumn"—are some of the responses perhaps not so poetically stated, that the teacher praised, and accepted with marked approval. Her aim was to give the children delight in, and confidence through, the utterances of their own genuine feelings.

During the course of the discussion and the responses, appropriate descriptive words were offered by the teacher, whenever it grew evident that the child was hampered in his contribution because of his limited vocabulary. Before the tree pictures were set aside, the class had added many descriptive words, pertaining to trees and parts of trees, to the teacher's list of words. These were all placed on the blackboard that the children might become really familiar with them.

Proceeding, the class agreed with the teacher that it might be interesting fun to find out what beauty others outside of the classroom group had found in trees. The teacher read with as much feeling as she could express various poems and stories that dealt with trees and the out-of-doors. Among the selections was Joyce Kilmer's "Trees" and a selected story from *Stories in Trees* by Mary I. Curtis.[1] Poems and stories written by other children were also read to the group. The Victrola record, "Wind Among the Trees," was played for the children to find out what beauty about trees the composer's story revealed.

The teacher then asked the children to find a tree that they should like to call their very own. Pictures of the oak, fir, elm, and pine were again displayed. The children were led on an imaginary journey to the foot of the most beautiful tree they had ever seen.

Intermittent directing and questioning by the teacher, as follows, led to written creative responses:

> Stand back and look at your tree as though you were an artist and wished to paint it.
> Walk up and feel of its bark. Run your fingers up and down and around it.
> Reach up for a sprig of leaves. Examine them, feel them, smell them.
> Now stand back again and see your tree as a whole.
> What lives near it? Above? To either side? Below?
> How do they look to you? To the tree? How do you suppose your tree feels about these neighbors?
> How does your tree feel about you?
> How does your tree feel about God?
> What do you wonder about your tree?
> Ask it questions so the rest of us may hear.

The teacher paused for responses of which some follow:

> "I wonder who spoke to you before I did and I wonder what they told you?"
> "I wonder how old you are?"
> "I wonder how you feel when the wind tosses your branches about?"
> "I wonder if you grow afraid when the north wind blows or if that is your merry-go-round ride?"
> "Does your tree tell you anything?"

---

[1] Mary I. Curtis. *Stories in Trees*. Chicago: Lyons and Carnahan, 1925.

The teacher then said:

> Now perhaps you would like to go off by yourself with your tree. Some of you will want to tell just what you see. Some will want to tell a story about it. Some of you will want to tell just how your tree feels and how you feel. Some of you will want to talk right to that tree. Let's put it down on paper.

The poems and parts of poems listed below show some of the results of the experience with trees:

> Then climbing trees so mossy green,
> They shape and hang the leaves
> So they will sing a melodious tune
> As they ruffle in the breeze.

TO YOU, O FIR TREE!

> O fir tree, standing on yon lone peak,
> Standing there amid the whirling snow,
> Why are you content to stay there alone;
> Why do you not join your brothers far below?
> Do I hear your answer?
>
> Borne upon the wild wind,
> Howling like a lost soul,
> You call that you have your duty to perform
> To God and man;
> You prolong the snowflakes,
> And gather and hold them under your branches,
> To keep them from flooding the valley below.
>
> The birds build their nests in your arms,
> And entrust you with their loved ones,
> What a wonderful thing you are,
> O fir tree!

THE TREE

> O tree on yonder peak,
> Brave sentinel
> For the valley below,
> How I love to hear you sing at night
> When the wind combs your bushy hair!
>
> When the moon peeks over your head,
> What a silky cloak you wear!
> Then your creepy shadow starts
> Coming down the hillside,
> To look up at you from below.
> You do so much for all of us,
> I wish I were you!

THE SONG OF HARVEST

Oh, what a tranquil spot, filled with the beauty of nature!
Weeping willows drooping emerald leaves mournfully
Over a brook of sapphire blue
That danced gaily down its twisted, rock-dotted bed,
While soft cypress moss trimmed its banks
To make it more beautiful.
Listening, I heard a soft, sweet melody;
Quickly a thought came to slip off my shoes.
Oh, how good it felt to lie there
In the shade of this sad old tree,
To dip my hot feet in the brook's cool and soothing waters
And to listen to an unseen musician-friend nearby!
Softly, softly, softly it went, then died away,
Then—louder, louder, louder; and nearer and nearer it came.
More distinct; more clear at last.
I heard it plainly—made out the words,
And there I saw tiny Mr. Cricket fiddling the hours away!
His melody, so clear, very gently said:
"Cheeree, cheeree-cheer up, rejoice ye, rejoice ye,
Fine harvest, good harvest, plenty of food,
We have our share—
Good harvest, Cheeree! Cheeree!"

MY PLUM TREES

Last week when I looked at my plum trees,
Their limbs were shivering and bare;
Not even a sign of a blossom,
Like babies who have no hair.
But when I looked this morning,
What do you think I saw?
My plum trees had white lace dresses,
As soft and as white as snow.
The rain fairies had done it,
But how, I do not know.

TREES

I saw one day on a hill a scarlet tree,
It was beautiful to see
In its crimson dress of yellow and gold,
It reminded me of a king upon a throne.

THE LEAF BABIES

I went a-walking one bright day,
In a forest green,
I was hunting Fairyland,
But nowhere was it seen.

Soon I heard a wee sweet voice,
Calling from above,
It was a little leaf baby,
Sending down its love.

He wanted me to play with him,
There 'neath the azure sky,
I was afraid I would fall off,
Way up there so high.

He said his was a leaf of joy,
And only good could be,
So soon I climbed beside him,
Where all things I could see.

I saw many other leaf babies
In their cradles fair,
They were bright and blithe and chubby,
For happy leaves, trees bear.

ENGLISH EXPRESSION IN RESPONSE TO MUSIC

The music of Rossini's "William Tell Overture" was presented to a fifth grade class for appreciation and furnished the incentive for a number of worthwhile phases of creative expression.

Many poems were inspired as the records created a mood which suggested such titles as "Awakening of Nature," "Song of Freedom," "Freedom is a Word of Joy," and "Dawn in the Alps" which is given below:

DAWN IN THE ALPS

See the sun's very first gleam
O'er the bluest mountain stream
Amid the dark outline of trees
Huge evergreen branches wave in the breeze.

Our fairest fancy or our dream
Can not equal the sun's first beam.
Silence lifts from dawn's early light
Day is just breaking from a long starlit night.

Some of these poems were set to music and many were delightfully illustrated in water colors, while others found expression in word pictures.

The story of the opera was so fascinating that everything available on the life of William Tell was read with keen interest, and led directly to the study of Switzerland.

The dramatic possibilities of the story also roused a desire to write a play to be presented with marionettes, in which the songs and poems previously written found an appropriate setting. The scenery was painted by the ones who illustrated their poems most beautifully. Many books were consulted to learn what kind of costumes would be suitable for the characters represented by the marionettes.

When the play was ready for performance, correctly worded invitations to parents and friends were thought necessary and were composed and written carefully.

Thus the response to Rossini's music led to many excursions into the realm of English. While it is impossible to tell just how far-reaching were the effects of this adventure, the visible results testify to its value.

RECORDING FACTUAL EXPERIENCES

Each classroom offers many situations for expression that are dominated by fact rather than by fancy. Such situations as recording and relating experiences, sharing discoveries, introducing book-friends, and writing letters occur frequently. Here too, children need encouragement in the expression of their own individuality rather than being led to reproduce in their own words the thought and feeling of other persons. No matter how brief his expression may be, it is all important that it belong to each pupil's own world. The sincerity and the originality of his expression should be stressed.

It is true each pupil must be taught correct form, paragraphing, proper usage, and the enrichment by the use of colorful words, yet he must be left free to develop his own style. He must be led to originate a captivating title, and to create beauty through clarity of thought, through variety in word choice and word sound, so setting his own

Courtesy of Yolo County Schools

Items from the Class Newspaper Must Be Broadcast in Clear and Distinct Tones rhythm. He may show his ingenuity in his manner of approach and in his ability to sound a fitting terminating note.

The friendly letter should express this self as naturally as when one visits a friend personally. All formality should be reduced to the minimum and show itself only in the terms of friendliness and respect in which such a message should be written. Chatty moments, bits of fun, news, common interests, and questioning may all be utilized to keep a natural quality. This, toned by each child's own unique expression, choice of words, and charm of statements should disclose the individual, unique and original always.

LEARNING TO USE THE TOOLS EFFECTIVELY

When children grow eager to write because of the joy experienced or the satisfaction gained by doing so, be it story or letter, poetry or drama; when they have created, have sensed ownership, and are carried on by their own growing power as well as by their teacher's whole-hearted enthusiasm and sympathetic approval, they will become interested in working over their efforts to perfect or more fully beautify the content. They will strive more nearly to parallel their attempts with the exact experience that prompted the expression.

Children, at this stage, may most profitably be introduced to proper form. The teacher, by the use of story books, may show them that fitting vocabulary, proper form, and accurate punctuation, are essential to convey accurately to others one's thoughts or inner feelings, and that through such use, the whole beauty which has been one's experience may be recaptured, revealed, communicated and permanently recorded.

The teacher should point out that all authors use definite "signposts" to guide them over word-paths and, by so doing, make the journey easy and pleasurable.

It is at this stage of their growth when children feel their own needs, that the teacher should show that the striving for the following mechanics in writing will bring increased power and accompanies an unselfish desire to share experiences in written form. It is surprising how little drill will be found necessary if these essentials are properly presented by the teacher and if the children write frequently and willingly from their own vivid, everyday experiences, so giving opportunity for the repeated use of the presented forms.

It is necessary for the teacher to provide correction periods, aside from the creative period, for the reclothing and repolishing of individual efforts. Here, forms may be reviewed, punctuation again discussed, and teacher-help given. The cautious, appreciative teacher will never force mere mechanics of form into the creative period lest a world of beauty be sacrificed.

Words

Boys and girls will feel themselves handicapped unless they have at their command a growing vocabulary of words that will convey their feeling accurately. They may be assisted to become more word-conscious as their desire to write grows. The teacher will find them eager to enlarge their vocabularies to meet their growing needs. It is helpful to some children to attempt to capture in word-lists the familiar wonders of nature; such as, the brooks, the trees, the winds, the mountains, and the stars. Children may well be encouraged to contribute descriptive words—such words as will make us see the image more clearly, make us feel it, smell it, or taste it.

The class may be led to feel the need of words to meet daily happenings and daily living. They may be guided to appraise their own vocabularies in terms of "word-power." Friendly competitive games and schemes may be set up to measure, in a child-like way, approximate growth in that power. A comparison with the motive-power of automobiles may be drawn. Proper spelling, too, would grow to be imperative as "go-power" or "word-power" would be lost when the written identification of the word became questionable. So proper spelling and word usage would unite as word-power and the child's hoarding instincts, coupled with his needs, will help him to capture for himself accurately spelled word-helpers.

Sentences

Reference to prose material in the child's reader or story book will give an opportunity to impress the child with the fact that, whether oral or written, thought is clarified for others when the author's words are grouped in definite, complete statements. The alert teacher will call attention once again to some story or article that has been previously enjoyed. Pupils may be shown what has made it readable, understandable, and consequently enjoyable.

Paragraphs

The paragraph content may be examined so that the group may become aware of the fact that similar ideas are grouped together in paragraphs, wherein there is order and sequence.

Punctuation

Punctuation marks may be compared to the traffic signals, guiding one's eye in its travels over word-paths. The "stop and go" signs that the author uses safeguards his thought and assures the reader of a smooth, uninterrupted "thought-getting" journey.

The wise teacher will present the use of punctuation slowly. She will ask children to strive for perfection in the *usage of but one mark during a given correction period*. She may present a new punctuation mark when she feels that the majority use the previous one with fair accuracy or ease. This method will reap results more rapidly than will a disconnected drill period when the teacher expects "carry over" and fails to get it.

By the time a child has reached the sixth grade, he should be familiar with, and able to use capitals, periods, commas, question marks, quotation marks, and apostrophes. Other terminal marks may be presented.

Good Usage

Correct usage or the employment of socially acceptable forms of construction may be difficult at first. Indeed, in some rural communities and some neighborhoods where foreign children are attending school, the socially accepted correct form may be slow in developing. If oral practice precedes any written work whatever, the gradual establishment of correct forms will come about in a natural manner. Always the spontaneous expression of genuine feeling should be regarded as of primary importance. The power to use correct forms can only be established through gradual, tactful, and kindly reminders. It is suggested that one error at a time be attacked and eliminated and that in no case spontaneous expression be driven out by hard and fast insistence on rules and regulations for speech and written expression if the child discovers a need for them in his own writing.

If the child can be led to see that the author shapes the beauty of his thought into a form that has beauty because of its clarity, that his foundation is strong because his idea is sound and complete, that his "word-mansion" hangs together under one roof and is connected by "thought-rooms" or paragraphs in which only the proper "thought-furniture" is found, that within these rooms, he punctuates to place his "thought-furniture" to lend charm and ease to make his "thought-home" and inviting one to many a reader-visitor, this child shall strive also to build such a mansion that *to him* will compare favorably with the thought and feeling that it is to hold.

Recognized and acclaimed by the teacher as young authors and made to feel that each contribution has been meritorious, in part if not as a whole, the group will accept and grasp the presented forms and will show a decided attempt to give the author's finish to their own creations; so with this need, this interest and definite aim, if the teacher frequently engineers her group through the polishing or correction period she will help to fix for them, in a surprisingly short time the mechanics of written English. Arduous drill will be unnecessary because significant practice will take its place.

WRITING STORIES

Some children are willing to communicate their imaginative experiences only in story form, even though they are exposed to poetry through the teacher's reading and through the work of the class group and individuals. Some few pupils prefer to avoid the form of poetry in their own attempts at written expression. Such pupils should never be forced to express themselves in verse form. It is well to remember and to point out to children that prose form will also convey beauty and depth of feeling.

It is wise to lead the group to the discovery that there is no set form for the telling of any short incident or story, that there are as many ways as there are authors, as varied beginnings, paragraphs and sentences as there are individuals. No two need be alike. Indeed no two should be alike.

Often a search through story books to find different types of introductions will reveal the fact that freedom of expression is necessary and that originality or freshness of view-point belongs to every good story. No set pattern or recipe for a story should ever be provided young people, for such a stereotype is sure to kill the first urge toward individual and unique expression.

The brief story with vivid familiar incidents expressed in simple, child-like language is the product the teacher hopes for. In these days of radio mystery stories and sensational moving picture narratives, it is more necessary than ever for the teacher to guide boys and girls in the choice of wholesome everyday themes for their story telling.

The retelling of stories which have been read, no matter how good they may be, can never be substituted for the fresh spontaneous expression of everyday experiences or imaginative flights of fancy.

Group Story Writing

Following is an account of story writing by a fourth grade group based on their experiences in growing Easter lilies. The story was entitled, "A Bulb that Decided to Grow."

The bulbs which were planted in January were supposed to bloom for mother's Easter gift. They were attended faithfully and lovingly. Each spike of green that poked through the soil brought exclamations of delight. The aphis caused genuine consternation. All the factors that enter into successful raising of bulbs were discussed with animation and their care became almost a ritual.

But alas! Some bloomed early in February, some were just getting a start in March, and some looked as if they would bear nothing but leaves. They simply refused to blossom by the calendar. So to relieve the distress it was suggested that an Easter story be written about the bulbs which would be the real Easter gift and the flowers could be taken home as they were ready. The idea was hailed with enthusiasm.

It took about twenty minutes a day for eight weeks to compose the story. It was written on the board sometimes by the teacher, sometimes one of the class as the boys and girls dictated their thoughts. After an incident was completed, it was read aloud and criticized. Words or phrases that were repeated were eliminated or synonyms were found. Often in order to find the happiest choice of words or phrases, they stopped and made a list of words or groups of words having the same or similar meanings, and then chose the one that was most helpful in expressing their thought.

When there was a question as to whose sentence was best or as to what turn the story should take, the class voted to see which met with the approval of the greatest number. Usually the majority were captured at once by one outstanding thought or theme and the movement of the story was never long delayed.

The story was mimeographed and each child made his copy into a book which was illustrated with his own drawings. The tender care with which these books were assembled, the sincere and spiritual feeling with which the story was composed, and the glowing pride with which each child carried his treasure away, were proof enough that with the flowers the souls of these boys and girls had likewise blossomed at Easter.

The story follows:

THE BULB THAT DECIDED TO GROW

CHAPTER I

THE BULB'S HELPERS

Once there was a bulb that wouldn't grow. He was afraid to grow because when he had beautiful flowers someone would pick them.

He said, "I have to work hard to make my flowers. First, I give them the food that is packed up in me. Then I have to send my roots into the ground to get more food. I have to take part of this food and make it into green leaves. Then I take some more of it and make it into stems. I take another part of my food and after a while it makes buds. By and by, my buds turn into beautiful flowers. They have such sweet perfume and such lovely colors."

Just then a voice said, "Why stay in the ground? It's very dark down there. Come out and play with the sunny breezes."

"Who are you?" asked the bulb.

"It is I, the sun. I will help you grow. I will give you warmth and light. That will make you have a pretty green gown. You will grow big and strong and healthy and will have beautiful flowers."

Just then the sun said, "Here comes a cloud. I will have to be leaving. I'll be seeing you again by and by."

The bulb felt lonely for a little while. All of a sudden he heard pitter-patter on the brown earth.

"Why, what is that? I wonder who is coming to visit me now. How damp the earth is getting! I believe this drink will help me grow. Maybe that's the rain coming."

A thousand little voices answered, "Yes, we are the raindrops coming to make the earth soft and give you a drink."

Pretty soon he felt something crumbling the earth around him.

"I wonder what that could be," said the bulb.

"It is I, your friend, the earthworm."

"What are you doing here?" said the bulb to the earth worm. "Why are you plowing the earth around me?"

"Why, don't you know?" asked the earthworm. "I am softening the earth so that it will be nice and easy for you to send your roots down to get food and water."

"Oh, are you helping me too?" replied the bulb. "I believe I'll begin to grow; because the sun gives me sunshine, the raindrops give me water, the earthworm crumbles up the earth, and I think I'd better do my part."

CHAPTER II

THE EASTER SURPRISE

The bulb thought and thought and finally he said, "First I'll send my roots down deep into the ground to hunt for food and water. Then I will take off my brown coat and put on my green gown and peep out and see the beautiful wide world. Yes, I think I'll do that as soon as my roots bring up the food and water."

One day a boy and girl came walking in the garden. It was a nice, sunny day.

All of a sudden the little girl said, "Oh, I see a little green leaf peeping out of the ground. I wonder what kind of a plant it is."

"Oh, it looks like a tulip," said the boy, "because its leaves are curled around each other."

The children danced for joy and cried, "Oh! spring is coming. Now we have something to take care of. Hurrah! hurrah!"

"It is such a hot day and the earth is so dry around it, the plant needs water," said the boy.

So the boy and girl ran to get their watering can. When they came back they saw a caterpillar crawling on the little plant's leaf.

"Oh," said the little girl, "we had better get a jar and put the caterpillar in it. Then we can watch it spin its cocoon and turn into a butterfly. For, if we leave it there, it will eat the tender leaves."

"Yes," said the boy, "I think we had better do that. I will go and get the jar."

The little girl thought, "I'll find a stick and lift the caterpillar off and when brother comes back I will slip it into the jar."

Just as she got back to the plant, she saw a big snail crawling toward it.

She called to her brother, "Oh, what shall I do now? There's a big snail coming to eat our tulip leaves."

"Of all the things that's happening," said her brother. "First I go to get the water and when I come back there's a caterpillar on our tulip. After that I go to get a jar and when I come back there's a big snail coming to eat our plant. Now, I'll have to get some lime to kill the snail. You watch that he doesn't get on the plant while I'm gone."

"My goodness!" said the bulb to himself, "What a racket is going on above, all about one little plant."

While her brother was gone the little girl, named Betty, said, "Now, I'll take this stick and put the caterpillar in the jar; then I'll water the plant."

Just when she had finished, her brother called, "Why, there isn't any lime!"

"Oh, dear! what are we going to do now?" cried Betty.

The two children thought for awhile. Suddenly the little boy, whose name was Bobby, said, "Oh, I have an idea! You go and ask mother if she has any work for us to do. Then we can earn some money to buy some lime."

So Betty went into the house and asked her mother if they could do some work to earn some money.

"Why yes, Betty, Bobby can pull some weeds out of the garden and you can wash the dishes. I will give each one of you five cents for doing the work. And then, when I give you the money, what will you spend it for?"

"Mother, I can't tell you now," said Betty. "It's a secret. You will find out on Easter morning."

So the children earned their money. Bobby went to the store and bought the lime. While Bobby was gone, Betty watched the plant and kept the snail away with a stick. Soon Bobby came running back with the lime.

"First, we had better put some lime on the snail and put him in the garbage can," said Bobby.

And they did it.

Then they formed a circle around the plant with the lime. They made the circle about a foot away from the plant. That would keep all the other snails from coming to eat the tulip leaves.

Every day the children watered the plant and took care of it, except one day they forgot to water it. But it rained.

The bulb said, "I am glad it rained or my leaves would have withered."

A few weeks later, on Easter morning, the children took their father and mother into the garden to show them their Easter gift. The plant had bloomed. On it was a gorgeous red tulip and a bud that was almost ready to open.

When she saw the plant the mother said, in a very happy voice, "Oh, is this what the secret was? What beautiful tulips!"

"Oh, thank you," said the father. "What a lovely Easter gift!"

"We'll have to go and get your surprise now," said father and mother.

Soon they came back. Each of them was carrying a basket of Easter eggs and a beautiful white rabbit.

The children jumped for joy and kissed their father and mother. They cried, "Now we have something new to take care of!"

The bulb said, "I am so glad I grew, because I made other people happy and besides I can see the beautiful wide world."

Beginning Written English in a Foreign Neighborhood

A group of girls and boys in the fourth grade of a school which is situated in the cotton mill district found their work in English expression difficult. Some came from foreign homes where no English was spoken. Others were accustomed to hearing only broken English. Their reading, as well as their language, was a problem.

Their teacher determined that all of their language work should be living, vital, close to their own immediate experience. The boys and girls with their teacher explored their own neighborhood in East Oakland to make some records of their discoveries so that other people might share them. They enjoyed their adventures in a whole-hearted fashion. Then they came back to their classroom and told of their discoveries, first in words and sentences, then later, in colored pictures made from bright papers pasted together in pleasing designs.

When the stories and the pictures were finally assembled and displayed by the class group, any one of the thirty children could "tell you all about it." There follows a list of single words that the girls and boys selected to use in telling of their experiences; then the words as they were combined in sentences to tell of the actual surprises and discoveries during their explorations. Time and again the girls and boys recalled their neighborhood journeys reading over and over proudly the "stories" which their group had made together. The young writers found all the joy of authorship in recording their discoveries. Their colorful pictures illustrated each experience giving it a special meaning and a certain humorous turn which they treasure.

FROM OUR WINDOWS

NOVEMBER

A beautiful clear day.
Mt. Tamalpais in the distance.
City Hall—Tribune Tower
Church Tower
Factories—tanks—chimneys—
   smoke
Flour elevator
   blue water of estuary
   ships—masts—piers
Homes—(roofs)
   yards—(washing on line)
   streets—telephone poles
   lines—trees
School

OUR NEIGHBORHOOD

A Survey

Estuary

Boat houses
Buildings
    Flour elevator
    Factories—chimneys—smoke
      (color, form)
    Montgomery-Ward
    Del Monte Cannery
    Oil Stations
      Auto repair
Depot—signal arch
Ice house
Tower
    Church—Schools—Homes
Stores—awnings—signs
    Fire hydrants
    Mail boxes
    Telephone posts
    Windmills—tanks
Roofs

Trains

Signal arch
Engine
Freight cars
Street cars
    "End of the line"
Passenger
Flat cars
Oil cars
Circus cars
Ice cars
Fruit cars

Airport

Airplanes (aviators)
Hangars
Cement Mixers
Tanks—posts
Cranes
Steam shovels
Steam rollers
Derricks
Trucks (oil, fruit, dump, lumber,
    moving vans, towing car)
Bus (To Alameda—To San Jose)
Peanut wagon
Ice wagon

Bridges

(Study steel construction)

Open and closed
Bridge tender's house

Boats

Launch
Motor
Lumber
Tug
Pilot
"Bear"
Whalers
Rafts

Barges
Sail
Fire boat
Row boat
Racing boat
    (crew)
Liners
Dredgers

Sea-gulls

Persons

Cannery workers
    (unemployed men on corners)
School children—Housewives
    (woman carrying boxes on
      head)
Policeman—Balloon man—
    Crowds
Mail man—linemen
Pop-corn man—Tamale man
Junk man—Taxi cab driver
Sailors
Nuns
Procession of Holy Ghost
Newsboys
Flagman (23d Avenue)
Painters (on cannery chimneys)

23d Avenue

Street car (No. 9)
Stores
Cotton mill
Foundry
Station (San Francisco cars)
Flagman
Laundry
Meat and fish market
Flower store
Taxi stand

Airport—Continued

Fruit wagon
Junk wagon
Fish wagon
Bakery wagon
Laundry wagon
Milk wagon
Garbage wagon
Tamale wagon
Vegetable wagon

Children

Skating
Fishing
On scooters
Running to store
With balloons
On bicycles
At carnival

Neptune Beach

Hot dog stands
Tents—flags
Swimming tank
Swings—slides—whoopees
Pop-corn wagon
Swimmers
Ferris wheel
Merry-go-round

Carnival

Springtime
    meadow—wild flowers
Tents—wagons—flags
Freaks
Merry-mix-up
Ponies
Ferris wheel
Ticket booths
Pennants

Our School

Sun Class (milk)
Miss Fredenburg's—Holland
Mrs. Moynes'—Circus
Mrs. Lesser's—Russian play
Perry Dilley's—Puppet Show
Our Walks—Our Games—Our Songs—Our Toys
Mrs. Mac Lean's—"Ark"
Our Goldfish
Cactus Garden
Our Chinese Lilies
May Day Festival

The Train

Cars

Passenger car
Dining car
Sleeping car (Pullman)
Mail car
Ice car
Baggage car
Oil car
Flat car
Fruit car
Freight car

Persons

Engineer
Fireman
Flagman
Baggageman
Expressman
Conductor
Switchman
"Butcher" boy
Pullman porter—maid
Diner—cook, waiters, manager

The Engine

Piston rod (oil wheels and piston
    rod)
Sander
Cowcatcher
Headlight
Cab
Whistle
Station

Bell
Window (in cab)
Switch track
Signal lights
Train shed
Depot

THE STEAM SHOVEL

PART I

We went for a nice walk.
The class went to see the steam shovel.
It was digging a ditch.
The steam shovel is a big machine.
The engine makes a loud noise.
We waved at the driver.
The driver was in the cab.
He was working the levers.
The driver asked Joe to climb into the cab.
Joe laughed, but he climbed into the cab.
Joe worked the levers.
The big boom moved up and down.
The body turned on its tractor base.
The shovel bit into the earth with its sharp teeth.

PART II

This is a story about the steam shovel.
Our class took a walk to watch the steam shovel at work.
It was digging a ditch.
It is a big thing.
It is made of steel and iron.
We watched it swing around on its tractor base.
The engine made a great noise.

PART III

Our class went to see the steam shovel today.
It was digging a ditch in the street.
We waved at the driver.
The driver called out, "Hello boys and girls."
Joe walked up to the machine.
The driver asked Joe to climb up into the cab.
Joe looked very small in the cab.
The driver showed Joe how to work the levers.

PART IV

The big body moved on its tractor base.
Joe was very happy.
He felt like a big man.
The big boom moved up and down.
The boys and girls ran out of the way.
The big shovel with its sharp teeth was coming our way.
The big shovel bit into the earth with its sharp teeth.
Walter made a sketch of the steam shovel.
Here it is. Do you like it?

THE ENGINE'S STORY

We saw sheep in a big freight car.
We saw a tractor on a flat car.
We saw a man on top of a freight car.
He was the brakeman.
The brakeman carried a flag.
I saw a man wave a flag.
He was the flagman.
We enjoyed our walk to the depot.
We were very happy.
I shall draw the engineer in his cab.
I shall draw the fireman too.

THE ENGINE

We saw the green light.
We saw the red light.
We saw the orange light too.
The green light means go.
The red light means stop.
The orange light means go slowly.
Our class counted the freight cars.
We counted ten freight cars.
The big engine pulled the long train.
We studied the freight cars.
I can draw a freight car.
We will draw the engineer.
We will draw the fireman too.
We will draw the big engine.
We will draw the freight cars.
We enjoyed our walk to the depot.

OCTOBER

We went for a nice walk.
It is October.
All the leaves are falling.
Some trees have yellow leaves.
Some trees have red leaves.
The ground is covered with leaves.
Joe said, "Let us walk through the leaves."
Manuel said, "Let us kick the fallen leaves."
The class will gather the leaves.
We will help Dad rake up the leaves.
We will help the farmer gather the fallen leaves.
I will take the big rake.
We will put the leaves in a pack.
The farmer will burn the dry leaves.
The farmer has elm trees on his farm.
The farmer has oak trees on his farm.
I have a poplar tree in my back yard.

⚹END OF THE LINE

1. This is the end of the street car line.
2. This is a one-man street car.
3. The motorman gets out and changes the trolley wire.
4. The motorman turns the seats around too.
5. The people are standing on the corner.
6. They are waiting for the street car.
7. They enter the car and put seven cents in the money box.
8. Some ask for transfers to another car.
9. The motorman is very kind and polite to the passengers.

OUR NEIGHBOR

This is the house across the street.
Mrs. Souza lives in this house.
She did a big washing this morning.
Her washing is always clean and very white.
Mrs. Souza is talking to the fish man.
The fish man comes around in a white wagon every Wednesday
    and Friday.
He blows his horn.
The woman comes to the front door.
Mrs. Souza is buying some fresh fish.
She has a platter for the fish in her hands.
The cats smell the fish.
They say, "Meow, meow."
Their tails stand straight up.
The cats like fish.
The fish man will give them the heads and tails from the fish.

THE STEEL BRIDGE

I saw a street car go over the bridge.
The bridge is made of steel.
The bridge is painted orange.
I saw many autos go over the bridge.
I saw boats go under the bridge.
I saw many boats in the canal.

⚹THE ENGINE

We saw the big engine.
I waved at the engineer.
Our class walked to the depot.
We saw many trains at the depot.
We saw the fireman in the cab of the engine.
We saw the engineer too.
The engineer waved at us.
He called, "Hello, hello" to us.
We laughed and waved at him.
We saw the signal lights.

THE CUTTER BEAR

Our class took many walks to see the Cutter Bear.
The Cutter Bear is a very strong boat.
It has sailed in frozen seas.
It can cut its way thru ice.
It has a tiny wooden Bear on its prow.
Mr. Richard Byrd bought the Cutter Bear.
Mr. Byrd bought it from the City of Oakland.
Mr. Byrd will take the Cutter Bear to the South pole with him.
The Cutter Bear will carry food for Mr. Byrd and his men and dogs.
The Cutter Bear was painted and repaired before it left.
The Cutter Bear is a famous boat.

THE ROWING CREW

This is a story about the rowing crew.
We saw them down by the bridge.
These boys come from a big school.
This big school is called a University.
The University of California is in Berkeley.
The crew boys go to the estuary in a big bus.
The boys practice rowing.
The boys row in a long slim boat.
This boat is called a shell.
It is called a shell because it is so light.
They can make it go very fast.
There are nine in the crew.
Eight men pull the oars.
One man sits in front. He is the coxswain.

THE BRIDGE

Our class took a long walk today.
We went to the bay.
We saw many boats.
We saw the bridge open and close.
Our class saw a big lumber boat.
We saw a red fire boat in the canal.
Nancy saw a little tug boat.
We sketched the boats in our notebook.

THE TAXICAB STAND

PART I

There is a Taxicab Stand on 23d Avenue.
Pete is the taxicab driver.
Pete stands near a telephone.
When the telephone rings, Pete goes after his passenger.
Pete has a nice taxicab.
It is painted bright orange and black.

PART II

We were walking on 23d Avenue yesterday.
We saw a lady with many bundles.
She wanted a taxicab to take her home.
The lady waved at Pete.
Pete is the taxicab driver.
Pete went over and helped her across the Avenue.

WE SHALL

I shall walk to the depot.
I shall see the trains.
I shall talk to the engineer.
I shall talk to the fireman.
He will show me the engine.
I shall climb into the cab of the engine.
I shall look out the window of the cab.
I shall wave to my class.
We had a good time.
We shall write a story about our walk.
We shall write the story in our note-book.
We shall read the story to Miss Cotter.
She will enjoy our story.

NEPTUNE BEACH

PART I

I went to Neptune Beach Sunday afternoon.
Neptune Beach is in Alameda.
Alameda is an island near our school.
We took street car number nine.
It took us right to the Beach.

PART II

David and I had a good swim.
We stayed in the tank for one hour.
We had lots of fun.
When we came out we bought peanuts and hot dogs.
David and I met Joe and Manuel by the peanut wagon.
Then, we all went on the Merry-go-round.

PART III

The ticket man told us this Merry-go-round came from England.
It came from England many years ago.
It came around Cape Horn.
We found Cape Horn on the map.
In the olden days boats came to California that way.

PART IV

The tickets cost five cents each.
Manuel bought five tickets.
I climbed on a white horse.
David and Joe rode black horses.
Manuel rode in a big seat.
He talked to the ticket man.
The music was gay, like gypsy music.

PART V

I took my swimming suit.
David and I went swimming in the tank.
I dived from the high diving board.
David tried to ride a rubber play horse.
He always fell off. I played with a rubber tire.

Examples of Children's Original Stories

The following are examples of brief, original stories written by boys and girls in the high fifth grade:

TALENTED FOLK OF THE GRASSES

'Twas noon, and circus day in Bugville! Myriad bug-folk came from afar, and gathered 'round the clearing to see the talented bugs perform.

Mrs. Spider had woven her stage and made a low curtsy upon it with a smile. Then she leaped upon a silver spoke and from one to the other she gracefully swung—a risking act, indeed!

Soon she deftly dropped to the leaf-covered ground. Ah, how stunning she did look in her dazzling vesture of silver! She was applauded by everyone as she vanished behind the leaf-curtain.

All then was quiet, in readiness for the rest of the performance. 'Twas to be gay Mr. Cricket who had been booked to play upon his violin, for a great violinist was he!

He fiddled away about the rippling brooks and falling autumn leaves, about flower chalices filled with dew, and about the gentle breezes that swayed the flower heads—holding everyone spellbound with his music. Not an antenna in the throng quivered.

Then Anthony Ant respectfully reached the center of the clearing. He and others were going to run a race, for great marathon runners were they among bug-folk.

The signal was given. Up a bulrush they went. Adolphus Ant soon gained the lead. Then feeler to feeler they excitedly ran on. Anthony Ant was running ahead; and reached the top of the bulrush, in the cheering of the shouting crowd, who anxiously had been jumping up and down in a great state of excitement.

Then came the last, the final one. It was Mr. Grasshopper playing the web. He played a march, a merry tune, while all bug-folk marched away—away to their homes in meadows, fields, and woods, gossiping about the performance and thinking about next circus day.

EGGS

It was the week before Easter and Colonel Egg was worried about the safety of his troops because the rabbit pirates had captured Eggly Fort and were sailing up the Eggleston River.

Suddenly Humpty-Dumpty ran up and told brave Colonel Egg that the pirates had captured the village and were boiling the citizens alive.

The brave Colonel made a valiant resolution. He would charge the pirates! He told the courageous soldiers what they were to do.

One old hard-boiled Egg cried out, "Let our cry be eggs!"

"Aye, Aye," the brave troopers shouted.

"Charge!" rang out on the quiet air.

They did. Eggs, Eggs, and more Eggs covered the heroic field when those soldiers charged that Easter time.

PRIMROSE CRADLES

Tip-Toe had gone off by herself to a tranquil spot. She had been thinking a lot as to where the other fairies kept their babies. She would ask Bell to go with her to find them. Bell agreed to go if Tip-Toe would bring her back. So they started out on their gay trip.

"Isn't it just wonderful here," said Bell, laughingly.

"It surely is. But see! What is in this primrose?" said Tip-Toe excitedly.

"It's a fairy baby! Isn't it cute," Tip-Toe cried.

"It's just getting its tiny wings!" said Bell.

"Don't awaken it, please," they both said together.

They both flew away quickly and quietly, each with a happy, loving feeling inside. Each was thinking, "A Primrose Cradle!"

EVALUATION OF AN EXPERIENCE IN CREATIVE COMPOSITION

One day something happened in a low fourth grade that revealed a new and delightful world to a surprised group of nine-year olds and to an amazed teacher.

Veritably it seemed to the teacher that Pegasus himself cantered into the classroom and bore forty-four youngsters off to his high pastures of delight. Imagination, his winged power, lifted them all easily—joyfully.

The teacher wanted to have the class write original fairy stories for each unit of work on life of peoples of many lands.

In preparation for writing the stories for Alaskan children, the class visited an Alaskan exhibit at the Oakland Public Museum. Certainly the mode of life of the Eskimo was made real by this trip. They saw everything from the bone needle and sinew for the thread to the model of the type of sledge used by the Eskimos.

Two scenes, one of musk oxen grazing on lichens on a rocky, snow-covered cliff, the other of massive polar bears treading upon the cracking ice floes, transported the children to a new world—the northern lands.

After this excursion the study of Alaska and Eskimos was most animated. Facts were demanded, sought after, and seized upon by both class and teacher.

One day after the study had been eagerly pursued for about three weeks, a child suddenly remarked to the teacher that she had not told them any Eskimo fairy stories. The teacher recognized in this remark her opportunity.

She had a real motive for developing what she knew was recorded in the mind of each child. She knew that these sensitive plates had been exposed. The year before they had been saturated with much children's literature of an imaginative type. The atmosphere of the North had permeated deeply from experiencing Eskimo life at the museum.

The teacher told her class that her trips to the library were futile.

Then one child challenged the room. "Maybe we could write our own!"

One Alaskan legend was told by the teacher. Again the class didn't fail. "What happened under the sea?" reverberated through the room.

"That's the fault I had with the story too," said the teacher. "It doesn't tell." From that point on it's easy to see what happened. "What would you do under the sea if you were the boy? How did you get under the sea? Pretend that you are a little Eskimo boy and that Mittling, the Giant of the Sea, has you under the sea."

The class was told to think quietly for awhile and to make up a story about an Eskimo boy under the sea.

At last they began to tell their stories. The teacher saw and heard child after child who had never before revealed a glimmer of imagination wax fluent with inventiveness and power. Matter of fact, stolid, James and Charles vied with those who had always been the stars in the room.

Of course, the teacher couldn't conceal that she was delighted with the stories, *but the children knew themselves that the stories of their classmates were good.* Children who rarely had much more than a few sentences to offer seemed literally to have their tongues untied. The stories were all long in their original oral form, taking from two to seven minutes to relate. They held the attention. The last hour in the day was spent in illustrating the stories.

Results of that joyous day are bound up in a book entitled "Adventures Under Arctic Seas." In this class book appears a story from each child and a picture from each child. Each story has its own originality. Each picture is different and is an expression of its owner's individuality.

For teaching material in composition, the class was confronted with the real need for paragraphs. They were faced with an incentive for title making because each one must have a different title. The pictures also had to be named. Both of these problems were satisfied in a living manner.

This experience in creative composition has caused the teacher to shift her emphasis away from the end result—from the work produced—*to the act and experience of creating.* The book, attractive though it is, the teacher recognizes as a superficial result of this experience.

Here are some excerpts from the class book.

ADVENTURES UNDER ARCTIC SEAS

INTRODUCTION

A week after school started our class went to the museum. We went to see the Alaskan exhibits. When we saw the musk ox scenes and polar bears at the Snow museum we felt as if we were in Alaska. Miss Farnum could not find any Alaskan fairy tales in the Library.

We always have stories about what we are studying. Our teacher said we would have to write our own fairy tales this time, for she couldn't find any. That is how we came to write these stories.

A Visit Under the Sea

Once there was a poor widow who had a little boy. One day when they were eating supper they heard a loud roar.

"Who is it?" said the woman.

"It is I," something roared.

Then, they saw some hair. My goodness this couldn't be a talking beast. Then, they saw some eyes.

"I am going to eat you," it roared.

"Are you a giant?" said the woman in a low tone.

"What?" it roared.

"Are you a giant?" she said louder.

"Yes," he roared.

"Please don't eat us," she asked.

"I won't if you will let me have your boy for six months."

"All right," said the woman.

Then, she was sorry. The giant's name was Lylo. The boy's name was Tittoo.

He took Tittoo across the ice in one step. He said it was the smallest step he ever took. He knocked on the ice. A door opened.

"It's dark," Tittoo said. At the end of the passage the giant knocked three times. A beautiful carriage made of pearls appeared.

Oh, what a good time Tittoo had!

Lylo's castle was beautiful. It was made of big pearls decorated with shells of all colors of the rainbow.

One day Tittoo told Lylo he wanted something to ride but the giant only said, "Go to bed."

When Tittoo woke up beside his bed was a beautiful carriage made of pearls. A whale pulled it.

Tittoo had a playmate named Seagreen. They would play ball with a pearl. Another game they played was racing. Tittoo very often won. If they won they would get a pearl. They tried to get the most pearls.

The servants were fish. The nurse was a clam. If Tittoo was bad she would pinch him.

A Lively Fish

Tuska was an Eskimo of the north seas. One day when he was out fishing a hand came out of the water and seized him. Then, Tuska felt himself being pulled through the water.

Suddenly he bumped on the bottom of the sea. Now standing in front of him was the sea giant.

"Who are you?" said the boy.

"I am _____."

He had a fish on his line and it pulled so hard it woke him up.

The Sea Giant's Magic

Once there was a little boy. His mother wanted him to get some snow to melt. He started to cry. She said that the Giant of the Sea would come to steal him away.

He started to get some snow to melt. Then, out of the gloomy mist suddenly came the Giant of the Sea. He blew a magic vapor. The boy fell asleep.

When he awoke he was down at the bottom of the sea. It was very queer down there at first. You couldn't imagine how strange it was.

The giant's castle was made of large pearls. The giant made him a carriage out of a clam. It had little windows in it.

Football Under the Sea

I am a little boy. My name is Coro. One night I heard a swishing noise. Then, I went to bed. Then, two blocks of ice fell from the side of the igloo. Then, two hands pulled me outside.

I could see a head, but not the body nor the feet. But the head had large bushy hair and red cheeks and black eyes. It was a giant. He pulled me out. He took one big step and he went down to sea.

There I met a sword fish. It said, "Can you play football?" I said, "No."

So then he told me how. I asked the Giant to make me a football. He said he would. He killed a whale and skinned it. Then, he sewed it together. He blew it up. I took it outside. Then, I threw it at the sword fish. He popped it with his sword. But I did not cry; so the Giant made me another football.

Courtesy of Los Angeles City Schools

The Development of Expressive Speech Results from Dramatic Activity

The well-written play written by adults and specifically planned for children's presentation is one type of dramatic activity that appeals especially to girls and boys in the sixth grade. The development of expressive speech, social cooperation, courage and confidence as well as the growth of appreciative powers result from this type of dramatic activity.

The following outline for the development of dramatic activities in the elementary grades has been worked out by Oakland teachers in the intermediate grades with the Supervisor of English and Dramatic Art.

Concrete Suggestions for Making Magic in the Classroom Theater

COME—LET'S PRETEND!

Dress you up then, make a stage
Be a king, a knight, a page,
Fairy princess, swineherd rude,
Monk or merry Robin Hood.
Take your choice, whate'er it be,
Play your part right merrily.

Surely whoever speaks to me in the right voice, him or her I shall follow as the waters follow the moon, silently with fluid steps, anywhere around the globe.

—Walt Whitman

Success in our dramatic activities is measured in terms of *spiritual values,* those human values which a wholesome play reveals to the boys and girls who bring it to life.

The final production is not our concern. If the plays or the poems which we bring to life minister to spiritual needs, if they awaken within the pupils some affirmative response to the good, the true, or the beautiful as they are revealed in the lives of everyday people, then the activity may be said to be successful in the highest sense.

The following outline presents a number of the more important aims of dramatic presentation together with a list of rather specific procedures through which the aims may be realized.

Aims	*Suggested Procedures*
1. To provide a constructive channel for the joyous expression of play impulse, the dramatic urge, which belongs to every boy and girl.	1. Choose dramatic material that is wholesome in content and well expressed; material which stimulates constructive emotional responses from boys and girls. Take care that the ideals expressed are of lasting value for building character, avoid the merely sensational or melodramatic.
2. To awaken and develop the fine constructive emotions of boys and girls; to direct the expression of those emotions through the use of wholesome material which build fine ideals and constantly lifts the level of taste.	2. Plan frequent informal short productions, based on material of excellent quality for small audiences rather than waiting for finished, polished productions of long plays.
	3. Plan to use dramatic poetry, favorite stories, and meaningful dramatic situations created by the pupils as well as plays that have been planned for production.
	4. Provide each boy and girl with a complete copy of the play, poem, or dramatic story so that the entire unit may be brought to life for all the participants.
3. To establish courage and confidence with girls and boys in their own expressive speech.	5. Hold informal round-table reading in a quiet setting so that every pupil may understand and enjoy the entire story.

Aims

4. To provide opportunities for social development and adaptation through participation in the group activities that are involved in informal play production.

5. To afford a genuine "practice ring" for living in which young players may try out the feelings and the experience of many characters in manifold situations to the end that they may direct their own life's action with more vision.

6. To provide an opportunity for boys and girls to become sympathetic, courteous members of an interested audience enjoying informal dramatic activities suited to their age.

7. To foster active appreciation of expressive reading and wholesome dramatic activity so that leisure time may be increasingly well employed.

Suggested Procedures

6. Clear up preliminary questions as to interpretation, pronunciation, and character types. Picture and discuss the persons and the situations so that they take on the color of life.

7. See to it that the fine underlying message of the play is understood.

8. Develop reading rehearsals slowly, allowing many pupils to try different parts so that originality and variety in interpretation are encouraged. Let this growing process go forward until the expression of genuine feeling emerges. Question players to bring out meaning, but give no directions for the inflection of lines.

9. Encourage pupils to use simple, natural, conversational voices.
"Let us talk to one another, let us listen to one another,
Let us feel every idea before we utter it,
Let us make sure we are sincerely living each situation as we speak.
Let us think each thought, feel each emotion, hear each sound with our inward mind, our inward feeling, and our inward ears,
Let us keep the total situations alive every minute."

10. Continue reading rehearsals with the gradual introduction of stage movement.
Place doors, windows, entrances, and exits allowing players to discuss and choose stage pictures, movement, etc.

11. Rehearse different casts with manuscripts many times before the lines are learned by heart.

12. Arouse the imagination of players and lead them to find their own way into the most expressive conversational form.
Be willing to wait patiently for results, keeping the social values of the process in mind rather than the end production.

13. Keep the self-confidence and the joyous spirit of the players awake. Commend the good and wait for growth.

14. Establish with the players an absolute **rule that each one must appreciate the** effort of his fellow workers. Permit no negative blighting words from players during rehearsals.

The urge to make plays or to create incidents in dialogue results from a desire to share some experience that has been enjoyable. The actual creation of a play is valuable and memorable when mimicry and imitation are banished completely by the wide awake enjoyment resulting from the actual personal recreation of interesting characters and situations through the use of familiar words.

Because of the very nature of plays, their changing scenes, their numerous characters and their unfolding stories, the original dramas that are attempted are perhaps best developed through group effort. The teacher's leadership is needed every step of the way in order to insure the selection of significant incidents which are taken from

Courtesy of Los Angeles City Schools

Spontaneous Conversation Rather Than Memorized Lines Are Possible When Situations Have Child Interest

appropriate themes rather than from the sensational moving picture or radio impressions of the boys and girls.

When the theme is once selected and the element of beauty is gradually introduced into the undertaking, boys and girls will keep the air alive with fresh imaginative ideas. The search for the expressive word and the choice of significant picture background is sure to lead to growth in vocabulary that will satisfy the most exacting teacher.

As brief plays and dramatic incidents are captured in words, speech and the expression of the feeling naturally follow. The informal playing of a dramatic incident with spontaneous conversation rather than memorized lines become possible when the situations have been selected with care and have been made a part of each pupil's own world.

SUMMARY OF ACTIVITIES INVOLVING ORAL AND WRITTEN EXPRESSION

Ability in oral and written expression will develop most naturally and most effectively from those group activities which are rich in their opportunities for vital communication.

The selection and the preparation of a well chosen play to be presented for parents and pupils, the making and giving of a group of puppet plays from a collection of favorite stories, or the arrangement of an auditorium festival presentation where original verse and story are combined with music and art, industrial arts and social studies, to create a school program, are examples of such undertakings.

Such activities challenge the interests and abilities of an entire class group. The children are given not only an opportunity for oral and written expression, but for physical expression as well. The outcome of their cooperative undertaking can be made so satisfying that each pupil realizes his own part in the group work and feels a genuine pride in the outcome.

The activities in the following lists are rich in possibilities for pupils to gain experience in oral and written expression.

Oral Language Activities

1. Presentation of appropriate childlike plays in simple settings.
2. Participation in group discussion when plans are made or when work is evaluated.
3. Presentation of puppet shows in simple settings with class planning and class evaluation.
4. Arrangement and presentation of broadcasts where selected poetry and story contributions are given careful interpretation.
5. Play making with groups from favorite stories or interesting appropriate incidents.
6. Participation in assemblies, school, class or group club organizations.
7. Presentation of exchange programs with neighboring class groups in the interpretation of poetry and selected dramatic incidents.

Written Language Activities

1. Writing original poems or brief stories alone or with class group.
2. Writing records of programs or keeping diary of incidents.
3. Writing puppet plays.
4. Writing "continuity" for broadcast programs. Interpreting the moods of music in short descriptive paragraphs.
5. Keeping class story book.
6. Keeping brief records of dramatic episodes in stories that have been enjoyed.
7. Arranging for programs through notes to neighboring class or club organizations.

8. Organizing and conducting story tellers' clubs.

9. Participation in clubs for young authors in verse or prose. Sharing and recording work.

10. Exploration and reporting on neighborhood bird life, flowers, trees and streams.

11. Reporting real journeys relived for the group including home experiences and school experiences.

12. Reporting imaginary journeys taken **through books or on other "magic** carpets."

13. Reporting and discussing wholesome happenings in current events.

14. Giving descriptions of **people or** places, real or imaginary for the purpose of having children guess identity. (Vocabulary exercise.)

15. Selecting and reading expressively favorite quotable lines from books that have been enjoyed.

16. Completing stories partially read.

17. Reading aloud the poetry and prose written by members of the class group.

8. Conducting treasure hunts and explorations for words, phrases and sentences that are expressive.

9. Recording work from author's clubs in class, magazine or newspaper.

10. Authors' writing clubs to encourage writing at leisure moments.

11. Keeping vacation diaries.

12. Arranging for and keeping up a vital exchange correspondence in a genuine situation where friendly relations are established.

14. Writing brief "guess it" descriptions of people and places.

15. Keeping a written collection of treasured words and phrases to be used as a dictionary for creative writing.

16. Completing in writing stories partially read.

HANDWRITING [1]

Since society expects of each person an ability to live cooperatively in his community, it becomes necessary for the individual to acquire such skills as are needed to meet adequately the daily demands made upon him by social situations.

The willingness to recognize a legible form of handwriting and to strive for it in order that others may get the message without undue strain, is a desirable attitude for each boy and girl who is a member of the social group in school. A willingness not only to communicate his ideas but to make that communication readily readable by his fellows is the attitude we should expect to secure.

It is necessary from the very outset to establish this social attitude because actual skill in handwriting is difficult to acquire and it will

[1] This section on Handwriting is intended only to set forth in very brief form a point of view on handwriting instruction. For detailed suggestions or instructional method the teacher is referred to the chapter Several Methods in Handwriting in *Suggested Course of Study in Oral and Written Expression for Elementary Schools.* State of California Department of Education Bulletin No. 15, November 1, 1933; pp. 39–72; and to the Teachers Manual on Handwriting of the California State Textbook Series.

take time and repeated practice before muscular control becomes sufficiently automatic to be made wholly subordinate to the expression of thought.

Because of the fact that there is an accepted standard for the formation of the letters of the alphabet and the reader anticipates a set form, size, slant and alignment of the letters, it is necessary for every child to aim for this standard in order that his writing may be legible. For his own health, comfort and ease in writing, he should know and use the correct position whenever he is actually practicing to acquire skill, and as far as possible at all other times when he is writing or copying notes for someone else to read.

At the very outset when boys and girls are attempting to capture their fleeting thoughts and feelings in written words all the mechanics of writing and language forms will doubtlessly be forgotten. At this point it is definitely destructive to creative effort for the teacher to insist upon conformity to the established standards in language usage or handwriting which are to be expected when the material is to be passed to other readers. While the children are writing, the teacher may herself make note of those who do not apply the handwriting and language standards easily, helping them later on during the revision period.

The aim for attaining the standard in legible penmanship should be emphasized in the correction period where it rightly belongs, when the reclothing of each child's thoughts for sharing with his associates leads him to put it into presentable form and makes him genuinely proud of his completed effort. It is well for us to remember that when a pupil is creating he is all intent on pouring out his feelings and his ideas in words that sometimes all but elude him if he does not set them down quickly, but after he has once captured his thought, he is ready to give his whole mind to the process of rewriting it so that others may enjoy his communication.

SPELLING[1]

Just as the teaching of language in the modern school demands a change from stereotyped mass methods to individualization and an adjustment of our methods and materials to the nature of our pupils, so

---

[1] The content of this section is adapted from Helen Miller, S. A. Courtis, and Garnette Watters. *Creative Teaching in the Field of Spelling.* Des Moines, Iowa: Wallace Publishing Company, 1931, and is used by permission of the authors and publisher.

For more detailed suggestions on spelling instructions the teacher is referred to the following: *Suggested Course of Study in Oral and Written Expression for Elementary Schools.* State of California Department of Education Bulletin No. 13, November 1, 1933, Chapter III, General Methods in Spelling, pp. 19–38; Fred C. Ayer, E. E. Oberholtzer, and Robert H. Lane. *Golden State Speller.* California State Series, Sacramento: California State Department of Education, 1935; J. R. Croad, E. P. O'Reilly, and W. J. Burkhard. *Pupils Individual Spelling Book.* California State Series. Sacramento: California State Department of Education, 1935.

too in the teaching of spelling. The work to be socially serviceable must be planned and fitted to meet the needs of individual persons.

Each pupil is entitled to his choice as to the way of study that is best for him and since each child has a natural rate of growth, he will succeed best when he is allowed to progress at his own rate. Furthermore, childrens' interests differ so widely that each one will move forward as he grows in experience developing his own distinctive vocabulary. To be sure the vocabularies of all children have some basic words in common and these words must be *completely mastered* as the need for written expression is felt.

No slip-shod half measures will do. These words are necessary tools. He must master them for all time when he is ready to use them. However, the differences that each child displays from his neighbors in the choice of words and the rate of learning is of the utmost significance for the teacher.

The teacher who capitalizes these differences increases the efficiency of school work by making it possible to adjust the subject matter and the method to fit the needs of each pupil.

In the teaching of spelling no less than in the teaching of oral expression and written expression, the purpose is to develop expressive persons who are able to live satisfactory lives in a somewhat complicated society.

As one group of authors have phrased it, "successful living" so far as spelling situations are concerned means that boys and girls should:

1. Be able to see the spelling problems in their own lives and in the group life of which they are a part.
2. Be able to solve those problems successfully.
3. Will to take the necessary steps to achieve the solution.

The methods used to achieve these purposes should be those which will develop in the children in the largest measure:

1. The ideals of worthy individual and social purposes.
2. Powers of self-direction, self-appraisal and self-control.
3. Desire and ability to work cooperatively with others in the solution of social problems.

The teaching of spelling is successful only as it contributes to the development of persons who are able to live successfully in a democracy.

This can not be achieved if boys and girls are taught merely to memorize the spelling of groups of words under teacher direction. Rather, the modern teacher, all of whose work in the class room functions in the building of integrated personalities, is at work, earnestly helping the boys and girls:

1. To see their own spelling problems.
2. To purpose and plan to solve those problems.
3. To cooperate with others in solving those problems.
4. To appraise the success of their own efforts.
5. To control themselves while making effort.

The old methods of routine memorization do not produce the desired results in teaching spelling for then "test passing" was the goal and mere achievement was the criterion of success.

When we accept the new point of view, which conceives of learning in spelling as growth in power and control, pupils are led to look upon tests as an opportunity to appraise their own power. As they become definitely conscious of their power and begin to take pride in it, they will desire to add new words to their vocabularies. From this point of view, it is not the achievement but growth and the desire for further growth which are all important.

It is evident that when pupils themselves are stimulated as a result of their language expression to work for the development of their own power in spelling, they ought not to study words they know how to spell, neither should they *pass by, without complete mastery,* any word which they have once undertaken to learn to spell. The successful teacher will lead her pupils, step by step, to accept full responsibility for their work, selecting the words to be studied and testing themselves to be absolutely sure they have succeeded in mastering the words selected.

Purpose is the key term for this enlightened type of teaching in spelling. The teacher's role in stimulating and in assisting in their final realization can be outlined briefly.

It will be the responsibility of the teacher to:

1. Present spelling situations to the children in such a way that they, themselves, will form purposes in those situations which seem worth while to them and make them self-active. The degree to which boys and girls become self-active is a measure of the success of this part of the teacher's work.

2. Assist children to achieve their purposes. This involves helping them plan, execute, judge and generalize. A self-active person desires help, not domination. Choice remains with him. This statement applies to the teacher's efforts in teaching spelling the new way, quite as much as to helping the pupils write a poem or interpret a play.

3. Interpret the results of action, pointing out the benefits secured.

Perfect mastery of a selected group of words common to all children's vocabularies is the first concern of elementary pupils working with the help of their teachers. The reason for this aim is clear. The social value of such a mastery is so important that boys and girls need to achieve it. No grade standard is suggested here. Each pupil should be given the opportunity to progress at his own rate. But from the very first, his aim should be absolute though slow mastery.

Drill work in the basic list should not occupy all of the pupils' or teachers' time. Learning to spell the words by transfer, will be most profitable. Playing games, and inventing methods for conquering difficulties will constitute a series of enjoyable activities giving much practice in spelling but not having spelling as their chief aim.

Group work for the class will include pronunciation, sharing and interpreting meanings, using words in sentences, word building and other such activities by which pupils make words a part of themselves and a ready tool for the expression of their ideas.

Each pupil will probably find some peculiar difficulties with specific words. These problem words of his own should be added to his one hundred per cent list and should be made his particular concern. Each pupil's "exception" list will, in all probability, differ from every other child's list.

A final concern in spelling instruction which is linked with oral and written expression is the habitual use of the dictionary as a standard of spelling, pronunciation and meaning. In all cases of doubt or difference of opinion, the dictionary should be consulted and, as a source of new words, its constant use should be general. Dictionary games for discovery of the meanings of new words and their use in paragraphs will stimulate interest.

The growth of power in spelling will develop if teachers throughout a school, stress constantly the social importance of mastery in spelling. A minimum of required work and a maximum of adjustment to meet the needs and conditions of individual pupils is suggested in the development of work in spelling that will contribute to the growth of persons.

MAKING MAGIC IN THE CLASSROOM THEATER

Dramatic experiences with girls and boys may be developed as a significant and a memorable part of the language program by any teacher who realizes the universal presence of the dramatic urge, a part of each person's "drive to action," and who lives with a group of pupils in a friendly informal relationship that fosters confidence and courage in cooperative undertakings. Dramatic activities lend them-

Courtesy of Los Angeles City Schools

Dramatic Experiences Should Be a Part of the Language Program for Every Child

selves constantly to informal daily use in the classroom for the development of power in speech and oral expression.

When once the teacher has sensed the primitive simplicity which characterized the beginnings of real theatre in the world, she will no longer think of children's presentations as ordeals in which polished, finished adult-directed "shows" are given for critical audiences, she will rather think of them as opportunities for girls and boys to relive and to share their experiences, real and imagined, in a sort of magic world where people and incidents are brought to life and endowed with feeling. Here, surely is "The Kingdom of the Child" as Alice Hertz Henniger has termed it. For in this world of the theatre every child is at home and at ease when adult artificialities are not thrust upon him.

Robert Edmond Jones, one of the foremost leaders in the American theater, has given us the following profound interpretation of the very beginning of drama in the dawn of civilization. His picture leads us to realize that any classroom may be transformed into that "circle" around the "fire" where thrilling events may be brought instantly to life through the magic-maker, a child, awake to the wonder of re-creation.

By looking at the theatre of the past we may come to see our own theatre more clearly. The theatre of every age has something to teach us if we are sensitive enough and humble enough to learn from it.

I am going to ask you to do the most difficult thing in the world—to imagine. Let us imagine ourselves back in the Stone Age, in the days of the cave man and the mammoth. It is night. We are all sitting together around a fire—Ook and Pow and Pung and Glup and little Zowie and all the rest of us. We sit close together. We like to be together. It is safer that way, if wild beasts attack us. And besides, we are happier when we are together. We are afraid to be alone. Over on that side of the fire the leaders of the tribe are sitting together—the strongest men, the men who can run fastest and fight hardest and endure longest. They have killed a lion today. We are excited about this thrilling event. We are all talking about it. We are always afraid of silence. We feel safer when somebody is talking. There is something strange about silence, strange like the black night around us, something we can never understand.

The lion's skin lies close by, near the fire. Suddenly the leader jumps to his feet. "I killed the lion! I did it! I followed him! He sprang at me! I struck at him with my spear! He fell down! He lay still!"

He is telling us. We listen. But all at once an idea comes to his dim brain. "I know a better way to tell you. See! It was like this! *Let me show you!*"

In that instant drama is born.

The leader goes on. "Sit around me in a circle—you, and you, and you—right here, where I can reach out and touch you all." And so with one inclusive gesture he makes—a theatre! From this circle of eager listeners to Reinhardt's great Schauspielhaus in Berlin is only a step in time. In its essence a theatre is only an arrangement of seats so grouped and spaced that the actor—the leader—can reach out and touch and hold each member of his audience. Architects of later days have learned how to add convenience and comfort to this idea. But that is all. The idea itself never changes.

The leader continues: "You, Ook, over there—you stand up and be the lion. Here is the lion's skin. You put it on and be the lion and I'll kill you and we'll show them how it was." Ook gets up. He hangs the skin over his shoulders. He drops on his hands and knees and growls. How terrible he is! Of course he isn't the real lion. We know that. The real lion is dead. We killed him today. Of course Ook isn't a lion. Of course not. He doesn't even look like a lion. "You needn't try to scare us, Ook. We know you. We aren't afraid of you!" And yet, in some mysterious way, Ook *is* the lion. He isn't like the rest of us any longer. He is Ook all right, but he is a lion too.

And now these two men—the world's first actors—begin to show us what the hunt was like. They do not tell us. They *show* us. They *act* it for us. The hunter lies in ambush. The lion growls. The hunter poises his spear. The lion leaps. We all join in with yells and howls of excitement and terror—the first community chorus! The spear is thrown. The lion falls and lies still.

The drama is finished.

Now Ook takes off the lion's skin and sits beside us and is himself again. Just like you. Just like me. Good old Ook. No; not quite like you or me. Ook will be, as long as he lives, the man who can be a lion when he wants to. Pshaw! A man can't be a lion! How can a man be a lion? But Ook can make us believe it, just the same.

Something queer happens to that man Ook sometimes. The lion's spirit gets into him. And we shall always look up to him and admire him and perhaps be secretly a little afraid of him. Ook is an actor. He will always be different from the rest of us, a little apart from us. For he can summon spirits.

Now we are in 1927 once more. Many thousands of years have passed since that first moment of inspiration when the theatre sprang into being. But we still like to get together, we still dread to be alone, we are still a little awed by silence, we still like to make believe, and when an artist like Duse or Chaliapin or Pauline Lord speaks aloud in our midst a thing that is in the minds of all of us and fuses our various moods into one common mood, we are still lost in wonder before this magical art of the theatre. It is really a kind of magic, this art. We call it glamour or poetry or romance, but that doesn't explain it. In some mysterious way these old, simple, ancestral moods still survive in us, and an actor can make them live again for a while. We become children once more. We believe! [1]

When we lead children into this mood, sharing their dramatic play with them when we truly "believe" with them there is a reality and a sincerity in the experience that is inexplicably significant.

The human desire to communicate may be captured and focussed through development of short dramatic dialogues in the classroom or through somewhat longer plays in which the incidents are vividly significant to the group.

When the themes selected for these dramatic experiences are vital and the situations are appropriate and interesting rather than merely informational, the enthusiasm of the group is sure to awaken the creative urge of the individuals and their work together will unfold until they are actually ready for presentation.

BIBLIOGRAPHY

Written Expression

*BLAISDELL, THOMAS CHARLES. *Ways to Teach English.* Garden City, New York: Doubleday, Doran & Company, 1930.

CARPENTER, GEORGE RICE; BAKER, F. T.; and SCOTT, F. N. *Teaching of English in the Elementary and the Secondary Schools.* New York: Longmans, Green and Company, 1913.

CHUBB, PERCIVAL. *Teaching of English in the Elementary and the Secondary Schools.* Revised. New York: The Macmillan Company, 1929.

COOK, HENRY CALDWELL. *Play Way; an Essay in Educational Method.* New York: Frederick A. Stokes Company, 1917.

Creative Expression. Edited by Gertrude Hartman and Ann Shumaker. New York: The John Day Company, 1932.

EASTMAN, MAX FORRESTER. *Enjoyment of Poetry.* Revised. New York: Charles Scribner's Sons, 1921.

Experience in English Composition and Literature. Vol. I. Chicago: Francis W. Parker School, 1932.

GULLAN, MARJORIE. *Speech Training in the School.* London: Evans Bros., 1929.

---

[1] Robert Edmond Jones. "The Theatre As It Has Been and As It Is." *Theatre Arts Monthly.* XI (September, 1927), 661–663.
* Outstanding titles are starred. These books are suggested for first purchase in building a library for reference.

HAYWARD, FRANK HERBERT. *Lesson in Appreciation.* New York: The Macmillan Company, 1915.

HERTS, ALICE MINNIE. *The Children's Educational Theatre.* New York: Harper and Brothers, 1911.

HITCHCOCK, ALFRED MARSHALL. *Bread Loaf Talks on Teaching Composition.* New York: Henry Holt & Company, 1927.

HOSIC, JAMES FLEMING. *Elementary Course in English.* Chicago: University of Chicago Press, 1911.

KLAPPER, PAUL. *Teaching English in Elementary and Junior High Schools.* New York: D. Appleton and Company, 1925.

*MEARNS, HUGHES. *Creative Youth.* Garden City, New York: Doubleday, Doran & Company, 1925.

*MEARNS, HUGHES. *Creative Power.* Garden City, New York: Doubleday, Doran & Company, 1929.

TROXELL, ELEANOR. *Language and Literature.* New York: Charles Scribner's Sons, 1927.

WARD, WINIFRED LOUISE. *Creative Dramatics for the Upper Grades and Junior High School.* New York: D. Appleton and Company, 1930.

WUNSCH, WILLIAM R., and SMITH, M. R. *Studies in Creative Writing.* New York: Henry Holt & Company, 1933.

YOUNG, NELL J., and MEMMOTT, F. W. *Methods in Elementary English.* New York: D. Appleton and Company, 1923.

Oral Expression

Another Treasury of Plays for Children. Edited by Jonas Montrose Moses. Boston: Little, Brown and Company, 1926.

BROWN, ABBIE FARWELL. *The Lantern, and Other Plays for Children.* Boston: Houghton Mifflin Company, 1928.

*BROWN, CORINNE. *Creative Drama in the Lower School.* Chapters V, VI, XIV. New York: D. Appleton and Company, 1930.

COOK, HENRY CALDWELL. *Play Way; an Essay in Educational Method.* New York: Frederick A. Stokes Company, 1917.

Creative Expression. Edited by Gertrude Hartman and Ann Shumaker. New York: The John Day Company, 1932.

DOLMAN, JOHN. *Art of Play Production.* New York: Harper and Brothers, 1928.

*GRIMBALL, ELIZABETH B., and WELLS, RHEA. *Costuming a Play.* New York: The Century Co., 1925.

GULLAN, MARJORIE, and GURREY, PERCIVAL. *Poetry Speaking for Children.* Part I and Part II. London: Methuen & Co., 1931.

GULLAN, MARJORIE. *Speech Training in the School.* London: Evans Bros., 1929.

HENIGER, ALICE MINNIE HERTS. *The Kingdom of the Child.* New York: E. P. Dutton and Company, 1918.

HERTS, ALICE MINNIE. *The Children's Educational Theatre.* New York: Harper and Brothers, 1911.

HOLT, ROLAND. *A List of Music for Plays and Pageants.* New York: D. Appleton and Company, 1925.

JAGENDORF, MORITZ A. *One-Act Plays for Young Folks.* London: Brentano's Ltd., 1924.

*LAMKIN, NINA B. *Good Times for All Times.* New York: Samuel French & Company, 1929.

*LE COMPTE, PEARLE. *Dramatics.* New York: A. S. Barnes & Co., 1931.

LINNELL, ADELAIDE. *The School Festival.* New York: Charles Scribner's Sons, 1921.

MAJOR, CLARE TREE. *Playing Theatre.* New York: Oxford University Press, 1930.

McKAY, CONSTANCE D'ARCY. *Costumes and Scenery for Amateurs.* New York: Henry Holt & Company, 1915.

---

* Outstanding titles are starred. These books are suggested for first purchase in building a library for reference.

MERRILL, JOHN. *Play-making and Plays.* New York: The Macmillan Company, 1930.

MITCHELL, ROY. *Creative Theatre.* New York: The John Day Company, 1929.

SHAY, FRANK. *The Appleton Book of Christmas Plays.* New York: D. Appleton and Company, 1930.

SKINNER, ELEANOR L. *Tales and Plays of Robin Hood.* New York: American Book Company, 1915.

SMITH, MILTON MYERS. *Book of Play Production.* New York: D. Appleton and Company, 1926.

A Treasury of Plays for Children. Edited by Jonas Montrose Moses. Boston: Little, Brown and Company, 1921.

*WARD, WINIFRED LOUISE. *Creative Dramatics for the Upper Grades and Junior High School.* New York: D. Appleton and Company, 1930.

Spelling

GATES, ARTHUR. "An Experimental Comparison of the Study Test and Study Methods in Spelling." *Journal of Educational Psychology,* XXII (January 1931), 1–19.

MILLER, HELEN; COURTIS, S. A.; and WATTERS, GARNETTE. *Creative Teaching in the Field of Spelling.* A Manual of Instruction. Des Moines: Wallace Publishing Co., 1931.

PINTNER, RUDOLF; RINSLAND, HENRY E.; ZUBIN, JOSEPH. "Evaluation of Self-Administering Spelling Tests." *Journal of Educational Psychology,* XX (February, 1929), 107–111.

PREHM, HAZEL. "Developing a Spelling Morale." *Elementary English Review.* VIII (January, 1931), 10–13.

WALLACE, ALBERTA. "First Semester in Spelling." *Educational Method,* IX (January, 1930), 206–210.

Dramatic Activities Through Puppets and Marionettes

MILLS, W. H., and DUNN L. M. *Marionettes, Masks and Shadows.* Garden City, New York: Doubleday, Page & Company, 1927.

PETTEY, EMMA. *The Puppet As An Elementary Project.* Fort Worth: Pioneer Publishing Co., 1925.

SMITH, MILTON MYERS. *A Book of Play Production.* New York: D. Appleton and Company, 1926.

WALTERS, MAUDE OWENS. *Puppet Shows for Home and School.* New York: Dodd, Mead & Company, Inc., 1929.

---

* Outstanding titles are starred. These books are suggested for first purchase in building a library for reference.

CHAPTER XIX

ARITHMETIC[1]

GENERAL CONSIDERATIONS

Introduction

The scientific study of the arithmetic curriculum has presented evidence that much of the traditional matter commonly taught in the schools of the past generation is of little social utility, and much too difficult for many children in the grades in which it has been taught. The elimination of cumbersome, difficult, useless processes and topics has greatly reduced the complexity of the skills that the pupils are now expected to acquire. At the same time the work in arithmetic has been greatly enriched and vitalized by stressing its application in meaningful activities and situations.

The learning of arithmetic furnishes an opportunity for developing some of the fundamental phases of character such as honesty, persistence, self-reliance and accuracy. Arithmetic holds before the pupil an ideal of truth. Number may be thought of as a mode of thinking. Habits of orderly procedure are necessary, and should result in an appreciation of the value of precise and accurate information.

Arithmetic may be considered to have four special functions, (1) the computational, (2) the informational, (3) the sociological, and (4) the psychological.[2] With these functions in mind arithmetic is seen to have broad objectives.

THE OBJECTIVES OF ARITHMETIC INSTRUCTION

It is the function of arithmetic to give pupils not only the elementary number ideas that they may use in their daily dealings but also the ability to understand the larger quantitative aspects of social needs and activities.[3]

By common agreement, one of the major aims of arithmetic in the elementary school is that the first six grades will prepare the child to use the four fundamental operations in integers, fractions and decimals with accuracy.

Stated simply the general objectives are:

---

[1] Prepared by Raymond T. Neideffer, Director of Elementary Education, Bakersfield City Schools, under the direction of Lawrence E. Chenoweth, Superintendent of Schools.

[2] *Report of the Society's Committee on Arithmetic.* Twenty-ninth Year Book of the National Society for the Study of Education. Bloomington, Illinois: Public School Publishing Company, 1930, p. 686.

[3] S. C. Parker. *Types of Elementary Teaching and Learning.* Boston: Ginn and Company, 1923, pp. 182-3.

1. To develop ease, accuracy, speed and neatness in computation.
2. To give such mathematical knowledge as an intelligent citizen ought to have ready for instant use.
3. To develop habits of neatness, accuracy, logical procedure, perseverance and self-reliance.
4. To develop the ability to apply mathematical knowledge to real situations in life.

Grade Placement of Subject Matter

The grade placement of subject matter in the California State Series arithmetic textbooks represents a significant departure from traditional practice. Formal work in learning arithmetic combinations comes now in the third grade. But this is preceded with a hundred pages of easy reading material based upon children's interest and experience wherein the child is introduced to number concept and number vocabulary. The usual work supplied by arithmetic texts is advanced one half year throughout the third, fourth, and fifth grades. Long division, for example comes in the beginning half of the fifth instead of in the second half of the fourth grade. This adjustment conforms to considerable extent to the recommendations contained in the Fourth Yearbook of the Department of Superintendence.[1] It is also noted that a comparison of the grade placement of the different processes compares favorably in the main with the recent investigation of the Committee of Seven.[2] There are some striking exceptions. These are found mostly in the fifth grade and in the sixth grade.

This extensive experiment finds both the minimum mental age and the optimum mental age for the teaching of complete long division to be 12 years and 7 months which would correspond to about the last half of the sixth grade. The optimum age for division of fractions would place it in the seventh or eighth grade.

To meet the conditions of optimum grade placement, as determined by this experiment would require considerable reorganization of textbooks. It could not be made without due consideration of the logical sequence of arithmetic processes.

Time Allotments

The discussion of time allotments immediately involves method of instruction and the view point in relation to the objectives. "If the

---

[1] *The Nation at Work on the Public School Curriculum.* Department of Superintendence Fourth Yearbook. Washington: Department of Superintendence of the National Education Association, 1926, p. 182.
[2] Carleton W. Washburne. *Adjusting the School to the Child.* Yonkers-on-Hudson, New York: World Book Company, 1932. Also "The Grade Placement of Arithmetic Topics: A 'Committee of Seven' Investigation." *Report of the Society's Committee on Arithmetic.* Twenty-Ninth Yearbook of the National Society for the Study of Education. Bloomington, Illinois: Public School Publishing Company, 1930, pp. 641–670.

curriculum is organized even in part on an activity basis a definite amount of time cannot be set aside for arithmetic, since number will be an inherent part of the total situation in which the need arises naturally in the course of the activity."[1]   To meet the broad objectives of arithmetic and to consider arithmetic one of the important social studies would require an increase in customary time allotments rather than a decrease which has been the tendency for several years. The time required for the computational phase of arithmetic has been the governing factor in determining time allotments.   There is a general hesitancy to give daily or weekly time allotments because of the inconsistency with the idea of adjusting the work to meet the varying conditions of classes as well as individuals.

Following are time allotments for arithmetic in the elementary grades suggested in previous studies and a recommended time allotment which is based on the growing tendency to displace formal instruction in arithmetic for the primary grades and the tendency to include application of arithmetic in units of work centering about other subjects.

Weekly Time Allotments for Arithmetic

Study	Grades					
	I	II	III	IV	V	VI
Bagley & Kyte, 1924 [2]	0	140	215	215	220	220
Brueckner's Summary, 1927 [3]	90	150	200	225	225	225
Mann Investigation, 1926 [4]	80	146	196	211	215	215
Twenty-Ninth Yearbook [5]	75 to 100	125 to 150	175 to 200	200 to 225	200 to 225	200 to 225
RECOMMENDED	0	0–75	150	200	200	200

The teacher will be interested in time allotments as a guide in organizing her program.   She must divide the time allotted among the various aspects of instruction, such as presenting new work, practice, review drill, problem solving and discussion.

SOCIAL VALUES

Guiding Principles

Developing the informal phase of arithmetic will include such items as the following, as a basis:

---

[1] *Report of the Society's Committee on Arithmetic.*   Twenty-Ninth Yearbook of the National Society for the Study of Education.   Bloomington, Illinois: Public School Publishing Company, 1930, p. 695.
[2] William C. Bagley, and George C. Kyte.   *The California Curriculum Study.* Berkeley: University of California Printing Office, 1926, p. 105.
[3] *The Supervision of Elementary Subjects.*   Edited by William H. Burton. New York: D. Appleton and Company, 1929, p. 21.
[4] C. H. Mann.   *How Schools Use Their Time.*   New York: Teachers College, Columbia University, Contributions to Education, Number 333, 1928, pp. 19-23.
[5] *Report of the Society's Committee on Arithmetic, op. cit.,* p. 77.

1. Developing an appreciation of the informational function of arithmetic.
2. Developing an appreciation of number as a means of precise and accurate thought.
3. Assisting pupils to understand quantitative references in readings.
4. Developing adequate concepts of units of measurements.
5. Providing conditions in which the growth of desirable social characteristics, attitudes and ideals will take place.
6. Enriching and vitalizing the experience of pupils.
7. Recognizing arithmetic applications in other subjects such as history, geography, science and health work.
8. Using experiences and activities that arise in connection with local conditions and situations.

Arithmetic in the Activities of Children

Investigations have shown that a surprisingly large amount of arithmetic is used in the activities of children in the first six grades both in school and out of school. There are many splendid opportunities to develop number concepts and to use arithmetical knowledge, especially the quantitative values. The teacher will be alert to recognize such opportunities. No one can tell in advance exactly what they may be. In general these opportunities will arise:

1. In the study of various units of work

   a. Measurement for construction or sewing
   b. Figuring amounts of materials needed
   c. A grocery store
   d. A market
   e. Problems growing out of geography work; (1) area and population of countries, population of cities compared, length of rivers, height of mountains, area of basins; (2) comparison of countries in output of cattle, hogs, wheat, coal, silk, and flax, and (3) comparison of water and railroad transportation, length of trade routes.
   f. Farming, wheat industry, size of wheat farms, amount of wheat produced, selling price of wheat, cost of production, amount gained, size and capacity of wheat bins.

2. Out of school projects

   a. School garden problems. Renting a garden for one season, plan a garden drawn to scale, amount and cost of fertilizer, amount of seeds and plants, cost of fencing.

    b. Operating the school savings system, deposits, figuring interest.

    c. Making change in the lunch room.

    d. Operating a candy sale, profit. Record of expenditures and receipts.

3. Out of excursions taken to various industries or places of business.

    a. What arithmetic does a grocer use?

    b. The cost of upkeep of the park.

4. Out of home situations

    a. Family budget. Adopt an imaginary family, size and income of family, items of budget such as rent, clothing, food, savings, amusements, education, incidentals.

    b. Running errands for mother, small purchases, weight, cost, change.

    c. Furnishing a girl's room.

SCHOOL ACTIVITIES INVOLVING ARITHMETIC

Following are presented two lists of specific activities involving arithmetic, the first centering primarily about the school and the second about the home.

Recording and comparing ages and birth dates of pupils
Recording and comparing size of families
Learning addresses and telephone numbers
Learning system of house numbering
Figuring distance of each child from home to school
Comparing distances from home to school
Computing carfare
Computing cost of school lunches
Keeping attendance records
Making and using calendar
Observing and recording number of clear and cloudy days in a week, a month
Recording temperature, indoors and out
Telling time of intermissions, classes
Computing length of school periods
Planning weekly order of milk, crackers
Computing cost of milk, crackers
Budgeting and arranging supplies
Passing books, papers
Buying personal school supplies from store
Planning window or outdoor gardens
Ordering seeds or bulbs from catalogues
Computing postage for letters and packages
Buying food for school pets
Making maps of schoolroom, suggesting rearrangements
Making maps of school grounds
Making maps of school neighborhood
Planning size, number, and arrangement of material for bulletin boards
Measuring materials used in practical arts
Computing cost of materials used

Using measures in recipes
Scoring arithmetic and spelling papers
Comparing individual and class scores
Making graphs to show progress
Finding pupil and class averages
Selling tickets for school entertainments
Keeping scores for games and contests
School banking

HOME ACTIVITIES INVOLVING ARITHMETIC

a. Activities arising from provision of food

Buying and selling of groceries, milk, meat, fruit, and vegetables
Computing daily, weekly, and monthly grocery bills
Comparing cost of groceries at different stores
Planning wholesome, inexpensive meals
Planning picnic lunches; refreshments for parties
Comparing cost of meals in cafeteria, restaurant and at lunch counter
Substituting inexpensive dishes for more expensive ones
Computing wages of clerks, cashiers, and deliverymen in grocery stores and
meat markets
Computing wages of cooks, waiters, waitresses, bus boys in restaurants
Computing savings from growing one's own vegetables; from keeping poultry
Using dry and liquid measures
Comparing the cost of baking one's own cakes and pies with cost of buy-
ing them

b. Activities arising from provision of clothing

Buying and selling of clothing, shoes
Computing cost of wardrobes for various members of family
Comparing cost of wardrobes of different seasons
Buying from advertised sales in newspapers
Ordering from catalogues
Writing money order; paying postage
Comparing cost of making clothing at home with cost of buying them ready-
made
Measuring amount of material needed for various garments
Selecting least expensive and most serviceable materials
Making family budget for clothing
Computing cost of cleaning, pressing and laundry
Computing wages of dressmaker; of milliner; of shoemaker; of employees in
dry goods store

c. Activities arising from provision of shelter

Computing cost of renting a house
Computing upkeep of property; such as, taxes, fire insurance, repairs
Buying furniture for various rooms
Comparing prices at sales
Estimating cost of fuel, gas, light, water
Computing cost of lawn, garden, flowers
Computing wages of carpenters, bricklayers, and other building artisans
Computing cost of apartments of rooms
Computing wages of janitors, gardeners, chambermaids, laundresses, domestic
labor

d. Activities arising from care of health
  Keeping height and weight records
  Recording weekly or monthly gain or loss in weight
  Budgeting time for sleeping, playing, working
  Computing cost of illness, doctor, nurse, hospital, loss of time

e. Activities arising from planning recreation
  Computing cost of movies, parties, picnics, concerts
  Computing cost of playground equipment
  Computing budget for magazines, books, newspapers
  Computing cost of music or radio in the home
  Buying musical instruments
  Computing expense of musical education
  Computing cost of celebrating various holidays
  Planning Christmas presents within a certain sum
  Computing cost of automobile and upkeep
  Planning auto trips and sharing of expenses
  Computing cost of trips by train
  Planning vacations for certain sums
  Computing wages of men on train crew
  Figuring game scores, baseball percentages

f. Activities arising from saving money
  Planning to visit a bank
  Opening a savings account
  Buying savings stamps
  Using a check book
  Budgeting children's allowance so saving is possible

THE TEXTBOOK

Advantages in Following the Plan of the Text

There are several advantages to be derived from following the textbook rather closely. A textbook that is worthy of adoption should not conflict in method, content and organization with the findings in research and modern practices. It should present adequate assistance to both teacher and pupil. Aid in presenting new processes, systematically arranged drill material, inventory and practice exercises and written problems should all be provided as needed.

Coördination of the program in arithmetic will follow adherence to the general plan of the series. Children who transfer from school to school and their teachers will be assisted in making the proper adjustments in the new situation. "As the work of each process has been developed systematically and scientifically, it is important that the order, method, and language of the text be followed very closely."[1] It is futile and needless for a teacher to attempt to develop a process without the aid of the textbook which has given attention to step by step development and the major causes of pupil difficulty.

---

[1] Leo J. Brueckner; C. J. Anderson; G. O. Banting; and Elda L. Merton. *The Triangle Arithmetics*. Grade III. California State Series. Sacramento: California State Department of Education, 1932, p. 4.

To get the author's plan the teacher should study carefully the introduction in her book. She should then become familiar with the plan of the book to see just how the different provisions of instruction are carried out.

Essential Teaching Tools

The essential teaching tools for instruction in the processes of arithmetic are:

1. Survey tests to provide a picture of the status of the class from time to time, preferably given at regular intervals during the year.
2. Diagnostic tests for locating the steps in processes in which pupils may be deficient, or the places at which difficulties exist.
3. Carefully constructed remedial exercises and instructional units, to be used to overcome the weaknesses revealed by the diagnosis.
4. Tests for measuring the effectiveness of the remedial work.
5. Exercises and drills for cumulative practice, to insure retention of the acquired skills.
6. Carefully graded exercises in which there is step by step development of the processes new to the grade and through which the pupil acquires correct concepts and ideas.
7. Ample problem material in which the need of such process is illustrated when it is presented, and in which the pupil is given practice in solving problems that are based upon situations such as arise in life in which the process is used.

Determining Goals of Attainment for Each Grade

The teacher should study the book as a whole for its content in new processes. The frequent interspersion of problem scales, diagnostic tests and drill exercises will not be confusing if a tabulation of the work of the year is made. A careful tabulation will provide the goals of attainment for the grade. The content of the fourth grade book[1] is tabulated as an example.

1. Review of addition, substraction, multiplication and division facts taught in the third grade.
2. Multiplication and division facts up to and including the 9's.
3. Multiplication of two, three and four digit numbers by a one-figure multiplier.
4. Introduction of multiplying by a two-figure multiplier.
5. Short division of two, three and four-digit numbers with all of the different difficulties involved.

---

[1] *Ibid.* Grade IV.

6. Two and three column addition usually limited to 3-5 addends.
7. Subtraction limited to 3 and 4 place numbers.
8. Reading and writing numbers usually less than 10,000, limited to millions.
9. Telling time, using time.
10. Roman numerals.
11. Value of pieces of United States money.
12. Making change.
13. Using the dollar sign and decimal point in addition, subtraction, multiplication and division of money values. Copying and solving examples.
14. The quantitative meaning of $\frac{1}{2}$, $\frac{1}{3}$, $\frac{1}{4}$.
15. The meaning of $\frac{1}{6}$, $\frac{5}{6}$, etc., as an application of the division tables.
16. Liquid measure, linear measure, inches, feet, yards, time, dozen.
17. Using numbers in addresses and telephone numbers.
18. Application of these facts and the processes of addition, subtraction, multiplication or division in the solution of one step problems.
19. Use of the ordinary names of the terms in the processes, language for correct explanations of steps in a process and the automatic use of signs: $+$, $-$, $\times$, $\div$, $=$.

The emphasis upon following the method and plan of the author should not be construed to mean that the book must be covered by all pupils at the rate of so many pages taken in numerical order per day or week. The following statements found in the preface to *The Triangle Arithmetic*, show conclusively that the plan of the author conceives using the text as a teaching tool to obtain certain definite goals:

> Differentiated assignments of practice and test material make it possible to adapt the work to the abilities of the pupils.
> Special practice exercises are provided to give special work for pupils weak in problem solving.
> The ample problem material provides suitable content for enriching the work of superior and advanced classes.[1]

THE LANGUAGE OF ARITHMETIC

Adequate Expression Requires the Use of Arithmetic Vocabulary

When children begin the study of arithmetic they are confronted with a vocabulary that is new to them. A working knowledge of this vocabulary is essential. Terms used must be understood. The children will have occasion to read and to write and to use in conversation some vocabulary peculiar to arithmetic. In connection with the funda-

---

[1] *Ibid.*, p. vi.

mental processes the pupil will need to be able to express himself adequately and to use correctly such expressions as "divided by," "multiply," and "product," and "remainder." An attempt to get the pupil to "think aloud" the steps of a process of diagnostic purposes will often reveal the lack of adequate arithmetic vocabulary. It is helpful for the pupil to be able to use the names of a process in telling the kind of work that he is doing such as "multiplying a whole number by a fraction."

Children learn the language by imitation and through use. It is imperative that the teacher have the habit of using simple, correct and adequate language. Such expressions as "goes into," "time it by" and "divided into" are inexcusable. To say 7 divided into 637 as an expression of $7/637$ is a gross error. It confuses the idea of the process and will not assist in its application in problem solving later. In stating the problem it is read 637 divided by 7. In solving the example it is correct and preferable to say, "The number of 7's in 63 is 9," or more briefly "7's in 63 are 9."

In teaching a child to say, "5 times 7 are 35," he is given a meaningless verbalism. If this fact is taught in the form, "five 7's are 35," we have expressed the multiplication idea in a form which is readily understood. Five 7's means exactly what it says.

Improving the Vocabulary

The vocabulary that will require special attention may, for convenience, be divided in groups:

1. Arithmetic terms used with processes, sum, quotient, product, denominator, fraction, divide, remainder, subtract, add and others.

2. Terms denoting quantitative values, acre, foot, mile, thousand, million, tenths, month, ton, ounce, dozen.

3. Terms used in problems and to express number relationships: buy, sell, loan, profit, loss, area, more than, less than, dealer, salary, rent, wages, merchant.

4. Terms used to give directions: numbers, solve, practice, review, answer, problem.

Development of ability to use and understand arithmetic vocabulary will be aided by thoughtful consideration and definite practices:

1. Directed practice in careful reading.
   a. Using material in the text especially the first part of the book for grade three.

b. Study-type readers contain material designed to develop com-prehension of arithmetic problems.

c. Practice in reading problems with "true," "false" or multiple choice exercises. For example:

> Eggs cost 48 cents a dozen. Mary buys 2 dozen. How much change should she receive from a dollar?
> 1. Mary buys 3 dozen eggs.
> 2. The eggs cost 48 cents a dozen.
> 3. Divide to find the cost of the eggs.
> 4. Mary spent less than a dollar for the eggs.
> 5. You are to find what Mary spent for the eggs.

d. Reading problems with facts missing. For example:

> "Mary bought bread at 12 cents a loaf. She gave the clerk 50 cents. What change should she receive?"

2. List the words for the grade, using some classification such as is given above for the different chapters in the book, so that organized attention may be given vocabulary development.

3. Habits of using the necessary vocabulary in the daily work in the natural situations in which they arise.

4. Exercises of the objective kind dealing with vocabulary. For example:

MATCHING EXERCISE

Put the phrases under the proper heading:

Add +	Subtract —	Multiply ×	Divide ÷

Which costs more	Find the products
Say the sums	Find the area
Subtract from	What is the difference
Which is larger	Write the product
How many times	Find the cost

COMPLETION EXERCISE

½ is called a _____ fraction.
The answer in addition is called the _____.
3¾ is a _____ number.
The number, .5 is a _____ fraction.

CLASSROOM PROCEDURE

The Levels of Instruction

Various levels of instruction in arithmetic may be differentiated, ranging from teaching which has a very narrow vision of the possibilities of the function of the subject to teaching which is enriched, socialized, vitalized, and significant. Brueckner has prepared a chart[1],

---

[1] Leo J. Brueckner. "A Chart for the Analysis of the Teaching of Arithmetic." *Journal of Educational Method.* IX (December, 1929), 130-137. Also Leo J. Brueckner, and Ernest O. Melby. *Diagnostic and Remedial Teaching.* Boston: Houghton Mifflin Company, 1931, p. 161.

including descriptions of seven levels in the teaching of arithmetic in which the methods of achieving the functions of the subject are briefly described and the place of diagnostic and remedial teaching is made clear. Use of this interesting scale to determine the level of instruction would doubtless find teaching on every level. There is a wide variance in enrollment in grades, working conditions, ability of classes, supervisory influences and other factors. Because of the wide variation in many factors different plans are being used.

Three Plans of Procedure

A modified class and study plan, the group plan and the individual plan, or a combination of these are used. Many will agree when using a textbook as the tool of instruction that a most advantageous plan of procedure will be the use of class instruction that is profitable to all of the class, temporary groups selected because of particular needs or abilities and individual practice and checking upon the mastery of each process and in the retention of skills. Any kind of plan will prove inadequate unless there is the necessary organization of material that provides for diagnostic teaching and some independence of the individual in attacking his work and checking his results.

The class plan. The use of uniform study, recitation, drill periods and assignments for the entire class is rarely satisfactory. Small units

Courtesy of Lassen County Schools

These Children Keep Individual Records of Their Progress in the Mastery of the Multiplication Tables

of work may be designated with some provision for variation in assignment. All of the pupils are given the introductory assignment of each unit, at the same time. Alternate days or other periods are designated for study. Certain periods of the week are used for clearing up difficulties, checking results and discussion. The scientifically prepared self help material in the textbooks is essential in providing for individual needs.

The individual plan. In most classes are pupils whose abilities range over four or five grades. To treat children whose abilities range through four or five grades as if they were alike, giving them all the same assignment and the same time to accomplish that assignment is preposterous. Individualizing the instruction allows each child to work at his own rate of progress. It is a substitution of piece work for time work. The teacher moves about the room observing the work, giving help as needed.

The first step in individualized teaching requires the teacher or some one to set down in black and white exactly what it is each child is expected to master. The second requirement is complete diagnostic tests to cover the objectives specified. The third necessity is the making or attainment of materials which are self-instructive and self-corrective. To individualize the text for instruction will require the preparation of an assignment manual. Additional explanations, practice material and diagnostic tests in some instances will be necessary. The answers are in the text. It will be especially helpful to secure some of the most carefully prepared self-instructive materials that are available for suggested organization and some book that outlines the basic principles of individual instruction.[1]

The group plan. The teacher works with groups of nearly equal ability. Survey tests given early in the term give sufficient information for the formation of two, three or four groups. Three groups are frequently used. Two groups may prove to be adequate. Occasionally four are used. The arithmetic period is frequently divided so that the teacher works with each group in turn. The teacher can contact the individual more easily in a small group than in the class. The instruction is individual to considerable extent. Each group will have the rate and content adjusted to its level. Assignments can be differentiated among the groups. The fast group may have briefer assignments in practice work for skill but an enriched program in problem situations and special investigations. The slow group will cover a minimum course simplified whenever possible, but with more exercises to acquire fundamental skills.

---

[1] Carleton W. Washburne. *Adjusting the School to the Child.* Yonkers-on-Hudson, New York: World Book Company, 1932.

DIAGNOSTIC TEACHING

Definition

Diagnostic teaching may be considered to be based on the broad definition of diagnosis, which is "scientific determination." Diagnostic teaching includes the whole act of teaching in acquiring and maintaining skills in computational arithmetic. Being scientific it is governed by the laws of learning. Scientific experimentation is done in accordance with psychological principles. From the results of such study have come the factors of diagnostic teaching.

The technique of diagnostic teaching is a definite professional approach to educational problems.

1. It determines the knowledge and ability the pupil brings to a given situation.
2. It considers attitudes and habits of work in analyzing the responses and thought processes.
3. It determines the probable causes of error or difficulties to be encountered.
4. It indicates the method of using instruction material that has been prepared as a result of the analysis of the numerous steps or skills in each process.
5. It measures the extent of learning and determines the practice and reteaching needed.

One of the most significant contributions of the Twenty-Ninth Yearbook [1] is considered to be the discussion of diagnostic and remedial teaching. Therein it is pointed out that the present emphasis on remedial work is a reflection on the lack of good teaching. The end toward which the schools should work is prevention rather than correction. With an adequate program of tests to use during teaching, the difficulties in arithmetic can be checked so promptly that they will be corrected during the original teaching procedure rather than allowed to accumulate to make a problem for remedial procedure. An attitude of checking every step of the work on the part of both the pupil and teacher is essential. Pupil and teacher alike must purpose, plan, execute and evaluate.

Diagnostic teaching does not mean merely testing at intervals to see if faults of procedure have been allowed to accumulate and then giving remedial exercise. But it is the orderly acquiring of skills that are checked step by step and at the conclusion of each unit.

---

[1] *Report of the Society's Committee on Arithmetic.* Twenty-Ninth Yearbook of the National Society for the Study of Education. Bloomington, Illinois: Public School Publishing Company, 1930, pp. 269-316.

Method of Organizing Work

1. The basic concepts involved must first be established by concrete illustrations.

2. The new process must be presented to the pupil one step at a time, no new step being added until the previous one has been fixed.

3. The amount of practice needed in the processes will vary widely among the pupils. Therefore, materials adapted to individualizing instruction should be used.

4. Reasonable speed of work and 100 per cent accuracy should be insisted upon in the initial practice periods in order that correct habits of work may be established from the beginning.

5. The pupil should apply the new process in problems and other activities.

6. After a process has been presented tests should be given to locate pupils who must be given additional help because of faulty habits of work, lack of understanding of the process, and other difficulties.

7. Provision must be made for the continuous review of processes that have been previously taught to offset possible loss of skill due to disuse.

Methods of Presentation

One of the first requisites in teaching arithmetic is that the teacher be familiar with the learning process in arithmetic. There are questions of whether to add up or down, how to present each process, and devices to use to aid learning. Fortunately the present textbooks give the actual presentation and generally contain the necessary method. Only a few general suggestions will be presented to serve as examples.

The use of study charts for the various steps of the processes that have been taught in a preceding grade, that are not reproduced in the books for the present grade will be found valuable and economical in the necessary reteaching. They may be prepared on large pieces of cardboard for use of groups or individuals. Often it will be convenient to have them on standard sizes of heavy paper so that they may be filed and used individually. A key list of practice exercises should be prepared in connection with each chart. Independent attack by each pupil upon his own particular deficiencies is economical and effective. The use of the small flash cards provides a means of independent checking and study. In connection with any facts requiring automatic response they are valuable for original learning and review.

The incomplete picture is found on one side of the card and the complete picture on the other. Pupils make their own as needed but a few carefully made sets prepared by the teacher on serviceable tag board should be on hand. A suitable size is about two by three inches.

Brueckner in his investigation to determine transfer in number combinations [1] as an interesting and valuable by-product of the main study, found the use of drill cards with groups of combinations to be an effective addition to usual methods of teaching.

Steps in the Teaching of a Process [2]

a. Establishing the need of the new step. We are advised to present each new step in some situation in which it functions in life. Finding situations in the activities of children is an unquestionable aid in making the work more meaningful. It should not be understood that each step within the process, such as division, requires such motivation.

b. Presenting the new step. The teacher explains by means of carefully selected models the particular step of the process to be learned. Charts such as are found in the book should be used in this connection so that they are available for future use. They give the pupil a definite source of reference. Having the children work alone the examples used in demonstration in the chart and by the teacher is an excellent idea and gives illumination regarding the effectiveness of the introduction. Next the pupils practice on new examples. While the teacher is observing the practice she will be gaining a general impression of the success of the class. The teacher will give a helpful word where it is needed as she moves about the room, but she must guard carefully against allowing the children to expect her to reteach the step to every individual and develop habits of dependence and loss of time through lack of effort. Each pupil is checking his own work with the answers in the back of the book. The individual report to the teacher of progress, coupled with her own observation, will probably be an adequate test to show those in need of reteaching. Rarely will the entire class need reteaching.

c. Reteaching as needed. Effective procedure will now segregate temporary groups according to needs. Six or eight children in a group will be taken over the work of the study chart again. Prob-

[1] Leo J. Brueckner, and E. A. Beito. "A Measurement of Transfer in the Learning of Number Combinations." *Report of the Society's Committee on Arithmetic.* Twenty-Ninth Yearbook of the National Society for the Study of Education. Bloomington, Illinois: Public School Publishing Company, 1930, pp. 569-587.

[2] Adapted from Leo J. Brueckner's "Supervision of Arithmetic." *The Supervision of Elementary School Subjects.* New York: D. Appleton and Company, 1929, pp. 43-45.

ably this group will be taken to the blackboard and there each pupil will work a different example under the teacher's direction. The difficulties will be observed and individual correction made. There may be individual cases that must be taken alone so that they may give orally every thought used in this particular step. Practice is continued for control of the process until each pupil feels and shows evidence to the teacher of some independence in the process and ability to refer to the study chart for help.

d. Testing. Testing has been going on all the time with the completion of each example and each list of examples in the text which provides carefully graded units of work suited to practice for mastery. By this process the pupil does not make "wild" errors to be discovered later when the teacher has had time to check his answers, but he has a means of control during his work. The teacher will administer brief tests at the end of each step that must be done without reference to answers. After several steps in a process have been practiced the pupils will then take a graded test, without the use of answers until after the test, and check the previous steps to see if further practice or reteaching is necessary. An example of this type of test will be found on page 54 of *The Triangle Arithmetics,* Grade Four,[1] in connection with the process of division. This test includes separate sets of examples that test ability in dividing by two, three, four and five respectively in problems involving remainders, carrying, and zeroes in the quotient. A mixed test of these three abilities using all three of the tables is also included. The results of such test may again refer individuals to the multiplication and division facts for practice or to any one of the specific abilities or difficulties in division. In either case the teacher will give such reteaching as may be required.

Acquiring and Maintaining Skills

Many different notions exist concerning the meaning of drill. Conclusions from consideration of the subject will be that much time and many activities in the school room have been used as "drill" that possessed very little, if any, of the characteristics of effective provision for acquiring or maintaining skills. Drill must constitute purposeful exercise at regular intervals. There may be a lack of drill, but quantity is not the sole consideration. Drill with the quality of meeting certain specific functions is of major importance. One of the most pernicious causes of incorrect habits of work in arithmetic is the application of drill exercises on processes which the pupil has not yet learned to do

[1] Leo J. Brueckner, C. J. Anderson, G. O. Banting, and Elda L. Merton. *The Triangle Arithmetics.* Grade IV. California State Series. Sacramento: California State Department of Education, 1932, pp. 52-54.

correctly. Consequently, drill exercises tend to "set" the bad habits of a pupil. Drill is thought of as serving two major purposes: (1) drill to build a skill, and (2) drill to maintain a skill.

Drill to build a skill will be limited in scope and diagnostic in nature. Skills are individual matters. The material to be used and the time required can be determined only by diagnostic procedure. Adequate individualized material of systematically arranged exercises with provision for self-checking is essential.

Drill to maintain a skill must be sufficiently frequent so that the habit begun in one period does not die out before the second period of practice begins. The textbooks supply materials for this purpose at regular intervals. Knight in the Third Yearbook of the Department of Superintendence gives these specifications to maintain acquired skills:

> a. Drill should be on the entire process
> b. Drill should come frequently in small amounts
> c. Each drill unit should be a mixed drill
> d. Drills should have time limits
> e. Drills should have accuracy standards
> f. Examples in a drill unit should be in the order of difficulty [1]

Games are frequently employed with the apparent idea of acquiring and maintaining skills. A critical analysis of the activity will very often reveal that they do not provide a learning situation, neither is there any effective practice. The actual time of practice per individual will be negligible and there is no systematic effort. Games are largely for motivation and should be understood as such. They may develop interest and add pleasure to the number work.

Games to be effective:

1. Should generally involve every member of the class for almost all of the time
2. Should make the child feel the need for knowing the number facts required to play the game
3. Should involve no waste of time
4. Should cause no great commotion
5. Should not eliminate the slow pupil
6. Should add pleasure and interest to class work

Speed should not be stressed in the initial stages of the learning process. Speed of response should increase with mastery of the operation. It is also a function of maturity. Too much stress has in many cases been placed upon speed of work with the result that accuracy has

---

[1] *Research in Constructing the Elementary School Curriculum.* Department of Superintendence Third Yearbook. Washington: The Department of Superintendence of the National Education Association, 1925, pp. 63-64.

been made a minor objective. Children have at times been working under unnecessary stress because of time limits.

Timed exercises will aid primarily in giving answers to combinations to impress upon the child that they are facts to be made automatic. The time limit will not permit the use of any of the numerous schemes of counting and will therefore aid in establishing correct habits. Exercises with time limits will hold up a standard of speed to the teacher and pupil. Teachers may differ considerably as to speed requirements. Speed standards for the arithmetic processes at different grade levels have been determined by experiment.[1] Unfortunately, some are not carefully determined.

TESTS IN ARITHMETIC [2]

Survey Tests

Survey tests may be considered under four main headings: (1) rate tests, (2) scales, (3) general survey tests and (4) curriculum tests.[3]

1. Rate tests. Rate may be interpreted either as the number of exercises attempted or as the number of exercises correct. The number of examples attempted gives a measure of the speed of work; the number of examples correct gives the speed for correct work. The Courtis Standard Research Test, Series B, is mentioned in this connection. It has standards of both rate and accuracy.

2. Scales. Scales are designed to measure the altitude or level of the pupil's development in arithmetic computation and problem solving. Among these are, (1) Woody-McCall Mixed Fundamentals, (2) Los Angeles Diagnostic Arithmetic Tests, (3) Stanford Achievement Tests, (4) Woody-VanWagenen Mixed Fundamentals, (5) Buckingham Scale for Problems in Arithmetic. In these tests the items are arranged in the order of their difficulty. They are adapted to survey purposes.

3. General survey tests. Several general survey tests are available that are neither pure rate tests nor scales. They usually contain examples in several processes and are used to secure a general measure of the level of achievement of a school. Examples are Courtis Supervisory Tests and Stones Reasoning Test.

---

[1] Carleton W. Washburne. *Adjusting the School to the Child.* Yonkers-on-Hudson, New York: World Book Company, 1932, p. 19.
[2] *Report of the Society's Committee on Arithmetic.* Twenty-Ninth Yearbook of the National Society for the Study of Education. Bloomington, Illinois: Public School Publishing Company, 1930, pp. 269-316.
[3] Leo J. Brueckner, and Ernest O. Melby. *Diagnostic and Remedial Teaching.* Boston: Houghton Mifflin Company, 1931, p. 167.

4. Curriculum tests.   Brueckner's curriculum tests have been mentioned before.   Supervisors and teachers should read the manual explaining the tests and become familiar with the possibilities of the tests.   The idea can be included in using the material of the text if the actual test booklets are not used.

The content of the tests for each of the ten months consists of a careful sampling of the new processes or portion of the curriculum taught during the corresponding month.   They have standard ratings of 1 to 8.   The tests are uniform in length.   Various kinds of analytical records and a progress chart for motivation are provided.   This kind of testing closely connects the results with the teaching and learning process and are recommended.

Diagnostic Tests

These tests vary widely in the theories underlying their construction and use.   Many of them have serious limitations for the teacher's use.   Some of them have limited sampling.   In most cases they show the kind of process causing difficulty but they do not always show the cause of difficulty.   Among these are mentioned (1) The Compass Diagnostic Tests, (2) The Brueckner Diagnostic Tests, (3) The Spencer Diagnostic Tests, and (4) The Monroe Diagnostic Test.

Teaching Tests

The necessity of adapting instructions to the individual differences in rates of learning and difficulties in computation revealed by test scores has resulted in the development of instruction techniques which have greatly increased the efficiency of teaching.   Tests that are diagnostic that show the difficulty and the cause of difficulty and have keyed remedial or practice exercises are of primary interest to the teacher. They are not only valuable in reteaching but they provide excellent material for individualized instruction in learning the process.   The Compass Diagnostic Tests and the Economy Remedial Exercise cards are mentioned.   Complete in one booklet are the Diagnostic Tests and Practice Exercises of Brueckner and others.   A study of these will be tremendously helpful to the teacher in using this style or type of material which is also found in the textbooks, *The Triangle Arithmetics* [1] but is not keyed nor so clearly presented.

DIAGNOSIS
Suggestions for Diagnosis and Remedial Work

The following general suggestions relating to the selection and use of arithmetic tests may be of some value in beginning a program of diagnosis and remedial work.

---

[1] *Op. cit.*

1. Read the literature on diagnostic teaching suggested in the bibliography.

2. Secure diagnostic material such as the "Diagnostic Tests and Practice Exercises" and study the procedure.

3. Study the charts of the most common difficulties in the fundamental operations. They may be used as individual diagnostic charts.[1]

4. Study the charts of specific abilities involved in each of the processes in fractions and decimals.

5. Examine the description of these different difficulties and skills with the examples that explain them. Notice the diagnostic tests given to be used that will show these difficulties.[2]

6. Plan
   a. If convenient use a standardized survey test to determine the general level of ability.
   b. Use the tests in your arithmetic to determine the process in which there may be a deficiency.
   c. Use a graded test to determine the level at which pupil has mastery of a process.
   d. Study the same test or use a keyed diagnostic test to discover the particular element as skill in a process that is causing the deficiency.
   e. Use reteaching charts and practice exercises on each specific skill of the process that requires it.
   f. Test each skill.
   g. Use a graded test on the entire process similar to the one used at the beginning.

7. Methods of individual diagnosis
   a. Analyze the written work of the pupil.
   b. Observe the pupil at work at his desk or at the blackboard.
   c. Observe the pupil's mental processes in working examples, by requiring him to do all of the work aloud.

The Most Common Faults in the Fundamental Operations

The following classification of faults in the four operations with whole numbers will suggest the types of errors teachers should expect to find present in the work of pupils deficient in the processes.

---

[1] *Report of the Society's Committee on Arithmetic.* Twenty-Ninth Yearbook of the National Society for the Study of Education. Bloomington, Illinois: Public School Publishing Company, 1930, p. 304.
[2] Leo J. Brueckner. *Diagnostic and Remedial Teaching in Arithmetic.* Philadelphia: The John C. Winston Company, 1930.

Addition Difficulties

1. Weakness in combinations
2. Counting
3. Vocalizes his work
4. Bridging the tens
5. Zero difficulty
6. Breaks up combinations
7. Roundabout methods
8. Carrying difficulty
   a. Forgets to carry
   b. Adds carried number irregularly
   c. Carried wrong number
9. Column addition
   a. Adds large numbers first
   b. Trouble with second addition in column
   c. Forgets sum and repeats work
   d. Adds by tens
   e. Loses place in column
   f. Inspects example to find starting point

Subtraction Difficulties

1. Weakness in combinations
2. Counting
3. Zero difficulty
   a. Zero in minuend
   b. Zero in subtrahend
4. Borrowing difficulty
   a. Does not allow for borrowing
   b. Does not borrow but gives zero as answer
   c. Borrows when borrowing is not necessary
   d. Deducts two from minuend digit after borrowing
   e. Does not reduce minuend digit after borrowing
   f. Errors due to minuend and subtrahend digits being the same
5. Subtracting minuend from subtrahend
6. Uses same digit in two columns
7. Roundabout methods
8. Splits up numbers
9. Reverses digits in remainder
10. Confuses processes with division
11. Skips one or more decades

Multiplication Difficulties

1. Weakness in combinations
2. Counting
   a. To carry
   b. To get combinations
3. Zero difficulty
   a. Zero in multiplier
   b. Zero in multiplicand
4. Carrying
   a. Carries wrong number
   b. Forgets to carry
   c. Error in carrying with zero
5. Errors in adding
   a. In partial products
   b. In carried number
6. Errors in multiplying
   a. Confuses products when multiplier has two or more digits
   b. Splits multiplier
   c. Uses multiplicand as multiplier
   d. Multiplies by adding
7. Omits digit in
   a. Multiplier
   b. Multiplicand
   c. Product
8. Uses wrong process (adds)
9. Errors in position of partial products

Division Difficulties

1. Weakness in combinations
2. Difficulty with remainders
   a. Within the example
   b. With final remainder
3. Zero difficulty
   a. Within the quotient
   b. Within dividend
4. Difficulty with quotient
   a. Trial quotient
   b. Counts to get quotient
   c. Derives quotient from a similar example
5. Roundabout methods
6. Difficulty with subtraction
7. Difficulty with multiplication
8. Repeats tables for results
9. Uses digits of divisor separately
10. Brings down digit in dividend twice
11. Faulty statements
12. Interchanges long and short division

PROBLEM SOLVING

Provision for Problem Solving

The teachers will note with satisfaction that written problems used for the application of the various arithmetical processes are tending to become more simplified in the newer arithmetic textbooks. The problems are more directly related to life situations. Suggestions are also made for applying arithmetic to actual situations.

In this phase of the work as in the fundamental processes provision is made for practice on a single type of problem until the pattern of thought in such application may be established. At first, addition problems and subtraction problems are not thrown together nor are one and two step problems thrown together until adequate preliminary work has been given. Lessons designed to introduce each type of problem and to aid in acquiring systematic methods in problem solving are provided.

Answers as an Aid in Problem Solving

The answers to be found in the book will render valuable assistance in this connection as well as in other phases of the work. Perhaps the inclusion of anwers in the text will do more than any other single thing to focus attention upon the process where it belongs rather than upon the answer. There are indications that an "answer complex" has been developed among teachers and pupils. The chief concern is in getting the answer. Generally the answer is to be used as an aid in developing processes. Children must think why they did or didn't get the answer and even though given in a different form ($.12\frac{1}{2}$ or $.125$), must know why their answer is correct. The pupil's work must be so organized and sufficiently neat so that he may show why the answer that is given is correct.

Reasons for Difficulty in Solving Problems

Numerous investigations have been made to determine the cause of pupil's inabilities to solve verbal problems. "The failure on the part of pupils to solve arithmetic problems is due to poor reading and consequent inability to understand the problems," was reported by Estaline Wilson[1] in 1922. According to Osburn[2] the most frequent difficulty in problem solving is inability to identify the proper process to use. Errors in computation have been shown to cause 20 to 40 per cent of the errors in problem solving. A noticeable cause reported among the investigations was "carelessness"—carelessness in reading, carelessness in arrangement of work, and carelessness in computing.

---

[1] Estaline Wilson. "Improving the Ability to Read Arithmetic Problems." *Elementary School Journal*, XXII (January, 1922), 380–386.
[2] W. J. Osburn. *Corrective Arithmetic.* Boston: Houghton Mifflin Company, 1924, p. 38.

The chief causes revealed by the investigation are:

1. Lack of ability to perform the necessary computations accurately or to select the operation needed.
2. Failure to comprehend the problem in whole or in part:
   a. General inability in reading
   b. Vocabulary difficulty
   c. Carelessness in reading
   d. Insufficient experience—vague quantitative concept
3. Lack of systematic method of attack:
   a. Failure to try to reason
   b. Lack of training
4. Lack of knowledge of essential facts, data, tables, or principles involved.

Improving Ability in Problem Solving

Investigations differ as to the effectiveness of various methods of teaching pupils to apply the mechanics of arithmetic to the solution of problems. Several studies show the value of a systematic procedure such as that in the following outline as a means of increasing the ability to solve verbal problems.

1. Apply methods of testing, diagnosis and remedial work.
2. Systematic work to develop the vocabulary of pupils.
3. Exercises in careful reading.
4. Practice in giving the process or processes to be used.
5. Improve accuracy in computation.
6. Drill on the value of units of measure.
7. Practice a definite method of attack:
   a. Reading the problem over carefully and thoughtfully
   b. What is the question asked by the problem
   c. What processes must be used
   d. Estimate the answer
   e. Carefully check or evaluate the final answer
8. Complete problems with missing numbers.
9. Finishing problems.
10. Constructing problems.
11. Practice in estimating answers.
12. Give practice in recognizing solution patterns involved in the problem by providing adequate experience in the eleven types of problem patterns.[1]

---

[1] Leo J. Brueckner. *Diagnostic and Remedial Teaching of Arithmetic.* Philadelphia: The John C. Winston Company, 1930, p. 327.

13. Use the Problem Scales in the text and keep a graphic record of the results.

Undoubtedly, the best way to teach the pupil how to apply arithmetic is to give him the opportunity to apply arithmetic in real life situations.   A large part of the training that pupils are given in this aspect of the subject is by means of the verbal problems found in textbooks.   A pupil may be able to find the area of a floor or the perimeter of a room when all of the data is given in a verbal problem and yet be unable to gather the data and solve the problem in an actual situation.

The real task is to utilize the possibilities of normal activities to give the pupil practice in thinking quantitatively in a normal way and to apply number as it is applied in life.

BIBLIOGRAPHY

BRUECKNER, LEO J. *Diagnostic and Remedial Teaching in Arithmetic.* Philadelphia: The John C. Winston Company, 1930.

BRUECKNER, LEO J., and MELBY, ERNEST O. *Diagnostic and Remedial Teaching.* Boston: Houghton Mifflin Company, 1931.

BUSWELL, GUY THOMAS, and JUDD, CHARLES HUBBARD. "Summary of Educational Investigation Relating to Arithmetic." *Supplementary Educational Monographs* XXVII (June, 1925). Chicago: University of Chicago Press, 1925.

BUSWELL, GUY THOMAS. "Summary of Arithmetic Investigations (1926)." I. *Elementary School Journal*, XXVII (May, 1927), 685–694.

BUSWELL, GUY THOMAS. "Summary of Arithmetic Investigations (1926)." II. *Elementary School Journal*, XXVII (June, 1927), 731–744.

BUSWELL, GUY THOMAS. "Summary of Arithmetic Investigations (1927)." I. *Elementary School Journal*, XXVIII (May, 1928), 702–709.

BUSWELL, GUY THOMAS. "Summary of Arithmetic Investigations (1927)." II. *Elementary School Journal*, XXVIII (June, 1928), 730–742.

BUSWELL, GUY THOMAS. "Summary of Arithmetic Investigations (1928)." I. *Elementary School Journal*, XXIX (May, 1929), 691–698.

BUSWELL, GUY THOMAS. "Summary of Arithmetic Investigations (1928)." II. *Elementary School Journal*, XXIX (June, 1929), 737–747.

BUSWELL, GUY THOMAS. "Summary of Arithmetic Investigations (1929)." *Elementary School Journal*, XXX (June, 1930), 766–775.

BUSWELL, GUY THOMAS. "Summary of Arithmetic Investigations (1930)." *Elementary School Journal*, XXXI (June, 1931), 756–766.

BUSWELL, GUY THOMAS. "Summary of Arithmetic Investigations (1931)." *Elementary School Journal*, XXXII (June, 1932), 766–773.

MORTON, R. L. *Teaching Arithmetic in the Primary Grades.* New York: Silver, Burdett and Company, 1927.

MORTON, R. L. *Teaching Arithmetic in the Intermediate Grades.* New York: Silver, Burdett and Company, 1927.

The Nation at Work on the Public School Curriculum. Department of Superintendence Fourth Yearbook. Washington: Department of Superintendence of the National Education Association, 1926, pp. 173–220.

OSBURN, W. J. *Corrective Arithmetic.* Boston: Houghton Mifflin Company, 1924.

Research in Constructing the Elementary School Curriculum. Department of Superintendence Third Yearbook. Washington: Department of Superintendence of the National Education Association, 1925, pp. 35–109.

Report of the Society's Committee on Arithmetic. Twenty-Ninth Yearbook of the National Society for the Study of Education. Bloomington, Illinois: Public School Publishing Company, 1930, pp. 1–408.

The Supervision of Elementary Subjects. Edited by William Henry Burton. New York: D. Appleton and Company, 1929.

WASHBURNE, CARLETON W. *Adjusting the School to the Child.* Yonkers-on-Hudson, New York: World Book Company, 1932.

Chapter XX

MUSIC [1]

PLACE OF MUSIC IN THE CURRICULUM

Music has held for the past few years a recognized place in the curriculum as one of the subjects essential to the development of the child's educational potentialities. Through the participation in, the knowledge of, and the inspiration gained from listening to good music, he may enter into a new world of beauty, self-expression, and spiritual enjoyment. It is the responsibility of the teacher so to guide him in his various musical experiences that the child's natural interest and enjoyment may find ever increasing satisfaction and development.

Dykema maintains [2] that the chief purpose of music instruction in the schools is to increase pleasure in life through contact with music. All through the primary grades this contact consists mainly of the development within the child of the desire and ability to sing many beautiful songs and to feel a free bodily response to the simple, fundamental rhythms. The joyous freedom felt by the primary child in his singing should be maintained through the intermediate grades. Much of the time should still be spent in singing, with the addition of only enough theoretical and structural knowledge of music and its instruments as will foster the more intelligent appreciation, and intellectual enjoyment which children of these grades are educationally ready to experience. Too often, during the intermediate grades, the spontaneous joy and freedom of singing is smothered beneath a wet blanket of theory and drill. This is the result of a mistaken idea that children will learn to love music by the acquisition of skill in sight reading and by storing up knowledge about music and musicians.

A balanced music program for the intermediate grades should include the following phases: (1) singing, (2) music reading, (3) music appreciation, (4) creative expression, (5) instrumental participation, (6) integration with other curricular activities.

SINGING

Need for Much Singing

Kwalwasser [3] believes that fully fifty per cent of the music period in the upper grades should be devoted to the singing of songs. These

---

[1] Contributed by Helen M. Barnett, Santa Barbara State College.
[2] Peter Dykema. "Music in the School Survey." *Music Supervisors Journal,* XVII (October, 1930), 20–21.
[3] Jacob Kwalwasser. "A Few Changes That Would Result in a Better Balanced Program." *Journal of Proceedings.* Music Supervisors National Conference, 1921, pp. 237–240.

songs should be inherently interesting and beautiful and should be largely of the art and folk song types, selected for their artisic appeal and interpretive possibilities. They should contain the same basic principles of design found in all great musical compositions; namely, balance in structure with repetition and contrast in melody and rhythm.

The words of the songs should be appropriate to the interests and experiences of each group. Alma Norton, in her study of the music of intermediate grades[1] finds that many children lose their interest in music after reaching the fourth grade, partly because of too much emphasis on technique and drill, and partly because of the use of texts

Courtesy of Oakland City Schools

Singing to an Accompaniment on Flower Pots

unrelated to the interests of the children. This lack seems to be particularly noticeable with the experiences of boys of intermediate age. Some of the newer music books, however, have recognized this problem and contain definite provision for sustaining the interests of the growing boy, with songs of the sea, the plains, and outdoor activities.

Care of the Voice

The voice of the growing child is a very delicate instrument and demands careful and constant attention. Strain during this period of

[1] Alma Norton. *Teaching School Music.* C. C. Crawford, University of Southern California, Los Angeles, 1932, Chapter V.

development will sometimes cause permanent injury to the vocal chords. Emphasis should be placed on beauty and purity of tone rather than on volume. There is no place in real singing for the coarse, raucous tone so often heard among boys who force the chest tones up to the higher notes in place of the floating head tones. They will even growl out the melody of a song an octave lower than it is written, fondly imagining that they are singing "bass". One teacher was able to overcome a dislike for singing high on the part of her fifth and sixth grade boys who thought it "sissy" to sing their songs up in the proper register, by telling them about Roland Hays, the famous negro tenor, and his beautiful *mezzo voce*. She then taught the boys a few of the more appropriate negro spirituals sung by Hays, and is most enthusiastic over the resultant improvement in the boys' attitude and in their tone quality.

Vocalizing

A few minutes of vocalizing several times a week will do much toward developing the desired tone quality. Following are a few suggestions:

(1) The children may sing *down* the scale, lightly and rapidly with some neutral syllable such as *loo, noo, lo* or *no,* beginning on C above middle C, going up a half step for each successive scale as far as F.

(2) Vocalizing smoothly flowing melodies with any of the neutral syllables suggested above is beneficial; also the sustained chanting of the words to a song all on one pitch.

(3) Singing in one breath as much of some chosen song as is possible will help to lighten and purify the tone and improve the breath control.

(4) Another exercise for improving the breath control is the singing of short phrases with a pause between each phrase, but no breathing. Some song with sustained tones might be chosen for this exercise, the tone being sung staccato, but the breath held for the required number of beats before passing on to the next tone.

The teacher needs to be careful not to develop too "hushed" a type of singing, in her desire for a light, sweet head tone. It is possible to secure this result but at the same time to suppress all natural spontaneity and life. The vibrant, joyous tones accompanying a keen enjoyment and appreciation of the mood and text of a song are much to be desired and must not be confused with the coarse, throaty tones of wrong production. If the jaw is relaxed, the mouth open, the facial expression pleasant, with the neck muscles showing no sign of tension or strain, and the tone quality good, there is little chance of the production being at fault. When the child once gains command of his head tones, he may be allowed considerable freedom in his expression.

Enunciation

Another important consideration is correct and pure enunciation. Final *d*'s and *t*'s should be brought to the front of the mouth and clearly enunciated and initial *l*'s and *h*'s definitely sounded. Where the vowel has a double sound, as in "light", "bright", etc., the initial "ah" part should be sustained during the time value of the note with the *"ee"* sound of the vowel used merely as a vanish, to round out the word. The same principle should be applied to the *"ay-ee"* sound of words such as "late", "hate"; to the *"oh-oo"* sound in such words as "go", "slow", "know"; and to the *"ee-oo"* sound in words like "new", "dew", and "tune." A common error in pronunciation is giving a "un" sound to words ending in "en" such as "lighten", "open", "happen", "pilgrim", etc. Close attention to a few of these common errors will result in a marked improvement not only in the enunciation but also in the tone quality of the group. Words properly enunciated tend to bring the vowel production forward into the correct resonating cavities.

Part Singing

Beginning with the fourth grade, after the children have gained independence in melody reading they are ready for the joy of experiencing a conscious pleasure in harmony through two-part singing. This may be introduced in several ways.

(1) The class may sing with neutral syllable a tone of the scale, perhaps the third, while the teacher sings the first of the scale.

(2) The class may then sing the fifth, the eighth and back to the fifth, the teacher holding the third of scale.

(3) The class may sing three, four, five, six and back to five, while the teacher sings one, two, three, four and back to three.

(4) Exercises similar to the above carried out in sixths instead of thirds are also good for initial drill.

(5) Half the class may then take the teacher's part in any of the above exercises and harmonize with the rest of the class. Little sections may be lifted out of two-part songs and used for initial drill.

(6) The children may be encouraged to make up their own little duets, perhaps using some familiar melody for one part and a second part added which "sounds well" with it. This type of work furnishes valuable background for chordal and harmonic feeling.

(7) Some authorities believe the singing of two-part rounds furnishes valuable background and introduction to two-part singing.

It is advisable to keep these simple exercises in definite groups, contained in two measure sections, as the rhythmic swing will help to carry along the melodic flow.

The following examples serve to illustrate the idea:

$$2/4 \quad \begin{array}{c|c|c} 5 & 8 & 5 & - \\ \hline 3 & 3 & 3 & - \end{array} \quad 4/4 \quad \begin{array}{c|c|c} 3\ 4\ 5\ 6 & 5 & - \\ \hline 1\ 2\ 3\ 4 & 3 & - \end{array} \quad 3/4 \quad \begin{array}{c|c|c} 5\ 8\ 6 & 5 & -\ - \\ \hline 3\ 3\ 4 & 3 & -\ - \end{array}$$

Many children have a tendency to put their fingers in their ears when first experiencing part singing, so that they may hear only the sound of their own voices, and *shut out* the other part. This procedure should never be allowed, as the joy of part singing lies in hearing the harmony created when the two parts are being sung. Each child should learn to *feel* his own part as it harmonizes with the other. There would be much less singing off pitch in both school and adult choruses if each singer were made definitely conscious of the relation his part bears to the harmonic structure of the whole composition. Children singing alto for the first time often have a tendency to sing with heavy chest tones, in order to hear their own part distinctly. This condition may be helped by asking the altos to sing softly while the sopranos merely hum their part. If songs with simple natural progressions and definite melodic flow are selected, the two parts should be sung simultaneously, drilling separately only when the need arises.

As soon as two-part singing becomes a free and natural expression, three-part music of simple melody and rhythm, may be introduced. This experience generally occurs in the sixth grade and may be introduced by the singing of three-part rounds. The children should be encouraged to sing in small group ensembles; duets, trios, sextettes, etc. This procedure will emphasize, in a most desirable manner, the amateur spirit in music, and will stimulate the memorization of many delightful songs for various occasions. With the wide-spread interest developing throughout the country for a cappella singing there has been a revival of sixteenth and seventeenth century music. It is possible to get attractive, simple madrigals, folk and sacred songs for the use of upper grade children, many of which have a quaintness of musical and literary expression most appealing to their interests. The English folk song *Mayday Carol*, arranged by Deems Taylor is good, as are the *Canzonets for Two Voices*, by Thomas Morley.[1] *The Little*

---

[1] Galaxy Music Corporation, New York.

Dustman,[1] *Now Is the Month of Maying,*[2] *Trip It, Trip It In a Ring,*[3] and *It Was a Lover and His Lass,*[4] are all good examples of this type of music.

The problem of the changing voice is rarely found as early as the sixth grade, hence it is seldom necessary to keep a child or a group of children singing the same part in song after song. The group should be divided into equal sections with a frequent interchange of parts. For memorization purposes it is perhaps advisable to have the same section always sing the alto to a given song, changing to soprano on the next song, etc.

Interpretation

In the fifth and six grades more exacting demands may be made on the children in the finish and interpretation of their songs. The vocal mechanism has developed and strengthened to such an extent that there is less danger of straining the delicate chords and the children have learned to sing with an easy flow of tone. Precision of attack and release, smooth phrasing and definite shading may be insisted upon, always keeping in mind, however, that adult volume of tone and mass effects are still impossible. The words and music of the songs themselves will suggest the appropriate spirit and mood and will also develop desirable tone qualities. The Foresman *Books of Songs*[5] and the *Music Education Series*[6] suggest the mood with a word above the first measure of each song, and the latter series uses expression marks suggesting the desirable light and shade.

A careful reading of the words aloud to the rhythm of the music will help in determining the proper dynamics necessary for enhancing the poetic meaning of the song. In all desirable songs the words and melody should blend together to produce a beauty of interpretation, each one accurately reproducing the feeling of the other and both within the emotional comprehension of the children. Mabelle Glenn, Director of Music, Kansas City, Missouri, considers the esthetic beauty of music all important. She encourages the children to question themselves continually as to whether their songs are becoming ever more beautiful and their enunciation and shading more perfect. This procedure is a splendid stimulation for the experience of independent thinking, continually increasing the capacity for feeling tonal beauty and rhythmic structure.

---

[1] Archibald T. Davison, and Others. *A Book of Songs,* for Grades 4–6. (Concord Series No. 14.) Boston: E. C. Schirmer Music Co., 1924, p. 199.
[2] *Ibid.,* p. 103.
[3] *Ibid.,* p. 256.
[4] *Ibid.,* p. 255.
[5] Robert Foresman. *Books of Songs.* New York: American Book Company, n.d.
[6] T. P. Giddings, and Others. *Music Education Series.* Boston: Ginn and Company, 1927.

Courtesy of Burbank City Schools

Folk Dances Offer an Opportunity for Rhythmic Expression

Throughout the singing period the teacher should remain in the background as much as possible. She may offer criticism and suggestion from time to time, but the children's singing should be the outward expression of the mood and beauty of the music felt within their own souls. In the classroom there need be little, if any, formal beating of time, or formal instruction in dynamics when once the children have been awakened to the idea that the music and words carry within themselves adequate suggestions for suitable interpretation.

MUSIC READING

Use for Notation

Considerable differences of opinion exist among music educators as to just where the music reading program should begin in the elementary grades; some would introduce it before the end of the second grade, while others insist that a formal reading program should be postponed until the fourth or even the fifth grade. After considerable research and experiment, thoughtful educators have come to the conclusion that far too much of the music period is being spent on the technique of music and too little on the actual experiences of music itself. Music has been called a universal language, and it is essentially the channel or mouthpiece for emotional expression. It then seems reasonable that much of the child's music experiences should be of a more esthetic nature gained through the singing of many songs of musical merit, and having a wide range of emotional expression, and through intelligent listening to music which he himself cannot perform.

In spite of the rigid reading program adhered to in many school systems, few children have become skillful sight-readers by the time they have completed the sixth grade. Many, on the other hand, because of undue stress on the mechanics of music, have acquired an actual antipathy toward the subject in general. Since the average adult has no need for a thorough technical training in his music experiences, does it not seem inadvisable to force all children through a strict technical routine, which after all does not provide for even a future need? Kwalwasser[1] believes that since a high degree of technical proficiency is most needed by those who will follow music as a vocation, this training should not be required in any grade, but might be offered in junior and senior high schools on an elective basis. The reading of the average child seems to be partly rote and partly note, following the lead of a few really good readers. This practice is almost universally true, even in chorus choirs and other choral organizations. Why then waste so much of the short time allotted to music in the curriculum trying to force all children to become skillful music readers, a type of music education for which few will have need and for which some have neither aptitude nor desire? The *why* rather than the *how* of music should be emphasized. Mursell[2] believes that the child must find in music an opportunity for happiness and a fuller life *in the present*. The child must be helped to really live his music, not to spend most of his time preparing for a possible future need.

When to Introduce Notation

Before introducing the children to the symbols of notation, it is most desirable that they have a wealth of auditory experiences in both the rhythmic and melodic idioms, and the natural sequential progressions found in all good music, just as they must become familiar with the idioms of speech before the written symbols can have meaning. Great care must be exercised in the building up of a musical background which will function in the process of music reading. Many folk songs and the music of composers of recognized merit should be emphasized. This music should include the rhythmic and melodic patterns and themes which the child will recognize later in his reading. For these reasons most children will not have a readiness for the real experience of notation before the third or even the beginning of the fourth grade.

[1] Jacob Kwalwasser. *Problems in Public School Music.* New York: M. Witmark and Sons, 1932, p. 113.
[2] James Mursell and Mabelle Glenn. *The Psychology of School Music Teaching.* New York: Silver, Burdett and Co., 1931, p. 366.

The richer and fuller the musical background, the more readily will the child recognize in the music symbols those idioms with which he has already become familiar through sound. There will be a feeling of *expectancy* in reading the rhythmic and melodic pattern which will help the child to know *what comes next* and greatly facilitate his speed in reading.

The various problems in the theory of music should be introduced only as the need for their use arises. These situations, of course, should be at all times under the careful control of the teacher. The children may be stimulated to feel a curiosity for finding out for themselves what the music has to say, just as they may be led to read a story or poem. Interesting, attractive texts are strong stimulants; so also is the desire to learn songs suitable for special programs or units of activity. Another fine stimulus for developing facility in staff and key notation is through creative melody activities. An understanding of the *up and down* of melody, key signatures, staff placements, and note values are all necessary for recording the original melodies created by the children. If accidentals or chromatics should be used in the melody through a natural desire on the part of the children to have it *sound that way,* then is the time to explain their use, whether the grade below or high. Some children may be more interested in the technicalities of music than others, and these should be given opportunities for satisfying their curiosity. They might be allowed to enter into more extensive creative work, to help some of the other members of the class with sympathetic understanding, or perhaps to search out and present to the class music suitable for various class activities.

Use of Syllables

Music educators disagree as to whether the movable *do* system of syllable reading, the scale numbers, or staff-placement should be used in the development of notation. Reading by staff-placement has the advantage of direct translation of note into sound but requires musical background and musical feeling. Anne L. Beck[1] believes that if individual instruction were possible, there would be no need for syllables. However, since a large number of teachers who are poorly prepared musically must take charge of the music lesson, she believes that syllables are necessary. They furnish most convenient "handles" with which to manipulate the various tones, and provide very definite interval relationships. The use of scale numbers has the same advantages as syllables, but the sounds of the numbers are not musically satisfying. The reading program should never be stressed at the expense of good singing. The child's attention needs at all times to

[1] Anne L. Beck. "Syllables," *Music Supervisors Journal,* XVII (February, 1931).

be centered upon the music and its expression. The phrase feeling and rhythmic swing should be maintained even at the expense of the syllables.

The aim of music reading might well be the establishing of a pleasurable response to the beauty of music and a conscious recognition of the various factors uniting to cause it. This aim is best realized through the use of much easy reading material, just as the language class reads many stories to develop facility in reading. The use of two or three music texts would accomplish much better results than one book, as even the best series available are lacking in sufficient material to adequately "pin down" any one reading problem. The teacher should be careful to follow the regular graded order in the music books as they have been compiled according to the order of technical difficulty. An occasional transgression is allowable, however, if there is sufficient interest in the text or the melodic beauty to overshadow the technical difficulties.

Music Writing

The writing of music should function in the music program as an activity whenever there is definite need for its use, and never simply as an exercise. For instance, if the children should be making a book of their favorite song, they would be interested in learning how to write music correctly. Otherwise, it becomes more strictly a vocational aim and as such it would not function in the experience of all children. Recent investigation shows no positive correlation between the ability to read at sight and facility in music writing.

MUSIC APPRECIATION

Need for Music Appreciation

While it is a recognized fact that every music lesson should stress appreciation and while much keen appreciation and musical understanding is derived from the singing of beautiful songs, there is still a vast wealth of wonderful music containing material beyond the vocal expression of the child and not within his ability to perform. To confine his musical contact to that music only which he himself could execute, would limit his experience to the simple rhythms, melodies and moods of musical expression. Much of our adult musical experience consists of listening to the performance of others, either in solo recital programs, or in choral and instrumental groups. The development of sympathetic and intelligent listening to music, then, becomes a most important as well as enjoyable phase of music education.

It seems most essential in this modern age, when the exquisite beauty of the music of such composers as Ravel and Stravinsky, played by the world's finest orchestras, are separated from the cheap blaring of trombones and the shrill whine of cornets by only a few numbers on the dials of our radios, that our children need to be led to establish habits of preferring good music through the growth of feeling for beauty and symmetry. This feeling will become ever more discriminating and the capacity for esthetic enjoyment will grow ever greater and more keen as desirable music experiences increase in scope and as the children learn to recognize and to evaluate for themselves the best of musical works of art. Music appreciation can never be *taught* in the formal sense of the word. Passive listening to any number of fine phonograph records will never arouse a response deep within the soul of the child, there to become a part of his own experience. Knowledge *about* music and composers is not sufficient to kindle the vital spark. The teacher may provide the desirable atmosphere and materials, but can only lead each child into a joyous, satisfying experience through the love, understanding and sympathy she herself feels for both the music and the child. A real appreciation for the message of music must come from a hearing and rehearing of the music itself.

Transition From Sensory to Mental Activities

In the primary grades the sensing of rhythm, melody and mood is developed through singing many beautiful songs, through quiet listening to instrumental melodies, and through active participation in the rhythm band and in creative steps and dances. These activities emphasize the sensory and motor impulses so dominant in the little child's experiences. He is then led to sense phrase, meter and simple form through folk songs and dances. With this well established background on which to build, music appreciation in the intermediate grades tends to be confined more to the feeling and mental activities. Discriminating judgments and musical standards are developed through a definite understanding of instrumental color, form or pattern, and nationalism as expressed in folk songs and dances. As the child's musical experiences widen and his interest becomes centered on the definite materials of music, so will his intelligent enjoyment of the best in music develop. It is suggested that listening lessons should be planned for one period a week throughout the whole year.

Aims for Music Appreciation in the Intermediate Grades

The aims for the development of appreciation in the three intermediate grades are about the same, with a gradual increase in the difficulty and maturity of the material used, as it is suited to the various interests and development of each grade. The aims might be expressed as follows:

1. To develop musical taste through an ever increasing delight in singing and listening to good music.

2. To become familiar with the orchestra as a whole and with the individual instruments.

3. To understand and appreciate the difference between pure and descriptive music, including major and minor modes.

4. To recognize by style the march, waltz, minuet, and gavotte and to recognize the different movements in the suite, sonata, and symphony.

5. To understand the principles of simple form, developed from the recognition of a single theme to three-part song form, rondo, and theme with variations.

6. To become acquainted with some of the most famous composers through familiarity with their music and through interesting, appropriate biographical incidents.

7. To become acquainted with national characteristics of various countries as expressed in their folk music.

Elaboration of Aims

The singing of many folk songs will be continued during the intermediate grades with the addition of the simpler art songs of the great masters and some of the best of the more modern composers. Then too, the children have had sufficient interpretative experience and have reached a stage in their emotional development where they may be encouraged to decide for themselves the manner in which their songs should be sung in order that the mood of both words and music may be adequately expressed. Some time should also be devoted to quiet listening to beautiful music just for the pleasure its moods may convey and with no special thought of analysis or detailed account of the impression it may make on different individuals.

When first introducing the orchestra as a whole, the familiar instruments should be stressed and the leading instruments of each family should be compared, one with the other. In the fifth and sixth grades the characteristic tone quality and expressiveness of individual instruments already known may be discussed and the less familiar instruments introduced by music written especially for that instrument by well known composers. There is a very good set of charts on the market[1] picturing the different instruments of the orchestra and show-

---

[1] *Instruments of the Orchestra.* Camden, N. J.: Educational Department, R. C. A.-Victor Company.

ing how each is played. These charts will serve as splendid visual aids when hearing records of their tone quality.

The study of pure as compared with descriptive and program music must of necessity start with the expression of very definite moods within the experiences of the children in the grade. The descriptive music should consist of short musical descriptions of events. As the child himself matures in his ability to discriminate between a variety of moods, the music used may become more involved and elaborate, expressed through both major and minor modes.

The development of the ability to distinguish a composition by its style and rhythmic qualities begins with a simple analysis of marches of various kinds, the waltz, the minuet, and the gavotte. The analysis is gradually extended to include recognition of the separate movements of the suite, sonata, and symphony. The detailed analysis of these styles is left for more mature consideration in the secondary schools. The use of the overture and the characteristics of opera and oratorio are interesting studies for the sixth grade.

A pleasant introduction to the study of phrases and simple song form would be a review of some of the familiar folk songs. "Falling Leaves" of *The Music Hour,* Third Book,[1] is a good example of simple phrasing and also of the song form A-B-A-B. "A Cheerful Song,"[2] is similar, A-A-B-A. "For the Peas Porridge"[3] is a little more extended, A-B-A-C. "George Washington"[4] has the same form. In *Intermediate Music* of the Music Education Series, "Calm Flowing River"[5] is a good illustration, A-A'-B-A'. "Songs of Sweden"[6] is rather odd, A-B-C-B. Still another good example is found in "In Siberia",[7] A-B-C-A'. "Believe Me If All Those Endearing Young Charms," "All Through the Night," "Should Old Acquaintance Be Forgot," "Old Folks at Home" are all good examples of simple song form with good balance and contrast. The children will enjoy making their own charts to picture the patterns of these songs.[8]

Anecdotes and incidents from the boyhood lives of some of the famous composers are splendid mediums through which to stimulate wide-awake interest in their lives and works. Many of the great composers wrote, during their childhood, music which has stood the test of

---

[1] Osbourne McConathy, and Others. *The Music Hour,* Third Book. California State Series. Sacramento: California State Department of Education, 1931, p. 36.
[2] *Ibid.,* p. 37.
[3] *Ibid.,* p. 38.
[4] *Ibid.,* p. 71.
[5] T. P. Giddings, and Others. *Intermediate Music.* Music Education Series. Boston: Ginn and Company, 1928, p. 124.
[6] *Ibid.,* p. 138.
[7] *Ibid.,* p. 93.
[8] Good examples of the procedure to be followed in the development of form are found in: Osbourne McConathy, and Others. *Intermediate Teachers Book* (Music Hour Series), California State Series. Sacramento: California State Department of Education, 1931, p. 23, and in: Mabelle Glenn and Margaret Lowry. *Music Appreciation for Every Child* (Intermediate Grades). New York: Silver, Burdett and Company, 1927, pp. 14 and 22.

time, and some have written music especially for children. The compositions chosen should express the individuality of the composer and when possible, reflect the national characteristics of the composer's own land. *Music Appreciation for Children* [1] contains some very interesting stories from the early lives of some of the famous composers.

> Nationality as expressed through folk music will have an especial appeal to the child in the sixth grade. Mabelle Glenn [2] says: He is now on the threshold of adolescence where very definite new appeals stimulate his interests and imagination. His social instinct is just awakening and he finds a deep interest in other lands and other people. Folk music, therefore, makes its greatest appeal at this period because it gives an impression of the people more vivid than words. Familiar folk songs may be reviewed at this time, special attention being called to those moods and customs in the songs which are typical of a particular country. This study will stimulate a strong correlation with the history and geography of the grade.

Suggested Music for the Appreciation Program [3]

MATERIALS FOR THIRD GRADE

For Rhythmic Development: Folk games and dances.

For Development of feeling for measure and pulse, and for stepping note values: any marches and folk tunes already familiar.

Descriptive music: Of a Tailor and a Bear (MacDowell); To a Water Lily (MacDowell); Witches' Dance (MacDowell); At the Brook (Boisdeffre); Funeral March of Marionette (Gounod); Spinning Song (Mendelssohn); Nutcracker Suite (Tschaikowsky).

For Quiet Listening: Traumerei (Schumann); Evening Song (Schumann); The Swan (Saint Saens); Melody in F (Rubenstein); Largo (Handel); On Wings of Song (Mendelssohn); Album Leaf (Wagner); Meditation from Thais (Massenet).

For Recognition of Waltz and Minuet: Waltz No. 2 (Brahms); Waltz of the Flowers from the Nutcracker Suite (Tschaikowsky); Minuet (Bach); Minuet (Boccherini).

MATERIALS FOR FOURTH GRADE

For Recurring Themes or Sections: Morning (Grieg); In the Hall of the Mountain King (Grieg); Of a Tailor and a Bear (MacDowell); Farandole (Bizet); Ecossaises (Beethoven); Amaryllis (Ghys); Humoresque (Dvorak); Hungarian Dance No. 7 (Brahms); Music Box (Liadow).

For Recognition of Returning Sections forming Pattern A B A (Repetition after Contrast): Narcissus (Nevin); To a Wild Rose (MacDowell); To a Water Lily (MacDowell); March of the Dwarfs (Grieg); Pizzicato (Delibes); To Spring (Grieg); At the Brook (Boisdeffre); March Militaire (Schubert).

For Recognition of Different Types of Marches: March Militaire (Schubert); Soldiers Changing Guard, from "Carmen" (Bizet); Turkish March, from "Ruins of Athens" (Beethoven); Soldiers' Chorus, from "Faust" (Gounod); Grand March, from "Aida" (Verdi); Toy Soldiers' March (Kreisler); Wedding March (Mendelssohn); Funeral March (Chopin); Pomp and Circumstance (Elgar); War March of Priests, from "Athalia" (Mendelssohn).

For Dance Types: Minuet in D (Mozart); Minuet (Gluck); Minuet Antique (Boccherini); Gavotte from "Mignon" (Thomas); Gavotte (Gluck-Brahms);

---

[1] *Music Appreciation for Children.* Camden, N. J.: Educational Department, R. C. A.-Victor Company, 1930, pp. 261-296.

[2] *Ibid.*, p. 41.

[3] *Music Appreciation for the First Six Grades.* Report of subcommittee of Music Supervisors National Conference, Lenora Coffin, Chairman. Ithaca, N. Y.: Cayuga Press, 1930, pp. 235-245.

Amaryllis (Gavotte) ; Waltz of the Flowers (Tschaikowsky) ; Blue Danube Waltz (Strauss) ; Vienna Woods (Strauss) ; Valse from "Coppelia" (Delibes) ; Waltz from "Faust" (Gounod).

For Descriptive Music: March of the Dwarfs (Grieg) ; In the Hall of the Mountain King (Grieg) ; Naiads at the Spring (Juon) ; Spring Song (Mendelssohn) ; Dance of the Flutes and Chinese Dance, from "Nutcracker Suite" (Tschaikowsky) ; Waltzing Doll (Poldini) ; The Swan (Saint-Saens) ; Spinning Song (Mendelssohn) ; Dance of the Hours (Ponchielli) ; At the Brook (Boisdeffre).

For Pure Music: Andante from "Orpheus" (Gluck) ; Musette (Gluck) ; Andante from "Raymond" (Thomas) ; Prelude in A Major (Chopin).

For Tone Color of Instruments: Records "Instruments of the Orchestra"; *Strings,* Vormeland (Swedish Folk Song) ; Anitra's Dance (Grieg) ; *Woodwinds and Brasses,* Soldiers Changing Guard (Bizet) ; March of Little Lead Soldiers (Pierne) ; *Woodwinds,* Music Box (Liadow) ; Chinese Dance and Dance of the Flutes (Tschaikowsky) ; In the Hall of the Mountain King (Grieg) ; *Strings and Woodwinds,* Farandole (Bizet) ; *Harp, Brasses, Woodwinds, Strings,* Waltz of the Flowers (Tschaikowsky).

For Quiet Listening: On Wings of Song (Mendelssohn) ; Ave Maria (Schubert) ; Serenade (Schubert) ; Nocturne from Midsummer Night's Dream (Mendelssohn) ; The Swan (Saint-Saens) ; To Spring (Grieg) ; Melody in F (Rubenstein).

Famous Composers: Schubert: Moment Musicale, March Militaire, Serenade, The Brooklet; Mendelssohn: Spring Song, Spinning Song, Midsummer Night's Dream, On Wings of Song; Tschaikowsky: Nut Cracker Suite, March of the Tin Soldiers, Humoresque; Grieg: Peer Gynt Suite, To Spring, Elfin Dance, March of the Dwarfs.

MATERIALS FOR FIFTH GRADE

For Recognition of Minor Mode: In the Hall of the Mountain King (Grieg) ; Funeral March (Chopin) ; Prelude in C Sharp minor (Rachmaninoff) ; Waltz in C Sharp minor (Chopin) ; March of the Caucasian Chief (Ippolitoff-Ivanoff).

For Recognition of Major Mode: Spring Song (Mendelssohn) ; Blue Danube Waltz (Strauss) ; Waltz of Flowers from "Nutcracker Suite" (Tschaikowsky).

Compositions in Both Major and Minor: Amaryllis (Ghys) ; Humoresque (Dvorak) ; Marche Militaire (Schubert) ; Funeral March of a Marionette (Gounod) ; Andante from "Surprise Symphony" (Haydn) ; Minuet from G-Minor Symphony (Mozart) ; Waltz Op. 34 No. 2 (Chopin).

For Recognition of Patterns and Form: Pattern by Phrases, A A B A; Believe Me If All Those Endearing Young Charms; All Thru the Night; etc. *Pattern by Sentences (Periods) A A B A,* Ash Grove; *A B A,* Nobody Knows de Trouble I See; etc. *Pattern by sections (Three-part Song-form) A B A,* Minuet from "Toy Symphony" (Haydn) ; Mazurka Op. 33 No. 2 (Chopin) ; Minuet from G-Minor Symphony (Mozart) ; Prelude in C-Sharp minor (Rachmaninoff) ; Waltz in D Flat (Minute Waltz) (Chopin) ; Prelude Op. 28 No. 15 (Chopin) ; etc.; also compositions listed under Fourth Year. *Rondo:* Rondino (Beethoven-Kreisler) ; Spanish Dance (Moszkowski) ; Rondo from Trio No. 3 (Haydn) ; Music Box (Liadow) ; Ecossaises (Beethoven) ; Hungarian Dance No. 7 (Brahms) ; etc. *Theme and Variations:* Harmonious Blacksmith (Handel) ; Andante from "Surprise Symphony" (Haydn) ; Shepherd's Hey (Grainger).

For Recognition of Different Types of Music: Suite: Henry VIII Suite (German) ; Scheherazade Suite (Rimsky-Korsakoff) ; Peer Gynt Suite (Grieg) ; Nutcracker Suite (Tschaikowsky) ; Moldau (Smetana) ; Petite Suite (Bizet) ; Caucasian Sketches (Ippolitoff-Ivanoff). *Overture:* Midsummer Night's Dream (Mendelssohn) ; Mignon (Thomas) ; William Tell (Rossini) ; Fingal's Cave (Mendelssohn) ; Oberon (Weber). *Scherzo* from "Midsummer Night's Dream" (Mendelssohn) ; Scherzo from "Trout Quintet" (Schubert). *Nocturne* from "Midsummer Night's Dream" (Mendelssohn) ; Nocturne in E Flat (Chopin) ; etc. *Prelude* Op. 28 No. 15 (Raindrop) (Chopin) ; Prelude in C sharp minor (Rachmaninoff). *Art*

Song: Serenade (Schubert) ; Hark! Hark the Lark (Schubert) ; The Brooklet (Schubert) ; Lo Hear the Gentle Lark (Bishop) ; Solveig's Sunshine Song (Grieg) ; Swiss Echo Song (Eckert).

For Discrimination between Descriptive and Pure Music: Descriptive: At Dawn, Storm, Calm, from "William Tell" Overture (Rossini) ; Danse Macabre (Saint-Saens) ; Omphale's Spinning Wheel (Le Rouet d'Omphale) (Saint-Saens). *Pure:* Largo (Handel) ; Largo from "New World Symphony" (Dvorak) ; Andante from "Surprise Symphony" (Haydn) ; Rondo from Trio No. 3 (Haydn).

For Tone Color of Instruments of Orchestra: The Young Prince and Princess (Rimsky-Korsakoff) (strings, woodwinds) ; William Tell Overture (Rossini), At Dawn (cello, tympani), The Storm (strings, brasses, flute), The Calm (English horn, flute), Finale (brasses) ; Nocturne (Mendelssohn) (French horn) ; Scherzo (Mendelssohn) (flutes, strings) ; Overture to "Mignon" (Thomas) (French horn, harp).

For Quiet Listening: Largo (Handel) ; Largo (Dvorak) ; Berceuse from "Jocelyn" (Godard) ; Nocturne (Mendelssohn) ; Nocturne in E flat (Chopin) ; Prelude Op. 28 No. 15 (Raindrop) (Chopin) ; At Dawn and Calm from "William Tell Overture" (Rossini).

Famous Composers: Handel: Harmonious Blacksmith, Largo, Joy to the World. Haydn : Andante from "Surprise Symphony", Rondo from Trio No. 3, Minuet in D, Toy Symphony. Chopin : Nocturne in E flat, Prelude Op. 28 No. 15 (Raindrop), Military Polonaise, Waltz in D flat (Minute Waltz), Waltz in C sharp minor. Saint-Saens : Spinning Wheel of Omphale, Danse Macabre, Carnival of the Animals.

MATERIALS FOR SIXTH GRADE

Selections from Opera: Prelude, Wedding March, Prelude Act III from "Lohengrin" (Wagner) ; Overture, Pilgrims' Chorus, Evening Star, from "Tannhauser" (Wagner) ; Prize Song, from "Mastersingers" (Wagner) ; Ride of Valkyries, Magic Fire Music, from "Valkyries" (Wagner) ; Overture to "Flying Dutchman" (Wagner) ; Overture to "Mignon" (Thomas) ; Overture to "William Tell" (Rossini) ; Barcarolle (Offenbach) ; Soldiers' Chorus from "Faust" (Gounod) ; Grand March, Celeste Aida, from "Aida" (Verdi) ; Anvil Chorus, from "Trovatore" (Verdi) ; Soldiers Changing the Guard, Gypsy Dance, Habanera, from "Carmen" (Bizet) ; Intermezzo, from Cavalleria Rusticana (Mascagni) ; etc. *Oratorio:* I Know That My Redeemer Liveth, He Shall Feed His Flock, Hallelujah Chorus, from "Messiah" (Handel) ; Oh, Rest in the Lord, from "Elijah" (Mendelssohn).

Separate Movements from Sonata: First Movement from "Moonlight Sonata" (Beethoven) ; Allegro Molto from Sonata in A major (Mozart).

Chamber Music: Andante Cantabile (String Quartet Op. 11) (Tschaikowsky) ; Andante from "Emperor Quartet" (Haydn) ; Scherzo from "Trout Quintet" Op. 114 (Schubert) ; Rondo (Finale from Trio No. 3) (Haydn) ; Pastorale from "Christmas" Concerto Grosso No. 8 (Corelli).

Symphony: First movement from "Unfinished Symphony" (Schubert) ; Second movement from Fifth Symphony (Beethoven) ; Largo from Symphony "From the New World" (Dvorak) ; Andante from "Surprise Symphony" (Haydn) ; First, Second and Third Movements of "Toy Symphony" (Haydn) ; Third Movement (Minuet) from G minor Symphony (Mozart) ; Second Movement from Symphony No. 8 (Beethoven) ; Finale from Symphony No. 4 (Tschaikowsky) ; Finale from Symphony No. 1 (Beethoven).

For Tone Color of Instruments: In the Village (Ippolitoff-Ivanoff) (viola, English horn, oboe) ; March of Caucasian Chief (Ippolitoff-Ivanoff) (piccolo, bassoon, clarinet) ; Largo from "New World Symphony" (Dvorak) (English horn) ; Hungarian Rhapsody No. 2 (Liszt) (basses, clarinet, flute, brasses) ; Song of India (Rimsky-Korsakoff) (strings, woodwinds) ; The Moldau (Smetana) (woodwinds, strings) ; Danse de la Fee Dragee (Sugar Plum Fairy) (Tschaikowsky) (celeste, bass clarinet) ; Marche Slav (Tschaikowsky) (bassoons, double basses, oboe, brasses) ; 1812 Overture (Tschaikowsky) (orchestra bells, chimes) ; Ride of Valkyries (Wagner) (strings, piccolo, brasses) ; Largo (Handel) (orchestra and organ) ; Spanish Rhapsody (Chabrier) (orchestra, castanets) ; Spanish Serenade (Bizet) (castanets) ; Nocturne from "Midsummer Night's Dream" (Mendelssohn) (French horn) ; Overture "Mignon" (Thomas) (French horn).

Famous Composers: Bach: Minuet (Bach-Winternitz), Musette, Air for G String, Ave Maria (Bach-Gounod) ; Beethoven: Minuet in G, Moonlight Sonata (First Movement), Country Dance, Second Movement from Symphony No. 5; Liszt: Hungarian Rhapsody No. 2, Liebestraum ; Verdi: Grand March from "Aida," Anvil Chorus and Miserere from "Trovatore"; Wagner: Prelude to Act III from "Lohengrin," Pilgrims' Chorus, Song to the Evening Star from "Tannhauser," Overture to "Flying Dutchman," Ride of the Valkyries from "Valkyries"; Dvorak: Largo from "New World Symphony," Indian Lament, Humoresque, Songs My Mother Taught Me.

MUSIC FROM OTHER LANDS [1]

Russian: In the Village (Ippolitoff-Ivanoff) ; In a Three Horse Sleigh (Tschaikowsky) ; Andante Cantabile (Tschaikowsky) ; Song of the Volga Boatman.

Gypsy: Spanish Rhapsody (Chabrier) ; Hungarian Dance No. 5 (Brahms) ; Gipsy Airs (Espejo).

Italian: A Merry Life ; Santa Lucia.

English: Shepherd's Hey (Grainger) ; Pomp and Circumstance (Elgar).

Irish: Molly on the Shore (Grainger).

Norse: In the Hall of the Mountain King (Grieg) ; March of the Dwarfs (Grieg) ; Triumphal March (Grieg).

American: My Old Kentucky Home ; Old Black Joe, Massa's in de Cold, Cold Ground (Foster) ; Nobody Knows de Trouble I See, etc.

CREATIVE EXPRESSION

The spirit of creative activity seems to be especially well adapted to the field of music, because of the plasticity and direct emotional appeal of its materials. It is a natural step in the artistic growth of the child, but until recently there has been a tendency to foster and develop only the indications of unusual musical talent in the child with a disregard for the educational growth and enjoyment possible through a development of the lesser talent. Miss Beckman[2] states:

> There is a conviction in the minds of many that Mother Nature has played favorites in the endowment of her sons and daughters with crea- tive ability—yet within each of God's creatures there is at least a yearning of one kind or another. Sometimes it is buried so deep that it is almost impossible to bring it to the surface. Again it is closer to the surface and more definite, but groping for a means of expression.

The child with the lesser talent may not have a musical offering of interest to the rest of the world, but for the sake of his own individual enjoyment and educational growth he has a right to experience the glorious sense of power and achievement gained through this avenue of self expression. Just as he is encouraged to mould words into original

[1] Mabelle Glenn and Margaret Lowry. *Music Appreciation for Every Child, Intermediate Grades.* New York: Silver, Burdett and Company, 1927, p. 43.

[2] Anita T. Beckman. *Creative Activities Through Literature.* Department of Classroom Teachers, Fifth Year Book. Washington: National Education Association 1930.

ideas in poem and story, he may be stimulated to weave tones into melodic and rhythmic patterns for the articulate expression of longings and emotions not brought to the surface in the more factual activities of the curriculum, yet which are vital in determining his emotional adjustment to the bewildering demands of modern living. Frances Clark [1] believes that creative music in a true sense will inspire dreams, suggest delicate imagery, transport the listener into strange lands, and into heights of emotional delights not hitherto experienced.

Preparation of the Teacher

Many alert teachers who are feeling the need for creative music activities hesitate to experiment in this newer field, because of a feeling that only expert musicians are capable of directing these activities. Musicians themselves have been responsible in a measure for the development of this attitude, as their attention has been centered on the musical results rather than on the educational growth in terms of child experience. The development of creative activities in music within the school room has been carried on successfully by teachers with no specialized training in music or unusual native endowment.

It seems advisable, however, that the teacher undertaking creative music activities have a knowledge of the rudiments of music. Her sense of pitch should be accurate and she should have a feeling for the pulse and sway of rhythm. She needs to know something of notation and should be able to recognize simple song form, cadences, sequences, imitation, and variation. The works of Handel, Haydn, Mozart, and Schumann are easy to analyze as their form is generally simple, the rhythm regular and the balance excellent. Such books as *Music Appreciation for the Student*,[2] by Erb and *The Appreciation of Music* [3] by Welch will prove helpful to the teacher wishing to get information on the points listed. Both books are written in a straight forward, easily understood and interesting manner.

The personal equation is nowhere so important as in this field of creative activity. The teacher must be imbued with the spirit of adventure, willing to break away from the well worn path of established routine and to strike out fearlessly into the newer, less tried field where the greater joy and keener appreciation experienced will be ample reward for the effort expended. She must have confidence in her own ability; be sympathetic with the children in their first rather awkward attempts at creative effort; and above all, use common sense and tact in determining just when to stimulate creative activity and

[1] Frances Clark. "The Radio and Music Appreciation." *Music Supervisors Journal*, February, 1930.
[2] J. Lawrence Erb. *Music Appreciation for the Student*. New York: G. Schirmer, Inc., 1926.
[3] Roy Dickinson Welch. *The Appreciation of Music*. New York: Harper and Brothers, 1927.

Intermediate Grade Children Composing Original Songs

push a project to completion and when to let it drop, even though it be but half finished.

When to Engage in Creative Work

Much of the creative effort of children in the primary grades is devoted to expressing the mood of music through free rhythmic interpretation, as it is desirable to have them learn to feel the pulse and rhythm of music through the muscles of the whole body. For most of the children in the intermediate grades, however, musical impressions become more of a mental than a physical process and are expressed creatively through song and melody writing. The approach is more definite and methodical with the older children than with the primary tots. The majority of children from third grade on have had a rich experience with a great variety of type songs and have had contact with notation. They are ready to make a more serious study of composition and should use definite patterns in outlining their melodies. Unless the teacher is skillful and confident of her own ability in dealing with unexpected situations, she should have her procedure definitely worked out.

A teacher can not force her class to create melodies. There must be a strong desire on the part of the children to compose music before spontaneous and satisfactory results can be expected. The creative muse is a shy creature and must be coaxed into activity. The very word "creation" suggests something spontaneous and beautiful, something not made to order or measured by minutes. If a class is not ready to respond when the teacher suggests creative work, it must be dropped until the opportune moment arrives. The great Wagner is said to have been ashamed to accept two thousand dollars paid to him by an organization in America for writing a composition to their order to be used in some convention. He felt that the music fell far short of his standard, because he was forced to complete a prescribed musical work within a given period of time.

Any interest which has the immediate attention of the children is apt to provide stimulation for creative activity. The various seasonal holidays or some project being carried on in the classroom are generally good incentives for interesting work. The inspiration for creative writing in one sixth grade came from seeing a medieval play put on by another school. The children asked if they could write such a play and when their scenes had been worked out, they decided some incidental music would give added interest to the production. They searched through several song books and could find nothing which seemed appropriate, so they decided to write their own songs. Through this experience they were encouraged to write a number of plays, using their own music.

Children may be led to sense the importance of form and balance in music through a study of simple folk songs. Their attention should be called to the similarity and repetition found in the various phrases of the songs. There will also be some sort of dissimilar or contrasting phrase to keep the song from becoming too monotonous and to secure variety. Good examples for this sort of study are found in the following folk songs:

"Bohemian Lullaby"[1]
"All Through the Night"[2]
"The Owl and the Moon"[3]
"A Cheerful Song"[4]
"Who Has Seen My Little Maiden"[5]
"Deep in a Wood"[6]
"The Stars"[7]
"Spinning Song"[8]

[1] Thaddeus P. Giddings, and Others. *Elementary Music.* Music Education Series. Boston: Ginn and Company, 1923, p. 29.
[2] *Ibid.,* p. 2.
[3] Osbourne McConathy, and Others. *The Music Hour,* Third Book. California State Series. Sacramento: California State Department of Education, 1931, p. 26.
[4] *Ibid.,* p. 37.
[5] Robert Foresman. *Second Book of Songs.* New York: American Book Company, 1925, p. 16.
[6] *Ibid.,* p 28.
[7] Archibald T. Davidson, and Others. *A Book of Songs,* for Grades 4–6 (Concord Series No. 14). Boston: E. C. Schirmer Music Co., 1924, p. 8.
[8] *Ibid.,* p. 24.

Another interesting study is that of the motives and figures of various songs and instrumental melodies. It is the motive or theme of a composition which causes one to distinguish it from all other melodies. This motive is sometimes melodic and sometimes rhythmic, while at other times the melodic and rhythmic figures appear together. These little figures often appear in sequence with rhythmic repetition. Good examples may be found in the books listed.

Procedures for Creating Melodies

An interesting start in the creation of melodies is sometimes made by talking about famous composers, some of their well known melodies and how they wrote their tunes. The composers in their work might be compared with makers of buildings. There must be the same balance and proportion observed in the creating of music as in the designing of buildings or the painting of a picture. There are certain established rules to follow in getting this balance, an important one being a good beginning and a good ending. The birds in their nest building offer splendid examples of symmetry and balance, while their work is beautifully exact and well finished. This discussion will naturally lead to a desire for experimenting with some original work.

Again the teacher may discuss with the class the purpose for which the song is to be written, and then select a title for it. After having established the general atmosphere of the song, whether it is to be

happy or sad, fast or slow, loud or soft, the children then decide on a rhythm pattern to be used. This rhythm is tapped on the desks, next clapped and then intoned on some neutral syllable such as *loo*, with strong accent. After the rhythm is definitely established, the words for the entire song are written, different members of the class making suggestions. Bars are placed before the accents to show the measure divisions, and then melodies are suggested for the various lines of the poem.

If the class is slow and hesitant about starting a poem, the teacher might make up the first line and then call for suggestions from the class for a second line to rhyme with the first. Most of the poems will consist of four phrase stanzas as the children's natural feeling for rhythm seems to hold them to four measure phrases and four phrase stanzas in their melodic creations. Sometimes a line suggested by one of the children may be put on the board and the class decide whether or not it embodies the idea they wish to express and is well worded. When it has been altered to meet the satisfaction of the class, the rhythm may be then worked out and other lines composed to fit the same pattern. If the number of syllables in the new line do not conform to the pattern of the first line, the class may search for similes and synonyms containing the right number of syllables and they are

5th and 6th Grade Girls   Milk Song (HEALTH PLAY)   Elementary School State Teachers College Santa Barbara, Calif.

I have a cow, her milk is pure, She gives us milk that's good I'm sure, Come buy my milk, its *chorus* fresh and clean, its pure and sweet and rich with cream. with this good milk there's no-thing wrong, it makes us health-y clean and strong. We drink one quart of milk a day and I can tell you it does pay.

substituted for other words in the line. Incidentally, this plan correlates well with the English work and might be worked out during the English lesson rather than the music period. After the poem has been written the children might chant the words so as to get the rhythmic swing and then suggest music for the first line. The various suggestions could then be put on the board, the class choosing the one to be developed, perhaps changing a note or two. A discussion would then follow as to how many musical phrases would be needed and whether the second phrase could be a repetition of the first. Perhaps the words in the second line of the poem would not fit the music created for the first line, in which case there should be a variation with the repetition used later in the stanza.

A different approach might be made by using a poem of four phrases, perhaps from a familiar selection or something written by the class. The teacher could create the music to the first section of each phrase and the children make up various endings. The rhythm in the words would suggest the note values to be used. Again the first two phrases might be supplied and the children add both the third and fourth lines. Gradually they would be emboldened to write a whole four phrase song.

One way of securing good form and clearly defined pattern would be to use a well known folk song, the children supplying various original phrases to alternate with the ones already known. The old folk song *All Through the Night* is a splendid one for this purpose, as are *The*

Last Rose of Summer and *Way Down Upon the Swanee River*. Many other simple songs such as these, with decided rhythm and beauty of form, will suggest themselves to the teacher.

One class of boys seemed to be having difficulty in thinking of a tune for their poem, so the teacher discussed with them the difference between the singing and speaking voice. She pointed out that in speaking the consonants are emphasized while in singing the vowels sustain the tone and provide the flow of melody. The class then read the poem over aloud several times, the rise and fall of the voices suggesting the melody for the first phrase to one of the students. Another group could not seem to get away from the theme of a song they had finished recently. This song started with the keynote, so the teacher suggested trying the *sol-mi* combination for the new song. With this suggestion as a starting point, the children quickly responded with one of their best songs. Their recent study of musical form was reflected in the little sequences of the song, the second phrase starting with *sol-fa* and the third with *sol-sol*. (See Milk Song.)

The Addition of a Second Part

A certain proportion of the singing in the upper grades is in two and three parts. The children have become accustomed to the general line of a second part, moving as it so often does in thirds and sixths, and they will put a second part to their melodies without much effort. Some good singer in the class might be asked to sing the melody through slowly, while another child supplies a second part, something that seems to "go well" with the melody. Perhaps several different alto parts might be improvised. The teacher should have the suggestions written on the board and the class may then decide on the one they wish to add to their song.

Transferring the Melodies to Notation

All the melodies approved by the class should be written on the staff before the project is declared complete. This is not only to preserve the creative efforts of the children but also to stimulate the work in notation. The teacher herself might put the notes on the staff at the blackboard directed by the children. Some of them will not be so quick or fertile as others in suggesting original melodies and these children might be asked to help in recording the songs, so that they will feel a more integral part of the activity. Then again, each child might make his own record of the songs, the teacher checking to see that they are correctly done. When the work is put on the board, some one should be designated to make a permanent copy of each song.

One method for transferring the melodies into notation, used in the Francis W. Parker School of Chicago, suggests that the children use cards containing notes of different values with which to arrange their own melodies in the rhythmic pattern. This plan gives each child a tactual experience with notes and makes the transfer to the staff a simple matter. Another teacher suggests a discussion with the children to determine the scale syllable on which the song begins. They then decide whether it starts on a strong or weak beat and are left to work out the rest of the problem individually, adding the title of the song and the name of the author of the words. A third plan is to put the staff on the board and write the words below it. As the class sings the song through with a strong accent, the teacher draws a bar before each accented word. The class repeats the song while the teacher puts notes with small heads on the staff. The unit of the beat is then determined, the signature placed, and the proper note values given. Still another plan for transferring the song to notation is to find the highest and lowest notes in the song and let the class decide where these notes should be placed on the staff in order to be easily within the proper voice range. The syllable names of the notes are then determined and the key fixed accordingly. The children might try out several keys in order to find the most suitable one if they are not sure just where the range of the song should be. If, during the writing of the song, a problem in musical theory should arise, which is in advance of the course of study, there need be no hesitancy in using it. The time to explain and make use of the technicalities of music is when the need for their use arises.

The following illustration serves to show how one fourth grade [1] composed an original Thanksgiving hymn to use on their Harvest program. The children decided that each of them should write a verse. These were read aloud and Roger's verse was chosen as the one most suitable for the occasion. This verse was then put on the board, criticized and changed slightly to suit the ideas of the group, and then was brought to the music class to be set to music:

> For food, for home, for loving care;
> For peace we're having everywhere;
> For our dear country brave and strong
> We're thankful all year long.

The whole class repeated the first line aloud several times to get the rhythmic swing of the words, and then the teacher asked the children to close their eyes and think the words over and over until they seemed to sing themselves into a little tune. When a tune came to a child he raised his hand and when the teacher came to him he hummed it to her

[1] Fourth Grade, Jefferson School, Santa Barbara, California.

softly, so as not to disturb the rest of the class. Some of the melodies
suggested for the first line were:

5 8 2 3 1 2 1 6
5 8 5 8 5 3 2 1
5 8 5 6 5 8 5 6
3 5 3 2 3 4 3 1 2

It is interesting to note that although no child heard another's
melody while they were being thought out, three of the examples given
begin with the same two notes. The teacher jotted the suggestions down
on the board as they were given to her, and then sang them over several
times to the children. The first example was liked the best by the
majority of the children, so it was selected for the first line of the song.
The teacher then asked the class to sing the line several times, suggesting
that anyone who could go right on and sing music to fit the second line
of the verse might do so. Suggestions were recorded as before, and a
second line chosen. At first the second line was just like the first, but
one child objected to it because, as he expressed it, "it goes over and
over like a record when the needle sticks." When the third line was
first suggested it ended down instead of up, "making the song sound
finished when there was still another line," according to one child's
criticism. With the third line ending up, it was an easy step to bring
the last line down to *do.*

THANKSGIVING SONG – *Fourth Grade*

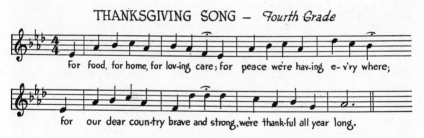

For food, for home, for lov-ing care; for peace we're hav-ing e-v'ry where;

for our dear coun-try brave and strong, we're thank-ful all year long.

After having sung the song through several times, the children
asked if it might be written on a staff on the board so that each one
could make a copy to keep. The teacher then put a staff on the board,
had the children decide which notes of the song were on *do,* and from
that start syllabilize the whole song. They found that the highest note
was *fa,* and the lowest one was *sol* below *do,* a range of about an octave,
and then decided to have *sol* on *e,* the first line of the staff, and *fa* on
d above. This put *do* on *a,* which would put the song in the key of A.
When deciding on the signature the children seemed to prefer the key
of A flat rather than that having three sharps. One of the children
put the signature on the staff and another one placed dots on the lines
and spaces as the class again sang the syllables. Next the children
decided that the first accent came after the first note, so a bar was drawn

and the time quickly determined as being four quarter notes to each measure.   They were puzzled for a bit when they realized that they wanted to pause on the words *care, where,* and *strong,* but could only use a quarter note on each word in order to keep the accent right, until someone finally remembered the use of the hold in this need.   The desire for a permanent record of their original song furnished the teacher with a splendid chance to show the children a practical need for a knowledge of the lines and spaces of the staff, key signatures, note values and measure divisions.

INSTRUMENTAL MUSIC

Need for Instrumental Experience

The voice is the most universal instrument by means of which varying shades of emotional feeling may be expressed, and singing is the most natural and spontaneous avenue for this expression, adaptable to even the small child's limitations.   In the intermediate grades, however, this form of musical expression may be augmented or superseded by instrumental experience with those children who seem to show a special aptitude or desire for this sort of activity, and who may find in the playing of an instrument a greater opportunity for self expression than in singing.   This is especially true of those children who have

Courtesy of Oakland City Schools

Fifth Grade Boys Making Their Own Marimbas

not been blessed with pleasing voices or who have difficulty reproducing melody vocally and yet have a keenness of ear and a sense of rhythm adequate for performance on an instrument. The orchestral instrument rather than the voice thus becomes the means through which to translate the beauty of music into a real experience in the life of the child. Through his instrument he becomes the maker of music and is free to feel the joy of creative experience denied him in the field of vocal expression.

Selection of Instruments

Dykema[1] suggests that piano, string, wood, and brass wind classes should begin in the fifth grade and continue through the grades and high school. Some schools, however, have had good results in fourth grade, especially with the piano classes. Children are generally admitted to these classes without any previous experience, and are usually required to furnish their own instruments. Educators are beginning to realize, however, that the children incapable of expressing themselves adequately in song have a right to free education in another field of musical expression, and many schools are furnishing instruments to those children not able to buy their own, for a minimum yearly or semester rental. Children wishing to join the orchestra should be examined by some one qualified to pass judgment as to their lung capacity and the shape of their lips, teeth, and fingers, with a recommendation of the instrument best suited to their individual qualifications. Because of their popular use, most children seem to want to learn to play the cornet or the saxophone, but through this method of examination many may be encouraged to study some of the less popular instruments which are necessary to the well balanced orchestra as well as interesting and enjoyable in themselves.

The different instruments should be taught in separate classes until the children become fairly sure of the fingering and tone production and are able to play simple scale and melodic passages, then they may be combined into an orchestra.

Selection of Music

Only the best music should be used in the orchestra, whatever its state of development may be. The practice followed in many school orchestras of playing nothing but cheap marches and waltzes under the delusion that they must be used because of their simplicity and rhythmic appeal is very much to be deplored. Some of the most charming music of Handel, Mozart, Beethoven, Schumann, and other such composers may be secured in simple enough arrangements to meet

---

[1] Peter W. Dykema. *Music for Public School Administrators.* New York: Bureau of Publications, Teachers College, Columbia University, 1931.

the needs of even beginning orchestras. Many folk songs and dances lend themselves to interesting orchestral arrangements. Children should be led to expect and desire only the best of instrumental music in their orchestral experience. Any reputable music publisher will furnish the teacher with names of collections containing this type of music. The teacher should not be too ambitious to play difficult music. The technical and esthetic satisfaction to be derived from a simple classic, well played, is infinitely better than the ambitious but unsatisfactory attempts to play music too difficult technically and too involved emotionally for the child's understanding. The writer remembers attending a music festival where the playing of an all-city fifth and sixth grade orchestra was much more pleasing and impressive than that of the junior high school, simply because the music for the grade orchestra consisted of simple classics which were well played tonally and rhythmically, with precision of attack and release, while the junior high school ensemble attempted music more suitable for high school performance. Though the attempt was heroic, the result was inferior in tone quality, accuracy of pitch, and technique. The children themselves must have been conscious that their work was not well done, and consequently they must have felt a sense of failure and dissatisfaction, a condition which is pedagogically and psychologically unsound.

Qualifications for Directing Instrumental Classes

In most city systems there is a special music teacher to take charge of the instrumental classes and to direct the orchestra. It sometimes happens, however, especially in rural districts, that the regular classroom teacher is called upon to undertake this activity. In order to direct instrumental groups it is necessary that the teacher have an accurate sense of pitch and time and some interpretive ability. She should know how to tune both string and wind instruments, and should understand fingering and bowing. If the classroom teacher feels it necessary that she undertake to direct an orchestra and cannot play any instrument herself, she should take enough lessons from a reputable teacher on both string and wind instruments to enable her to understand the fundamental points listed above. This being impossible, she will find the study of a good text book on instruments helpful. Should the children be allowed to constantly play on instruments which are out of tune, using wrong positions and fingering, the instrumental experience is productive of far more harm than good. In such cases it would be wiser to eliminate instrumental experience from the classroom! The teacher does not necessarily need to be a proficient player herself, but she must understand the method of playing each instrument used.

If in the beginning of the children's instrumental experience the teacher is able to arrange simple parts for violin, clarinet, and so forth, to some of the songs and folk tunes already familiar to them, she will be able to furnish them with much satisfaction and pleasure. The sense of cooperation and unity gained through even very small instrumental groups is an important part of every instrumentalist's musical education, and cannot be started too early in his musical experience.

Integration With Other Curricular Activities

The music period will be a greater joy to the child and his music will become a more rich and vital part of his individual experience if it is made to function definitely as a real part of his other curricular activities. This correlation will serve not only to give greater meaning to the music period, but also vitalize and enrich the other activities.

Music and Physical Education

Correlation between music and physical education is obvious. This is evidenced in folk dancing, natural dancing, pageantry, singing games, gymnastic activities, and often in athletic training. Many of man's physical activities have been performed with some type of music throughout the period of recorded history.

Music and Art

Drawings might be made to illustrate the texts of songs, and copies of famous pictures used to help develop mood and atmosphere in connection with phonograph records.

The picture of the *Loggia of the Vatican* which was painted under the direction of Raphael is a beautiful illustration of balance, proportion, and unity. Such pictures make the conception of form in music more clear to the child. *The Mill,* painted by Hobbema, *In the Gloaming,* by Buttersack, and *A Landscape,* by Crome, are good examples of serene beauty, and might be used with such records as *To a Wild Rose,* by MacDowell, *Melody in F,* by Rubinstein, and others of the same type. The Colonial Art Company [1] has inexpensive copies of many paintings and pictures of musicians, and a perusal of their catalogue might prove helpful. *Apollo,* [2] a well illustrated manual of the history of art throughout the ages, is also good reference material.

Music and the Social Studies

Perhaps the greatest opportunity for definite integration will be found in the social studies, forming as they do the core of the whole intermediate grade program. Here the teacher has a splendid chance to make the children vividly conscious of the customs, emotions, and

[1] The Colonial Art Company, 1336 North West First Street, Oklahoma City.
[2] S. Reinach. *Apollo.* New York: Charles Scribner's Sons, 1924.
30—17050

Courtesy of Oakland City Schools

**Fourth Grade Pupils Using Homemade Tom-Toms to Accompany a
Class Singing Indian Songs**

aspirations of other peoples through an acquaintance with their folk
songs and dances which so truly reflect their everyday life. When
developing a unit on California, for instance, a much more intimate
picture of the gaiety, the spontaneity, the warm-hearted hospitality,
and the love for dancing and singing prevalent among the Spanish
and Mexican people can be gained by singing and listening to their
music than by much discussion and reading about their habits. The
children will feel an added thrill and interest in their study if they
are allowed to sing some of the songs in Spanish. The graceful, flowing melodies seem to demand the soft consonants and liquid beauty of
vowel elision found in the Spanish language. The classified index of
The Music Hour, Intermediate Teacher's Book,[1] of the Foresman *Books
of Songs*,[2] and the *Song Source Material for the Activity Curriculum*[3]
will be found most helpful with suggestions for songs suitable for the
development of the various social study units. *The American Song-*

[1] Osbourne McConathy, and Others. *Intermediate Teacher's Book* (Music Hour
Series) California State Series. Sacramento: California State Department of Education, 1931.
[2] Robert Foresman. *Books of Songs*. New York: American Book Company.
[3] Frances Wright and Laverna L. Lossing. *Song Source Material for the
Activity Curriculum*. New York: Teachers College, Columbia University, 1932.

bag[1] is rich in material for use with any unit on American life from the pioneer days to the present. The following additional material has been found useful by the writer.

SPANISH AND MEXICAN UNIT

HAGUE, ELEANOR. *Early Spanish-Californian Folk Songs*, arranged by Gertrude Ross. New York: J. Fischer and Brother, 1922.
FARWELL, ARTHUR. *Spanish Songs of Old California*, collected and translated by Charles F. Lummis. New York: G. Schirmer, Inc., 1929.

INDIAN UNIT

The Land of the Sky Blue Water, *Cadman*.
By the Waters of Minnetonka, *Lieurance*.
Pale Moon, *Logan*.

WESTERN PLAINS UNIT

LOMAX, JOHN A. *Cowboy Songs*. New York: The Macmillan Company, 1922.
ALLEN, JULES V. *Cowboy Lore*. San Antonio, Texas: Naylor Printing Company, 1933.
LARKIN, MARGARET. *The Singing Cowboy*. New York: Alfred A. Knopf, Inc., 1931.

The following groups are suggestive of the manner in which songs may be used for various class activities. The songs may be tied together to form a unit with a thread of dialogue developed from the social studies program so as to give glimpses into the lives and customs of a particular people. These groups make interesting material for school assemblies and parent-teacher programs.

THE SOUTHERN NEGRO AT HOME (Fifth and Sixth Grades)

"Way Down Upon the Swanee River." McConathy, Osbourne, and Others. *Music Hour Series*, Fifth Book. New York: Silver, Burdett and Company, 1928.
"Carry Me Back to Old Virginny." *Twice 55 Community Songs; The Green Book*. Boston: C. C. Birchard and Company.
"Swing Low, Sweet Chariot." McConathy, Osbourne, and Others. *Music Hour Series*, Fifth Book. New York: Silver, Burdett and Company, 1928.
"All God's Chillun Got Wings." Newell, George. *Girl Scout Song Book*. New York: Girl Scouts Inc., 1929.
"One More River to Cross." Newell, George. *Girl Scout Song Book*. New York: Girl Scouts Inc., 1929.
"Waterboy," Avery Robinson (sheet music).
"Deep River." *Twice 55 Community Songs; The Green Book*. Boston: C. C. Birchard and Company.
"Nobody Knows de Trouble I See." *Twice 55 Community Songs; The Green Book*. Boston: C. C. Birchard and Company.
"Old Black Joe." McConathy, Osbourne, and Others. *Music Hour Series*, Fifth Book. New York: Silver, Burdett and Company, 1928.

THE GYPSY TRAIL (Fifth and Sixth Grades)

"The Gypsy Trail." Giddings, T. P., and Others. *Intermediate Music*. Music Education Series. Boston: Ginn and Company, 1928.

---

[1] Carl Sandburg. *The American Songbag*. New York: Harcourt, Brace and Company, 1930.

"The Spanish Gypsy." Giddings, T. P., and Others. *Two Part Music*. Music Education Series. Boston: Ginn and Company, 1927.

"The Gypsy Dancers." Giddings, T. P., and Others. *Intermediate Music*. Music Education Series. Boston: Ginn and Company, 1928.

"The Bolero." McConathy, Osbourne, and Others. *The Music Hour*, Fifth Book. California State Series. Sacramento: California State Department of Education, 1931.

"Song of the Plain." Foresman, Robert. *Fifth Book of Songs*. New York: American Book Co.

"The Gypsy Seer." Giddings, T. P., and Others. *Two Part Music*. Music Education Series. Boston: Ginn and Company, 1927.

"Just Like a Gypsy," from "The Fortune Teller," by Victor Herbert.

IN THE FAIRIES COURT (Fourth and Fifth Grades)

This program was developed from a study of the countries of Europe, the songs listed being combined with folk dances of the countries chosen for the program. The play opens with a boy and girl on their way home from school. They sit down to rest, and tell each other how interesting it would be to go to all the countries about which they have been reading. They fall asleep and are taken by the dream fairy to the fairies' court where people of the various nations are called in to sing and dance for them. At the close of the program the singers and dancers all disappear and the children wake to continue on their way home.

PROGRAM

France

"La Belle Demoiselle." Giddings, T. P., and Others. *Intermediate Music*. Music Education Series. Boston: Ginn and Company, 1928.

"Are You Sleeping?" McConathy, Osbourne, and Others. *Music Hour Series*, Fourth Book. New York: Silver, Burdett and Company.

Spain

"Mandolin Song." Foresman, Robert. *Fourth Book of Songs*. New York: American Book Co.

China

"Flower of China." Foresman, Robert. *Fifth Book of Songs*. New York: American Book Co.

"The Jasmine Flower." *The Music Hour*, Third Book. California State Series. Sacramento: California State Department of Education, 1931.

Russia

"The Volga Boat Song." Foresman, Robert. *Fifth Book of Songs*. New York: American Book Company.

"Cossack Dance." McConathy, Osbourne, and Others. *The Music Hour*, Third Book. California State Series. Sacramento: California State Department of Education, 1931.

Indian

"Wah Wah Tay See." Foresman, Robert. *Fourth Book of Songs*. New York: American Book Company.

"Nai-No-Otz." McConathy, Osbourne, and Others. *The Music Hour*, Fourth Book. New York: Silver, Burdett and Company.

American
"The Minuet." Parker, H. W. and Others. *Progressive Music Series*, Book 3.
New York: Silver, Burdett and Company.

BIBLIOGRAPHY

COFFIN, LENORA, AND OTHERS. *Report of the Sub-Committee on Music for the
First Six Grades.* Ithaca, N. Y., Music Supervisors National Conference,
1930 Year Book, pp. 229-245.
ERB, J. LAWRENCE. *Music Appreciation for the Student.* New York: G. Schirmer,
Inc., 1926.
GEHRKENS, KARL W. *Music in the Grade Schools.* Boston: C. C. Birchard and
Company, 1933.
GLENN, MABELLE, AND LOWRY, MARGARET. *Music Appreciation for Every Child,*
(Intermediate Grades, Teachers' Manual). New York: Silver, Burdett and
Company, 1927.
KINSCELLA, HAZEL G. *Music and Romance.* Camden, N. J., R. C. A. Victor Company, 1930.
KWALWASSER, JACOB. *Problems in Public School Music.* New York: M. Witmark
and Sons, 1932.
MCCONATHY, OSBOURNE, AND OTHERS. *Intermediate Teachers Book* (Music Hour
Series). California State Series. Sacramento: California State Department
of Education, 1931.
MURSELL, JAMES, AND GLENN, MABELLE. *Psychology of Public School Music.*
New York: Silver, Burdett and Company, 1931.
NORTON, ALMA. *Teaching School Music.* University of Southern California, Los
Angeles: C. C. Crawford, 1932.
SANDBURG, CARL. *The American Songbag.* New York: Harcourt, Brace and
Company, 1927.
WELCH, ROY D. *The Appreciation of Music.* New York: Harper and Brothers,
1927.
WRIGHT, FRANCES, AND LOSSING, LAVERNA L. *Song Source Material for the
Activity Curriculum.* New York: Teachers College, Columbia University, 1932.

Chapter XXI

ART [1]

PURPOSE AND SCOPE OF ART INSTRUCTION

The purpose of teaching art is to help people to derive pleasure from the act of seeing, to know the exhilaration that is inherent in the act of creating, and to enjoy the independence that comes with the ability to make one's own decisions in all matters in which art qualities are concerned. It is the responsibility of the school to help people to see, to create, and to appreciate.

Seeing

Eyes help us with the routine of living. With their aid we earn our livelihood, we find our way about, we read the billboards and the newspapers. Only a few of us, however, take the time to marvel at the world that we see through these eyes. We go sight-seeing by car, rail, or plane; we absorb, through quick glances, an infinitesimal part of what we pass by. In our haste and blindness we fail to see around us the miracles that could color our lives and personalities. Those few persons who do take time to cultivate the art of seeing discover a source of lasting pleasure which the rest of humanity completely overlooks.

We appreciate the value of a language in enabling us to converse with one another. When we travel in a foreign country, we are convinced that the command of several spoken languages is most desirable. We realize, nevertheless, that a knowledge of even six or seven languages cannot bring us into contact with all of the people of the world, nor can it help us to converse with the inanimate things about us—the trees, the flowers, the hills. The fine art of significant seeing demands the use, and therefore the knowledge, of another language. A beautiful thing speaks to us in this language in terms more stimulating than the spoken word. It speaks to the Egyptian and the Japanese, to the German and the Frenchman, in the same terms; if it is understood by them, it can unite them all through a common admiration and devotion. We use this language ourselves when we live beautifully; when we make ourselves attractive; when we give our patronage to the fine and the beautiful in any field of our civilization, whether it be the theatre, literature, music, art, or any of the kindred forms; when, in a foreign

[1] Contributed by Ella Moen, Fresno State College, with editorial assistance by Frances Robert Nugent, Los Angeles. The section on Industrial Arts was contributed by Ethel I. Salisbury, Associate Professor of Elementary Education, University of California at Los Angeles, and Educational Consultant, Santa Monica Public Schools.

land, even though ignorant of the language, we silently show our admiration by noticing, by contemplating joyfully, and by respecting the beauty that we find; when we make some spot on earth more beautiful than it was before, or when we show respect for the beautiful in nature by conserving and increasing what is already there.

The one common constructive bond of all the people of all the ages seems to have been some degree of love for what is beautiful. By an intensification of this attitude, by the development of a sincere respect and protective veneration for beauty even when it is expressed with an accent different from our own, we could prevent the destruction by war, neglect, and ignorance of some of the world's most valuable possessions.

In a lecture, William John Cooper, former United States Commissioner of Education, compared the present use of our libraries with that of our art galleries. During the depression, although the libraries of the country have increased their circulation sixty-seven per cent, art galleries have shown no great increase in attendance. This disparity was due, he thought, to the relative preparation given in our schools for the enjoyment of the two institutions. People with a good deal of leisure time at their disposal can now enjoy our libraries, for they have learned to read at school; not so many, as we well know, have learned there the universal language which is used in the art of all countries. The only way to learn this language is to use it. It is doubtful whether a person has really seen a place, or an object, or a quality, until he has tried to put into concrete form with words, paint, or other vehicle his feeling about that place, object, or quality. For this reason, many people say that the road to real appreciation is through creation.

Creating

General progress in our civilization is dependent upon inventiveness. In the field of art, inventiveness is replaced by creative imagination. Only through the exercise of this creative imagination can the art of any country flourish. The students who become producing artists should be able, through their creative ability, to advance the art of their time, instead of merely to restate the art of the past. The rest of the students should become intelligent consumers, supporting genuine artists (architects, furniture designers, textile designers, as well as painters) who will keep our art developing and truly expressive of our age. They should all, artists and consumers alike, be able to apply their creative abilities to their own and to community art problems.

What are the ways of stimulating creative imagination? Certainly not through dictation, or by the use of formula, can the rare quality of individual creation be evoked as part of a child's habitual expression.

The following paragraph by Miss Sallie B. Tannahill illustrates the futility of copying:[1]

> Slavish reproduction or imitation of another's work has little value as an art experience for children. Copying, without constructive thought, tends to deaden the creative sense, leads to a dull, lifeless kind of expression, hinders initiative, and develops little or no art sensitivity. No true art has ever resulted from copying. Art expression demands activity of mind; to be told step by step just what to do, to draw exactly what forty other children are attempting to draw at the same time and in the same way, requires little thought or feeling. The whole process is mechanical, lacking in any value from the point of view of art. . . . No art, either fine or industrial, can result from motions of the hand unless those motions are accompanied by creative thinking and feeling.

Many years ago, Emerson stressed the need for independent thought in his essay, *Self-reliance*, in which he says, "A man should learn to detect and watch that gleam of light that flashes across his mind from within, more than the firmament of bards and sages." Suggestions for promoting creativeness in the classroom may be found in the *Teachers' Guide to Child Development*.[2]

We should be able to feel, when we have looked at the work of forty different children, or when we have seen a collection of paintings by forty different artists, that we have met and talked with forty distinctly different personalities. All too often this impression is not gained. Many exhibits are full of uninteresting, painstaking pictures, made, like the druggist's pills, according to a formula. The artist endangers no one if he takes liberties with accepted formulas. In spite of this fact, many artists are just as afraid of deviating from current formulas as are the druggists. Not only painters, but also architects and even shoe designers cling steadfastly to approved conceptions. If we really believe that art must be personal, then a painting which is merely a mechanically accurate recording of some spot in nature is not creative work. A description of a house, in terms of the numbers of rooms and numbers of windows, of the brand of roofing and wall materials, and of other details of interest to the contractor—such a description as this is far less significant to us than one which, making no effort to enumerate for purposes of identification, gives instead the spirit of the place in so striking a fashion that a lasting impression is made on us. In the same way, a painting which is an interpretation of life rather than a realistic representation of it, and which has spontaneity, freedom, and daring boldness of treatment rather than meticulous, dull delineation of uninteresting detail, will give pleasure. A child will paint symbolically with verve and dash and joy if the teacher does not force him to do otherwise.

[1] Sallie B. Tannahill. *Fine Arts for Public School Administrators*. New York: Bureau of Publications, Teachers College, Columbia University, 1932, pp. 2-3.
[2] *Teachers' Guide to Child Development*. Compiled by the State Curriculum Commission. Sacramento: California State Department of Education, 1930, pp. 360-65.

Courtesy of San Diego City Schools

Creative Art Stimulates Imagination

Appreciating and Enjoying

A group of persons were listening to some records. When some Chinese music was introduced, many in the group laughed so loudly that those who were eager to hear were unable to do so. Those who laughed were so amused at the strange sounds that they made no real attempt to listen or to understand. Similarly, a large number of people, when confronted by the unfamiliar in art, in literature, in countries, in personalities, never go beyond the first stage, amusement. They are suspicious of and prepared to dislike a different race, a stranger, or a new line of thought. In order to enjoy, we must understand. In order to understand, we must take time to consider other points of view. Although international understanding seems to be still beyond reach, great interest can be developed in a country whose art one has learned to admire. Some individuals claim that the material in museums is dead, and that we should be interested primarily in the art that is being introduced around us today. No one should advocate a thoughtless worship of the past; everyone, on the other hand, should recognize the point of entry into the spirit and philosophy of an age that is offered in its art. The danger of worshipping the art of the past lies in our tendency to imitate what we worship; the benefits to be derived from the study of the art of various civilizations consist partly in a growing respect for races other than our own, and partly in less complacency over the art accomplishments of our own country.

The ability to appreciate and to create not only is the basis for more sane and satisfying production of art in this country, but also is the best of prepartion for leisure. Since in all probability people will be retiring from the active business of earning a living at an earlier age than ever before, surely they should be making some intelligent preparation for the last twenty or thirty years of their lives. Leisure hours should be looked forward to as a means of enriching one's life. People with art training get more from their environments, find a greater number of enriching experiences, and develop more natural and significant outlets for those experiences, than do the men and women without such art training.   As a result, their characters and personalities grow stronger and finer.[1]

Fields Covered by the Study of Art

There is a good deal of misunderstanding as to just what problems and questions come within the realm of art.   The following situations, which may be extremely unfortunate in their outcomes, occur because of the popular unawareness of what decisions should legitimately be made either by an artist or by one well-versed in art standards.

1. Repainting the school building. The attractiveness of the building is enhanced by the selection of paint of appropriate color. The teacher may advise in this regard. If the suggestion is tactfully made, it will usually be welcomed. The redecoration of a school building can frequently be based on practical plans developed by the children as an art project under the teacher's guidance.

2. Building new equipment for the classrooms. Cabinets, tables, shelves, and other extra articles are frequently built without consideration for their proportions or the relationship of their shapes to the spaces they are to occupy. The plans for these pieces might well be approved by the art instructor or supervisor before construction begins.

3. Buying accessories for the school building and grounds. In practically every school, minor additions are made from time to time to the physical equipment of the buildings and grounds. Trees and shrubbery are placed, gates built, curtains bought for classrooms and rugs for offices, changes made in the buildings, and innumerable other things done without due consideration of the art principles involved. Decisions made on the basis of art judgments—decisions which may greatly increase the functional as well as the art merit of the things in question—should occur as a matter of course.

---

[1] A more complete discussion of the reasons for teaching appreciation is presented in the section, Objectives in Teaching Art, pp. 482–491.

4. Selection of class gifts to the school. Many ugly, useless things have been given to schools by persons unable to select wisely. If money is to be spent for sculpture, pictures, and furniture, why should there not be a consultation with the principal about what is needed, and with the art instructor about the character, shape, size, and color of such gifts? Even though the final decision may rest with the teacher, all of these matters should be discussed with the children.

5. Planning the school annual. Both the cover design and the layout of pages for the annual are often turned over to engravers and printers. These art problems should be worked out by students of the school if they are to be representative of the school. The selection of binding materials, cover designing, layout of pages, selection of photographs, selection of type, and any other problems related to the appearance of the book should be worked out under the supervision of the art teacher.

Inasmuch as attractive surroundings help to develop good taste, the art teacher should be consulted about any changes to be made in the surroundings.

Significance of the Social Values of Art

Although the decisions involved in school situations may seem to be of relatively small importance, they really signify much of what may happen on a much larger scale in the city and state government. If the children are aided to appreciate the increased satisfaction resulting from a choice esthetically sound as well as practically acceptable, they may later be influential in remedying some of the unhappy situations that constantly occur in public affairs. People who know nothing about art are often the ones who, when some spot is to be beautified, manage to have their ideas carried out. To many untrained in art, beautifying means ornamenting, decorating with superficial adornments, rather than the refining of proportion in structural parts and the careful use of harmonious embellishment in form and color. As a result, cities abound in buildings with false fronts and false decorations. There should be art commissions in each city to control the architecture and the other factors which make up its appearance. And, until a public educated to realize the value of art authority is finally developed, there can be no effective cooperation. The social values of art lie in the voluntary contribution of each individual of his own measure of taste to the leadership of trained artists in all fields.[1]

---

[1] The numerous art problems that confront every individual are discussed under Art Activities and Discussion Topics for Social Studies, pp. 466–481.

The Teacher's Directly Controlled Field

Every teacher has under her direct control two fields or channels of artistic development for the pupils in her classes. The first field is concerned with the external factors of the room environment; that is, with the teacher's own appearance from day to day, and with the appearance of the classroom from day to day. The second bears on the type of thinking in relation to art that the children do under the teacher's conscious or unconscious guidance; that is, on their perception of the validity of their art problems, and their understanding of the fundamental art qualities involved in the immediate and the associated questions that arise from their class experiences.

External Factors of the Room Environment

Personal taste of the teacher. Angelo Patri in one of his syndicated newspaper articles says:

> Children note the details of the teacher's dress and these stay with them. They become standards for the children when they are good. They become pivots upon which to hang personal dislike when they are not good.

If the classroom walls could be lined with mirrors for a week, the teacher would be convinced in half that time that attractive costuming and careful grooming makes up her first real personal responsibility as an art teacher. In this imaginary situation, she would have suffered with the children if the effect of her clothes were not pleasing. A full-length mirror in the home of every teacher would help the development of art appreciation in the schools. An immaculate person whose costume is an inspiration to the children will create an impression and exert an influence whose effects will still be growing long after most of what that teacher said has been forgotten. The ability to judge the effect of one's own costume, to evaluate properly the appearance of the classroom, to recognize other art qualities besides neatness in judging a student's work—such ability on the part of the teacher requires taste, feeling, an understanding of art theories, and a growing familiarity with art in general. The time still spent by some teachers in making hectographed designs for the children to fill in with color, or in drawing animal patterns for the children to trace, or in making stencils for the borders of blackboards, might be much better spent on self-improvement. That person is valuable as an art teacher who not only reads the best books and magazines on art, but also spends some time in painting, modeling, and designing for his own pleasure. Designing can mean the arrangement of objects or materials of any kind in terms of line, color, and pattern, whether the scale be that of a garden or of the objects on a mantel.

Appearance of the classroom. The next responsibility of the art teacher lies in the field of equipment and materials. No construction work or painting can be carried on smoothly in a limited space. Furniture should be moved around until there is plenty of room for large sheets of paper, for paint jars, and for children moving about freely. The teacher needs to see that each child has sufficient materials to work with, that they are accessible, that larger equipment is conveniently arranged—in short, that all working conditions be as favorable as possible. The schoolroom should be a stimulating place in which to work. When it is attractive, it exerts the same influence over a child that a carefully costumed teacher does. In art it is especially true that appreciation can be developed more effectively by example than by words. The responsibility for the room, of course, must be shared with the children.

It has been obvious for a long time that sympathy and encouragement are necessary parts of a child's working conditions. The teacher whose taste is sufficiently well developed to permit him to feel as well as to wonder about the work of his children has a great advantage over the one who is uncertain in his own appreciation. It is much easier for the teacher to be enthusiastic about a child's painting if he knows enough about art qualities to recognize all that are actually present there. In even the poorest work there is to be found some one quality which can be developed by commendation and interest. It is the art teacher's responsibility to find that quality.

Guided Thinking About Art

The many difficulties and genuine art problems that arise in the classroom no longer call for only the teacher's solution. With the children, the teacher must approach and solve them. Isolated principles, remote from significant practice, like dictated lessons have vanished from the modern classroom. The following examples of guided thinking link the teacher and the pupil in a joint attack on the challenges that meet them.

Teaching art principles through purposeful activities. Art teachers have been criticized for teaching, year after year, a set list of art problems which bear no relationship whatsoever to other activities going on in the classroom. Many of them still teach autumn leaves for the first week of school, Thanksgiving posters for Thanksgiving, block alphabets for the fourth week, perspective for the twelfth week, and so on. A teacher in an untidy room cannot urge children to apply their art to their own lives and their own homes, and ignore the environment that she is permitting in the school. The art teacher is always preaching against ugliness. What of the students who leave everything where they finish with it, feeling no further responsibility for materials or room? What of the "sore spots" in the room—spots which the teacher becomes so accustomed to overlooking that she does so without remembering why? A multitude of such vague, guilty feelings as these about desk-tops, files, shelves, cupboards, bulletin boards, and unfinished construction work in every corner can make a person feel very unhappy. There is no reason why homes may not have the efficiency of offices where everything is filed away systematically and where one can in a few seconds put his finger on anything he needs. Construction supplies in school could profitably be organized under a similar system. The pupil's interest in sorting and labeling should be utilized.

Courtesy of Alameda County Schools

In the Modern School Some Problem in Construction Is Always Under Way

Two teachers once took their classes to hear a concert in Hollywood Bowl. The next day, one class drew all the instruments which they had seen. The other class discussed the things that had impressed them on the evening before. One boy told how he had admired the rapidity with which the thousands of cars parked around the bowl were on their way within five minutes after the concert was over. The people and the cars all disappeared in an orderly, quiet, and efficient manner. All of this comment led the children to a discussion of order in all things. The children, of their own accord, decided that a good art problem would be cleaning their own art cupboards and then planning a system for them. The plan was carried out with enthusiasm. It should not take very much self- and class-discipline to keep cupboards orderly and paint jars washed. The children may be led to see that the chairs, dishes, newspapers, working tools, and supplies of all kinds might be considered the materials which they juggle around to produce their pictures. They can create a harmony with those materials, instead of with pigment, that is just as capable of giving pleasure as is the picture. They may learn to get joy from these seemingly ordinary activities if they can anticipate the satisfactions that lie in the results.

Courtesy of San Diego City Schools

A Trip Around the World to Find Out How Other People Live

Integration. Integrating art with the rest of the school program does away with the artificial art problems and the untimely bringing in of drill exercises—especially formal perspective and some of the too numerous color charts. Art lessons never getting any farther than the paper need no longer be forced on disinterested children. The teacher need not spend time planning different problems each day for the art period—problems sure to produce finished looking specimens which the mothers will approve. There need be no more sorry attempts to hold the quick students in check during a dictation lesson while the slow ones catch up with the directions.   There need be no more monotonous exhibitions on the walls, with each piece exactly like its neighbor.   The art problems naturally grow out of the rest of the school program if the children feel the presence of problems which need some art help for their solution.   Since, in the modern school, something is always being constructed, there are plenty of art problems found in the placing of the work in the school room, in choosing the colors for the object, and in relating them to the rest of the colors in the room.

Oftentimes, when the art studies grow out of the class interest in a particular country or age, children are encouraged to copy the designs and forms of its pottery or weaving or other art expressions. Too much copying may lead the group to feel that the copying is in itself an art.   Copying in composition is recognized for what it is; copying in art is frequently rewarded with prizes.   A painting that is a direct imitation of another's work may receive a prize at a county fair; an honest piece of child-work next to it may pass unnoticed because the subject matter is not easily figured out.

Whenever any object is made in the class, the child who creates it should be helped to consider whether the article can be used for the purpose it is meant to serve, whether its shape is as good as it can be, and whether it really needs some decoration.   Every child needs to do some thinking of his own in art as well as in arithmetic.   Just the arrangement of the classroom and the construction problems carried out for the social studies provide dozens of genuine art problems for the children.

An outlet for emotional urge.   Although art functions effectively in connection with the social studies program, it serves an equally fundamental purpose in child development by serving as an outlet for an emotional urge.   Art has a two fold function; it is a hand-maiden to all fields and is a means of expressing beauty for its own sake.   It is a purposeful activity to recreate a fleeting vision of a beautiful bit of landscape, to record the memory of an exquisite mood in music, or express in clay a beautiful form.   Children should be encouraged in these individual expressions of thought and emotion.   The child gifted in art will probably be discovered by such a procedure.

Decoration and beauty.   The art teacher says that anything that is made must, when it is finished, look as attractive as possible.   Many people interpret that statement to mean that everything must be decorated.   Do ribbons, feathers, and flowers placed on hats necessarily improve the appearance of them?   Does a dress, in order to be beautiful, have to be trimmed with a lot of buttons, or bead-work, or ruffles? Does the furniture have to have painted flowers or scenes, or dozens of shiny tacks?   Do knives and forks need to have elaborate patterns on the handles? The fact that it is often impossible to buy a lampshade that is absolutely plain is evidence that people think that articles must be decorated to be beautiful. Elaborate decorations on a poorly designed shade can do nothing for that shade. Decoration is often only something applied to a surface, a veneer, structurally unrelated to the surface or the object. Excellent definitions of structural and decorative design, with a list of the requirements of each, can be found in *Art in Everyday Life*.[1]

Functional appropriateness and beauty. A room which is so arranged that it is possible to carry on the activities of the class easily and smoothly, so organized that supplies are readily accessible, and so situated that plenty of light and sunshine are available, is well on its way to being a beautiful room. A room which does not fulfill these conditions will look inharmonious no matter how much decoration is hung on the wall. A chair richly carved and upholstered with gorgeous materials would still be a ridiculous thing if it were so constructed that it would not stand. A flower vase which could not support the flowers placed in it, a pitcher with a handle so weak that it could not be used for lifting, a toy which could not survive strenuous play, a street dress so narrow that one could not walk in it—all these articles, though they might be highly decorative, would be useless.

It is foolish to put decorations into a room which is inconvenient, disorderly, and poorly organized. Any articles or place so constructed cr arranged that it cannot completely serve the purpose for which it was planned, can never be really beautiful, no matter how dextrously the artist juggles colors or designs. In connection with the furniture that they construct, children can understand this fact from the first grade up; it must stand, and it must stay together. Vases and figures made out of clay must be able to stand alone. Toys must be so strong that they can be played with. In connection with their own clothing, children can understand that in winter they dress to keep warm, or that any dress, no matter how beautiful in color or material, tends to look badly if the wearer is uncomfortable in it. Appropriateness in costume can be taught from the first grade.

Planning for desired effects. The visual effect is another purpose to be considered in most cases, before colors and patterns can be planned. A poster, for instance, is supposed to attract attention; in order to produce a good poster, one must know how to secure an arresting effect. A wallpaper is supposed to make a background for persons in the room; in order to design a satisfactory wallpaper, one must know how to produce a quiet effect. When the child asks the teacher,

[1] Harriet Goldstein, Irene Goldstein, and Vetta Goldstein. *Art in Everyday Life.* New York: The Macmillan Company, 1930, pp. 6-20.

"What color shall I use?" he needs to be helped to realize the effect that he wants to get. If he wants something gay, then he chooses gay colors; if he wants something startling, then he chooses contrasting colors; if he wants something quiet, he chooses closely related colors. The desired result is brought about by a relationship of colors and shapes. A discussion of these effects and how to secure them is easily understood in the third grade.

ART AND THE SOCIAL STUDIES

In studying any people teachers and children are interested in their clothing, their homes, their furnishings, their cities, their public buildings, their industrial plants, and their products. Noticing how differently and how imaginatively various countries and civilizations have used form, color, line, and pattern in these fields brings about extensive growth in appreciation. Noticing, too, how they played with and experimented with materials at hand, such as feathers, seeds, and shells, provokes resourceful use of our own local materials.

Courtesy of Edom School, Riverside County

Children Show Their Weaving and Basketry in an Out-Door Dramatization

Imitation Versus Adaptation in Art

The question of why Indians or Eskimos dress as they do may lead to the question as to why we dress as we do, and eventually to a realization that the style and appearance of clothing is largely dependent on climate and on the activities of the people wearing it, and on the materials at hand with which to make it. That any style not based on the activities of the people using it is likely to be inappropriate, is a fact easily understood. The same thinking might well be applied to architecture. Why has the Eskimo home the shape it has? Why did the Greek temple have its characteristic shape? And why is making our steel buildings superficially like Greek temples as absurd as trying to play tennis in an Eskimo's furs? What is the actual danger in such imitation? Buildings which have stone columns and pillars and porticoes piled up in front of the steel and stone structure, are a potential menace in times of earthquakes or explosions.

Courtesy of Edom School, Riverside County

Costumes Made for Indian Play

Designers seem eager to disguise the honest concrete and steel of modern buildings with a coat of stone in front. In other forms, too, a new product is often made to look like the material which it is replacing. Linoleum imitates brick and tile and wood; electric light fixtures imitate candles; oilcloth looks like leather; celluloid resembles marble; and metal walls of railway coaches appear to be grained wood. This attitude does not show a respect for the material being used; no decoration of an object should be used as a disguise for either the material or the object. Both of these latter should grow out of the material and the process used in building the object. An attitude of sincerity and honesty in the use of materials is necessary if art is to kept alive. The other approach—the imitation of previous forms—is due to timidity and to lack of imagination.

Adaptation

No intelligent person, on the other hand, wishes to reject all that the study of what has gone before can teach him. Do the homes of other countries perhaps have qualities with which the American home would be improved? Our homes, for example, need badly some of the simplicity and flexibility of the Japanese house. In studying Japan, emphasis should be placed on the simplicity which the Japanese embody, not only in their art, but also in their everyday life. In no other art are examples of rhythm so easily understood and enjoyed by children as in that of the Chinese and Japanese.

In reliving the life of any period, there should be as much opportunity as possible given for imaginative expression. The Japanese and Chinese made beautiful pottery, the best of their potters creating new forms as they worked; in living as the Japanese do, therefore, the class need not try to produce forms that imitate Japanese vases, but instead to create new forms, keeping in mind the principles of simplicity, rhythm, and balance, as their Japanese prototypes did. While they work as the Romans did, the class need to try to feel the Roman love of splendor, but to control with underlying restraint the bombastic magnificance that permeated most of the art of that time. Roman art, except in Pompeian painting, perhaps, is an example of what happens when one country imitates another country in its outward manner of doing things.

In studying Indian pottery and basketry, and in pretending to be Indian potters and weavers children may be taught some of the artistic philosophy of the Indian, instead of being made to copy the final product of this philosophy. The Indians used symbols for Indian men and women, for birds, animals, lightning, and other natural forces and phenomena. The symbols were ideas rather than photographic images, simpler than the Japanese symbols that were used the same way. Since it takes a great deal more imagination to produce a satisfactory and artistic idea drawing or symbol of an object than it does to draw an accurate representation of it, these new symbols are likely to be more stimulating to the children than copied ones would be. Then, after the children have been originators, as the Indians were, they can compare their symbols with real Indian forms, gaining much from the contrasts in the two arrangements.

The Eskimos carved figures out of bones or tusks, the final product being more or less long and cylindrical, with no projections, because the limits of the shape of bone or tusk forced the artist to hold to a simple treatment. The Gothic artists, although for a different reason, apparently kept the same idea in mind when they made their figures long and slender to fit on the side of a long stone column or to take the place of the column. When the children carve on a broomstick or a piece of soap, they too have limitations that hold them to simple forms. Although they may not be able to duplicate the actual working materials of all the places which they study, the children may interpret the other conditions in terms of their own experiences. In all the imaginative entries into the life of other people that the children attempt, the purpose of the teacher must be to help them think sincerely in terms of the simplest philosophy and the material problems of the time and place.

Art Activities and Discussions Common to Many Social Studies Units

In almost any social studies unit there may arise a need for any one of the following activities: developing a personal costume (selecting, assembling, and grooming); building (including planning and furnishing the interior of a building); landscaping, city planning and building; staging and costuming plays for children or puppets; decorating for parties; editing the school or class newspaper; making books, posters, charts, maps, toys; painting, modeling, and weaving.[1]

Developing a Personal Costume

The study of the child's present day problems in personal costume should not be restricted to the clothing unit suggested for the fifth grade. Since one of the most important art problems in which we all share is that of selecting and combining the parts that make up our daily apparel, and since children are tremendously interested in their own clothing, time should be devoted to discussing this problem whenever there is occasion for it. Suggestions for organizing the work are made under the clothing unit; objectives to be kept in mind are listed under the general objectives.

Building

Several fundamental matters need to be considered before any actual construction can be successfully carried through. The following topics offer fruitful discussions:

a. Consideration of what the building is to be used for and of how this use will affect the plan, e. g.; a house, a store, a railway station.

b. Sincerity in construction—having the house show the way in which it is made.

c. Fineness of outside shape and proportions.

d. Determination of number of rooms. (If there is to be more than one room in the building, there is the additional problem

---

[1] For art standards, refer to Objectives in Teaching Art, pp. 482–491.

of arranging windows to look well from the outside and the inside both.)

e. Placing and proportion of openings, extensions, projections. (Relative sizes of doors and windows, wall spaces, and their relative niceties of proportion; shape of roof, porches.)

f. Determination of color relationships between building and room, building and other buildings, parts of the building. (Color of roof, walls, trimming around doors and windows; relationship of colors in the class-room and those of the separate building or the village, etc.)

Color schemes may be worked out by making test combinations, of which the best will be chosen. Since bright colors do not ordinarily look well in large areas, it would be unwise to choose bright red or green, for instance, for the roof or wall colors. Sample houses might first be made from paper boxes. On these, colored paper windows might be pinned to determine right proportions and colors. Then all the colors could be tried out in the proportions in which they would be used on the larger house—a large amount of wall color, a small amount of trimming color, and a medium amount of roof color. Combinations pleasing to the senses and quiet enough so that they do not distract from the rest of the classroom are essential.

In making small houses for an indoor village, attractive ones covering about a square foot can be made in forty-five minutes by piling up small colored blocks of various shapes. The child can study, through these, the balance of shapes, contour, simplicity of effect (the most difficult of all), placing of doors and windows, and selection of colors. The study of fine homes which should follow construction can bring out solutions which the children are not able to make for themselves.

Furnishing the interior of a building involves a consideration of many individual problems in construction, as well as a constant regard for harmonious combinations of form and color. The making of chairs, tables, beds and benches, shelves, lamps, rugs, textiles, and pottery gives wide range for creative imagination and for practical resourcefulness.

Chairs must be strong enough to stand actual use. The children can ask themselves the following questions about each chair they make. Is it comfortable, or does it hurt one's back? Does it have rough edges that tear the clothes? Is it simple and pleasing in shape and color? Is it enough like the other chairs in the playhouse to look well with them? Is the pattern for an upholstered chair small enough to suit the chair? Have several patterns been tried out to permit the best solution? Are the decorations and upholstery subordinate to the shape of the chair? For practical reasons, children should not attempt to make thin legs for chairs or tables. Since the children cannot fasten on such members, they can devise ways of using boards for the whole side of a chair, for the end of a bed, or for the supports under a table.

Tables bring up the question of decoration, after all problems of structure and design have been satisfactorily solved. Should tables be decorated? Under what circumstances?

Rugs, of a good size, can be made out of flannel or any soft rags on a heavy cardboard loom. Although such a loom is fairly satisfactory for children, since the cardboard gives as the strings tighten, the box-and-broomstick loom, which can be made by pupils in the upper grades, is much better.[1] The necessity for some system in the color arrangement of even a rag rug can be demonstrated to the class. Colored warp threads will appeal to them as one means of achieving unity. Pattern weaving is better left for wall hangings and table textiles than rugs, for fear of getting too much excitement into the furnishings of the room.

Textile decoration of other types may be produced by embroidering on coarse material like burlap with a crochet hook, or by stamping patterns with large blocks of wood or with potatoes cut into simple shapes. Wallpaper, if it needs decoration, can be stamped or stenciled. A discussion of the different types of pattern suitable for wallpapers, curtains, and rugs is helpful to the children. From their own designs, or from the pieces they find, the pupils may study the different kinds of pattern used—dotted, striped, plaid, irregular, and complex. The textiles need not be made, if the children can find appropriate designs, because wise selection is as much an art expression as is the making of new combinations. A study of fine furniture and textiles, in connection with this construction work, is appropriate and helpful. The furniture for the playhouse may be kalsomined and shellacked to bring it into harmony with the color scheme employed in the textiles and the rest of the room.

Arrangement of the furnishings demands a further consideration of the amounts and kinds of patterns to be used together. The confusing effects of too much pattern; the greater adaptability of simple and small patterns instead of large, bold patterns; the selection of groups of two patterns that may be used with each other—these matters provide good material for discussion. In regard to colors, too, many questions arise. The children may discover that there are too many

---

[1] See Frederick G. Bonser, and Lois Coffey Mossman. *Industrial Arts for Elementary Schools.* New York: The Macmillan Company, 1923. This book contains a description of the box-and-broomstick loom.

colors in the room, or that they are so bright that they are dizzying to see. They will notice that they like large spots of soft colors and small spots of bright.   Then they will find that some colors are gloomy, heavy, and ugly; that others are gay and pleasing. They may ask the following questions of themselves: Are there more pieces of furniture in the room than are actually necessary? Are there things on the wall that could be eliminated? Have different arrangements of furniture been tried? Do the flowers in the room contribute to the beauty of the color scheme? Is the vase less important than the flowers? Can the flowers, leaves, and vase make a fine design? Are there any new and different ways of arranging flowers that the children might have seen in homes that they have visited? How can they make the playhouse and the schoolroom more attractive to live in?[1]

Landscaping

Gardening is appropriate around a playhouse if it is outdoors; if it is indoors, then potted plants may be used.[2] Arranging flowers and bushes around the house requires thought for the massing of colors, perhaps to get some spots of pure colors or perhaps to get a combination of harmonious colors. The formal versus the informal garden, and the right use of each, is another matter for discussion. The practical matter of leaving sufficient space around windows, in order not to cut off the light, likewise demands attention.

City Planning and Building

Organizing an art commission in the class is a good early step in this series of experiences. Laying out the streets, passing on the plans for all the large buildings, condemning the block houses which are not satisfactory from an art standpoint, and taking charge of all matters of civic planning and construction are all problems for the art commission to approve or disapprove. They can insure that the public buildings like the library and the courthouse are not hidden by lots of ugly houses crowded up against them, but have large, clear spaces around them to permit long views from all directions. Such problems as these relate closely to typical civic questions that must arise in any town. The children can answer them in terms of their own city. Have billboards been placed where they cover up fine views of buildings or countryside? Do telephone poles mar an otherwise attractive street? Are streets wide enough to meet future needs, or will trees have to be cut down later on, and lawns sacrificed? Are there open spaces set apart

---

[1] For excellent suggestions for schoolroom arrangements, see *Art in the Elementary Schools*, published by the Los Angeles City Schools, and also Chapter V, The School Environment, in the *Teachers' Guide to Child Development*. Sacramento: California State Department of Education, 1930.
[2] See *School and Home Gardens*. Science Guide for Elementary Schools, I (March, 1935).

for parks and playgrounds? Do the electric signs in the streets and
the shops, the decorations over the midle of the street, and the sidewalk stands make a badly confused medley of lights and forms? Are
the street lights, the trolley cars, the railroad stations, and the oil stations goodlooking or ugly additions? Art in the community is well
discussed in *Art Appreciation,* by Collins and Riley.[1]

Staging and Costuming Plays

Sets and costumes for plays need be made for effect only, without
overcareful workmanship or small details that would not contribute to
the impression gained by the audience. Since the costumes should, by
their shape and color, strengthen the mood of the play, the children
may decide whether the contrasts of color and pattern and material
make the great king seem greater, and the villain wickeder. They can

Courtesy of San Diego City Schools

Painting the Scenery for a Class Play

decide whether the costumes are to be symbolic, or historically correct.
Similar consideration has to be given to the background, which must be
subordinate to the actors. After these early decisions have been made,
the children should be allowed to work directly with materials, draping
without cutting until the costume is planned. If they make a standard
approximating the shape of an average-sized child for that grade, then
each one can drape his costume on the form, working with cut lengths
of a suitable size. Besides the material in the school, the children can
bring scraps to supplement. Crepe paper, since it cannot be used over
again like cloth, is often less satisfactory. All fastening can be done
with little safety pins, obviating the need of much stitching. Pleated

---

[1] M. Rose Collins and Olive L. Riley. *Art Appreciation.* New York: Harcourt,
Brace and Company, 1932, pp. 107-48.

and folded newspapers can also be used at times. Wrapping paper, paper bags, and cereal boxes are good for masks. Many other waste articles found around the home or the school can be utilized for effective headdresses, jewelry, and other decoration. When costumes cannot be made by draping, the teacher needs to have on hand some tagboard patterns of jackets, blouses, and trousers. After several plays have been given, there will be on hand an accumulation of various garments of different colors and kinds, which, if sorted away in labelled uniform boxes, will be easily accessible for brand-new combinations. A skirt, for example, may be used plain, with bright polka dots basted on, or

Courtesy of Butte County Schools

A Marionette Theater in a Rural School

with contrasting stripes sewed on around the bottom. A jacket may serve as part of a Santa Claus costume, or as the foundation for a princess costume to which puffed sleeves can be added.

Puppet plays offer children nearly all the principles of stage designing and stage costuming, with less consumption of time and material than is required in a regular production. Hand puppets, which many professionals prefer for their performances, are the ones most easily manipulated by children. Marionettes are much more trying to a child's patience because they take more time for construction and because the strings of the finished doll constantly get tangled.

Simple paper dolls on sticks, operated from below like the Japanese puppets, although not necessarily as shadow puppets, would be extremely easy to make, although they are less fun to operate than the hand type. The children can be encouraged to make their puppet heads just as grotesque or exaggerated as they like, interpreting qualities of gayety, age, goodness, wickedness, weirdness, and mystery rather than facts of normal proportions of eyes, nose, and mouth. Puppet heads, since they are on a scale to make normal proportions difficult to obtain, are better when they are purely symbolical. Primitive ceremonial masks offer finely expressed examples of vividly interpreted feelings. The heads should be made as simply as possible. In the lower grades they may be merely stuffed rag forms with crayola features. In the upper grades, fired heads of adobe or other clay can be quickly made; papier mâché or carved soap are also satisfactory. Sallie B. Tannahill's book, *Fine Arts for the Public School Administrator*,[1] gives a good list of books on puppets and puppeteering.

Puppet stage sets may be rapidly painted in kalsomine; crayons make the decorating drudgery. For a puppet stage, a doorway with a curtain drawn across it, above which the dolls perform, does very nicely. Another possibility is presented in the frame of an old screen, which can be covered with paper. An opening of the right height for the children, cut in the central panel, makes an ideal stage.

Decorating for Parties

Unless the children are already studying a country intensively, the complete conversion of a room into a Dutch scene or an Oriental garden, for instance, is foolish. If the room has been made as colorful and attractive as it can be with its usual colored maps and hangings; if the tables have been made gay with place cards, doilies, and carefully arranged flowers; if the refreshments have been attractively placed in the dishes—if these things have all been done, then the children have made adequate preparation. A preliminary discussion of table manners rounds out the experience of getting ready for a party.

Editing the School or Class Newspaper

The newspaper can be made more attractive if the children have access to a typewriter set with large type than if they are limited to the usual size of type or to a hand printing set. Headlines made with a stamping outfit are effective. Interesting experiments are quite possible in the matters of margins and blocks of type. Decoration, if any is necessary, can easily grow out of certain letter combinations on the typewriter.

---

[1] Sallie B. Tannahill. *Fine Arts for the Public School Administrator.* New York: Columbia University Press, 1932.

Cartooning and caricaturing, since they are an integral part of all modern newspapers, will inevitably creep into the school newspaper. If the children study the work of such fine caricaturists and draughtsmen as Wanda Gag, Yasuo Kuniyoshi, Covarrubias, and Cotton, and if they collect examples of the work of the best cartoonists from different periodicals, they might work out fresh, original, and well-presented comic strips for their newspaper. Many artists could profit by studying the works of the best cartoonists. Recognition of the cartoonist's strict economy of line, of his careful selection of essentials, of his courage in using extreme exaggeration, of his frequent use of symbols, all offer a profitable field for study. Although to make a genuinely amusing picture of a thing or of a person requires discrimination and skill, children with this ability usually find their efforts ignored or frowned upon. The ability to caricature, an enviable and remunerative attribute, deserves cultivation just as much as ability in other of the fields allied to art. Since so many children delight in this activity, they should be helped to do it well.

Advertisements in the newspapers must fulfill the same requirements that posters demand.[1] To aid their own designing, the children might make collections of the advertisements in the finer magazines, noting their variety of letter types, their legibility, and their appropriateness to the articles advertised. Perhaps the children would like to write letters to the local companies doing the most artistic advertising, expressing their enjoyment; perhaps they might even like to write to some of the firms doing fine advertising in the nationally circulated magazines, commending them. The judgment of people who hire fine designers in any line of work should certainly be recognized.

Photographs for advertising or any other purposes in newspapers and magazines should be studied critically for their composition. The pupils, asking the following questions, can test them for their merit as art: Are they simple? Do they have too many line directions, objects, and patterns? Have they variety in dark and light? Is the photographing done from an interesting or a commonplace point of view? By experimenting with blue print paper in making prints of photographs which they have taken for their own newspaper, the children can get a good idea of how photographs are printed. Combining their experiences of cartooning, advertising layouts and design, and photography with careful organization of the printed matter of the newspaper, the class has an opportunity to learn much from getting out their own sheet.

---

[1] The requirements are listed later under Posters, p. 464.

Books

Making books brings up many art problems. Is the book large enough to encourage large illustrations, and bold lettering with a flat $\frac{1}{8}$ or $\frac{1}{4}$ inch lettering brush? (Children make letters more easily with a brush than with a pen, which is always getting out of condition anyway. For smaller letters, they can use blunt sticks.) Is the binding of the book trim and complete, or does it have brass fasteners that scratch surfaces and catch in other books? Japanese bindings are simple, neat, and easy. Is the cover design simple and effective? Are the words legible? The lettering can be massed to make patterns like some of the Mohammedan designs to be found on vases, tiles, and walls. Are there end-pages to contribute to the appearance of the book when it is opened? These pages might be of colored paper, or of paper decorated with stick printing, potato printing, or starch designs. The title page takes careful planning. The empty pages at the beginning and end of books serve as transition between the covers and the text of the volume. Again, when printed material and illustrations are found facing each other, do they make a unit? There should be so much harmony about them in color, in the character of lettering and illustration, and in the page layouts that they seem to need to be together. Miss Tannahill's *P's and Q's*[1] offers excellent material on book making, lettering, and poster making.

Illustrations for the books may be painted in color, or done in line with a wide lettering brush to correspond with the pages of lettering. Cut paper can be used for illustration. When a number of copies are to be made of the same book, illustrations can be duplicated from linoleum block prints. A simpler process for reproducing a large number of copies consists of rubbings made from a design incised with a pencil on a smooth, damp, clay tile. Wax crayons can be used for rubbings from this, just as pencils are used for coin rubbings. Photographs or stencils offer still other possibilities for book illustration.

If the book pages are double, with the fold along the outer edge, it is possible to paste or paint on side of the page, and to letter on the other. If the books are to contain clippings, then the scrap material should be so trimmed that its edges parallel the edge of the page. Even for scrapbooks, all lettering needs to be carefully done. Many ineffective, untidy looking books (and posters) are made by cutting pictures out of magazines, letting the edge be the irregular outline of the object, and then pasting them—probably with a number of other ragged clippings, in each corner of the page, finishing up with some illegible, feeble handwriting in hard pencil in the center.

---

[1] Sallie B. Tannahill, *P's and Q's.* Garden City, New York: Doubleday, Doran and Company, 1923.

There are now in libraries a large number of beautiful children's books which supply fine material for real appreciation of all the art aspects of a book—illustrations, type, layout, and related ensemble. Book jackets, too, can sometimes be borrowed from the county libraries. In studying book illustrations, the children will see that symbolic rather than realistic designs often suit the lettering better. Fine illustrations are often more like posters than they are like photographic drawings. For realism, photography is far better than an attempted realistic painting. Well designed illustrations should try, in general, to do more than the photograph can do. On the other hand, some books are improved by photographs for illustrations. The type of book suitable for each style of illustration can be determined by the children.

Posters

Posters are made to advertise an event, a product, or an idea, such as "keeping clean" or "being a good citizen." Since they must be read in a glance, and frequently from a distance, they must be extremely simple—so simple that they could be reduced to the size of a postage stamp without losing their effectiveness. In order to attract attention, they must have contrast of color, or dark and light, and of line direction. Much that was said about book illustration applies also to posters. It is unwise to use clippings on school posters, because pictures found in magazines are usually too detailed and small for good, effective design. The time consumed in looking for suitable material for clipping is sufficient to make a satisfactory design in paint directly on the poster.[1]

Charts

Children, if rightly guided, are capable of making attractive wall decorations with the charts that they need for their class work. Like some of the excellent decorative maps that have been made, charts have material just as suitable for manipulation into a balanced design. Deciding how to make a fine layout of the contents of a chart is a searching and profitable art problem. Added decorations are usually unnecessary. The names along the top, for instance, can be of one color, forming a wide stripe; the words down the side can be another; the squares laid off can be repetitions of the two colors in use. Additional information can make a block or band, perhaps underscored with color. The placing of these charts in the room, and the choosing of colors harmonious with the environment are again material for art discussions.

---

[1] Sallie B. Tannahill. *P's and Q's.* Garden City, New York: Doubleday, Doran and Company, 1923.

Maps

Maps would be far more fun to study if they were colorful, pictorial, and well-designed. They should be always and easily accessible, but not always in sight, or else they become customary to the children, and, finally, unnoticed. A big screen in the form of a large book which is firmly fastened to its base, with castors to facilitate its being rolled to any part of the room, would be most useful to hold the maps. It could always be available, it could be consulted by the children without the aid of the teacher, and it could serve, when closed, as a bulletin board.

Toys

Like clay, wood offers children a chance to think in three dimensions. It is unfortunate, then, to limit toy-making in wood to the cutting out of silhouettes. The pupils, if they are encouraged to work with solid form, have an opportunity to learn about the balance of forms which underlies the arts of architecture and sculpture. Such an experience also gives added richness to their work in paint and pencil. If the children compare a fine toy, a work of sculpture, and a building they will discover that all have three dimensions. They become conscious of the outside contours of each, of the manner in which each has its outside parts so balanced that the whole can stand well, and of the arrangement of all parts to be interesting when viewed from any angle. All sorts of scraps of wood (and by scraps is meant material small enough so that toys can be put together with very little sawing or changing of the shapes found) can be secured from a planing mill. These blocks, cylinders, half-cylinders, pyramid forms, cones, and half-cones, nailed together in different arrangements, with just a little cutting of edges and sandpapering, work up easily into the shape of animals, known or imaginary. With such a procedure as this to follow, the children are forced into symbolic, simplified treatment. These articles, after a coat of paint in some one or two gay colors, make attractive playthings. Decoration can be applied to indicate imaginative wings, feathers, and fur. Paper boxes, wire, pipe cleaners, papier mâché, cloth, clay, rope; newspapers twisted, wrapped, or braided; rags treated in the same way; tin cans; old leather; and odds and ends of all sorts are suitable for the construction of toys.[1] Kalsomine paint and shellac finish up the articles. There would, of course, be absolutely no point in activities like these if the children did not have a chance to experiment with their materials before deciding how to use them. There would be little point in the activity if some of the qualities of art were not incorporated into the toys.[2]

---

[1] Evadna Kraus Perry. *Art Adventures with Discarded Materials.* 336 South Broadway, Los Angeles, California: Wetzel Publishing Co., Inc., 1933.
[2] Painting and modeling are considered under Development of Skill.

ART ACTIVITIES AND DISCUSSION TOPICS FOR SOCIAL STUDIES

In studying art in connection with any of the specific units of elementary work, there are a number of questions and suggestions that apply to all of them with equal pertinence, and then there are other groups that apply individually to particular units. A general effort to characterize the art expression connected with the unit is helpful to children, since it focuses their random impressions. They might try to decide, for instance, whether the art in question is *bold, vigorous, and strong; quiet, subtle, and delicate; formal, dignified, and simple; rich, detailed, and elaborate; or weird, strange, and mysterious.*

General Questions and Suggestions

The following questions will apply to practically all of the countries or ages studied by the children. The determination of answers to them will afford the class a skeleton for their work on the art of that place or period.

What art element or principle predominates in this expression? Are the people a group of imitators, or independent creators? Are they realists, or do they have a symbolic art? In what fields do they excel—pottery, architecture, theater design, et cetera? Is art practiced by the few, or by everyone; is it for the rich, or for the poor as well? What can be learned from them to help the child in his own creative expressions? What are the similarities between their art and modern American art?

In addition to following through questions such as these, the children can study the homes, the clothing, and the formal and informal art expressions of the people, collecting illustrations and examples whenever possible for comparison with other groups.[1]

Specific Questions and Suggestions

The customary units for elementary school study naturally lead into particular fields of activity and discussion. Under the topics which follow, many specific recommendations or possibilities are discussed. The arbitrary organization under such main headings as Historic Civilization, Modern Civilization, with the further subdivision into national groups and industrial fields, has no relationship to the sequences that might be used in the elementary program.

Historic Civilizations

The great periods that have marked the forward stride of civilization include, among others, the civilizations or cultures centering chiefly

---

[1] General art standards for the discussions are mentioned in connection with the Objectives in Teaching Art.

around the Mediterranean Sea and in what is now modern Europe, and the developments in the two Americas. The Oriental cultures, although of vast importance to the progress of the world, can perhaps best be understood by the children in terms of their contemporary expressions.

Prehistoric life. In connection with this unit, the children might study the cave paintings of southern France and Spain, and the drawings that have been found in different parts of the world, scratched on the rocks of the hill-sides. Ancient stone implements, and the few pieces of bronze that have been found, afford rich material for discussion and speculation. A comparison of qualities of prehistoric art with those of any known art will help to reveal the attributes of the earliest expressions. A Japanese brush drawing of an animal, and a child's painting may both share in the common quality of simplicity and vigor of interpretation. Carvings on bones and tusks are often similar to incised lines scratched on pottery for decoration. The work of the archeologist and museum field worker is fascinating to children, making good supplementary material to use with this unit.

Egyptian life. The Egyptian unit offers a particularly wide range of activities. Egyptian architecture exhibits great simplicity, restraint, and permanence. Scale models of characteristic types of buildings, such as the adobe hut, the temple, and the tomb would demonstrate the structural problems and methods of the times, and lead to a realization of the engineering feats of the architects and builders. A comparison with other civilizations would reveal the peculiar, massive beauty of Egyptian architecture. One feature closely related to architecture was the use of sculpture in connection with it. Heroic figures in the round, as well as bas-relief, offer further material for comparison, for the Greeks, the East Indians, and the Europeans of Gothic times, to mention a few of many possibilities, used these same methods of decoration, although in different ways, in their building. Chinese sculpture, too, has some features in common with Egyptian. The solidity, the symmetry, the extreme simplicity, and the symbolism of Egyptian sculpture all suggest points that may be incorporated into the work of the children in the classroom. To gain the real effect of bas-relief the boys might even, in places where clay is plentiful, build an adobe wall, washing it down with water to smooth the surface. On this they might incise designs that would be symbolic in spirit, registered (placed in tiers or rows) like the Egyptian, treated with the same or corresponding formalities of drawing. Although this procedure would not give experience in the Egyptian material, stone, it would give an opportunity to plan and carry out large areas of decoration characteristic of the civilization.

The Egyptians painted some of the fine murals of the world. Their process was not only fresco (painting in water-mixed paints on fresh, wet plaster) but also distemper or tempera (painting with sized pigments on a dry surface of plaster, clay, wood, and so forth). Some large scale tempera or kalsomine painting on the walls of a frame and cardboard playhouse would give the children some fine experiences with large scale color organization. Their subjects might well be taken from class or club interests that would correspond to the Egyptians' illustration of the events of daily life.

Egyptian crafts offer a particularly profitable field for study. In pottery, flower pots of well-designed shapes are a good problem. An incised line, like the engraving line the Egyptians used for bas-relief, suggests an appropriate and simple kind of decoration. In jewelry, the Egyptians followed many of the same processes that later primitive civilizations developed, but frequently with far greater refinement and beauty. In the process of making adobe beads, pendants, and other decorative forms, the children would find a study of modern jewelry stimulating. Modern design owes much to the Egyptians.

Assyrian life. Assyrian civilization is notable for its use of large sculptured figures—the winged bulls—and its bas-relief decoration in the form of mosaics of glazed bricks. Both of these were used only in connection with architecture. The interest in animals of both the Babylonians and Assyrians might suggest a variation of the Egyptian experiences, carried out in wall decorations of sculptured, glazed tile. (A study of later Persian developments might reach far into the course of history, touching on the rugs, textiles, and illuminated manuscripts of that country during Europe's period of medieval emergencies.)

Greek life. The description of Greek life in *Creative Expression*,[1] supplies excellent material for this topic. A study of Greek architecture, archaic sculpture, terra-cotta figurines, vase-painting, furniture, and clothing gives a rich background for creative work. Comparison of the imitations of Greek buildings with what remains of the originals may show the children the beauty of finely proportioned, simply treated forms. Cretan pottery and frescoes and metal-work, especially in repoussé, are good for the children to study because of their fresh, vigorous treatment.

The Roman life. A comparison of the art of Greece with that of Rome brings out the changed point of view of the latter country. Interest in organization, in problems of engineering and construction, supersedes the simpler, more esthetic attitudes of Greece. Bridges, acqueducts, roads; the development of the barrel vault and intersecting vaults leading to entirely new forms of building; the dome—all these new developments suggest immediate contributions to modern times, offering

---

[1] *Creative Expression.* Edited by Gertrude Hartman and Ann Shumaker. New York: The John Day Company, 1932.

good points for study and comparison. In the more restricted art fields, the Roman sculptured portraits, coins, and medallions are interesting, as are the Pompeian homes with their gay, architectural frescoes. A comparative study of coins might be developed. For larger work, the children might make portrait busts of each other.

The Vikings. The Vikings offer to the modern boy and girl the study of ships, of costume, and of wood-carving and tapestry weaving. A simple type of architecture and furniture, that can be effectively presented in the schoolroom, suggests the possibility of building a Viking hall, complete with decorative shields to hang on the wall; rude, solid table and bench; chair or throne for the chieftain; rude table utensils of wood or even of bone; straw or rushes on floor.

Medieval life. The Medieval unit has so many possibilities, most of which have already been described many times, that they scarcely need to be suggested. Apart from the customary life of the manor, there are: Cathedral architecture, enrichment through stained glass windows, sculpture, mosaics, and carved wood; craft guilds, with their divisions of labor; training of apprentices, patron saints and processions; and many individual crafts, such as tapestry weaving, for instance.

Courtesy of Burbank City Schools

A Viking Ship Made for Use in an Original Play "Europe Gets the News." The Children Represent the Indians Brought Back to Europe by the Explorers

Modern Civilizations

The modern civilizations in this outline will be considered to be those which have been known since the great ancient and medieval civilizations. Most of them can now be studied in some contemporary form. They will be considered in groups: the national groups of Europe; the two great present civilizations of the Orient; the civilizations of the Americans. A study of modern industry and social life should be considered in connection with the United States.

European Civilizations

European life. A general unit of this nature suggests a comparative study of the different styles of architecture that have developed since the Greek and Roman times. The most important painters of

Courtesy of Chico State College

Castles and Costumes in Medieval Life

Italy, Spain, France, Germany, Holland and Belgium, and England are likewise natural material for a comprehensive study. Perhaps nearer to the children, because simpler, is the peasant art of the different countries. This is a most profitable field for exploration.

The Dutch. Art correlatives of the Dutch unit might well include a study of the architecture, the home interiors, the costume, the painting of both Dutch and Flemish schools, and the Flemish tapestries. In painting, the Dutch chose subjects particularly interesting to children— scenes in the home: people eating at the table, kitchen scenes, people playing some instrument; pictures of sheep, cows, and horses. The children can compare this art with what they know of the art of other countries; the Japanese, for instance, used subject matter and techniques very different from the Dutch. The children then might look around their own homes for new and interesting subjects for their own paintings. They might, too, paint flower or animal compositions of their own.

The Swiss. California and Switzerland offer fine comparisons in their farms and homes. The two typical kinds of interiors could be brought out by collections of illustrations of Swiss architecture and decoration. The Swiss costumes, too, offer colorful material for class use. A comparison of the Swiss with the Indian loom with which the children are familiar would be helpful. The interest in cleanliness and order characteristic of this people is worth turning to class account by discussions of the value of a clean place to work in, and of the possibilities of keeping the room orderly even while work is in progress. Possibly even a system, complete with labels and inventory, for using desks and cupboards and storeroom might come from this unit.

Other European peoples. Each country offers individual points of interest that may develop into genuine art problems. Homes, costumes, markets, vehicles, pastimes—from some of these sources the children will surely be able to find interests and suggestions for their own work in art.

Oriental Civilizations

The Japanese. The Japanese unit has been so well developed by frequent repetition that it is particularly rich material. The class may find good reference material on costumes, homes, temples, gardens, flower arrangement, pottery, theatre art, dancing and dance costumes, weaving, books, masks, dolls, toys, fans, umbrellas, embroideries, prints, mounting and showing of pictures. These topics immediately suggest comparisons—Indian and Japanese costumes and masks, for instance, or pottery. Similarly, the poses of the Japanese dances are remarkable like those portrayed in their prints; a study of the line patterns produced in the dances shows that they resemble carefully designed pictures. The children, after a survey of the topics mentioned, might easily feel moved to make toys, kites, masks, a flower garden, or to prepare an original pantomime with their own masks and costumes. Possibly the Japanese children of the neighborhood might give a demonstration of Japanese dances. If the girls like the kimonos, they might make a collection of samples of appropriate materials.

An alert class, in addition to doing some of the obvious things just mentioned, can draw many profitable lessons from their observation and study of this country. They might ask themselves the following questions: What can the Japanese teach them about the arrangement of articles in a room? What can the Japanese artist teach them about painting? (This question would naturally arise after a demonstration of the pose, technique, and materials of the Japanese artist.) What is the attitude of the Japanese artist toward the things that he sees about in his daily activities? From the answers to such questions as these, and from the attendant discussions, the children can easily appreciate some of the generous contributions of Japanese civilization and culture to Occidental art forms.

The Chinese. Although the Japanese took most of their art forms from the Chinese, adapting them to their own national temperament, most people are less familiar with the Chinese prototypes than with the adaptations. Particularly valuable for art study in connection with the Chinese unit are the sculpture in stone and semi-precious materials, the terra-cotta and porcelain work, pottery, painting, embroideries, and costume and furniture. The terra-cottas made first of red clay and painted over with white clay recall the Indians' use of colored clays in painting their pottery and animal figures. The Chinese were very fond of modeling terra-cotta horses, of which the children might like to collect illustrations. They might also like to use the combination of different colors of clay to decorate their own pottery. The Chinese temple dogs or lions offer another amusing and delightful form of the potter's art. A study of the Chinese potter, his hillside kiln, and his world famous art would prove most illuminating to the class. Then a comparison of the many imitations of Chinese pottery would show the superiority of the original products.

Other phases of the art that are stimulating for group study are the street festivals (compared to the New Orleans Mardi Gras, for instance, or the California street parades), and the theatre with its simple setting, properties, and property man. Costumes, masks, and poses again become significant. Chinese clothes for ordinary wear, as well as for festivals, may suggest several improvements in American clothes. In modeling and painting, the large, simple rhythms and movements evidenced in monumental sculpture and all painting can be emphasized for inclusion in the children's own work.

American Civilizations

The cultures included in the study of the art of the American civilizations are those of the North American Indians, the Alaskan Indians, the Mexican Indians, and the South American Indians; of the pioneers; of the Californians; of the modern United States; and, finally, of some of the industrial and social phases of the United States.

The American Indians. The general range of topics suitable for
art study in this unit includes personal and ceremonial costumes,
masks, homes, pottery, beadwork, weaving, dolls, carving on utensils
and in homes, totem poles, old and contemporary painting, symbolism,
use of available local materials, such as feathers, fur, gourds, and seeds.
Out of this wide range might come a problem in which a child would
develop his own symbols and designs for his pottery or weaving. He
might find modern symbols in posters and illustrations for man, tree,
house, speed, and so forth. Some children might make decorative maps
of the Indian civilizations, locating each with a characteristic symbol.
Modeling and painting of animals, with comparisons with Indian
modeling and painting, would develop naturally. Pottery, too, with
original designs, would lead to the need of a kiln. An outdoor kiln,
like the Indians', might suggest an exhibition of all the Indian work
completed by the class, together with all of the Indian things that could
be borrowed from the surrounding homes. Out of this might even
develop an exchange of the painting, modeling, and pottery with an
Indian school. The culmination of the study might be a masked
party, at which all costumes would be imaginative (not based on any
Indian national costumes primarily) and made of articles to be found

Children in the Warm Springs School Study About Life in Alaska

at home, such as paper bags, newspapers, ropes, small rugs, and so forth. Afterward, the costumes could be compared with some Indian costumes to discover their points in common.

Alaskan life. Alaska offers the study of some revealing and constructive comparisons. Totem poles can be compared with the monuments in the city squares of other countries. The Indians' wooden houses with their carved decoration can be compared with Scandinavian and Russian houses. The children then may try to find out if any houses in the United States have such decoration as this, and whether the decoration is a structural part of the house, or fastened on afterward. Plaster decoration, such as is common here, may or may not improve a house. The children can make collections of illustrations of decorated houses, deciding on their beauty, or lack of it, and listing some of the precautions to be observed in using it.

The utensils of the Alaskan Indians may be compared with American utensils; perhaps the children will carve some, using original motifs of similar types. Pottery and weaving motifs can be developed too. Low relief serves for the designs on pottery. Jewelry can be made from bits of thread, buttons, seeds, and other available scraps.

Mexican life. Mexican art divides itself into ancient and modern forms. The class, after studying the ancient art of the Mayas, Toltecs, and Aztecs, with its impressive architecture and sculpture, can compare it with that of the Pueblo Indians. Then the Spanish art brought over by the conquerors can be compared, and its influence noted. The churches and miracle paintings will prove valuable, too.

In *Idols Behind Altars,*[1] Anita Brenner tells of Mexico's present painters—Diego Rivera, Orozco, and others. The original of some of their murals may be seen in this country; reproductions are many and easily available, and might lead to a general study of murals of several countries. The present method of teaching art in the open-air schools of Mexico may be compared with American methods; illustrations of collections of such toys as painted clay pigs, fruits, horses, and pottery; of glassware, basketry, weaving, and costumes will prove popular with the children. Reports on the exhibitions in this country of the work of Mexican artists may lead to the painting of a mural for the school, on which the master-painter and his assistants would all work. Reading of *The Painted Pig*[2] may lead naturally to the making and painting of pottery.

South American life. Peruvian pottery may be compared to other Indian clay forms, or even with early Cretan pottery. The children

---

[1] Anita Brenner. *Idols Behind Altars.* New York: Harcourt, Brace & Company, 1929.
[2] Elizabeth Morrow. *The Painted Pig.* New York: Alfred A. Knopf, Inc.. 1930.

can find by observation the dominant characteristic of the designs for both pottery and weaving, judging them for their beauty and their other interest. The architecture of modern South American cities can be compared with that of North America. The children may make an illustrated descriptive folder, containing drawings or paintings of the inside and the outside of their homes, of their clothing for different events, of their toys, of automobiles, airplanes, and other interesting objects, to send to some South American school in exchange for a similar book from them.

The Pioneers. Study of the pioneers brings out the enforced simplicity of their homes, their furniture, their crafts, suggesting a comparison of their forms with the more ornate, machine-made forms of today—hooked and braided rugs versus linoleum in large, bold patterns, or imitation Oriental rugs, or modern domestic rugs in bright, intricate

Courtesy of Los Angeles City Schools

The Westward Movement Shown in Children's Frieze

patterns. Clothing, now, is simpler than pioneer clothes were. With the home crafts of the pioneer, the home crafts of European countries might be studied. The children undoubtedly could collect from their families many examples of laces, knitting, crocheting, and embroideries; old silver, pewter, and china; samplers, and other handcrafts of past generations to compare with the embroidered mittens and caps, stockings, coverlets, carved bowls and chests, and furniture from other lands.

For their own creation, children might make applique wall decorations for a playhouse, rugs, covers for doll beds, embroideries on burlap carried out with rags or heavy yarn and large crochet hooks to give a bold and quick result. Illustrations of stories for a pioneer book is always suitable.

California. Besides the study of the missions, and the finding of forms similar to them in the architecture of the world, the class may consider the most beautiful California cities, many of which have an art commission regulating building. The typical farm can be studied, the children working out a plan for building and grounds that would be attractive as well as practical. Gardens and parks and flowers offer another range of interest; art colonies, artists, architects, museums, and Indian art, still another. The movies and animated cartoons offer many varied opportunities.

The children may paint landscapes, outdoor markets, oil derricks and tanks, fruit packing scenes; they may make real moving pictures with 8 mm. film of their own pantomime; they may take pictures with their own cameras, printing their films on blueprint paper; they may experiment with the various uses of adobe, firing beads, puppet heads, and pottery in their own home-made kiln. For their picture collections they can find designs and illustrations for markets, oil stations, theatres, auto courts, and roadside stands. They may design labels for canned fruit and vegetables.

The United States.[1] Houses in the United States vary a great deal in design. A collection of illustrations would show the structural honesty of some, the dishonesty of others; false fronts, roof structure disguised, materials made to imitate other materials, handsome fronts and ugly backs—such insincerity the children can identify. The derivation of designs in houses—English, colonial, Spanish, in the main—and the comparison of the originals with the adaptations can bring out the pleasing features of each. Different kinds of furniture, as shown in the homes and on the screen, and varying standards of interior decoration offer opportunity for discriminating judgments.[2]

Lighting of the homes, from colonial times until today; home implements like stoves; household machinery like sewing machines, vacuum cleaners, telephones, and refrigerators—these offer good contrast in their changing designs and efficiency.

Civic responsibilities in the field of art, treated previously under City Planning and Building, can be expanded to include the consideration of the usual American attitude toward beauty. How should public parks, camp grounds, rented houses, libraries, and so forth be treated? Should cars be abandoned beside the road, or in empty lots? Should tin cans, bottles, and waste paper be thrown into unoccupied yards? Do American school buildings, in comparison with those of other countries, represent merely ostentation and display, as many critics, foreign and domestic, claim most American art forms do? Are such critics justified in their general condemnation of the country's attitude, or is the complacent tourist a misleading indication of the mass of the people? Does

---

[1] See also topics under Pioneers, California, The American Indians, The Home, Clothing, The City.

[2] Some standards for judging interiors, furniture, etc., are listed under Objectives in Teaching Art.

the ordinary citizen really enjoy fine music, fine dance recitals, fine painting and architecture? Does he feel that his civic responsibility includes ability to recognize and promote the beautiful, and to reject the ugly? Is the criticism leveled at the county fair justified? Who should judge the art exhibits? Who usually judges them? All of these questions can be raised for class discussion, to determine, within the limits of the children's experience, their individual responsibilities toward civic art.

Art in industrial forms and inventions is well discussed by Norman Bel Geddes in his new book, *Horizons*.[1] He gives many illustrations of the evolutions occurring in their designs. Automobiles, airplanes, trains; radios; kitchen utensils; skyscrapers; store-fronts; soda fountains, drug stores; ready made houses—all of these diversified manifestations contain material for discussions and explorations for the art class. Posters, bill-boards, labels for packaged merchandise, electric signs are other forms related to the field of art, and worthy of class notice.

Organized art activities in the museums of the country have been stimulating to the entire field of art. The class might discuss the museum at Santa Fe and its contributions to Indian art of today. National exhibitions and expositions are similarly stimulating to a larger group of artists, and therefore important. American painters have worked in many different styles since they first began to form a distinct group in colonial days. The children would profit from selecting the types of work and the artists that most appeal to them from the entire group. A comparison of the work of the best American artists with the best Chinese and Japanese artists would bring out many differences and a few similarities. Do American artists try to paint what they see, or what they feel? After thinking along these lines, the class may begin to appreciate the fundamental likeness of all the arts, and the enrichment they offer each other. They might, too, be more ready than before to consider the natural beauty of their country, and to wish to share in it and preserve it.

For their creative activities in this unit, the class may build a playhouse incorporating some of the fine features of the houses studied, but not imitating any one. They might have an art colony—writing and producing plays, composing music for their concerts, exhibiting their arts and crafts. They might have a county fair, displaying all the various community activities—preserving, baking, crafts, and so on, and perhaps even a side show with puppet performers. They might make a set of travel posters for the United States. If the school can arrange loans of fine reproductions to the homes, then the families might enjoy the pictures that the children study in school, profiting by

---

[1] Norman Bel Geddes. *Horizons*. Boston: Little, Brown and Company, 1932.

the class discussions retailed to them. Further activities, almost endless in their variety, are suggested in relation to specific social and
industrial topics.

Social and Industrial Topics

The home.[1] Material suitable for this unit has already been discussed under Building. In addition to house building and furnishing,
many small articles can be made for individual creative work. Some of
these are fountains and sculpture for the garden, bird baths, garden pottery; door stops, book ends, paper weights, flower holders for vases,
knobs for table drawers, flower pots; single tiles for hot dishes, or group

Courtesy of Alameda County Schools

Happy Experiences in Creative Expression in Pleasanton Grammar School

tiles for a whole table top. Wall paper sample books are good for discussions of designs and paint samples for color. Samples of textiles are
really necessary for discussions or decisions about draperies and uphol-
steries. The children would do well to collect fine examples of tables
well set for lunch or dinner. Visits to lovely gardens will prove
inspirational to the class, perhaps making them wish to write letters to
the people whose gardens delight them.

---

[1] Stimulating suggestions on this subject will be found in an *Autobiography of
Frank Lloyd Wright.* New York: Longmans, Green and Company, 1932.

Food. Art interest in foods may lead to a discussion of the different shapes and surface qualities of certain fruits and vegetables, and of how artists have used them in pictures. Market men frequently experiment with different combinations to get striking and beautiful effects in their displays. The children may experiment similarly with bowls for their tables, for party decoration, or for displays in their play store. They may make up gift boxes of fruits and nuts. If they have a store, they may plan and execute displays, posters, labels, smocks for the clerks, and other accessories of store activities. They may plan and pack picnic boxes for their own picnic.

Clothing. A clothing store offers many opportunities for creative art activities. If the children can each bring a few garments and accessories for stock, they can then select complete costumes for various occasions. The staff of the store can consist of the display man, the sign painter, and the salesmen. After discussion, new selections can be made. A factory for doll's clothes would call for costume designers, pattern makers, tailors, and salesmen. A fashion magazine for dolls, with appropriate pictures of what to wear to the mountains, to the beach, to the party, and to school might lead to a fashion show for the dolls, or even for the children, would be fun. Perhaps the class might put on plays about proper costuming for the whole school, or make posters about the value of simplicity and good grooming.

Workers. Discussions dealing with any of the semi-professions or trades can be developed in much the same way, whether they relate to the postman, the policeman, the soldier, nurse, conductor, engineer, barber, milkman, porter, or grocer. The study of their costumes, of the places in which they work, of the design aspects of the forms and supplies with which they work, of the ramifications of their connections, of the systems which they use in their activities—all these can be interpreted in any one of the branches. The postoffice and its systems, the milkman and his dairy farm suggest interests in design, in painting, in modeling, in construction, and in discussion. Interests might range from the shape of the milk bottle to the design of the stamp.

Transportation. Since boats, automobiles, trains, bicycles, roller skates, wagons, stations, piers, and airports are all made according to some design, the children can hunt for the best designs. They can discuss the need for better ones for streetcars, gasoline stations, road maps, and railroad tickets. They know that attractive cars sell sooner than unattractive ones, and that the same truth holds in other objects. They may make travel posters, stickers, and advertising folders for railways and steamship lines. They can collect and study the fine European travel posters, and the Japanese prints made for the same purpose.

They can read and hear about new plans for railroad yards. They can realize their personal responsibility in traveling for the appearance of the aisle and seats on the train, knowing that some European countries fine people who put their feet on the seats. They may plan a travel wardrobe, or investigate and discuss traveling bags.

Frieze of Pioneers Crossing the Mountains

The farm. Creative activities in relation to the farm are discussed under California, The Pioneers, and Building. Additional activities might include the discovery of the crafts still carried on about some farms, and the possibilities inherent in such materials as quills, feathers, pine needles, straw, and other accessible farm materials. They may discuss the beauty of farm scenery—of the growing crops; of the orchards, haystacks, and ploughed fields; of the grazing cattle and other farm animals—all of them interesting material for painting. Farm machinery has its fascinations, too, in form and rhythm. The children may also discuss clothes suitable for farm use.

Manufacturing. Discussion among the members of the class will soon bring out the merit of machine-made objects which are well designed and of good material. Only because manufactured articles are frequently ugly and cheap in appearance are they rejected by discriminating people. Good, appreciative consumers show their approval by purchasing only the well designed objects. The things that make for fine design in any article should be discussed at this point. Homemade art appreciation tests, composed of several series of clippings of similar objects from magazines, can be administered to each other by the children. Standardized tests, like the Christensen and McAdory forms, can also be given to make the class realize the nature of art appreciation. The class might make a collection of well designed articles costing not more than ten or fifteen cents. They exhibit these articles, advertising them appropriately. They might organize a toy factory, dividing the labor into special fields. They might also consider the appearance of factory districts, and plan for their improving. They might decide on the characteristics that make a place pleasant to work in, writing to factories that seem to be so planned.

The city. This topic is discussed in the sections City Planning and Building, and California. The children can assemble for discussion all the elements that enter into city planning—people, home, walks, streets, trees, telephone and lamp posts, public buildings, parks, playgrounds, theatres, railway stations, street cars, buses, stores, factories, news stands, street signs and advertising, mail boxes, disposal cans. With all of these they have art responsibilities. They may make maps of their own city, and then decide on better layouts, after studying plans for the cities of the future. They may make an ideal, uncrowded play village, incorporating their best thoughts on civic art.

Records. Records include books, magazines, newspapers, movies, and photographs. Some of these have been previously discussed. A print shop, equipped with a large typewriter with large type, and several stamping outfits, will permit experiments on book jackets, magazine covers, book illustrations, layouts on various types of printed sheets, and other activities.

OBJECTIVES IN TEACHING ART

Art in the elementary grades should develop in the child a pleasure in seeing, and should urge him to find, while giving him every opportunity for it, the satisfaction that lies in playing with what he sees through the use of certain materials, colors, lines, and forms.

Since the development of taste (appreciation) and the cultivation of the creative spirit are the two most important objectives, they should receive the greatest amount of emphasis from the beginning of the first year. Taste develops more slowly than skill; training in it should begin before the child has acquired many prejudices from people lacking in taste. Encouragement and preservation of creative ability should be uppermost in the teacher's mind, especially during the first three years while the child still shows daring and fearlessness in expressing his ideas. In the fourth grade because there is self-consciousness in regard to results, if the proper attitude toward honest creative work has not already been established it will be difficult to keep the child from copying and imitating work he sees around him.

Appreciation

The child should be helped toward an enjoyment of seeing and looking, not merely at painting and sculpture, but at all things about him. His teachers should develop in him the habit of exploring, examining, and thinking imaginatively about the shapes, colors, patterns, trees, flowers, mountains, and houses that he sees. Having taught him a few skills, and having given him the experience of expressing with paint, clay, or cloth, the things (not necessarily objects) he has seen and felt, she can more easily arouse in him a curiosity and a critical interest in what other people have seen and expressed through similar materials. She can help to develop taste by giving the child an opportunity to make constant choices between arrangements of lines, shapes, and colors, first of all in those things with which everyone is concerned, such as our clothing and our homes. Continual thoughtful observation and frequent choices will grow into independent judgment and discrimination. Each child should establish the habit of criticising his own work, his clothes, and all appearances with which he is concerned; to consider his own ideas, and to take pride in making his own decisions. The importance of independent choice should be emphasized to the class, together with the fact that fine judgment and taste is far more essential than money in producing pleasant, comfortable, and beautiful surroundings.

Creative Ability

In every grade the work produced should be completely the child's own. The teacher should not touch the child's work, or allow him to

Courtesy of Butte County Schools

Children Should Be Given Many Experiences in Handling a Variety of Materials

copy directly from any illustrative material. Copying some design that is generally accepted as fine in quality is sometimes considered as an excellent exercise in observation and appreciation. If it is used in this way the exercise should be accompanied by a complete explanation of the purpose of the exercise and by a discussion of the quality of the design. Giving the child patterns of animals, or persons, and of automobiles to follow, only makes him dependent. Strange to say, these patterns do not help much; work made from patterns suffers in comparison with work done without them. Although patterns for difficult, standard construction problems such as those needed for making a coat, blouse, or pair of trousers are time savers, they should not be relied upon entirely in costuming either. The correct way of using patterns for costumes is discussed later. Too much art is imitative. It will continue to be so until the children are taught to respect their own ideas and to rely on their own inventiveness. Individual creative expression will not be developed by having designs dictated step by step by the teacher.

Skills

The children should be taught enough about handling materials and processes to be encouraged by satisfying results. The processes involved in drawing, lettering, modeling, painting, and construction; and the use of all material and tools involved, such as clay, wood, cloth, yarn, paper, and paint, should be introduced in the first grade and used regularly until they can be controlled easily. Though dictation and drill can be used here, there should be a certain amount of experimentation by the child with different ways of using materials.

Habits and Attitudes

Habits and attitudes which should be constantly emphasized through all the grades include:

1. Pride in original, honest work and finished products.
2. Willingness and eagerness to experiment.
3. Willingness and patience to repeat worthwhile experiments until fine results are secured.
4. Confidence in individual ability and in the value of individual ideas.
5. Interest in, and tolerance, sympathy, and respect for, the work of other people, countries, and civilizations.
6. Respect for materials and fine craftmanship.
7. Application of art principles to everything that is made; and realization that any thing that is not beautifully made, well made, and suited to its use, is a waste of material and time, and a source of constant irritation to those who must see and use it.

8. Independence in working and in making his personal evaluation of his own work and the work of others.

The principles of design, which are discussed under the following objectives, and the skills with which the teacher wants to familiarize the child are merely aids to help him express his reaction to his environment and his experiences. They should never usurp a more important place. Over-emphasis on technical skill and a too conscious and constant drill on principles will take the attention of the child away from the experience he is trying to express, and will perhaps kill all spontaneity and pleasure in working. Guiding principles need not destroy the feeling of freedom that the child must have in order to do vigorous and fearless work. Since children are not capable of producing technically finished articles, holding up adult standards of workmanship will not only deaden all creative tendencies but will result in a dislike for art. Nearly every child comes to school with a natural liking for all art activities; this attitude can be preserved with but the slightest show of encouragement and sympathy. All discussion of technique and other aids should come after the creation has taken place. The teacher should see that the child has experiences which he is anxious to put into some concrete form, or should revive his memories of such experiences; then, after he has painted or modeled or constructed these ideas in some form, she should get him to look critically at his results, to decide how he can better his performance another time. To experience, to express, to evaluate—that seems to be the most satisfactory procedure. No teacher should ever laugh at any attempts that were not intended to be funny; every teacher should educate the parents of her group to regard with respect, before the child, work which has been seriously done, no matter how amusing it is. Many a child has lost his frank joy in painting through a sense of inadequacy built up in him by thoughtless remarks.

The appreciative teacher demands something in a painting or in a piece of modeling quite different from photographic accuracy. The vitality, the freshness, and the spirit in a child's work gives far more real pleasure than any amount of dull perfection in methodical drawing or painting. The child is content at first with painting an idea, a symbol of a bird or a man. But the adult has difficulty in getting beyond the detail and the actual dimensions. If one keeps in mind the thought that a painting or drawing or bit of modeling is meant to interpret the spirit of the object, instead of to make a dull impersonal record of it, then adult criticism of children's work will become more complimentary and less condescending.

Some Specific Objectives in Art

These objectives which have not been allocated to specific grades, are listed somewhat in the order of their difficulty. They should all have been covered to a large degree by the end of the sixth year. From each division as much work should be covered each year as the children *understand, want* and *need.*

1. Clothing

Emphasis should be placed only on those points for which the child can take some responsibility.

a. Pride in having clothes clean, shoes dusted, hair brushed, hands and finger nails clean; an appreciation of the effect of all this on one's personal appearance, no matter how richly dressed.

b. Realization of the effect of posture on the appearance of beautiful costumes or ordinary ones, on the appearance one makes when standing, walking, or sitting.

c. Appreciation of lovely color apparent in the clothes of the children.

d. Appreciation of colorful patterns in dress materials worn by the children.

e. Recognition of appropriateness in clothes for playing, for school, for special occasions. (This includes appropriateness of accessories, shoes, purses, handkerchief, jewelry).

f. Appreciation of simplicity—the greatest aid in making anyone look well—secured through avoiding too many different colors, too many different patterns, too many accessories, or too complicated a style.

g. Appreciation of fine textile design—especially of those suitable for personal costumes.

h. Recognition of the social pressure of fashions—comparing that which is fashionable but good, with that which is bizarre—selecting what is both fashionable and fine.

i. Study of fashions of different periods.

j. Appreciation of suitability in hair dressing—simple, following contour of head, natural in appearance, and tidy.

k. Recognition of appropriateness of various color effects for different occasions.

l. Appreciation of validity of applying design principles and art elements to personal appearance—simplicity, emphasis, balance, unity, repetition, variety of spacing, dark, and light pattern—stressing especially unity of effect in combinations of shoes, hat, hose, dress, coat, necktie, handkerchief, and all accessories.

m. Developing of the habit of observing costumes on street and in shop windows, critically; reasons for their beauty or ugliness.

n. Appreciation of all fine textile patterns.

2. Immediate surroundings

a. Pride in appearance of class room and feeling of responsibility for the appearance of it.

b. Recognition of the elements of order—cleanliness, keeping floor and tables clear, keeping materials in their places.

c. Observation of shapes, colors, and decoration of objects that make up environment, such as furniture, pottery, textiles, rugs, pictures, sculpture, buildings, books, machines, and tools.

d. Appreciation of the art and beauty in painting.

e. Application of art principles to room arrangement

(1) Simplicity—leaving large plain spaces on wall, keeping things on walls on a level with the eye as nearly as possible.

(2) Spacing—careful arrangement of material on bulletin boards, construction work and furniture in the room.

(3) Repetition of color, forms, and motifs.

(4) Unity through repetition and simplicity—not showing too many different kinds of pictures at the same time on the walls, not having too many different types of patterns and objects.

f. Appreciation of appropriateness and fine design in home furnishings.

g. Appreciation of and desire for fine color in home and class room.

h. Recognition of the effects of different types of color on different people.

i. Developing of habit of observing attractive homes analytically.

j. Recognition of the value of system in filing all materials used, and of practice in organizing cupboards, shelves and files.

3. General environment

This includes architecture, landscaping and city planning.

a. Observation of the proportions and colors of details of house and setting, shapes of houses, shapes and placement of doors and windows, colors used in painting houses, arrangement in planting gardens, flowers, trees, and arrangement of walks around houses.

b. Recognition of community responsibilities, such as keeping backyards clean, keeping roads and walks clear, feeling personal responsibility for all public parks, picnic places, school grounds, and the country side.

c. Enjoyment of the beauty of the buildings around, pride in keeping them attractive, and respect for the yards and houses of others.

d. Appreciation of the differences of design found in buildings of this country and in those of other countries.

e. Appreciation of the complexity of problems in city planning.

4. Fundamentals of art

Recognition of simple art elements and principles and the application of them to everything that is made. Line, color, and dark and light pattern, are the three elements of art. The introduction of these elements in their simplest forms should come as soon as the children can understand them.

a. Appreciation of beauty in line or space breaking.
  (1) Emphasis—bringing out some part of composition by
      (a) Making that part larger than other shapes
      (b) Making that part brighter than other shapes
      (c) Making that part lighter or darker than the background
      (d) Adding more detail to the most important part
      (e) Having lines lead in to most important part
      (f) Giving that part the most important position on the page
  (2) Rhythm of movement.
      (a) Curved lines, flowing lines, diagonal lines all help to add movement, and many lines going in the same direction will carry the eye along in their direction.
  (3) Simplicity and variety in space-breaking—dangers in going to the extreme in either. (The extreme of simplicity is confusion. Make use of simplicity in order to keep design quiet, and introduce just enough variety to make it interesting).

b. Appreciation of beauty in color.
  (1) Knowledge of the names of colors.
  (2) Ability to make colors seem right for purpose.
  (3) Ability to distinguish and to make both dark and light colors, and both bright and dull colors.

(4) The ability to make pleasing color combinations by
    (a) Using a few, well chosen hues
    (b) Using contrast of value and chroma
    (c) Using colors which are related to one another because of a hue held in common, such as red and orange, and blue and green

(5) Ability to produce effects desired in play productions, such as mystery, gaiety, sorrow, goodness, and dignity by combinations of appropriate colors.

c. Appreciation of beauty in dark and light pattern.

(1) Ability to secure a variety of contrasts in values.

(2) Knowledge of what contrast does for design, and when to use it.

Development of Skill

The processes and experiences necessary to the child in developing skills may include:

1. Painting with water color poster paint
    a. Care of materials, tools, and place of work.
    b. Convenient arrangement of work materials.
    c. Use of brush in the paint box and on paper.
    d. Ability to get rich and clear colors with the right amount of water.
    e. Direct painting, without later fussing.
    f. Ability to mix colors directly on paper to get the desired color, such as brown or grayed blue.
    g. Ability to use proper amount of water to get color light or dark.
    h. Ability to model surfaces by grading colors from dark to light or light to dark, and to make edges soft or sharp.
    i. Ability to get strong fresh colors without repainting. This includes ability to use variety of colors, and to change color within a small area, red orange changing to yellow orange and then to grayish orange.
    j. Ability to suggest texture.

2. Modeling
    a. Making vases and figures stand, because of large enough base and balanced shape.
    b. Making forms solid and simple in outlines so that they do not break.

    c. Getting form by exaggerating shapes and accenting shapes such as very round, extremely sharp.

    d. Keeping in mind the limitations of the clay; avoiding long thin projections and making all projecting parts solid and heavy.

    e. Getting definite form and well designed contours.

    f. Getting unity of lines within contour.

    g. Getting movement and detail in figures, within a simple contour.

    h. Use of symbolic rather than realistic treatment of persons and animals.

    i. Working with sufficient material (about two handfuls of clay). Shaped models should be large enough to permit of large free work.

    j. Making primitive outdoor kiln for clay objects.

    k. Learning to fire outdoor primitive kiln.

3. Drawing

    a. Making direct lines with no redrawing of the first lines, and no erasing.

    b. Use of pencil, crayolas and brush in drawing.

    c. Use of contour and memory drawing as aids to closer observation.

    d. Ability to show thickness of forms.

    e. Ability to use simple perspective—objects in the distance made smaller than those close by.

    f. Use of good organization of lines in a drawing, considering figures as shapes in a design.

    g. Economy of line. Using no more lines than are absolutely necessary for the description of the object.

    h. Close observation of objects, and selection of the significant peculiarities of line direction and shape.

    i. Use of appropriate proportions in hands and feet, head, legs and shoulders.

    j. Making a great quick drawing stressing line quality, which may be delicate, vigorous, direct, strong, and heavy; or thin and tremulous, flowing, or straight and rigid.

4. Lettering with flat one-fourth inch brush

    a. Use of capital letters.

    b. Making letters vertical and uniformly tall.

c. Considering letters and masses of letters as shapes in a design.

d. Spacing and grouping of letters, relationship between letters and illustrations, use of decoration with the letters.

e. Avoidance of distortion or over-decoration of letters which might destroy legibility.

5. Construction in wood, paper or cloth

a. Fastening things carefully and neatly so that they will be usable.

b. Allowing no loose ends to protrude.

c. Leaving no part unfinished to destroy the appearance of the article.

d. Simplicity of structural forms.

e. Use and care of tools.

f. Consideration of the strength of the wood in constructing shapes.

g. Recognition of the function of the object in determining material and design.

h. Recognition of the character of material in determining design.

i. Construction of the stage costumes for show and effect instead of permanence and finish.

j. Construction of stage sets with large effective details but with the least expenditure of time and money.

INDUSTRIAL ARTS [1]

Nature and Purpose of Industrial Arts

As a subject for educative purposes industrial arts is a study of the changes made by man in the forms of materials to increase their values, and of the problems of life related to these changes.[2]

Industrial arts is one of the social studies, and has a distinct subject matter of its own organized under the major headings of food, shelter, clothing, tools and utensils, and records. Like other content subjects it is regarded from the modern point of view as a source of material upon which the teacher and children draw as needs arise in their activities rather than as "subject-matter to-be-learned."

Industrial arts by the very nature of its content and the activities it suggests has a special contribution to make to the development of children in the intermediate grades.

Integration of personality by means of industrial arts activities. Modern education seeks to develop the integrated personality. Such

[1] Contributed by Ethel I. Salisbury, Associate Professor of Elementary Education, University of California at Los Angeles, and Educational Consultant, Santa Monica Public Schools.
[2] Frederick G. Bonser and Lois Coffey Mossman. *Industrial Arts for the Elementary Grades.* New York: The Macmillan Company, 1923.

a personality is one which is able to make thoughtful decisions in line with a steadfast purpose or ideal. Inner control rather than outer compulsion determines the acts of the integrated personality.

The constructive and investigative activities of industrial arts utilize the natural impulses of children to work toward their own purposes and to make decisions appropriate to their maturity.

Integration of the social group by means of industrial arts activities. The coming era promises to be one in which man for his own survival must see and act in accordance with the fact that individual welfare is an inseparable part of all human welfare. An integrated society is one in which each person thinks and acts in relation to the whole rather than as an isolated element. This interaction of the individual and the group progressing toward a common goal is an ideal of democracy.

Children who engage in industrial arts activities in informal situations cooperating and finding satisfaction in group work constitute a miniature integrated society. Modern psychology points to the conclusion that participation in the activities of such a society under wise guidance through the period of infancy is the best training to establish the habits and develop the understandings which characterize the good citizen.

Integration of the curriculum through industrial arts activities. Integration as an educational objective is primarily a matter of pupil responses. In considering the integrated program and the integrated curriculum, it should be emphasized that these two pieces of machinery which occupy so much of the time and attention of educators are but means to an end—the integrated individual in the integrated society.

Integration of the curriculum is in recent years being brought about by resolving the traditional subjects into curriculum units which afford the teacher more definite help in carrying on a program of child purposing than does the subject matter organization. Each unit is designed to develop basic or major understandings by suggesting educative experiences and providing a block of subject matter to be drawn upon for the support and enrichment of those experiences.

Industrial arts which emphasizes the study of modern industries such as production and distribution and suggests activities that involve not only content from industrial arts, but other subjects as well, is a major influence toward integration of the curriculum.

General Principles of Industrial Arts Instruction [1]

Industrial arts should be the same, in the elementary school, for all children, regardless of sex or future vocation.

---

[1] Adapted from Frederick G. Bonser and Lois Coffey Mossman, *op. cit.*

The things made are not so important as the purposes of the children, their habits of work, and the meanings they associate with what they are doing.

Children think and create best in an atmosphere of freedom, but not of chaos.

In studying the evolution of industries children should be led to see the relationship of the beginnings of things to their later development.

Children should be guided to an appreciation of the interdependence of all mankind for supplies and markets.

Criteria for Evaluating Work With Materials

Following are several essential characteristics of pupils' activities in industrial arts which conform to the foregoing principles:

1. The pupil makes something he can use.
2. The making of an article clarifies ideas for the child.
3. Frequently the work of each pupil is part of a common purpose.
4. There is evidence of interest in work at hand and a general spirit of cooperation.
5. The construction work is easy enough to assure some measure of success to the pupil and difficult enough to challenge him to think.
6. Appropriate materials and tools are available.
7. The pupils organize for the maximum efficiency in the use of a limited number of tools.
8. The values to be derived from making an article are commensurate with the time necessary for completion.
9. The product is disposed of when it is no longer useful.
10. The product conforms in a reasonable degree to principles of art construction.
11. The project is feasible for the space available.

The Evaluation and Planning Period

The success of the construction period is largely the result of what goes on from day to day in the evaluation period. In the latter period the children report individually or in small groups to the whole class what they have accomplished. Each tries to evaluate his own efforts. If he fails to have a clear perspective on his achievements or manner of working he is aided by suggestions from his classmates and teacher. It is excellent training in social understanding and discrimination for children to learn how to offer comments which are impersonal and genuinely helpful and withhold those which are expressions of condemnation or of their own over confidence.

The child reporting often uses the article he has been constructing for purposes of illustration, thereby losing some of his self-consciousness and helping the discussion to go forward informally. Frequently the child reporting indicates at this time what the next steps in his work will be. Sometimes, however, all planning is left until the latter part of the period. Children vary in ability to think through their problems, in inclination to take responsibility and therefore in need to be included in a final summary of the work of the following day.

Besides affording opportunities for constructive thinking, for judging and for organizing, the evaluation period is important for another reason. It is in this period that the teacher establishes a unity of thinking and of purpose. This unity is an essential part of the good life in the classroom. It is developed, not by preaching, but by the practical application of such universal principles as the need for cooperation, self-control, safety and the like. In addition to the intellectual application of the principles, the children at this time should also discover the genuine pleasure that results from working with others toward common purposes.

There are some very definite points of technique in conducting a profitable evaluation period. Those who are successful in guiding the children through the evaluation period in general conform to the following suggestions:

1. The teacher tries to keep the spirit and tone of the period one of interest, enjoyment and helpfulness by

   a. Keeping the management of the period herself rather than delegating it to a child chairman;

   b. Making it a time for solving problems that have actually come up in the previous period, rather than hypothetical problems which are not real to children;

   c. Insisting on constructive suggestions rather than criticism;

   d. Being selective in the material to be evaluated; avoiding long monotonous fruitless reports of the obvious;

   e. Making the period a time when interesting related information is shared. The teacher, as well as the child, contributes whatever may enrich the subject at hand;

   f. Avoiding in general the discussion of disciplinary problems, particularly in such a way as to develop priggishness on the part of those who are only too willing to sit in judgment on their fellows.

2. A child undertaking a task is led to set standards for himself and later check to recognize whether or not he has attained those standards and if not why not.

3. The children take responsibility for the clean up period and any evasion or neglect of this responsibility is discussed in the evaluation period.

4. Poor English is unobtrusively corrected by the teacher if in her judgment a child will not be deterred from further expression. Later proper forms are made the basis of practice.

5. In planning for the next work period, each child decides what he is to do. In the upper grades, the child decides upon the materials needed and knows whether he is to furnish them or they will be supplied. Sometimes he writes this information on a slip of paper and files it with the teacher.

SUGGESTED INSTRUCTIONAL MATERIALS

The following paintings, drawings, and pieces of sculpture are interesting to children in subject matter, and fine in color and design. They are worthy of study and discussion. Those in color will be effective on the class room walls if they are reasonably large.

Paintings and Prints for Appreciation

JAPANESE

Hokusai	*The Wave, Figure of a Seated Woman, Galloping Horse*
Hiroshige	*The Shower, The Treasure Ship with Seven Gods of Good Fortune*
Masayoshi	*Geese*
Okio	*Young Dogs*
Korin	*Deer*

ITALIAN

Giotto	*Flight into Egypt, Adoration of the Shepherds*
Simone Martini	*St. George and the Dragon, Annunciation*
Piero della Francesca	*Visit of the Queen of Sheba to King Solomon*
Fra Angelico	*Flight into Egypt, Annunciation, Angels*
Botticelli	*Magnificat*

DUTCH

Rubens, Peter Paul	*Helena Fourment and her Children*
Vermeer, Jan	*Young Woman at Casement Window*
Van Gogh, Vincent	*Crows over a Corn Field, The Artist's Room, Street in Arles, Garden in Arles*

SPANISH

El Greco	*The Garden of Gethsemane, The Holy Family, The Nativity*
Goya, Francisco Jose de	*Family of Charles IV, Blind Man's Buff, Stilts*
Velasquez, Diego	*Don Balthazar Carlos, Portrait of Infanta Margarita*

ENGLISH

Gainsborough, Thomas	*Morning Walk, Portrait of a Child, Portrait of Mrs. Morley and her Children*
Morris, Cedric	Paintings of Birds

FRENCH

Corot, Jean Baptiste Camille	*Reveille*, Early Portraits
Degas, Edouard	*Ballet Girls Dancing*
Seurat, Georges	*The Circus, The Ile de la Grand Jatte*
Renoir, August	*Children at the Piano, The Umbrellas*
Cezanne, Paul	*Railway Cut, Woman Sewing*
Gauguin, Paul	*Ta Matete*
Rousseau, Henri	*Rain in the Jungle*
Matisse, Henri	*The Young Sailor*
Laurencin, Marie	*Girls*

SWEDISH

Zorn, Anders	*On the Stairs*
Larrsen, Carl	*Ladagaarden* (The barn, with cows in a stall), *Gaarden* (The farm, with artist, cow and dairymaid)

GERMAN

Marc, Franz	*Deer in the Forest*
Peckstein, Max	*Boats in Canal*
Hofer, Carl	*Mountain Village*
Schmidt, Rottluff	*Cats* (Wood Cut)

AMERICAN

Stuart, Gilbert	*Portrait of George Washington*
Ryder, Albert	*Toilers of the Sea*
Whistler, James McNeil	*Portrait of Miss Alexander*
Cassatt, Mary	*The Bath*
Marin, John	Landscapes, Schooner Yachts
McFee, Henry Lee	Portraits
Benton, Thomas	*Speeding Train*, (Lithograph)
Klitgaard, Georgina	*Girls Swinging on Play Ground*
Blume, Peter	*Show Boat*
Kuniyoshi, Yasuo	*Boy with Fruit, The Cock*
Diederick, Hunt	Horses and Dogs in cutouts of black paper
Ulreich, Nura	Pictures of Children

MEXICAN

Rivera, Diego	*Festival of the Gathering of Corn, Dancers at Tehuantepec, While the Poor Sleep, Cane Workers*
Orozco, Jose Clemente	*Revolution* (Lithograph)

GREEK

Chirico, Giorgio de	*Three Horses*

Sculpture for Appreciation

Gaudier, Brzeska	*Cat*
Lehmbreuck, Wilhelm	*Portrait*
Gill, Eric	*Statuette*
Epstein, Jacob	*Pigeons*
Archipenko, Alexander	*Maternity*
Laurent, Robert	*The Flame*
Faggi, Alfeo	*Stations of the Cross*
Mestrovic, Ivan	*Madonna and Child, Distant Chords, Archangel Gabriel*
Michael Angelo	*David* (Unfinished)
Assyrian Reliefs	
Minoan Porcelain figures	
Egyptian Reliefs and Free Standing Sculpture	*Hawk, Ibis, Seated Personage in Bronze*

Japanese	*Kwannon*, Wood—672-686 A.D.
Chinese	Chinese figures in wood—A.D. 600 T'ang. Bronze Lions; Figures of Ming tombs—huge camels, elephants, and monsters in stone. Marble tiger guardians
Javanese	*Temple of Boro-Boudour*—details in bas-relief from the life of Buddha
Siamese	*Bronze Lion before a Temple*
East Indian	Palace of Angor-Vat-Procession in bas-relief Rowers in bas-relief *Pagoda of Sriringam*, the court of the horses Sculptured elephants *Man Milking*—Eighth Century relief
African	Helmets, Fetishes, Idols, War and Dance Masks, Weapons
Archaic Greek	*Votive Statue, Man and Calf, Athens—Sixth Century, Archaic Greek Priest, Tanagra figurines,* Fourth Century
Gothic	*Royal Doorway—Chartres, Western Portal of Chartres*

Architecture for Appreciation

Homes of various countries	Japan, China, America, India, England, Switzerland, Germany
Public Buildings, Cathedrals, Palaces	
Egyptian Temples	Temple of Abu Simhel (This is a good example of a rock cut temple), rock-cut tomb Touthmes III at Karnak, Denderah, Amon Luxor
Early Greek Temples	
European Cathedrals	Chartres, Notre Dame in Paris, St. Mark's in Venice, Cathedral and Tower of Pisa
Venetian Palaces on Grand Canal in Venice	
Oriental Architecture	Taj Mahal, India; Chinese and Japanese Temples
American Skyscrapers	Empire State Building (Reproductions costing only a few cents of buildings in the modern functional style can be secured from the University Prints, Boston Massachusetts)

Architects of the United States

Hugh Ferris	Author of *The City of the Future*
Major Pierre Charles L'Enfant	French architect who planned our national capitol
Frank Lloyd Wright	Originator of the modern movement in architecture
Louis Sullivan	Responsible for the skyscraper in its new form
Arthur Loomis Harmon	Shelton Hotel, New York City
Shreve, Lamb, and Harmon	Empire State Building, New York City
Bertram Grosvenor Goodhue	Nebraska State Capitol, Lincoln Los Angeles Public Library

Sources of Illustrative Material

Firms from whom reproductions of paintings, and photographs of sculpture and architecture, can be obtained, are listed in the chapter on Textbooks and Other Instructional Materials. In addition to those listed, there is also the fine collection of Mrs. Vera Jones Bright, 165 Post Street, San Francisco. If the picture wanted is not in the catalogue of a firm, the firm is usually able to get a reproduction from some source.

Illustrations of Costumes
Illustration of Rugs, Pottery, Furniture, and Textiles

National Geographic Magazine

Day Color Reproductions "Pertaining to Man," "Pertaining to Animals," "Pertaining to Birds."

School Arts, Design, Creative Arts. New York: Brown, Robertson and Company

The Doris Rosenthal Portfolios. New York: Brown, Robertson and Company

BIBLIOGRAPHY

Books for Teachers

BERRY, ANNA M. *Art for Children.* London, England: The Studio, Ltd., 44 Leicester Square, London, 1929.

BOAS, BELLE. *Art in the School.* Garden City, New York: Doubleday, Doran & Company, 1924.

COLLINS, M. ROSE, and RILEY, OLIVE L. *Art Appreciation for Junior and Senior High Schools.* New York: Harcourt, Brace and Company, 1931.

COX, GEORGE J. *Art for Amateurs and Students.* Garden City, New York: Doubleday, Doran & Company, 1926.

Creative Expression. Edited by Gertrude Hartman and Ann Shumaker. New York: John Day Company, 1932.

DEWEY, JOHN. *Construction and Criticism.* New York: Columbia University Press, 1930.

DOW, ARTHUR WESLEY. *Composition.* Garden City, New York: Doubleday, Page & Company, 1926.

ECKFORD, EUGENIA. *Wonder Windows.* New York: E. P. Dutton and Company, 1931.

GARDNER, HELEN. *Art Through the Ages.* New York: Harcourt, Brace and Company, 1926.

GARDNER, HELEN. *Understanding the Arts.* New York: Harcourt, Brace and Company, 1933.

GOLDSTEIN, HARRIET, IRENE, and VETA. *Art in Everyday Life.* New York: The Macmillan Company, 1925.

KNOX, ROSE B. *School Activities and Equipment.* Boston: Houghton Mifflin Company, 1927.

RUGG, HAROLD, and SHUMAKER, ANN. *The Child-Centered School.* Yonkers-on-Hudson, New York: World Book Company, 1928, Chapters IV, V, VI, XI, XV, XVI.

TANNAHILL, SALLIE B. *Fine Arts for Public School Administrators.* New York: Bureau of Publications, Teachers College, Columbia University, 1932.

TANNAHILL, SALLIE. *P's and Q's.* Garden City, New York: Doubleday, Doran & Company, 1923.

WELLING, JANE BETSEY. *More Color for You.* Chicago: Abbott Educational Company, 1927.

WHEELER, IDA. *Playing With Clay.* New York: The Macmillan Company, 1927.

Periodicals

Cox, GEORGE J. "Art Teacher Training for the Changing Curriculum," *Teachers College Record.* XXXIII (October, 1931), 52–62.

Cox, GEORGE J. "The Educational Value of Art," *Teachers College Record.* XXXIV (October, 1932), 29–33.

KERSEY, VIERLING. "Teaching Children to Live Art," *Proceedings of the Pacific Arts Association.* 8th annual meeting, April, 1932.

MANGRAVITE, PEPPINO. "Art in Education," *Arts Magazine.* XIII (March, 1928), 145–152.

Progressive Education, references from:

BARNES, EMILY ANN, and YOUNG, BESS M. "Children and Architecture," IX (January, 1932), 29-38.

BLAI, BORIS. "Working in Wood, Stone and Clay," VIII (February, 1931), 120–125.

D'AMICO, VICTOR. "The Modern Art Room," VIII (November, 1931), 575–577.

"Creative Expression Through Dramatics," (entire number), VIII (January, 1931).

HASBROUCK, ELSA. "The Conditions for Creative Work," VIII (December, 1931), 648-655.

AIN, GREGORY. "Progressive Architecture for the Progressive School," IX (March, 1932), 195-202.

YOUTZ, PHILIP N. "School Buildings That Educate," IX (March, 1932), 189-194.

Books for Children

The following books for children can be used in the teaching of appreciation of beautiful books. These have well-designed illustrations, covers, title pages, and the printed pages, in most cases, have been laid out in an interesting manner.

CAMPBELL, RUTH. *The Cat Whose Whiskers Slipped.* New York: P. E. Volland Company. n. d.

COATSWORTH, ELIZABETH. *The Cat Who Went to Heaven.* New York: The Macmillan Company, 1930.

CRAIG, GIMMAGE. *The Picture Book of Ships.* New York: The Macmillan Company, 1930.

DAUTEUR, MAY. *Joan and Pierre.* Garden City, New York: Doubleday, Doran & Company, 1931.

GARWAITHE, JIMMY. *Zoo Book.* New York: Harper and Brothers, 1929.

MORROW, ELIZABETH. *The Painted Pig.* New York: Alfred A. Knopf, Inc., 1930.

MOESCHLIN, ELSA. *The Red Horse.* New York: Coward-McCann Company, 1929.

McNEIL, MARION L. *The Little Green Cart.* Akron, Ohio: Saalfield Publishing Company, 1931.

PETERSHAM, MAUD and MISKA. *Auntie and Celia Jane and Miki.* Garden City, New York: Doubleday, Doran & Company, 1932.

SEWELL, HELEN. *A Head for Happy.* New York: The Macmillan Company, 1931.

WHITE, GWEN. *A Picture Book of Ancient and Modern Dolls.* New York: The Macmillan Company, 1928.

These books are written for children about art or artists.

LOWNSBERY, ELOISE. *The Boy Knight of Reims.* Boston: Houghton Mifflin Company, 1927. (Story of medieval craftsman, not illustrated.)

MORLEY, MARGARET. *Donkey John of the Toy Valley.* Chicago: A. C. McClurg & Company, 1909. (Story of a Swiss toy maker, not illustrated.)

WHEELER, IDA W. *Playing with Clay.* New York: The Macmillan Company, 1927.

Standardized Tests in Art Appreciation

CHRISTENSEN, ERWIN O. *Art Appreciation Test.* Cambridge, Massachusetts: Harvard University Press.

MCADORY, MARGARET. *Art Appreciation Test.* Bureau of Publications, Teachers College, Columbia University.

CHAPTER XXII

CREATIVE PLAY AS AN INTEGRATING ACTIVITY [1]

CREATIVE PLAY AS A SCHOOL ACTIVITY

Inner Values as Essential as Objective Results

It is now generally recognized among thoughtful people that the world has been too much occupied with the material aspects of life and too little concerned with inner values. Wealth, machinery and commodity have been accorded an importance quite out of proportion to any corresponding degree of inner satisfaction and spiritual well being. The schools seem to have reflected the tendency of the day with an emphasis on facts, perceived knowledge, and objective results. This tendency is revealed in the widespread movement for measuring facts and skills apart from their significance and use to the child; in the annual exhibits of articles many of which have served no child's own need; in entertainments which are performances rather than honest, however simple, expressions of inner values which children themselves associate with character and events.

The best school practice today registers the influence of a counter movement in which the way a child views a character, an event, a situation or a fact at successive stages in his life is considered a more reliable index of growth than his ability to give photographic description of these aspects of life. The philosophy which places the values of persons above things *per se* is as old as Plato, but has been made most articulate in a comprehensive way for the present generation by John Dewey.

School practice has lagged far behind philosophy for the reason that the techniques for the guidance of children so that they may gain values are obviously and necessarily less clearly defined than the rules for getting a standardized product by a direct and fairly mechanized teaching procedure. There are no fixed specifications for teaching the child to make wise choices, to take right attitudes and to adjust satisfactorily to a variety of conditions.

The behavior of an individual in the continuous stream of choice-making is determined by his sense of values. If the child is to attain a socially acceptable sense of values he must first have practice in expressing things as he sees them. It is then in the province of the

---

[1] Contributed by Ethel I. Salisbury, Associate Professor of Elementary Education, University of California at Los Angeles, and Educational Consultant, Santa Monica Public Schools.

teacher to lead him into new experiences that he may gain deeper insight and so revise his values.

To illustrate, a group of children have the notion that the Chinese are all queer people who do everything backward and eat rats and mice. In their play they express just these ideas which seem to have registered for the reason that they appeal to the interests of children— have value for them.

After the children, however, have revealed the values they associate with the Chinese, they are led into further reading of informational material and stories bringing out many characteristics and customs of the Chinese, until their play shows an entirely new conception of these people. As a result the attitude of the children is changed from one of derision to one of respect and interest.

In many phases of traditional schoolroom practice children take over the values set for them by adults. The sad predicament of society today is ample evidence that the values upon which the elders set great store are often the wrong values—individual achievement quite apart from the good of society, development of industry without a plan for distributing its products, advertisement and sales instead of quality and fair exchange.

The point cannot be overemphasized that the child needs to learn to arrive at his own values for things. He does so by going through many experiences in which he has an opportunity to distinguish between that which really has value for him and that which someone else has told him has value. For the child to have to take the evaluations of his elders actually prevents him from appraising things for himself. When the individual acquires facts without feeling that they are worthwhile, goes through forms which express nothing for him, puts on a semblance of emotion without feeling that emotion, he becomes a hollow personality. The educational task is to find the way in which the child naturally arrives at human values and then seek to organize and guide that tendency.

Free Play

Probably the little child's most natural way of gaining values is through his free imaginative play. Some person, animal, or thing enlists his interest and curiosity. He observes its more apparent characteristics and behaviors and before long begins to identify himself with the object of his interest. He becomes according to his environment, policeman, farmer, pony, rabbit, train, automobile or other animated object. This procedure on his part is a spontaneous reaction and also a way of study whereby he becomes more intimately acquainted with the object itself. The best way, indeed the only way, to know what an experience is, is to live through that experience. To become acquainted with the many aspects of his environment the child proceeds to multiply his experiences through imagination. In doing thus he is reconstructing the world about him in the light of what he sees in it. He is working back from the way people behave to what they think and how they feel.

Little children in their block play constantly carry out the adult activities they see in progress about them to comprehend better these activities. The child of the intermediate grade level also engages in creative play. One has only to observe these children in park, in barn, or attic, to see them living in an imaginary world of their own. Adults recall their own participation in imaginative play.

> I do not remember dramatizing before I was old enough to read for myself. Then we read stories for the sole purpose of acting them out. We never played if anyone could see us or hear us—we were afraid that someone would make fun of us. From the age of ten to fourteen, we played whenever we could go to some part of the house where we should not have an audience. We often performed the same thing over and over for three or four hours at a time, and every day at that. We were apt to be five different characters in a single hour. When we studied our real school lessons, we pretended we were girls at boarding school. I shall always remember the intense pleasure we derived from these impersonations. I often wondered whether other children played in this way and was surprised when I first learned that it was natural for all.[1]

The play of the older children differs from that of the younger children in several particulars. The older children demand more in the way of plot; little children are satisfied with short disconnected characterizations while older children see the relation and sequence of events and express themselves in a continuous stream of related experiences. The older children attempt more complex situations than do the younger children.

The play of the older children is more realistic. They feel that costumes and setting are essential. They do not go in for fairies so much and they choose their characters from among men and women of their environment from history and from fiction. Stranger and bolder characters are portrayed. The older children do not identfy themselves with characters as do the younger children but consciously pretend to be those characters. During all their play the intermediate grade children as well as the primary children are dealing with values—ways of seeing characters and events and expressing what they see rather than the literal facts. Between their interpretations of an event or a character and a recitation of the facts about an event or a character, there is as much difference as there is between the artist's painting of a home and an architect's specifications.

---

[1] John Merrill and Martha Fleming. *Play-making and Plays.* New York: The Macmillan Company, 1930, p. 11.

Courtesy of Los Angeles City Schools

Home Life in Holland Played by Intermediate Grade Children

History, biography, and fiction afford instances of this natural tendency of children to express a thing as they see it.

A bowshot or so north of the church there lay by the roadside a great block of stone, and around it a thick small grove of birch and aspen. Here the children were wont to play at church, and Tomas, the youngest son of Eirik's priest's daughter, stood up in the person of his grandfather and said mass, sprinkled holy-water, and even baptized, when there was rain-water in the hollows of the rock. But once, the autumn before, this game had fallen out but sadly for them. For first Tomas had married Kristin and Arne—Arne was not so old but he would go off and play with the children when he saw a chance. Then Arne caught a baby pig that was going by, and they brought it into church to be baptized. Tomas anointed it with mud, dipped it into a pool of water, and, copying his grandfather, said mass in Latin and chid them for the smallness of their offerings—and at this the children laughed, for they had heard their elders talk of Eirik's exceeding greed for money. But the more they laughed the worse Tomas got in the things he hit on; for next he said that this child had been gotten in Lent, and they must pay penalty for their sin to the priest and the church. The great boys shouted with laughter at this; but Kristin was so ashamed that she was all but weeping, as she stood there with the little pig in her arms. And just as this was going on who must choose to come that way but Eirik himself riding home from a sick-visit. When he understood what the young folks were about, he sprang from his horse, and handed the holy vessels to Bentein, his eldest grandson, who was with him, so suddenly that Bentein nearly dropped the silver dove with God's body on it on the hillside, while the priest rushed in among the children belabouring all he could reach. Kristin let slip the little pig, and it rushed shrieking down the road with the christening robe trailing after it, while Eirik's horses reared and plunged with terror; the priest pushed her, too, so that she fell down, and he knocked against her with his foot so hard that she felt the pain in her hip for many days after. Lavrans had thought when he heard of this, that Eirik had been too hard with Kristin, seeing she was but a little child. He said he would speak to the priest of it, but Ragnfrid begged him not to do so, for the child had gotten but what she deserved for joining in such a blasphemous game. So Lavrans said no more of the matter; but he gave Arne the worst beating the boy had ever had.[1]

Here the play of Kristin, Tomas, and Arne illustrates the way in which children create an imaginative world out of fragments of the little comprehended adult world in which they live in order to get at its meaning and values. The "great boys" having no doubt but recently put away childish things themselves express their superior maturity in their laughter. Eirik typifies the adult who has no understanding of the function of play in childhood and sees it as blasphemy or a waste of time.

It is through the child's free imaginative play that he reveals himself in all his naivete. He reconstructs the world about him in terms of what it means to him. He is not relaying facts to an audience but expressing inner values for himself regardless of audience. "This is what a horse means to me" is what the kindergarten boy is saying as he gallops by on a broomstick. He is not primarily concerned with the fact that a horse has four legs, two ears, and a tail.

"This is what baptism and marriage mean to us" say Kristin and her playmate. "This is what school means to us" say the children whose free play at one time seemed to include little more than the antics of obstreperous pupils and the tirades of an irate teacher.

Play Not a Means of Making Dull Things Interesting

Christopher Morley describes an incident recorded in Thomas Fuller's *Holy State and Profane State* published in 1642 which illustrates the procedure of making hard things easy by dramatic play. Quoting Morley:

Fuller tells the marvelous story, a perfect fable for teachers, of the gentleman who took a number of children for a walk into the country, and forgetting they were so much younger than himself, he led them farther than he intended to. They began to "grutch", complained that they were tired and began to whine. I can't accurately quote Fuller's language, but he describes that this gentleman cut a big stick from the hedge as a nag for himself, and little switches as ponies for the children, and told them that they were horses, and thus mounted, he says, "Fancy," (or what we would call imagination), "Fancy put metal into their legs and they came cheerfully home."[2]

---

[1] Sigrid Undset. *Kristin Lavransdatter.* New York: Alfred A. Knopf, Inc., 1923, p. 8.

[2] Christopher Morley. *Ex Libris Carissimis.* Philadelphia: University of Pennsylvania Press, 1932, pp. 72–73.

Mr. Morley goes on to comment:

> And I often think to myself, if only teachers would remember that,
> if they would just enliven our pedestrianism now and then with a little
> more imagination, how much longer journeys we could take, and how
> much more cheerfully we would get home.[1]

The purpose of dramatic play in the schools is not to enliven a weary pedestrianism, and Mr. Morley would find if he observed children whose teacher had used it more than once to get disagreeable tasks done agreeably, a great lack of enthusiasm for that sort of hoax.

There is a nice distinction between capitalizing the natural tendency of children for dramatic play and trying to make a given item of subject matter interesting by tricks of instruction. In the first instance a natural appetite is being supplied with wholesome food, while in the latter situation the appetite is being stimulated artificially for unpalatable food.

Play in the Intermediate Grades Neglected

In the kindergarten and primary grades the free imaginative play of the children has been capitalized for educational purposes. In the intermediate grades, however, it has not been a legitimate part of the curriculum for several reasons. First a puritanic inheritance on the part of many adults is the general conviction that play in school is not only a waste of time but positively detrimental to the child's character because it is not "hard." They point out the fact that many tasks which adults must undertake are hard and they argue that the child should have a rigorous training in doing "hard" things. These people lose sight of the fact that the adult in his task has a leverage of purpose behind the hard work such as gaining a livelihood, expressing an art, achieving fortune or fame and they deny the right of the child to the leverage of a purpose vital to him at his age. They fail to recognize that the work which has an intrinsic value for the man partakes of the nature of play in that it completely absorbs him, not for the end of achievement alone but for the joy of the doing. They approve the adult's whole-souled interest in and devotion to work, science, art or profession but gainsay the child's right to lose himself in activities which have meaning for him.

Another reason that play has not been utilized in the public schools lies in the fact that the machinery of the school is built chiefly to accomplish tangible ends, thus making conditions in which even gifted teachers find it very difficult to carry on any activity which is not more or less formalized. Crowded classrooms, lack of materials, the presence of atypical children, administrative regulations, a curriculum packed

---
[1] *Ibid.*

with requirements of many unrelated items, are all a part of the machinery. Those who are responsible for the execution of plans always find that it requires far more time to go through the necessary and educative stages of experimentation and the handling of materials, than is ordinarily allotted.

Last but not least, the guidance of children in creative play, the related research and industrial arts activities is a task for the teacher who herself is creative and willing to give arduous hours to the preparation necessary.

Courtesy of Los Angeles City Schools

Richer and Deeper Insights of People, Objects and Events Are Gained by Children Through Creative Play

TECHNIQUES OF GUIDING DRAMATIC PLAY

Study of Free Play

Since children in their creative play reveal something of the inner values which they associate with people, objects and events, it is there that they should be studied by those who would guide them into gaining richer and deeper insights. Any study of free play is best carried on when the children are unconscious of critical observation. The intermediate grade child is especially shy of those who might be skeptical

or who might laugh at his interpretations.   It is perhaps because the
child of the intermediate grade age has come to know that in his
inner life he does not place the same values as do adults on many
things, that he becomes reticent about revealing his own values.   The
school instead of establishing a situation to make him delight in his
creative play, directs him into organized games where he goes according to the rules and where values are pretty much already determined.

Observation of any particular group of children at their free play
will afford the teacher many clues regarding individual interests, abilities and background of culture.   It will give an index also to the
various personal traits, such as kindliness, patience, fairness, ambition,
determination and the like.

Courtesy of Los Angeles City Schools

Ceremonial Dance of the Pueblos

Releasing the Spirit of Children for Play

How can the spirit of children be released for free play in the
class room where outer semblance of a conventional order has long
been the legitimate goal rather than the child's honest expression of
inner values?   It is difficult to say which comes first of the many
factors which make children willing to carry on free play in the schoolroom.   Long before it is suggested to them as a part of the school day,
a spirit of love must be established—love not in any sentimental sense

—but in a sense which gives children the security of knowing that their beliefs, thoughts and feelings are taken as seriously by the teacher as by the children themselves. The creative spirit in dramatic play is a delicate, sensitive one which needs to be fostered without too much attention and always with understanding.

Sometimes the teacher plays with the children. If she enters into the spirit of the play, many of the barriers of diffidence and shyness are removed. She does not play to show the children, but plays to become part of their recreated world.

Frequently the free play begins with some story of dramatic interest related to the social studies unit, and purposely introduced early by the teacher, such as *Sokar and the Crocodile*,[1] for Egypt, *Red Howling Monkey*[2] for the South American Jungle, or *One Day with Manu*[3] for the South Seas.

In the fourth grade the play may begin with puppetry. Stories from the best of literature offer opportunities for the integration of English, art and construction.

Organization for Play

The very practical problem of organization appears early. How can free play be carried on with 35 or 40 children in a room? Obviously the numbers complicate the situation but with careful organization and planning the children can learn to have their fun without disturbing others. Sometimes a small group is permitted to play quietly in the house or the boat, or market which has been constructed, for the purpose of actual use, while the remainder of the class go on with their other work of reading, research and the like. Sometimes part of the class play actively while others observe in order to be able to suggest improvements. One group may carry through some custom typical of the life of a people, such as using the Mexican metate, making tortillas, selling in a market stall, trekking to a fiesta and the like. Whatever has come to the children vividly in discussion, moving picture or reading, may be translated into action. Sometimes the whole class may participate in playing out certain scenes, for example, a Chinese wedding or a market day. The more the content of what they study appeals to them the more it will appear in their play. This works the other way around, too. The more the children *play the more they demand.* For example, a child in a Chinese play says: "I wanted to be a fisherman today but I didn't know how the Chinese fish." Another asks, "Does any one know whether the Chinese use nets or fishing-poles?"

[1] Alice Howard. *Sokar and the Crocodile.* New York: The Macmillan Company, 1928.
[2] Helen Tee-Van. *Red Howling Monkey.* New York: The Macmillan Company, 1926.
[3] Armstrong Sperry. *One Day With Manu.* Philadelphia: The John C. Winston Company, 1933.

A group playing Early Days in America carry out their versions of how an Indian trapped deer or how a Forty-niner dug gold. The play is earnest to the extent to which the teacher is able to establish a spirit of genuine delight in interpretation and creative thinking.

Any procedure in which there is a discussion for improvement is best carried out when the children have come to feel at home playing creatively in the classroom. After the more or less fragmentary play has established a certain amount of initiative, organization must be introduced to make it go forward profitably. The free play is developed into a second stage, dramatic play. Discussion and organization usually precede this play. The teacher plans with the group so that they may maintain some sort of unity of theme by deciding on the general nature of the play for the day. At this time they organize themselves as mother, father, Daniel Boone, or other leading characters. Children naturally in their play out-of-doors plan and organize. Unless this step is taken, a hodge-podge follows. While there is entire freedom in the continuity, conversation, and business of the free play, so that creative thinking can go on, there must be some definite structure of plot or incident in the minds of the children participating. Sometimes children make up their own plot, sometimes they borrow one.

Teachers often ask if the children just get up and begin playing without plans beforehand. The children do so during the first few days of the play when left to their own devices, and they also do so after their play has set into a pattern with only minor variations of business, conversation, incident, and the like. During the growing, evolving, creative states, as has been said, some organization and guidance is essential. It is a matter for delicate discrimination on the part of the teacher to know when to offer suggestions and when to remain quiet. Obviously long, wasteful, digressions get nowhere and are to be avoided but good thinking, even though slow, should not be short-circuited. One teacher in starting a study of the Westward Movement presented visual materials on the subject. The children had in the previous grade participated in dramatic play and many industrial arts activities. The teacher now asked what they would like to do in relation to the study. Following are some of the requests:

May we have a play? May I be Daniel Boone? May I be Jemima Boone? May I be Buffalo Bill? May I be a cowgirl in a cowboy play? May we build a ranch house? May we have a play about some of the forts? May I be Francis in the story? May I be one of Daniel Boone's followers? May I be Hawkeye? May I be an Indian? May I be Chief Sitting Bull? May I be George Washington? May I be Betsy? When are we going to have a play? May we have a play of pioneers? May we draw some pictures?

It is easy to see that from such a multiplicity of ideas some unity of theme must be developed or the children must be divided into groups to play out different stories.

Play, the Integrating Activity for Study and Work

At the beginning of the term, before a social studies unit has gotten under way, there is little of setting in the classroom about which the play can center. This fact is a very good reason why the play should begin as soon as the children, through reading, study and discussion, have acquired some information about the lives of a given people. As they relive the lives of a people, playing out the incidents, customs and characters of those people, they find a need for appropriate setting, for costumes, tools and implements, and for additional information about the lives of people. If their plan really grows the children are continuously seeking an ever-increasing knowledge of the ways of the people whose lives they are reliving. If they answer these needs by constructing articles with attention to standards, the industrial arts become an organic part of the play life of the children. Indeed it often seems that the child of the middle grades finds as much satisfaction in the artistic construction of articles with which to carry on the play as in the play itself.

Play, Not Dramatization in the Old Sense

Playing a story creatively for fun and expression without the constant direction of the teacher is, of course, a very different procedure from the dramatizing of a story by liberal adherence to the author's words. From the beginning dramatization is designed for an audience. Dramatic play does not thrive before an audience until it has set into a pattern.

When the children play a story or fragments from the life of a people according to their own interpretation, they begin with values they see and by means of action, tone, and words express those values not for others but for themselves. Often, as with primitive peoples, mood is expressed by song rhythm and dance. The children in playing Chinese life were carrying the rice bags. Spontaneously they formed a procession and as they carried their burdens, broke into a grunting chant. Several days previously they had read that the Chinese often grunt and groan at their labors.

Method of Dramatic Play

The method of expression is through setting, characterization and plot. The application of these terms can be illustrated in the following account of dramatic play as it developed in a fourth grade.

The children had learned something of the river life in China, the work of the coolies in the rice fields, and the home customs of wealthy Chinese. A junk and a back drop showing appropriate background of water, land and pagodas, furnished the setting for the river life. For the play, which centered about the home of a wealthy Chinese, a black teakwood table, high benches, a screen and a few other articles of furniture constituted the setting. The only available space in the room furnished a setting for the rice field. Atmosphere was added when big bags of what was supposed to be rice were scattered about. The coolies merely stood by the radiator as they stamped on the rice. Characterization was employed by the children when, as coolies, they stolidly tramped the rice; as wealthy Chinese they assumed a domineering manner when visiting the rice fields; and as inhabitants of the junk they patiently mended sails and caught fish.

How completely a child identifies himself with a character he has assumed for play is illustrated in the following incident.

While studying the everyday life of the Hebrews, a phase of old world background, a group of sixth grade children came to the conclusion that Abram must have called a council of his men to discuss ways and means of carrying out the Lord's command to leave the land

Courtesy of Los Angeles City Schools

Children Live the Life of the Pueblo Indians

of his fathers. The class decided to relive this council meeting in dramatic play. A group of boys was selected to enact the parts of Hebrew characters. In the meantime Sarai organized the women to make plans for the journey. While Abram was presiding over the men's council several of the boys tittered, whereupon someone suggested that plans should be made to discipline any who misbehaved on the journey to the Promised Land. In reply to this suggestion the young leader, quite in keeping with the wisdom of Abram, said, "I think that I shall be able to manage those problems as they arise."

The development of plot is less obvious. Plot is extended action. It is action which has become a complete whole with beginning, climax and end. The children who were living the three phases of Chinese life as mentioned before combined them in something of a story in which the wealthy Chinese man was taken in a sedan by his coolies to go by the boat to the rice fields where he transacted some business after which he returned to his home to recount the experiences of the day to his family.

Development of plot is usually the result of discussion where the teacher's part is to bring about an awareness of problems and to stimulate the proposal of possible solutions.

Courtesy of Los Angeles City Schools

Miniature Replica of Pueblo House

Enrichment of Free Play

While care should be taken not to require a long, wearisome recital by the children of what they have played, it is well to create a situation in which the children do recount some of their imaginary experiences. Often these will be fragmentary and lacking in content, and here lies one of the tasks of the teacher. By leading the children into reading about peoples, industry, history, and contemporary social and national groups, she stimulates them to acquire a wealth of ideas which, in turn, they soon are ready to express in their dramatic play. Indeed, the social studies and literature afford the chief sources of content for the dramatic play after it has become a natural part of the schoolroom. As the children read of Egypt they become Egyptians and relive the life of these people in a certain sense. As they study Pioneers they play out the habits and customs of these people. What is more natural than that they should suggest the building of a pioneer home with its simple furnishings and all of the little details which enlist the interest of children and add to a body of information from which they may derive principles of geography and history. For example, they learn that the activities, mode of dress, and experiences of people in the hot climate differ greatly from those of a temperate climate; that people are, to a certain extent, the product of their environment; that civilization brings about certain fundamental changes in the mode of life of a people; that superstition and ignorance are responsible for lack of progress. They gain these conceptions in a way that has values for themselves, not as the parrot repetition of something stated by elders.

Often inaccuracies appear in the play and construction work and here the teacher has an opportunity skillfully to correct misconceptions, to bring in fresh information in order that new elements will be added to the play. Care should be taken not to suggest a literal adherence to facts when the child is concerned with expressing a human value. A correction of fact may be made in another period.

Causes of Failure

It is true that play in the classroom with the inexperienced teacher frequently seems to fall flat or result in pandemonium. It may do so for any of several reasons:

(1) the children have not enough background of information or story interest;

(2) they do not feel free to go ahead;

(3) they have worn out the subject because new elements have not been introduced;

(4) the spirit which fosters creative thinking is lacking;

(5) there has been no organization among the children and no discussion of the general trend of the play;

(6) there has been no check-up following the play during consecutive days to analyze their mistakes; and

(7) the children have not learned the techniques of using many books to get information in regard to the necessary detail and come to their play lacking the required knowledge.

In general it may be said, just as with every other activity, children learn to play by playing. Some teachers provide a regular time for the play, while others find that the best play follows very spontaneously the reading of a story or a discussion of a report. For example, after one child had told the class what he had read about a Chinese wedding, a child exclaimed: "Let's have a Chinese wedding now!" A little organization followed and very soon the children had lost themselves in living the lives of the Chinese bride, groom, and guests. The teacher said: "Had we waited for the regular play period, I doubt if there would have been the same keen interest in playing out a wedding." Very much depends upon seizing the moment when the children are in the spirit of the thing. Of course the spirit can be built up by proper stimulation, but often it is a long, arduous process and shows the result of a set stage. Free play certainly requires a flexible program.

Courtesy of Los Angeles City Schools

As Children Relive the Lives of People They Find a Need for Appropriate Setting, Costumes, and Implements

Creative Play Important in the School of Today

Education can no longer concern itself exclusively with teaching children to acquire fixed and definite facts and skills even though these be integrated in meaningful activities. It has another task. Children must be led into experience in which they will gain some of the techniques of creative response to changing life situations. Today the ability to experiment and arrive at the best way of proceeding is important. At a time when budgets for concrete materials are limited, dramatic play is perhaps the activity best adapted to the development of the technique of experimentation.

If children are to learn to live in a planning society instead of a planned society they must participate in activities which give them practice in sharing in creative thinking and in maintaining some balance between the extremes of personality characteristics. Self-effacement is no more desirable than utter selfishness. Over-ambition is as detrimental both to the individual and society of which he is a part as is laziness. Only in the stream of active experience working on common problems with his fellow can the child learn to float and let his companions float by maintaining, in the long run, a near equilibrium. Dramatic play is an activity which offers innumerable opportunities for children to use judgment as to the right amount of cooperation, initiative, leadership, followership, ambition, and the like to employ in many types of situations.

Surely continuous practice in meeting the infinite variety of conditions presented in play will better fit the children to live successfully and happily than an education that calls only for ready made responses.

BIBLIOGRAPHY

BROWN, CORRINE. *Creative Drama in the Lower School.* New York: D. Appleton and Company, 1929.

COOK, H. CALDWELL. *The Play Way.* New York: Frederick A. Stokes Company, 1917.

CURTI, MARGARET WOOSTER. *Child Psychology.* New York: Longmans, Green and Company, 1930.

LEHMAN, HARVEY C., and WITTY, PAUL A. *The Psychology of Play Activities.* New York: A. S. Barnes and Company, 1927.

MERRILL, JOHN, and FLEMING, MARTHA. *Play-making and Plays.* New York: The Macmillan Company, 1930.

SMITH, HILDA WORTHINGTON. "A Post Office in Fairyland." *Atlantic Monthly.* CLIV (August, 1934), 231-239.

BIBLIOGRAPHY ON CURRICULUM UNITS [1]

The references included in this bibliography have been carefully selected to include those books which have been found most useful and helpful by children and teachers in connection with a wide variety of curriculum units. The books have been classified under the headings Books for Pupils and Books for Teachers. Children's books are classified as Reference Books and Story Books. The bibliography is divided into major sections according to general subject arranged in the following order:

Animals	Foods	Pioneers
Arctic Region	Forestry	Pottery
British Empire	France	Prehistoric Life
California	Germany	Records
Canada	Greece	Rome
China	Holland	Russia
Clothing	Homes	Ships and Cargoes
Communication	Honey Bees	South America
Deserts	Indians of the Southwest	Spain and Portugal
Dogs	Italy	Switzerland
Earth, Sun, Moon, and Stars	Japan	Time
	Magnets	Transportation
Egypt	Medieval Life	United States
Electricity	Mexico	Vikings
Farm Life	Miners and Mining	Weather
	Money	

ANIMALS

Books for Pupils

REFERENCE BOOKS

DOPP, KATHERINE E. *The Early Cave Men.* Chicago: Rand McNally & Company, 1904.

DOPP, KATHERINE E. *Early Herdsmen.* Chicago: Rand McNally & Company, 1923.

DOPP, KATHERINE E. *The Tree Dwellers.* Chicago: Rand McNally & Company, 1926.

DUNCAN, FRANCIS MARTIN, and DUNCAN, L. T. *Animal Life in Africa.* Book II New York: Oxford University Press, 1921.

---

[1] The references included in this bibliography were selected by Jasmine Britton, Supervising Librarian, Los Angeles City Schools, working under the general direction and at the request of Ethel I. Salisbury, Associate Professor of Elementary Education, University of California at Los Angeles, and Educational Consultant, Santa Monica City Schools, who acted as chairman of the subcommittee of the State Curriculum Commission on the preparation of this volume. The arrangement and form of this bibliography was developed by Helen Heffernan, Chief of the Division of Elementary Education and Rural Schools, Gladys L. Potter, Assistant Chief of the Division of Elementary Education and Rural Schools, and Ivan R. Waterman, Chief of the Division of Textbooks and Publications.

DUNCAN, FRANCIS MARTIN, and DUNCAN, L. T. *Animal Life in the East.* Book III. New York: Oxford University Press, 1921.

DUNCAN, FRANCIS MARTIN, and DUNCAN, L. T. *Animal Life in the New World.* Book IV. New York: Oxford University Press, 1921.

DUNCAN, FRANCIS MARTIN, and DUNCAN, L. T. *Animal Friends.* New York: Oxford University Press, 1921.

DUNN, FANNIE W., and TROXELL, ELEANOR. *Baby Animals.* Evanston, Illinois: Row, Peterson and Company, 1928.

Elephant Stories Retold. New York: The Century Co., 1919.

GHOSH, SARATH KUMAR. *Wonders of the Jungle.* Vol. I-II. Boston: D. C. Heath and Company, 1915.

KNECHT, KLARA E. *Wild Animals as I Know Them.* Akron, Ohio: The Saalfield Publishing Company, 1933.

LORD, ISABEL ELY. *Picture Book of Animals.* New York: The Macmillan Company, 1931.

MCNALLY, GEORGIA MAUD. *Baby Animals.* New York: George H. Doran Company, 1917.

MOHR, LOUISE MAUDE. *Days Before Houses.* Chicago: Rand McNally & Company, 1928.

MORSE, GEORGE F. *Wild Animals of America in Picture Strip.* Chicago: Follett Publishing Company, 1931.

MORSE, GEORGE F. *The Life of Baby Animals.* Chicago: Wilcox and Follett Company, 1930.

NIDA, WILLIAM L., and NIDA, STELLA H. *Animal Life.* Science Reader for Silent Reading, Book IV. Boston: D. C. Heath and Company, 1926.

NIDA, WILLIAM L., and NIDA, STELLA H. *The Baby Animal Zoo.* Science Readers for Silent Reading. Book III. Boston: D. C. Heath and Company, 1926.

NIDA, WILLIAM LEWIS, and NIDA, STELLA. *Trailing Our Animal Friends.* Boston: D. C. Heath and Company, 1928.

PATCH, EDITH M., and HOWE, H. E. *Hunting.* Nature and Science Readers. Book I. New York: The Macmillan Company, 1932.

PATCH, EDITH M., and HOWE, H. E. *Surprises.* Nature and Science Readers. Book III. New York: The Macmillan Company, 1933.

WEIMER, TERESA, and JONES, R. G. *Chats in the Zoo.* Chicago: Rand McNally & Company, 1914.

STORY BOOKS

ASHBROOK, FRANK G. *Furry Friends.* Racine, Wisconsin: Whitman Publishing Company, 1930.

CARRICK, VALERY. *Tales of Wise and Foolish Animals.* New York: Frederick A. Stokes Company, 1928.

DOUGLAS, ROBERT DICK; MARTIN, DAVID R., and OLIVER, DOUGLAS L. *Three Boy Scouts in Africa.* New York: G. P. Putnam's Sons, 1928.

GALE, ELIZABETH. *Circus Animals.* Chicago: Rand McNally & Company, 1927.

GRAHAM, C. E. *Furry Friends.* Four Footed Friends Series. Newark, New Jersey: Charles E. Graham & Company. n. d.

GREEN, FITZHUGH. *Martin Johnson, Lion Hunter.* New York: G. P. Putnam's Sons, 1928.

KIPLING, RUDYARD. *Jungle Book.* Garden City, New York: Doubleday, Doran & Company, 1932.

KIPLING, RUDYARD. *Just So Stories.* New York: The Macmillan Company, 1930.

LEWIS, MARY R. *At the Zoo.* New York: Thomas Nelson & Sons, 1927.

MUKERJI, DHAN GOPAL. *Kari the Elephant.* New York: E. P. Dutton and Company, 1922.

Lion and Tiger Stories, Retold. New York: The Century Co., 1925.

SERL, EMMA. *In the Animal World.* New York: Silver, Burdett and Company, 1931.

SMITH, LAURA ROUNTREE. *The Circus Book.* Chicago: A. Flanagan Company, 1930.

WIESE, KURT. *Ella the Elephant.* New York: Coward, McCann & Company, 1931.

WIESE, KURT. *Karoo the Kangaroo.* New York: Coward, McCann & Company, 1927.

Books for Teachers

COOPER, COURTNEY RYLEY. *Lions 'n' Tigers 'n' Everything.* Boston: Little, Brown and Company, 1924.

GASK, LILIAN. *All about Animals A to Z.* London: George G. Harrap & Co., Ltd., 1932.

HORNADAY, W. T. *Tales from Nature's Wonderland.* New York: Chas. Scribner's Sons, 1924.

KNIGHT, CHARLES ROBERT. *Animals of the World for Young People.* New York: Frederick A. Stokes Company, 1908.

MILLS, ENOS ABIJAH. *Watched by Wild Animals.* Boston: Houghton Mifflin Company, 1932.

MUKERJI, DAHN GOPAL. *Jungle Beasts and Men.* New York: E. P. Dutton & Company, 1923.

NELSON, EDWARD WILLIAM. *Wild Animals of North America.* Washington: National Geographic Society, 1930.

SCHWARTZ, JULIA AUGUSTA. *Wilderness Babies.* Boston: Little, Brown and Company, 1906.

ARCTIC REGION

Books for Pupils

REFERENCE BOOKS

ALLEN, NELLIE B. *How and Where We Live.* Boston: Ginn and Company, 1924.

AITCHISON, ALISON E., and UTTLEY, MARGUERITE. *Across Seven Seas to Seven Continents.* Indianapolis: Bobbs-Merrill Company, 1925.

ATWOOD, W. W. and ATWOOD, THOMAS. *Home Life in Far Away Lands.* Boston: Ginn and Company, 1928.

CARPENTER, FRANK G. *Around the World With the Children.* New York: American Book Company, 1917.

CARPENTER, FRANCES. *Our Little Friends of Eskimo Land, Papik and Natsek.* New York: American Book Company, 1931.

CARPENTER, FRANCES. *Our Neighbors Near and Far.* New York: American Book Company, 1933.

CHANCE, L. M. *Little Folks of Many Lands.* Boston: Ginn and Company, 1904.

CHAMBERLAIN, J. F. *How We Are Sheltered.* New York: The Macmillan Company, 1924.

GILMAN, ISABEL AMBLER. *Alaska, The American Northland.* Yonkers-on-Hudson, New York: World Book Company, 1923.

GIST, A. S.; EIDE, A. H.; and GIST, R. P. *New Stories from Eskimo Land.* San Francisco: Harr Wagner Publishing Co., 1930.

HEADLEY, E. A. *How Other People Travel.* Chicago: Rand McNally & Company, 1926.

PEARY, JOSEPHINE. *Children of the Arctic.* New York: Frederick A. Stokes Company. n. d.

PEARY, ROBERT EDWIN. *Snowland Folk.* New York: Frederick A. Stokes Company. n. d.

PERDUE, HANNAH AVIS. *How Other Children Live.* Chicago: Rand McNally & Company, 1927.

PERDUE, HANNAH AVIS. *Child Life in Other Lands.* Chicago: Rand McNally & Company, 1918.

SCANTLEBURY, ELIZABETH ELLIS. *Little World Children.* Boston: Ginn and Company, 1928.

SMITH, MARY ESTELLA. *Eskimo Stories.* Chicago: Rand McNally & Company. n. d.

STEFÁNSSON, VILHJÁLMUR, and IRWIN, V. M. *Kak, The Copper Eskimo.* New York: The Macmillan Company, 1927.

STEFÁNSSON, VILHJÁLMUR. *My Life with the Eskimo.* New York: The Macmillan Company, 1913.

THOMPSON, RUTH. *Our Neighbors Near and Far.* San Francisco: Harr Wagner Publishing Company, 1926.

THOMPSON, RUTH. *Type Stories of the World for Little Folk.* San Francisco: Harr Wagner Publishing Company, 1922.

STORY BOOKS

CHAFFEE, ALLEN. *Sitka, The Snow Baby.* Springfield, Mass.: Milton Bradley Company, 1923.

HADER, BERTA and ELMER. *Chuck-A-Luck and His Reindeer.* Boston: Houghton Mifflin Company, 1933.

HADER, BERTA and HADER, ELMER. *Tooky.* New York: Longmans, Green & Company, 1931.

LOMEN, HELEN and FLACK, MARJORIE. *Taktuk, An Arctic Boy.* Garden City, New York: Doubleday, Doran & Company, 1928.

MULETS, LENORE ELIZABETH. *Little People of the Snow.* Chicago: A. Flanagan Company, 1925.

PEARY, JOSEPHINE. *Snow Baby.* New York: Frederick A. Stokes Company. n. d.

PEARY, MARIE AHNIGHTO (Stafford, M. A.). *Snowbaby's Own Story.* New York: Frederick A. Stokes Company, 1934.

PERKINS, LUCY. *Eskimo Twins.* Boston: Houghton Mifflin Company. n. d.

STEFÁNSSON, VILHJÁLMUR. *Northward Ho!* New York: The Macmillan Company, 1928.

WIESE, KURT. *Wallie the Walrus.* New York: Coward, McCann & Company, 1930.

BRITISH EMPIRE

Books for Pupils

REFERENCE BOOKS

ALLEN, NELLIE B. *The New Europe.* Boston: Ginn and Company, 1920.

ATWOOD, WALLACE W., and THOMAS, H. G. *Nations Beyond the Seas.* Boston: Ginn and Company, 1930.

BARNARD, HOWARD CLIVE. *British Empire in Pictures.* New York: The Macmillan Company, n. d.

BARROWS, H. H.; PARKER, E. P.; and PARKER, M. T. *Europe and Asia.* New York: Silver, Burdett and Company, 1930.

BLAISDELL, ALBERT F., and BALL, FRANCIS K. *English History Story Book.* Boston: Little, Brown and Company, 1912.

BEST, SUSIE M. *Merry England.* World Famous Stories in Historic Settings, V. 3. New York: The Macmillan Company, 1918.

BRYANT, LORINDA. *Children's Book of Celebrated Bridges.* New York: The Century Co., 1925.

BRYANT, LORINDA. *Children's Book of Celebrated Towers.* New York: The Century Co., 1926.

BRYANT, LORINDA. *Children's Book of European Landmarks.* New York: The Century Co., 1928.

CARPENTER, FRANK G. *Africa.* New York: American Book Company, 1924.

CARPENTER, FRANK G. *Australia, New Zealand and some islands of the South Seas.* Garden City, New York: Doubleday, Page & Co., 1924.

CARPENTER, FRANK G. *Europe.* New York: American Book Company, 1922.

CHAMBERLAIN, J. F., and CHAMBERLAIN, F. H. *Europe.* New York: The Macmillan Company, 1916.

CLARK, MARION G., and GORDY, WILBUR F. *What Men Brought from Europe to America.* New York: Chas. Scribner's Sons, 1929.

CORNEY, EVIE, and DORLAND, G. W. *Great Deeds of Great Men.* Boston: D. C. Heath and Company, 1930.

CURTIS, MARY ISABEL. *England of Song and Story.* Boston: Allyn and Bacon, 1931.

DARK, SIDNEY. *Book of Scotland for Young People.* New York: George H. Doran Company, 1924.

DARK, SIDNEY. *The Book of England for Young People.* New York: George H. Doran Company, 1923.

DAVIS, WILLIAM STEARNS. *Life in Elizabethan Days.* New York: Harper and Brothers, 1930.

DICKENS, CHARLES. *Child's History of England.* New York: E. P. Dutton and Company, 1907.

FAIRGRIEVE, JAMES. *Homes Far Away.* New York: D. Appleton and Company, 1927.

FINNEMORE, JOHN. *England and Wales.* New York: The Macmillan Company, 1921.

FOX, SIR FRANK. *Australia.* Peeps at Many Lands. New York: The Macmillan Company, 1929.

GOLDING, VAUTIER. *Story of Stanley.* Children's Heroes Series. New York: E. P. Dutton and Company, 1906.

GREGORY, J. W. *Africa, A Geographic Reader.* Chicago: Rand McNally & Company, 1928.

GRIERSON, ELIZABETH WILSON. *Scotland; and Ireland.* Peeps at Many Lands. New York: The Macmillan Company, 1921.

GUERBER, HÉLÈNE ADELINE. *Story of the English.* Guerbers Historical Readers. New York: American Book Company, 1924.

HAGEDORN, HERMANN. *Book of Courage.* Philadelphia: The John C. Winston Company, 1929.

HANCOCK, MARY S. *Children of History; Early Times.* Boston: Little, Brown & Company, 1909.

HILLYER, VIRGIL M. *Child's Geography of the World.* New York: The Century Co., 1929.

HILLYER, VIRGIL M. *A Child's History of the World.* New York: The Century Co., 1931.

HUNTINGTON, ELLSWORTH; BENSON, C. B.; and McMURRY, F. M. *Living Geography.* Book I. New York: The Macmillan Company, 1932.

HUNTINGTON, ELLSWORTH; BENSON, C. B.; and McMURRY, F. M. *Living Geography.* Book II. New York: The Macmillan Company, 1932.

JORDAN, DAVID STARR, and CATHER, K. D. *Europe.* Highlights of Geography. Yonkers-on-Hudson, New York: World Book Company, 1925.

LAMPREY, LOUISE. *In the Days of the Guild.* New York: Frederick A. Stokes Company, 1918.

LANG, ANDREW. *Tartan Tales.* New York: Longmans, Green & Company, 1928.

METHLEY, ALICE A. *Happy Homes in Foreign Lands.* New York: Frederick A. Stokes Company, 1922.

MITTON, GERALDINE EDITH. *London; and Paris, by Margery Williams.* Peeps at Many Lands Series. New York: The Macmillan Company, 1921.

PACKARD, LEONARD O., and SINNOTT, C. P. *Nations as Neighbors.* Revised Edition. Part II. New York: The Macmillan Company, 1931.

PECK, ANNE MERRIMAN. *Storybook, Europe.* New York: Harper & Brothers, 1929.

PHILLIPS, GRACE DARLING. *Far Peoples.* Chicago: University of Chicago Press, 1929.

POWER, EILEEN E., and POWER, R. D. *Boys and Girls of History.* New York: The Macmillan Company, 1927.

POWER, EILEEN E., and POWER, R. D. *Cities and Their Stories.* Boston: Houghton Mifflin Company, 1927.

PYLE, HOWARD. *Merry Adventures of Robin Hood of Great Renown, in Nottinghamshire.* New York: Chas. Scribner's Sons, 1902.

QUENNELL, MARJORIE, and QUENNELL, C. H. B. *Everyday Life in Anglo-Saxon, Viking and Norman Times.* New York: G. P. Putnam's Sons, 1927.

QUENNELL, MARJORIE, and QUENNELL, C. H. B. *Everyday Life in Roman Britain.* New York: G. P. Putnam's Sons, 1925.

QUENNELL, MARJORIE, and QUENNELL, C. H. B. *History of Everyday Things in England.* London: Batsford, B. T., Ltd., 1930.

QUENNELL, MARJORIE, and QUENNELL, C. H. B. *A History of Everyday Things in England, The Rise of Industrialism, 1733–1851.* New York: Chas. Scribner's Sons, 1934.

QUENNELL, MARJORIE, and QUENNELL, C. H. B. *A History of Everyday Things in England, Age of Production, 1851–1934.* New York: Chas. Scribner's Sons, 1935.

SCALES, LAURA WOOLSEY. *Boys of the Ages.* Boston: Ginn and Company, 1922.

SINGLETON, ESTHER. *Great Cities of Europe.* Garden City, New York: Doubleday, Page & Company, 1913.

SMITH, SUSAN. *Made in England.* New York: Thomas Nelson and Sons, 1932.

STUART, DOROTHY MARGARET. *Young Folk's Book of Other Lands.* Boston: Little, Brown and Company, 1927.

STUART, DOROTHY MARGARET. *Boy Through the Ages.* New York: George H. Doran Company, 1926.

STULL, DE FOREST, and HATCH, ROY W. *Our World Today.* Boston: Allyn and Bacon, 1931.

TAPPAN, EVA MARCH. *In the Days of William the Conqueror.* Boston: Lothrop, Lee & Shepard Company, 1901.

TAPPAN, EVA MARCH. *In the Days of Queen Victoria.* Boston: Lothrop, Lee & Shepard Company, 1903.

TAPPAN, EVA MARCH. *In the Days of Queen Elizabeth.* Boston: Lothrop, Lee & Shepard Company, 1902.

TAPPAN, EVA MARCH. *In the Days of Alfred the Great.* Boston: Lothrop, Lee & Shepard Company, 1900.

TAPPAN, EVA MARCH. *England's Story.* Boston: Houghton Mifflin Company, 1928.

TAYLOR, T. G. *Australia, Including Chapters on New Zealand and Neighboring Islands.* Chicago: Rand McNally & Company, 1931.

TERRY, ARTHUR GREY. *Tales from Far and Near.* Evanston, Illinois: Row, Peterson and Company, 1926.

TERRY, ARTHUR GREY. *Tales of Long Ago.* Evanston, Illinois: Row, Peterson and Company, 1926.

TERRY, ARTHUR GREY. *The Beginnings.* Book III. Evanston, Illinois: Row, Peterson and Company, 1926.

TERRY, ARTHUR GREY. *Lord and Vassal.* Evanston, Illinois: Row, Peterson and Company, 1926.

WHITE, GWEN. *Picture Book of Ancient and Modern Dolls.* New York: The Macmillan Company, 1928.

WILLIAMS, LAWRENCE S. *Robin and Jean in England.* New York: American Book Company, 1929.

WILLIAMSON, MARGARET. *John and Betty's English History Visit.* Boston: Lothrop, Lee & Shepard Company, 1910.

STORY BOOKS

ADAMS, KATHARINE. *Wisp; A Girl of Dublin.* New York: The Macmillan Company, 1922.

BLAND, EDITH. *Five Children.* New York: Coward, McCann & Company, 1930.

CASSERLEY, ANNE T. *Michael of Ireland.* New York: Harper and Brothers, 1927.

CLEMENS, SAMUEL L. *Prince and the Pauper.* New York: Harper and Brothers, 1917.

COLUM, PADRAIC. *Road Round Ireland.* New York: The Macmillan Company, 1926.

COLUM, PADRAIC. *Island of the Mighty; being the Hero Stories of Celtic Britain Retold from Mabinogion.* New York: The Macmillan Company, 1924.

COLUM, PADRAIC. *Boy in Eirinn.* Little Schoolmates Series. New York: E. P. Dutton and Company, 1929.

CREW, HELEN C. *Alanna.* New York: Harper and Brothers, 1929.

CREW, HELEN C. *Saturday's Children.* Boston: Little, Brown and Company, 1927.

DANIEL, HAWTHORNE. *Gauntlet of Dunmore.* New York: The Macmillan Company, 1926.

DIX, BEULAH MARIE. *Merrylips.* New York: The Macmillan Company, 1906.

GREEN, FRANCES N., and KIRK, D. W. *With Spurs of Gold.* Boston: Little, Brown and Company, 1905.

GRIERSON, ELIZABETH WILSON. *Tales from Scottish Ballads.* New York: The Macmillan Company, 1912.

HARTLEY, GEORGE INNESS. *Boy Hunters in Demerara.* New York: The Century Co., 1921.

HAWES, CHARLES B. *Dark Frigate.* Boston: Little, Brown and Company, 1925.

HORNE, RICHARD HENRY. *Memoirs of a London Doll.* New York: The Macmillan Company, 1922.

Irish Fairy Book. Compiled by Graves, Alfred P. New York: Frederick A. Stokes Company, 1909.

JACOBS, JOSEPH. *English Fairy Tales.* New York: G. P. Putnam's Sons, 1911.

Jataka Tales. Edited by Francis, H. T., and Thomas, E. J. New York: The Macmillan Company, 1916.

KIPLING, RUDYARD. *Jungle Book.* Garden City, New York: Doubleday, Doran & Company, 1932.

KIPLING, RUDYARD. *Puck of Pook's Hill.* Garden City, New York: Doubleday, Doran & Company, 1906.

KIPLING, RUDYARD. *Rewards and Fairies.* Garden City, New York: Doubleday, Doran & Company, 1911.

McDONALD, ETTA AUSTIN, and DALRYMPLE, JULIA. *Kathleen in Ireland.* Little People Everywhere. Boston: Little, Brown and Company, 1909.

MACMANUS, SEUMAS. *Donegal Fairy Stories.* Garden City, New York: Doubleday, Doran & Company, 1900.

MARSHALL, HENRIETTA ELIZABETH. *Island Story.* New York: Frederick A. Stokes Company, 1920.

MARSHALL, BERNARD GAY. *Torch Bearers.* New York: D. Appleton and Company, 1923.

MASEFIELD, JOHN. *Jim Davis.* New York: Thomas Nelson & Sons, 1932.

MASON, ARTHUR. *Wee Men of Ballywooden.* Garden City, New York: Doubleday, Doran & Company, 1930.

MUKERJI, DAHN GOPAL. *Chief of the Herd.* New York: E. P. Dutton and Company, 1929.

MUKERJI, DAHN GOPAL. *Gay-neck, the Story of a Pigeon.* New York: E. P. Dutton and Company, 1928.

MUKERJI, DAHN GOPAL. *Kari, the Elephant.* New York: E. P. Dutton and Company, 1922.

NEUMANN, DAISY. *Timothy Travels from the Mediterranean to the North Sea.* New York: Coward, McCann & Company, 1928.

OLCOTT, FRANCES JENKINS. *Wonder Tales from Fairy Isles.* New York: Longmans, Green and Company, 1929.

PERKINS, LUCY. *Irish Twins.* Boston: Houghton Mifflin Company, 1913.

PERKINS, LUCY. *Scotch Twins.* Boston: Houghton Mifflin Company, 1919.

PYLE, HOWARD. *Men of Iron.* New York: Harper and Brothers, 1930.

PYLE, HOWARD. *Story of King Arthur and His Knights*. New York: Chas. Scribner's Sons, 1903.

ROSS, MARGARET ISABEL. *Back of Time*. New York: Harper & Brothers, 1932.

RANSOME, ARTHUR. *Swallows and Amazons*. Chicago: J. B. Lippincott Company, 1931.

SCOTT, SIR WALTER. *Ivanhoe*. Boston: Allyn and Bacon, 1916.

STEEL, FLORA ANNIE. *Adventures of Akbar*. New York: Frederick A. Stokes Company, 1913.

STEEL, FLORA ANNIE. *Tales of the Punjab*. New York: The Macmillan Company, 1894.

STEPHENS, JAMES. *Irish Fairy Tales*. New York: The Macmillan Company, 1920.

STEVENSON, ROBERT LOUIS. *Kidnapped*. Boston: Allyn and Bacon, 1925.

STEVENSON, ROBERT LOUIS. *Treasure Island*. Boston: Allyn and Bacon, 1915.

TAPPAN, EVA MARCH. *Old Ballads in Prose*. Boston: Houghton Mifflin Company, 1901.

TENNYSON, ALFRED. *Idylls of the King*. London: J. M. Dent & Sons, Ltd., 1929.

WARREN, MAUDE LAVINIA. *Robin Hood and his Merry Men*. Chicago: Rand McNally & Company, 1914.

WARREN, MAUDE LAVINIA. *King Arthur and his Knights*. Chicago: Rand McNally & Company, 1916.

WAYMAN, HERBERT E. *Bemol and Kusum, Children of Bengal*. Yonkers-on-Hudson, New York: World Book Company, 1925.

WHITHAM, GRACE I. *Captive Royal Children*. New York: Frederick A. Stokes Company, 1911.

WHITNEY, ELINOR. *Tod of the Fens*. New York: The Macmillan Company, 1928.

WIESE, KURT. *Karoo the Kangaroo*. New York: Coward, McCann & Company, 1929.

WILLIAMS, WILBUR H. *The Traveling Tingles*. Boston: Marshall Jones Company, 1931.

YONGE, CHARLOTTE MARY. *Prince and the Page*. New York: The Macmillan Company, 1925.

YOUNG, ELLA. *Tangle-coated Horse, and Other Tales*. New York: Longmans, Green & Company, 1929.

Books for Teachers

HARTLEY, DOROTHY, and ELLIOT, M. M. V. *Life and Work of the People of England*. 6v. New York: G. P. Putnam's Sons, 1931.

CALIFORNIA

Books for Pupils

REFERENCE BOOKS

ALLEN, NELLIE B. *How and Where We Live*. Boston: Ginn and Company, 1924.

ARMSTRONG, MARGARET. *Field Book of Western Wild Flowers*. New York: G. P. Putnam's Sons, 1915.

ATWOOD, WALLACE W. *United States Among the Nations*. Boston: Ginn and Company, 1929.

BANDINI, HELEN ELLIOTT. *History of California*. New York: American Book Company, 1908.

BASS, FLORENCE. *Stories of Early Times in the Great West*. Indianapolis: Bobbs-Merrill Company, 1927.

CARPENTER, FRANK G., and CARPENTER, FRANCES. *Foods We Eat*. New York: American Book Company, 1925.

CARPENTER, FRANK G. *How the World is Housed*. New York: American Book Company, 1930.

CHAMBERLAIN, J. F. *How We are Fed*. New York: The Macmillan Company. n.d.

CORWIN, MAE JOHNSON. *The Pioneer's Pathway.* Western Nature Science Series. San Francisco: Harr Wagner Publishing Company, 1932.

CORWIN, WALLING. *Trails Today.* Western Nature Science Series. San Francisco: Harr Wagner Publishing Company, 1932.

FAIRBANKS, HAROLD WELLMAN. *Home and Its Relations to the World.* San Francisco: Harr Wagner Publishing Company, 1921.

FAIRBANKS, HAROLD WELLMAN. *Southern California.* San Francisco: Harr Wagner Publishing Company, 1929.

FISHER, ELIZABETH FLORETTE. *Resources and Industries of the United States.* Boston: Ginn and Company, 1928.

FORBES, HARRIE REBECCA PIPER. *California Missions and Landmarks.* Los Angeles: The Author, 1925.

FOX, EDITH KIRK. *In Old California.* New York: The Macmillan Company, 1927.

FULTZ, FRANCIS MARION. *Out of Door Studies in Geography.* Bloomington, Illinois: Public School Publishing Company, 1908.

HIGGINS, ETHEL BAILEY. *Our Native Cacti.* New York: A. T. De La Mare Company, Inc., 1931.

HILL, LAURANCE L. *La Reina, Los Angeles in Three Centuries.* Los Angeles: Security First National Bank of Los Angeles, 1931.

HOFFMAN, LOLA B. *California Beginnings.* San Francisco: Harr Wagner Publishing Company, 1933.

HOLWAY, HOPE. *Story of Water Supply.* New York: Harper and Brothers, 1929.

HORNADAY, WILLIAM TEMPLE. *Tales from Nature's Wonderland.* New York: Chas. Scribner's Sons, 1924.

HOUGHTON, ARTHUR D. *The Cactus Book.* New York: The Macmillan Company, 1931.

HUNT, ROCKWELL DENNIS. *California.* Boston: D. C. Heath and Company, 1931.

HUNT, ROCKWELL DENNIS. *New California The Golden.* New York: Silver Burdett and Company, 1933.

HUNT, ROCKWELL DENNIS, and SANCHEZ, NELLIE. *Short History of California.* New York: T. Y. Crowell Company, 1929.

JAEGER, EDMUND C. *The California Desert.* Stanford University, California: Stanford University Press, 1933.

JAEGER, EDMUND C. *Denizens of the Desert.* Boston: Houghton Mifflin Company, 1922.

KINSEY, DON J. *The Romance of Water and Power.* Los Angeles, California: The Department of Water and Power, 1928.

KNOWLTON, PHILIP ARNOLD. *First Lessons in Geography.* New York: The Macmillan Company, 1929.

LEETCH, DOROTHY LYMAN. *Benito and Loreta Delfin.* Boston: Lothrop, Lee and Shepard Company, 1932.

LEFFERTS, WALTER. *Our Own United States.* Chicago: J. B. Lippincott Company, 1925.

LUMMIS, CHARLES F. *Spanish Songs of Old California.* New York: G. Schirmer, Inc., 1923.

MCSPADDEN, JOSEPH WALKER. *California.* New York: George Sully and Company, 1926.

MARCY, C. A., and MARCY, FERNE L. *The Indians' Garden.* San Francisco: Harr Wagner Publishing Company, 1932.

MARCY, C. A. *Padres' Garden.* San Francisco: Harr Wagner Publishing Company, 1932.

MELLEN, IDA M. *Young Folks' Book of Fishes.* New York: Dodd, Mead & Company, Inc., 1927.

NIDA, WILLIAM LEWIS, and WEBB, V. L. *Our Country Past and Present.* Chicago: Scott, Foresman and Company, 1930.

NORTON, HENRY KITTREDGE. *Story of California.* Chicago: A. C. McClurg & Co., 1913.

OTIS, JAMES. *Martha of California.* New York: American Book Company, 1913.

PADEN, WILLIAM G., and RICE, F. A. *Seeing California.* New York: The Macmillan Company, 1926.

PETERSHAM, MAUD and MISKA. *The Story Book of Gold.* Philadelphia: The John C. Winston Company, 1935.

RAMSAY, ELLEN M. *Story of Citrus Fruits.* Dansville, N. Y.: F. A. Owen Publishing Company, 1928.

RICHARDS, IRMAGARDE. *Our California Home.* California State Series. Sacramento: California State Department of Education, 1930.

ROBINSON, W. W. *Beasts of the Tar Pits.* New York: The Macmillan Company, 1932.

ROLFE, MARY A. *Our National Parks. Book II.* Chicago: Benj. H. Sanborn and Company, 1931.

SHEPHERD, EDITH P. *Geography for Beginners.* Chicago: Rand McNally & Company, 1930.

SMITH, JOSEPH RUSSELL. *Home Folks.* Philadelphia: The John Winston Company, 1930.

SNEDDEN, GENEVRA SISSON. *Docas.* Boston: D. C. Heath and Company, 1899.

TAPPAN, EVA MARCH. *Diggers in the Earth.* Boston: Houghton Mifflin Company, 1916.

WAGNER, HARR, and KEPPEL, MARK. *Lessons in California History.* San Francisco: Harr Wagner Publishing Company, 1922.

WYMAN, LUTHER E., and BURNELL, ELIZABETH F. *Field Book of Birds of Southwestern United States.* Boston: Houghton Mifflin Company, 1925.

Books for Teachers

ARMER, LAURA ADAMS. *Cactus.* New York: Frederick A. Stokes Company, 1934.

CHAPMAN, CHARLES E. *A History of California: Spanish Period.* New York: The Macmillan Company, 1921.

CLELAND, ROBERT GLASS. *A History of California: American Period.* New York: The Macmillan Company, 1926.

JAY, GLADYS. *Twins in Fruitland.* Chicago: Beckley-Cardy Company, 1929.

JEPSON, WILLIS LINN. *The Trees of California.* Berkeley, California: Sather Gate Book Shop, 1923.

MADISON, ELIZABETH. *Child of the Sea.* San Francisco: Suttonhouse Publishers, 1932.

MUIR, JOHN. *The Mountains of California.* New York: The Century Company, 1898.

TAPPAN, EVA MARCH. *Farmer and His Friends.* Boston: Houghton Mifflin Company, 1929.

TRESIDDER, MARY CURRY. *The Trees of Yosemite.* Stanford University, California: Stanford University Press, 1932.

CANADA

Books for Pupils

REFERENCE BOOKS

AITCHISON, ALISON E., and UTTLEY, MARGUERITE. *Across Seven Seas to Seven Continents.* Indianapolis: Bobbs-Merrill Company, 1931.

AITCHISON, ALISON E., and UTTLEY, MARGUERITE. *North America by Plane and Train.* Indianapolis: Bobbs-Merrill Company, 1931.

ALLEN, NELLIE, *United States.* Boston: Ginn and Company, 1925.

ALLEN, NELLIE. *North America.* Boston: Ginn and Company, 1922.

ATWOOD, WALLACE W., and THOMAS, H. G. *Americas. Earth and its People. Book II.* Boston: Ginn and Company, 1929.

BARROWS, H. H., and PARKER, E. P. *Geography: United States and Canada.* New York: Silver, Burdett and Company, 1925.

BEALBY, JOHN THOMAS. *Canada.* Peeps at Many Lands. New York: The Macmillan Company, 1921.

BENGSTON, NELS AUGUST, and GRIFFITH, DONEE. *Wheat Industry, For Use In Schools.* New York: The Macmillan Company, 1915.

CARPENTER, FRANK G. *Around the World With The Children.* New York: American Book Company, 1917.

CARPENTER, FRANK G. *North America.* New York: American Book Company, 1922.

CHAMBERLAIN, J. F., and CHAMBERLAIN, A. H. *North America.* New York: The Macmillan Company, 1927.

CLARK, MARION G., and GORDY, WILBUR F. *What Men From Europe Brought to America.* New York: Chas. Scribner's Sons, 1929.

CLARK, MARION G., and GORDY, WILBUR F. *First Three Hundred Years in America.* New York: Chas. Scribner's Sons, 1931.

DUNCAN, FRANCIS MARTIN, and DUNCAN, L. T. *Animal Life in the New World.* Wonders of Animal Life, v. 4. New York: Oxford University Press, 1921.

DUNN, FANNIE W., and TROXELL, ELEANOR. *In Fields and Forest.* Evanston, Illinois: Row, Peterson and Company, 1928.

FAIRFORD, FORD. *Newfoundland.* New York: The Macmillan Company, 1921.

FOOTE, ANNA E., and SKINNER, A. W. *Explorers and Founders of America.* New York: American Book Company, 1907.

GEORGE, MARIAN M. *Little Journeys to Alaska and Canada.* Chicago: A. Flanagan Company, 1928.

HOME, BEATRICE. *Canada.* Peeps at History. New York: The Macmillan Company, 1911.

HUNTINGTON, ELLSWORTH; BENSON, C. B.; and McMURRY, F. M. *Living Geography.* Book I. New York: The Macmillan Company, 1932.

HUNTINGTON, ELLSWORTH; BENSON, C. B.; and McMURRY, F. M. *Living Geography.* Book II. New York: The Macmillan Company, 1932.

Lands and Peoples. Canada and the United States. New York: The Grolier Society, 1930.

LEFFERTS, WALTER. *Neighbors, North and South.* Philadelphia: J. B. Lippincott Company, 1926.

MARSHALL, HENRIETTA E. *Canada's Story.* Our Empire Story Series. New York: Thomas Nelson & Sons, 1932.

MARSHALL, HENRIETTA E. *Our Empire Story.* New York: Frederick A. Stokes Company, 1909.

MITCHELL, LUCY. *North America.* New York: The Macmillan Company, 1931.

NICHOLS, MARIE LOUISE. *Science for Boys and Girls.* Lippincott's School Text Series. Chicago: J. B. Lippincott Company, 1924.

PACKARD, LEONARD O., and SINNOTT, C. P. *Nations as Neighbors.* Revised Edition. Part II. New York: The Macmillan Company, 1931.

Pageant of America. Vol. 1, Pt. 5, "Adventures in the Wilderness." Edited by R. Henry Gabriel. New Haven: Yale University Press, 1929.

PATCH, EDITH M. *First Lessons in Nature Study.* New York: The Macmillan Company, 1932.

QUINN, VERNON. *Beautiful Canada.* New York: Frederick A. Stokes Company, 1925.

SMALLIDGE, OLIVE E., and PAXSON, F. L. *Finding America.* Boston: Houghton Mifflin Company, 1929.

SMITH, EDITH LILLIAN. *Everyday Science Projects.* Boston: Houghton Mifflin Company, 1925.

TALBOT, FREDERICK A. A. *Canadian Pacific Railway.* Peeps at Great Railways. New York: The Macmillan Company, 1915.

WEAVER, EMILY POYNTON. *Book of Canada, for Young People.* Garden City, New York: Doubleday, Doran & Company, 1928.

WRIGHT, SIDNEY H. *Marvels of the World's Fisheries.* Philadelphia: J. B. Lippincott Company, 1923.

STORY BOOKS

COBB, BERTHA B., and COBB, ERNEST. *Andre.* New York: G. P. Putnam's Sons, 1930.

CRUMP, IRVING. *Boys' Book of Mounted Police.* New York: Dodd, Mead & Company, Inc., 1917.

DUNCAN, NORMAN. *Adventures of Billy-Topsail.* New York: Fleming H. Revell & Company. 1906.

DUNCAN, NORMAN. *Doctor Luke of the Labrador.* New York: Fleming H. Revell & Company, 1904.

GRENFELL, SIR WILFRED T. *Adrift on an Ice-Pan.* London: Jarrolds, Publishers, 1929.

KIPLING, RUDYARD. *Captains' Courageous.* New York: The Macmillan Company, 1930.

LOGIE, ALFRED ERNEST. *Canadian Wonder Tales.* Evanston, Illinois: Row, Peterson and Company, 1925.

McDONALD, ETTA AUSTIN, and DALRYMPLE, JULIA. *Betty in Canada.* Little People Everywhere. Boston: Little, Brown and Company, 1910.

MacDONALD, ELIZABETH ROBERTS. *Our Little Canadian Cousin.* Boston: L. C. Page & Company, 1904.

MACMILLAN, CYRUS. *Canadian Wonder Tales.* New York: Dodd, Mead & Company, Inc., 1918.

MONTGOMERY, LUCY MAUD. *Anne of Avonlea.* London: George G. Harrap & Co., Ltd., 1931.

MONTGOMERY, LUCY MAUD. *Anne of Green Gables.* London: George G. Harrap & Co., Ltd., 1931.

MURPHY, EMILY GOWAN. *Our Little Canadian Cousin of the Great Northwest.* Boston: L. C. Page & Company, 1923.

PHILLIPS, ETHEL CALVERT. *Gay Madelon.* Boston: Houghton Mifflin Company, 1931.

PHILLIPS, ETHEL CALVERT. *Jean-Marie and Her Golden Bird.* Boston: Houghton Mifflin Company, 1934.

POLLOCK, FRANK LILLIE. *Northern Diamonds.* Boston: Houghton Mifflin Company, 1917.

SAXE, MARY S. *Our Little Quebec Cousin.* Little Cousin Series. Boston: L. C. Page & Company, 1919.

SKINNER, CONSTANCE LINDSAY. *Beaver, Kings and Cabins.* New York: The Macmillan Company, 1933.

SKINNER, CONSTANCE LINDSAY. *Roselle of the North.* New York: The Macmillan Company, 1927.

STEFÁNSSON, VILHJÁLMUR. *Northward Ho!* New York: The Macmillan Company, 1925.

WALLACE, DILLON. *Story of Grenfell of the Labrador.* New York: Fleming H. Revell & Company, 1922.

WALLACE, DILLON. *Ungava Bob.* Every Boy's Library. New York: Fleming H. Revell & Company, 1907.

WHITE, STEWART EDWARD. *Magic Forest.* Little Library. New York: The Macmillan Company, 1923.

Books for Teachers

British America. The nations of today; a new history of the world. Edited by John Buchan. Boston: Houghton Mifflin Company, 1923.

HAWORTH, PAUL L. *Trailmakers of the Northwest.* New York: Harcourt, Brace & Company, 1921.

JOHNSON, WILLIAM HENRY. *French Pathfinders in North America.* Boston: Little, Brown and Company, 1905.

PARKMAN, FRANCIS. *Pioneers of France in the New World.* Boston: Little, Brown and Company, 1887.

WILLIAMS, MABEL BERTA. *Jasper National Park.* Ottawa: The Department of Interior, 1928.

WRONG, GEORGE MCKINNON. *The Conquest of New France.* New Haven: Yale University Press, 1921.

CHINA

Books for Pupils

REFERENCE BOOKS

BUNKER, FRANK F. *China and Japan.* Philadelphia: J. B. Lippincott Company, 1928.

CARPENTER, FRANK G. *Around The World With The Children.* New York: American Book Company, 1917.

CARPENTER, FRANCES. *Our Neighbors Near and Far.* New York: American Book Company, 1933.

CHAMBERLAIN, J. F. *How We Travel.* New York: The Macmillan Company, n. d.

COFFMAN, RAMON. *Child's Story of the Human Race.* New York: Dodd, Mead & Company, Inc., 1927.

DUNHAM, EDITH. *Jogging Around the World.* New York: Frederick A. Stokes Company, 1905.

FAIRGRIEVES, JAMES, and YOUNG, ERNEST. *World.* New York: D. Appleton and Company. n. d.

FRANCK, HARRY A. *Marco Polo, Junior.* New York: The Century Company, 1929.

GEORGE, MARIAN M. *A Little Journey to China and Japan.* Chicago: A. Flanagan Company, 1928.

HALL, KATHERINE STANLEY. *Children at Play in Many Lands.* Missionary Education Movement. New York: Friendship Press, 1912.

HEADLEY, E. A. *How Other People Travel.* Chicago: Rand McNally & Company, 1926.

JEAN, SALLY LUCAS, and HALLOCK, GRACE T. *Spending the Day in China, Japan and the Philippines.* New York: Harper & Brothers, 1932.

PERDUE, HANNAH AVIS. *How Other Children Live.* Chicago: Rand McNally & Company, 1927.

PERDUE, HANNAH AVIS. *Child Life in Other Lands.* Chicago: Rand McNally & Company, 1918.

PIPER, WATTY. *Little Folks of Many Lands.* New York: The Platt & Munk Company, 1929.

PRICE, OLIVIA. *Middle Country.* Yonkers-on-Hudson, New York: The World Book Company, 1926.

SCANTLEBURY, ELIZABETH ELLIS. *Little World Children.* Boston: Ginn and Company, 1928.

THOMPSON, RUTH. *Our Neighbors Near and Far.* San Francisco: Harr Wagner Publishing Company, 1926.

THOMSON, JOHN STUART. *Bud and Bamboo.* New York: D. Appleton and Company, 1912.

TIETJENS, EUNICE. *China.* Burton Holmes Travel Stories. Chicago: Wheeler Publishing Company, 1930.

VAN BERGEN, ROBERT. *The Story of China.* New York: American Book Company, 1902.

STORY BOOKS

CHRISMAN, ARTHUR BOWIE. *Shen of the Sea.* New York: E. P. Dutton and Company, 1925.

CHRISMAN, ARTHUR BOWIE. *The Wind That Wouldn't Blow.* New York: E. P. Dutton and Company, 1927.

DAVIS, MARY HAYES, and CHOW-LEUNG. *Chinese Fables and Folk Stories*. New York: American Book Company, 1908.

FLACK, MARJORIE, and WIESE, KURT. *The Story About Ping*. New York: The Viking Press, 1933.

HEADLAND, ISAAC TAYLOR. *Our Little Chinese Cousin*. Boston: L. C. Page & Company, 1903.

HEADLAND, ISAAC TAYLOR. *Chinese Mother Goose Rhymes*. New York: Fleming H. Revell & Company, 1900.

HEADLAND, ISAAC TAYLOR. *Chinese Boy and Girl*. New York: Fleming H. Revell & Company. n. d.

LATTIMORE, ELEANOR FRANCES. *Jerry and the Pusa*. New York: Harcourt Brace and Company, 1932.

LATTIMORE, ELEANOR FRANCES. *Little Pear*. New York: Harcourt, Brace & Company, 1931.

LEE, YAN PHOU. *When I Was a Boy in China*. Boston: Lothrop, Lee and Shepard Company, 1887.

LEWIS, ELIZABETH FOREMAN. *Ho-Ming, Girl of New China*. Philadelphia: Junior Literary Guild and The John C. Winston Company, 1934.

LEWIS, ELIZABETH FOREMAN. *Young Fu of the Upper Yangtze*. Philadelphia: The John C. Winston Company, 1932.

METZGER, BERTA. *Picture Tales from the Chinese*. New York: Frederick A. Stokes, 1934.

OLCOTT, FRANCES JENKINS. *Wonder Tales from China Seas*. New York: Longmans, Green and Company, 1925.

PITMAN, NORMAN HINSDALE. *Chinese Fairy Tales*. New York: T. Y. Crowell Company, 1924.

PITMAN, NORMAN HINSDALE. *Chinese Wonder Book*. New York: E. P. Dutton and Company, 1919.

ROWE, DOROTHY. *Moon's Birthday*. New York: The Macmillan Company, 1932.

ROWE, DOROTHY. *Rabbit Lantern*. New York: The Macmillan Company, 1925.

ROWE, DOROTHY. *Traveling Shops*. New York: The Macmillan Company, 1929.

SCHWARTZ, JULIA AUGUSTA. *Five Little Strangers and How they Came to Live in America*. New York: American Book Company, 1904.

SHERWOOD, MERRIAM, and MANTZ, H. E. *Road to Cathay*. New York: The Macmillan Company, 1928.

WIESE, KURT. *Liang and Lo*. Garden City, New York: Doubleday, Doran & Company, 1930.

YAN PHOU, LEE. *When I Was a Boy in China*. Boston: Lothrop, Lee & Shepard Company. n. d.

Books for Teachers

ALLEN, NELLIE B. *Asia*. Boston: Ginn and Company, 1929.

AYSCOUGH, FLORENCE. *Firecracker Land*. Boston: The Junior Literary Guild, and Houghton Mifflin Company, 1932.

CARPENTER, FRANK G. *Asia*. New York: American Book Company, 1924.

CHAMBERLAIN, J. F., and CHAMBERLAIN, A. H. *Asia*. Revised Edition. New York: The Macmillan Company, 1925.

FRANCK, HARRY A. *China*. Dansville, New York: F. A. Owen Publishing Company, 1927.

HOKE, GEORGE WILSON. *Russia and the Old East*. Richmond, Virginia: Johnson Publishing Company, 1924.

SEEGER, ELIZABETH. *The Pageant of Chinese History*. New York: Longmans, Green and Company, 1934.

WIESE, KURT. *Chinese Ink Stick*. Garden City, New York: Doubleday, Doran & Company, 1929.

CLOTHING

Books for Pupils

REFERENCE BOOKS

AITCHISON, ALISON E., and UTTLEY, MARGUERITE. *North America By Plane and Train.* Indianapolis: Bobbs-Merrill Company, 1931.

ALLEN, NELLIE B. *Cotton and Other Useful Fibers.* Boston: Ginn and Company, 1929.

ALLEN, NELLIE B. *How and Where We Live.* Boston: Ginn and Company, 1924.

AMERICAN LEATHER PRODUCERS, INC. *Romance of Leather and Its Importance to Mankind.* New York: American Leather Producers, Inc.

AMERICAN WOOLEN COMPANY. *From Wool to Cloth.* Boston: American Woolen Company, 1911.

BONSER, EDNA M. *How The Early Hebrews Lived and Learned.* New York: The Macmillan Company, 1924.

BROOKS, EUGENE CLYDE. *Story of Cotton.* Chicago: Rand McNally & Company. n. d.

BROOKS, EUGENE CLYDE. *Story of Cotton and the Development of the Cotton States.* Chicago: Rand McNally & Company, 1911.

BUNKER, FRANK F. *China and Japan.* Chicago: J. B. Lippincott Company, 1928.

BURNS, ANNIE JOHNSON. *Stories of Shepherd Life,* A Social Science Reader. New York: American Book Company, 1934.

CARPENTER, FRANK G. *How the World is Clothed.* New York: American Book Company, 1908.

CARPENTER, FRANK G. *North America.* New York: American Book Company, 1922.

CARPENTER, FRANK G., and CARPENTER, FRANCES. *Clothes We Wear.* New York: American Book Company, 1926.

CHAMBERLAIN, J. F. *How We Are Clothed.* Revised Edition. New York: The Macmillan Company. n. d.

COOKE, ARTHUR O. *Visit to a Woolen Mill.* New York: George H. Doran Company, 1912.

COOKE, ARTHUR O. *Visit to a Cotton Mill.* New York: George H. Doran Company, 1912.

DEARBORN, FRANCES R. *How the Indians Lived.* Boston: Ginn and Company, 1927.

DOPP, KATHERINE E. *Early Cave Men.* Chicago: Rand McNally & Company, 1904.

DOPP, KATHERINE E. *Early Herdsmen.* Chicago: Rand McNally & Company, 1923.

EARLE, ALICE MORSE. *Home Life in Colonial Days.* New York: The Macmillan Company, 1898.

FAIRGRIEVE, JAMES, and YOUNG, ERNEST. *World.* New York: D. Appleton & Company, 1925.

FISHER, ELIZABETH F. *Resources and Industries of the United States.* Boston: Ginn and Company, 1928.

HAIRE, FRANCES H. *Folk Costume Books.* New York: A. S. Barnes & Co., 1926.

HALL, JENNIE. *Weavers and Other Workers.* Chicago: Rand McNally & Company, 1917.

HUNTINGTON, ELLSWORTH; BENSON, C. B.; and McMURRY, F. M. *Living Geography.* Book II. New York: The Macmillan Company, 1932.

HUNTINGTON, ELLSWORTH, and CUSHING, S. W. *Modern Business Geography.* New York: World Book Company, 1932.

JENKINS, OLIVER P. *Interesting Neighbors.* Philadelphia: P. Blakiston's Son & Co., 1922.

KEIR, MALCOLM. *The Epic of Industry.* The Pageant of America. V. 5. New Haven: Yale University Press, 1926.

KNOWLTON, PHILIP A. *First Lessons in Geography.* New York: The Macmillan Company, 1924.

McFEE, INEZ NELLIE. *World About Us.* Philadelphia: Macrae Smith Co., 1931.

36—17050

MAYNE, EVA. *Story of Flax.* Dansville, New York: F. A. Owen Publishing Company, 1910.

MOHR, LOUISE MAUDE. *Palestine and Syria.* Chicago: Rand McNally & Company, 1931.

NIDA, WILLIAM LEWIS, and WEBB, V. L. *Our Country Past and Present.* Chicago: Scott, Foresman and Company, 1930.

PATCH, EDITH M. *First Lessons in Nature Study.* New York: The Macmillan Company, 1932.

PEIRCE, W. M. *Story of Leather.* Dansville, New York: F. A. Owen Publishing Company, 1918.

PERDUE, HANNAH AVIS. *Child Life in Other Lands.* Chicago: Rand McNally & Company, 1918.

PETERSHAM, MAUD and MISKA. *The Story Book of Clothes.* Philadelphia: The John C. Winston Company, 1933.

PRESCOTT, DELLA R. *Day in a Colonial Home.* Boston: Marshall Jones Company, 1921.

REYNOLDS, MINNIE J. *How Man Conquered Nature.* New York: The Macmillan Company, 1914.

RUSH, CHARLES EVERETT, and WINSLOW, AMY. *Science of Things About Us.* Boston: Little, Brown and Company, 1927.

SAGE, ELIZABETH. *Textiles and Clothing.* New York: Chas. Scribner's Sons, 1930.

SCARBOROUGH, DOROTHY. *The Story of Cotton.* New York: Harper & Brothers, 1933.

SHEPARD, EDITH P. *Geography for Beginners.* Books I-II. Chicago: Rand McNally & Company, 1927–1930.

SHILLIG, ELNORA E. *Four Wonders, Cotton—Wool—Linen—Silk.* Chicago: Rand McNally & Company, 1913.

SMITH, JOSEPH RUSSELL. *Home Folks.* Philadelphia: The John C. Winston Company, 1930.

TAPPAN, EVA MARCH. *Farmer and His Friends.* Boston: Houghton Mifflin Company, 1916.

TAPPAN, EVA MARCH. *Makers of Many Things.* Boston: Houghton Mifflin Company, 1916.

THOMPSON, RUTH. *Type Stories of the World for Little Folk.* San Francisco: Harr Wagner Publishing Company, 1922.

WATSON, ELIZABETH. *Story of Textiles.* New York: Harper and Brothers, 1928.

WINSLOW, ISAAC OSCAR. *Europe.* Boston: D. C. Heath and Company, 1922.

WORTHINGTON, JOSEPHINE, and MATTHEWS, C. V. *Our Clothing.* Dansville, New York: F. A. Owen Publishing Company, 1931.

STORY BOOKS

NIDA, STELLA H. *Letters of Polly, The Pioneer.* New York: The Macmillan Company, 1916.

PERKINS, LUCY. *Mexican Twins.* Boston: Houghton Mifflin Company, 1915.

Books for Teachers

BONSER, FREDERICK G., and MOSSMAN, L. C. *Industrial Arts for Elementary Schools.* New York: The Macmillan Company, 1923.

COMMUNICATION

Books for Pupils

REFERENCE BOOKS

AMERICAN TELEPHONE and TELEGRAPH CO. *Things Worth Knowing About The Telephone.* New York: American Telephone & Telegraph Co., 1931.

BACHMAN, FRANK P. *Great Inventors and Their Inventions.* New York: American Book Company, 1918.

BEEBY, DANIEL J., and BEEBY, DOROTHEA. *How The World Grows Smaller.* Community-Life History Series. Book I. New York: Charles E. Merrill Company, 1924.

BOY SCOUTS of AMERICA. *Official Handbook for Boys.* New York: Boy Scouts of America, 1927.

BRADLEY, GLENN DANFORD. *Story of the Pony Express.* Chicago: A. C. McClurg & Co., 1913.

BRIDGES, T. C. *The Young Folks' Book of Invention.* Boston: Little, Brown and Company, 1926.

BUSH, MAYBELL G., and WADDELL, JOHN F. *How We Have Conquered Distance.* New York: The Macmillan Company, 1934.

CALDWELL, OTIS WILLIAM, and MEIER, W. H. D. *Open Doors to Science, with Experiments.* Boston: Ginn and Company, 1926.

CARPENTER, FRANK G. *Ourselves and Our City.* New York: American Book Company, 1928.

CARPENTER, FRANK G. *The Ways We Travel.* New York: American Book Company, 1929.

CHAMBERLAIN, J. F. *How We Travel.* New York: The Macmillan Company, 1924.

CHASE, ANNIE, and CLOW, E. *Stories of Industry.* Vol. I. New York: Educational Publishers, 1913.

CLARK, MARION G., and GORDY, WILBUR F. *The Early Story of Mankind.* New York: Chas. Scribner's Sons, 1929.

CLODD, EDWARD. *Story of the Alphabet.* New York: D. Appleton and Company, 1915.

COLEMAN, SATIS N. *Bells.* Chicago: Rand McNally & Company, 1928.

CRAIG, GERALD S., and JOHNSON, GOLDIE M. *Our Earth and Its Story.* Boston: Ginn and Company, 1932.

CRUMP, IRVING. *Boys' Book of the United States Mails.* New York: Dodd, Mead & Company, Inc., 1926.

DARROW, FLOYD LAVERN. *Masters of Science and Invention.* New York: Harcourt, Brace & Company, 1923.

DARROW, FLOYD LAVERN. *Thinkers and Doers.* New York: Silver, Burdett and Company, 1925.

DUKELOW, JEAN H., and WEBSTER, HANSON H. *The Ship Book.* Boston: Houghton Mifflin Company, 1931.

DU PUY, WILLIAM ATHERTON. *Odd Jobs of Uncle Sam.* Factual Reading. Boston: D. C. Heath Company, 1927.

EARLE, ALICE MORSE. *State Coach and Tavern Days.* New York: The Macmillan Company, 1900.

FORMAN, SAMUEL E. *Stories of Useful Inventions.* New York: The Century Co., 1914.

FOX, F. C. *How the World Rides.* New York: Chas. Scribner's Sons., 1929.

FRANKLIN, BENJAMIN. *Autobiography.* Boston: Allyn and Bacon, 1929.

GEORGE, LLOYD, and GILMAN, JAMES. *Modern Mercuries.* New York: Robert M. McBride and Company, 1932.

HARTMAN, GERTRUDE. *World We Live In and How It Came To Be.* New York: The Macmillan Company, 1931.

HILLYER, VIRGIL M. *A Child's History of the World.* New York: The Century Co., 1924.

HOLLAND, RUPERT S. *Historic Inventions.* Historic Series for Young People. Philadelphia: Macrae Smith Co., 1911.

KEELOR, KATHERINE LOUISE. *Working with Electricity.* New York: The Macmillan Company, 1929.

KUH, CHARLOTTE. *Postman.* Happy Hour Books. New York: The Macmillan Company, 1929.

LANSING, MARION FLORENCE. *Great Moments in Science.* Garden City, New York: Doubleday, Doran & Company, 1926.

LEEMING, JOSEPH. *Peaks of Invention.* New York: The Century Co., 1929.

McMILLEN, WHEELER. *Young Collector.* New York: D. Appleton and Company, 1928.

McSPADDEN, JOSEPH WALLSER. *How They Carried the Mail.* New York: J. H. Sears & Co., 1930.

MARSHAK, I. I. *Black on White; The Story of Books.* Chicago: J. B. Lippincott Company, 1932.

MEADOWCROFT, WILLIAM HENRY. *Boys' Life of Edison.* New York: Harper and Brothers, 1929.

MERIWEATHER, SUSAN. *Story of the Telephone and the Genie Called Electricity.* New York: Harper and Brothers, 1927.

MILLS, JOHN. *Magic of Communication.* Revised Edition. New York: American Telephone & Telegraph Co., 1926.

MORRIS, CHARLES. *Heroes of Progress in America.* Chicago: J. B. Lippincott Company, 1919.

MOWRY, W. A. *American Inventions and Inventors.* New York: Silver, Burdett and Company, 1900.

Pageant of America. Edited by R. Henry Gabriel. Vol. 4, Pt. 4. Communications. New Haven: Yale University Press, 1925–1927.

PARKER, ARTHUR C. *The Indian How Book.* Garden City, New York: Doubleday, Doran & Company, 1927.

PARKER, BERTHA MORRIS. *Book of Electricity.* Boston: Houghton Mifflin Company, 1928.

A Popular History of American Inventions. Vol. I. Edited by Waldemar B. Kaempffert. New York: Chas. Scribner's Sons, 1924.

PERRY, FRANCES MELVILLE. *Four American Inventors; Robert Fulton, Samuel F. B. Morse, Eli Whitney, Thomas A. Edison.* New York: American Book Company, 1901.

ROLT-WHEELER, FRANCIS WILLIAM. *Boy with the United States Radio.* Boston: Lothrop, Lee & Shepard Company, 1924.

ROLT-WHEELER, FRANCIS WILLIAM. *News-hunters.* Boston: Lothrop, Lee & Shepard Company, 1926.

ROMER, ANDREW RALPH, and ROMER, M. T. *Sky Travel.* Chicago: Rand McNally & Company, 1930.

RUGG, HAROLD. *Introduction to American Civilization.* Boston: Ginn and Company, 1929.

RUSH, CHARLES EVERETT, and WINSLOW, AMY. *Science of Things About Us.* Boston: Little, Brown and Company, 1927.

SHENTON, EDWARD. *Couriers of the Clouds.* Philadelphia: Macrae Smith Co., 1930.

SIEGEL, WILLIAM. *Around the World in a Mail Bag.* New York: Robert M. McBride and Company, 1932.

STONE, GERTRUDE LINCOLN, and FICKETT, M. G. *Famous Days in the Century of Invention.* Boston: D. C. Heath and Company, 1920.

TAPPAN, EVA MARCH. *Travelers and Traveling.* Industrial Readers, Book IV. Boston: Houghton Mifflin Company, 1930.

TAPPAN, EVA MARCH. *Wonders of Science.* Boston: Houghton Mifflin Company, 1927.

VAN METRE, THURMEN WILLIAM. *Trains, Tracks and Travel.* New York: Simmons-Boardman Publishing Company, 1931.

WADE, MARY H. *Light-bringers.* Boston: Little, Brown and Company, 1914.

WEBSTER, HANSON HART. *The World's Messengers.* Boston: Houghton Mifflin Company, 1934.

DESERTS

Books for Pupils

REFERENCE BOOKS

AITCHINSON, ALISON E., and UTTLEY, MARGUERITE. *Across Seven Seas to Seven Continents.* Indianapolis: Bobbs-Merrill Company, 1931.

ATWOOD, WALLACE, and THOMAS, H. G. *Home Life in Far Away Lands.* Boston: Ginn and Company, 1928.

BURNS, ANNIE JOHNSON. *Stories of Shepherd Life.* New York: American Book Company, 1934.

CARPENTER, FRANCES. *Our Neighbors Near and Far.* New York: American Book Company, 1933.

CARPENTER, FRANCES. *Our Little Friends of the Arabian Desert.* New York: American Book Company, 1934.

CARPENTER, FRANK. *Around the World With the Children.* New York: American Book Company, 1917.

HALL, JENNIE. *Weavers and Other Workers.* Chicago: Rand McNally & Company, 1917.

HEADLEY, E. A. *How Other People Travel.* Chicago: Rand McNally & Company, 1926.

MOHR, LOUISE MAUD. *Palestine and Syria.* Chicago: Rand McNally Company, 1931.

PIPER, WATTY. *Little Folks of Other Lands.* New York: The Platt & Munk Co., 1929.

SCANTLEBURY, ELIZABETH ELLIS. *Little World Children.* Boston: Ginn and Company, 1928.

STORY BOOKS

HIMES, VERA CAROLA. *Pepi and the Golden Hawk.* New York: T. Y. Crowell Company, 1932.

HOWARD, ALICE WOODBURY. *Sokar and the Crocodile.* New York: The Macmillan Company, 1930.

MANSFIELD, BLANCHE. *Our Little Arabian Cousin.* Boston: L. C. Page and Company, 1907.

PALMER, WINTHROP B. *Abdul.* New York: The Macmillan Company, 1928.

PURNELL, IDELLA. *Little Yusuf.* New York: The Macmillan Company, 1931.

STARR, LAURA B. *Mustafa, the Egyptian Boy.* Chicago: A. Flanagan Company, 1930.

TIETJENS, EUNICE. *Boy of the Desert.* New York: Coward, McCann & Company, 1928.

WELLS, RHEA. *Ali, the Camel.* Garden City, New York: Doubleday, Doran and Company, 1931.

DOGS

Books for Pupils

REFERENCE BOOKS

ALDIN, CECIL C. W. *Dogs of Character.* New York: Chas. Scribner's Sons, 1927.

ALEXANDER, CHARLES. *Bobbie, a Great Collie.* New York: Dodd, Mead & Company, Inc., 1926.

BIANCO, MARGERY. *All About Pets.* New York: The Macmillan Company, 1929.

DUNCAN, FRANCIS MARTIN, and DUNCAN, L. T. *Animal Friends.* Book VI. New York: Oxford University Press, n. d.

FUERTES, LOUIS AGASSIZ, and OTHERS. *Book of Dogs.* Washington: National Geographic Society, 1919.

KING, JULIUS. *Dogs.* New York: Thomas Nelson & Sons, 1927.

LAWSON, JAMES GILCHRIST. *The Book of Dogs.* Chicago: Rand McNally and Company, 1934.

MUIR, JOHN, and OTHERS. *Good Dog Book.* Boston: Houghton Mifflin Company, 1924.

NIDA, WILLIAM LEWIS, and NIDA, STELLA. *Trailing Our Animal Friends.* Science Readers Book II. Boston: D. C. Heath and Company, 1928.

THORNE, DIANA. *Dogs.* Akron, Ohio: The Saalfield Publishing Company, 1932.

STORY BOOKS

ATKINSON, ELEANOR. *Greyfriars Bobby.* New York: Harper & Brothers, 1912.

BAYNES, ERNEST HAROLD. *Polaris.* New York: The Macmillan Company, 1927.

BROWN, JOHN. *Rab and His Friends.* Chicago: Rand McNally and Company, 1902.

BRYAN, DOROTHY, and BRYAN, MARGUERITE. *Fun with Michael.* Garden City, New York: Doubleday, Doran and Company, 1934.

BRYAN, DOROTHY, and BRYAN, MARGUERITE. *Michael Who Missed His Train.* Garden City, New York: Doubleday, Doran and Company, 1933.

CALDWELL, FRANK. *Wolf, the Storm Leader.* New York: Dodd, Mead and Company, 1929.

DARLING, ESTHER BIRDSALL. *Baldy of Nome.* Philadelphia: The Penn Publishing Company, 1923.

DE LA RAMÉE, LOUISE. *Dog of Flanders.* Chicago: M. A. Donohue & Company, n. d.

FIELD, RACHEL LYMAN. *Little Dog Toby.* New York: The Macmillan Company, 1928.

FITZPATRICK, PERCY. *Jock of the Busaveld.* New York: Longmans, Green and Company, 1918.

FLACK, MARJORIE. *Angus and the Ducks.* Garden City, New York: Doubleday, Doran & Company, 1930.

FLACK, MARJORIE. *Topsy.* Garden City, New York: Doubleday. Doran and Company, 1935.

GEHRES, ETHEL MALTBY. *Wag, a Friendly Dog.* Philadelphia: The John C. Winston Company, 1934.

HORN, ERNEST, and McBROOM, MAUDE. *Learn to Study Readers. Book II.* Boston: Ginn and Company, 1924.

KENT, FRANCES. *Puppy Dog Tales and Stories of Other Animal Friends.* New York: The Macmillan Company, 1922.

LONDON, JACK. *The Call of the Wild.* New York: Grosset and Dunlap, 1903.

MILLS, ENOS A. *Story of Scotch.* Boston: Houghton Mifflin Company, 1909.

MUIR, JOHN. *Stickeen.* Boston: Houghton Mifflin Company, 1923.

OLLIVANT, ALFRED. *Bob, Son of Battle.* Garden City, New York: Doubleday, Page and Company, 1925.

ORTON, HELEN. *Prince and Rover of Cloverfield Farm.* New York: Frederick A. Stokes Company, 1921.

PYLE, KATHERINE. *Black-Eyed Puppy.* New York: E. P. Dutton and Company, 1923.

ROBINSON, MABEL L. *Little Lucia and Her Puppy.* New York: E. P. Dutton and Company, 1923.

SAUNDERS, MARSHALL. *Beautiful Joe.* Philadelphia: The Judson Press, 1893.

SEELY, EVA BRUNELL, and LANE, M. A. *Chinook and His Family.* Boston: Ginn and Company, 1930.

TERHUNE, ALBERT PAYSON. *Lad: A Dog.* New York: E. P. Dutton and Company, 1919.

WHITE, MARGARET L., and HAWTHORN, ALICE. *Interesting Things to Know.* Do and Learn Readers. New York: American Book Company, 1930.

WHITNEY, ELINOR. *Tyke-y.* New York: The Macmillan Company, 1925.

EARTH, SUN, MOON, AND STARS

Books for Pupils

ATWOOD, WALLACE W. *The World at Work.* Boston: Ginn and Company, 1931.

BAKER, ROBERT HORACE. *When the Stars Come Out.* New York: Junior Literary Guild and The Viking Press, 1934.

CLARK, ELIOT C. *Astronomy from a Dipper.* Boston: Houghton Mifflin Company, 1909.

COLLINS, ARCHIE FREDERICK. *Book of Stars.* New York: D. Appleton and Company, 1920.

COLLINS, A. FREDERICK. *The Boy Astronomer.* Boston: Lothrop, Lee & Shepard Company, 1923.

CRAIG, GERALD S., and HURLEY, BEATRICE DAVIS. *The Earth and Living Things.* Boston: Ginn and Company, 1932.

CRAIG, GERALD S., and CONDRY, MARGARET G. *Learning About Our World.* Boston: Ginn and Company, 1932.

CRAIG, GERALD S., and BALDWIN, SARA E. *Our Wide, Wide World.* Boston: Ginn and Company, 1932.

GRIFFITH, ALICE MARY MATLOCK. *The Stars and Their Stories.* New York: Henry Holt and Company, 1913.

HALE, GEORGE ELLERY. *The New Heavens.* New York: Charles Scribner's Sons, 1922.

JOHNSON, GAYLORD. *The Sky Movies.* New York: The Macmillan Company, 1922.

JOHNSON, GAYLORD. *The Star People.* New York: The Macmillan Company, 1928.

KINNEY, MURIEL. *Stars and Their Stories.* New York: D. Appleton and Company, 1926.

LEWIS, ISABEL ELEANOR (Martin). *Astronomy for Young Folks.* New York: Dodd, Mead & Company, Inc., 1932.

McKAY, HERBERT. *The Sun and the Moon.* First Steps in Science. London: Oxford University Press, n.d.

MARKOWITZ, WILLIAM. *Planets.* A Century of Progress Wonder Library. Chicago: Colortext Publications, 1933.

MARTIN, MARTHA EVANS. *The Friendly Stars.* New York: Harper & Brothers, 1907.

MARTIN, MARTHA EVANS. *The Ways of the Planets.* New York: Harper & Brothers, 1912.

OLCOTT, WILLIAM TYLER. *The Book of Stars For Young People.* New York: G. P. Putnam's Sons, 1923.

PATCH, EDITH M., and HOWE, HARRISON E. *Surprises.* New York: The Macmillan Company, 1934.

PROCTOR, MARY. *Legends of the Stars.* Philadelphia: David McKay Company, n.d.

PROCTOR, MARY. *The Young Folk's Book of the Heavens.* Boston: Little, Brown and Company, 1926.

REED, W. MAXWELL. *The Earth for Sam.* New York: Junior Literary Guild, 1930.

REED, W. MAXWELL. *The Stars for Sam.* New York: Harcourt, Brace and Company, 1931.

SCHWARTZ, JULIA AUGUSTA. *Little Star Gazers.* New York: Frederick A. Stokes Company, 1917.

SWEZEY, GOODWIN DELOSS. *Boys' Book of Astronomy.* New York: E. P. Dutton & Co., Inc., 1929.

WARNER, GERTRUDE CHANDLER. *Star Stories for Little Folks.* Boston: The Pilgrim Press, 1918.

WASHBURNE, CARLETON W., and WASHBURNE, HELUIZ CHANDLER. *The Story of Earth and Sky.* New York: The Junior Literary Guild and The Century Co., 1933.

EGYPT

Books for Pupils

REFERENCE BOOKS

ALLEN, NELLIE. *Africa, Australia, and the Islands of the Pacific.* Boston: Ginn and Company, 1924.

ATWOOD, WALLACE W., and THOMAS, H. G. *Home Life in Far Away Lands.* Boston: Ginn and Company, 1928.

ATWOOD, WALLACE W., and THOMAS, H. G. *Nations Beyond the Seas.* Boston: Ginn and Company, 1930.

BARROWS, H. H.; PARKER, E. P., and PARKER, M. T. *Geography. Southern Lands.* New York: Silver, Burdett and Company, 1929.

BEST, SUSIE M. *Egypt and Her Neighbors* New York: The Macmillan Company, 1918.

BLUNT, ALFRED W. F. *Ancient World and Its Legacy to Us.* New York: Oxford University Press, 1928.

BREASTED, JAMES HENRY. *Ancient Times, A History of the Early World.* Boston: Ginn and Company, 1916.

CARPENTER, FRANK G. *Around the World With the Children.* New York: American Book Company, 1917.

CARPENTER, FRANK G. *Africa.* New York: American Book Company, 1924.

CHAMBERLAIN, J. F., and CHAMBERLAIN, A. H. *Africa.* New York: The Macmillan Company, 1925.

CHAPMAN, H. S. *Stories of the Ancient Peoples.* Boston: Houghton Mifflin Company, 1929.

CHURCH, ALFRED JOHN. *Stories of the East from Herodotus.* New York: Dodd, Mead & Company, Inc., 1880.

CLARK, MARION G., and GORDY, WILBUR F. *The Early Story of Mankind.* New York: Chas. Scribner's Sons, 1929.

COFFMAN, RAMON. *Child's Story of the Human Race.* New York: Dodd, Mead & Company, Inc., 1927.

DAKIN, WILSON S. *Great Rivers of the World.* New York: The Macmillan Company, 1925.

ERLEIGH, EVA VIOLET. *In the Beginning.* Garden City, New York: Doubleday, Doran & Company, 1926.

HALL, JENNIE. *Weavers and Other Workers.* Chicago: Rand McNally & Company, 1917.

HEADLEY, E. A. *How Other People Travel.* Chicago: Rand McNally & Company, 1926.

HICHENS, ROBERT SMYTHE. *Egypt and Its Monuments.* New York: The Century Co., 1908.

HILLYER, VIRGIL M. *Child's Geography of the World.* New York: The Century Co., 1929.

HILLYER, VIRGIL M. *A Child's History of the World.* New York: The Century Co., 1924.

HODGDON, J. R. *The Enchanted Past.* Boston: Ginn and Company, 1922.

KELLY, ROBERT TALBOT. *Egypt; and the Holy Land.* Peeps at Many Lands. New York: The Macmillan Company, 1921.

KUMMER, FREDERIC ARNOLD. *First Days of Knowledge.* New York: George H. Doran Company, 1923.

LAMPREY, LOUISE. *Children of Ancient Egypt.* Boston: Little, Brown and Company, 1926.

LANSING, MARION FLORENCE. *Man's Long Climb.* Boston: Little, Brown and Company, 1933.

MILLS, DOROTHY. *Book of the Ancient World for Younger Readers.* New York: G. P. Putnam's Sons, 1923.

MOHR, LOUISE MAUDE. *Palestine and Syria.* Chicago: Rand McNally & Company, 1931.

MOHR, LOUISE MAUDE. *Egyptians of Long Ago.* Chicago: Rand McNally & Company, 1926.

PACKARD, LEONARD OSCAR, and SINNOTT, C. P. *Nations as Neighbors.* New York: The Macmillan Company, 1930.

PERRY, WALTER SCOTT. *With Azir Girges in Egypt.* New York: Mentzer, Bush & Company, 1913.

SALISBURY, ETHEL IMOGENE, and STEDMAN, LULU M. *Our Ancestors in the Ancient World.* Boston: Little, Brown and Company, 1935.

SMALL, SIDNEY AYLMER. *Boys' Book of the Earth.* New York: E. P. Dutton and Company, 1924.

SOUTHWORTH, GERTRUDE, and SOUTHWORTH, J. VAN D. *What the Old World Gave the New.* Syracuse, New York: Iroquois Publishing Company, 1924.

STUART, DOROTHY MARGARET. *Boy Through the Ages.* New York: George H. Doran Company, 1926.

TIETJENS, EUNICE STRONG. *The Boy of the Desert.* New York: Coward, McCann & Company, 1928.

VAN LOON, HENRIK W. *Ancient Man.* New York: Boni & Liveright, 1922.

VAN LOON, HENRIK W. *The Story of Mankind.* New York: Boni & Liveright, 1921.

VAUGHAN, DOROTHY M. *Great Peoples of the Ancient World.* New York: Longmans, Green and Company, 1925.

WELLS, MARGRET E. *How the Present Came From the Past.* Book II. New York: The Macmillan Company, 1932.

WEST, RUTH, and WEST, W. M. *New World's Foundations in the Old.* Boston: Allyn and Bacon, 1929.

STORY BOOKS

HIMES, VERA C. *Pepi and the Golden Hawk.* New York: T. Y. Crowell Company, 1932.

HOWARD, ALICE. *Sokar and the Crocodile.* New York: The Macmillan Company, 1928.

JEWETT, ELEANOR M. *Egyptian Tales of Magic.* Boston: Little, Brown and Company, 1924.

MANSFIELD, BLANCHE. *Our Little Arabian Cousin.* Boston: L. C. Page & Company, 1907.

MCDONALD, ETTA AUSTIN, and DALRYMPLE, JULIA. *Hassan in Egypt.* Boston: Little, Brown and Company, 1911.

MIRZA, YOUEL BENJAMIN. *Myself When Young.* Garden City, New York: Doubleday, Doran & Company, 1929.

MIRZA, YOUEL BENJAMIN. *Children of the Housetops.* Garden City, New York: Doubleday, Doran & Company, 1931.

PALMER, W. B. *Abdul, Story of an Egyptian Boy.* New York: The Macmillan Company, 1928.

PURNELL, IDELLA. *Little Yusuf.* New York: The Macmillan Company, 1931.

STARR, LAURA B. *Mustafa, The Egyptian Boy.* Chicago: A. Flanagan Company, 1905.

WELLS, RHEA. *Ali, The Camel.* Garden City, New York: Doubleday, Doran & Company, 1931.

ELECTRICITY

Books for Pupils

ABBOT, CHARLES GREELEY. *Everyday Mysteries.* New York: The Macmillan Company, 1923.

BACHMAN, FRANK P. *Great Inventors and Their Inventions.* New York: American Book Company, 1918.

BAXTER, LEON H. *Electro-craft in Theory and Practice.* Milwaukee, Wisconsin: The Bruce Publishing Company, 1925.

BOLTON, SARAH K. *Famous Men of Science.* New York: Thomas Y. Crowell & Company, 1889.

BRIDGES, T. C. *The Young Folk's Book of Inventions.* Boston: Little, Brown and Company, 1929.

CALDWELL, OTIS W., and MEIER, W. H. D. *Open Doors to Science.* Boston: Ginn and Company, 1925.

CARPENTER, FRANK G., and CARPENTER, FRANCES. *The Houses We Live In.* New York: American Book Company, 1926.

CARPENTER, FRANK G. *How the World is Housed.* New York: American Book Company, 1930.

CHAMBERLAIN, JAMES F. *How We Are Sheltered.* New York: The Macmillan Company, 1929.

CHAMBERLAIN, JAMES F. *How We Travel.* New York: The Macmillan Company, 1927.

CRAIG, GERALD S., and HURLEY, BEATRICE DAVIS. *The Earth and Living Things.* Boston: Houghton Mifflin Company, 1932.

CRAIG, GERALD S., and JOHNSON, GOLDIE M. *Our Earth and Its Story.* Boston: Ginn and Company, 1932.

DARROW, FLOYD L. *The Boy's Own Book of Science.* New York: The Macmillan Company, 1931.

DARROW, FLOYD L. *Masters of Science and Inventions.* New York: Harcourt, Brace and Company, 1923.

DARROW, FLOYD L. *Thinkers and Doers.* New York: Silver, Burdett and Company, 1925.

DOWNING, ELLIOT ROWLAND. *Our Physical World.* Chicago: The University of Chicago Press, 1924.

EATON, JEANETTE. *The Story of Light.* New York: Harper & Brothers, 1928.

FARIS, JOHN T. *Real Stories from Our History.* Boston: Ginn and Company, 1916.

FRYER, JANE EAYRE. *Community Interest and Public Spirit.* Philadelphia: The John C. Winston Company, 1919.

GEORGE, LLOYD, and GILMAN, JAMES. *Modern Mercuries.* New York: Robert M. McBride & Company, 1932.

GIBSON, CHARLES ROBERT. *Electrical Amusements and Experiments.* Philadelphia: J. B. Lippincott Company, 1925.

HOLLAND, RUPERT S. *Historic Inventions.* Philadelphia: Macrae Smith Company, 1911.

HOUGH, WALTER. *The Story of Fire.* Garden City, New York: Doubleday, Doran & Company, 1930.

KEELOR, KATHERINE L. *Working With Electricity.* New York: The Macmillan Company, 1933.

KEIR, MALCOLM. *The Epic of Industry.* The Pageant of America, Vol. 5, Part 1. New Haven: Yale University Press, 1926.

LACEY, IDA BELLE. *Light Then and Now.* New York: The Macmillan Company, 1931.

LANSING, MARION FLORENCE. *Great Moments in Science.* Garden City, New York: Doubleday, Doran & Company, 1931.

MEADOWCROFT, WILLIAM H. *The Boy's Life of Edison.* New York: Harper & Brothers, 1911.

MERIWETHER, SUSAN. *The Story of the Telephone.* New York: Harper & Brothers, 1927.

MILLS, JOHN. *The Magic of Communication.* New York: American Telephone & Telegraph Company, 1928.

MOWRY, WILLIAM A., and MOWRY, ARTHUR MAY. *American Inventions and Inventors.* New York: Silver, Burdett and Company, 1910.

NICHOLS, M. LOUISE. *Science for Boys and Girls.* Philadelphia: J. B. Lippincott Company, 1924.

NIDA, WILLIAM L., and NIDA, STELLA H. *Makers of Progress.* Science Readers for Silent Reading. Book V. Boston: D. C. Heath and Company, 1926.

PARKER, BERTHA MORRIS. *The Book of Electricity.* Boston: Houghton Mifflin Company, 1928.

PARKMAN, MARY R. *Conquests of Invention.* New York: The Century Co., 1921.

PIEPER, CHARLES JOHN, and BEAUCHAMP, WILBUR LEE. *Everyday Problems in Science.* Chicago: Scott, Foresman and Company, 1925.

ROLT-WHEELER, FRANCIS. *The Boy With the U. S. Inventors.* Boston: Lothrop, Lee & Shepard Company, 1920.

RUSH, CHARLES E., and WINSLOW, AMY. *The Science of Things About Us.* Boston: Little, Brown and Company, 1928.

SMITH, EDITH LILLIAN. *Everyday Science Projects.* Boston: Houghton Mifflin Company, 1925.

STONE, GERTRUDE L., and FICKETT, M. GRACE. *Famous Days in the Century of Invention.* Boston: D. C. Heath & Co., 1920.

TAPPAN, EVA MARCH. *Heroes of Progress.* Boston: Houghton Mifflin Company, 1928.

TOWER, SAMUEL F., and LUNT, JOSEPH R. *Science of Common Things.* Boston: D. C. Heath & Co., 1922.

VAN BUSKIRK, EDGAR F., and SMITH, EDITH LILLIAN. *The Science of Everyday Life.* Boston: Houghton Mifflin Company, 1925.

FARM LIFE

Books for Pupils

REFERENCE BOOKS

AITCHISON, ALISON E., and UTTLEY, MARGUERITE. *Across Seven Seas to Seven Continents.* Indianapolis: Bobbs-Merrill Company, 1931.

AITCHISON, ALISON E. and UTTLEY, MARGUERITE. *North America by Plane and Train.* Indianapolis: Bobbs-Merrill Company, 1931.

ALLEN, NELLIE B. *Cotton and Other Useful Fibers.* Boston: Ginn and Company, 1929.

ALLEN, NELLIE B. *How and Where We Live.* Boston: Ginn and Company, 1924.

ALLEN, NELLIE B. *Our Cereal Grains.* Boston: Ginn and Company, 1928.

ALLEN, NELLIE B. *United States.* Boston: Ginn and Company, 1925.

BARROWS, H. H., and PARKER, E. P. *Geography: United States and Canada.* New York: Silver, Burdett and Company, 1925.

BASS, FLORENCE. *Stories of Pioneer Life.* Boston: D. C. Heath and Company, 1900.

BEATY, JOHN Y. *The Farmer at His Work.* Akron, Ohio: The Saalfield Publishing Company, 1933.

BROOKS, EUGENE C. *Story of Corn and the Westward Migration.* Chicago: Rand McNally & Company, 1916.

BROOKS, EUGENE C. *Story of Cotton.* Chicago: Rand McNally & Company. n. d.

BURNS, ANNIE JOHNSON. *Stories of Shepherd Life.* New York: American Book Company, 1934.

CAMP, RUTH ORTON. *Story of Markets.* New York: Harper and Brothers, 1929.

CARPENTER, FRANK G. *Around the World with the Children.* New York: American Book Company, 1917.

CARPENTER, FRANK G., and CARPENTER, FRANCES. *Clothes We Wear.* New York: American Book Company, 1926.

CARPENTER, FRANK G., and CARPENTER, FRANCES. *Foods We Eat.* New York: American Book Company, 1925.

CARPENTER, FRANK G. *How the World is Clothed.* New York: American Book Company, 1908.

CARPENTER, FRANK G. *How the World is Fed.* New York: American Book Company, 1923.

CARPENTER, FRANK G. *North America.* New York: American Book Company, 1922.

CURTIS, MARY ISABEL. *Stories in Trees.* Chicago: Lyons and Carnahan, 1925.

DORRANCE, JOHN GORDON. *Story of the Forest.* New York: American Book Company, 1916.

DU PUY, WILLIAM A. *Our Plant Friends and Foes.* Philadelphia: The John C. Winston Company, 1930.

DU PUY, WILLIAM A. *Our Insect Friends and Foes.* Philadelphia: The John C. Winston Company, 1925.

FAIRBANKS, HAROLD WELLMAN. *Southern California.* San Francisco: Harr Wagner Publishing Company, 1929.

FISHER, ELIZABETH F. *Resources and Industries of the United States.* Boston: Ginn and Company, 1928.

HALIFAX, JEAN. *Story of Wheat.* Dansville, New York: F. A. Owen Publishing Company, 1906.

HUNTINGTON, ELLSWORTH; BENSON, C. B.; and McMURRY, F. M. *Living Geography.* Book I. New York: The Macmillan Company, 1932.

HUNTINGTON, ELLSWORTH; BENSON, C. B.; and McMURRY, F. M. *Living Geography.* Book II. New York: The Macmillan Company, 1932.

HUNTINGTON, ELLSWORTH, and CUSHING, S. W. *Modern Business Geography.* Yonkers-on-Hudson, New York: World Book Company, 1932.

JOHNSON, CLIFTON. *New England.* New York: The Macmillan Company, 1917.

KELLER, A. G., and BISHOP, A. L. *Commercial and Industrial Geography.* Boston: Ginn and Company, 1912.

KNOWLTON, PHILIP ARNOLD. *First Lessons in Geography.* New York: The Macmillan Company, 1924.

LEFFERTS, WALTER. *Our Own United States.* Chicago: J. B. Lippincott Company, 1925.

NATHAN, ADELE GUTMAN. *The Farmer Sows His Wheat.* New York: Minton, Balch and Company, 1932.

NICHOLS, MARIE LOUISE. *Science for Boys and Girls.* Chicago: J. B. Lippincott Company, 1924.

NIDA, WILLIAM LEWIS, and NIDA, STELLA. *Trailing Our Animal Friends.* Boston: D. C. Heath and Company, 1928.

NIDA, WILLIAM LEWIS, and WEBB, V. L. *Our Country Past and Present.* Chicago: Scott, Foresman and Company, 1930.

PACKARD, LEONARD O., and SINNOTT, C. P. *Nations as Neighbors.* New York: The Macmillan Company, 1925.

PARKER, BERTHA MORRIS, and COWLES, H. C. *Book of Plants.* Science Readers. Boston: Houghton Mifflin Company, 1925.

PATCH, EDITH M. *First Lessons in Nature Study.* New York: The Macmillan Company, 1932.

PIEPER, CHARLES J., and BEAUCHAMP, W. L. *Everyday Problems in Science.* Chicago: Scott, Foresman and Company, 1925.

QUINN, VERNON. *Picture Map Geography of the United States.* New York: Frederick A. Stokes Company, 1931.

SANDERS, ALVIN H. *Cattle of the World.* Washington: National Geographic Society, 1926.

SCARBOROUGH, DOROTHY. *Story of Cotton.* City and Country Series. New York: Harper and Brothers, 1933.

SHEPARD, EDITH P. *Geography for Beginners.* Books I-II. Chicago: Rand McNally & Company, 1927-1930.

SHILLIG, ELNORA ELIZABETH. *Four Wonders.* Chicago: Rand McNally & Company, 1913.

SKILLING, WILLIAM THOMPSON. *Nature-study Agriculture.* Yonkers-on-Hudson, New York: World Book Company, 1929.

SMITH, EDITH LILLIAN. *Everyday Science Projects.* Boston: Houghton Mifflin Company, 1925.

SMITH, JOSEPH RUSSELL. *Home Folks*. Philadelphia: The John C. Winston Company, 1930.

TAPPAN, EVA MARCH. *Farmer and His Friends*. Boston: Houghton Mifflin Company, 1929.

WATSON, ELIZABETH. *Story of Milk and How It Came About*. New York: Harper and Brothers, 1927.

WORTHINGTON, JOSEPHINE, and MATTHEWS, C. V. *Our Food*. Dansville, New York: F. A. Owen Publishing Company, 1930.

WORTHINGTON, JOSEPHINE, and MATTHEWS, C. V. *Our Clothing*. Dansville, New York: F. A. Owen Publishing Company, 1931.

STORY BOOKS

CANFIELD, HENRY S. *Boys of the Rincon Ranch*. New York: The Century Co., 1902.

DOUBLEDAY, RUSSELL. *Cattle Ranch To College*. New York: Grosset & Dunlap, 1930.

FOLGER, DORIS, and NICOL, NINA. *Rusty Pete of the Lazy AB*. New York: The Macmillan Company, 1929.

GRINNELLI, GEORGE BIRD. *Jack, The Young Cowboy*. New York: Frederick A. Stokes Company, 1913.

HADER, BERTA, and HADER, ELMER. *Farmer in the Dell*. New York: The Macmillan Company, 1931.

HESS, FJERL. *Buckaroo*. New York: The Macmillan Company, 1933.

HOUGH, EMERSON. *Story of the Cowboy*. New York: Grosset & Dunlap, 1925.

INMAN, HENRY. *Ranche on the Oxhide*. New York: The Macmillan Company, 1923.

JAMES, WILL. *Smoky, the Cow Horse*. New York: Chas. Scribner's Sons, 1929.

KNOX, ROSE B. *Marty and Company*. Garden City, New York: Doubleday, Doran Company, 1933.

MEANS, FLORENCE CRANNELL. *Ranch and Ring*. Boston: Houghton Mifflin Company, 1932.

McNEELY, MARIAN. *Jumping-off Place*. New York: Longmans, Green and Company, 1929.

NIDA, STELLA H. *Letters of Polly the Pioneer*. New York: The Macmillan Company, 1916.

ROLLINS, PHILLIP A. *Cowboy*. New York: Chas. Scribner's Sons, 1922.

STONG, PHIL. *Farm Boy*. Garden City, New York: Doubleday, Doran and Company, 1934.

TOUSEY, SANFORD. *Cowboy Tommy's Roundup*. Garden City, New York: Doubleday, Doran and Company, 1934.

WELLS, RHEA. *An American Farm*. Garden City, New York: Doubleday, Doran and Company, 1928.

Books for Teachers

BONSER, FREDERICK G., and MOSSMAN, L. C. *Industrial Arts for Elementary Schools*. New York: The Macmillan Company, 1923.

CRISSEY, FORREST. *The Story of Foods*. Chicago: Rand McNally & Company, 1917.

FOODS

Books for Pupils

REFERENCE BOOKS

AITCHISON, ALISON E., and UTTLEY, MARGUERITE. *Across Seven Seas to Seven Continents*. Indianapolis: Bobbs-Merrill Company, 1931.

AITCHISON, ALISON E., and UTTLEY, MARGUERITE. *North America by Plane and Train*. Indianapolis: Bobbs-Merrill Company, 1931.

ALLEN, NELLIE B. *United States.* Boston: Ginn and Company, 1925.

ALLEN, NELLIE B. *Our Cereal Grains.* Boston: Ginn and Company, 1928.

ALLEN, NELLIE B. *How and Where We Live.* Boston: Ginn and Company, 1924.

ATWOOD, WALLACE W., and ATWOOD, THOMAS. *Home Life in Far Away Lands.* Boston: Ginn and Company, 1928.

BAILEY, EDGAR H., and BAILEY, H. S. *Food Products from Afar.* New York: The Century Co., 1922.

BARROWS, H. H.; PARKER, E. P.; and PARKER, M. T. *Europe and Asia.* New York: Silver, Burdett and Company, 1930.

BARROWS, H. H., and PARKER, E. P. *Geography: United States and Canada.* New York: Silver, Burdett and Company, 1925.

BROOKS, EUGENE C. *Story of Corn and the Westward Migration.* Chicago: Rand McNally & Company, 1916.

CAMP, RUTH ORTON. *Story of Markets.* New York: Harper and Brothers, 1929.

CARPENTER, FRANK G. *How the World is Fed.* New York: American Book Company, 1923.

CARPENTER, FRANK G. *North America.* New York: American Book Company, 1922.

CARPENTER, FRANK G., and CARPENTER, FRANCES. *Foods we Eat.* New York: American Book Company, 1925.

CHAMBERLAIN, J. F. *How We are Fed.* New York: The Macmillan Company. n.d.

CRISSEY, FORREST. *Story of Foods.* Chicago: Rand McNally & Company, 1917.

CRUMP, IRVING. *The Boys' Book of Fisheries.* New York: Dodd, Mead and Company, Inc., 1933.

FAIRGRIEVE, JAMES, and YOUNG, ERNEST. *World.* New York: D. Appleton and Company, 1925.

FISHER, ELIZABETH F. *Resources and Industries of the United States.* Boston: Ginn and Company, 1928.

FRANCK, HARRY A. *China.* Dansville, New York: F. A. Owen Publishing Company, 1927.

FRANCK, HARRY A. *The Japanese Empire.* Dansville, New York: F. A. Owen Publishing Company, 1927.

FRANCK, HARRY A. *Mexico and Central America.* Dansville, New York: F. A. Owen Publishing Company, 1927.

GILMAN, ISABEL A. *Alaska, the American Northland.* Yonkers-on-Hudson, New York: World Book Company, 1923.

HALIFAX, JEAN. *Story of Wheat.* Dansville, New York: F. A. Owen Publishing Company, 1906.

HUNTINGTON, ELLSWORTH; BENSON, C. B.; and McMURRY, F. M. *Living Geography.* Book I. New York: The Macmillan Company, 1932.

HUNTINGTON, ELLSWORTH; BENSON, C. B.; and McMURRY, F. M. *Living Geography.* Book II. New York: The Macmillan Company, 1932.

HUNTINGTON, ELLSWORTH, and CUSHING, S. W. *Modern Business Geography.* Yonkers-on-Hudson, New York: World Book Company, 1932.

JAY, GLADYS. *Twins in Fruitland.* Chicago: Beckley-Cardy Company, 1929.

KNOWLTON, PHILIP ARNOLD. *First Lessons in Geography.* New York: The Macmillan Company, 1924.

LEFFERTS, WALTER. *Neighbors North and South.* Philadelphia: J. B. Lippincott Company, 1926.

MITCHELL, LUCY. *North America.* New York: The Macmillan Company, 1931.

NIDA, WILLIAM LEWIS, and WEBB, V. L. *Our Country Past and Present.* Chicago: Scott, Foresman and Company, 1930.

PACKARD, LEONARD O., and SINNOTT, C. P. *Nations as Neighbors.* New York: The Macmillan Company, 1925.

PACKARD, LEONARD O., SINNOTT, P., and OVERTON, BRUCE. *The Nations at Work.* New York: The Macmillan Company, 1933.

PARKER, BERTHA MORRIS, and COWLES, H. C. *Book of Plants.* Science readers. Boston: Houghton Mifflin Company, 1925.

PATCH, EDITH M. *First Lessons in Nature Study.* New York: The Macmillan Company, 1932.

PETERSHAM, MAUD and MISKA. *The Storybook of Food.* Philadelphia: The John C. Winston Company, 1933.

PUMPHREY, MARGARET BLANCHE. *Stories of the Pilgrims.* Chicago: Rand McNally & Company, 1912.

SALISBURY, ETHEL I. *From Panama to Cape Horn.* Yonkers-on-Hudson, New York: World Book Company, 1927.

SHEPHERD, EDITH P. *Geography for Beginners.* Books I-II. Chicago: Rand McNally & Company, 1927-1930.

SKILLING, WILLIAM THOMPSON. *Nature-Study Agriculture.* Yonkers-on-Hudson, New York: World Book Company, 1929.

SMITH, JOSEPH RUSSELL. *Home Folks.* Philadelphia: The John C. Winston Company, 1930.

TAPPAN, EVA MARCH. *Farmer and His Friends.* Boston: Houghton Mifflin Company, 1916.

THOMPSON, RUTH. *Type Stories of the World for Little Folk.* San Francisco: Harr Wagner Publishing Company, 1922.

TRAFTON, GILBERT HAVEN. *Nature Study and Science for Intermediate Grades.* New York: The Macmillan Company, 1927.

WATSON, ELIZABETH. *Story of Bread.* New York: Harper and Brothers, 1927.

WATSON, ELIZABETH. *Story of Milk and How It Came About.* New York: Harper and Brothers, 1927.

WORTHINGTON, JOSEPHINE, and MATTHEWS, C. V. *Our Food.* Dansville, New York: F. A. Owen Publishing Company, 1930.

STORY BOOKS

McDONALD, ETTA AUSTIN, and DALRYMPLE, JULIA. *Marta in Holland.* Boston: Little, Brown and Company, 1911.

NIDA, STELLA HUMPHREY. *Letters of Polly the Pioneer.* New York: The Macmillan Company, 1916.

OLCOTT, VIRGINIA. *Anton and Trini.* New York: Silver, Burdett and Company, 1930.

PERKINS, LUCY. *Mexican Twins.* Boston: Houghton Mifflin Company, 1915.

PERKINS, LUCY. *Eskimo Twins.* Boston: Houghton Mifflin Company. n. d.

Books for Teachers

BONSER, FREDERICK G., and MOSSMAN, L. C. *Industrial Arts in the Elementary Schools.* New York: The Macmillan Company, 1923.

Curriculum Making in an Elementary School. Columbia University Teachers College. Boston: Ginn and Company, 1927.

FORESTRY

Books for Pupils

REFERENCE BOOKS

AITCHISON, ALISON E., and UTTLEY, MARGUERITE. *North America by Plane and Train.* Indianapolis: The Bobbs-Merrill Company, 1931.

ALLEN, NELLIE B. *United States.* Boston: Ginn and Company, 1925.

ATWOOD, WALLACE W. *The World at Work.* Boston: Ginn and Company, 1931.

BARROWS, H. H., and PARKER, E. P. *Geography: United States and Canada.* New York: Silver, Burdett and Company, 1925.

CARPENTER, FRANK G. *North America.* New York: American Book Company, 1922.

CARPENTER, FRANCES. *The Houses We Live In*. New York: American Book Company, 1926.

CHAMBERLAIN, J. F. *How We Are Sheltered*. New York: The Macmillan Company, 1924.

CHASE, ANNIE, and CLOW, E. *Stories of Industry*. Book I. New York: Educational Publishers, 1913.

CORWIN, MAE JOHNSON. *The Pioneer's Pathway*. San Francisco: Harr Wagner Publishing Company, 1932.

CRAIG, GERALD S., and CONDREY, MARGARET G. *Learning About Our World*. Pathways in Science, V. 5. Boston: Ginn and Company, 1932.

CRUMP, IRVING. *Boys' Book of Forest Rangers*. New York: Dodd, Mead & Company, Inc., 1924.

CURTIS, MARY ISABEL. *Stories in Trees*. Chicago: Lyons and Carnahan, 1925.

DORRANCE, JOHN GORDON. *Story of the Forest*. New York: American Book Company, 1916.

FRASER, CHELSEA CURTIS. *Heroes of the Wilds*. New York: T. Y. Crowell Company, 1923.

JORDAN, DAVID STARR, and CATHER, K. D. *North America*. Yonkers-on-Hudson, New York: World Book Company, 1925.

McFEE, INEZ NELLIE. *Gifts of the Forest*. Dansville, New York: F. A. Owen Publishing Company. n. d.

MADDOX, RUFUS S., and PARKINS, A. E. *Our Trees and How They Serve Us*. New York: Chas. Scribner's Sons, 1925.

MITCHELL, LUCY. *North America*. New York: The Macmillan Company, 1931.

PACK, CHARLES LATHROP. *Forestry Primer*. Washington, D. C.: American Tree Assn., 1926.

PACK, CHARLES LATHROP. *School Book of Forestry*. Washington, D. C.: American Tree Assn., 1922.

PACK, CHARLES LATHROP. *Trees as Good Citizens*. Washington, D. C.: American Tree Assn., 1922.

PACKARD, LEONARD OSCAR, and SINNOTT, C. P. *Nations as Neighbors*. New York: The Macmillan Company, 1925.

PATCH, EDITH M. *First Lessons in Nature Study*. New York: The Macmillan Company, 1926.

ROCHELEAU, WILLIAM FRANCIS. Great American Industries, Vol. 2. *Products of the Soil*. Chicago: A. Flanagan Company, 1928.

RUSH, CHARLES EVERETT. *Science of Things About Us*. Boston: Little, Brown and Company, 1927.

SMITH, JOSEPH RUSSELL. *Home Folks*. Philadelphia: The John C. Winston Company, 1927.

TAPPAN, EVA MARCH. *Farmer and His Friends*. Boston: Houghton Mifflin Company, 1929.

TRESIDDER, MARY CURRY. *Trees of Yosemite*. Stanford University, California: Stanford University Press, 1932.

STORY BOOKS

MEADER, STEPHEN W. *Lumberjack*. New York: Harcourt, Brace and Company, 1934.

MEIGS, CORNELIA. *Swift Rivers*. New York: The Junior Literary Guild, 1932.

WADSWORTH, WALLACE. *Paul Bunyan and His Great Blue Ox*. New York: George H. Doran Company, 1926.

FRANCE

Books for Pupils

REFERENCE BOOKS

ALLEN, NELLIE B. *The New Europe.* Boston: Ginn and Company, 1920.

ATWOOD, WALLACE W., and THOMAS, H. G. *Nations Beyond the Seas.* Boston: Ginn and Company, 1930.

BARROWS, H. H.; PARKER, E. P.; and PARKER, M. T. *Europe and Asia.* New York: Silver, Burdett and Company, 1930.

BEURET, GEORGETTE. *When I was a Girl in France.* Boston: Lothrop, Lee & Shepard Company, 1925.

BOUTET DE MONVEL, LOUIS M. *Joan of Arc.* New York: The Century Co., 1907.

BRYANT, LORINDA. *Children's Book of Celebrated Bridges.* New York: The Century Co., 1925.

BRYANT, LORINDA. *Children's Book of Celebrated Buildings.* New York: The Century Co., 1924.

BRYANT, LORINDA. *Children's Book of Celebrated Towers.* New York: The Century Co., 1926.

BRYANT, LORINDA. *Children's Book of European Landmarks.* New York: The Century Co., 1928.

CARPENTER, FLORA LEONA. *Stories Pictures Tell.* Book I. Chicago: Rand McNally & Company.

CARPENTER, FLORA LEONA. *Stories Pictures Tell.* Book II. Chicago: Rand McNally & Company.

CARPENTER, FLORA LEONA. *Stories Pictures Tell.* Book III. Chicago: Rand McNally & Company.

CARPENTER, FLORA LEONA. *Stories Pictures Tell.* Book IV. Chicago: Rand McNally & Company.

CARPENTER, FLORA LEONA. *Stories Pictures Tell.* Book V. Chicago: Rand McNally & Company.

CARPENTER, FLORA LEONA. *Stories Pictures Tell.* Book VI. Chicago: Rand McNally & Company.

CARPENTER, FRANK G. *Europe.* New York: American Book Company, 1924.

CHAMBERLAIN, J. F., and CHAMBERLAIN, F. H. *Europe.* New York: The Macmillan Company, 1916.

CLEMENT, M. *Once in France.* Garden City, New York: Doubleday, Page & Company, 1927.

CORTELLEMONT, GERVAIS. "Chateau Land." *National Geographic Magazine.* LVIII (October, 1930). Washington: National Geographic Magazine.

CREIGHTON, LOUISE. *Tales of Old France.* New York: Longmans, Green and Company, 1924.

DICKENS, CHARLES. *Tale of Two Cities.* Boston: Allyn and Bacon, 1922.

DALKEITH, LENA. *Stories from French History.* New York: E. P. Dutton and Company, 1909.

DARK, SIDNEY. *Book of France for Young People.* New York: George H. Doran Company, 1923.

FINNEMORE, JOHN. *France. Peeps at Many Lands.* London: A. and C. Black, 1912.

GUERBER, HELENE ADELINE. *Story of Modern France.* New York: American Book Company, 1910.

GUERBER, HELENE ADELINE. *Story of Old France.* New York: American Book Company, 1910.

HAAREN, JOHN HENRY, and POLAND, A. B. *Famous Men of the Middle Ages.* New York: American Book Company, n. d.

HANCOCK, MARY S. *Children of History, Later Times.* Boston: Little, Brown and Company, 1909.

HILLYER, VIRGIL M. *Child's Geography of the World.* New York: The Century Co., 1929.

37—17050

HUNTINGTON, ELLSWORTH; BENSON, C. B.; and MCMURRY, FRANK M. *Living Geography*. Book I. New York: The Macmillan Company, 1932.

HUNTINGTON, ELLSWORTH; BENSON, C. B.; and MCMURRY, FRANK M. *Living Geography*. Book II. New York: The Macmillan Company, 1932.

Lands and Peoples. British Isles and Western Europe. New York: The Grolier Society, 1929.

LAUGHLIN, CLARE E. *Where it All Comes True in France*. Boston: Houghton Mifflin Company, 1929.

LESTER, KATHERINE MORRIS. *Great Pictures and Their Stories*. Book I. New York: Mentzer, Bush & Company, 1927.

LESTER, KATHERINE MORRIS. *Great Pictures and Their Stories*. Book II. New York: Mentzer, Bush & Company, 1927.

LESTER, KATHERINE MORRIS. *Great Pictures and Their Stories*. Book III. New York: Mentzer, Bush & Company, 1927.

LESTER, KATHERINE MORRIS. *Great Pictures and Their Stories*. Book V. New York: Mentzer, Bush & Company, 1927.

LESTER, KATHERINE MORRIS. *Great Pictures and Their Stories*. Book VI. New York: Mentzer, Bush & Company, 1927.

LINNELL, GERTRUDE B. *Behind the Battlements*. New York: The Macmillan Company, 1931.

MACGREGOR, MARY. *The Story of France Told to Boys and Girls*. New York: Frederick A. Stokes Company, 1920.

MARSHALL, HENRIETTA E. *History of France*. New York: George H. Doran Company, 1925.

MULETS, LENORE ELIZABETH. *Sunshine Lands of Europe*. Yonkers-on-Hudson, New York: World Book Company, 1918.

PACKARD, LEONARD O., and SINNOTT, C. P. *Nations as Neighbors*. New York: The Macmillan Company, 1925.

PECK, ANNE MERRIAM. *Storybook Europe*. New York: Harper and Brothers, 1929.

PORTOR, LAURA SPENCER. *Genevieve*. Little Schoolmate Series. New York: E. P. Dutton and Company, 1914.

PRICE, ELEANOR C. *Stories from French History*. New York: Dodd, Mead & Company, Inc., 1921.

RICHARDS, LAURA ELIZABETH. *Joan of Arc*. New York: D. Appleton and Company, 1919.

SCALES, LAURA WOOLSEY. *Boys of the Ages*. Boston: Ginn and Company, 1922.

SMITH, SUSAN C. *Made in France*. New York: Alfred A. Knopf, 1931.

STUART, DOROTHY M. *Young Folks Book of Other Lands*. Boston: Little, Brown and Company, 1927.

STULL, DE FOREST, and HATCH, ROY W. *Our World Today*. Boston: Allyn and Bacon, 1931.

TAPPAN, EVA MARCH. *Hero Stories of France*. Boston: Houghton Mifflin Company, 1920.

TERRY, ARTHUR GREY. *The Beginnings*. Evanston, Illinois: Row, Peterson and Company, 1926.

TERRY, ARTHUR GREY. *Lord and Vassal*. Evanston, Illinois: Row, Peterson and Company, 1926.

UPJOHN, ANNA MILO. *Friends in Strange Garments*. Boston: Houghton Mifflin Company, 1927.

WILLIAMS, MARGERY. *Paris*. Peeps at Great Cities Series. New York: The Macmillan Company, 1910.

WILLIAMS, LAWRENCE S. *Robin and Jean in France*. New York: American Book Company, 1931.

WINSLOW, ISAAC OSCAR. *Europe*. Boston: D. C. Heath and Company, 1921.

STORY BOOKS

ADAMS, KATHERINE. *Red Caps and Lilies.* New York: The Macmillan Company, 1924.

AULNOY, MARIE C. *White Cat.* New York: The Macmillan Company, 1928.

BALDWIN, JAMES. *Story of Roland.* New York: Chas. Scribner's Sons, 1930.

BAZIN, RENE. *Juniper Farm.* New York: The Macmillan Company, 1928.

BILL, ALFRED H. *Clutch of the Corsican.* Boston: Little, Brown and Company, 1925.

BRANN, ESTHER. *Nanette of the Wooden Shoes.* New York: The Macmillan Company, 1929.

BROOKS, ELBRIDGE S. *A Boy of the First Empire.* New York: The Century Co., 1908

EATON, JEANETTE. *Daughter of the Seine.* New York: Harper and Brothers, 1929.

ECHOLS, ULA W. *Knights of Charlemagne.* New York: Longmans, Green and Company, 1928.

HILL, HELEN, and MAXWELL, VIOLET. *Little Lost Shepherd.* New York: The Macmillan Company, 1931.

HILL, HELEN, and MAXWELL, VIOLET. *Little Tonino.* New York: The Macmillan Company, 1928.

HUGO, VICTOR. *Les Miserables.* An adaptation by Ettie Lee. New York: Boni & Liveright, 1924.

LANSING, MARION F. *Page, Esquire and Knight.* Boston: Ginn and Company, 1910.

LISLE, CLIFTON. *Hobnails and Heather.* New York: Harcourt, Brace & Company, 1929.

LOWNSBERY, ELOISE. *Boy Knight of Reims.* Boston: Houghton-Mifflin Company, 1927.

LOWNSBERY, ELOISE. *Lighting the Torch.* New York: Longmans, Green and Company, 1934.

LOWNSBERY, ELOISE. *Out of the Flame.* New York: Junior Literary Guild, 1931.

MALOT, HECTOR H. *Nobody's Boy.* New York: Cupples & Leon Co., 1930.

MALOT, HECTOR H. *Nobody's Girl.* New York: Cupples & Leon Co., 1929.

MARTINEAU DES CHESNEZ, ELIZABETH. *Lady Green Satin and Her Maid Rosette.* New York: The Macmillan Company, 1927.

MARTINEAU, HARRIET. *Peasant and the Prince.* Boston: Ginn and Company, 1917.

MULVANY, MAY MELANIE. *Joan and Pierre.* Garden City, New York: Doubleday, Doran & Company, 1931.

OLCOTT, VIRGINIA. *Jean and Fanchon.* New York: Silver, Burdett and Company, 1931.

ROBIDA, ALBERT. *Treasure of Carcassonne.* New York: Longmans, Green and Company, 1928.

SEAMAN, AUGUSTA. *When a Cobbler Ruled the King.* New York: Sturgis & Walton Co., 1911.

STEIN, EVALEEN. *Gabriel and the Hour Book.* Boston: L. C. Page & Company, 1906.

STEIN, EVALEEN. *The Little Count of Normandy.* Boston: L. C. Page & Company, 1911.

STEIN, EVALEEN. *Little Shepherd of Provence.* Boston: L. C. Page & Company, 1910.

STEVENSON, ROBERT LOUIS. *Travels With a Donkey in the Cevennes.* New York: Dodd, Mead & Company, Inc., 1931.

STRATTON, CLARENCE. *Paul of France.* New York: The Macmillan Company, 1927.

WILLIAMS, ANNE. *National Traits and Fairy-lore.* New York: Chas. Scribner's Sons, 1928.

GERMANY

Books for Pupils

REFERENCE BOOKS

ALLEN, NELLIE B. *The New Europe.* Boston: Ginn and Company, 1920.

ATWOOD, WALLACE W., and THOMAS, H. G. *Nations Beyond the Seas.* Boston: Ginn and Company, 1930.

BACON, MARY SCHELL. *Operas Every Child Should Know.* Garden City, New York: Doubleday, Page & Company, 1911.

BARROWS, H. H.; PARKER, E. P., and PARKER, M. T. *Geography: Europe and Asia.* New York: Silver, Burdett and Company, 1927.

BLAICH, LYDIA R. *Three Industrial Nations.* New York: American Book Company, 1918.

BRYANT, LORINDA. *Children's Book of Celebrated Bridges.* New York: The Century Co., 1925.

BRYANT, LORINDA. *Children's Book of Celebrated Towers.* New York: The Century Co., 1926.

BRYANT, LORINDA. *Children's Book of European Landmarks.* New York: The Century Co., 1928.

CARPENTER, FLORA LEONA. *Stories Pictures Tell.* Book VII. Chicago: Rand McNally & Company, n. d.

CARPENTER, FRANK G. *Europe.* New York: American Book Company, 1924.

CATHER, KATHERINE DUNLAP. *Boyhood Stories of Famous Men.* London: George G. Harrap & Co., Ltd., 1932.

CHAMBERLAIN, J. F., and CHAMBERLAIN, F. H. *Europe.* New York: The Macmillan Company, 1916.

CRICHTON, FRANCES ELIZABETH. *Peep-in-the-world.* New York: Longmans, Green and Company, 1929.

CROSS, DONZELLA. *Music Stories for Girls and Boys.* Boston: Ginn and Company, 1926.

DAKIN, WILSON S. *Great Rivers of the World.* New York: The Macmillan Company, 1927.

FINNEMORE, JOHN. *Germany.* London: A. & C. Black, 1913.

GORDY, WILBUR F. *American Beginnings in Europe.* New York: Chas. Scribner's Sons, 1925.

HALL, JENNIE. *Our Ancestors in Europe.* New York: Silver, Burdett and Company, 1916.

HALLECK, REUBEN POST, and FRANTZ, JULIETTE. *Our Nation's Heritage.* New York: American Book Company, 1925.

HILLYER, VIRGIL M. *Child's Geography of the World.* New York: The Century Co., 1929.

HILLYER, VIRGIL M. *A Child's History of the World.* New York: The Century Co., 1924.

HUNTINGTON, ELLSWORTH; BENSON, C. B.; and McMURRY, F. M. *Living Geography.* Book I. New York: The Macmillan Company, 1932.

HUNTINGTON, ELLSWORTH; BENSON, C. B.; and McMURRY, F. M. *Living Geography.* Book II. New York: The Macmillan Company, 1932.

LESTER, KATHERINE MORRIS. *Great Pictures and Their Stories.* Book III. New York: Mentzer, Bush & Company, 1927.

LESTER, KATHERINE MORRIS. *Great Pictures and Their Stories.* Book V. New York: Mentzer, Bush & Company, 1927.

McFEE, INEZ NELLIE. *Boys and Girls of Many Lands.* New York: T. Y. Crowell Company, 1917.

McSPADDEN, JOSEPH W. *Stories from Wagner.* New York: T. Y. Crowell Company, 1905.

PACKARD, LEONARD OSCAR, and SINNOTT, C. P. *Nations as Neighbors.* New York: The Macmillan Company, 1925.

PECK, ANNE MERRIMAN. *Roundabout Europe.* New York: Harper and Brothers, 1931.
PERDUE, HANNAH AVIS. *Child Life in other Lands.* Chicago: Rand McNally & Company, 1918.
PERDUE, HANNAH AVIS. *How Other Children Live.* Chicago: Rand McNally & Company, 1927.
SCHWIMMER, FRANCISKA. *Great Musicians as Children.* Garden City, New York: Doubleday, Doran & Company, 1929.
STULL, DE FOREST, and HATCH, R. W. *Our World Today.* Boston: Allyn and Bacon, 1931.
TAYLOR, BAYARD. *Boys of Other Countries.* New York: G. P. Putnam's Sons, 1904.
TIPPETT, JAMES S. *Toys and Toy Makers.* New York: Harper and Brothers, 1931.
WEST, RUTH, and WEST, W. M. *New World Foundations in the Old.* Boston: Allyn and Bacon, 1929.
WHITCOMB, IDA P. *Young People's Story of Music.* New York: Dodd, Mead & Company, Inc., 1908.

STORY BOOKS

ANDREWS, JANE. *Seven Little Sisters.* Boston: Ginn and Company, 1924.
BALDWIN, JAMES. *Story of Siegfried.* New York: Chas. Scribner's Sons, 1931.
BARRINGER, MARIE. *Martin the Goose Boy.* Garden City, New York: Doubleday, Doran and Company, 1932.
BROOKS, EDWARD. *Story of Siegfried.* Philadelphia: Penn Publishing Company, 1903.
CHAPIN, ANNA ALICE. *Story of the Rhinegold.* New York: Harper and Brothers, 1897.
DE LA RAMÉE, LOUISE. *Nürnberg Stove.* New York: The Macmillan Company, 1928.
GRIMM, JAKOB L., and GRIMM, W. K. *Fairy Tales.* New York: Grosset & Dunlap, 1931.
GUERBER, HELENE ADELINE. *Legends of the Rhine.* New York: A. S. Barnes & Co., 1910.
HILL, HELEN, and MAXWELL, VIOLET. *Rudi of the Toll Gate.* New York: The Macmillan Company, 1932.
KASTNER, ERICH. *Emil and the Detectives.* Garden City, New York: Doubleday Doran & Company, 1930.
KNAPP, ADELINE. *Boy and the Baron.* New York: The Century Co., 1902.
LEBERMANN, NORBERT. *New German Fairy Tales.* New York: Alfred A. Knopf, 1930.
LEHMANN, AGNES C. *Milly and Her Village.* New York: The Macmillan Company, 1931.
MCDONALD, ETTA AUSTIN, and BLACKBURNE, M. F. *Fritz in Germany.* Little People Everywhere. Boston: Little, Brown and Company, 1910.
MULLER, MARGARETHE. *Elsbeth.* Little Schoolmate Series. New York: E. P. Dutton and Company, 1914.
NEUMANN, DAISY. *Sperli the Clockmaker.* New York: The Macmillan Company, 1932.
OLCOTT, FRANCES JENKINS. *Wonder Tales from Baltic Wizards.* New York: Longmans, Green and Company, 1928.
OLCOTT, FRANCES JENKINS. *Wonder Tales from Goblin Hills.* New York: Longmans, Green and Company, 1930.
OLCOTT, VIRGINIA. *Karl and Gretel.* New York: Silver, Burdett and Company, 1932.
PLEASANTON, LOUISE M. *Fairyland of Opera.* Philadelphia: Penn Publishing Company, 1923.

PYLE, HOWARD. *Otto of the Silver Hand.* New York: Chas. Scribner's Sons, 1905.
SIEBE, JOSEPHINE. *Kasperle's Adventures.* New York: The MacMillan Company, 1929.

Books for Teachers

BOWMAN, ISAIAH. *New World.* Yonkers-on-Hudson, New York: World Book Company, 1928.
GOOCH, GEORGE P. *Germany.* New York: Chas. Scribner's Sons, 1925.
HUNTINGTON, ELLSWORTH, and CUSHING, S. W. *Modern Business Geography.* Yonkers-on-Hudson, New York: World Book Company, 1932.
NEWMAN, EDWARD M. *Seeing Germany.* New York: Funk & Wagnalls, 1929.

GREECE

Books for Pupils

REFERENCE BOOKS

AKER, HOMER FERRIS, and NELSON, D. LLOYD. *Yesterday the Foundation of Today.* San Francisco: Harr Wagner Publishing Company, 1933.
ALLEN, NELLIE B. *New Europe.* Boston: Ginn and Company, 1920.
ATWOOD, WALLACE W., and THOMAS, HELEN GOSS. *Nations Beyond the Seas.* Boston: Ginn and Company, 1930.
BAKER, EMILIE. *Stories of Old Greece and Rome.* New York: The Macmillan Company, 1913.
BALDWIN, JAMES. *Story of the Golden Age.* New York: Chas. Scribner's Sons, 1897.
BAUER, MARION, and PEYSER, E. R. *How Music Grew.* New York: G. P. Putnam's Sons, 1925.
BEST, SUSIE M. *Glorious Greece and Imperial Rome.* New York: The Macmillan Company, 1918.
BLUMMER, HUGO. *Home Life of the Ancient Greeks.* New York: Funk & Wagnalls, 1914.
BROWNE, EDITH A. *Greece.* Peeps at Many Lands. London: A. & C. Black, 1930.
BRYANT, LORINDA. *Children's Book of Celebrated Sculpture.* New York: The Century Co., 1923.
BRYANT, LORINDA. *Children's Book of European Landmarks.* New York: The Century Co., 1928.
CARPENTER, FRANK G. *Europe.* New York: American Book Company, 1922.
CHAMBERLAIN, J. F., and CHAMBERLAIN, F. H. *Europe.* New York: The Macmillan Company, 1916.
CHAPMAN, HENRY SMITH. *Stories of the Ancient Peoples.* Boston: Houghton Mifflin Company, 1929.
CLARK, MARION G., and GORDY, WILBUR F. *Early Story of Mankind.* New York: Chas. Scribner's Sons, 1929.
COLEMAN, SATIS N. *Bells.* Chicago: Rand McNally & Company, 1928.
CORNEY, EVIE, and DORLAND, G. W. *Great Deeds of Great Men.* Boston: D. C. Heath and Company, 1919.
ERLEIGH, EVA V. *In the Beginning.* Garden City, New York: Doubleday, Doran & Company, 1926.
EVANS, LAWTON BRYAN. *Our Old World Beginnings.* Chicago: Benj. H. Sanborn & Co., 1927.
FAIRGRIEVE, JAMES, and YOUNG, ERNEST. *Homes Far Away.* New York: D. Appleton and Comapny, 1927.
FARJEON, ELEANOR. *Mighty Men.* New York: D. Appleton and Company, 1926.
FOWLER, HAROLD NORTH. *Picture Book of Sculpture.* New York: The Macmillan Company, 1929.
GRANT, GORDON H. *Story of the Ship.* Springfield, Massachusetts: McLoughlin Bros., Inc., 1919.

GUERBER, HELENE ADELINE. *Myths of Greece and Rome.* New York: American Book Company, 1893.

HAAREN, JOHN HENRY, and POLAND, A. B. *Famous Men of Greece.* New York: American Book Company, 1904.

HALL, JENNIE. *Our Ancestors in Europe.* New York: Silver, Burdett and Company, 1916.

HALL, JENNIE. *Men of Old Greece.* Boston: Little, Brown and Company, 1906.

HALL, JENNIE. *Buried Cities.* New York: The Macmillan Company, 1922.

HALL, JENNIE. *Four Old Greeks.* Chicago: Rand McNally & Company, 1933.

HALLOCK, GRACE TABER. *Boy Who Was.* New York: E. P. Dutton and Company, 1928.

HILLYER, VIRGIL M. *Child's History of the World.* New York: The Century Co., 1924.

HUNTINGTON, ELLSWORTH; BENSON, C. B.; and MCMURRY, F. M. *Living Geography.* Book I. New York: The Macmillan Company, 1932.

HUNTINGTON, ELLSWORTH; BENSON, C. B.; and MCMURRY, F. M. *Living Geography.* Book II. New York: The Macmillan Company, 1932.

KING, MARIAN. *Story of Athletics.* New York: Harper and Brothers, 1931.

KINGSLEY, CHARLES. *Heroes.* New York: Robert M. McBride & Co., 1930.

KROUT, JOHN ALLEN. *Annals of American Sport.* Pageant of America. V. 15. New Haven: Yale University Press, 1929.

LAMPREY, LOUISE. *Children of Ancient Greece.* Boston: Little, Brown and Company, 1924.

LANSING, MARION FLORENCE. *Man's Long Climb.* Boston: Little, Brown and Company, 1933.

MACGREGOR, MARY. *Story of Greece Told to Boys and Girls.* New York: Frederick A. Stokes Company, 1914.

MILLS, DOROTHY. *Book of the Ancient Greeks.* New York: G. P. Putnam's Sons, 1925.

MOHR, LOUISE M. *Greeks and Persians of Long Ago.* Chicago: Rand McNally and Company, 1933.

NIDA, WILLIAM LEWIS. *Pilots and Pathfinders.* New York: The Macmillan Company, 1928.

PACKARD, LEONARD O., and SINNOTT, C. P. *Nations as Neighbors.* New York: The Macmillan Company, 1925.

PEABODY, JOSEPHINE PRESTON. *Old Greek Folk Stories, Told Anew.* Boston: Houghton Mifflin Company, 1897.

PERDUE, HANNAH AVIS. *Child Life in Other Lands.* Chicago: Rand McNally & Company, 1918.

PYLE, KATHERINE. *Tales from Greek Mythology.* Chicago: J. B. Lippincott Company, 1928.

QUENNELL, MARJORIE, and QUENNELL, C. H. B. *Everyday Life in Homeric Greece.* New York: G. P. Putnam's Sons, 1930.

QUENNELL, MARJORIE, and QUENNELL, C. H. B. *Everyday Things in Archaic Greece.* New York: G. P. Putnam's Sons, 1931.

SALISBURY, ETHEL I., and STEDMAN, LULU M. *Our Ancestors in the Ancient World.* Boston: Little, Brown and Company, 1935.

SCALES, LAURA WOOLSEY. *Boys of the Ages; Their Dreams and Their Crafts.* Boston: Ginn and Company, 1922.

SHAW, CHARLES DANNELLY. *Stories of the Ancient Greeks.* Boston: Ginn and Company, 1903.

Stories of Greece and Rome. New York: The Century Co., 1909.

STUART, DOROTHY MARGARET. *A Boy Through the Ages.* New York: George H. Doran Company, 1926.

STUFF, HARRY SPENCER. *Story of the Olympic Games.* Los Angeles: Times-Mirror Press, 1931.

TAPPAN, EVA MARCH. *Story of the Greek People.* London: George G. Harrap & Co., 1929.

TAPPAN, EVA MARCH. *Old World Hero Stories*. Boston: Houghton Mifflin Company, 1911.

STORY BOOKS

BURT, MARY ELIZABETH, and RAGOZIN, Z A. *Herakles, The Hero of Thebes*. New York: Chas. Scribner's Sons, 1900.

CHURCH, ALFRED JOHN. *Three Greek Children*. New York: G. P. Putnam's Sons, 1903.

COLUM, PADRAIC. *Golden Fleece and the Heroes Who Lived Before Achilles*. New York: The Macmillan Company, 1921.

CRUSE, AMY. *Young Folk's Book of Myths*. Boston: Little, Brown and Company, 1926.

DAVIS, WILLIAM STEARNS. *Day in Old Athens*. Boston: Allyn and Bacon, 1914.

DRAGOUMIS, JULIA D. *Under Greek Skies*. Little Schoolmate Series. New York: E. P. Dutton and Company, 1913.

HAWTHORNE, NATHANIEL. *Wonder-book and Tanglewood Tales*. Philadelphia: The John C. Winston Company, 1930.

HODGDON, JEANNETTE RECTOR. *Enchanted Past*. Boston: Ginn and Company, 1922.

HOMER. *Adventures of Ulysses, by Charles Lamb*. New York: The Platt & Munk Co., 1928.

HOMER. *Boy's Iliad, by Walter Copeland Perry*. New York: The Macmillan Company, 1925.

HOMER. *Boys' Odyssey, by Walter Copeland Perry*. New York: The Macmillan Company, 1925.

HOMER. *Iliad for Boys and Girls, by Alfred J. Church*. New York: The Macmillan Company, 1907.

HOMER. *Story of the Iliad, by E. Brooks*. Philadelphia: Penn Publishing Company, 1890.

HOMER. *Story of the Odyssey, by E. Brooks*. Philadelphia: Penn Publishing Company, 1892.

HOMER. *Story of Troy, by M. Clarke*. New York: American Book Company, 1897.

HUTCHINSON, WINIFRED M. L. *Golden Porch*. New York: Longmans, Green and Company, 1925.

HUTCHINSON, WINIFRED M. L. *Orpheus with his Lute*. New York: Longmans, Green and Company, 1926.

PERKINS, LUCY. *Spartan Twins*. Boston: Houghton Mifflin Company, 1920.

SNEDEKER, CAROLINE DALE. *Theras and his Town*. Garden City, New York: Doubleday, Doran & Company, 1924.

TANNER, EDWIN PLATT. *Yesterday's Children*. Chicago: Rand McNally & Company, 1927.

Books for Teachers

GARDNER, HELEN. *Art Through the Ages*. New York: Harcourt, Brace & Company, 1926.

GRIMBALL, ELIZABETH B., and WELLS, RHEA. *Costuming a Play*. New York: The Century Co., 1925.

HINMAN, MARY WOOD. *Gymnastic and Folk Dancing*. Vol. 1, 2, and 5. New York: A. S. Barnes & Co., 1921-1923.

HOFER, MARI RUEF. *Festival and Civic Plays*. Chicago: Beckley-Cardy Company, 1926.

HOLLAND

Books for Pupils

REFERENCE BOOKS

CARPENTER, FRANK G. *Around the World with the Children*. New York: American Book Company, 1917.

CARPENTER, FRANCES. *Our Neighbors Near and Far*. New York: American Book Company, 1933.

CHANCE, L. M. *Little Folks of Many Lands.* Boston: Ginn and Company, 1904.

DUNHAM, EDITH. *Jogging Round the World.* New York: Frederick A. Stokes Company, 1905.

FAIRGRIEVE, JAMES, and YOUNG, ERNEST. *World.* New York: D. Appleton and Company, n. d.

HEADLEY, E. A. *How Other People Travel.* Chicago: Rand McNally & Company, 1926.

PERDUE, HANNAH AVIS. *Child Life in Other Lands.* Chicago: Rand McNally & Company, 1918.

PERDUE, HANNAH AVIS. *How Other Children Live.* Chicago: Rand McNally & Company, 1927.

PIPER, WATTY. *Little Folks of Other Lands.* New York: The Platt & Munk Co., 1929.

SCANTLEBURY, ELIZABETH ELLIS. *Little World Children.* Boston: Ginn and Company, 1928.

SMITH, MARY ESTELLA. *Holland Stories.* Chicago: Rand McNally & Company, 1932.

THOMPSON, RUTH. *Our Neighbors Near and Far.* San Francisco: Harr Wagner Publishing Company, 1926.

STORY BOOKS

CAMPBELL, HELEN G. *Story of Little Jan, the Dutch Boy.* New York: Educational Publishers, n. d.

DE GROOT, CORNELIA. *When I Was a Girl in Holland.* Boston: Lothrop, Lee & Shepherd Company, 1917.

DODGE, MARY. *Hans Brinker or The Silver Skates.* Garden City, New York: Garden City Publishing Company, 1932.

GRANT, MAUDE MARGARET. *Windmills and Wooden Shoes.* Dallas, Texas: Southern Publishing Co., 1919.

HALL, MAY EMERY. *Dutch Days.* New York: Dodd, Mead & Company, Inc., 1927.

HALL, MAY EMERY. *Jan and Betje.* New York: Charles E. Merrill Company, 1914.

KING, MARIAN. *Kees.* New York: Harper and Brothers, 1930.

KING, MARIAN. *Kees and Kleintje.* New York: The Junior Literary Guild, and Albert Whitman and Company, 1934.

LE MAIR, HENRIETTE WILLEBECK. *Old Dutch Nursery Rhymes.* Philadelphia: David McKay Company, 1917.

MACDONALD, ETTA AUSTIN, and DALRYMPLE, JULIA. *Marta in Holland.* Boston: Little Brown and Company, 1911.

MILLER, OLIVE KENNON. *Tales Told in Holland.* Vol. 3. My Travelship. Chicago: Book House for Children, 1925-1926.

OLCOTT, FRANCES JENKINS. *Wonder Tales from Windmill Lands.* New York: Longmans, Green and Company, 1926.

OLCOTT, VIRGINIA. *Klaas and Jansje.* New York: Silver, Burdett and Company, 1933.

OLMSTEAD, EMMA. *Ned and Nan in Holland.* Evanston, Illinois: Row, Peterson and Company, 1916.

PERKINS, LUCY. *Dutch Twins.* Boston: Houghton Mifflin Company, 1911.

PERKINS, LUCY. *Kit and Kat.* Boston: Houghton Mifflin Company, 1929.

SMITH, LAURA ROUNTREE. *Hans and Hilda in Holland.* Chicago: A. Flanagan Company, n. d.

VAN STOCKUM, HILDA. *A Day on Skates.* New York: The Junior Literary Guild, and Harper & Brothers, 1934.

HOMES

Books for Pupils

REFERENCE BOOKS

AITCHISON, ALISON E., and UTTLEY, MARGUERITE. *Across Seven Seas to Seven Continents.* Indianapolis: Bobbs-Merrill Company, 1931.

ALLEN, NELLIE B. *How and Where We Live.* Boston: Ginn and Company, 1924.

ATWOOD, WALLACE W., and THOMAS, H. G. *Home Life in Far Away Lands.* Boston: Ginn and Company, 1928.

BARROWS, H. H.; PARKER, E. P., and PARKER, M. T. *Europe and Asia.* New York: Silver, Burdett and Company, 1930.

BASSETT, SARA WARE. *Story of Lumber.* Philadelphia: Penn Publishing Company, 1912.

BASSETT, SARA WARE. *Story of Glass.* Philadelphia: Penn Publishing Company, 1916.

BROWN, ELIZABETH V. *When the World was Young.* Yonkers-on-Hudson, New York: World Book Company, 1913.

CARPENTER, FRANCES. *Our Neighbors Near and Far.* New York: American Book Company, 1933.

CARPENTER, FRANCES. *Ourselves and Our City.* New York: American Book Company, 1928.

CARPENTER, FRANK G., and CARPENTER, FRANCES. *Houses We Live In.* New York: American Book Company, 1926.

CARPENTER, FRANK G. *How the World is Housed.* New York: American Book Company, 1930.

CHAMBERLAIN, J. F. *How We are Sheltered.* New York: The Macmillan Company, 1924.

CHASE, ANNIE, and CLOW, E. *Stories of Industry.* V. 1. New York: Educational Publishers, 1913.

CURTIS, MARY ISABEL. *Stories in Trees.* Chicago: Lyons and Carnahan, 1925.

DEARBORN, FRANCES ROSS. *How the Indians Lived.* Boston: Ginn and Company, 1927.

DOPP, KATHERINE E. *Early Cave Men.* Chicago: Rand McNally & Company, n. d.

DORRANCE, JOHN GORDON. *Stories of the Forest.* New York: American Book Company, 1916.

FRANCK, HARRY A. *Japanese Empire.* Dansville, New York: F. A. Owen Publishing Company, 1929.

FRANCK, HARRY A. *Mexico and Central America.* Dansville, New York: F. A. Owen Publishing Company, 1929.

FRANCK, HARRY. *China.* Dansville, New York: F. A. Owen Publishing Company, 1929.

McFEE, INEZ NELLIE. *Gifts of the Forest.* Dansville, New York: F. A. Owen Publishing Company, n. d.

METHLEY, ALICE A. *Happy Homes in Foreign Lands.* New York: Frederick A. Stokes Company, 1922.

MOHR, LOUISE MAUDE. *Days Before Houses.* Chicago: Rand McNally & Company, 1928.

NIDA, WILLIAM LEWIS. *Following the Frontier.* New York: The Macmillan Company, 1924.

PACKARD, LEONARD OSCAR, and SINNOTT, C. P. *Nations as Neighbors.* New York: The Macmillan Company, 1925.

PERDUE, HANNAH AVIS. *Child Life in Other Lands.* Chicago: Rand McNally & Company, 1918.

PERDUE, HANNAH AVIS. *How Other Children Live.* Chicago: Rand McNally & Company, 1927.

PETERSHAM, MAUD and MISKA. *Storybook of Houses.* Philadelphia: The John C. Winston Company, 1933.

PRESCOTT, DELLA R. *A Day in a Colonial Home.* Boston: Marshall Jones Company, 1921.

RUSH, CHARLES EVERETT, and WINSLOW, AMY. *Science of Things About Us.* Boston: Little, Brown and Company, 1927.

SCANTLEBURY, ELIZABETH ELLIS. *Little World Children.* Boston: Ginn and Company, 1928.

SHEPARD, EDITH P. *Geography for Beginners.* Books I-II. Chicago: Rand McNally & Company, 1927-1930.

SMITH, JOSEPH RUSSELL. *Home Folks.* Philadelphia: The John C. Winston Company, 1930.

TAPPAN, EVA MARCH. *Makers of Many Things.* Boston: Houghton Mifflin Company, 1916.

THOMPSON, RUTH. *Our Neighbors Near and Far.* San Francisco: Harr Wagner Publishing Company, 1926.

VERPILLEUX, E. A. *The Picture Book of Houses.* New York: The Macmillan Company, 1931.

WELLS, MARGARET ELIZABETH. *How the Present Came from the Past.* Book I. New York: The Macmillan Company, 1932.

STORY BOOKS

NIDA, STELLA H. *Letters of Polly, the Pioneer.* New York: The Macmillan Company, 1916.

TEE-VAN, HELEN. *Red Howling Monkey.* New York: The Macmillan Company, 1926.

Books for Teachers

BONSER, FREDERICK GORDON, and MOSSMAN, L. C. *Industrial Arts for Elementary Schools.* New York: The Macmillan Company, 1923.

HONEY BEES
Books for Pupils

BONSELS, WALDEMAR. *The Adventures of Maya the Bee.* New York: Thomas Seltzer, 1922.

CORWIN, WALLING. *Trails Today.* Western Nature Science Series. San Francisco: Harr Wagner Publishing Company, 1932.

CRAIG, GERALD S., and HURLEY, BEATRICE DAVIS. *The Earth and Living Things.* Boston: Ginn and Company, 1932.

DAULTON, AGNES McCLELLAND. *Wings and Stings.* Chicago: Rand McNally and Company, 1903.

DuPUY, WILLIAM ATHERTON. *Our Insect Friends and Foes.* Philadelphia: The John C. Winston Company, 1925.

DUNCAN, F. MARTIN, and DUNCAN, L. T. *Bees, Wasps and Ants.* London: Oxford University Press, 1931.

FABRE, JEAN HENRI. *Mason Bees.* New York: Dodd, Mead & Company, Inc., 1914.

HALE, ETHEL M. *Stories of Men and Nature.* Philadelphia: J. B. Lippincott Company, 1927.

MORLEY, MARGARET WARNER. *The Bee People.* Chicago: Atkinson, Mentzer and Grover, 1899.

MORLEY, MARGARET WARNER. *Butterflies and Bees.* Boston: Ginn and Company, 1905.

PATCH, EDITH M. *First Lessons in Nature Study.* New York: The Macmillan Company, 1927.

PATCH, EDITH M. *Hexapod Stories.* Boston: The Atlantic Monthly Press, 1920.

PATCH, EDITH M., and HOWE, HARRISON E. *Surprises.* New York: The Macmillan Company, 1934.

TAPPAN, EVA MARCH. *The Farmer and His Friends.* Boston: Houghton Mifflin Company, 1929.

Books for Teachers

The Classroom Teacher. V. 8. Chicago: The Classroom Teacher, Inc., 1927–28.

COMSTOCK, ANNA BOTSFORD. *Handbook of Nature Study.* Ithaca, New York: Comstock Publishing Company, 1912.

MAETERLINCK, MAURICE. *The Life of the Bee.* New York: Dodd, Mead & Company, Inc., 1922.

INDIANS OF THE SOUTHWEST

Books for Pupils

REFERENCE BOOKS

CHAMBERLAIN, J. F. *How We Are Sheltered.* New York: The Macmillan Company, 1924.

CHANCE, L. M. *Little Folks of Other Lands.* Boston: Ginn and Company, 1904.

DEARBORN, FRANCES R. *How The Indians Lived.* Boston: Ginn and Company, 1927.

FISH, ELEANOR. *Tepee and Wigwam in Picture Strip.* Chicago: Follett Publishing Company, 1931.

MADISON, HAROLD LESTER. *Indian Homes.* Cleveland: Cleveland Museum Natural History, 1925.

PERDUE, HANNAH AVIS. *Child Life in Other Lands.* Chicago: Rand McNally & Company, 1918.

SALOMON, JULIAN HARRIS. *Book of Indian Crafts and Indian Lore.* New York: Harper and Brothers, 1928

STARR, FREDERICK. *American Indians.* Boston: D. C. Heath and Company, 1899.

VERPILLEUX, EMILE ANTOINE. *Picture Book of Houses.* New York: The Macmillan Company, 1931.

WISSLER, CLARK. *Indian Costumes in the United States.* New York: American Museum of Natural History, 1928.

STORY BOOKS

ARMER, LAURA ADAMS, and ARMER, SIDNEY. *Waterless Mountain.* New York: Longmans, Green and Company, 1931.

BAYLESS, CLARA. *Little Cliff Dweller.* Bloomington, Illinois: Public School Publishing Company, 1908.

BROCK, EMMA LILLIAN. *One Little Indian Boy.* New York: Alfred A. Knopf, 1931.

CANNON, CORNELIA JAMES. *Pueblo Boy.* Boston: Houghton Mifflin Company, 1926.

CANNON, CORNELIA. *Pueblo Girl.* Boston: Houghton Mifflin Company, 1929.

COOLIDGE, FLORENCE CLAUDINE. *Little Ugly Face and Other Indian Tales.* New York: The Macmillan Company, 1925.

DE HUFF, ELIZABETH WILLIS. *Swift Eagle of the Rio Grande.* Chicago: Rand McNally & Company, 1928.

DE HUFF, ELIZABETH WILLIS. *Taytay's Memories.* New York: Harcourt, Brace & Company, 1924.

DE HUFF, ELIZABETH WILLIS. *Taytay's Tales.* New York: Harcourt, Brace & Company, 1922.

GRIMES, KATHERINE ATHERTON, *Kwasa, The Cliff Dweller.* Dansville, New York: F. A. Owen Publishing Company, n. d.

HARRINGTON, ISIS. *Eagles Nest.* New York: The Macmillan Company, 1930.

HARRINGTON, ISIS L. *Komoki of the Cliff.* New York: Chas. Scribner's Sons, 1934.

HODGE, ZAHRAH PREBLE. *Tomar of Siba.* Los Angeles: Suttonhouse Publishing Company, 1933.

JAMES, AHLEE. *Tewa Firelight Tales.* New York: Longmans, Green and Company, 1927.

JEWETT, MARTHA. *Hopi the Cliff Dweller.* Philadelphia: David McKay Company, 1929.

LUMMIS, CHARLES FLETCHER. *Pueblo Indian Folk Stories.* New York: The Century Co., 1910.

MALKUS, ALIDA SIMS. *Dragon Fly Zuni.* New York: Harcourt, Brace & Company, 1928.

MOON, GRACE. *Chi-Wee and Loki.* New York: Frederick A. Stokes Company, 1917.

MOON, GRACE. *Chi-Wee.* Garden City, New York: Doubleday, Doran & Company, 1925.

MOON, GRACE, and MOON, CARL. *Book of Nah-Wee.* Garden City, New York: Doubleday, Doran & Company, 1932.

MOON, GRACE. *Runaway Papoose.* Garden City, New York: Doubleday, Doran & Company, 1928.

MOON, GRACE. *Missing Katchina.* Garden City, New York: Doubleday, Doran & Company, 1930.

MOON, GRACE. *Magic Trail.* Garden City, New York: Doubleday, Doran & Company, 1929.

MORAN, GEORGE NEWELL. *Kwahu, The Hopi Indian Boy.* New York: American Book Company, 1913.

NUSBAUM, AILEEN. *Zuni Indian Tales.* New York: G. P. Putnam's Sons, 1929.

NUSBAUM, AILEEN. *Seven Cities of Cibola.* New York: G. P. Putnam's Sons, 1926.

NUSBAUM, DERIC. *Deric With the Indians.* New York: G. P. Putnam's Sons, 1927.

NUSBAUM, DERIC. *Deric in Mesa Verde.* New York: G. P. Putnam's Sons, 1929.

WILEY, BELL, and EDICK, G. W. *Children of the Cliff.* New York: D. Appleton and Company, 1905.

WILSON, GILBERT LIVINGSTONE. *Myths of the Red Children.* Boston: Ginn and Company, 1907.

Books for Teachers

BONSER, FREDERICK GORDON, and MOSSMAN, L. C. *Industrial Arts for Elementary Schools.* New York: The Macmillan Company, 1923.

COOLIDGE, MARY ELIZABETH BURROUGHS. *Rain Makers.* Boston: Houghton Mifflin Company, 1929.

GODDARD, PLINY EARL. *Indians of the Southwest.* New York: American Museum of Natural History, 1931.

HORRIGAN, OLIVE KATHERINE. *Creative Activities in Physical Education.* New York: A. S. Barnes & Co., 1929.

HOUGH, WALTER. *The Hopi Indians.* Cedar Rapids, Iowa: The Torch Press, 1915.

ICKES, ANNA. *Mesaland.* Boston: Houghton Mifflin Company, 1933.

LUMMIS, CHARLES FLETCHER. *Mesa Cañon and Pueblo.* New York: The Century Co., 1925.

SEDGWICK, MARY KATRINE. *Acoma, The Sky City.* Cambridge, Mass.: Harvard University Press, 1926.

SEYMOUR, FLORA WARREN. *Story of the Red Man.* New York: Longmans, Green and Company, 1929.

WISSLER, CLARK. *American Indian.* New York: Oxford University Press, 1922.

ITALY

Books for Pupils

REFERENCE BOOKS

ALLEN, NELLIE B. *The New Europe.* Boston: Ginn and Company, 1920.

ATWOOD, WALLACE W. *Nations Beyond the Seas.* Boston: Ginn and Company, 1930.

BARROWS, H. H.; PARKER, E. P.; and PARKER, M. T. *Europe and Asia.* New York: Silver, Burdett and Company, 1930.

BOTSFORD, FLORENCE H. *Picture Tales from the Italian.* New York: Frederick A. Stokes Company, 1929.

BRYANT, LORINDA. *Children's Book of Celebrated Bridges.* New York: The Century Co., 1925.

BRYANT, LORINDA. *Children's Book of Celebrated Buildings.* New York: The Century Co., 1924.

BRYANT, LORINDA. *Children's Book of Celebrated Towers.* New York: The Century Co., 1926.

BRYANT, LORINDA. *Children's Book of European Landmarks.* New York: The Century Co., 1928.

CARPENTER, FRANK G. *Europe.* New York: American Book Company, 1924.

CARPENTER, FLORA LEONA. *Stories Pictures Tell.* Book V. Chicago: Rand McNally & Company, 1918.

CARPENTER, FLORA LEONA. *Stories Pictures Tell.* Book VII. Chicago: Rand McNally & Company, 1918.

CATHER, KATHERINE D. *Boyhood Stories of Famous Men.* London: George G. Harrap & Co., Ltd., 1932.

CHAMBERLAIN, J. F., and CHAMBERLAIN, F. H. *Europe.* New York: The Macmillan Company, 1916.

CHAMBERLAIN, J. F. *How We Travel.* New York: The Macmillan Company. n. d.

CROSS, DONZELLA. *Music Stories for Girls and Boys.* Boston: Ginn and Company, 1926.

FINNEMORE, JOHN. *Italy; and Greece.* New York: The Macmillan Company, 1921.

HAAREN, JOHN HENRY, and POLAND, A. B. *Famous Men of Modern Times.* New York: American Book Company, 1909.

HEADLEY, E. A. *How Other People Travel.* Chicago: Rand McNally & Company, 1926.

HILLYER, VIRGIL M. *Child's Geography of the World.* New York: The Century Co., 1929.

HILLYER, VIRGIL M. *Child's History of the World.* New York: The Century Co., 1924.

HUNTINGTON, ELLSWORTH; BENSON, C. B.; and McMURRY, F. M. *Living Geography.* Book I. New York: The Macmillan Company, 1932.

HUNTINGTON, ELLSWORTH; BENSON, C. B.; and McMURRY, F. M. *Living Geography.* Book II. New York: The Macmillan Company, 1932.

LAUGHLIN, CLARA ELIZABETH. *Where It All Comes True, in Italy and Switzerland.* Boston: Houghton Mifflin Company, 1928.

LESTER, KATHERINE MORRIS. *Great Pictures and Their Stories.* Book I. New York: Mentzer, Bush & Company, 1927.

LESTER, KATHERINE MORRIS. *Great Pictures and Their Stories.* Book II. New York: Mentzer, Bush & Company, 1927.

LESTER, KATHERINE MORRIS. *Great Pictures and Their Stories.* Book III. New York: Mentzer, Bush & Company, 1927.

LESTER, KATHERINE MORRIS. *Great Pictures and Their Stories.* Book IV. New York: Mentzer, Bush & Company, 1927.

McDONALD, ETTA AUSTIN, and DALRYMPLE, JULIA. *Rafael in Italy.* Boston: Little, Brown and Company, 1909.

McFEE, INEZ N. *Boys and Girls of Many Lands.* New York: T. Y. Crowell Company, 1917.

MULETS, LENORE ELIZABETH. *Sunshine Lands of Europe.* Yonkers-on-Hudson, New York: World Book Company, 1918.

PACKARD, LEONARD OSCAR, and SINNOTT, C. P. *Nations as Neighbors.* New York: The Macmillan Company, 1925.

PECK, ANNE MERRIMAN. *Storybook Europe.* New York: Harper and Brothers, 1929.

PLEASANTON, LOUISE M. *Fairyland of Opera.* Philadelphia: Penn Publishing Company, 1923.

PERDUE, HANNAH AVIS. *Child Life in Other Lands.* Chicago: Rand McNally & Company, 1918.

SCALES, LAURA WOOLSEY. *Boys of the Ages; Their Dreams and Their Crafts.* Boston: Ginn and Company, 1922.

STUART, DOROTHY MARGARET. *Young Folk's Book of Other Lands.* Boston: Little, Brown and Company, 1927.

STULL, DE FOREST, and HATCH, R. W. *Our World Today.* Boston: Allyn and Bacon, 1931.

UPJOHN, ANNA MILO. *Friends in Strange Garments.* Boston: Houghton Mifflin Company, 1928.

WHITCOMB, IDA PRENTICE. *Young People's Story of Music.* New York: Dodd, Mead & Company, Inc., 1908.

WILLARD, MARY FRANCES. *Along Mediterranean Shores.* New York: Silver Burdett and Company, 1914.

WILLIAMS, ANNE. *National Traits and Fairy Lore.* New York: Chas. Scribner's Sons, 1928.

WILLIAMS, LAURENCE S. *Robin and Jean in Italy.* New York: American Book Company, 1934.

STORY BOOKS

AMBROSI, MARIETTA. *When I Was a Girl in Italy.* Boston: Lothrop, Lee & Shepard Company, 1906.

AMICIS, EDMONDO DE. *Cuore.* Boston: D. C. Heath and Company, 1925.

BARTON, FLORENCE. *Mary and Peter in Italy.* New York: Thomas Nelson & Sons, 1928.

BRANN, ESTHER. *Nicolina.* New York: The Macmillan Company, 1931.

CAPUANA, LUIGI. *Italian Fairy Tales.* New York: E. P. Dutton and Company, 1929.

CAPUANA, LUIGI. *Nimble-Legs.* New York: Longmans, Green and Company, 1927

COLLOLDI, C. (pseudonym for Carlo Lorenzini). *Pinocchio.* Garden City, New York: Garden City Publishing Co., 1926.

CROMMELIN, EMELINE G. *Famous Legends Adapted for Children.* New York: The Century Co., 1904.

DELLA CHIESA, CAROLYN M. *Three of Salu.* Yonkers-on-Hudson, New York: World Book Comapny, 1923.

DE LA RAMÉE, LOUISE. *Moufflon, the Dog of Florence.* Chicago: A. Whitman & Co., 1931.

FARJEON, ELEANOR. *Italian Peep-show, and Other Tales.* New York: Frederick A. Stokes Company, 1926.

FORBES, HELEN CADY. *Mario's Castle.* New York: The Macmillan Company, 1928.

GIBSON, KATHARINE. *Goldsmith of Florence.* New York: The Macmillan Company, 1929.

HALLOCK, GRACE TABER. *Boy Who Was.* New York: E. P. Dutton and Company, 1928.

LORENZINI, CARLO. (C. Collodi, pseudonym). *Pinocchio.* Garden City, New York: Garden City Publishing Co., 1932.

MACDONNELL, ANNE. *Italian Fairy Book.* New York: Frederick A. Stokes Company, 1914.

MEIKLEJOHN, NANNINE. *Cart of Many Colors.* New York: E. P. Dutton and Company, 1919.

OLCOTT, VIRGINIA. *Concetta, the Coral Girl.* New York: Frederick A. Stokes Company, 1928.

OLCOTT, VIRGINIA. *Dino of the Golden Boxes.* New York: Frederick A. Stokes Company, 1930.

OLCOTT, VIRGINIA. *Beppo and Lucia.* New York: Silver, Burdett and Company, 1934.

PERKINS, LUCY. *Italian Twins.* Boston: Houghton Mifflin Company, 1920.

JAPAN

Books for Pupils

REFERENCE BOOKS

ALLEN, NELLIE B. *Asia.* Boston: Ginn and Company, 1929.

BUNKER, FRANK F. *China and Japan.* Chicago: J. B. Lippincott Company, 1928.

CARPENTER, FRANK G. *Asia.* New York: American Book Company, 1924.

CARPENTER, FRANK G. *Around the World With the Children.* New York: American Book Company, 1917.

CHAMBERLAIN, J. F., and CHAMBERLAIN, A. H. *Asia.* New York: The Macmillan Company, 1925.

CHAMBERLAIN, J. F. *How We Are Sheltered.* New York: The Macmillan Company, 1924.

CHANCE, L. M. *Little Folks of Many Lands.* Boston: Ginn and Company, 1904.

EDWARDS, EVA D. *Haruko, Child of Japan.* San Francisco: Harr Wagner Publishing Company, 1933.

FRANCK, HARRY A. *The Japanese Empire.* Dansville, New York: F. A. Owen Publishing Company, 1927.

GEORGE, MARIAN M. *Little Journey to China and Japan.* Chicago: A. Flanagan Company, 1928.

HEADLEY, E. A. *How Other People Travel.* Chicago: Rand McNally & Company, 1926.

JEAN, SALLY LUCAS, and HALLOCK, GRACE T. *Spending the Day in China, Japan and the Philippines.* New York: Harper & Brothers, 1932.

PERDUE, HANNAH AVIS. *How Other Children Live.* Chicago: Rand McNally & Company, 1927.

PERDUE, HANNAH AVIS. *Child Life in Other Lands.* Chicago: Rand McNally & Company, 1918.

PIPER, WATTY. *Little Folks of Many Lands.* New York: The Platt & Munk Co., 1929.

SCANTLEBURY, ELIZABETH ELLIS. *Little World Children.* Boston: Ginn and Company, 1928.

SCHWARTZ, JULIA AUGUSTA. *Five Little Strangers.* New York: American Book Company, 1904.

SUGIMOTO, CHIYONO WILSON. *Picture Tales from the Japanese.* New York: Frederick A. Stokes Company, 1928.

THOMPSON, RUTH. *Our Neighbors Near and Far.* San Francisco: Harr Wagner Publishing Company, 1926.

STORY BOOKS

COATSWORTH, ELIZABETH J. *Cat Who Went to Heaven.* New York: The Macmillan Company, 1930.

DUNHAM, EDITH. *Jogging Round the World.* New York: Frederick A. Stokes Company, 1905.

McDONALD, ETTA AUSTIN, and DALRYMPLE, JULIA. *Ume San in Japan.* Boston: Little, Brown and Company, 1909.

MILLER, OLIVE KENNON. *Little Pictures of Japan.* My Travelship. Vol. II. Chicago: Book House for Children, 1926.

Norton, Edith Constance. *Little Black Eyes; The Story of a Little Girl in Japan.* New York: The Macmillan Company, 1927.

Perkins, Lucy. *Japanese Twins.* Boston: Houghton Mifflin Company, 1912.

Rowe, Dorothy. *The Begging Deer.* New York: The Macmillan Company, 1928.

Sugimoto, Etsu. *Daughter of the Samurai.* Garden City, New York: Doubleday, Doran & Company, 1925.

Sugimoto, Etsu, and Austen, N. V. *With Taro and Hana in Japan.* New York: Frederick A. Stokes Company, 1926.

Williston, Teresa Peirce. *Japanese Fairy Tales.* Chicago: Rand McNally & Company, 1904.

Yule, Emma Sarepta. *In Kimono Land.* Chicago: Rand McNally & Company, 1927.

Books for Teachers

Tietjens, Eunice Strong. *Japan, Korea and Formosa.* Burton Holmes Travel Stories. Chicago: Wheeler Publishing Company, 1924.

MAGNETS
Books for Pupils

Caldwell, Otis W., and Meier, W. H. D. *Open Doors to Science.* Boston: Ginn and Company, 1925.

Craig, Gerald S., and Hurley, Beatrice Davis. *The Earth and Living Things.* Boston: Ginn and Company, 1932.

Craig, Gerald S., and Condry, Margaret G. *Learning About Our World.* Boston: Ginn and Company, 1932.

Craig, Gerald S., and Baldwin, Sara E. *Our Wide, Wide World.* Boston: Ginn and Company, 1932.

Craig, Gerald S., and Burke, Agnes. *We Look About Us.* Boston: Ginn and Company, 1932.

Keelor, Katherine L. *Working With Electricity.* New York: The Macmillan Company, 1933.

Morgan, Alfred Powell. *Boy Electrician.* Boston: Lothrop, Lee & Shepard Co., 1929.

Parker, Bertha Morris. *The Book of Electricity.* Boston: Houghton, Mifflin Company, 1928.

Patch, Edith M., and Howe, Harrison E. *Surprises.* New York: The Macmillan Company, 1934.

Reed, W. Maxwell. *And That's Why* . . . New York: Harcourt, Brace and Company, 1932.

Smith, Edith Lillian. *Everyday Science Projects.* Boston: Houghton Mifflin Company, 1925.

Books for Teachers

Parker, Bertha Morris. *An Introductory Course in Science in the Intermediate Grades.* Chicago: University of Chicago, 1931.

Stevens, Bertha. *Child and the Universe.* New York: The John Day Company, 1931.

MEDIEVAL LIFE
Books for Pupils
REFERENCE BOOKS

Bulfinch, Thomas. *Age of Chivalry.* Boston: Lothrop, Lee & Shepard Company, n. d.

Church, Alfred J. *Heroes of Chivalry and Romance.* New York: The Macmillan Company, 1898.

CLARK, MARION G., and GORDY, WILBUR F. *What Men Brought from Europe to America.* New York: Chas. Scribner's Sons, 1929.

DAVIS, WILLIAM S. *Life on a Medieval Barony.* New York: Harper and Brothers, 1923.

ECHOLS, ULA W. *Knights of Charlemagne.* New York: Longmans, Green and Company, 1928.

GORDY, WILBUR F. *American Beginnings in Europe.* New York: Chas. Scribner's Sons, 1925.

GUERBER, HELENE ADELINE. *Legends of the Middle Ages.* New York: American Book Company, n. d.

HAAREN, JOHN H., and POLAND, A. B. *Famous Men of the Middle Ages.* New York: American Book Company, n. d.

HALL, JENNIE. *Our Ancestors in Europe.* New York: Silver, Burdett and Company, 1916.

HALLECK, R. P., and FRANTZ, J. *Our Nation's Heritage.* New York: American Book Company, 1925.

HARDING, CAROLINE HIRST. *Story of the Middle Ages.* Chicago: Scott, Foresman and Company, n. d.

HARTMAN, GERTRUDE. *World We Live In.* New York: The Macmillan Company, 1931.

HILLYER, VIRGIL M. *Child's History of the World.* New York: The Century Co., 1924.

KELTY, MARY G. *Old World Beginnings of America.* Boston: Ginn and Company, 1932.

LAMPREY, LOUISE. *In the Days of the Guild.* New York: Frederick A. Stokes Company, 1918.

LAMPREY, LOUISE. *Masters of the Guild.* New York: Frederick A. Stokes Company, 1920.

LANSING, MARION F. *Barbarian and Noble.* Boston: Ginn and Company, 1911.

LANSING, MARION F. *Page, Esquire and Knight.* Boston: Ginn and Company, 1910.

LINNELL, GERTRUDE B. *Behind the Battlements.* New York: The Macmillan Company, 1931.

PARKER, CORNELIA. *Watching Europe Grow.* New York: Horace Liveright Company, 1930.

PECK, ANNE MERRIMAN. *Storybook Europe.* New York: Harper and Brothers, 1929.

PYLE, HOWARD. *Men of Iron.* New York: Harper and Brothers, 1930.

QUENNELL, MARJORIE, and QUENNELL, C. H. B. *History of Everyday Things in England.* London: B. T. Batsford, Ltd., 1930.

SMALLIDGE, OLIVE E., and PAXSON, F. L. *Finding America.* Boston: Houghton Mifflin Company, 1929.

SMITH, SUSAN C. *Made in France.* New York: Alfred A. Knopf, 1931.

Stories of the Middle Ages. New York: The Century Co., 1909.

TAPPAN, EVA MARCH. *Old Ballads in Prose.* Boston: Houghton Mifflin Company, 1911.

TAPPAN, EVA MARCH. *When Knights Were Bold.* Boston: Houghton Mifflin Company, 1911.

TERRY, ARTHUR GREY. *Lord and Vassal.* History Stories of Other Lands. Book IV. Evanston, Illinois: Row, Peterson and Company, 1915.

TIPPETT, JAMES S. *Toys and Toymakers.* New York: Harper and Brothers, 1931.

VERIPILLEUX, EMILE A. *Picture Book of Houses.* New York: The Macmillan Company, 1931.

STORY BOOKS

BALDWIN, JAMES. *Stories of the King.* New York: American Book Company, 1910.

BALDWIN, JAMES. *Story of Roland.* New York: Chas. Scribner's Sons, 1930.

CROMMELIN, EMELINE G. *Famous Legends Adapted for Children.* New York: The Century Co., 1904.

GIBSON, KATHERINE. *Goldsmith of Florence.* New York: The Macmillan Company, 1929.

HOLLAND, RUPERT S. *Knights of the Golden Spur.* New York: The Century Co., 1912.

LOWNSBERY, ELOISE. *Boy Knight of Reims.* Boston: Houghton Mifflin Company, 1927.

LOWNSBERY, ELOISE. *Lighting the Torch.* New York: Longmans, Green and Company, 1934.

LOWNSBERY, ELOISE. *Out of the Flame.* New York: Longmans, Green and Company, 1931.

PYLE, HOWARD. *Merry Adventures of Robin Hood of Great Renown, in Nottinghamshire.* New York: Chas. Scribner's Sons, 1902.

PYLE, HOWARD. *Otto of the Silver Hand.* New York: Chas. Scribner's Sons, n. d.

PYLE, HOWARD. *Story of King Arthur and His Knights.* New York: Chas. Scribner's Sons, 1903.

PYLE, HOWARD. *Story of Sir Launcelot and His Companions.* New York: Chas. Scribner's Sons, 1907.

PYLE, HOWARD. *Story of the Champions of the Round Table.* New York: Chas. Scribner's Sons, 1926.

RICHARDS, LAURA E. *Our Little Feudal Cousin of Long Ago.* Boston: L. C. Page & Company, 1922.

Seven Champions of Christendom. Edited by Frederick J. H. Darton. New York: Frederick A. Stokes Company, 1913.

SCOTT, SIR WALTER. *Ivanhoe.* Boston: Allyn and Bacon, 1916.

STEIN, EVALEEN. *Gabriel and the Hour Book.* Boston: L. C. Page & Company, 1906.

WARREN, MAUDE LAVINIA. *King Arthur and His Knights.* Chicago: Rand McNally & Company, 1916.

MEXICO

Books for Pupils

REFERENCE BOOKS

AITCHISON, ALISON E., and UTTLEY, MARGUERITE. *North America by Plane and Train.* Indianapolis: Bobbs-Merrill Company, 1931.

ALLEN, NELLIE B. *North America.* Boston: Ginn and Company, 1922.

ATWOOD, WALLACE W., and THOMAS, H. G. *The Americas.* Boston: Ginn and Company, 1929.

BANKS, HELEN W. *Story of Mexico.* New York: Frederick A. Stokes Company, 1926.

BARROWS, H. H.; PARKER, E. P.; and PARKER, M. T. *Geography: Southern Lands.* New York: Silver, Burdett and Company, 1929.

CARPENTER, FRANK G. *North America.* New York: American Book Company, 1922.

CHAMBERLAIN, J. F., and CHAMBERLAIN, A. H. *North America.* New York: The Macmillan Company, 1927.

CLARK, MARION G., and GORDY, WILBUR F. *What Men Brought From Europe to America.* New York: Chas. Scribner's Sons, 1929.

FRANCK, HARRY A. *Mexico and Central America.* Dansville, New York: F. A. Owen Publishing Company, 1929.

GEORGE, MARIAN M. *Little Journey to Mexico and Central America.* Chicago: A. Flanagan Company, 1929.

JANVIER, THOMAS A. *Aztec Treasure House.* New York: Harper and Brothers, 1918.

LANG, ANDREW. *The Conquest of Montezuma's Empire.* New York: Longmans, Green and Company, 1928.

LEFFERTS, WALTER. *Neighbors, North and South.* Philadelphia: J. B. Lippincott Company, 1926.

MARTEN, WILLIAM S. *Inexpensive Basketry.* Peoria, Illinois: Manual Arts Press, 1912.

MITCHELL, LUCY. *North America.* New York: The Macmillan Company, 1931.

MORRIS, ANN. *Digging in Yucatan.* Garden City, New York: Doubleday, Doran & Company, 1931.

Pageant of America. V. I. Pt. III. "Spain and the New World." Edited by R. H. Gabriel. New Haven: Yale University Press, 1925.

PAN AMERICAN UNION. *Mexico.* Washington: The Union, 1932.

PAN AMERICAN UNION. *Mexico City.* Washington: The Union, 1932.

PECK, ANNE MERRIMAN. *Young Mexico.* New York: Robert M. McBride and Company, 1934.

PERDUE, HANNAH AVIS. *How Other Children Live.* Chicago: Rand McNally & Company, 1927.

RICHARDS, IRMAGARDE, and LANDAZURI, E. *Children of Mexico.* San Francisco: Harr Wagner Publishing Company, 1935.

SMALLIDGE, OLIVE E., and PAXSON, F. L. *Finding America.* Boston: Houghton Mifflin Company, 1929.

SMITH, SUSAN C. *Made in Mexico.* New York: Alfred A. Knopf, 1930.

SPINDEN, HERBERT J. *Ancient Civilization of Mexico and Central America.* New York: American Museum of Natural History, 1928.

THOMPSON, RUTH. *Our Neighbors Near and Far.* San Francisco: Harr Wagner Publishing Company, 1926.

WINSLOW, ISAAC O. *Our American Neighbors.* Boston: D. C. Heath and Company, 1922.

WINTERBURN, ROSA V. *The Spanish in the Southwest.* New York: American Book Company, 1903.

STORY BOOKS

BAYLOR, FRANCES C. *Juan and Juanita.* Boston: Houghton Mifflin Company, 1926.

GAINES, RUTH L. *Lucita; a Child's Story of Old Mexico.* Chicago: Rand McNally & Company, 1913.

GAINES, RUTH L., and READ, G. W. *Village Shield.* New York: E. P. Dutton and Company, 1917.

GAY, ZHENYA, and GAY, JAN. *Pancho and His Burro.* New York: William Morrow Co., Inc., 1930.

GODOY, MERCEDES. *When I Was a Girl in Mexico.* Boston: Lothrop, Lee & Shepard Company, 1919.

MACDONALD, ETTA AUSTIN, and DALRYMPLE, JULIA. *Manuel in Mexico.* Boston: Little, Brown and Company, 1909.

MOON, GRACE. *Nadita.* Garden City, New York: Doubleday, Doran & Company, 1927.

MOON, GRACE. *Tita of Mexico.* New York: Frederick A. Stokes Company, 1934.

MORROW, ELIZABETH R. *The Painted Pig.* New York: Alfred A. Knopf, 1930.

PERKINS, LUCY. *Mexican Twins.* Boston: Houghton Mifflin Company, 1915.

PURNELL, IDELLA, and WEATHERWAX, J. M. *Talking Bird.* New York: The Macmillan Company, 1930.

PURNELL, IDELLA. *Wishing Owl.* New York: The Macmillan Company, 1931.

THOMAS, MARGARET LORING. *The Burro's Moneybag.* New York: Abingdon Press, 1931.

Books for Teachers

BEST-MAUGARD, ADOLFO. *Method for Creative Design.* New York: Alfred A. Knopf, 1926.

BIART, LUCIEN. *Aztecs.* Chicago: A. C. McClurg & Co., n. d.

CHASE, STUART, and TYLER, MARIAN. *Mexico.* New York: The Macmillan Company, 1932.

HASBROUCK, LOUISE S. *Mexico, From Cortez to Carranza.* New York: D. Appleton and Company, 1918.

QUINN, VERNON. *Beautiful Mexico.* New York: Frederick A. Stokes Company, 1924.

CARR, HARRY. *Old Mother Mexico.* Boston: Houghton Mifflin Company, 1931.

WHEELER, IDA WILLSEA. *Playing With Clay.* New York: The Macmillan Company, 1927.

MINERS AND MINING

Books for Pupils

REFERENCE BOOKS

AITCHISON, ALISON E., and UTTLEY, MARGUERITE. *North America by Plane and Train.* Indianapolis: Bobbs-Merrill Company, 1931.

ATWOOD, WALLACE W. *United States Among the Nations.* Boston: Ginn and Company, 1930.

CARPENTER, FRANK G., and CARPENTER, FRANCES. *Houses We Live In.* New York: American Book Company, 1926.

CARPENTER, FRANK G. *How The World is Housed.* New York: American Book Company, 1930.

CARPENTER, FRANK G. *North America.* New York: American Book Company, 1922.

CHAMBERLAIN, J. F. *How We are Sheltered.* New York: The Macmillan Company, 1924.

COE, FANNY E. *Heroes of Everyday Life.* Boston: Ginn and Company, 1911.

EATON, JEANNETTE. *Story of Light.* New York: Harper and Brothers, 1928.

ELIOT, ETHEL A. *Little Black Coal.* New York: Frederick A. Stokes Company, 1923.

FAIRBANKS, HAROLD WELLMAN. *Stories of Rocks and Minerals.* New York: Educational Publishers, n. d.

GRUENING, MARTHA. *Story of Mining.* New York: Harper and Brothers, 1931.

HUNTINGTON, ELLSWORTH; BENSON, C. B., and MCMURRY, F. M. *Living Geography.* Book I. New York: The Macmillan Company, 1932.

HUNTINGTON, ELLSWORTH; BENSON, C. B., and MCMURRY, F. M. *Living Geography.* Book II. New York: The Macmillan Company, 1932.

HUNTINGTON, ELLSWORTH, and CUSHING, S. W. *Modern Business Geography.* Yonkers-on-Hudson, New York: World Book Company, 1932.

LACY, IDA BELLE. *Light Then and Now.* New York: The Macmillan Company, 1930.

LOOMIS, FREDERIC B. *Field Book of Common Rocks and Minerals.* New York: G. P. Putnam's Sons, 1923.

PACKARD, LEONARD O., and SINNOTT, C. P. *Nations as Neighbors.* Revised Edition. Part II. New York: The Macmillan Company, 1931.

PETERSHAM, MAUD and MISKA. *The Storybook of Coal.* Philadelphia: The John C. Winston Company, 1935.

PETERSHAM, MAUD and MISKA. *The Storybook of Iron and Steel.* Philadelphia: The John C. Winston Company, 1935.

PETERSHAM, MAUD and MISKA. *The Storybook of Oil.* Philadelphia: The John C. Winston Company, 1935.

PRICE, OVERTON W. *Land We Live In.* New York: Dodd, Mead & Company, Inc. n.d.

RUSH, CHARLES EVERETT, and WINSLOW, AMY. *Science of Things About Us.* Boston: Little, Brown and Company, 1927.

SMITH, JOSEPH RUSSELL. *Home Folks.* Philadelphia: The John C. Winston Company, 1930.

STORY BOOKS

ROLT-WHEELER, FRANCIS W. *Boy With the United States Miners.* Boston: Lothrop, Lee & Shepard Company, 1922.

MONEY

Books for Pupils

REFERENCE BOOKS

AUSTIN, OSCAR P. *Uncle Sam's Secrets.* New York: D. Appleton and Company, 1917.

BASS, FLORENCE. *Stories of Pioneer Life.* Boston: D. C. Heath and Company, 1900.

CAMP, RUTH O. *Story of Markets.* New York: Harper and Brothers, 1929.

CARPENTER, FRANK G. *North America.* New York: American Book Company, 1922.

CARTER, MARY DUNCAN. *The Story of Money.* New York: Farrar & Rinehart, Inc., 1932.

CLARK, MARION G. *Westward to the Pacific.* New York: Chas. Scribner's Sons, 1932.

DEARBORN, FRANCIS R. *How the Indians Lived.* Boston: Ginn and Company, 1927.

FRASER, CHELSEA C. *Secrets of the Earth.* New York: T. Y. Crowell Company, 1921.

HARTMAN, GERTRUDE. *These United States and How They Came To Be.* New York: The Macmillan Company, 1932.

HAYWARD, WILLIAM R. *Money, What It Is and How To Use It.* Boston: Houghton Mifflin Company, 1917.

HILLYER, VIRGIL M. *Child's History of the World.* New York: The Century Co., 1931.

HOKE, GEORGE W. *Lands and Life.* Richmond, Virginia: Johnson Publishing Co., 1924.

HOLBROOK, FLORENCE. *Cave, Mound, and Lake Dwellers.* Boston: D. C. Heath and Company, 1911.

HOLLAND, RUPERT S. *Sons of Seven Cities.* Philadelphia: Macrae Smith Co., 1929.

HUNTINGTON, ELLSWORTH, and CUSHING, S. W. *Modern Business Geography.* Yonkers-on-Hudson, New York: World Book Company, 1925.

KEIR, ROBERT M. *March of Commerce.* Pageant of America, Vol. 4, Pt. 5. New Haven: Yale University Press, n. d.

McMILLEN, WHEELER. *Young Collector.* New York: D. Appleton and Company, 1928.

NICOLAY, HELEN. *Boys' Life of Alexander Hamilton.* New York: The Century Co., 1927.

QUENNELL, MARJORIE, and QUENNELL, C. H. B. *Everyday Life in the New Stone, Bronze, and Early Iron Ages.* New York: G. P. Putnam's Sons, 1923.

REYNOLDS, MINNIE J. *How Man Conquered Nature.* New York: The Macmillan Company, 1914.

ROCHELEAU, WILLIAM F. *Minerals.* Great American Industries, Vol. 1. Chicago: A. Flanagan Company, 1929.

TAPPAN, EVA MARCH. *Diggers in the Earth.* Boston: Houghton Mifflin Company, 1916.

WILLIAMS, ARCHIBALD. *How It Is Made.* New York: Thomas Nelson & Sons, 1908.

STORY BOOKS

Colonial Stories, Retold. New York: The Century Co., 1905.

NIDA, STELLA H. *Letters of Polly the Pioneer.* New York: The Macmillan Company, 1916.

SNEDDEN, GENEVRA. *Leif and Thorkel.* Yonkers-on-Hudson, New York: World Book Company, 1922.

Books for Teachers

Du Puy, William Atherton. "Geography of Money." *National Geographic.* LII (December, 1927), 744–68. Washington: National Geographic Magazine.

Hughes, Ray O. *Community Civics.* Boston: Allyn and Bacon, 1927.

PIONEERS

Books for Pupils

REFERENCE BOOKS

Baldwin, James. *Four Great Americans.* New York: American Book Company, 1897.

Bailey, Carolyn Sherwin. *Boys and Girls of Colonial Days.* Chicago: A. Flanagan Company, 1917.

Barker, Eugene Campbell, and Others. *Story of Our Nation.* Evanston, Illinois: Row, Peterson and Company, 1929.

Bass, Florence. *Stories of Early Times in the Great West.* Indianapolis: Bobbs-Merrill Company, 1927.

Bass, Florence. *Stories of Pioneer Life for Young Readers.* Revised Edition. Boston: D. C. Heath and Company, 1928.

Blaisdell, Albert F., and Ball, Frances K. *American History for Little Folks.* Boston: Little, Brown and Company, 1927.

Blaisdell, A. F., and Ball, F. K. *Log Cabin Days.* Boston: Little, Brown and Company, 1921.

Blaisdell, Albert F., and Ball, Francis K. *Pioneers of America.* Boston: Little, Brown and Company, 1919.

Brooks, Ellridge S. *The True Story of George Washington.* Boston: Lothrop, Lee and Shepard Company, 1895.

Burns, Annie Johnson. *Stories of Shepherd Life.* New York: American Book Company, 1934.

Clark, Marion G., and Gordy, Wilbur F. *First Three Hundred Years in America.* New York: Chas. Scribner's Sons, 1931.

Cody, William Frederick. *Adventures of Buffalo Bill.* New York: Harper & Brothers, n. d.

Colonial Stories Retold. New York: The Century Co., 1905.

Dalgliesh, Alice. *American Travels.* New York: The Macmillan Company, 1934.

Earle, Alice Morse. *Home Life in Colonial Days.* New York: The Macmillan Company, 1898.

Earle, Alice Morse. *Child Life in Colonial Days.* New York: The Macmillan Company, 1898.

Hale, Ethel M. *Stories of Men and Nature.* Chicago: J. B. Lippincott Company, 1927.

Heard, Sarah Dow, and King, M. W. *Stories of American Pioneers.* Philadelphia: The John C. Winston Company, 1929.

Kaler, James Otis. *Calvert of Maryland.* New York: American Book Company, 1910.

Kaler, James Otis. *Mary of Plymouth.* New York: American Book Company. n.d.

Kaler, James Otis. *Ruth of Boston.* New York: American Book Company. n. d.

Kaler, James Otis. *Richard of Jamestown.* New York: American Book Company, n. d.

Kaler, James Otis. *Stephen of Philadelphia.* New York: American Book Company, n. d.

Lamprey, L. *Days of the Colonists.* New York: Frederick A. Stokes Company, 1922.

Livingstone, Cora Luetta. *Glimpses of Pioneer Life.* Chicago: A. Flanagan Company, 1904.

McGOWAN, ELLEN AMELIA. *Soap Bubbles.* New York: The Macmillan Company, 1929.

MULLIKEN, SARAH ELIZABETH. *Boys and Girls of Colonial Times.* Boston: Ginn and Company, 1928.

NIDA, WILLIAM LEWIS. *Following the Frontier.* New York: The Macmillan Company, 1924.

NIDA, WILLIAM LEWIS, and WEBB, V. L. *Our Country Past and Present.* Chicago: Scott, Foresman and Company, 1930.

PRESCOTT, DELLA R. *A Day in a Colonial Home.* Boston: Marshall Jones Company, 1921.

PUMPHREY, MARGARET BLANCHE. *Pilgrim Stories.* Chicago: Rand McNally & Company, 1910.

SMITH, SUSAN COWLES. *Made in America.* New York: Alfred A. Knopf, 1929.

STONE, GERTRUDE LINCOLN, and FICKETT, M. G. *Everyday Life in the Colonies.* Boston: D. C. Heath and Company, 1905.

TILLINGHAST, L. MORTON, and COLEMAN, E. M. *Colonial Life in America.* Dansville, New York: F. A. Owen Publishing Company, 1928.

WARREN, MAUDE LAVINIA. *Little Pioneers.* Chicago: Rand McNally & Company, 1916.

WHITE, STEWART EDWARD. *Daniel Boone.* Garden City, New York: Doubleday, Page and Company, 1925.

STORY BOOKS

ALBERT, EDNA. *Little Pilgrim to Penn's Woods.* New York: Longmans, Green and Company, 1932.

BENNETT, JOHN. *Barnaby Lee.* New York: The Century Company, 1902.

BUSH, BERTHA E. *A Prairie Rose.* Boston: Little, Brown and Company, 1910.

CARR, MARY JANE. *Children of the Covered Wagon.* New York. Junior Literary Guild, and Thomas Y. Crowell Company, 1934.

COATSWORTH, ELIZABETH. *Away Goes Sally.* New York: The Macmillan Company, 1934.

DARBY, ADA CLAIRE. *Gay Souerette.* New York: Frederick A. Stokes Company, 1933.

DIX, BEULAH MARIE. *Blithe McBride.* New York: The Macmillan Company, 1916.

DIX, BEULAH MARIE. *Soldier Rigdale.* New York: The Macmillan Company, 1899.

FIELD, RACHEL. *Calico Bush.* New York: The Junior Literary Guild, and the Macmillan Company, 1931.

GARDINER, ALICE CUSHING. *Father's Gone A-whaling.* Garden City, New York: Doubleday, Doran and Company, 1926.

GREY, KATHERINE. *Hills of Gold.* Boston: Little, Brown and Company, 1933.

GREY, KATHERINE. *Rolling Wheels.* Boston: Little, Brown and Company, 1933.

HOUGH, EMERSON. *The Covered Wagon.* New York: D. Appleton and Company, 1926.

LEETCH, DOROTHY L. *Annetje and Her Family.* Boston: Lothrop, Lee and Shepard Company, 1926.

MEANS, FLORENCE CRANNELL. *A Candle in the Mist.* Boston: Houghton Mifflin Company, 1931.

MEDARY, MARJORIE. *Prairie Anchorage.* New York: Longmans, Green and Company, 1934.

MEIGS, CORNELIA LYNDE. *Master Simon's Garden.* New York: The Macmillan Company, 1925.

MEIGS, CORNELIA LYNDE. *Willow Whistle.* New York: The Macmillan Company, 1931.

MEIGS, CORNELIA LYNDE. *Wind in the Chimney.* New York: The Macmillan Company, 1934.

MORROW, HONORÉ WILLSIE. *On to Oregon.* New York: William Morrow and Company, 1926.

NIDA, STELLA H. *Letters of Polly the Pioneer.* New York: The Macmillan Company, 1916.

ORTON, HELEN. *Treasure In the Little Trunk.* New York: Frederick A. Stokes Company, 1932.

PERKINS, LUCY FITCH. *The Colonial Twins of Virginia.* Boston: Houghton Mifflin Company, 1924.

PERKINS, LUCY FITCH. *The Puritan Twins.* Boston: Houghton Mifflin Company, 1921.

SCHWARTZ, JULIA AUGUSTA. *Five Little Strangers.* New York: American Book Company, 1904.

SKINNER, CONSTANCE LINDSAY. *Debby Barnes. Trader.* New York: The Macmillan Company, 1932.

WILDER, LAURA. *Little House in the Big Woods.* New York: Harper and Brothers, 1932.

Books for Teachers

MEIGS, CORNELIA LYNDE. *Willow Whistle.* New York: The Macmillan Company, 1931.

POTTERY

Books for Pupils

REFERENCE BOOKS

BALDWIN, JAMES. *Old Greek Stories.* New York: American Book Company, 1895.

BASSETT, SARA WARE. *Story of Porcelain.* Philadelphia: Penn Publishing Company, 1919.

CARPENTER, FRANK G., and CARPENTER, FRANCES. *House We Live In.* New York: American Book Company, 1926.

DEARBORN, FRANCES ROSS. *How the Indians Lived.* Boston: Ginn and Company, 1927.

DOPP, KATHERINE E. *Early Cave-men.* Chicago: Rand McNally & Company.

FRANCK, HARRY A. *China.* Dansville, New York: F. A. Owen Publishing Company, 1929.

HAAREN, JOHN HENRY, and POLAND, A. B. *Famous Men of Greece.* New York: American Book Company, 1904.

HALL, JENNIE. *Men of Old Greece.* Boston: Little, Brown and Company, 1906.

HALLECK, REUBEN POST, and FRANTZ, JULIETTE. *Our Nation's Heritage.* New York: American Book Company, 1925.

HILLYER, VIRGIL M. *Child's History of the World.* New York: The Century Co., 1924.

HOLLAND, ROBERT W., and NIXON, ALFRED. *Historic Inventions.* Philadelphia: Macrae Smith Co., 1911.

KELLY, ROBERT T. *Egypt.* New York: The Macmillan Company, 1931.

MEAD, CHARLES W. *Old Civilizations of Inca Land.* New York: American Museum of Natural History, 1924.

MOHR, LOUISE MAUDE. *Egyptians of Long Ago.* Chicago: Rand McNally & Company, 1926.

PERDUE, HANNAH AVIS. *Child Life in Other Lands.* Chicago: Rand McNally & Company, 1918.

SMITH, SUSAN COWLES. *Made in America.* New York: Alfred A. Knopf, 1929.

SMITH, SUSAN COWLES. *Made in England.* New York: Thomas Nelson and Sons, 1932.

SMITH, SUSAN COWLES. *Made in France.* New York: Alfred A. Knopf, 1931.

SMITH, SUSAN COWLES. *Made in Germany and Austria.* New York: Minton, Balch & Company, 1933.

SMITH, SUSAN COWLES. *Made in Mexico.* New York: Alfred A. Knopf, 1930.

TAPPAN, EVA MARCH. *Makers of Many Things.* Boston: Houghton Mifflin Company, 1916.

TAPPAN, EVA MARCH. *Story of the Greek People.* London: George G. Harrap & Co., 1929.

TERRY, ARTHUR GREY. *Tales from Far and Near.* Evanston, Illinois: Row, Peterson and Company, 1926.

VAN LOON, HENRIK W. *Story of Mankind.* New York: Boni and Liveright, 1923.

WELLS, MARGARET E. *How the Present Came from the Past.* Book II. New York: The Macmillan Company, 1932.

WILLIAMS, ARCHIBALD. *How it is Made.* New York: Thomas Nelson & Sons, 1908.

STORY BOOKS

Aesop's Fables. New York: Thomas Nelson & Sons, 1933.

Arabian Nights. New York: T. Y. Crowell Company, 1917.

BALDWIN, JAMES. *Story of Roland.* New York: Chas. Scribner's Sons, 1930.

DE LA RAMÉE, LOUISE. *Nürnberg Stove.* New York: The Macmillan Company, 1928.

HAWTHORNE, NATHANIEL. *Wonder Book.* Garden City, New York: Doubleday, Doran & Company, 1930.

HILL, HELEN, and MAXWELL, VIOLET. *Little Tonino.* New York: The Macmillan Company, 1928.

HOWARD, ALICE. *Sokar and the Crocodile.* New York: The Macmillan Company, 1928.

MALKUS, ALIDA S. *Dragon Fly of Zuni.* New York: Harcourt, Brace & Company, 1928.

OLMSTEAD, EMMA. *Ned and Nan in Holland.* Evanston, Illinois: Row, Peterson and Company, 1916.

PALMER, WINTHROP B. *Abdul.* New York: The Macmillan Company, 1928.

PERKINS, LUCY. *Cave Twins.* Boston: Houghton Mifflin Company, 1916.

PERKINS, LUCY. *Dutch Twins.* Boston: Houghton Mifflin Company, 1911.

ROWE, DOROTHY. *Rabbit Lantern.* New York: The Macmillan Company, 1925.

VAN DYKE, HENRY. *The Blue Flower.* New York: Chas. Scribner's Sons, 1902.

Books for Teachers

BINNS, CHARLES F. *The Potter's Craft.* New York: D. Van Nostrand Company, Inc., 1922.

BONSER, FREDERICK GORDON, and MOSSMAN, L. C. *Industrial Arts for Elementary Schools.* New York: The Macmillan Company, 1923.

COX, GEORGE JAMES. *Pottery for Artists, Craftsmen, and Teachers.* New York: The Macmillan Company, 1926.

MEAD, CHARLES W. *Peruvian Art.* New York: American Museum of Natural History, 1919.

MOORE, N. HUDSON. *Old China Book.* New York: Frederick A. Stokes & Company, 1903.

RINGO, FREDONIA J. *China and Glassware.* Merchandise Manual. London: McGraw-Hill Book Company, Inc., 1925.

WHEELER, IDA WILLSEA. *Playing with Clay.* New York: The Macmillan Company, 1931.

WINSLOW, LEON L. *Elementary Industrial Arts.* New York: The Macmillan Company, 1922.

PREHISTORIC LIFE

Books for Pupils

REFERENCE BOOKS

CLARK, MARION G., and GORDY, WILBUR F. *Early Story of Mankind.* New York: Chas. Scribner's Sons, 1929.

COFFMAN, RAMON. *Child's Story of the Human Race.* New York: Dodd, Mead & Company, Inc., 1927.

DOPP, KATHERINE E. *The Early Cave-men.* Chicago: Rand McNally & Company, 1904.

DOPP, KATHERINE E. *Early Herdsmen.* Chicago: Rand McNally & Company, 1923.

DOPP, KATHERINE E. *Story of the Early Sea People.* Chicago: Rand McNally & Company, 1913.

DOPP, KATHERINE E. *Later Cave-men.* Chicago: Rand McNally & Company.

DOPP, KATHERINE E. *The Tree Dwellers.* Chicago: Rand McNally & Company, 1903.

ERLEIGH, EVA VIOLET. *In the Beginning; a First History for Little Children.* Garden City, New York: Doubleday, Doran & Company, 1926.

GORDY, WILBUR F. *American Beginnings in Europe.* New York: Chas. Scribner's Sons, 1925.

HALLECK, R. P., and FRANTZ, J. *Our Nation's Heritage.* New York: American Book Company, 1925.

HIBBEN, THOMAS. *The Carpenter's Tool Chest.* Philadelphia: The Junior Literary Guild and J. B. Lippincott Company, 1933.

HILLYER, VIRGIL M. *Child's History of the World.* New York: The Century Co., 1924.

KUMMER, FREDERIC A. *First Days of Man.* New York: George H. Doran Company, 1922.

LAMPREY, LOUISE. *Children of Ancient Britain.* Boston: Little, Brown and Company, 1921.

LANSING, MARION FLORENCE. *Man's Long Climb.* Boston: Little, Brown and Company, 1933.

MIX, JENNIE IRENE. *Mighty Animals.* New York: American Book Company, 1912.

MOHR, LOUISE MAUDE. *Days Before Houses.* Chicago: Rand McNally & Company, 1928.

O'HARA, ELIZABETH FORBES. *From Hunters to Herdsmen.* New York: The Macmillan Company, 1932.

O'HARA, ELIZABETH FORBES. *Taming the Wild Grasses.* New York: The Macmillan Company, 1932.

QUENNELL, MARJORIE, and QUENNELL, C. H. B. *Everyday Life in the Old Stone Age.* New York: G. P. Putnam's Sons, 1922.

ROBINSON, W. W. *Ancient Animals.* New York: The Macmillan Company, 1934.

ROBINSON, W. W. *Beasts of the Tar Pits.* New York: The Macmillan Company, 1932.

SALISBURY, ETHEL I., and STEDMAN, LULU M. *Our Ancestors in the Ancient World.* Boston: Little, Brown and Company, 1935.

STUART, DOROTHY MARGARET. *Boy Through the Ages.* New York: George H. Doran Company, 1926.

VAN LOON, HENDRIK W. *Ancient Man.* New York: Boni & Liveright, 1920.

WASHBURNE, CARLETON W., and WASHBURNE, H. C. *Story of the Earth.* New York: The Century Co., 1916.

WELLS, MARGARET ELIZABETH. *How the Present Came From the Past.* Book I. New York: The Macmillan Company, 1932.

WEST, RUTH, and WEST, W. M. *The New World's Foundations in the Old.* Boston: Allyn and Bacon, 1929.

STORY BOOKS

CRUMP, IRVING. *Og, Son of Fire.* New York: Dodd, Mead & Company, Inc., 1922.

PERKINS, LUCY. *Cave Twins.* Boston: Houghton Mifflin Company, 1916.

WATERLOO, STANLEY. *Ab, the Cave Man.* New York: Educational Publishers, 1911.
WATERLOO, STANLEY. *Story of Ab.* Garden City, New York: Doubleday, Doran & Company, 1897.

RECORDS

Books for Pupils

REFERENCE BOOKS

ADAMS, JOSEPH H. *Harper's Indoor Book for Boys.* New York: Harper and Brothers, 1908.

AMERICAN COUNCIL ON EDUCATION. *The Story of Writing.* Washington: The American Council on Education, 1932.

BACHMAN, FRANK P. *Great Inventors and Their Inventions.* New York: American Book Company, 1918.

BALDWIN, JAMES. *Thirty More Famous Stories Retold.* New York: American Book Company, 1905.

BRIDGES, T. C. *The Young Folk's Book of Invention.* Boston: Little, Brown and Company, 1926.

BUNKER, FRANK F. *China and Japan.* Chicago: J. B. Lippincott Company, 1928.

CHASE, ANNIE, and CLOW, E. *Stories of Industry.* Book I. New York: Educational Publishers, 1913.

CHASE, ANNIE, and CLOW, E. *Stories of Industry.* Book II. New York: Educational Publishers, 1913.

CHURCH, ALFRED J. *Stories from English History.* New York: The Macmillan Company, 1898.

CLARK, MARION G., and GORDY, WILBUR F. *Early Story of Mankind.* New York: Chas. Scribner's Sons, 1929.

CLARK, MARION G., and GORDY, WILBUR F. *What Men Brought from Europe to America.* New York: Chas. Scribner's Sons, 1929.

CLODD, EDWARD. *Story of Primitive Man.* New York: D. Appleton & Company. n. d.

COFFMAN, RAMON. *Child's Story of the Human Race.* New York: Dodd, Mead & Company, Inc., 1927.

COLLINS, A. F. *Handicraft for Boys.* New York: Frederick A. Stokes Company, 1918.

CURTIS, MARY ISABEL. *Stories in Trees.* Chicago: Lyons and Carnahan, 1925.

DARROW, FLOYD L. *Thinkers and Doers.* New York: Silver, Burdett and Company, 1925.

DEARBORN, FRANCES ROSS. *How the Indians Lived.* Boston: Ginn and Company, 1927.

DORRANCE, JOHN G. *Story of the Forest.* New York: American Book Company, 1916.

DUTTON, MAUDE. *Little Stories of England.* New York: American Book Company, 1911.

EARLE, ALICE MORSE. *Child Life in Colonial Days.* New York: The Macmillan Company, 1899.

EGE, OTTO F. *Story of the Alphabet.* Baltimore: Norman T. A. Munder & Co., 1921.

ERLEIGH, EVA VIOLET. *In the Beginning.* Garden City, New York: Doubleday, Doran & Company, 1926.

FABRE, JEAN H. *Storybook of Science.* New York: The Century Co., 1917.

FRANKLIN, BENJAMIN. *Autobiography.* Chicago: Rand McNally & Company, 1912.

HAAREN, JOHN H., and POLAND, A. B. *Famous Men of the Middle Ages.* New York: American Book Company. n.d.

HALL, JENNIE. *Buried Cities.* New York: The Macmillan Company, 1922.

HARDING, CAROLINE HIRST. *Story of the Middle Ages.* Chicago: Scott, Foresman and Company. n.d.

HARTMAN, GERTRUDE. *World We Live in and How it Came to Be.* New York: The Macmillan Company, 1931.

HILLYER, VIRGIL M. *Child's History of the World.* New York: The Century Co., 1924.

HODGON, JEANETTE R. *Enchanted Past.* Boston: Ginn and Company, 1922.

HOLLAND, RUPERT S. *Historic Adventures.* Philadelphia: Macrae Smith Co., 1913.

HOLLAND, RUPERT S. *Historic Inventions.* Philadelphia: Macrae Smith Co., 1911.

ILIN, M. (Pseudonym for Ilia I. Marshak.) *Black on White.* Chicago: J. B. Lippincott Company, 1932.

KUMMER, FREDERICK ARNOLD. *First Days of Knowledge.* New York: George H. Doran Company, 1923.

LAMPREY, LOUISE. *In the Days of the Guild.* New York: Frederick A. Stokes Company, 1918.

LANSING, MARION FLORENCE. *Great Moments in Science.* Garden City, New York: Doubleday, Doran & Company, 1926.

McFEE, INEZ NELLIE. *Stories of American Invention.* New York: T. Y. Crowell Company, 1921.

MARKSHAK, ILIA I. (M. Ilin, pseudonym). *Black on White.* Chicago: J. B. Lippincott Company, 1932.

MAXWELL, MARJORIE. *Story of Books Up Through the Ages.* New York: Harper and Brothers, 1928.

MILLS, DOROTHY. *Book of the Ancient World.* New York: G. P. Putnam's Sons, 1923.

MITCHELL, DONALD G. *About Old Story Tellers.* New York: Chas. Scribner's Sons. n. d.

MOHR, LOUISE MAUDE. *Babylonia and Assyria.* Chicago: Rand McNally & Company, 1928.

MOHR, LOUISE MAUDE. *Days Before Houses.* Chicago: Rand McNally & Company, 1928.

MOHR, LOUISE MAUDE. *Egyptians of Long Ago.* Chicago: Rand McNally & Company, 1926.

MOWRY, W. A. *American Inventions and Inventors.* New York: Silver, Burdett and Company, 1900.

Pageant of America. Vol. V. Pt. III. "Making of America." Edited by R. H. Keir. New Haven: Yale University Press, 1925.

PARKMAN, MARY R. *Conquests of Invention.* New York: The Century Co., 1921.

RAWLINGS, GERTRUDE B. *Story of Books.* New York: D. Appleton and Company, 1901.

ROLT-WHEELER, FRANCIS W. *Boy with the United States Inventors.* Boston: Lothrop, Lee & Shepard Company, 1920.

RUSH, CHARLES EVERETT, and WINSLOW, AMY. *Science of Things About Us.* Boston: Little, Brown and Company, 1927.

SMITH, DAVID E. *Number Stories of Long Ago.* Boston: Ginn and Company, 1919.

STANLEY-BROWN, KATHARINE. *Story of Printed Pictures.* New York: Harper and Brothers, 1931.

STONE, GERTRUDE L., and FICKETT, M. G. *Famous Days in the Century of Invention.* Boston: D. C. Heath and Company, 1920.

Stories from English History. Edited by Henry P. Warren. Boston: D. C. Heath and Company, 1923.

TAPPAN, EVA MARCH. *Makers of Many Things.* Boston: Houghton Mifflin Company, 1916.

TAPPAN, EVA MARCH. *World's Story.* V. I. Boston: Houghton Mifflin Company, 1914.

TAPPAN, EVA MARCH. *World's Story.* V. VII. Boston: Houghton Mifflin Company, 1914.

TERRY, ARTHUR GREY. *New Liberty.* History Stories of Other Lands. Book V. Evanston, Illinois: Row, Peterson and Company, 1915.

VAN LOON, HENRIK W. *The Story of Mankind.* New York: Boni & Liveright, 1923.

WELLS, H. G. *Short History of Mankind.* New York: The Macmillan Company, 1925.

WELLS, MARGARET ELIZABETH. *How the Present Came from the Past.* New York: The Macmillan Company, 1932.

WIESE, KURT. *Chinese Inkstick.* Garden City, New York: Doubleday, Doran & Company, 1929.

STORY BOOKS

GIBSON, KATHRINE. *Goldsmith of Florence.* New York: The Macmillan Company, 1929.

KIPLING, RUDYARD. *Just So Stories.* New York: The Macmillan Company, 1930.

OLCOTT, FRANCES JENKINS. *Story Telling Poems.* Boston: Houghton Mifflin Company, 1928.

STEIN, EVALEEN. *Gabriel and the Hour Book.* Boston: L. C. Page & Company, 1906.

Books for Teachers

BEAN, FLORENCE O., and BROADHEAD, J. C. *Book Binding for Beginners.* Worcester, Mass.: Davis Press, 1924.

BONSER, FREDERICK GORDON, and MOSSMAN, L. C. *Industrial Arts for Elementary Schools.* New York: The Macmillan Company, 1923.

CLODD, EDWARD. *Story of the Alphabet.* New York: D. Appleton and Company, 1915.

COCKERELL, DOUGLAS. *Book Binding and the Care of Books.* New York: Pitman Publishing Corporation, 1920.

Curriculum Making in an Elementary School. Columbia University Teachers College. Lincoln School. Boston: Ginn and Company, 1927.

FAY, LUCY ELLA, and EATON, A. T. *Instruction in the Use of Books and Libraries.* Boston: F. W. Faxon Co., 1919.

GOODYEAR, FREDERICK. *Printing and Bookcraft for Schools.* New York: Frederick A. Stokes Company, 1926.

HUNTER, DARD. *Paper Making in the Classroom.* Peoria, Illinois: Manual Arts Press, 1931.

JOHNSTON, EDWARD. *Writing, Illuminating, and Lettering.* New York: Pitman Publishing Corporation, 1925.

MADDOX, H. A. *Paper, Its History, Sources, and Manufacture.* New York: Pitman Publishing Corporation, 1930.

MASON, WILLIAM A. *History of the Art of Writing.* New York: The Macmillan Company, 1928.

WESTON, HARRY E. *Book on Paper.* Syracuse, New York: Syracuse University Book Store, 1927.

WINSLOW, LEON LOYAL. *Elementary Industrial Arts.* New York: The Macmillan Company, 1922.

ROME

Books for Pupils

REFERENCE BOOKS

AKER, HOMER FERRIS, and NELSON, D. LLOYD. *Yesterday, the Foundation of Today.* San Francisco: Harr Wagner Publishing Company, 1933.

ANDREWS, JANE. *Ten Boys who Lived on the Road from Long Ago to Now.* Boston: Ginn and Company, 1924.

ATKINSON, ALICE M. *European Beginnings to American History.* Boston: Ginn and Company, 1912.

BALDWIN, JAMES. *Thirty More Famous Stories Retold.* Eclectic Readings. New York: American Book Company, 1905.

BEST, SUSIE M. *Glorious Greece and Imperial Rome.* World Famous Stories in Historic Settings. V. II. New York: The Macmillan Company, 1918.

BULWER-LYTTON, EDWARD GEORGE EARLE. *Last Days of Pompeii.* New York: T. Y. Crowell Company, 1912.

BURNHAM, S., and WHIPPLE, W. *Hero Tales from History.* Philadelphia: The John C. Winston Company, 1922.

CLARK, MARION G., and GORDY, WILBUR F. *The Early Story of Mankind.* New York: Chas. Scribner's Sons, 1929.

COFFMAN, RAMON. *Child's Story of the Human Race.* New York: Dodd, Mead & Company, Inc., 1927.

DALKEITH, LENA. *Stories from Roman History.* Told to the Children Series. New York: E. P. Dutton and Company, n. d.

Egypt, Greece and Rome. Compiled by Celia Richmond. Boston: Ginn and Company, 1913.

ERLEIGH, EVA VIOLET. *In the Beginning; a First History for Little Children.* Garden City, New York: Doubleday, Doran & Company, 1926.

EVANS, LAWTON BRYAN. *Our Old World Beginnings.* Chicago: Benj. H. Sanborn & Co., 1927.

FARJEON, ELEANOR. *Mighty Men.* New York: D. Appleton and Company, 1925.

GORDY, WILBUR F. *American Beginnings in Europe.* New York: Chas. Scribner's Sons, 1925.

GUERBER, HELENE ADELINE. *Story of the Romans.* New York: American Book Book Company, 1920.

HAAREN, J. H., and POLAND, A. B. *Famous Men of Rome.* New York: American Book Company, 1909.

HALL, JENNIE. *Buried Cities.* New York: The Macmillan Company, 1922.

HALL, JENNIE. *Our Ancestors in Europe.* New York: Silver, Burdett and Company, 1916.

HALLECK, R. P., and FRANZ, J. *Our Nation's Heritage.* New York: American Book Company, 1925.

HALLOCK, GRACE TABER. *Boy Who Was.* New York: E. P. Dutton and Company, 1928.

HANCOCK, MARY S. *Children of History.* Boston: Little, Brown and Company, 1909.

HARDING, S. B., and HARDING, MARGARET. *Old World Background to American History.* Chicago: Scott, Foresman and Company, 1919.

HILLYER, VIRGIL M. *A Child's History of the World.* New York: The Century Co., 1924.

HODGON, JEANNETTE R. *Enchanted Past.* Boston: Ginn and Company, 1922.

KUMMER, FREDERIC ARNOLD. *First Days of History.* Garden City, New York: Doubleday, Doran & Company, 1925.

LAMPREY, LOUISE. *Children of Ancient Rome.* Boston: Little, Brown and Company, 1922.

MACGREGOR, MARY. *Story of Rome.* New York: Frederick A. Stokes Company, 1909.

NIDA, WILLIAM LEWIS. *The Dawn of American History in Europe.* New York: The Macmillan Company, 1921.

POWER, EILEEN E., and POWER, R. D. *Cities and Their Stories.* Boston: Houghton Mifflin Company, 1927.

SALISBURY, ETHEL I., and STEDMAN, LULU M. *Our Ancestors in the Ancient World.* Boston: Little, Brown and Company, 1935.

SCALES, LAURA WOOLSEY. *Boys of the Ages; Their Dreams and Their Crafts.* Boston: Ginn and Company, 1922.

SCHWARTZ, JULIA. *From Then Till Now.* Yonkers-on-Hudson, New York: World Book Company, 1929.

SOUTHWORTH, GERTRUDE, and SOUTHWORTH, J. VAN D. *What the Old World Gave the New.* Syracuse, New York: Iroquois Publishing Company, 1924.

Stories of Greece and Rome. New York: The Century Co., 1909.

STUART, DOROTHY MARGARET. *Boy Through the Ages.* New York: George H. Doran Company, 1926.

TAPPAN, EVA MARCH. *Old World Hero Stories.* Boston: Houghton Mifflin Company, 1911.

TAPPAN, EVA MARCH. *Story of the Roman People.* Boston: Houghton Mifflin Company, 1910.

TERRY, ARTHUR GREY. *Tales from Far and Near.* Evanston, Illinois: Row, Peterson and Company, 1926.

TERRY, ARTHUR GREY. *Tales of Long Ago.* Evanston, Illinois: Row, Peterson and Company, 1926.

VAN LOON, HENRIK W. *The Story of Mankind.* New York: Boni and Liveright, 1923.

WEST, RUTH, and WEST, W. M. *New World's Foundations in the Old.* Boston: Allyn and Bacon, 1929.

STORY BOOKS

CHURCH, ALFRED JOHN. *Stories from Livy.* New York: Dodd, Mead & Company, Inc., 1883.

KIPLING, RUDYARD. *Puck of Pook's Hill.* Garden City, New York: Doubleday, Doran & Company, 1906.

MACAULEY, THOMAS BABINGTON. *Lays of Ancient Rome.* Philadelphia: Henry Altemus Company, n. d.

PRICE, MARGARET. *Enchantment Tales for Children.* Chicago: Rand McNally & Company, n. d.

Books for Teachers

BAILSIE, JAMES. *Ancient Rome. Peeps at Many Lands.* New York: The Macmillan Company, 1917.

DAVIS, WILLIAM STEARNS. *Day in Old Rome; A Picture of Roman Life.* Boston: Allyn and Bacon, 1925.

JOHNSTON, HAROLD WHETSTONE. *Private Life of the Romans.* Chicago: Scott, Foresman and Company, 1903.

MILLS, DOROTHY. *Book of the Ancient Romans.* New York: G. P. Putnam's Sons, 1927.

SCUDDER, HORACE ELISHA. *Children's Book: A Collection of the Best and Most Famous Stories and Poems in the English Language.* Boston: Houghton Mifflin Company, 1910.

VIRGIL. (Publius Virgilius Maro.) *Story of the Aeneid,* by E. Brooks. Classic Stories for Boys and Girls. Philadelphia: Penn Publishing Company, 1899.

RUSSIA

Books for Pupils

REFERENCE BOOKS

ALLEN, NELLIE B. *The New Europe.* Boston: Ginn and Company, 1920.

ATWOOD, WALLACE W., and THOMAS, H. G. *Nations Beyond the Seas.* Boston: Ginn and Company, 1930.

BARROWS, H. H.; PARKER, E. P.; and PARKER, M. T. *Europe and Asia.* New York: Silver, Burdett and Company, 1930.

BLUMENTHAL, VERA. *Folk Tales from the Russian.* Chicago: Rand McNally & Company, 1903.

CARPENTER, FRANK G. *Europe.* New York: American Book Company, 1922.

CHAMBERLAIN, J. F., and CHAMBERLAIN, A. H. *Europe.* New York: The Macmillan Company, 1912.

CROSS, DONZELLA. *Music Stories for Boys and Girls.* Boston: Ginn and Company, 1926.

CURTIN, JEREMIAH. *Wonder Tales from Russia.* Boston: Little, Brown and Company, 1921.

FAIRGRIEVE, JAMES, and YOUNG, ERNEST. *World.* Human Geography. Book III. New York: D. Appleton and Company, 1925.

HAAREN, JOHN H., and POLAND, A. B. *Famous Men of Modern Times.* New York: American Book Company, 1909.

HEADLEY, E. A. *How Other People Travel.* Chicago: Rand McNally & Company, 1926.

HILLYER, VIRGIL M. *Child's History of the World.* New York: The Century Co., 1924.

HOKE, GEORGE WILSON. *Russia and the Old East.* Lands and Life. Book I. Richmond, Va.; Johnson Publishing Co., 1924.

KREHBIEL, HENRY E. *Second Book of Operas.* Garden City, New York: Garden City Publishing Company, 1926.

MCFEE, INEZ N. *Boys and Girls in Many Lands.* New York: T. Y. Crowell Company, 1917.

PACKARD, LEONARD O., and SINNOTT, C. P. *Nations as Neighbors.* New York: The Macmillan Company, 1925.

PHILLIPS, GRACE D. *Far Peoples.* Chicago: University of Chicago Press, 1929.

SCHWIMMER, FRANCISKA. *Great Musicians as Children.* Garden City, New York: Doubleday, Doran & Company, 1929.

SMITH, FREELOVE. *Trading East.* Boston: Little, Brown and Company, 1930.

STONE, KATHRYN EMILIE. *Lessons in Music Understanding.* 3441 S. Flower St., Los Angeles, California: The Author.

TAPPAN, EVA MARCH. *Old World Hero Stories.* Boston: Houghton Mifflin Company, 1911.

TAYLOR, BAYARD. *Boys of Other Countries.* New York: G. P. Putnam's Sons, 1904.

TERRY, ARTHUR GREY. *Tales of Long Ago.* History Stories of Other Lands. Book II. Evanston, Illinois: Row, Peterson and Company, 1915.

VAN LOON, HENRIK W. *Story of Mankind.* New York: Boni & Liveright, 1923.

WALTER, EDNA; HAENON, F. DE; and OTHERS. *Russia.* New York: The Macmillan Company, 1917.

WHEELER, POST. *Russian Wonder Tales.* New York: The Century Co., 1912.

WHITCOMB, IDA P. *Young People's Story of Music.* New York: Dodd, Mead & Company, Inc., 1908.

WHITE, WILLIAM C. *Made in Russia.* New York: Alfred A. Knopf, 1933.

STORY BOOKS

BRESHKOOSKY, CATHERINE. *Little Grandmother of the Russian Revolution.* Boston: Little, Brown and Company, 1917.

CARRICK, VALERY. *More Russian Picture Tales.* New York: Frederick A. Stokes Company, 1920.

CARRICK, VALERY. *Picture Tales from the Russian.* New York: Frederick A. Stokes Company, 1920.

CHARSKAYA, LIDIYA A. *Little Princess Nina.* New York: Henry Holt & Company, 1924.

CHEVALIER, JULIER C. *Noalis Grandchildren.* Garden City, New York: Doubleday, Doran & Company, 1929.

DAUGHERTY, SONIA. *Mashinka's Secret.* New York: Frederick A. Stokes Company, 1932.

DEBOGORY-MOKRIEVITCH, V. *When I Was a Boy in Russia.* Boston: Lothrop, Lee & Shepard Company, 1916.

GRISHINA-GIVAGO, N. J. *Peter Pea.* New York: Frederick A. Stokes Company, 1926.

GRISHINA-GIVAGO, N. J. *Shorty.* New York: Frederick A. Stokes Company, 1924.

GRISHINA-GIVAGO, N. J. *Sparrow House.* New York: Frederick A. Stokes Company, 1928.

HASKELL, HELEN E. *Katrinka.* New York: E. P. Dutton and Company, 1915.

HASKELL, HELEN E. *Peter, Katrinka's Brother.* New York: E. P. Dutton and Company, Inc., 1933.

HOLLAND, RUPERT S. *Historic Girlhoods.* Philadelphia: Macrae Smith Co., 1910.

HOUGHTON, LOUISE. *Russian Grandmother's Wonder Tales.* New York: Chas. Scribner's Sons, 1906.

KARAZIN, NIKOLAI N. *Cranes Flying South.* Garden City, New York: Doubleday, Doran & Company, 1931.

KLENOVA, VARIA, and LAMPREY, LOUISE. *Natalia and Nikolai, Children of Russia.* Yonkers-on-Hudson, New York: World Book Company, 1928.

LUSTIG, SONIA. *Roses of the Winds.* Garden City, New York: Doubleday, Doran & Company, 1926.

McDONALD, ETTA AUSTIN, and DALRYMPLE, JULIA. *Boris in Russia.* Boston: Little, Brown and Company, 1910.

MAZER, SONIA. *Maska, a Little Russian Girl.* Garden City, New York: Doubleday, Doran and Company, 1932.

MAZER, SONIA. *Yossele's Holiday.* Garden City, New York: Doubleday, Doran and Company, 1934.

PHELPS, FRANCES BROWN. *Nikita.* New York: Harcourt, Brace and Company, 1932.

ZEITLIN, IDA. *Skazki.* New York: George H. Doran Company, 1926.

Books for Teachers

BOWMAN, ISAIAH. *New World.* Yonkers-on-Hudson, New York: World Book Company, 1922.

EDDY, GEORGE S. *Challenge of Russia.* New York: Farrar & Rinehart, Inc., 1931.

MARSHAK, I. I. (M. Ilin, pseudonym.) *New Russia's Primer.* Boston: Houghton Mifflin Company, 1931.

SHIPS AND CARGOES

Books for Pupils

REFERENCE BOOKS

ADAMS, PETER. *Cork Ships and How to Make Them.* New York: E. P. Dutton and Company, 1928.

ADAMS, PETER. *Clipper Ships Done in Cork Models.* New York: E. P. Dutton and Company, 1929.

ABBOT, WILLIS J. *Story of Our Navy.* New York: Dodd, Mead & Company, Inc., 1910.

AITCHISON, ALISON E., and UTTLEY, MARGUERITE. *Across Seven Seas to Seven Continents.* Indianapolis: Bobbs-Merrill Company, 1931.

ALLEN, NELLIE B. *Europe.* Boston: Ginn and Company, 1928.

BALDWIN, JAMES, and LIVINGOOD, W. W. *Sailing the Seas.* New York: American Book Company, 1920.

BARNARD, EUNICE FULLER. *How the Old World Found the New.* Boston: Ginn and Company, 1929.

BARNES, JAMES. *Yankee Ships and Yankee Sailors.* New York: The Macmillan Company, 1922.

BLAISDELL, ALBERT F., and BALL, F. K. *Heroic Deeds of American Sailors.* Boston: Little, Brown and Company, 1915.

BRIDGES, THOMAS C. *Young Folk's Book of the Sea.* Boston: Little, Brown and Company, 1928.

BUSH, MAYBELL G., and WADDELL, JOHN F. *How We Have Conquered Distance.* New York: The Macmillan Company, 1934.

CARPENTER, FRANCES. *Ways We Travel.* New York: American Book Company, 1929.

CARTWRIGHT, CHARLES E. *Boys' Book of Ships.* New York: E. P. Dutton and Company, 1925.

CARTWRIGHT, CHARLES E. *Tale of Our Merchant Ships.* New York: E. P. Dutton and Company, 1924.

CHASE, ANNIE, and CLOW, E. *Stories of Industry.* New York: Educational Publishers, 1913.

CHATTERTON, EDWARD K. *Sailing Ships and Their Story.* Chicago: J. B. Lippincott Company, 1923.

COLLINS, FRANCIS A. *Naval Heroes of Today.* New York: The Century Co., 1918.

COLLINS, FRANCIS A. *Our Harbors and Inland Waterways.* New York: The Century Co., 1924.

COLLINS, FRANCIS A. *Sentinels Along Our Coast.* New York: The Century Co., 1922.

CURTIS, NELL C. *Boats.* Chicago: Rand McNally & Company, 1927.

DUKELOW, JEAN H., and WEBSTER, H. H. *The Ship Book.* Boston: Houghton Mifflin Company, 1931.

EVANS, ERNESTINE. *The Story of the Harbor.* New York: Harper & Brothers, 1928.

FOX, F. C. *How the World Rides.* New York: Chas. Scribner's Sons, 1929.

FRASER, CHELSEA C. *Heroes of the Sea.* New York: T. Y. Crowell Company, 1924.

FROTHINGHAM, JESSIE P. *Sea Wolves of Seven Shores.* New York: Chas Scribner's Sons, 1904.

GIMMAGE, PETER. *Picture Book of Ships.* New York: The Macmillan Company, 1930.

GRANT, GORDON. *Story of the Ship.* Springfield, Mass.: McLoughlin Bros., Inc., 1931.

GREEN, FITZHUGH. *Uncle Sam's Sailors.* New York: D. Appleton and Company, 1926.

HALL, JENNIE. *Viking Tales.* Chicago: Rand McNally & Company, 1902.

HILLYER, VIRGIL M. *Child's Geography of the World.* New York: The Century Co., 1929.

HILLYER, VIRGIL M. *Child's History of the World.* New York: The Century Co., 1931.

HOBBS, EDWARD W. *Sailing Ships at a Glance.* New York: G. P. Putnam's Sons, 1926.

HOLLAND, RUPERT S. *Historic Ships.* Philadelphia: Macrae Smith Co., 1926.

HOTCHKISS, CAROLINE W. *Representative Cities of the United States.* Boston: Houghton, Mifflin Company, 1913.

INGERSOLL, ERNEST. *Book of the Ocean.* New York: The Century Co., 1898.

JACKSON, GEORGE G. *Book of the Ship.* New York: Robert M. McBride & Co., 1930.

JACKSON, ORTON P. *New Book of American Ships.* New York: Frederick A. Stokes Company, 1926.

JOHNSTON, CHARLES H. L. *Famous Privateersmen and Adventurers of the Sea.* Boston: L. C. Page & Company, 1911.

LEEMING, JOSEPH. *Ships and Cargoes.* Garden City, New York: Doubleday, Page & Company, 1926.

LENT, HENRY B. *Full Steam Ahead!* New York: The Macmillan Company, 1934.

MOHR, LOUISE MAUDE, and POWER, R. D. *Egyptians of Long Ago.* Chicago: Rand McNally & Company, 1926.

POWER, EILEEN E. *Cities and Their Stories.* Boston: Houghton Mifflin Company, 1927.

PRYOR, WILLIAM CLAYTON. *Steamship Book.* New York: Harcourt, Brace and Company, 1934.

QUENNELL, MARJORIE, and QUENNELL, C. H. B. *Everyday Life in Homeric Greece.* New York: G. P. Putnam's Sons, 1930.

QUENNELL, MARJORIE, and QUENNELL, C. H. B. *Everyday Things in Archaic Greece.* New York: G. P. Putnam's Sons, 1931.

SCOTT, JANET L. *Round the World We Sail.* Akron, Ohio: Saalfield Publishing Co., 1930.

SEAWELL, MOLLY E. *Twelve Naval Captains.* New York: Chas. Scribner's Sons, n. d.

SMALLIDGE, OLIVE E., and PAXSON, F. L. *Finding America.* Boston: Houghton Mifflin Company, 1929.

STEVENS, WILLIAM O. *Boyhoods of Our Navy Heroes.* New York: Harper and Brothers, 1924.

STOCKTON, FRANK R. *Buccaneers and Pirates of our Coast.* New York: Grosset & Dunlap, n. d.

SYNGE, MARGARET B. *A Book of Discovery.* New York: G. P. Putnam's Sons, 1925.

TALBOT, FREDERICK A. A. *Lightships and Lighthouses.* Chicago: J. B. Lippincott Company, 1913.

TAPPAN, EVA MARCH. *Travelers and Traveling.* Boston: Houghton Mifflin Company, 1916.

VAN METER, THURMAN WILLIAM. *Tramps and Liners.* Garden City, New York: Doubleday, Doran & Company, 1931.

WEBSTER, HANSON HART. *Travel by Air, Land and Sea.* Boston: Houghton Mifflin Company, 1933.

YATES, RAYMOND FRANCIS. *Boys' Book of Model Boats.* New York: The Century Co., 1920.

STORY BOOKS

BERNSTEIN, DORIS. *Judy's Ocean Voyage.* New York: American Book Company, 1932.

DALGLIESH, ALICE. *American Travels.* New York: The Macmillan Company, 1934.

DEFOE, DANIEL. *Robinson Crusoe.* New York: American Book Company, 1911.

FIELD, RACHEL L. *Hitty, her First Hundred Years.* New York: The Macmillan Company, 1929.

HAWES, CHARLES BOARDMAN. *Dark Frigate.* Boston: Little, Brown and Company, 1925.

HEWES, AGNES DANFORTH. *Glory of the Seas.* New York: Junior Literary Guild, and Alfred A. Knopf, 1933.

KIPLING, RUDYARD. *Captains Courageous.* New York: The Macmillan Company, 1930.

A Little Book of Vagabond Songs. Compiled by Frank Shay. New York: Harper and Brothers, 1931.

MEIGS, CORNELIA. *Rain on the Roof.* New York: The Macmillan Company, 1930.

MEIGS, CORNELIA. *The Trade Wind.* Boston: Little, Brown and Company, 1929.

MELVILLE, HERMAN. *Moby Dick.* Boston: Allyn and Bacon, 1928.

NORDHOFF, CHARLES, and HALL, JAMES NORMAN. *Mutiny on the Bounty.* Boston: Little, Brown and Company, 1934.

PYLE, HOWARD. *Book of Pirates.* New York: Harper and Brothers, 1921.

SEAWELL, MOLLY E. *Paul Jones.* New York: D. Appleton and Company, n. d.

SNEDDEN, GENEVRA. *Leif and Thorkel.* Yonkers-on-Hudson, New York: World Book Company, 1922.

SNEDEKER, CAROLINE D. *Theras and His Town.* Garden City, New York: Doubleday, Doran & Company, 1924.

STEVENSON, ROBERT LOUIS. *Treasure Island.* Boston: Allyn and Bacon, 1915.

WHITNEY, ELINOR. *Try All Ports.* New York: Longmans, Green and Company, 1932.

WYSS, JOHANN DAVID. *Swiss Family Robinson.* New York: William Collins Sons & Co., Ltd., 1930.

Books for Teachers

BERRY, ANA M. *Art for Children.* New York: Boni & Liveright, 1929.

BOND, ALEXANDER R. *On the Battlefront of Engineering.* New York: The Century Co., 1916.

Home Book of Verse. Compiled by Burton E. Stevenson. New York: Henry Holt & Company, 1922.

MASEFIELD, JOHN. *Salt Water Poems and Ballads.* New York: The Macmillan Company, 1926.

McCANN, ERNEST A. *Ship Model Making.* New York: Norman W. Henley Publishing Company, 1922.

Rainbow Gold. Compiled by Sara Teasdale. New York: The Macmillan Company, 1922.

This Singing World. Edited by Louise Untermeyer. New York: Harcourt, Brace & Company, 1923.

THOMPSON, BLANCHE JENNINGS. *Silver Pennies.* New York: The Macmillan Company, 1925.

SOUTH AMERICA

Books for Pupils

REFERENCE BOOKS

AITCHISON, ALISON E., and UTTLEY, MARGUERITE. *Across Seven Seas.* Indianapolis: The Bobbs-Merrill Company, 1931.

ALLEN, NELLIE B. *South America.* Boston: Ginn and Company, 1918.

ATWOOD, WALLACE W., and THOMAS, HELEN G. *The Americas.* Boston: Ginn and Company, 1929.

BARNARD, EUNICE FULLER, and TALL, LIDA LEE. *How the Old World Found the New.* Boston: Ginn and Company, 1929.

BARROWS, HARLAN H.; PARKER, EDITH PUTNAM; and PARKER, MARGARET TERRELL. *Geography: Southern Lands.* New York: Silver, Burdett and Company, 1929.

BOWMAN, ISAIAH. *South America.* Chicago: Rand McNally & Company, 1915.

BRANOM, FREDERICK K., and GANEY, HELEN M. *Geography of North America and South America.* New York: William H. Sadler, 1928.

BROOKS, E. C. *Stories of South America.* Richmond, Virginia: Johnson Publishing Co., 1922.

CARPENTER, FRANK G. *South America.* New York: American Book Company, 1921.

CLARK, MARION G., and GORDY, WILBUR F. *What Men From Europe Brought to America.* New York: Charles Scribner's Sons, 1929.

DAKIN, WILSON S. *Great Rivers of the World.* New York: The Macmillan Company, 1931.

DODGE, RICHARD ELWOOD, and LACKEY, EARL EMMETT. *Our Country and American Neighbors.* Chicago: Rand McNally & Company, 1932.

FRANCK, HARRY A. *South America.* Dansville, New York: F. A. Owen Publishing Company, 1928.

GUITTEAU, WILLIAM B., and WINTER, NEVIN O. *Seeing South America.* Evanston, Illinois: Row, Peterson and Company, 1929.

HUNTINGTON, ELLSWORTH; BENSON, C. BEVERLEY; and McMURRY, FRANK M. *Living Geography.* Book I. New York: The Macmillan Company, 1932.

HUNTINGTON, ELLSWORTH; BENSON, C. BEVERLEY; and McMURRY, FRANK M. *Living Geography.* Book II. New York: The Macmillan Company, 1932.

LEFFERTS, WALTER. *Our Neighbors in South America.* Philadelphia: J. B. Lippincott Company, 1927.

McNAB, ALLAN. *The Picture Book of Rivers.* New York: The Macmillan Company, 1932.

MEAD, CHARLES W. *Conventionalized Figures in Ancient Peruvian Art.* New York: The American Museum of Natural History, 1916.

MEAD, CHARLES W. *Old Civilizations of Inca Land.* New York: The American Museum of Natural History, 1932.

MEAD, CHARLES W. *Peruvian Art.* New York: The American Museum of Natural History, 1929.

PACKARD, LEONARD O., and SINNOTT, CHARLES P. *Nations as Neighbors.* New York: The Macmillan Company, 1925.

PACKARD, LEONARD O.; SINNOTT, CHARLES P., and OVERTON, BRUCE. *The Nations at Work.* New York: The Macmillan Company, 1933.

SALISBURY, ETHEL IMOGENE. *From Panama to Cape Horn.* Yonkers-on-Hudson, New York: World Book Company, 1927.

SMALLIDGE, OLIVE E., and PAXSON, FREDERIC L. *Finding America.* Boston: Houghton Mifflin Company, 1929.

WHITE, RUFUS AUSTIN. *South America Today.* Chicago: A. Flanagan Company, 1930.

STORY BOOKS

BROOKS, EVA CANNON. *Our Little Argentine Cousin.* Boston: The L. C. Page & Company, 1910.

COATSWORTH, ELIZABETH. *The Boy With the Parrot.* New York: The Macmillan Company, 1930.

EELLS, ELSIE SPICER. *Fairy Tales From Brazil.* New York: Dodd, Mead & Company, Inc., 1930.

EELLS, ELSIE SPICER. *The Magic Tooth.* Boston: Little, Brown and Company, 1930.

FERNALD, HELEN C., and SLOCOMBE, EDWIN M. *Scarlet Fringe.* New York: Longmans, Green and Co., 1932.

FINGER, CHARLES J. *Tales From Silver Lands.* Garden City, New York: Doubleday, Doran & Company, 1930.

HUDSON, W. H. *A Little Boy Lost.* New York: Alfred A. Knopf, 1931.

JEKYLL, GRACE B. *Two Boys in South American Jungles.* New York: E. P. Dutton & Co., Inc., 1929.

LAVARRE, WILLIAM J. *Up the Mazaruni for Diamonds.* Boston: Marshall Jones Company, 1922.

MALKUS, ALIDA SIMS. *A Fifth for the King.* New York: Harper & Brothers, 1931.

MILLER, LEO E. *Adrift on the Amazon.* New York: Charles Scribner's Sons, 1923.

MILLER, LEO E. *The Hidden People.* New York: Charles Scribner's Sons, 1925.

NIXON-ROULET, MARY F. *Our Little Brazilian Cousin.* Boston: The L. C. Page & Company, 1907.

OLCOTT, FRANCES JENKINS. *Good Stories for Great Birthdays.* Boston: Houghton Mifflin Company, 1922.

QUIROGA, HORACIO. *South American Jungle Tales.* New York: Duffield and Company, 1922.

TEE-VAN, HELEN. *Red Howling Monkey.* New York: The Macmillan Company, 1928.

THOMAS, MARGARET LORING. *Paulo in the Chilean Desert.* New York: The Junior Literary Guild and Bobbs-Merrill Company, 1934.

WIESE, KURT. *The Parrot Dealer.* New York: Coward, McCann & Company, 1932.

SPAIN AND PORTUGAL
Books for Pupils
REFERENCE BOOKS

ALLEN, NELLIE B. *New Europe.* Boston: Ginn and Company, 1920.

ALFAU, FELIPE. *Old Tales from Spain.* Garden City, New York: Doubleday, Doran & Company, 1929.

ATWOOD, WALLACE W., and THOMAS, H. G. *Nations Beyond the Seas.* Boston: Ginn and Company, 1930.

BARNARD, EUNICE F., and TALL, L. L. *How the Old World Found the New.* Boston: Ginn and Company, 1929.

BARROWS, H. H., PARKER, E. P., and PARKER, M. T. *Europe and Asia.* New York: Silver, Burdett and Company, 1930.

BROWNE, EDITH A. *Spain and Portugal.* New York: The Macmillan Company, 1921.

CARPENTER, FLORA L. *Stories Pictures Tell.* Book IV. Chicago: Rand McNally & Company, n. d.

CARPENTER, FLORA L. *Stories Pictures Tell.* Book VI. Chicago: Rand McNally & Company, n. d.

CARPENTER, FRANK G. *Europe.* New York: American Book Company, 1922.

Castles in Spain. Compiled by Bertha L. Gunterman. New York: Longmans, Green and Company, 1928.

CROMMELIN, EMELINE G. *Famous Legends.* New York: The Century Co., 1904.

GORDY, WILBUR F. *American Beginnings in Europe.* New York: Chas. Scribner's Sons, 1925.

HAAREN, JOHN H., and POLAND, A. B. *Famous Men of the Middle Ages.* New York: American Book Company, n. d.

HARDING, SAMUEL B., and HARDING, MARGARET. *Old World Background to American History.* Chicago: Scott, Foresman and Company, 1919.

HILLYER, VIRGIL M. *Child's Geography of the World.* New York: The Century Co., 1929.

HILLYER, VIRGIL M. *Child's History of the World.* New York: The Century Co., 1924.

LESTER, KATHERINE MORRIS. *Great Pictures and Their Stories.* Book I. New York: Mentzer, Bush & Company, 1927.

LESTER, KATHERINE MORRIS. *Great Pictures and Their Stories.* Book II. New York: Mentzer, Bush & Company, 1927.

LESTER, KATHERINE MORRIS. *Great Pictures and Their Stories.* Book IV. New York: Mentzer, Bush & Company, 1927.

MCFEE, INEZ NELLIE. *Boys and Girls of Many Lands.* New York: T. Y. Crowell Company, 1917.

MULETS, LENORE ELIZABETH. *Sunshine Lands of Europe.* Yonkers-on-Hudson, New York: World Book Company, 1918.

PACKARD, LEONARD O., and SINNOTT, C. P. *Nations as Neighbors.* New York: The Macmillan Company, 1925.

PECK, ANNE MERRIMAN. *Roundabout Europe.* New York: Harper and Brothers, 1931.

STUART, DOROTHY M. *Young Folk's Book of Other Lands.* Boston: Little, Brown and Company, 1927.

TAPPAN, EVA MARCH. *Old World Hero Stories.* Boston: Houghton Mifflin Company, 1911.

TERRY, ARTHUR GREY. *The Beginnings.* History Stories of Other Lands. Book III. Evanston, Illinois: Row, Peterson and Company, 1915.

WILLARD, MARY F. *Along Mediterranean Shores.* New York: Silver, Burdett and Company, 1914.

STORY BOOKS

BATES, KATHERINE L. *In Sunny Spain with Pilarica and Rafael.* New York: E. P. Dutton and Company. 1913.

BOLTON, IVY MAY. *Shadow of the Crown.* New York: Longmans, Green and Company, 1931.

BRANN, ESTHER. *Lupe Goes to School.* New York: The Macmillan Company, 1930.

CARPENTER, FRANCES. *Tales of a Basque Grandmother.* Garden City, New York: Doubleday, Doran & Company, 1930.

CERVANTES, SAAVEDRA M. *Don Quixote.* New York: Dodd, Mead & Company, Inc., 1929.

EL CID CAMPEADOR. *The Tale of the Warrior Lord.* New York: Longmans, Green and Company, 1930.

DUNHAM, EDITH. *Jogging Round the World.* New York: Frederick A. Stokes Company, 1905.

ELLS, ELSIE SPICER. *Tales of Enchantment from Spain.* New York: Harcourt, Brace & Company, 1920.

GREENE, FRANCES N., and KIRK, D. W. *With Spurs of Gold.* Boston: Little, Brown and Company, 1905.

HENDERSON, B. L. K., and CALVERT, C. V. *Wonder Tales of Ancient Spain.* New York: Frederick A. Stokes Company, 1925.

HEWES, AGNES D. *Spice and the Devil's Cave.* New York: Alfred A. Kopf, 1930.

IRVING, WASHINGTON. *Tales of the Alhambra.* Toronto: McClelland & Stewart, Ltd., n. d.

MUNTANER, RAMON. *Boys' Chronicle of Muntaner.* New York: D. Appleton and Company, 1926.

PERKINS, LUCY FITCH. *Spanish Twins.* Boston: Houghton Mifflin Company, 1934.

ROULET, MARY F. NIXON. *Our Little Spanish Cousin.* Boston: L. C. Page & Company, 1906.

SAWYER, RUTH. *Tono Antonio.* New York: The Viking Press, 1934.

WELLS, RHEA. *Coco the Goat.* Garden City, New York: Doubleday, Doran & Company, 1929.

WILDE, OSCAR. *Birthday of the Infanta.* New York: The Macmillan Company, 1929.

Books for Teachers

FRANCK, HARRY A. *Four Months Afoot in Spain.* New York: The Century Co., 1911.

PEIXOTTO, ERNEST C. *Through Spain and Portugal.* New York: Chas. Scribner's Sons, 1922.

SWITZERLAND

Books for Pupils

REFERENCE BOOKS

AITCHISON, ALISON E., and UTTLEY, MARGUERITE. *Across Seven Seas to Seven Continents.* Indianapolis: Bobbs-Merrill Company, 1931.

ALLEN, NELLIE B. *How and Where We Live.* Boston: Ginn and Company, 1924.

ALLEN, NELLIE B. *New Europe.* Boston: Ginn and Company, 1920.

ATWOOD, WALLACE W., and THOMAS, H. G. *Home Life in Far Away Lands.* Boston: Ginn and Company, 1928.

ATWOOD, WALLACE W. *Nations Beyond the Seas.* Boston: Ginn and Company, 1930.

BARROWS, H. H.; PARKER, E. P.; and PARKER, M. T. *Geography: Europe and Asia.* New York: Silver, Burdett and Company, 1927.

CARPENTER, FRANK G. *Around The World With The Children.* New York: American Book Company, 1917.

CARPENTER, FRANCES. *Our Neighbors Near and Far.* New York: American Book Company, 1933.

CARPENTER, FRANK G. *Europe.* New York: American Book Company, 1922.

CHAMBERLAIN, J. F., and CHAMBERLAIN, A. H. *Europe.* New York: The Macmillan Company, 1927.

FINNEMORE, JOHN. *Switzerland.* New York: The Macmillan Company, n. d.

HUNTINGTON, ELLSWORTH; BENSON, C. B.; and McMURRY, F. M. *Living Geography.* Book I. New York: The Macmillan Company, 1932.

HUNTINGTON, ELLSWORTH; BENSON, C. B.; and McMURRY, F. M. *Living Geography.* Book II. New York: The Macmillan Company, 1932.

LAUGHLIN, CLARA ELIZABETH. *Where It All Comes True in Italy and Switzerland.* Boston: Houghton Mifflin Company, 1928.

PACKARD, LEONARD OSCAR, and SINNOTT, C. P. *Nations as Neighbors.* New York: The Macmillan Company, 1925.

SCANTLEBURY, ELIZABETH ELLIS. *Little World Children.* Boston: Ginn and Company, 1928.

SMITH, JOSEPH RUSSELL. *World Folks.* Philadelphia: The John C. Winston Company, 1930.

STUART, DOROTHY M. *Young Folk's Book of Other Lands.* Boston: Little, Brown and Company, 1927.

THOMPSON, RUTH. *Type Stories of the World.* San Francisco: Harr Wagner Publishing Company, 1922.

THOMPSON, RUTH. *Our Neighbors Near and Far.* San Francisco: Harr Wagner Publishing Company, 1926.

WINSLOW, ISAAC OSCAR. *Europe.* Boston: D. C. Heath and Company, 1921.

STORY BOOKS

ADAMS, JULIA DAVIS. *Mountains are Free.* New York: E. P. Dutton and Co., 1930.

ANDREWS, JANE. *Seven Little Sisters.* Boston: Ginn and Company, 1924.

CREW, HELEN COALE. *Peter Swiss.* New York: Harper & Brothers, 1934.

KELLER, GOTTFRIED. *Fat of the Cat, and Other Stories.* New York: Harcourt, Brace & Company, 1925.

McGUCKIN, MILDRED CRISS. *Malou, a Little Swiss Girl.* Garden City, New York: Doubleday, Doran and Company, 1929.

MARSHALL, H. E. *Stories of William Tell and His Friends.* New York: E. P. Dutton and Company, 1907.

MORELEY, MARGARET WARNER. *Donkey John of the Toy Valley.* Chicago: A. C. McClurg & Co., 1909.

OLCOTT, VIRGINIA. *Anton and Trini.* New York: Silver, Burdett and Company, 1930.

PATTESON, SUSANNA LOUISE. *When I Was a Girl in Switzerland.* Boston: Lothrop, Lee & Shepard Company, 1921.

PERKINS, LUCY. *Swiss Twins.* Boston: Houghton Mifflin Company, 1922.

SPYRI, JOHANNA. *Heidi.* New York: A. L. Burt Company, Inc., 1932.

SPYRI, JOHANNA. *Moni.* Boston: D. C. Heath and Company, 1897.

TIME

Books for Pupils
REFERENCE BOOKS

ABBOT, CHARLES GREELEY. *Everyday Mysteries.* New York: The Macmillan Company, 1923.

BAILEY, ROY RUTHERFORD. *Through the Ages With Father Time.* Evanston, Illinois: The Author, 1922.

BASSETT, SARA WARE. *Christopher and the Clockmakers.* Boston: Little, Brown and Company, 1925.

BOYLE, MARGARET P. *Calendar Stories.* Chicago: A. Flanagan Co., 1900.

BREARLEY, HARRY CHASE. *Time Telling Through the Ages.* Garden City, New York: Doubleday, Page & Company, 1919.

BRIDGES, T. C. *The Young Folk's Book of Invention.* Boston: Little, Brown and Company, 1929.

BROWN, ELIZABETH V. *When the World Was Young.* Yonkers-on-Hudson, New York: World Book Company, 1918.

BRYANT, LORINDA MUNSON. *The Children's Book of Celebrated Towers.* New York: The Century Co., 1926.

BUSH, BERTHA E. *Stories of Time.* Dansville, New York: F. A. Owen Publishing Company, 1913.

CALDWELL, OTIS W., and MEIER, W. H. D. *Open Doors to Science.* Boston: Ginn and Company, 1925.

CHASE, A., and CLOW, E. *Stories of Industry.* Vol. 1. Boston: Educational Publishing Company, 1915.

CLARK, ELIOT C. *Astronomy from a Dipper.* Boston: Houghton Mifflin Company. 1909.

COLEMAN, SATIS N. *Bells.* Chicago: Rand McNally & Company, 1928.

COLLINS, ARCHIE FREDERICK. Book of Stars. New York: D. Appleton and Company, 1920.

DUPUY, WILLIAM ATHERTON. *Odd Jobs of Uncle Sam.* Boston: D. C. Heath and Company, 1927.

EARLE, ALICE MORSE. *Old Time Gardens.* New York: The Macmillan Company, 1922.

EARLE, ALICE MORSE. *Sundials and Roses of Yesterday.* New York: The Macmillan Company, 1922.

GORDON, BERTHA F. *Prove It Yourself.* Dansville, New York: F. A. Owen Publishing Company, 1928.

HALLECK, REUBEN POST, and FRANTZ, JULIETTE. *Our Nation's Heritage.* New York: American Book Company, 1925.

ILIN, M. *What Time Is It?* Philadelphia: J. B. Lippincott Company, 1932.

JOHNSON, GAYLORD. *The Star People.* New York: The Macmillan Company, 1928.

KINNEY, MURIEL. *Stars and Their Stories.* New York: D. Appleton and Company, 1926.

KINSCELLA, HAZEL GERTRUDE. *Conrad's Magic Flight.* Lincoln, Nebraska: The University Publishing Company, 1930.

KINSCELLA, HAZEL GERTRUDE. *Kinscella Music Appreciation Readers.* Book II. Lincoln, Nebraska: The University Publishing Company, 1928.

KINSCELLA, HAZEL GERTRUDE. *Kinscella Music Appreciation Readers.* Book III. Lincoln, Nebraska: The University Publishing Company, 1928.

KINSCELLA, HAZEL GERTRUDE. *Storyland.* Lincoln, Nebraska: The University Publishing Company, 1930.

KINSCELLA, HAZEL GERTRUDE. *Tales of Olden Days.* Lincoln, Nebraska: The University Publishing Company, 1930.

KUMMER, FREDERIC ARNOLD. *The First Days of Knowledge.* Garden City, New York: Doubleday, Doran & Company, 1929.

LANSING, MARION FLORENCE. *Great Moments in Science.* Garden City, New York: Doubleday, Doran & Company, 1931.

MARTIN, MARTHA EVANS. *The Friendly Stars.* New York: Harper & Brothers, 1907.

MARTIN, MARTHA EVANS. *The Ways of the Planets.* New York: Harper & Brothers, 1912.

MCFEE, INEZ. *The World About Us.* Philadelphia: Macrae Smith Company, 1931.

MCKAY, HERBERT. *Sound and Noise.* London: Oxford University Press, n.d.

MCKAY, HERBERT. *Sun and the Moon.* London: Oxford University Press, n.d.

MILLS, DOROTHY. *The Book of the Ancient World for Younger Readers.* New York: G. P. Putnam's Sons, 1923.

OLCOTT, WILLIAM TYLER. *The Book of Stars for Young People.* New York: G. P. Putnam's Sons, 1923.

PROCTOR, MARY. *The Young Folk's Book of the Heavens.* Boston: Little, Brown and Company, 1926.

QUENNELL, MARJORIE, and C. H. B. *Everyday Life in the New Stone, Bronze and Early Iron Ages.* New York: G. P. Putnam's Sons, 1923.

RUSH, CHARLES E., and WINSLOW, AMY. *The Science of Things About Us.* Boston: Little, Brown and Company, 1926.

ST. NICHOLAS. *Travel Stories.* New York: The Century Co., 1920.

SMITH, EDITH LILLIAN. *Everyday Science Projects.* Boston: Houghton Mifflin Company, 1925.

STONE, GERTRUDE L., and FICKETT, M. GRACE. *Everyday Life in the Colonies.* Boston: D. C. Heath & Co., 1905.

TAPPAN, EVA MARCH. *Makers of Many Things.* Boston: Houghton Mifflin Company, 1929.

Telling Time Throughout the Centuries. Achievements of Civilization Number 5. Prepared under the auspices of the Committee on Materials of Instruction of the American Council on Education. Washington: American Council on Education, 1933.

The Story of Our Calendar. Achievements of Civilization Number 4. Prepared under the auspices of the Committee on Materials of Instruction of the American Council on Education. Washington: American Council on Education, 1933.

WELLS, MARGARET E. *How the Present Came From the Past.* Book One. New York: The Macmillan Company, 1932.

WELLS, MARGARET E. *How the Present Came From the Past.* Book Two. New York: The Macmillan Company, 1932.

STORY BOOKS

BARRINGER, MARIE. *Martin the Goose Boy.* Garden City, New York: Doubleday, Doran & Company, 1932.

MOLESWORTH, MARY LOUISE. *The Cuckoo Clock and the Tapestry Room.* New York: The Macmillan Company, 1925.

NEUMANN, DAISY. *Sperli, the Clockmaker.* New York: The Macmillan Company, 1932.

OLCOTT, VIRGINIA. *Anton and Trini.* New York: Silver, Burdett and Company, 1930.

PERKINS, LUCY FITCH. *The Swiss Twins.* Boston: Houghton Mifflin Company, 1922.

ROLT-WHEELER, FRANCIS. *The Boy With the U. S. Inventors.* Boston: Lothrop, Lee & Shepard Co., 1920.

STOCKTON, FRANK R. *Fanciful Tales.* New York: Charles Scribner's Sons, 1894.

Books for Teachers

TIPPETT, JAMES S., and OTHERS. *Curriculum Making in an Elementary School.* Boston: Ginn and Company, 1927.

SLOSSON, EDWIN E. *Keeping Up With Science.* New York: Harcourt, Brace and Company, 1925.

TRANSPORTATION

Books for Pupils

REFERENCE BOOKS

AITCHISON, ALISON E., and UTTLEY, MARGUERITE. *North America by Plane and Train.* Indianapolis: Bobbs-Merrill Company, 1931.

BRADLEY, GLENN DANFORD. *Story of the Pony Express.* Chicago: A. C. McClurg & Co., 1913.

BUSH, MAYBELL G., and WADDELL, JOHN F. *How We Have Conquered Distance.* New York: The Macmillan Company, 1934.

CARPENTER, FRANCES. *Ways We Travel.* New York: American Book Company, 1929.

CHAMBERLAIN, J. F. *How We Travel.* New York: The Macmillan Company. n.d.

COLLINS, FRANCIS ARNOLD. *Boys' Book of Model Aeroplanes.* New York: The Century Co., 1929.

CRAIG, GERALD S., and JOHNSON, GOLDIE M. *Our Earth and Its Story.* Boston: Ginn and Company, 1932.

CRUMP, IRVING. *Boys' Book of Airmen.* New York: Dodd, Mead & Company, Inc., 1927.

CRUMP, IRVING. *Boys' Book of the United States Mails.* New York: Dodd, Mead & Company, Inc., 1926.

DUKELOW, JEAN H., and WEBSTER, HANSON HART. *The Ship Book.* Boston: Houghton Mifflin Company, 1931.

EARLE, ALICE MORSE. *Stage Coach and Tavern Days.* New York: The Macmillan Company, 1900.

EATON, JEANETTE. *Story of Transportation.* New York: Harper and Brothers, 1927.

EVANS, ERNESTINE. *Story of the Harbor.* New York: Harper and Brothers, 1928.

FLOHERTY, JOHN J. *'Board the Airliner.* Garden City, New York: The Junior Literary Guild and Doubleday, Doran and Company, 1934.

FOX, F. C. *How the World Rides.* New York: Chas. Scribner's Sons, 1929.

GRANT, GORDON. *Story of the Ship.* Springfield, Mass.: McLoughlin Bros., Inc., 1931.

GREEN, ELMER. *Pathfinders by Land and Sea.* Yonkers-on-Hudson, New York: World Book Company, 1932.

HADER, BERTA and ELMER. *The Picture Book of Travel.* New York: The Macmillan Company, 1928.

HEADLEY, EDIA A. *How Other People Travel.* Chicago: Rand McNally and Company, 1926.

HOLLAND, RUPERT S. *Historic Inventions.* Philadelphia: Macrae Smith Co., 1911.

HOLLAND, RUPERT S. *Historic Railroads.* Philadelphia: Macrae Smith Co., 1927.

HOLLAND, RUPERT S. *Historic Ships.* Philadelphia: Macrae Smith Co., 1926.

JONES, PAUL. *Alphabet of Aviation.* Philadelphia: Macrae Smith Co., 1928.

KEIR, ROBERT MALCOLM. *Pageant of America.* Vol. 4, Pt. 6, 7. New Haven: Yale University Press.

LENT, HENRY B. *Full Steam Ahead!* New York: The Macmillan Company, 1934.

LENT, HENRY B. *Wide Road Ahead!* New York: The Macmillan Company, 1934.

MEEKER, EZRA. *Ox Team Days on the Oregon Trail.* Yonkers-on-Hudson, New York: World Book Company, 1922.

METHLEY, ALICE A. *How the World Travels.* New York: Frederick A. Stokes Company, 1922.

MILLER, JOAQUIN. *Overland in a Covered Wagon.* New York: D. Appleton and Company, 1930.

MITCHELL, LUCY SPRAGUE. *North America.* New York: The Macmillan Company, 1931.

MORROW, HONORÉ WILLSIE. *On to Oregon!* New York: William Morrow Co., Inc., 1926.

NATHAN, ADELE G., and ERNEST, MARGARET. *Iron Horse.* New York: Alfred A. Knopf, 1931.

NIDA, WILLIAM LEWIS. *Following the Frontier.* New York: The Macmillan Company, 1924.

PETERSHAM, MAUD, and PETERSHAM, MISKA. *The Story Book of Transportation.* Philadelphia: The John C. Winston Company, 1933.

PRYOR, WILLIAM CLAYTON. *The Airplane Book.* New York: Harcourt Brace and Company, 1935.

PRYOR, WILLIAM CLAYTON. *The Steam Ship Book.* New York: Harcourt, Brace and Company, 1934.

PRYOR, WILLIAM CLAYTON. *The Train Book.* New York: Harcourt, Brace and Company, 1933.

ROMER, ANDREW RALPH. *Sky Travel.* Chicago: Rand McNally & Company, 1930.

RUGG, HAROLD O. *Introduction to American Civilization.* Boston: Ginn and Company, 1929.

RUSH, CHARLES EVERETT, and WINSLOW, AMY. *Science of Things About Us.* Boston: Little, Brown and Company, 1927.

SABIN, EDWIN LEGRAND. *Buffalo Bill and the Overland Trail.* Chicago: J. B. Lippincott Company, 1914.

SMALLIDGE, OLIVE E., and PAXSON, F. L. *Finding America*. Boston: Houghton Mifflin Company, 1929.

STEPHENSON, MARY BOWEN. *Wheel, Sail and Wing*. Chicago: Thomas S. Rockwell Company, 1930.

TAPPAN, EVA MARCH. *Travelers and Traveling*. Boston: Houghton Mifflin Company, 1930.

THOMAS, JAY EARLE. *Aviation Stories*. New York: Longmans, Green and Company, 1929.

VAN METRE, THURMAN WILLIAM. *Trains, Tracks, and Travel*. New York: Simmons-Boardman Publishing Company, 1931.

VAN METRE, THURMAN WILLIAM. *Tramps and Liners*. Garden City, New York: Doubleday, Doran & Company, 1931.

WALDEN, ARTHUR TREADWELL. *Harness and Pack*. New York: American Book Company, 1935.

WEBSTER, HANSON HART. *Travel by Air, Land and Sea*. Boston: Houghton, Mifflin Company, 1933.

STORY BOOKS

DALGLIESH, ALICE. *American Travels*. New York: The Macmillan Company, 1934.

HOUGH, EMERSON. *Covered Wagon*. New York: D. Appleton and Company, 1926.

KUH, CHARLOTTE. *A Train, a Boat and an Island*. New York: The Macmillan Company, 1932.

LENT, HENRY BOLLES. *Clear Track Ahead*. New York: The Macmillan Company, 1932.

PARKMAN, FRANCIS. *Boys' Parkman*. Boston: Little, Brown and Company, 1912.

Books for Teachers

MEIGS, CORNELIA LYNDE. *Willow Whistle*. New York: The Macmillan Company, 1931.

UNITED STATES

Books for Pupils

REFERENCE BOOKS

AITCHISON, ALISON E., and UTTLEY, MARGUERITE. *North America by Plane and Train*. Indianapolis: The Bobbs-Merrill Company, 1931.

ALLEN, NELLIE B. *United States*. Boston: Ginn and Company, 1925.

ALLEN, NELLIE B. *North America*. Boston: Ginn and Company, 1922.

ATWOOD, WALLACE W., and THOMAS, H. G. *The Americas*. Boston: Ginn and Company, 1929.

ATWOOD, WALLACE W. *United States Among the Nations*. Boston: Ginn and Company, 1930.

ATWOOD, WALLACE W. *The World at Work*. Boston: Ginn and Company, 1931.

BAILEY, CAROLYN SHERWIN. *Boys and Girls of Colonial Days*. Chicago: A. Flanagan Company, 1917.

BALDWIN, JAMES. *Four Great Americans*. New York: American Book Company, 1897.

BARKER, EUGENE CAMPBELL AND OTHER. *Story of Our Nation*. Evanston, Illinois: Row, Peterson and Company, 1929.

BARROWS, H. H., and PARKER, E. P. *Geography: United States and Canada*. New York: Silver, Burdett and Company, 1925.

BASS, FLORENCE. *Stories of Early Times in the Great West*. Indianapolis: Bobbs-Merrill Company, 1927.

BASS, FLORENCE. *Stories of Pioneer Life*. Boston: D. C. Heath and Company, 1928.

BEEBY, DANIEL J., and BEEBY, DOROTHEA. *How the World Grows Smaller*. New York: Charles E. Merrill Company, 1924.

BENET, ROSEMARY, and BENET, STEPHEN VINCENT. *A Book of Americans.* New York: Farrar and Rinehart, Inc., 1933.

BRIDGES, T. C. *Young Folks' Book of Inventions.* Boston: Little, Brown and Company, 1926.

BROOKS, ELBRIDGE S. *The True Story of George Washington.* Boston: Lothrop, Lee & Shepard Company, 1895.

CARPENTER, FRANK G. *North America.* New York: American Book Company, 1922.

CARPENTER, FRANCES. *Ourselves and Our City.* New York: American Book Company, 1928.

CHAMBERLAIN, J. F., and CHAMBERLAIN, A. H. *North America.* New York: The Macmillan Company, 1927.

CLARK, MARION G., and GORDY, WILBUR F. *First 300 Years in America.* New York: Chas. Scribner's Sons, 1931.

CLARK, MARION G. *Westward to the Pacific.* New York: Chas. Scribner's Sons, 1932.

DAKIN, WILSON S. *Great Rivers of the World.* New York: The Macmillan Company, 1927.

DARROW, FLOYD LAVERN. *Thinkers and Doers.* New York: Silver, Burdett and Company, 1925.

DEARBORN, FRANCES ROSS. *How the Indians Lived.* Boston: Ginn & Company, 1927.

EARLE, ALICE MORSE. *Home Life in Colonial Days.* New York: The Macmillan Company, 1898.

EGGLESTON, EDWARD. *Stories of Great Americans.* New York: American Book Company, 1895.

FAIRBANKS, HAROLD W. *Southern California, the Land and Its People.* San Francisco: Harr Wagner Publishing Company, 1929.

FAIRGRIEVE, JAMES, and YOUNG, ERNEST. *United States.* Human Geography by Grades. Book IV. New York: D. Appleton and Company, 1925.

FIELD, RACHEL. *American Folk and Fairy Tales.* New York: Junior Literary Guild, Inc., 1929.

FISHER, ELIZABETH FLORETTE. *Resources and Industries of the United States.* Boston: Ginn and Company, 1928.

FLOHERTY, JOHN J. *Fire Fighters!* Garden City, New York: Doubleday, Doran & Company, 1933.

GORDY, WILBUR F. *How the Colonies Grew Into States.* New York: Chas. Scribner's Sons, 1929.

GROSVENOR, GILBERT. *Washington Through the Years.* Washington: National Geographic Society, 1931.

HARTMAN, GERTRUDE. *These United States and How They Came to Be.* New York: The Macmillan Company, 1932.

HARTMAN, GERTRUDE. *World We Live In.* New York: The Macmillan Company, 1931.

HEARD, SARAH DOW, and KING, M. W. *Stories of American Pioneers.* Philadelphia: The John C. Winston Company, 1929.

HILL, LAURANCE L. *La Reina, Los Angeles in Three Centuries.* Los Angeles: Security First National Bank, 1929.

HILLYER, VIRGIL M. *Child's Geography of the World.* New York: The Century Co., 1929.

HINES, LEWIS. *Men at Work.* New York: The Macmillan Company, 1932.

HOTCHKISS, CAROLINE W. *Representative Cities of the United States.* Boston: Houghton Mifflin Company, 1913.

HUNT, ROCKWELL DENNIS. *New California The Golden.* New York: Silver Burdett and Company, 1933.

HUNTINGTON, ELLSWORTH; BENSON, C. B.; and McMURRY, F. M. *Living Geography.* Book I. New York: The Macmillan Company, 1932.

HUNTINGTON, ELLSWORTH; BENSON, C. B.; and McMURRY, F. M. *Living Geography*. Book II. New York: The Macmillan Company, 1932.

HUNTINGTON, ELLSWORTH, and CUSHING, S. W. *Modern Business Geography*. Yonkers-on-Hudson, New York: World Book Company, 1932.

KATES, HERBERT S. *Minute Glimpses of Great Cities*. New York: Grosset & Dunlap, 1933.

KELTY, MARY G. *Growth of the American People and Nation*. Boston: Ginn and Company, 1931.

LAMPREY, L. *All the Ways of Building*. New York: The Macmillan Company, 1933.

LATIMER, LOUISE P. *Your Washington and Mine*. New York: Chas. Scribner's Sons, 1924.

LEFFERTS, WALTER. *Our Own United States*. Chicago: J. B. Lippincott Company, 1925.

LENT, HENRY. *Diggers and Builders*. New York: The Macmillan Company, 1933.

McCONNELL, W. R. *Living in the Americas*. Chicago: Rand McNally and Company, 1934.

McFEE, INEZ NELLIE. *World About Us*. Philadelphia: Macrae Smith Co., 1931.

MITCHELL, LUCY. *North America*. New York: The Macmillan Company, 1931.

MORGAN, ALFRED. *The Story of Skyscrapers*. New York: Farrar and Rinehart, Inc., 1934.

NAUMBERG, ELSA H.; LAMBERT, CLARA; and MITCHELL, LUCY SPRAGUE. *Skyscraper*. New York: The Junior Literary Guild and The John Day Company, 1934.

NIDA, WILLIAM LEWIS, and WEBB, V. L. *Our Country Past and Present*. Chicago: Scott, Foresman and Company, 1930.

PACKARD, LEONARD O., and SINNOTT, C. P. *Nations as Neighbors*. Revised Edition. New York: The Macmillan Company, 1931.

PACKARD, LEONARD O., SINNOTT, C. P., and OVERTON, BRUCE. *The Nations at Work*. New York: The Macmillan Company, 1933.

PALMER, WINTHROP B. *American Songs for Children*. New York: The Macmillan Company, 1931.

PEARDON, CELESTE, and COMEGYS, Z. DE M. *Adventures in a Big City*. New York: The Macmillan Company, 1931.

PECK, ANNE MERRIMAN, and JOHNSON, ENID. *Roundabout America*. New York: The Junior Literary Guild and Harper & Brothers, 1933.

PRYOR, WILLIAM CLAYTON. *The Fire Engine Book*. New York: Harcourt, Brace and Company, 1934.

PUMPHREY, MARGARET BLANCHE. *Stories of the Pilgrims*. Chicago: Rand McNally & Company, 1912.

QUINN, VERNON. *Picture Map Geography of the United States*. New York: Frederick A. Stokes Company, 1932.

SMITH, JOSEPH RUSSELL. *Home Folks*. Philadelphia: The John C. Winston Publishing Company, 1930.

SOUTHWORTH, GERTRUDE, and KRAMER, S. E. *Great Cities of the United States*. Syracuse, New York: Iroquois Publishing Company, 1922.

STEVENSON, BURTON. *American History in Verse*. Boston: Houghton Mifflin Company, 1932.

STULL, DE FOREST, and HATCH, ROY W. *Our World Today*. Boston: Allyn and Bacon, 1931.

WINSLOW, ISAAC OSCAR. *The United States*. Boston: D. C. Heath and Company, 1921.

YARD, ROBERT STERLING. *Book of the National Parks*. New York: Chas. Scribner's Sons, 1928.

STORY BOOKS

BENNETT, JOHN. *Barnaby Lee.* New York: The Century Co., 1902.

CODY, WILLIAM FREDERICK. *Adventures of Buffalo Bill.* New York: Harper and Brothers, n. d.

CURTIS, ALICE. *Little Maid of Massachusetts Colony.* Little Maid's Historical Stories. Philadelphia: Penn Publishing Company, 1913-1925.

HOLLAND, RUPERT SARGENT. *Sons of Seven Cities.* Philadelphia: Macrae Smith Company, 1929.

KALER, JAMES OTIS. *Ruth of Boston.* New York: American Book Company, 1910.

KALER, JAMES OTIS. *Stephen of Philadelphia.* New York: American Book Company, 1910.

LEETCH, DOROTHY L. *Annetje and Her Family.* Boston: Lothrop, Lee & Shepard Company, 1926.

NIDA, STELLA H. *Letters of Polly the Pioneer.* New York: The Macmillan Company, 1916.

Books for Teachers

HAWTHORNE, HILDEGARDE. *New York.* Peeps at Cities. New York: The Macmillan Company, 1911.

HOTCHKISS, CAROLINE W. *Representative Cities of the United States.* Boston: Houghton Mifflin Company, 1913.

JOHNSTON, CLIFTON. *What to See in America.* New York: The Macmillan Company, 1925.

VIKINGS

Books for Pupils

REFERENCE BOOKS

ALLEN, NELLIE B. *The New Europe.* Boston: Ginn and Company, 1920.

BARROWS, H. H.; PARKER, E. P.; and PARKER, M. T. *Europe and Asia.* New York: Silver, Burdett and Company, 1930.

BRIDGES, T. C., and TILTMAN, H. H. *Heroes of Modern Adventure.* Boston: Little, Brown and Company, 1927.

CLARK, MARION G., and GORDY, WILBUR F. *Early Story of Mankind.* New York: Chas. Scribner's Sons, 1929.

HALL, JENNIE. *Viking Tales.* Chicago: Rand McNally & Company, 1902.

Heroes of Iceland. Edited by A. French. Translated by Sir George Webbe Dasent. Boston: Little, Brown and Company, 1905.

HOLBROOK, FLORENCE. *Northland Heroes.* Boston: Houghton Mifflin Company, 1905.

HOLLAND, RUPERT S. *Historic Ships.* Philadelphia: Macrae Smith Co., 1926.

JUDD, ALFRED. *Conquest of the Poles.* New York: Thomas Nelson & Sons, 1924.

KEARY, ANNIE, and KEARY, ELIZA. *Heroes of Asgard.* New York: The Macmillan Company, 1924.

LANSING, MARION FLORENCE. *Great Moments in Exploration.* Garden City, New York: Doubleday, Doran & Company, 1928.

PACKARD, LEONARD O., and SINNOTT, C. P. *Nations as Neighbors.* New York: The Macmillan Company, 1925.

QUENNELL, MARJORIE, and QUENNELL, C. H. B. *Everyday Life in Anglo-Saxon, Viking, and Norman Times.* New York: G. P. Putnam's Sons, 1927.

SMALLIDGE, OLIVE E., and PAXSON, F. L. *Finding America.* Boston: Houghton Mifflin Company, 1929.

TERRY, ARTHUR GREY. *The Beginnings.* History Stories of Other Lands. Book III. Evanston, Illinois: Row, Peterson and Company, 1925.

WILMOT-BUXTON, ETHEL M. *Stories of Norse Heroes.* New York: T. Y. Crowell Company, 1909.

STORY BOOKS

BALDWIN, JAMES. *Story of Siegfried.* New York: Chas. Scribner's Sons, 1888.

BORUP, GEORGE. *Tenderfoot with Peary.* New York: Frederick A. Stokes Company, 1911.

BROWN, ABBIE FARWELL. *In the Days of Giants.* Boston: Houghton Mifflin Company, 1902.

BULFINCH, THOMAS. *Golden Age of Myth and Legend.* New York: Frederick A. Stokes Company, 1915.

BURGLON, NORA. *Children of the Soil.* Garden City, New York: Junior Literary Guild and Doubleday, Doran and Company, 1933.

COLUM, PADRAIC. *Children of Odin.* New York: The Macmillan Company, 1926.

FRENCH, ALLEN. *Story of Rolf and the Viking's Bow.* Boston: Little, Brown and Company, 1924.

FRENCH, ALLEN. *Story of Grettir the Strong.* New York: E. P. Dutton and Company, 1908.

GREEN, FITZHUGH. *Dick Byrd, Air Explorer.* New York: G. P. Putnam's Sons, 1928.

GUERBER, HELENE ADELINE. *Myths of Northern Lands.* New York: American Book Company, n. d.

HANSON, LIDA SIBONI. *Eric the Red.* Garden City, New York: Doubleday, Doran and Company, 1934.

HARSHAW, RUTH. *Reindeer of the Waves.* Chicago: The Junior Literary Guild and Rand McNally and Company, 1934.

HOSFORD, DOROTHY G. *Sons of the Volsungs.* New York: The Macmillan Company, 1932.

JOHNSTON, CHARLES H. *Our Little Viking Cousin of Long Ago.* Boston: L. C. Page & Company, 1916.

LEIGHTON, ROBERT. *Olaf, the Glorious.* New York: The Macmillan Company, 1929.

MABIE, HAMILTON W. *Norse Stories Retold from the Edas.* New York: Dodd, Mead & Company, Inc., 1901.

PERKINS, LUCY FITCH. *The Norwegian Twins.* Boston: Houghton Mifflin Company, 1933.

SCHRAM, FRU CONSTANCE WIEL. *Olaf, Lofoten Fisherman.* New York: Longmans, Green and Company, 1929.

SNEDDEN, GENEVRA. *Leif and Thorkel.* Yonkers-on-Hudson, New York: World Book Company, 1922.

ZWILGMEYER, DIKKEN. *Johnny Blossom.* Boston: The Pilgrim Press, 1912.

ZWILGMEYER, DIKKEN. *What Happened to Inger Johanne.* Boston: Lothrop, Lee and Shepard Company, 1919.

WEATHER

Books for Pupils

REFERENCE BOOKS

ADAMS, JOSEPH H. *Harper's Outdoor Book for Boys.* New York: Harper and Brothers, 1908.

BARNEY, MAGINEL. *Weather, Signs and Rhymes.* New York: Alfred A. Knopf, 1931.

BROOKS, CHARLES FRANKLIN. *Why the Weather?* New York: Harcourt, Brace & Company, 1924.

CALDWELL, OTIS WILLIAM, and MEIER, W. H. *Open Door to Science.* Boston: Ginn and Company, 1926.

CRAIG, GERALD S., and HURLEY, BEATRICE DAVIS. *The Earth and Living Things.* Boston: Ginn and Company, 1932.

CRAIG, GERALD S., and BALDWIN, SARA E. *Our Wide, Wide World.* Boston: Ginn and Company, 1932.

CRAIG, GERALD S., and BALDWIN, SARA E. *Out of Doors.* Boston: Ginn and Company, 1932.

CRAIG, GERALD S., and BURKE, AGNES. *We Look About Us.* Boston: Ginn and Company, 1932.

CURTIS, MARY ISABEL. *Stories in Trees.* Chicago: Lyons and Carnahan, 1925.

DUVAL, ELIZABETH W. *This Earth We Live In.* New York: Frederick A. Stokes Company, 1927.

GORDON, BERTHA FRANCES. *Prove It Yourself.* Dansville, New York: F. A. Owen Publishing Company, 1929.

HARRINGTON, MARK W. *About the Weather.* New York: D. Appleton and Company, 1907.

HAZELTINE, KARL, and OTHERS. *Weather.* Science Guide for Elementary Schools. I (December, 1934). Sacramento, California: California State Department of Education.

HEILE, MARYANNA. *World's Moods.* New York: Oxford University Press, 1927.

HOLWAY, HOPE. *Story of Water Supply.* New York: Harper and Brothers, 1929.

KINSEY, DON JACKSON. *River of Destiny.* 207 South Broadway, Los Angeles: Department of Water and Power, 1928.

KINSEY, DON JACKSON. *Romance of Water and Power.* 207 South Broadway, Los Angeles: Department of Water and Power, 1926.

McKAY, HERBERT. *Air and the Wind.* First Steps in Science. Book IV. New York: Oxford University Press, 1929.

MUSSET, PAUL DE. *Mr. Wind and Madame Rain.* Glasgow: Blackie & Son, 1929.

Outline of Science. Edited by John Arthur Thompson. New York: G. P. Putnam's Sons, n. d.

PIEPER, CHARLES J., and BEAUCHAMP, W. L. *Everyday Problems in Science.* Chicago: Scott, Foresman and Company, 1925.

ROLT-WHEELER, FRANCIS WILLIAM. *Boy With the United States Weather Man.* Boston: Lothrop, Lee & Shepard Company, 1917.

SMITH, EDITH LILLIAN. *Everyday Science Projects.* Boston: Houghton Mifflin Company, 1925.

TAPPAN, EVA MARCH. *Wonders of Science.* Boston: Houghton Mifflin Company, 1927.

TRAFTON, GILBERT HAVEN. *Nature Study and Science for Intermediate Grades.* New York: The Macmillan Company, 1927.

TOWER, SAMUEL FRANCIS, and LUNT, J. R. *Science of Common Things.* Boston: D. C. Heath and Company, 1922.

VAN BUSKIRK, EDGAR FLANDREAU; SMITH, E. L., and NOURSE, W. L. *Science of Everyday Life.* Boston: Houghton Mifflin Company, 1931.

BIBLIOGRAPHY ON RECREATORY READING [1]

THIRD AND FOURTH GRADES

ADAMS, S. W. *Five Little Friends.* New York: The Macmillan Company, 1922.
About the good time that five children had at school, on the farm, and at the seashore.

AESOP. *Fables.* Selected by J. Jacobs. New York: The Macmillan Company, 1914.
A particularly satisfactory selection of eighty-two of the fables which are most interesting to children.

ALCOTT, LOUISA MAY. *Under the Lilacs.* Boston: Little, Brown and Company, 1928.
A story about a boy from a circus who finds friends for himself and his clever dog.

ALDIS, DOROTHY. *Everything and Anything.* New York: Minton, Balch & Company, 1927.
Gay little verses about happy children.

ANDERSEN, HANS C. *Fairy Tales.* Edited by J. H. Stickney. 2v. Boston: Ginn and Company, 1914.
The first volume of this edition contains twenty stories for younger readers, while the thirty tales in the second volume are for older readers.

ASBJÖRNSEN, P. C., and MOE, J. E. *East o' the Sun and West o' the Moon.* Translated by Gudrun Thorne-Thomsen. Evanston, Illinois: Row, Peterson and Company, 1912.
Twenty-two beautifully told Norwegian folk tales.

AULNOY, M. C. J. DE B., COMTESSE D'. *Children's Fairyland.* New York: Henry Holt & Company, 1919.
Not only excellent fairy stories but also a vivid picture of 17th century France.

BABBITT, E. C. *Jataka Tales.* New York: The Century Co., 1912.
Simple fables, chiefly about animals, retold from one of the sacred books of the East.

BACON, PEGGY. *Lion-hearted Kitten.* New York: The Macmillan Company, 1927.
Among these droll stories of animals, large and small, are tales of a brave kitten, a baby elephant, a lost zebra and a nightingale.

BAILEY, MARGERY. *Seven Peas in the Pod.* Boston: Little, Brown and Company, 1919.
Seven quaint fairy tales, one for each day in the week.

BAKER, MARGARET. *Black Cats and the Tinker's Wife.* New York: Duffield & Green, Inc., 1923.
How the wish of a tinker's wife broke the spell of a wicked witch and changed the black cats into what they ought to be.

---

[1] Prepared by Marion Horton, Traveling Librarian, Los Angeles Public Schools, under the direction of Jasmine Britton, Supervising Librarian, Los Angeles Public Schools.

The illustrations used in the following pages originally appeared in the books opposite or immediately following which they are here placed. The courtesy of the following publishers in loaning the engravings for these illustrations is gratefully acknowledged: E. P. Dutton and Company; Ginn and Company; Houghton, Mifflin Company; Little, Brown and Company; Longmans, Green & Company; Lothrop, Lee & Shepard Company; The Macmillan Company; Penn Publishing Company; and Charles Scribner's Sons.

BAKER, MARGARET. *Little Girl Who Curtsied.* New York: Duffield & Green, Inc., 1925.

This is the story of a little girl who never forgot to be polite. She always said "Good morning" and curtsied politely and did a kind deed whenever she could.

BALDWIN, JAMES. *Fairy Stories and Fables.* New York: American Book Company, 1895.

Folk tales very simply told.

BALDWIN, JAMES. *Fifty Famous Stories Retold.* New York: American Book Company, 1924.

This collection of legends and historical tales includes many old favorites.

BANNERMAN, HELEN. *Story of Little Black Sambo.* New York: Frederick A. Stokes Company, n.d.

Universally popular is this humorous account of a little black boy's adventure with a tiger in the jungle.

BARRIE, SIR JAMES. *Peter Pan and Wendy.* Edited by May Byron. New York: Charles Scribner's Sons, 1926.

The story of a boy who never grew up.

BARROWS, MARJORIE. *One Hundred Best Poems for Boys and Girls.* Racine, Wisconsin: Whitman Publishing Company, 1930.

Children like to buy this book for themselves at the ten cent store.

BERTELLI, LUIGI. *Prince and His Ants.* New York: Henry Holt & Company, 1910.

When a little boy wishes he could be an ant to escape studying his lessons, he is suddenly turned into a big black ant, and learns many things about the insects around him.

BESKOW, E. M. *Aunt Green, Aunt Brown and Aunt Lavender.* New York: Harper and Brothers, 1928.

A delightful picture book telling of three aunts, Aunt Green who always wore a green dress, Aunt Brown who always wore a brown dress, and Aunt Lavender who always wore a lavender dress, just as surely as dandelions are yellow and bluebells are blue.

BESKOW, E. M. *Buddy's Adventures in the Blueberry Patch.* New York: Harper and Brothers, 1931.

Charming, imaginative pictures of a little boy among elves and berry bushes.

BESKOW, E. M. *Pelle's New Suit.* New York: Harper and Brothers, 1929.

How Pelle's lamb is sheared, and how his grandmother spins the wool and his mother weaves the cloth for Pelle's new suit.

BESTON, HENRY. *Firelight Fairy Book.* Boston: Atlantic Monthly Press, 1919.

Modern fairy tales of wonder and enchantment.

BIANCO, M. W. *Little Wooden Doll.* New York: The Macmillan Company, 1925.

The old-fashioned wooden doll was forgotten in an attic until the mice and spiders helped a little girl to find her.

Blue Fairy Book. Edited by Andrew Lang. New York: Longmans Green and Company, n.d.

A favorite collection of standard fairy tales.

Book of Fables and Folk Stories. Compiled by H. E. Scudder. Boston: Houghton Mifflin Company, 1906.

One of the very best collections of folk tales.

BOWEN, W. A. *Merrimeg.* New York: The Macmillan Company, 1923.

A jolly story of a little girl who goes on everyday errands and meets chimney imps, appleseed elves and gnomes and fairies.

BOWEN, W. A. *Old Tobacco Shop.* New York: The Macmillan Company, 1921.

The fantastic adventures of Freddie who visits the tobacco shop and makes friends with Mr. Punch, the wooden man outside the door.

BROCK, E. L. *Runaway Sardine.* New York: Alfred A. Knopf, 1929.

Zacharie is a sardine who leaves his quiet life in the house of a peasant in Brittany and runs away to find the sea.

BROOKE, L. L. *Golden Goose Book.* New York: Frederick Warne & Co., Inc., n.d.

A most satisfactory picture story book which includes also "The Three Bears," "The Three Pigs," and "Tom Thumb."

BROOKS, W. R. *To and Again.* New York: Alfred A. Knopf, 1927.

An amusing story of farmyard animals who travel to Florida by way of Washington.

BROWN, A. F. *John of the Woods.* Boston: Houghton, Mifflin Company, 1909.

A story of a boy tumbler who escapes from his cruel masters and lives in a forest, where he makes friends with the animals.

BROWN, E. A. *Chinese Kitten.* Boston: Lothrop, Lee & Shepard Company, 1922.

Two little girls spend a week at the seashore and visit friends in Boston.

BROWNE, FRANCES. *Granny's Wonderful Chair.* New York: The Macmillan Company, 1924.

Modern fairy tales of unusual value.

BRYCE, C. T. *Fables from Afar.* New York: Newson & Company, 1910.

An interesting collection of animal stories.

CARRICK, VALERY *Picture Tales from the Russian.* New York: Frederick A. Stokes Company, n.d.

Amusing folk stories about animals, with delightful line drawings.

CARRICK, VALERY. *Valery Carrick's Picture Folk-Tales.* New York: Frederick A. Stokes Company, 1926.

Ten stories printed in large type with humorous illustrations. Among the stories are "The Three Billy Goats Gruff," and "Flounder, Flounder in the Sea."

CARRYL, C. E. *Davy and the Goblin.* Boston: Houghton, Mifflin Company, 1928.

After Davy read *Alice in Wonderland,* he went on a "believing voyage" with a goblin.

CASSERLY, A. T. *Michael of Ireland.* New York: Harper and Brothers, n.d.

Delightful Irish fairy tales which tell of Michael and his adventures with the apple woman, Flanagan's pig and the red-headed girl.

CHAMOUD, SIMONE. *Picture Tales from the French.* New York: Frederick A. Stokes Company, 1933.

Twenty-two short and amusing tales from France.

Children's Book. Edited by H. E. Scudder. Illustrated by George Cruikshank, Gustav Dore, and Arthur I. Keller. Boston: Houghton, Mifflin Company, 1910.

A collection of the best and most famous stories in the English language, still as good as when the great critic of children's literature made it fifty years ago.

Chimney Corner Poems. Edited by V. S. Hutchinson. New York: Minton, Balch & Company, 1929.

An interesting collection of poems new and old.

CLARK, MARGERY. *Poppy Seed Cakes.* Garden City, New York: Doubleday, Doran & Company, 1924.

Fascinating pictures in color adorn these stories about Andrewshek and his auntie and the goat which gave the milk for the poppy seed cakes.

COATSWORTH, E. J. *The Cat and the Captain.* New York: The Macmillan Company, 1927.

A jolly story of a sea captain, Susannah, the cook, and the big black cat who proves himself a hero.

COLLODI, CARLO. *Adventures of Pinocchio.* New York: The Macmillan Company, n.d.

Tells the amusing adventures of an Italian marionette.

COLOMA, LOUIS DE. *Perez the Mouse.* New York: Dodd, Mead & Company, Inc., n.d.

This story was first written to amuse a king when he was a little boy. It tells of little King Bubi who was changed into a mouse.

COLUM, PADRAIC. *Forge in the Forest.* New York: The Macmillan Company, 1925.

A forest blacksmith bargained to shoe a wild horse if the man who brought it to his forge would tell a story for each of the elements he used in his work—fire, water, earth, and air.

COLUM, PADRAIC. *Peep-show Man.* New York: The Macmillan Company, 1924.

Three stories—one for Midsummer Day, another for Hallowe'en, and a third for Easter—were told by the peep-show man who traveled the roads in Ireland.

CONKLING, HILDA. *Silverhorn.* New York: Frederick A. Stokes Company, 1924.

In this book are the special favorites from two books of poems written by a little girl.

CRAIK, DINAH M. *Little Lame Prince.* Chicago: Rand McNally & Company, 1909.

A magic traveling cloak, the gift of a fairy godmother, releases a little boy from his prison tower to many exciting journeys in the outside world.

CRANE, WALTER. *Beauty and the Beast Picture Book.* New York: Dodd, Mead & Company, Inc., n.d.

Here are three famous tales gorgeously illustrated by a great artist.

DALGLIESH, ALICE. *America Travels.* New York: The Macmillan Company, 1933.

Stories of transportation from stagecoaches to horseless carriages.

DALGLIESH, ALICE. *Relief's Rocker.* New York: The Macmillan Company, 1932.

Relief is a little girl in Nova Scotia who has a small brother, a kitten, a doll, and a rocking chair with a story.

D'AULAIRE, INGRI. *Ola.* Garden City, New York: Doubleday, Doran & Company, 1932.

Pictures of unusual distinction show how a little boy in Norway found codfish and eider-down and cod liver oil.

DIAZ, A. M. *Story of Polly Cologne.* Boston: Lothrop, Lee & Shepard Company, 1930.

A mystery story about a rag doll.

DIXON, MAYNARD. *Injun Babies.* New York: G. P. Putnam's Sons, 1923.

Tales for very little children of a little girl who wanted to run away, a greedy child, a fat little fish who did not mind, and a boy who was brave.

DJURKLOU, N. G. *Fairy Tales from the Swedish.* Tr. by H. L. Braekstad. New York: Frederick A. Stokes Company, 1901.

Homely folk tales, characterized by much humor, few of which are found in other collections.

DONALDSON, LOIS. *Karl's Wooden Horse.* Chicago: A. Albert Whitman & Company, 1932.

About the little wooden horse that Karl received for Christmas and how it carried him to the home of the princess.

DOOTSON, L. L. *Riddle Book for Silent Reading.* Chicago: Rand McNally & Company, 1925.

Riddles for beginners in reading, illustrated with delightful silhouettes.

DUSSAUZE, ALICE. *Little Jack Rabbit.* New York: The Macmillan Company, 1927.

This pretty story of a family of rabbits in a rabbit warren is told simply and with appreciation of the French countryside.

DE LA MARE, WALTER. *Peacock Pie.* New York: Henry Holt and Company, 1916.

Whimsical poems of distinction, rich with humor and fairy gold.

DE LA MARE, WALTER. *Songs of Childhood.* New York: Henry Holt and Company, 1923.

Delightfully fanciful poems for children.

EGGLESTON, EDWARD. *Stories of Great Americans for Little Americans.* New York: American Book Company, 1895.

Episodes in the life of Franklin, Washington, Lincoln, Daniel Boone, Audubon, Longfellow, and other famous Americans.

ELIOT, E. A. *Little Black Coal.* New York: Frederick A. Stokes Company, 1923.

A lump of coal in the scuttle tells its history from early geological ages to the time it was mined and used as fuel.

English Fairy Tales. Edited by Joseph Jacobs. New York: G. P. Putnam's Sons, 1911.

A favorite collection of old English folk tales, which includes "Jack and the Beanstalk," "Jack the Giant Killer," and other classics.

EVERSON, F. M. *Puppet Plays for Children.* Chicago: Beckley-Cardy Company, 1929.

An account of an actual school project in which children made their own puppets, wrote their plays, and presented them.

FARJEON, ELEANOR. *Italian Peep-show.* New York: Frederick A. Stokes Company, 1926.

Original stories and old Italian folk tales are interwoven in this charming collection.

FARJEON, ELEANOR. *The Old Nurse's Stocking-Basket.* New York: Frederick A. Stokes Company, 1931.

As she darns the children's stockings the nurse tells them stories of many countries, a long story for a large hole and a short story for a small hole.

FIELD, RACHEL. *Polly Patchwork.* Garden City, New York: Doubleday, Doran & Company, 1928.

A gay little book telling about a little girl in a patchwork dress and a spelling match in Maine.

FIELD, RACHEL. *Taxis and Toadstools.* Garden City, New York: Doubleday, Doran & Company, 1926.

Sprightly verses about taxis, thoroughfares, stores, and storekeepers suggest some of the interesting things to be seen in cities. Other verses about berries and branches, salty days, and toadstools tell about the country.

FISHER, D. F. C. *Made-to-order Stories.* New York: Harcourt, Brace and Company, 1925.

When the author's little boy demanded realistic stories about coal scuttles and door knobs, polar bears and burglars, his mother made these to order.

FLACK, MARJORIE. *The Story about Ping.* New York: The Viking Press, Inc., 1933.

An amusing tale, with bright pictures, of a Peking duckling that lived in a wise-eyed boat on the Yangtze River.

FLACK, MARJORIE. *Tim Tadpole and the Great Bullfrog.* Garden City, New York: Doubleday, Doran & Company, 1934.

A lively book which shows in pictures and simple text how a tadpole became a frog.

FOGLER, DORIS. *Rusty Pete of the Lazy A B.* New York: The Macmillan Company, 1929.

This story of a cow pony on a mountain ranch tells about a rodeo and Indians on the open range.

FORBES, H. C. *Araminta.* New York: The Macmillan Company, 1927.

What happened to a little girl eleven years old when she found a baby.

FYLEMAN, ROSE. *Fairies and Chimneys.* Garden City, New York: Doubleday, Doran & Company, 1920.

Poems of elfin humor and delicious fancy.

FYLEMAN, ROSE. *Forty Good Morning Tales.* Garden City, New York: Doubleday, Doran & Company, 1929.

Short, whimsical stories of fairies, goblins, magic brooms, Persian kittens, pirates, and other surprising characters.

GAG, ASTA. *Sue Sew-and-sew.* New York: Coward, McCann & Company, 1931.

Gives clear directions for clothes for a doll. Drawings show the different steps necessary for each article.

GAG, WANDA. *Millions of Cats.* New York: Coward, McCann & Company, 1928.

How the best cat of all was chosen from millions and billions and trillions of cats.

GALE, ELIZABETH. *Circus Animals.* Chicago: Rand McNally & Company, 1924.

Stories of animals in the great woods and how they are captured and brought to the circus.

GAYLORD, I. N. *Little Sea-folk.* Boston: Little, Brown and Company, 1923.

Describes and illustrates starfish and sea urchins, lobsters, crabs, and sponges.

GHOSH, S. K. *Wonders of the Jungle.* 2v. Boston: D. C. Heath and Company, 1915-1918.

True stories of jungle beasts and birds simply and clearly told.

GILKISON, GRACE. *Sparrow of Ulm, and Four Other Famous Birds.* New York: The Macmillan Company, 1931.

Five stories of birds taken from various sources and retold for children.

Golden Staircase. Compiled by Louey Chisholm. New York: G. P. Putnam's Sons, n.d.

The two hundred selections in this anthology are carefully selected and well graded.

GRANT, M. M. *Windmills and Wooden Shoes.* Dallas, Texas: Southern Publishing Co., 1919.

Very simple text telling of two Dutch children and their home near the big brown windmill.

GRIMM, J. L. K., and GRIMM, W. K. *Fairy Tales.* Edited by Frances Jenkins Olcott. Philadelphia: Penn Publishing Company, n.d.

Fifty-one of the famous stories delightfully illustrated by a Dutch artist.

GRIMM, J. L. K., and GRIMM, W. K. *Household Stories.* Illustrated by Walter Crane. New York: The Macmillan Company, 1912.

An attractive edition of the much beloved stories.

GRISHINA GIVAGO, N. J. *Peter Pea.* New York: Frederick A. Stokes Company, 1926.

A Russian tale about a little boy no bigger than a pea who journeyed to the king's palace and won the love of the beautiful princess.

GRISHINA GIVAGO, N. J. *Shorty.* New York: Frederick A. Stokes Company, 1924.

A droll Russian folk tale which shows what happened to one who always wanted to have his own way.

HADER, BERTA. *Farmer in the Dell.* New York: The Macmillan Company, 1931.

Here are charming pictures of spring, summer, autumn, and winter work and play for the farmer and his family in the dell.

HADER, BERTA. *Spunky.* New York: The Macmillan Company, 1933.

An interesting story about a white Shetland pony.

HALL, MAY EMERY. *Jan and Betje.* New York: Charles E. Merrill Company, 1914.

Tells of the everyday life of two children who lived on a flatboat on a Dutch canal.

HARRINGTON, ISIS. *Eagle's Nest.* New York: The Macmillan Company, 1930.

How two Nava:o boys spent the summer tending their sheep on the grassy slopes of Mt. Taylor and how they found the lost and fertile valley of their ancestors.

HARRINGTON, ISIS. *Komoki of the Cliffs.* New York: Chas. Scribner's Sons, 1934.

This story of a Hopi Indian boy is illustrated with pictures in color made by Indian children.

HAWTHORNE, NATHANIEL. *Wonder Book and Tanglewood Tales.* Illustrated by Maxfield Parrish. New York: Duffield & Green, Inc., n.d.

A gorgeously illustrated edition of the famous Greek stories.

HELLE, ANDRE. *Big Beasts and Little Beasts.* New York: Frederick A. Stokes Company, 1924.

Droll pictures and true descriptions of big and little beasts in a book which amuses and instructs at the same time.

HILL, HELEN. *Charlie and His Puppy Bingo.* New York: The Macmillan Company, 1923.

The amusing adventures of a five-year-old boy and his dog.

History Stories of Other Lands. Book I. Tales of Far and Near. Edited by A. G. Terry. Evanston, Illinois: Row, Peterson and Company, 1926.

Simply told stories of the heroes of many countries.

HOLBROOK, FLORENCE. *Book of Nature Myths.* Boston: Houghton, Mifflin Company, 1902.

Among these tales are the stories telling why the woodpecker's head is red, why the rabbit is timid, why the sea is salt, and how fire was brought to the Indians.

HOPKINS, W. J. *Sandman: His Farm Stories.* Boston: L. C. Page & Company, 1902.

Stories of the happenings on a farm.

HORNE, RICHARD H. *Good-Natured Bear.* New York: The Macmillan Company, 1927.

The jolly adventures of Mr. Bear and his friends, Dr. and Mrs. Littlepump and their children.

HORNE, RICHARD H. *Memoirs of a London Doll.* New York: The Macmillan Company, n.d.

A quaint story of a doll in the London of a century ago.

HOWARD A. W. *Sokar and the Crocodile.* New York: The Macmillan Company, 1928.

A fanciful story about a little boy in ancient Egypt.

HOWARD, ALICE WOODBERRY. *The Princess Runs Away, a Story of Egypt in 1900 B.C.* New York: The Macmillan Company, 1934.

Tells what happened when Meryt, the little Egyptian princess, ran away from the palace.

HOWARD, F. W. *Banbury Cross Stories.* New York: Charles E. Merrill Company, 1909.

Simple vocabulary and large print make this collection of retold favorites very useful for young readers.

HUNT, C. W. *About Harriet.* Boston: Houghton, Mifflin Company, 1916.
Tells of the good times Harriet had every day in the week.

HUNT, C. W. *Little House in the Green Valley.* Boston: Houghton, Mifflin Company, 1932.
When summer came, Roger and Gail joyfully left their city flat and spent their holidays in the country.

HUTCHINSON, V. S. *Chimney Corner Stories.* New York: Minton, Balch & Company, 1925.
Sixteen favorite folk tales beginning with "Henny Penny" and ending with "Cinderella."

INGELOW, JEAN. *Mopsa the Fairy.* Illustrated by Dorothy P. Lathrop. New York: Harper Brothers, n.d.
A little boy finds a nest of fairies and fills his pocket with them and then on the back of an albatross flies away to fairyland.

JONES, WILLARD. *How the Derrick Works.* New York: The Macmillan Company, 1930.
Illustrates the different parts of the derrick, such as the bull stick, the mast and boom, and explains how each part works.

KALER, J. O. *Toby Tyler.* New York: Harper Brothers, 1923.
A circus story that has fascinated two generations of readers.

KIPLING, RUDYARD. *Just So Stories.* Garden City, New York: Doubleday, Doran & Company, 1907.
In these amusing tales you will learn how the camel got his hump and how the whale got his small throat.

KNOX, R. B. *Marty and Company.* Garden City, New York: Doubleday, Doran & Company, 1933.
About a little girl and her particular pig and her superior chicken on a farm in the South.

LANSING, M. F. *Fairy Tales.* 2v. Boston: Ginn and Company, 1907–1908.
Simply and clearly told versions of the classic fairy stories.

LARUE, M. G. *Billy Bang Book.* New York: The Macmillan Company, 1927.
When the Rushing River carries Billy Bang's house down stream, he makes friends with Wolf, Squirrel, and Sammy Otter.

LARUE, M. G. *In Animal Land.* New York: The Macmillan Company, 1924.
Fanciful animal stories in which the animals talk and act as the chief characters. The action words are especially good and the detail is excellent.

LATHROP, D. P. *Fairy Circus.* New York: The Macmillan Company, 1931.
Charming pictures illustrate this tale of the fairies who set up their own circus with turtles for elephants, mice for horses, spiders to weave the trapezes and tight ropes, and fireflies to light it all.

LATTIMORE, E. F. *Little Pear.* New York: Harcourt, Brace and Company, 1931.
There was once a little Chinese boy called Little Pear. He was five years old and very mischievous. He had a round solemn face with eyes like apple seeds. After he ran away and fell into the river he decided to be a good boy. "Little Pear is growing up," his sister said.

LEAR, EDWARD. *Nonsense Books.* Boston: Little, Brown and Company, n.d.
Amusing rhymes, funny limericks, and laughable pictures.

LEDERER, CHARLOTTE. *Golden Flock.* New York: Farrar & Rinehart, Inc., 1931.
A Hungarian legend that through the charm and simplicity of the telling manages to retain in its English version something of the folklore quality of the original.

LEFEVRE, FELICITE. *The Cock, the Mouse and the Little Red Hen.* Philadelphia: Macrae Smith Co., n.d.
A popular folk tale retold for little children.

LEFEVRE, FELICITE. *Little Grey Goose.* Philadelphia: Macrae Smith Co., 1925.
An amusing story about a white duck who goes hunting for her yellow shoes and stockings to wear to the little red hen's birthday party.

LENT, H. B. *Diggers and Builders.* New York: The Macmillan Company, 1931.
Pictures and descriptions of the derrick builder, the steel worker, the road builder, the truck driver, and other men at work.

LENT, H. B. *Clear Track Ahead.* New York: The Macmillan Company, 1932.
Chapters on the duties of engineers, brakemen, conductors, railway postmen, and station agents.

LENT, H. B. *Full Steam Ahead.* New York: The Macmillan Company, 1933.
How a small boy spends six days on an ocean liner crossing the Atlantic. He talks to the Captain on the bridge, visits the engine room, discovers how the boat is steered, and other exciting things.

LEWIS, JANET. *Friendly Adventures of Ollie Ostrich.* Garden City, New York: Doubleday, Doran & Company, 1923.
An amusing story of the Pinocchio type for small children.

LIPPINCOTT, J. W. *Bun, a Wild Rabbit.* Philadelphia: Penn Publishing Company, 1918.
A true story of the happenings in the life of a rabbit.

LOFTING, HUGH. *Story of Doctor Dolittle.* New York: Frederick A. Stokes Company, 1920.
The first and best of several books about the famous doctor who is fond of animals and understands their language.

LOFTING, HUGH. *Story of Mrs. Tubbs.* New York: Frederick A. Stokes Company, 1923.
How Peter Punk, Polly Ponk, and Patrick Pink rescue Mrs. Tubbs from an unhappy fate.

LOMEN, HELEN. *Taktuk, an Arctic Boy.* Garden City, New York: Doubleday, Doran & Company, 1928.
Taktuk and his friends live on the edge of the Arctic circle near Bering Strait. This book tells of seal and walrus hunting, the great reindeer roundup and even of the school where Taktuk learns "the white man's words."

LUDMANN, OSCAR. *Hansi the Stork.* Chicago: Albert Whitman & Company, 1932.
An unusual picture book of quaint Alsace.

MACDONALD, GEORGE. *Light Princess.* New York: The Macmillan Company, 1926.
The adventures of a little princess who weighed nothing and floated as easily as a feather.

MAMIN, D. N. *Verotchka's Tales.* New York: E. P. Dutton and Company, 1922.
Charming and unusual Russian tales of birds, beasts, and insects.

MARTIN, D. B. *Awisha's Carpet.* Garden City, New York: Doubleday, Doran & Company, 1930.

The chief ambition of Awisha, a small Arab girl, was to weave rugs as skillfully as the other women of her family. The life and customs of the people of Tunisia are introduced as a background.

MARTIN, D. B. *Fatma Was a Goose.* Garden City, New York: Doubleday, Doran & Company, 1929.

Fatma was a goose, an Arabian goose who lived in Tunisia and had a great adventure with a camel, a coach, and an antique statue.

MARTINEAU DES CHESNEZ, E. L. *Lady Green Satin and Her Maid Rosette.* New York: The Macmillan Company, 1923.

A charming story of little Jean Paul and his two white mice.

MAXWELL, VIOLET, and HILL, HELEN. *Charlie and His Kitten, Topsy.* New York: The Macmillan Company, 1922.

Seven charmingly written little stories in which the moral is humorously suggested rather than pointed.

MEIGS, CORNELIA. *Willow Whistle.* New York: The Macmillan Company, 1931.

A lively story of pioneer children, Indians, and buffaloes.

MEIGS, CORNELIA. *Wonderful Locomotive.* New York: The Macmillan Company, 1928.

Tells of Peter's marvelous journey in Number 44, a rejuvenated old engine.

MILNE, ALAN A. *When We Were Very Young.* New York: E. P. Dutton and Company, 1924.

Imaginative poems for and about little children in most engaging rhyme and meter, with illustrations that match.

MILNE, ALAN A. *Winnie-the-Pooh.* New York: E. P. Dutton and Company, 1926.

Christopher Robin's father told his little boy these stories about his toy animals.

MOE, LOUIS. *Raggle Taggle Bear.* New York: Longmans, Green & Company, 1926.

Lively pictures illustrate these adventures of a poor old bear.

MOON, G. P. *Chi-Wee.* Garden City, New York: Doubleday, Doran & Company, 1925.

Tells the adventures of a little Indian girl who lived in a pueblo in New Mexico.

MORCOMB, M. E. *Red Feather Stories.* Chicago: Lyons & Carnahan, 1916.

Simply told stories of Indian children.

OLCOTT, VIRGINIA. *Anton and Trini.* New York: Silver, Burdett and Company, 1930.

Into this fascinating story of a Swiss family living in a mountain village is skillfully woven information about modern Switzerland—its geography, history, industries, and customs.

OLFERS, S. V. *When the Root Children Wake Up.* New York: Frederick A. Stokes Company, 1930.

A charming book which pictures the coming of spring.

OLMSTEAD, E. G., and GRANT, E. B. *Ned and Nan in Holland.* Evanston, Illinois: Row, Peterson & Company, 1916.

Tells of markets, canals, dikes, and all the other interesting things two children saw in Holland.

ORTON, H. F. *Bobby of Cloverfield Farm.* New York: Frederick A. Stokes Company, 1922.

Simple stories of everyday life on a farm.

ORTON, H. F. *Little Lost Pigs.* New York: Frederick A. Stokes Company, 1925.

A realistic story of two little pigs which ran away and were found by the farm dog.

ORTON, H. F. *Prancing Pat.* New York: Frederick A. Stokes Company, 1927.

A good story of a horse.

ORTON, H. F. *Twin Lambs.* New York: Frederick A. Stokes Company, 1931.

Pet lambs, tiny and weak when first given to the Baker children, soon grow lively and playful with the care they receive. They amuse everyone, especially the little sick girl from the city.

PAINE, A. B. *Arkansaw Bear.* Philadelphia: Henry Altemus Company, 1902.

The amusing adventures of a little boy and a big black bear.

PAINE, A. B. *Hollow Tree and Deep Woods Books.* New York: Harper Brothers, 1901.

Amusing stories of a crow, a 'coon and a 'possum.

PALM, AMY. *Wanda and Greta of Broby Farm.* New York: Longmans, Green and Company, 1930.

From Sweden comes this story of simple everyday life of two small girls on a shoreside farm.

PATCH, E. M. *Holiday Hill.* New York: The Macmillan Company, 1931.

Tells of the interesting things to be seen on a hill every day in the year.

PATCH, E. M. *Holiday Pond.* New York: The Macmillan Company, 1929.

Ten short stories about the flowers and grasses that grow near a pond and the frogs, turtles, sandpipers, dragon flies, ducks, and swallows found there.

PEARY, JOSEPHINE. *Children of the Arctic.* New York: Frederick A. Stokes Company, 1903.

Stories and pictures of the unusual sights little Marie saw when she lived with the Eskimos.

PEARY, JOSEPHINE. *Snow Baby.* New York: Frederick A. Stokes Company, 1901.

Little Marie was called the Snow Baby because she was born in Greenland.

PERDUE, H. A. *Child Life in Other Lands.* Chicago: Rand McNally & Company, 1918.

The stories, games, festivals, and everyday life of little children in Norway, Holland, Germany, Italy, Greece, Japan, China, and Armenia.

PERKINS, L. F. *Dutch Twins.* Boston: Houghton, Mifflin Company, 1912.

Here are the everyday doings of Kit and Kat in Holland.

PERKINS, L. F. *Eskimo Twins.* Boston: Houghton, Mifflin Company, 1914.

Stories of Menie and Monnie, aged five, and of their dogs, Nip and Tup.

PERKINS, L. F. *Japanese Twins.* Boston: Houghton, Mifflin Company, 1912.

The five year old twins celebrate doll day, the feast of the flags, and other happy festivals.

PETERSHAM, M. F. *Christ Child.* Garden City, New York: Doubleday, Doran & Company, 1931.

A beautiful picture book made by two American artists in Palestine.

PETERSHAM, M. F. *Miki.* Garden City, New York: Doubleday, Doran & Company, 1929.

Miki is a little boy who goes to Hungary and travels about with Sari, the green goose, and Matyi, the shepherd's dog with silver curls. They listen to the shepherd's folk tales, dance with the gypsies, and ride on the merry-go-round in Budapest.

PETERSHAM, M. F. *The Story Book of Things We Use*. Philadelphia: The John C. Winston Company, 1934.

Fascinating pictures in colors illustrate this outline of the history of everyday things. It is also published in four separate parts, about houses, food, clothing, and transportation.

PHILLIPS, E. C. *Black-eyed Susan*. Boston: Houghton, Mifflin Company, 1921.

A happy story of a little girl who lived with her grandfather and grandmother.

PHILLIPS, E. C. *Pretty Polly Perkins*. Boston: Houghton, Mifflin Company, 1925.

The adventures of a rag doll with three little girls, one American, one French, and one Scotch.

PHILLIPS, E. C. *Wee Ann*. Boston: Houghton, Mifflin Company, 1919.

Describes the delightful happenings that befell a little girl in the country.

Pinaforte Palace. Edited by K. D. S. Wiggin, and N. A. Smith. Garden City, New York: Doubleday, Doran & Company, 1910.

Delightful poems for very young persons.

PLIMPTON, EDNA. *Your Workshop*. New York: The Macmillan Company, 1926.

A simple book with drawings and designs that show how to make toys and marionettes.

Posy Ring. Edited by K. D. S. Wiggin. Garden City, New York: Doubleday, Doran & Company, 1913.

A charming collection for children a little older than those who enjoyed *Pinaforte Palace*.

POTTER, BEATRIX. *Roly-poly-pudding*. New York: Frederick Warne & Co., Inc., 1908.

Tom Kitten's adventures with the rats, Anna Maria and Samuel Whiskers, in the old English house make delightful reading.

POTTER, BEATRIX. *The Tailor of Gloucester*. New York: Frederick Warne & Co., Inc., 1903.

A Christmas story of rare charm.

POTTER, BEATRIX. *Tale of Jemina Puddleduck*. New York: Frederick Warne & Co., Inc., 1910.

One of the many small volumes by Beatrix Potter, who writes with a fascinating mixture of reality and fancy that has the flavor of real literature.

POTTER, M. S. C. *Sally Gabble and the Fairies*. New York: The Macmillan Company, 1929.

Sally Gabble lived in a wee brown cottage that had a little door for fairies.

PRYOR, W. C. *Train Book*. New York: Harcourt, Brace and Company, 1933.

Excellent photographs and simple text, describing a railroad journey and a visit to a freight yard.

PUMPHREY, M. B. *Stories of the Pilgrims*. Chicago: Rand McNally & Company, 1910.

This book begins with Queen Anne's visit to Scrooby Inn and tells of the Brewster children and other Pilgrim children in England, Holland and America.

PYLE, HOWARD. *Twilight Land*. New York: Harper and Brothers, 1922.

Characters of legend and fairy tale gather together in the Mother Goose Village of Twilight Town and take turns in telling stories.

PYLE, HOWARD. *Wonder Clock*. New York: Harper and Brothers, 1887.

These twenty-four magical tales, one for each hour of the day, are illustrated with pictures as enchanting as the stories.

PYLE, KATHERINE. *Black-eyed Puppy*. New York: E. P. Dutton and Company, 1923.

A simple story of the good and bad fortunes of a puppy named Muffins.

PYLE, KATHERINE. *Careless Jane and Other Tales.* New York: E. P. Dutton and Company, 1902.

Entertaining moral tales in verse.

PYLE, KATHERINE. *Six Little Ducklings.* New York: Dodd, Mead & Company, Inc., 1915.

Amusing story by an author who understands the interests of small children.

RANSOME, ARTHUR. *Old Peter's Russian Tales.* New York: Thomas Nelson & Sons, n.d.

These are the stories that a Russian grandfather told to two children.

RICHARDS, L. E. H. *Tirra Lirra.* Boston: Little, Brown and Company, 1932.

Rollicking nonsense verses that have charmed children for two generations.

RICKERT, EDITH. *Bojabi Tree.* Garden City, New York: Doubleday, Doran & Company, 1923.

An amusing story with much repetition, adapted from an African folk tale.

ROSSETTI, C. G. *Sing-Song.* New York: The Macmillan Company, 1924.

A nursery rhyme book unsurpassed for its lyric quality, technical workmanship, and birdlike spontaneity.

ROWE, DOROTHY. *Rabbit Lantern.* New York: The Macmillan Company, 1925.

Twelve simple stories about Chinese children and their quaint customs.

SAYERS, FRANCES C. *Bluebonnets for Lucinda.* New York: The Viking Press, Inc.

Lucinda lived on an island near the coast of Texas. One day she went to visit Frau Geranium on the mainland. There she saw a great field of bluebonnets and played a tune on her music box for the geese on the farm.

SCHRAM, C. W. N. *Olaf, Lofoten Fisherman.* New York: Longmans, Green and Company, 1929.

The story of a little Norwegian boy who spent the winter in a far north fishing village of the Lofoten Islands.

SCHWARTZ, J. A. *Little Star Gazers.* New York: Frederick A. Stokes Company, 1917.

Four star stories, one about Egypt, one about Greece, a third about the Renaissance and the last about modern times.

SCHWARTZ, J. A. *Wilderness Babies.* Boston: Little, Brown and Company, 1906.

Tells of elk, opossum, rabbit, beaver, squirrel, and bear babies.

SERL, EMMA. *In Fableland.* New York: Silver, Burdett and Company, 1911.

A supplementary reader which contains thirty-four of Aesop's fables retold in dramatic style.

SERL, EMMA. *Work-a-day Doings on the Farm.* New York: Silver, Burdett and Company, 1914.

An account of two bears who buy a farm and are plowing, planting, harvesting and caring for the stock.

SHANNON, MONICA. *Goose Grass Rhymes.* Garden City, New York: Doubleday, Doran & Company, 1930.

Whimsical fancies and jolly rhymes characterize these California verses.

Silver Pennies. Edited by B. J. Thompson. New York: The Macmillan Company, 1925.

An attractive collection of modern poems that have delighted many children.

SKINNER, E. L. *Merry Tales.* New York: American Book Company, 1915.

One of the most popular collections of humorous fairy tales and poems.

SKINNER, E. L. *Nursery Tales from Many Lands*. New York: Chas. Scribner's Sons, 1917.

Humorous folk tales, illustrated in black and white.

Sleeping Beauty in the Wood and Other Stories. Edited by Andrew Lang. New York: Longmans, Green and Company, 1912.

Two other stories are included here: "The Bronze Ring," and "East of the Sun and West of the Moon."

SMITH, L. R. *Circus Book*. Chicago: F. A. Flanagan Company, 1913.

The everyday life of the circus, reduced to the dimensions of the child's world.

SMITH, M. E. E. *Holland Stories*. Chicago: Rand McNally & Company, 1913.

About the dikes and windmills, canals and boats, fishing folk and the sea, dress and customs of the peasants, and the keeping of St. Nicholas' Day.

SNEDDEN, G. S. *Docas, the Indian Boy of Santa Clara*. Boston: D. C. Heath & Company, 1899.

Stories of a little Indian boy who lived long ago in California.

SPERRY, ARMSTRONG. *One Day with Manu*. Philadelphia: The John C. Winston Company, 1933.

Story and bright pictures of a little boy's life in the South Seas.

SPYRI, JOHANNA. *Heidi*. Illustrated by Marguerite Davis. Boston: Ginn and Company, 1901.

A classic which tells of a little girl in the mountains of Switzerland.

SPYRI, JOHANNA. *Moni, the Goat Boy*. Boston: Ginn and Company, 1906.

A sunny story of a boy's life high in the Alps.

STEVENSON, R. L. *Child's Garden of Verses*. New York: Chas. Scribner's Sons, 1909.

No one can afford to miss these perfect poems for children.

SUGIMOTO, C. W. *Picture Tales from the Japanese*. New York: Frederick A. Stokes Company, 1928.

A favorite collection of the stories that a Japanese girl heard her grandmother tell.

Sugar and Spice and All That's Nice. Edited by M. W. F. Tileston. Boston: Little, Brown and Company, 1928.

Contains Mother Goose melodies and other favorite verses.

Susanna's Auction. New York: The Macmillan Company, 1923.

A moral and amusing tale of a little French girl and the auction of her dolls.

Tales of Laughter. Edited by K. D. S. Wiggin, and N. A. Smith. Garden City, New York: Doubleday, Doran & Company, 1912.

Favorite folk and fairy tales illustrated with lively pictures.

This Singing World. Edited by Louis Untermeyer. New York: Harcourt, Brace and Company, 1923.

A refreshing collection of three hundred twenty-one unusual poems written by English and American poets.

TIPPETT, J. S. *I Live in a City.* New York: Harper and Brothers, 1927.

Verses about a little boy in New York City.

> "I'm glad that I
> Live near a park
> For in the winter
> After dark
> The park lights shine
> As bright and still
> As dandelions
> On a hill."

TIPPETT, J. S. *Singing Farmer.* Yonkers-on-Hudson, New York: World Book Company, 1927.

Rhymes about a farmer's work.

TIPPETT, J. S. *Toys and Toy Makers.* New York: Harper and Brothers, 1931.

Tells how toys are made and something about their makers in this country and in Europe. One chapter tells about the dolls and doll furniture, rattles and toy animals, that children played with centuries ago.

TROXELL, ELEANOR, and DUNN, F. W. *Baby Animals.* Evanston, Illinois: Row, Peterson and Company, 1928.

Stories and rhymes about puppies, fawns, opossums, bear cubs, and other baby animals.

WELLS, RHEA. *Ali, the Camel.* Garden City, New York: Doubleday, Doran & Company, 1931.

About the adventures of Ali, his master Bali, and his camel, who lived in the Bedouin country.

WELLS, RHEA. *Beppo, the Donkey.* Garden City, New York: Doubleday, Doran & Company, 1930.

A most attractive book about Sicily. Pictures and decorations give an excellent idea of the life of the people and archeological treasures.

WELLS, RHEA. *Coco, the Goat.* Garden City, New York: Doubleday, Doran & Company, 1929.

Describes the antics of a baby goat in Spain.

WELLS, RHEA. *Peppi, the Duck.* Garden City, New York: Doubleday, Doran & Company, 1927.

Pictures in color and in black and white add to the interest of this story of a duck hatched in a castle courtyard.

WHEELER, I. W. *Playing with Clay.* New York: The Macmillan Company, 1927.

This book contains directions for making clay bowls and tiles as well as stories of potters in many different countries and periods.

WHITE, E. O. *When Abigail Was Seven.* Boston: Houghton, Mifflin Company, 1931.

Abigail was seven in the year 1828. She lived in New Hampshire and this story tells of her cousin and her cats and her journey to Salem.

WHITNEY, ELINOR. *Tyke-y; His Book and His Mark.* New York: The Macmillan Company, 1925.

Adventures of a Welsh terrier puppy, "black and tan, mostly black." Written simply with many silhouettes of the active and amusing Tyke-y.

WIESE, KURT. *Chinese Inkstick.* Garden City, New York: Doubleday, Doran & Company, 1929.

An unusual inkstick tells stories of a letter writer, a bamboo painter, a brave riverman, a tea merchant and other interesting Chinese people.

WIESE, KURT. *Karoo, the Kangaroo.* New York: Coward, McCann & Company, 1929.

It was very fine to be a kangaroo in the spring of the year on the wide plains of Australia. Little Karoo lost his mother when the Dingos came barking, but he hopped east through the forest and west through the desert until he found the herd again.

WIESE, KURT. *Liang and Lo.* Garden City, New York: Doubleday, Doran & Company, 1930.

Liang, the son of a merchant, travels down the river until he finds Lo, a small boy who lives on the back of a water buffalo. Together they ride about; and one day they meet a dragon.

WILDER, LAURA. *The Little House in the Big Woods.* New York: Harper and Brothers, 1932.

A vivid picture of life in the Big Woods of Wisconsin sixty years ago.

WILEY, BELLE. *Mewanee, the Little Indian Boy.* New York: Silver, Burdett & Company, 1912.

The story of the son of an Indian chief.

WILLIAMSON, HAMILTON. *A Monkey Tale.* Garden City, New York: Doubleday, Doran & Company, 1929.

A delightfully funny picture book telling of Jocko's adventures in the jungle.

WILLISTON, T. P. *Japanese Fairy Tales.* 2v. Chicago: Rand McNally & Company, 1904, 1911.

Stories simply told and illustrated in color by a Japanese artist.

WODELL, H. P. *Beginning to Garden.* New York: The Macmillan Company, 1928.

An excellent book for young gardeners.

WYNNE, ANNETTE. *For Days and Days.* New York: Frederick A. Stokes Company, 1919.

Simple childlike poems for every day in the year.

YAP, WEDA. *Abigail's Private Reason.* New York: The Macmillan Company, 1932.

A sad and funny tale of the beautiful new slippers that Abigail wore before her birthday party.

YOUMANS, ELEANOR. *Skitter Cat.* Indianapolis, Indiana: Bobbs-Merrill Company, 1925.

Tells of a Persian kitten that lived in California.

YOUNG, ELLA. *Unicorn with Silver Shoes.* New York: Longmans, Green and Company, 1932.

For the child of poetic imagination and exceptional reading taste.

ZWILGMEYER, DIKKEN. *Johnny Blossom.* Boston: Pilgrim Press, 1912.

The amusing escapades of a Norwegian boy who is always getting into scrapes.

FIFTH AND SIXTH GRADES

AANRUD, HANS. *Lisbeth Longfrock.* Boston: Ginn and Company, 1907.

A vivid picture of Norwegian farm life during the wonderful summer on the mountain pastures.

ADAMS, KATHLEEN, and ATCHINSON, F. E. *Book of Giant Stories.* New York: Dodd, Mead & Company, Inc., 1926.

Seventeen entertaining stories, familiar and unfamiliar.

ALCOTT, LOUISA MAY. *Little Men.* Boston: Little, Brown and Company, 1924.

The jolly adventures of the children of Meg, Jo, and Amy at Plumfield.

ALCOTT, LOUISA MAY. *Little Women.* Boston: Little, Brown and Company, 1911.

This famous story of Louisa Alcott's own girlhood is loved by each generation of readers.

Arabian Nights. The Arabian Nights' Entertainments. Edited by Andrew Lang. New York: Longmans, Green & Company, n.d.

Twenty-six stories of glamor and enchantment.

ARMER, L. A. *Waterless Mountain.* New York: Longmans, Green & Company, 1931.

Tells of the life of a Navajo boy who lives in the shadow of the Waterless Mountain and takes a long journey to see the blue water.

ASBJÖRNSEN, P. C., and MOE, J. E. *East o' the Sun and West o' the Moon.* Translated by G. W. Dasent. Philadelphia: David McKay Company, n.d.

A collection of Norse folk tales, humorous and romantic.

AUSTIN, M. H. *Basket Woman.* Boston: Houghton, Mifflin Company, 1910.

Some of these stories are about the Indians of the Southwest and others are Indian folk tales.

AUSTIN, M. H. *Children Sing in the Far West.* Boston: Houghton, Mifflin Company, 1928.

Poems written to express the author's appreciation of the magic of the desert.

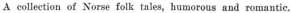

Baker's Dozen. Edited by M. G. Davis. New York: Harcourt, Brace and Company, 1930.

Thirteen story-hour favorites chosen from recent children's books for their literary quality, vitality and unusual plots.

BAKER, OLAF. *Shasta of the Wolves.* New York: Dodd, Mead & Company, Inc., 1919.

Shasta was an Indian boy who grew up in a wolf's den. When he was captured and about to be sacrificed in a sun dance, the wolves saved him.

BALDWIN, JAMES. *Story of Roland.* New York: Chas Scribner's Sons, 1911.

Recounts the glorious exploits of the perfect knight, who was the greatest hero of the middle ages.

BALDWIN, JAMES. *Story of Siegfried.* Illustrated by Howard Pyle. New York: Chas. Scribner's Sons, 1913.

Stirring tales of the wooing of Brunhilde, and the slaying of Fafnir the dragon.

BALDWIN, JAMES. *Story of the Golden Age.* Illustrated by Howard Pyle. New York: Chas. Scribner's Sons, 1915.

Ulysses is the hero of this story which includes legends about the Trojan War.

BAYLOR, F. C. *Juan and Juanita.* Boston: Houghton, Mifflin Company, 1915.

An exciting story of two Mexican children who were captured by the Comanches.

BAYNES, E. H. *Jimmie, the Story of a Black Bear Cub.* New York: The Macmillan Company, 1923.

Jimmie was a mischievous black bear who lived with the family of the author of this book.

BAYNES, E. H. *Polaris, the Story of an Eskimo Dog.* New York: The Macmillan Company, 1922.

The mother and father of this Eskimo dog were members of the train that drew Peary's sledge to the Pole. The book tells of Polaris' puppy days in New Hampshire before he was given to Dr. Grenfell for service in Labrador.

BENET, R. C. *Book of Americans.* New York: Farrar & Rinehart, Inc., 1933.

More than fifty poems telling of great Americans from Columbus to Woodrow Wilson. Some of the verses are amusing, others are serious; all illuminate the history of our country.

BEST, A. C. *Girls in Africa.* New York: The Macmillan Company, 1928.

The first story tells of an English girl's journey to Nigeria; and the others are about the girls of various negro tribes.

BEST, HERBERT. *Garram the Hunter.* Garden City, New York: Doubleday, Doran & Company, 1930.

The strange experiences of an African hill boy, an expert hunter, when he goes down to the city of the plains.

BIANCO, MARGERY. *All About Pets.* New York: The Macmillan Company, 1929.

An attractive book giving simple and reliable advice on the care of pets.

BLAISDELL, A. F., and BALL, F. K. *Log Cabin Days.* Boston: Little, Brown and Company, 1921.

Relates simply and dramatically stories of Columbus, Balboa, Israel Putnam, Nancy Campbell, Lydia Darrah, Mollie Pitcher, John Paul Jones, Daniel Webster, and other American heroes.

BLAND, EDITH. *Bastable Children.* New York: Coward, McCann & Company, n.d.

Tells of a family of English children who were always getting into mischief.

Book of Nonsense. Edited by Ernest Rhys. New York: E. P. Dutton and Company, 1928.

A good collection, containing poems from Edward Lear, Lewis Carroll, Mother Goose, and Struwwelpeter.

BORSKI, L. M., and MILLER, K. B. *Jolly Tailor and Other Fairy Tales.* New York: Longmans, Green & Company, 1928.

Among these merry tales from Poland is one of a tailor so thin that he could pass through the eye of his own needle.

BOUTET DE MONVEL, L. M. *Joan of Arc.* New York: The Century Co., 1907.

One of the most beautiful books ever printed. With exquisite simplicity it tells the story of the Maid who saved France.

Boy's Book of Verse. Compiled by H. E. Fish. New York: Frederick A. Stokes Company, 1923.

Old favorites and modern poems that appeal especially to boys.

BRANN, ESTHER. *Lupe Goes to School.* New York: The Macmillan Company, 1930.

A vivid story of a little girl in a boarding school in Spain.

BRANN, ESTHER. *Nanette of the Wooden Shoes.* New York: The Macmillan Company, 1929.

About a little girl who lived with her grandmother in a Breton village.

BRINK, CAROL RYRIE. *Anything Can Happen on the River!* New York: The Macmillan Company, 1934.

An exciting story of a French boy and a riverman who solve a mystery on the Seine.

BRONSON, W. S. *Fingerfins; the Tale of a Sargasso Fish.* New York: The Macmillan Company, 1930.

A little mouse fish was called Fingerfins because of the grasping properties of his fins. The book tells of his adventures in the sea and in the aquarium and of his escape from his captors.

BRONSON, W. S. *Paddlewings; the Penguin of Galapagos.* New York: The Macmillan Company, 1931.

Tells what happened to a solemn young penguin, full of curiosity, from the time he pecked his way out of the egg shell in Galapagos until he reached the New York aquarium.

BROOKS, E. S. *True Story of Abraham Lincoln.* Boston: Lothrop, Lee & Shepard Company, 1896.

An interesting account dealing chiefly with incidents of Lincoln's early life.

BROOKS. E. S. *True Story of Benjamin Franklin.* Boston: Lothrop, Lee & Shepard Company, 1898.

Tells entertainingly of the great American who was scientist, diplomat, and man of letters.

BROWN, A. F. *In the Days of Giants.* Boston: Houghton, Mifflin Company, 1902.

One of the most attractive collections of Norse myths.

BROWNING, ROBERT. *Pied Piper of Hamelin.* Illustrated by Hope Dunlap. Chicago: Rand McNally & Company, 1910.

A quaint tale of the magic that made rats and children follow the piper.

BRYANT, L. M. *Children's Book of Celebrated Pictures.* New York: The Century Co., 1922.

Fifty reproductions accompanied by descriptions of celebrated paintings.

BURGESS, T. W. *Burgess Bird Book for Children.* Boston: Little, Brown and Company, 1919.

Reliable information about common birds, presented in story form.

BURGLON. NORA. *Children of the Soil.* Garden City, New York: Doubleday, Doran & Company, 1932.

How good luck came to two children in Sweden.

CALDWELL, FRANK. *Wolf, the Storm Leader.* New York: Dodd, Mead & Company, Inc., 1910.

An Alaskan wolf which became the leader of a mail carrier's dog train tells the story.

Cambridge Book of Poetry for Children. Edited by Kenneth Grahame. New York: G. P. Putnam's Sons, 1933.

A delightful collection of verses, arranged in groups for little children, those a little older, and others still older.

CANNON, C. J. *Pueblo Boy.* Boston: Houghton, Mifflin Company, 1926.

Tyami lived in an Indian village on the mesa of Acoma. When the Spaniards under Coronado came, he saved his people from an attack by the explorers.

CAPUANA, LUIGI. *Golden-feather.* New York: E. P. Dutton and Company, 1930.

An attractive collection of fifteen modern fairy tales translated from the Italian.

CARPENTER, FRANCES. *Tales of a Basque Grandmother.* Garden City, New York: Doubleday, Doran & Company, 1930.

These stories "out of the past when animals talked and fairies, witches and ogres were abroad in the land" were told by a wise old grandmother as she sat in her low chair spinning yarn.

CARR, W. H. *Stir of Nature.* New York: Oxford University Press, 1930.

An excellent first book for boys and girls whose interest in wild creatures is awakening.

CARROLL, LEWIS. *Alice's Adventures in Wonderland.* Illustrated by John Tenniel. New York: The Macmillan Company, 1906.

A supreme childhood classic, with illustrations as unforgettable as the text.

CARRYL, C. E. *Admiral's Caravan.* Boston: Houghton, Mifflin Company, 1920.

Of the wooden images and Noah's ark animals that came to life in Wonderland.

CHEVALIER, RAGNHILD. *Wandering Monday and Other Days in Old Bergen.* New York: The Macmillan Company, 1931.

Stories of a happy Norwegian family in Bergen.

CHRISMAN, ARTHUR. *Shen of the Sea.* New York: E. P. Dutton and Company, 1925.

Amusing and original Chinese stories.

CHURCH, A. J. *Odyssey for Boys and Girls.* New York: The Macmillan Company, 1911.

An attractive edition of the famous story.

EL CID CAMPEADOR. *Tale of the Warrior Lord.* Translated by Merriam Sherwood. New York: Longmans, Green and Company, 1930.

Herein are chronicled the adventures and deeds of prowess of that invincible warrior and crusader of the eleventh century, Rodrigo Diaz of Vivar, more commonly known as The Cid.

CLARK, MARGERY. *Etiquette, Jr.* Garden City, New York: Doubleday, Doran & Company, 1926.

A sprightly book of suggestions for young people, including information useful for formal and informal occasions.

CLEMENS, S. L., (Mark Twain, pseudonym.) *The Prince and the Pauper.* New York: Harper and Brothers, n.d.

Of the strange adventures that befell the boy king, Edward VI, and Tom Canty when they exchanged their clothing.

CLEMENS, S. L. (Mark Twain, pseudonym.) *Adventures of Tom Sawyer.* New York: Harper and Brothers, 1920.

This story, based on Mark Twain's recollections of his boyhood in Missouri, is a perennial favorite.

CLEMENT, MARGUERITE. *Once in France.* Garden City, New York: Doubleday, Doran & Company, 1927.

Stories of old France which center around historical characters.

COATSWORTH, E. J. *The Boy with the Parrot.* New York: The Macmillan Company, 1930.

Sebastian was an Indian boy in Guatemala, who sold silks and beads from the pack he carried on his back. With his first earnings he bought a parrot which went everywhere with him.

COATSWORTH, E. J. *The Cat Who Went to Heaven.* New York: The Macmillan Company, 1930.

Good Fortune was a little cat, black, white and yellow, who lived with a

Japanese artist. He painted a picture of the great Buddha and of the animals who went to Heaven—the snail, the elephant, the horse, the buffalo, and last of all, by a miracle, the little spotted cat.

CODY, W. F. *Adventures of Buffalo Bill.* New York: Harper and Brothers, 1904.
Buffalo Bill's own story of his thrilling life.

COFFMAN, RAMON. *Child's Story of the Human Race.* New York: Dodd, Mead & Company, Inc., 1924.
A vivid history, in which customs, fashions, inventions, and interesting personalities play an important part.

COFFMAN, RAMON. *Our America.* New York: Dodd, Mead & Company, Inc., 1930.
A brief history of America from pre-historic times to the present day. Well illustrated.

COIT, DOROTHY. *Ivory Throne of Persia.* New York: Frederick A. Stokes Company, 1929.
Delightful quick-moving tales retold from the Shah-Nameh of Firdausi.

COLUM, PADRAIC. *Adventures of Odysseus and the Tale of Troy.* New York: The Macmillan Company, 1918.
The classic story is beautifully retold, with text and illustrations in the true Homeric spirit.

COLUM, PADRAIC. *Voyagers, Being Legends and Romances of Atlantic Discovery.* New York: The Macmillan Company, 1925.
Marvelous stories of the lost Atlantis, St. Brendan, Eric the Red, Ponce de Leon, Amerigo Vespucci, and other explorers.

COMMINS, D. B. *Making an Orchestra.* New York: The Macmillan Company, 1931.
Describes and pictures thirty-two orchestral instruments. A large folded chart showing the arrangement of an orchestra can be cut out and mounted.

CREW, H. C. *Alanna.* New York: Harper and Brothers, 1929.
Tells of Alanna Malone of Ballycooly, a fine little Irish girl whose eyes matched the harebells and her hair the raven's wing, and of how she wandered over the hills in Ireland and came to visit her aunt in America.

CRICHTON, F. E. *Peep-in-the-World.* New York: Longmans, Green and Company, 1925.
What happened to a little English girl when she went to visit her uncle in Germany.

CROTHERS, S. M. *Miss Muffet's Christmas Party.* Boston: Houghton, Mifflin Company, 1902.
Into the Muffet household on Christmas Eve came the spider, suggesting that Miss Muffet invite all the people she had read about, to come to a party.

CRUMP, IRVING. *Boys' Book of Firemen.* New York: Dodd, Mead & Company, Inc., 1919.
Describes the work and training of enginemen, hook and ladder boys, the fire patrol, the mile-a-minute rescue men, and the marine fire fighting force.

CRUMP, IRVING. *Boys' Book of Policemen.* New York: Dodd, Mead & Company, Inc., 1917.
Many thrilling anecdotes are included in this account of the work of patrolmen, mounted police, and detectives.

DARBY, A. C. *Gay Soeuretts.* New York: Frederick A. Stokes Company, 1933.
A vivid picture of life in a French village in the Mississippi Valley just before the Louisiana purchase.

DARK, SIDNEY. *Book of France for Young People.* Garden City, New York: Doubleday, Doran & Company, 1923.

A romantic and stirring account of French history.

DARLING, E. B. *Baldy of Nome.* Philadelphia: Penn Publishing Company, 1916.

A story of a real dog in Alaska.

D'AULAIRE, INGRI. *Conquest of the Atlantic.* New York: Viking Press, Inc., 1933.

Gorgeous pictures and readable text show how men have crossed the Atlantic from the days of the Vikings to the present time.

DEFOE, DANIEL. *Robinson Crusoe.* Illustrated by E. Boyd Smith. Boston: Houghton, Mifflin Company, n.d.

There are many editions of this famous book. Whether you read a copy with pictures or without, you will never forget the moment when Crusoe finds a human footprint on his lonely shore.

DE LA MARE, WALTER. *Down-adown-derry.* Illustrated by Dorothy P. Lathrop, New York: Henry Holt & Company, 1922.

Charming poems about fairies, witches, and the world of dreams.

DE LA MARE, WALTER. *Poems for Children.* New York: Henry Holt & Company, 1930.

Contains among other favorites "The Isle of Lone," "Bunches of Grapes," and "Tartary."

DICKENS, CHARLES. *Magic Fishbone.* New York: Frederick Warne & Co., Inc., 1922.

A gay holiday fantasy of the Princess Alicia, her seventeen children and the Fairy Grandmarina.

DOONE, RADKO. *Nuvat the Brave, an Eskimo Robinson.* Philadelphia: Macrae Smith Co., 1934.

Northern adventures are woven into this tale of a boy who became a great hunter.

DOUGLAS, R. D. *Three Boy Scouts in Africa.* New York: G. P. Putnam's Sons, 1928.

Three boys who went to Africa with Martin Johnson relate their adventures.

DRUMMOND, HENRY. *Monkey That Would Not Kill.* New York: Dodd, Mead & Company, Inc., n.d.

Tells of the mischievous pranks of a monkey that "won't hang, won't drown, won't shoot."

DU CHAILLU, P. B. *Country of the Dwarfs.* New York: Harper and Brothers, 1913.

Strange experiences among the African Pygmies and the great negro tribes among whom the little people live.

DU CHAILLU, P. B. *Stories of the Gorilla Country.* New York: Harper and Brothers, 1909.

Tales of wild men and wild beasts recounted by one of the first African explorers.

DUNCAN, NORMAN. *Adventures of Billy Topsail.* New York: Fleming H. Revell & Company, 1906.

Stories of the icebergs, seals, whales, and a giant squid that a Newfoundland boy and his dog met when the boy carried Her Majesty's mail.

EELLS, E. S. *Fairy Tales from Brazil.* New York: Dodd, Mead & Company, Inc., 1917.

"How the Tiger Got His Stripes," "How the Hen Got Speckles," and other animal tales remind one of the Uncle Remus stories.

EELLS, E. S. *Tales of Enchantment from Spain.* New York: Harcourt, Brace and Company, 1920.

Fifteen magical tales with a strange Spanish setting.

EGGLESTON, EDWARD. *Hoosier Schoolboy.* New York: Charles Scribner's Sons, 1918.

Tales of school days in Indiana in pioneer times.

English Fairy Tales. Edited by F. A. W. Steel. Illustrated by Arthur Rackham. New York: The Macmillan Company, 1918.

A popular collection of excellent stories.

EWING, J. H. G. *Jan of the Windmill.* New York: Harcourt, Brace and Company, n.d.

A story of a boy who, like Rembrandt, the painter, lived in a windmill.

Fairy Shoemaker, and other Fairy Poems. Illustrated by Boris Artzybasheff. New York: The Macmillan Company, 1928.

An exquisite book with pictures by a Russian artist for five fairy poems by William Allingham, Walter De La Mare, and Matthew Arnold.

Fairy Ring. Edited by K. D. S. Wiggin, and N. A. Smith. Garden City, New York: Doubleday, Doran & Company, 1913.

Sixty-two unusual fairy tales.

FARJEON, ELEANOR. *Mighty Men from Achilles to Julius Caesar.* New York: D. Appleton-Century Company, Inc., 1925.

Well written stories of the heroes of southern Europe.

FARJEON, ELEANOR. *Mighty Men from Beowulf to William the Conquerer.* New York: D. Appleton-Century Company, Inc., 1925.

This book includes vivid tales of the heroes of northern Europe.

FERNALD, H. C., and SLOCOMBE, E. M. *Scarlet Fringe.* New York: Longmans, Green and Company, 1931.

An exciting story of the Incas in Peru.

FIELD, R. L. *Hitty, Her First Hundred Years.* New York: The Macmillan Company, 1929.

Hitty is a wooden doll who was made from a piece of mountain ash more than a hundred years ago. She has seen the world from a stage coach and a whaling vessel. Through all her adventures she has kept her cheerful smile and her serene poise.

FILLMORE, P. H. *Czechoslovak Fairy Tales.* New York: Harcourt, Brace and Company, 1919.

Fifteen fanciful tales with Czech local color; for example, in the story of the charcoal burner's son who married a princess.

FILLMORE, P. H. *Mighty Mikko.* New York: Harcourt, Brace and Company, 1922.

An excellent version of tales chosen from the Kalevala, the Finnish epic.

FINGER, C. J. *Courageous Companions.* New York: Longmans, Green and Company, 1929.

Story of the adventures of a young English boy who shipped with Magellan on the first voyage around the world.

FINGER, C. J. *Tales from Silver Lands.* Garden City, New York: Doubleday, Doran & Company, 1924.

Nineteen stories based on the legends that the author heard from Indians in South America.

FISHER, D. F. C. *Understood Betsy.* New York: Henry Holt & Company, 1917.

Elizabeth Ann who has been too much coddled by an over-conscientious aunt goes to a wholesome Vermont farm and becomes a strong self-reliant small girl.

FITINGHOFF, L. M. B. *Children of the Moor.* Boston: Houghton, Mifflin Company, 1927.

A gallant picture of a little family of seven orphans who seek food and shelter in southern Sweden.

FRENCH, ALLEN. *Sir Marrók; a Tale of the Days of King Arthur.* New York: The Century Co., 1902.

This is a good story of sorcery and knightly valor in the days of King Arthur.

FRENCH, ALLEN. *Story of Rolf and the Viking's Bow.* Boston: Little, Brown and Company, n.d.

Old Icelandic sagas are the basis of this stirring tale.

FRENCH, H. W. *Lance of Kanana.* Boston: Lothrop, Lee & Shepard Company, 1920.

How the brave Bedouin boy, Kanana, gave his life to save the Arabians from their enemies.

GALE, ELIZABETH. *Katrina van Ost and the Silver Rose.* New York: G. P. Putnam's Sons, 1934.

Katrina came from Holland to New Amsterdam in the year 1638.

GEISTER, EDNA. *What Shall We Play.* New York: Richard R. Smith, Inc., 1924.

In this collection are Not Noisy Games, Very Noisy Games, Sick Abed Games, Sidewalk Games, Tag Games, and others for indoors and out.

GIMMAGE, PETER. *Picture Book of Ships.* New York: The Macmillan Company, 1930.

Among the ships pictured and described are the dinghy, dory, gig, punt, raft, skiff, bark, schooner, sloop, yawl, lugger, steamer, and motorboat. The book was written by a sailor to answer his son's questions.

Girl's Book of Verse. Compiled by M. G. Davis. New York: Frederick A. Stokes Company, 1922.

Grouped under the headings Pipes of Pan, Enchantment and Stories, are poems ranging from Solomon's "Song of Songs" to Hilda Conkling's "Tree Toad."

Golden Numbers. Edited by K. D. S. Wiggin, and N. A. Smith. Garden City, New York: Doubleday, Doran & Company, 1913.

A well balanced collection of poems for children in the upper grades.

GRUNDTVIG, S. H. *Danish Fairy Tales.* New York: T. Y. Crowell Company, n.d.

Eighteen charming tales, told with simplicity and grace.

HADER, BERTA, and HADER, ELMER. *Picture Book of Travel; the Story of Transportation.* New York: The Macmillan Company, 1923.

Here we see a cave man with a pack on his back, a litter, a palanquin, and a sedan chair, carts and carriages, a covered wagon, a stage coach, and a horse car.

HALE, L. P. *Peterkin Papers.* Boston: Houghton, Mifflin Company, 1914.

The Peterkin family was always having amusing adventures because they had every virtue except common sense.

HALL, JENNIE. *Buried Cities.* New York: The Macmillan Company, 1922.

Fascinating accounts of old cities—Pompeii, Olympia and Mycenae.

HALL, JENNIE. *Four Old Greeks.* Chicago: Rand McNally & Company, 1901.

Achilles, Herakles, Dionysos, and Alkestis are the four heroes whose stories are told here.

HALL, JENNIE. *Viking Tales.* Chicago: Rand McNally & Company, 1902.

An easy-to-read version of the northern sagas.

HAMILTON, E. T. *The Boy Builder.* New York: Harcourt, Brace and Company, 1933.

Careful directions for using tools and making all kinds of useful articles out of wood.

HANSON, L. S. *Eric the Red.* Garden City, New York: Doubleday, Doran & Company, 1933.

A stirring account of the Viking heroes who found new homes in Iceland and Greenland.

HARRIS, J. C. *Uncle Remus; His Songs and His Sayings.* New York: D. Appleton-Century Company, Inc., 1914.

These stories of Br'er Fox, Br'er B'ar, Br'er Rabbit, and the Tar Baby are often enjoyed most when they are read aloud.

HASKELL, H. E. *Katrinka: Story of a Russian Child.* New York: E. P. Dutton and Company, 1915.

Of a little Russian peasant girl who was trained for the Imperial ballet before the Revolution.

HERODOTUS. *Stories from the East, by Herodotus,* by A. T. Church. New York: Dodd, Mead & Company, Inc., n.d.

These adaptations from the histories of Herodotus are well-suited to young readers who prefer history to fairy tales.

HIBBEN, THOMAS. *The Carpenter's Tool Chest.* Philadelphia: J. B. Lippincott Company, 1933.

Tells of the evolution of tools from the stone age to the nineteenth century.

HILL, HELEN, and MAXWELL, VIOLET. *Little Tonino.* New York: The Macmillan Company, 1928.

Little Tonino and his sister Nanou lived in Provence. The story tells about the flower harvest and perfume making, Christmas customs and the big fair at Venice, but most of all, about how Tonino made clay bowls and cups and animals so that Tintourlet, his donkey, need not be sold.

HILLYER, V. M. *Child's History of the World.* New York: The Century Co., 1924.

An outline of events, century by century and epoch by epoch, told in colloquial style with breezy illustrations.

History Stories of Other Lands. Book II. Tales of Long Ago. Edited by A. G. Terry. Evanston, Illinois: Row, Peterson and Company, 1926.

This book tells of the heroes of many countries.

History Stories of Other Lands. Book IV. Lord and Vassal. Edited by A. G. Terry. Evanston, Illinois: Row, Peterson and Company, 1926.

Gives the background for tales of chivalry in the years 1066 to 1485.

Home Book of Verse for Young Folks. Edited by B. E. Stevenson. Decorations by Willy Pogany. New York: Henry Holt & Company, n.d.

A standard collection including many selections from recent poets.

HINE, L. W. *Men at Work.* New York: The Macmillan Company, 1932.

Unusual photographs show men building skyscrapers, or working on the railroads, in mines, or machine shops.

HOUGH, WALTER. *Story of Fire.* Garden City, New York: Doubleday, Doran & Company, 1928.

A dramatic account of the application of fire to various purposes, from the camp fires and torches of primitive man to the blazing furnaces and brilliant lights of today.

HOUGHTON, L. S. *Russian Grandmother's Wonder Tales.* New York: Charles Scribner's Sons, 1906.

An excellent collection of curious and fascinating stories.

HOWARD, A. W. *Ching-Li and the Dragons.* New York: The Macmillan Company, 1931.

An unusual tale of a Chinese boy who longed for adventure and found it in rescuing the greatest dragon of all.

HUDSON, W. H. *Little Boy Lost.* Illustrated by Dorothy P. Lathrop. New York: Alfred A. Knopf, 1920.

Written with a mysterious charm, this story tells of a little boy who is lured from his home by a vision of the false water and meets many strange people when he wanders through the wilderness.

HUTCHINSON, W. M. L. *Golden Porch.* New York: Longmans, Green and Company, 1925.

Beautifully told stories from Pindar.

ILIN, M. (pseudonym of Il'Ia I. Marshak.) *Black on White.* Philadelphia: J. B. Lippincott Company, 1932.

A most unusual and alluring history of the making of books in many countries and many ages.

JEWETT, SOPHIE. *God's Troubadour.* New York: T. Y. Crowell Company, 1910.

The story of St. Francis of Assisi is told with distinction of style in this book.

KELLY, E. P. *The Trumpeter of Krakow.* New York: The Macmillan Company, 1928.

An exciting story which relates the adventures of a fifteenth century Polish boy who saved his father's life and also the great Tarnov crystal.

KENNEDY, H. A. *New World Fairy Book*. New York: E. P. Dutton and Company, 1922.

Tales of Indian magic and of brave warriors and chiefs, of Indian youths and maidens, and of enchanted animals.

KENT, LOUISE ANDREWS. *Two Children of Tyre*. Boston: Houghton, Mifflin Company, 1932.

The two children, David and Esther, lived 3000 years ago, when Solomon ruled in Jerusalem and Hiram was King in Tyre.

KINGSLEY, CHARLES. *Heroes; or Greek Fairy Tales*. Illustrated by T. H. Robinson. New York: E. P. Dutton and Company, n.d.

In this book the stories of Perseus, Theseus and the Argonauts are told with steadfast simplicity.

KINGSLEY, CHARLES. *Water Babies*. Illustrated by Warwick Goble. New York: The Macmillan Company, n.d.

A classic which concerns a little chimney sweeper who was turned into a water baby.

KIPLING, RUDYARD. *Jungle Book*. Garden City, New York: Doubleday, Doran & Company, 1894.

Fascinating stories of Mowgli who lived in the jungle with wolves and a wise old bear and a panther.

KIPLING, RUDYARD. *Puck of Pook's Hill*. Garden City, New York: Doubleday, Doran & Company, 1906.

American readers who are familiar with Shakespeare and English history delight in these stories of prehistoric man, Celts, Romans, Saxons, Normans, Plantagenets, and Tudors.

KNEELAND, C. A. *Smuggler's Island and the Devil Fires of San Marcos*. Boston: Houghton, Mifflin Company, n.d.

The setting of this story is a desert island in the Gulf of California where a resourceful girl and her four small brothers and sisters lived for seven years.

KNOX, R. B. *Boys and Sally Down on a Plantation*. Garden City, New York: Doubleday, Doran & Company, 1930.

Sally visited her uncle who lived on a plantation in the south not long after the Civil War.

LABOULAYE, E. R. L. *Quest of the Four-leafed Clover*. Adapted by W. T. Field. Boston: Ginn and Company, 1910.

Gives a picture of Bedouin life among the tents, and in the bazaars, and of the mysterious desert with its half obliterated trails and its passing caravans.

LA GANKE, FLORENCE. *Patty Pans*. Boston: Little, Brown and Company, 1929.

Entertainingly written cook book for little cooks, giving practical directions for cooking and serving many dishes.

LAGERLÖF, SELMA. *Wonderful Adventures of Nils*. Translated by Velma Swanston Howard. Garden City, New York: Doubleday, Doran & Company, 1912.

An idle cruel boy, reduced to elfin size for malicious mischief, migrates with the wild geese and learns lessons of love and helpfulness.

LANSING, M. F. *Life in the Greenwood*. Boston: Ginn and Company, 1909.

A simple version of the Robin Hood ballads.

LANSING, M. F. *Magic Gold, a Story of the Time of Roger Bacon*. Boston: Little, Brown and Company, 1928.

An unusual tale of the thirteenth century in which Roger, the son of a baron, serves his apprenticeship to an alchemist, and learns the greatest law: to seek and speak the truth.

LANSING, M. F. *Page, Esquire and Knight.* Boston: Ginn and Company, 1910.
Well told stories of King Arthur, Charlemagne, and other knightly heroes.

LEETCH, D. L. *Annetje and Her Family.* Boston: Lothrop, Lee & Shepard Company, 1926.
A pleasant story of a little girl and her five brothers and sisters who lived in New Amsterdam before it became New York City.

LEETCH, D. L. *Tommy Tucker on a Plantation.* Boston: Lothrop, Lee & Shepard Company, 1925.
Much information about colonial life in Virginia is woven into this story of a little boy's visit to his uncle's plantation.

LEWIS, E. F. *Young Fu of the Upper Yangtze.* Philadelphia: The John C. Winston Company, 1932.
A young Chinese boy becomes a skilled coppersmith. Shows life today in war-torn China.

LIDE, A. A., and JOHANSEN, M. A. *Ood-le-uk the Wanderer.* Boston: Little, Brown and Company, 1930.
A story of olden times in the far north with an Eskimo boy as the center of interest.

LINDSAY, VACHEL. *Johnny Appleseed and Other Poems.* New York: The Macmillan Company, 1928.
Poems of swinging rhythm, grouped under four headings: Yellow Butterflies, Moon Poems, Stories and Heroes, and Nightingales.

LINNELL, GERTRUDE. *Behind the Battlements.* New York: The Macmillan Company, 1931.
Three good stories about Carcassonne, Avignon, and Mont St. Michel are accompanied by accounts of the history of the cities.

Little Book of Necessary Nonsense. Compiled by Burges Johnson. New York: Harper and Brothers, 1929.
A little book, full of funny poems by Samuel Johnson, Thackeray, Bret Harte, Lewis Carroll, Gelett Burgess, and other writers.

LOWNSBERY, ELOISE. *Boy Knight of Reims.* Boston: Houghton, Mifflin Company, 1927.
Of guilds and festivals, knights and craftsmen, soldiers and a bishop, and especially of a boy who helped to build a great cathedral.

LUCAS, E. V. *Slowcoach.* New York: The Macmillan Company, 1910.
The adventures of seven English children who traveled through the Shakespeare country in a caravan.

MACDONALD, GEORGE. *At the Back of the North Wind.* New York: The Macmillan Company, n.d.
The book tells of a dreamy little boy and his affection for the north wind.

MACMANUS, SEUMAS. *Donegal Fairy Stories.* Garden City, New York: Doubleday, Doran & Company, 1900.
Ten colorful, heroic, and humorous Celtic fairy tales.

MARRYAT, FREDERICK. *Children of the New Forest.* Illustrated by E. B. Smith. New York: Henry Holt & Company, n.d.
The adventures of the four children of a cavalier who were hidden in the New Forest in the time of Charles II and the Roundheads.

MARRYAT, FREDERICK. *Masterman Ready.* Philadelphia: Macrae Smith Co., n.d.
Classic sea story of a shipwreck on a desert island.

MARSHALL, H. E. *Stories of Beowulf.* New York: E. P. Dutton and Company, n.d.
Simply told versions of the great Saxon hero.

MARSHALL, H. E. *Stories of William Tell and His Friends.* New York: E. P. Dutton and Company, 1907.
A thrilling story of the Swiss hero and his struggle for freedom.

MASON, ARTHUR. *Wee Men of Ballywooden.* Garden City, New York: Doubleday, Doran & Company, 1930.
These two long tales are rich in humor and imagination and these qualities pervade the admirable illustrations.

McNEELY, M. H. *Jumping-off Place.* New York: Longmans, Green and Company, 1929.
When the four young Linvilles were left alone in the world, they showed their pluck and determination in making a home for themselves on the Dakota prairie.

MEANS, F. C. *Candle in the Mist.* Boston: Houghton, Mifflin Company, 1931.
A pioneer story of Wisconsin in the seventies. Janey Grant's faith in her foster brother was the candle that burned when he was suspected of theft.

MEIGS, CORNELIA. *Master Simon's Garden.* New York: The Macmillan Company, 1916.
A romantic story of a garden, a witch, and a treasure in England in colonial times.

MEIGS, CORNELIA. *The New Moon.* New York: The Macmillan Company, 1924.
The story of an Irish boy who crosses the Atlantic and walks across Pennsylvania with a flock of sheep.

MEIGS, CORNELIA. *Swift Rivers.* Boston: Little, Brown and Company, 1932.
The stirring adventures of two boys who succeeded in taking a raft of logs from Minnesota to St. Louis, in spite of rapids, sandbars, and hostile Indians.

MILLER, E. C. *Children of the Mountain Eagle.* Garden City, New York: Doubleday, Doran & Company, 1927.
A story of Bor and Marash who lived high in the mountain fastnesses of Albania.

MILLER, E. C. *Pran of Albania.* Garden City, New York: Doubleday, Doran & Company, 1929.
Mystery and romance are found in this story of primitive life in central Europe.

MILLER, E. C. *Young Trajan.* Garden City, New York: Doubleday, Doran & Company, 1931.
This story of peasant life in Rumania is gay with festivals, songs, and dancing despite the hardships of extreme poverty and oppression.

MIRZA, Y. B. *Children of the Housetops.* Garden City, New York: Doubleday, Doran & Company, 1931.
Shirin, a little Persian girl, plays with her brother and her pets and learns how to be a good housewife.

MITCHELL, L. S. *North America.* New York: The Macmillan Company, 1931.
A refreshing description which opens with an account of a modern ship entering the Golden Gate.

MOLESWORTH, M. L. *Cuckoo Clock.* Philadelphia: J. B. Lippincott Company, n.d.
A pleasing story of Griselda's adventures with the cuckoo in Butterfly Land.

MOON, G. P. *Nadita.* Garden City, New York: Doubleday, Doran & Company, 1927.
How a little Mexican girl visits a sugar plantation and is carried away by a traveling circus.

MORLEY, M. W. *Donkey John of the Toy Valley.* Chicago: A. C. McClurg & Co., 1909.
How a litle boy who lived in the Tyrol won a prize for the donkeys he carved out of wood.

MORROW, ELIZABETH. *The Painted Pig.* New York: Alfred A. Knopf, 1930.

The bright pictures by René d'Harnoncourt add much to the clever Mexican story.

MORROW, H. M. W. *Ship's Monkey.* New York: William Morrow Co., Inc., 1933.

An amusing tale of the antics of a lively monkey that proves to be the mascot of a sailing vessel in the Pacific.

MUKERJI, D. G. *Gay-Neck, the Story of a Pigeon.* Illustrated by Boris Artzy-basheff. New York: E. P. Dutton and Company, 1927.

Tells of Gay-Neck's training in India and of his part in the Great War.

MUKERJI, D. G. *Hari, the Jungle Lad.* New York: E. P. Dutton and Company, 1924.

An East Indian boy hunts with his father in the jungle and finds the famous elephant Kari.

MUKERJI, D. G. *Kari, the Elephant.* New York: E. P. Dutton and Company, 1922.

Something of the mystery of the jungle is found in this story a Hindu boy tells about his elephant.

NAUMBURG, E. H. *Skyscraper.* New York: The John Day Company, 1933.

Unusual photographs and readable descriptions of the erection of city buildings.

NORRIS, MARGARET. *Heroes and Hazards.* New York: The Macmillan Company, 1932.

The work of men like the Sandy Hook pilots, structural steel·workers, sandbags, locomotive engineers, is always hazardous and often heroic.

NUSBAUM, A. B. *Zuni Indian Tales.* New York: G. P. Putnam's Sons, 1926.

Colorful stories of the Zuni Indians.

NUSBAUM, DERIC. *Deric in Mesa Verde.* New York: G. P. Putnam's Sons, 1926.

Deric's father is an archeologist in New Mexico and this book tells much about the cliff-dwellers.

NYBLOM, H. A. *Jolly Calle and Other Swedish Fairy Tales.* New York: E. P. Dutton and Company, n.d.

Wholesome simplicity characterizes these fairy tales.

OLCOTT, F. J. *Wonder Tales from China Seas.* Illustrated by Dugald Stewart Walker. New York: Longmans, Green and Company, 1925.

Chinese folk tales told in singing prose.

Once There Was and Was Not. Edited by G. E. Dane, and B. J. Dane. New York: Junior Literary Guild, 1931.

Short rhymes and fourteen diverting folk tales, from Mallorca, each beginning, "Once there was and was not," and each ending, "and if we never meet together here again, may we all meet in glory."

PALM, AMY. *Wanda and Greta at Broby Farm.* Translated from the Swedish by Siri Andrews. New York: Longmans, Green and Company, 1930.

Tells of the interesting things that two little girls found to do on a farm in Sweden.

PALMER, W. B. *Abdul.* New York: The Macmillan Company, 1928.

A story of modern Egypt, which tells how Abdul's drawings of his camel brought him the friendship of an artist in Cairo.

PARRISH, ANNE. *Floating Island.* New York: Harper and Brothers, 1930.

An original tale of a family of dolls shipwrecked on a tropical island.

PECK, A. M. *Roundabout America.* New York: Harper and Brothers, 1933.

After traveling roundabout this country by plane, train, steamer, and car, the author describes many of the sights she saw.

PECK, A. M. *Roundabout Europe.* New York: Harper and Brothers, 1931.

A readable travel book which relates the traditions, history, and literary associations connected with many interesting places.

PERKINS, L. F. *Mexican Twins.* Boston: Houghton, Mifflin Company, 1915.

Two little Mexican peasant children are pictured in their everyday life at home, helping with the work, and enjoying their simple pleasures on the great feast day.

PHELPS, F. B. *Nikita.* New York: Harcourt, Brace and Company, 1932.

An interesting story of the journey made by a boy and his grandmother from a little Russian vllage to Siberia at the time of the war with Japan.

Picture Book of Animals. Compiled and translated by I. E. Lord. New York: The Macmillan Company, 1932.

One hundred and fifty unusual photographs of birds, beasts, fish, and other creatures from many parts of the world.

POTTER, EDNA. *Christopher Columbus.* New York: Oxford University Press, 1932.

Vivid account of the life of one whose courage and vision never failed.

PURNELL, IDELLA, and WEATHERWAX, J. M. *The Talking Bird, an Aztec Story Book.* New York: The Macmillan Company, 1930.

These are stories of the Axtecs of Old Mexico, as Grandfather Juan told them to little Paco.

PUTNAM, D. B. *David Goes Voyaging.* New York: G. P. Putnam's Sons, 1925.

Lucky David Putnam tells what happened when he went to the Galapagos Island with a scientific expedition under William Beebe.

PYLE, HOWARD. *Men of Iron.* New York: Harper and Brothers, 1904.

How Miles Falworth won his spurs and vanquished his father's enemy is told in this dramatic tale of the time of Henry IV.

PYLE, HOWARD. *Merry Adventure of Robin Hood of Great Renown in Nottinghamshire.* New York: Chas. Scribner's Sons, 1912.

The very best version of the ballads of the bold outlaw and his merry men in the greenwood.

PYLE, HOWARD. *Pepper and Salt; or, Seasoning for Young Folk.* New York: Harper and Brothers, 1913.

A clever and amusing concoction of stories, rhymes, and pictures.

PYLE, HOWARD. *Story of King Arthur and His Knights.* New York: Chas. Scribner's Sons, 1912.

A beautiful retelling of the heroic tales.

Rainbow Gold. Edited by Sara Teasdale. New York: The Macmillan Company, 1922.

A very beautiful collection of poems new and old. A poet's invitation to read poetry for its own sake.

RANSOME, ARTHUR. *Swallows and Amazons.* Philadelphia: J. B. Lippincott Company, 1931.

A joyo..s chronicle of the summer holiday of some English boys and girls.

REED, W. M.   *Earth for Sam*.   New York: Harcourt, Brace and Company, 1930.

Sam asked his uncle questions about the formation of rivers, mountains, clouds, stars, and the earth. His uncle told him how scientists have learned from fossils and rocks that the earth has changed from a white hot mass where nothing could exist to a place where plants, animals, and men live.

REED, W. M.   *Stars for Sam*.   New York: Harcourt, Brace and Company, 1931.

Explains the structure and evolution of the universe, from the sun to the farthest galaxy of stars.

ROBINSON, W. W.   *Beasts of the Tar Pits*.   With drawings by Irene Robinson.

New York: The Macmillan Company, 1932.

A picture book of prehistoric animals. Many of them fell into the La Brea pits in Los Angeles. Scientists came from far and near to study their bones while countless automobiles of today's civilization whirl by them.

ROOSEVELT, THEODORE. *Theodore Roosevelt's Letters to His Children*.   Edited by Joseph Bucklin Bishop.   New York: Charles Scribner's Sons, 1919.

Spontaneous and entertaining letters written by the energetic president when his children were young.

ROWE, DOROTHY.   *Begging Deer*.   New York: The Macmillan Company, 1928.

Attractive pictures of child life in Japan.

RUSSELL, W. C.   *Wreck of the Grosvenor*.   New York: Dodd, Mead & Company, Inc., n.d.

A famous story of a shipwreck.

SALTEN, FELIX.   *Bambi*.   New York: Simon & Schuster, Inc., 1929.

The life story of a forest deer, from fawn to full grown stag, told simply, tenderly, and poetically.

SANDBURG, CARL.   *Early Moon*.   New York: Harcourt, Brace and Company, 1930.

These seventy poems give pictures of Chicago and of Illinois farm life. They are prefaced by an interesting "Short Talk on Poetry."

SANDBURG, CARL.   *Rootabaga Stories*.   New York: Harcourt, Brace and Company, 1922.

Nonsense, fantasy, and reality are in these very original American stories.

SCHULTZ, J. W.   *With the Indians in the Rockies*.   Boston: Houghton, Mifflin Company, 1912.

Tells of the capture of a white boy and an Indian boy by hostile Indians, and of their escape.

SCOTT, EVELYN, and SCOTT, C. K.   *In the Endless Sands*.   New York: Henry Holt & Company, 1925.

The adventures of a little American boy and a little Arabian girl who were lost in the Sahara Desert.

SEGUR, SOPHIE.   *Memoirs of a Donkey*.   Translated from French by Marguerite Fellows Melcher.   New York: The Macmillan Company, 1924.

A very lively little French girl and her small playmates who are her able seconds in mischief hold the center of the stage. In the background hovers a sensible mother with a sense of humor.

Seven Champions of Christendom. Edited by F. J. H. Darton. New York: Frederick A. Stokes Company, n.d. •

A romantic account of knightly adventures.

SHANNON, MONICA. *California Fairy Tales.* Garden City, New York: Doubleday, Doran & Company, 1926.

A gay and original book about the little people of California forests and deserts.

SKINNER, C. L. *Silent Scot, Frontier Scout.* New York: The Macmillan Company, 1925.

Tells of the adventures of Andy and his Indian friend, Runner-on-the-Wind, in the days before Tennessee became a state.

SMITH, E. B. *Pocahontas and Captain John Smith.* Boston: Houghton, Mifflin Company, n.d.

Twenty-six full page pictures in color add to the attraction of the story.

SMITH, S. C. G. *Made in America.* New York: Alfred A. Knopf, 1929.

Sketches of Paul Revere as a silversmith, Duncan Phyfe as a cabinet maker, Thomas Jefferson as an architect, and other American craftsmen.

SNEDEKER, C. D. *Downright Dencey.* Garden City, New York: Doubleday, Doran & Company, 1927.

The story of an impulsive little Quaker girl who lived in Nantucket over a hundred years ago.

SNEDEKER, C. D. *Perilous Seat.* Garden City, New York: Doubleday, Doran & Company, 1923.

Ancient Greece is the background of this delightful story.

SNEDEKER, C. D. *Theras and His Town.* Garden City, New York: Doubleday, Doran & Company, 1924.

A good story of an Athenian school boy who lived for a short time in Sparta.

STEIN, EVALEEN. *Gabriel and the Hour Book.* Boston: L. C. Page & Company, 1906.

An appealing story of a French peasant who helped to illustrate a book of hours which was given by Louis XII to Anne of Brittany.

STEVENSON, R. L. *Treasure Island.* New York: Chas. Scribner's Sons, 1911.

One of the most famous of all books for boys, ranking first among tales of pirates.

STOCKTON, F. R. *Bee-man of Orn and Other Fanciful Tales.* New York: Chas. Scribner's Sons, 1915.

Charming fantasies, rich in delicate humor.

STOCKTON, F. R. *Buccaneers and Pirates of Our Coast.* New York: The Macmillan Company, 1898.

Exciting tales of the West Indies and the Spanish Main.

SWIFT, H. H. *Little Blacknose.* New York: Harcourt, Brace and Company, 1929.

Little Blacknose is the name given by the author to the De Witt Clinton engine that drew the first train from Albany to Schenectady.

SWIFT, JONATHAN. *Gulliver's Travels.* Edited by Padraic Colum. Illustrated by Willy Pogany. New York: The Macmillan Company, 1917.

A classic which tells of a giant among pygmies and of a pygmy among giants.

TAPPAN, EVA MARCH. *Old Ballads in Prose.* Boston: Houghton, Mifflin Company, 1901.

Well told versions of "King John and the Abbott," "Robin Hood," "Tamerlane," and other favorite English poems.

TARN, W. W. *The Treasure of the Isle of Mist.* New York: G. P. Putnam's Sons, 1934.

A charming fantasy for girls who appreciate imaginative literature.

THACKERAY, W. M. *The Rose and the Ring.* New York: The Macmillan Company, 1923.

An amusing tale of what happened to a prince and princess to whom the fairies gave a rose, a ring, and a little misfortune.

This Singing World. Edited by Louis Untermeyer. New York: Harcourt, Brace and Company, 1923.

An attractive anthology containing many modern poems.

TIETJENS, E. S. H. *Boy of the Desert.* New York: Coward, McCann & Company, 1928.

The lively adventures of Abdul Aziz, a little Arabian boy who lived in modern Tunisia, and of Son of Satan, the small donkey that brought him luck.

TIETJENS, E. S. H. *Boy of the South Seas.* New York: Coward, McCann & Company, 1931.

A beautifully told story of Teiki, a Polynesian boy.

TOPELIUS, ZAKARIAS. *Canute Whistlewinks and Other Stories.* New York: Longmans, Green and Company, 1927.

Topelius may be called the Hans Andersen of Finland. These tales, legends, and studies of child life in Finland and Lapland, are filled with delicate fancies and simple beauty.

TURNER, N. B. *In the Days of Young Washington.* Boston: Houghton, Mifflin Company, 1931.

An interesting story of country life in eighteenth century Virginia.

TURNER, N. B. *Magpie Lane.* New York: Harcourt, Brace and Company, 1927.

Delicate poems and dainty silhouettes of child life.

VAN METRE, T. W. *Trains, Tracks and Travel.* New York: Simmons-Boardman Publishing Company, 1926.

Nearly everything about American railroads may be found in this volume.

VERPILLEUX, E. A. *Picture Book of Houses.* New York: The Macmillan Company, 1931.

Pictures and explanations of the homes of lake dwellers, cliff dwellers, Greeks, Romans, knights and courtiers, orientals and nomads, and men of modern times.

WHITE, HERVEY. *Snake Gold: A Tale of Indian Treasure.* New York: The Macmillan Company, 1926.

A story of the search for Inca treasure, buried in the mountains of Mexico.

WHITE, S. E. *Daniel Boone, Wilderness Scout.* Illustrated by James Daugherty. Garden City, New York: Doubleday, Doran & Company, 1922.

A gorgeously illustrated and vividly written biography of the great frontiersman.

WHITE, S. E. *Magic Forest.* New York: The Macmillan Company, n.d.

The adventures of a little boy among friendly Indians in a Canadian forest.

WIGGIN, K. D. S. *Birds' Christmas Carol.* Boston: Houghton, Mifflin Company, 1918.

A sweet story of Carol Bird's Christmas party for the nine Ruggles children.

WIGGIN, K. D. S. *Rebecca of Sunnybrook Farm.* Boston: Houghton, Mifflin Company, n.d.

Tells what happened when a lively little girl went to live with her sedate aunts in a quiet brick house.

Wyss, Johann. *Swiss Family Robinson.* Illustrated by Louis Rhead. New York : Harper and Brothers, n.d.

A famous story of a family shipwrecked on a desert island.

Young, Ella. *Tangle-coated Horse and Other Tales.* New York : Longmans, Green and Company, 1929.

From the great cycle called the Fionn Saga the author has chosen stories which tell how the shaggy coated horse carried the friends of Fionn to the Land-underwave; how Fionn won the lordship of the Fionna ; and how he came to the Well of the Sacred Hazels and became himself the Salmon of Knowledge.

Zollinger, Gulielma. *Widow O'Callaghan's Boys.* Chicago : A. C. McClurg & Company, 1929.

How an Irish widow and her seven sons struggled for a livelihood.

Zwilgmeyer, Dikken. *What Happened to Inger Johanne.* Boston : Lothrop, Lee & Shepard Company, 1919.

An amusing story of a little Norwegian girl who was always in trouble.

K